Living With Śiva

शिवेन सह जीवनम्

சிவனோடு வாழ்தல்

Living With Śiva

Hinduism's Contemporary Culture

शिवेन सह जीवनम्

हिन्दूधर्म समकालीन संस्कृति

சிவனோடு வாழ்தல்

இந்து சமயத்தின் தற்கால கலாச்சாரம்

Satguru Sivaya
Subramuniyaswami

HIMALAYAN ACADEMY, INDIA • USA
AND
MOTILAL BANARSIDASS PUBLISHERS
PRIVATE LIMITED • DELHI

First Indian Edition: Delhi, 2013

ISBN: 978-81-208-3264-0

MOTILAL BANARSIDASS
41 U.A. Bungalow Road, Jawahar Nagar, Delhi 110 007
8 Mahalaxmi Chamber, 22 Bhulabhai Desai Road, Mumbai 400 026
203 Royapettah High Road, Mylapore, Chennai 600 004
236, 9th Main III Block, Jayanagar, Bengaluru 560 011
Sanas Plaza, 1302 Baji Rao Road, Pune 411 002
8 Camac Street, Kolkata 700 017
Ashok Rajpath, Patna 800 004
Chowk, Varanasi 221 001

Cover Art: Artist S. Rajam depicts life in a South Indian riverside village. Under Lord Śiva's blessed gaze, children play near a *tulsī* tree shrine, a cowherd brings his animals from the forest, women draw water at the well, and families carry on their household duties.

Gaṇeśa Dancing: Famed Indian artist Indra Sharma paints a gleefully dancing and somewhat portly Lord Gaṇeśa to bless the book's opening, mimicking in earthy tones the stone carving style of images found on temple walls throughout India.

Half Title Page: S. Rajam takes us inside a shrine room where husband and wife are worshiping a crystal Śivaliṅga. He passes the flame and will soon set the Liṅga on a metal base, as she prepares to bathe Śiva with fresh water. Both have Śiva alive in their hearts.

Printed in India

by RP Jain at NAB Printing Unit,
A-44, Naraina Industrial Area, Phase I, New Delhi–110028
and published by JP Jain for Motilal Banarsidass Publishers (P) Ltd,
41 U.A. Bungalow Road, Jawahar Nagar, Delhi-110007

உ

Dedication

Samarpaṇam

समर्पणम्

BURSTING FORTH ON THE POWER OF DIVINE INSPIRATION, *LIVING WITH ŚIVA* WAS WRITTEN FOR THE BENEFIT OF THE HIGHEST ATTAINMENT, PARAŚIVA, FOR ALL OF ŚIVA'S FOLLOWERS. WE DEDICATE THIS PROCLAMATION OF CULTURE TO SATGURU SIVA YOgaswami (1872-1964) and to all who preceded him in the holy Kailāsa Paramparā. We have received the blessings and authorization from Lord Gaṇeśa to proceed at a very special time in a very special way. We have received the power, the lightning flash, from Lord Murugan and His permission to proceed. May all souls live in the Grace of our Supreme God Śiva—creator, preserver and destroyer of all that is good, bad, confused and indifferent, the source of grace, the author of *dharma*, the giver of all good things, the light and love of the world—who has always, does always, will always spread His goodness and glory everywhere. The spirit of *Living with Śiva* was succinctly conveyed 2,200 years ago by weaver saint Tiruvalluvar in the following verses from his famed ethical scripture, the *Tirukural:*

> *Attach yourself to Him who is free from all attachments. Bind yourself to that bond so that all other bonds may be broken* (350).
>
> *It is said that all good things are natural to those who know their duty and walk the path of perfect goodness* (981).
>
> *Love, modesty, propriety, kindly look and truthfulness—these are the five pillars on which perfect goodness rests* (983).

Indra Sharma captures the powerful grace of Satguru Siva Yogaswami of Jaffna, Sri Lanka (1872-1964). He is proudly bearing the three lines of holy ash that every Śaivite honors and a simple, hand-woven cloth which he always wore.

Contents

Vishayasūchī

विषयसूची

PART FOUR: HINDUISM'S NANDINĀTHA SŪTRAS

Section 1: Right Living

Section 2: Ethics

Section 3: The Family Path

Section 7: The Monastic Path

RESOURCES

Author's Introduction

Granthakāra Bhūmikā

ग्रन्थकार भूमिका

MOST PEOPLE THINK OF THEMSELVES AS REMOTE FROM GOD, BUT THE HIGHEST SOULS ARE LIVING WITH HIM EVERY DAY, NO MATTER WHAT THEY ARE DOING. THEY ARE LIVING WITH GOD, WHOM WE CALL ŚIVA, WHILE WORKING, WHILE DRIVING OR performing ordinary chores. Śiva is, for these remarkable devotees, closer than their breath, nearer than their hands and feet. This is the true spiritual life, which recognizes that there is nothing that is not Śiva. Living with Śiva is Śiva consciousness. The reconciled past releases consciousness into the eternal moment in which we see Śiva as the life and light within everyone's eyes. Living with Śiva is living with everyone—every reptile, fish, fowl, animal and creature, to the very smallest—in a consciousness of the one life force within all of them that sustains this perfect universe. Truly, God Śiva is everywhere. He is the energy within our mind manifesting thought. He is the thought thus made manifest. He is the light within your eyes and the feel within your fingers. God Śiva is the ignorance which makes the One seem as two. He is the *karma,* which is the law of cause and effect, and He is the *māyā,* which is the substance of evolution in which we become so deeply immersed that we look upon the outside world as more real than God. God Śiva is all this and more. He is the Sun, the Earth and the spaces between. He is the revealed scriptures and those who have scribed the scriptures. He is all who seek the wisdom of scripture, too.

Śiva dances in every atom throughout this universe. Śiva dances energetically, ceaselessly, eternally. Śiva is perpetual movement. His mind is all-pervasive, and thus He sees and knows everything in all spheres simultaneously and without effort. Śiva is the Self, and He is the energy we put forth to know the Self. He is the mystery which makes us see Him as separate from us. He is the energy of life, the power in the wind. He is the dissolution called death, the peace of motionless air. He is the great force of the ocean and the stillness on a calm lake. Śiva is All and in all.

Our great God Śiva is beyond time, beyond space, beyond form and form's creation, and yet He uses time and causes form. He is in the sky, in the clouds, in the swirling galaxies. Śiva's cosmic dance of creation, preservation and dissolution is happening this very moment in every atom of the cosmos. Supreme God Śiva is immanent, with a beautiful human-like form which can actually be seen and has been seen by many mystics in visions. Śiva is also transcendent, beyond time, cause and space. Such are the mysteries of Śiva's being.

Read the holy scriptures and contemplate their description of our great God Śiva. They explain who Śiva is. They tell us that Śiva has three perfections: Paraśiva, Satchidānanda and Maheśvara. As Paraśiva, He is the Self, beyond time, form and space. As Satchidānanda, He is all-pervasive love, light and consciousness flowing through every atom of existence. As Maheśvara, He is the Primal Soul, the Supreme Being who creates, preserves and destroys what we term existence. They tell us that our Supreme Being has a body of light and a mind and will that reigns over His creations. They tell us that Supreme God Śiva created our individual soul, which is a body of light in which His uncreated mind resides. Lord Śiva's mind is called Satchidānanda. It is the all-pervasive, inner state of mind inherent in every person on this Earth, but to be realized to be known.

In chapter 45 I urge all Śaivites, devotees of God Śiva, to worship Him as the God of Love and in doing so to become beings of love. The great saints of our religion were Śiva *bhaktas.* They changed the world through their love of God. They did not need vast institutions to spread their message. They did not need riches or carts filled with books to spread their message. They did not need radio, television or the Internet. Their message spread because their minds and hearts were filled with direct knowledge, direct experience of God Śiva. Their message spread far and wide, though some perhaps never left their native village. They just evolved within it. You, too, are emissaries of God Śiva, and your love for Him is your greatest message. Simply love God Śiva and let that love radiate out into the world.

In those days, Śaivites, well schooled in knowledge of God Śiva, did not fear alien religious influences entering their minds. They were so knowledgeable that no amount of adverse propaganda could sway them away from Śiva. Rather, they converted the Jains back to God Śiva. They converted the Buddhists back to God Śiva. Such was the strength of the love of devotees in the old days. In this century, too, Śaivites strong in the love of God Śiva are bringing those Śaivites who have strayed into alien religions back to Śiva's feet. They are drawing back into Śaivism those who have been enthralled with Western notions or ensnared in atheistic, existential doubt. So strong is their adoration for God and their compassion for their fellow Śaivites.

From a psychological point of view, when the subconscious is at odds with soul qualities, with the basic laws of how we intuitively know what we should be doing, when the past of unsoulful deeds carries into the present, we are not able to live with Śiva. Instead, we are living with humans, living with problems, living with the conflicting forces of the world.

At this time in the Kali Yuga, ignorance is equally distributed worldwide, and wisdom has become an endangered species. People are confused as to the performance of their duties, and too often duty is no longer even taught. It is to liberate seekers after Truth from this confusion that this book has been written. Forbearance, tolerance and compassion are not as popular today as they once were and perhaps may be at some future time when the darkness of ignorance is removed from the hearts of all people. Therefore, *Living with Śiva* and its 365 Nandinātha Sūtras, translated into many languages for seekers living in various countries, will play an important part in bringing the best of traditional Hinduism forward in these modern times.

The first edition of *Living with Śiva* was addressed to my followers and did not contain the more than 800 pages of inspired talks that form the main body of this second edition. It was a book of aphorisms only, an in-house book of 365 *sūtras*, written for the large number of Tamil Śaiva followers from Sri Lanka who had, due to civil war, dispersed all over the world. As their hereditary *guru*, it was my duty to revive the standards that my *satguru*, Sage Yogaswami, worked so hard to maintain among their parents and grandparents.

Soon, however, we noticed that *Living with Śiva* began circulating among people of all religions and persuasions. The Tamils called it the "modern *Tirukural*," and non-Hindus took it as a lifeline from the past into the present to hang on to for a better and more productive life. Having realized that *Living with Śiva* had acquired its own identity and gained its own following of devotees and readers, we added many chapters about Hindu culture to this second edition.

These 365 *sūtras* make up Part Four in this second edition, and Parts One, Two and Three are drawn from my inspired talks, dictations and writings given since my international ministry began in 1957 to bring forth and clarify the *dharma,* and discuss the issues and problems faced all over the world in bringing Hinduism, particularly Śaivism, into the technological age as a system of knowledge, strength and solace to individuals and families in daily life. Especially potent in dealing with the challenges facing the modern Hindu were the series of talks I gave in the United States, Canada, Mauritius, India and Sri Lanka on Renaissance Tours from 1979 to 1983. In the past two decades, excerpts from this collection of talks on culture have touched the hearts and minds of thousands of seekers through my Publisher's Desk column in our international magazine, HINDUISM TODAY. All that is now captured in this book.

Today, and in every era, people young and old do want to discuss matters of the family. But all too often when questions arise, answers are avoided or, if given, are irrelevant. It was this urgent need for practical insights on family-oriented subjects that inspired this book. Here we frankly answer the eternal inquiries, openly discuss the problems and boldly show the noble path of *dharma* for those seeking insights into traditional ways of life that can and should be lived in these contemporary times.

Many things in the world are wrong, certainly, but they do not have to be that way, since Hindus do have a traditional, proven way to follow. We do. It is the ancient Hindu path of the wise *ṛishis,* so well articulated, though sometimes too well hidden, in our sacred scriptures. It is not always easy to discover where this path begins, in what direction it leads and where it will take us. But once we find the path, we also find answers to many family-related questions that have troubled us, about which the old cultures had not only generations of knowledge, but also practical, sensible solutions. So, we hope you enjoy this modern look at the ancient Hindu path and find here much to emulate in your own life.

Of course, now, as in ages past, there are those dedicated to being nonconformist, committed to noncommitment, who discipline themselves to avoid a disciplined life. This book may confound them, for they do not understand discipline's place on the spiritual path. Ardent, convinced seekers must be tolerant and understanding of the woes and wants of less-disciplined souls. In the final analysis, it is up to each individual to cultivate soul qualities that are already resident within. This is done in a way similar to how a garden is nurtured along into bud, blossom and beauty. The weeds and harmful insects must somehow be kept away. There must be proper light and shade, water and sun. When conditions are right, the intended results manifest of their own accord. The teachings expounded in the pages of *Living with Śiva* and succinctly codified in the Nandinātha Sūtras are similar to what a gardener needs to know to raise his plants successfully, for the soul is a bud that blossoms, blooms and shines out its beauty, but only if the conditions are right.

Proceed with confidence. Don't look back. Fear not what others say or do. There is a new world tomorrow, and you are a vital part of it. The yesterdays cannot be adjusted or corrected until we meet them with a new attitude born of knowledge and wisdom in the tomorrows of our future. We are bound together by bands of steel, as are all worshipers of our Supreme Lord Śiva. Following the culture, protocols and admonitions found in *Living with Śiva* will keep this bondage happy and rewarding, thus avoiding the tugs and pulls of impropriety, thus averting the pitfalls of humanness which can so often bring pain and remorse.

We feel that anyone of any culture, creed or belief can benefit from reading *Living with Śiva,* and will in his or her heart of hearts recognize the valid wisdom herein that has matured through the millennia. We feel this book will be especially appreciated by the elders of all communities where a few families are the central, functioning hub, where the head of the family looks to his *kulaguru* for advice, to the family priest for ceremony and sacraments, where children are raised as dependents until fully matured, well educated to eventually inherit the family wealth to maintain the traditions, culture and proprieties as they have been dutifully taught.

Love and blessings to you from this and inner worlds,

Satguru Sivaya Subramuniyaswami
162nd Jagadāchārya of the Nandinātha
Sampradāya's Kailāsa Paramparā
Guru Mahāsannidhānam
Kauai Aadheenam, Hawaii
Satguru Pūrṇimā, July 4, 2001
Hindu year of Vṛisha, 5103

The Master Course

Pradhāna Pāṭhyakramaḥ

प्रधान पाठ्यक्रमः

DRAWN FROM A LIFETIME OF WISDOM GIVEN FORTH TO SATISFY THE THIRST OF THOUSANDS OF SEEKERS, *LIVING WITH ŚIVA, HINDUISM'S CONTEMPORARY CULTURE* IS THE SECOND BOOK OF A REMARKABLE TRILOGY. THE FIRST BOOK IS *DANCING WITH Śiva, Hinduism's Contemporary Catechism,* and the third is *Merging with Śiva, Hinduism's Contemporary Metaphysics.* These three make up a *Master Course* to be studied daily, 365 days a year. It was in 1957 that the first edition of *The Master Course* was developed to serve the needs of devotees who worshiped at our temple, the first Hindu temple in America. Since then it has taken many forms: as lessons for personal study, a correspondence course and a series of tape recordings, twelve in all, recorded in the Guru Pīṭham at Kauai Aadheenam in 1970. A beautiful children's course on the Śaivite religion came out of it in 1993; and now, in the year 2001, after two decades of effort, *The Master Course* has emerged in its final form as three textbooks, *Dancing with Śiva, Living with Śiva* and *Merging with Śiva,* each with 1,000 or more pages of information, insight and *sādhanas. The Master Course* trilogy is a detailed summary and explanation of *ashṭāṅga yoga* according to the traditions of our lineage, the Nandinātha Sampradāya's Kailāsa Paramparā. *Ashṭāṅga yoga,* also called *rāja yoga,* has eight successive steps, each one dependent upon the one that precedes it. These eight successive steps are *yama* (restraint), *niyama* (observance), *āsana* (posture), *prāṇāyāma* (breath control), *pratyāhāra* (sense withdrawal), *dhāraṇā* (concentration), *dhyāna* (meditation) and *samādhi* (contemplation).

Often the uninformed prefer to start on their spiritual path at steps seven and eight, ignoring the other six, and more than often wonder why no immediate and lasting results are obtained. Drawing upon over half a century of teaching and explaining, the trilogy articulates in no uncertain terms why you must begin at the beginning, with a firm foundation of philosophical clarity and good character, and proceed from there.

Dancing with Śiva, the first book of the trilogy, lays out the philosophical, Vedic-Āgamic beliefs, attitudes and expectations of the Śaivite Hindu religion, which are so necessary to understand, adopt and uphold in order to make true progress in the areas discussed in the other two books. *Living with Śiva,* the second book of the trilogy, concerns itself with Śaivite lifestyle, culture, family life, character-building and the overcoming of uncomplimentary habits that disturb others as well as oneself. It focuses on *yama, niyama* and, in a lesser way, *āsana* and *prāṇāyāma (haṭha yoga).* For the entire system of *ashṭāṅga yoga* to work, a firm philosophical-cultural foundation, as found in *Dancing with Śiva* and *Living with Śiva,* must be subconsciously accepted by the devotee as his own way of looking at and living life, relating it to experience, solving problems, approaching worship and so forth. *Merging with Śiva,* the third book of the trilogy, encompasses steps five, six and seven, leading to eight, all of which is personally experiential once we learn to dance with Śiva and live with Śiva. This means having a good philosophical understanding, a solid commitment, as well as good character, and living the religion. Upon such a foundation, the yogic and metaphysical experiences described in *Merging* come naturally and are sustainable.

The Master Course trilogy is a daily, lifetime study for my devotees worldwide to be explored year after year after year, generation after generation. Through great effort we have summarized this entire study of more than 3,000 pages into 365 Nandinātha Sūtras of four lines each that make up Part Four of *Living with Śiva. The Master Course* is a life-transforming study organized in 365 daily lessons. Devotees may begin at any time—and whatever time lesson one is begun is the most auspicious time—then continue right around the year until 365 lessons are complete. If you are ready to change your life, begin *The Master Course* today. If not, then perhaps tomorrow. There are three ways to study *The Master Course:* 1) Internet Study; 2) Home Study; and 3) Formal Correspondence Study.

1. INTERNET STUDY: The Internet Study can be begun immediately at any time. The current lesson of the day is found on the Internet at www.gurudeva.org in the *The Master Course* Daily Lesson section. Or you can receive it via e-mail by sending a message to gurudeva-mastercourse-subscribe@jnanadana.org The lessons begin on the first day of the Tamil calendar year, in mid-April, but can be commenced on any day during the year. You need not wait for day one of the year to roll around. Start with the current lesson, which might be number 132—and consider

your year complete when you reach lesson 131. You will find the lessons filled with philosophical, practical and soul-stirring information potent enough to inspire even a skeptic to change his ways of thinking about life and the ultimate goal of existence on this planet. Begin now. Today is the most auspicious time.

2. **HOME STUDY:** The Master Course Home Study requires the ownership of the three books of the trilogy. Begin your daily reading on any Monday with *Dancing with Śiva, śloka* one and its *bhāshya.* Then open *Living with Śiva* and read Lesson 1. Next, turn to the Nandinātha Sūtras in Part Four of *Living with Śiva* and read the first *sūtra.* Lastly, open *Merging with Śiva* and read the first lesson. Reading each day's lesson from the three books takes about twenty minutes. Because there are only 155 lessons *(ślokas* and *bhāshyas)* in *Dancing with Śiva,* when you complete lesson 155 of this book, begin again at the beginning. Then, when you complete the second reading, totalling 310 days, begin again with lesson one, and continue reading until lesson 55, to coincide with lesson 365 of *Living with Śiva* and *Merging with Śiva.* If you study these lessons each day for a year, you will have completed a profound *sādhana,* a personal odyssey into the interior of you and on into the depths of Hinduism, a practice sufficient to transform your life by transforming the way you look at life itself. *The Master Course* trilogy of *Dancing, Living* and *Merging with Śiva* can be enjoyed by the entire family year after year after year, studied personally and read aloud at breakfast, dinner or in the shrine room after the morning *pūjā.* Proceed with confidence and without delay.

3. **FORMAL CORRESPONDENCE STUDY:** The Master Course Correspondence Study is for those who seek a personalized, supervised approach. This is a service offered by Himalayan Academy since 1957. It requires formal enrollment and qualification, openly describing the goals one wishes to accomplish and the details of one's background, education and experience. Correspondent students are required to purchase the color edition of all three books. They have access to regular e-mail news reports, discounts on Innersearch Travel-Study Programs and special attention when visiting the monastery in Hawaii. E-mail mastercourse@hindu.org for more information.

A word of advice: There is a strong tendency when a student first begins meditation to want to give up external things, to give up work and devote more time to making his meditation the perfect thing. But this is not the spirit of *The Master Course.* Many more forces that are negative would result from his turning away from the world as possibly already occurred in his work in the exterior world prior to his ever hearing about meditation. The thrust of The Master Course Correspondence Study is to improve all aspects of one's life. Step one is for the student to prove to himself that he can work positively in the world, performing his duties with full energy, intuiting how the whole mechanism of life is constructed—the exterior world, his mind, himself. Then ten, fifteen or twenty minutes of good, dynamic meditation a day and *The Master Course* studies to guide the mind along in a step-by-step manner are more than sufficient. It comes down to readjusting our thinking and making our point of reference the reality within ourselves instead of the reality and permanence of the external world of things, forms and fancy. Once our whole philosophical structure is in line with Śaiva Siddhānta thinking, it is easy to throw the mind into meditation. Then when we are working in our daily life, involved in external things and material affairs, the point of reference is that the energy within and the core of the energy and the Self itself are real.

The key is to put more energy into each activity you are engaged in. Rather than renouncing it, really work at it. Put your whole self in it. Get enthusiastic about it. Then you are flooding more life force through the body, right from the center of life itself. Having the Self as a point of reality reference and not the material things, with the life force constantly flooding through these nerve currents, you are actually seeing what you are doing as part of the cosmic dance of Śiva, as the energy of Śiva flows in and through you. Through this practice you can cut through many of your deep-rooted subconscious hang-ups that were provoked in past lives without having them come to the surface, simply by creating a new habit pattern of facing and looking at yourself as a divine being performing your *dharma* in God Śiva's perfect universe. You create the new habit patterns by doing everything as best you can, with as much forethought and as much energy as you can command. This approach will bring steady progress on the path of personal spiritual realization and transformation. Write or e-mail us for an application to begin the supervised *sādhanas* of The Master Course Correspondence Study. We welcome you. It won't be easy, but anything worthwhile is not easy.

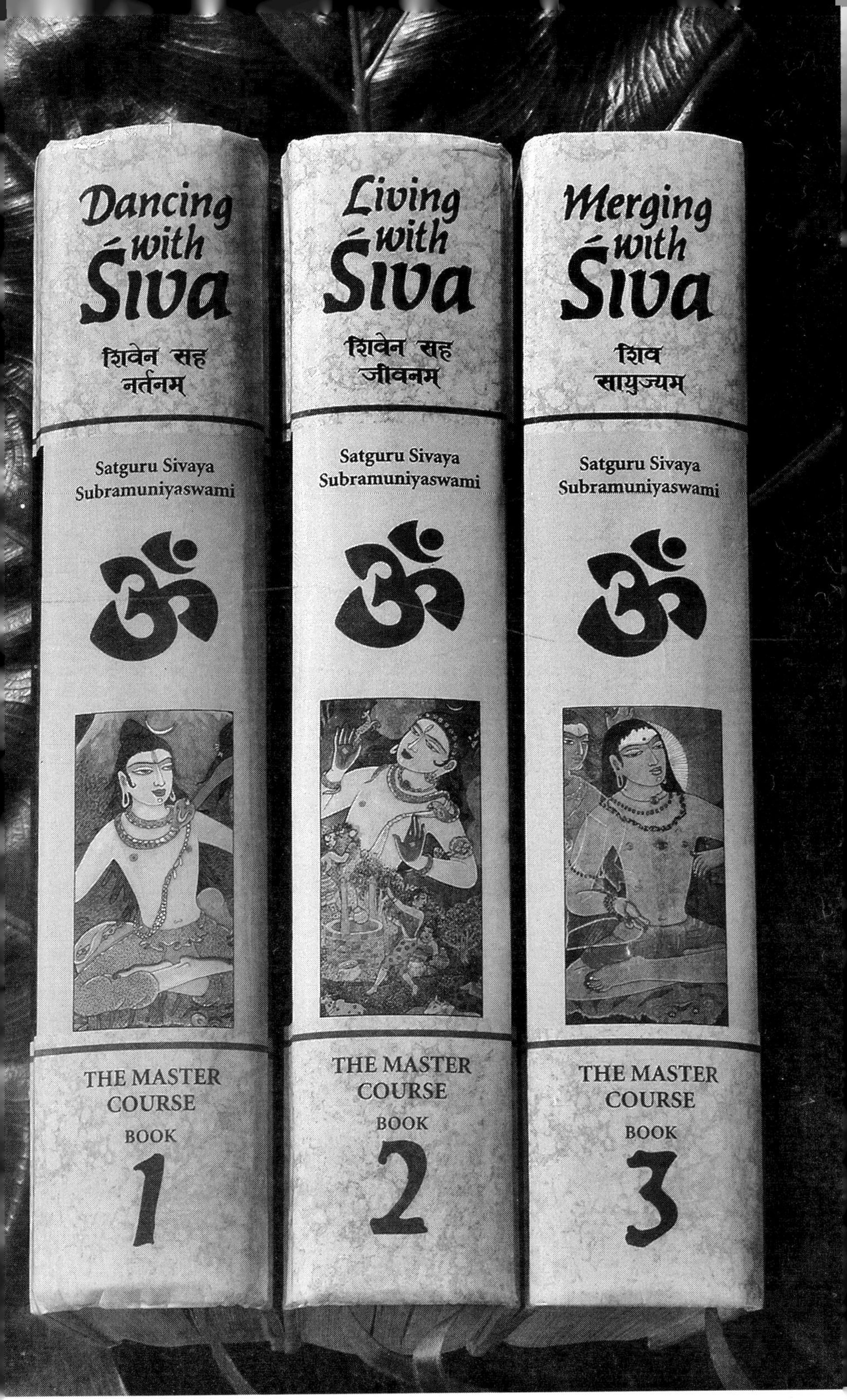
Dancing with Śiva
शिवेन सह नर्तनम्
Satguru Sivaya Subramuniyaswami
THE MASTER COURSE
BOOK
1
Living with Śiva
शिवेन सह जीवनम्
Satguru Sivaya Subramuniyaswami
THE MASTER COURSE
BOOK
2
Merging with Śiva
शिव सायुज्यम्
Satguru Sivaya Subramuniyaswami
THE MASTER COURSE
BOOK
3

Hindu Family Life

Hindu Gṛihastha Dharmaḥ

हिन्दूगृहस्थधर्मः

LEADERS OF THE UNITED NATIONS DEDICATED 1994 AS THE INTERNATIONAL YEAR OF THE FAMILY. THEY WERE SEEKING TO COUNTER A GLOBAL FAILURE OF THE FAMILY UNIT AND THE BY-PRODUCTS OF SUCH A BREAKDOWN: CRIME, DELINQUENT YOUTH, DISobedient children, divorce and other household miseries, in other words the basic problems of social instability. They decided to inquire of the major religions of the world as to what their views were and are today on family life, all planned for a multi-lingual United Nations publication, *Family Issues as Seen by Different Religions,* a unique vision of family from the point of view of Jews, Christians, Muslims, Buddhists, Hindus and Baha'is. The UN approached us at Hinduism Today magazine to define and describe the traditional family values of the Hindu. They also asked us to describe, honestly, the difficulties Hindus face and how the Sanātana Dharma is helping families in these difficult times. In creating the Hindu chapter to the UN book, we joined forces with two of our Hinduism Today correspondents, Archana Dongre of Los Angeles and Lavina Melwani of New York. Their comments provide the "voices" of personal experience interspersed throughout the text. We are happy to include the resulting article here as an apt prologue to *Living with Śiva.*

The Hindu View of Family

Here, now, are voices of Hindus sharing their vision of family. Not as family was lived by their ancestors for three-hundred generations (Hindu family history extends beyond most, 6,000 years and more). Here we encounter the Hindu experience as it exists today in many nations, under agreeable circumstances and adverse. Here we broadly survey threats to family integrity in the Hindu community. Then we summon the spiritual

Satguru Sivaya Subramuniyaswami speaks to 1,200 spiritual leaders at the United Nations Millennium Peace Summit in New York on August 25, 2000. He asked all to "Stop the war in the home." Gurudeva holds his UN U Thant Peace Award.

values which continue to sustain the traditional household and offer a pledge of well-being for family members and a promise of perpetuation of cultural ways and wisdoms.

Hindu families all over the world are struggling—some failing, most succeeding. Our experience is that those most rooted in their Hinduness cope better and are the better survivors. Hindu households, sheltering one-sixth of the human race, are being threatened. What if the concept of family itself were dying? What if the very institution, the cauldron of our cultural and spiritual consciousness, were struck by some fatal disease and perished? Who could measure such a tragedy? Who could weep sufficient tears? Yet, that is precisely the path which we are semiconsciously following, a path leading to the demise of the traditional Hindu family, the source of our strength, the patron of our spirituality, the sole guarantor of our future.

Is it our fault that the family is disintegrating? Perhaps. Does it portend uncertainty? Be certain that it does. Is it inevitable? Probably not. A final eulogy for the Hindu family may be premature. Yet this appraisal of problems may usefully be taken as a warning, a glimpse of the future in the making that all must heed so none may have to face it. With that in mind, let us embark on an exploration of some of the Hindu family's truly remarkable strengths, some of the most destructive forces arrayed against it and some of the hopeful signs we have seen of its ability to survive.

A typical case in point: Ramesh is a 25-year-old man from Bangalore, studying engineering in the US. While at the university, he fell in love with an American student and would soon marry her. The mother and father were torn apart by their only son's decision to marry an "outsider." To them it was the undoing of centuries of continuity, a break in the stream of tradition, a social calamity. Their friends would not understand. Their life would surely change. Their grandchildren would "be different" in color, in caste, in culture. Furthermore, the new wife came from another faith, and the couple declared, "We plan to raise our children in both faiths and allow them to make their own choices as young adults." To the strict-casted parents, this was not a welcome sign of interfaith harmony. Rather, it was a warning signal ringing to mourn a break in their lineage, a potential loss of their grandchildren to another religion, another country, another culture.

There are countless Rameshes and their female counterparts scattered about the globe. They are part of a growing Hindu diaspora which has brought with it the very real threat that many families may not persist, that in one or two generations all that Ramesh's grandfather knew and hoped to pass on would have been discarded and in its place would be other values or no values, other beliefs or disbeliefs, other ideals, ideologies and histories. This is a serious concern of millions of families, especially those living in the West or in urban India. The Hindu community in Texas told me that eighty percent of its young women are marrying outside of the Indian tradition, outside of Hinduism.

Or, consider this: Shanti was raised in America as an American, but her parents were from India. They used to go visiting there when she was young, but not anymore. Shanti is not comfortable leaving her American friends to go to a place where she feels she no longer fits in. At the same time, she feels bad for her father and mother and does not want to hurt them. In her Texas community, Shanti is frequently mistaken as Hispanic and has been dating a Mexican American named Juan. One day Shanti suddenly announced, "Father, I have met someone, and he is wonderful. We are going to get married." Father was startled. He yelled, "You are? Just like that? Married? How long have you been seeing that guy?" Shanti answered, "Well, I have been meaning to tell you, it's been over a year." The father said, "We had always agreed that you would marry an Indian boy of good breeding, from a proper family and caste." "But, Daddy, Juan and I love each other," Shanti cried and ran off to her room. She could be heard weeping softly. Her father sat in a dejected mood. His life was shattered. He knew only too well what was to come!

The Western materialistic goal is personal fulfillment, while the Eastern religious ideal is fulfillment of duty—duty to one's parents, one's society and one's country, which includes tradition. But when the children of Eastern families are raised up with Western values, personal fulfillment overrides duty, passion overrides society, personal freedom overrides tradition and sometimes even country.

Voices: *My grandma never tired of reminding us that the Hindu religion always glorified sacrifice. It was considered heroic to make sacrifice for the family members. Hindu epics like* Rāmāyaṇa *and* Mahābhārata *purport that even great beings like Lord Rāma and noble kings like the Paṇḍavas had to endure trying circumstances and make sacrifices. "So what's wrong if ordinary folks had to make some sacrifices?" she would say. Parents often make great sacrifices to give* *a good education to their children. Many Hindu parents have gone hungry to afford quality education for their children. The children in turn curtail their freedom and luxury when parents grow old and infirm and need support from the younger generation. A Hindu never pities a sacrifice, but glorifies it with appreciation. Grandma made a big point to us about hospitality. She took it as a spiritual duty to serve guests as if they were God. This helped a lot in tying her community together and gave the family a loving way to greet the outside world. If a guest comes to a family, even unannounced, he is invited in warmly and asked about his well being. He is also served the best food in the house, even to the extent that family members may go hungry to ensure that the guest is well fed. Hinduism taught us the love of all living creatures. At lunch time, my mother would say a silent prayer and set aside a portion to be fed to the cows. If a hungry man came to the door at mealtime, he was fed and given a few coins.*

It is now too late for the parents to say no to the Shantis and Rameshes who are driven by youthful emotions, know little about their religion and are impelled to live in a land where sex is a symbol of prowess, independence and esteem. Of course, Shanti and Ramesh did not want to hurt their parents, but they both did so nonetheless. Their parents are hurting and so are relatives and friends. These moms and dads will continue to hurt until they realize that they, without realizing it, relinquished their parental authority somewhere in the process of raising their children. Shanti did marry Juan, but not without a lot of trouble, almost too much for her to bear. First, mother threatened suicide. Her brother started a fast, though it ended at breakfast a few days later. Dad all but ordered her out of the house, but stopped short because he really did love her. Slowly, the parents adjusted, a quiet marriage took place, and with the first child came a softening of feelings.

Unlike Ramesh's wife, Shanti's husband was not affiliated with any religion. Because of this, he took great pride in attending the *nāmakāraṇa*, name-giving sacrament, for his first child. It was a boy! Her grandparents came from India, and his from Iowa, and all oo'd and awe'd over the beautiful child. Yes, the resulting family was different than all had expected, but as one insightful youth confronted his parents, "If you didn't want me to become an American, why did you bring me to the States?"

There are over 32,000 Indian nationals attending universities in the US today. Many are from wealthy families and know little about their religion, even though their parents may know quite a lot. This is what happened to Shanti and Ramesh. They know more about rock-and-roll, modern art and pop superstars than most Westerners, because they are struggling to fit in. Hindu families continue to leave Indian, Sri Lankan, Nepalese and other homelands for political, economic and educational reasons. Then, deprived of traditional support systems, they are faced with profoundly disturbing problems: teenage crises, violent games, divorce, abortion, suicide, mothers-in-law, dowry, drugs, free sex, paid sex, pornography and the growing challenges of cross-national marriages like those of Ramesh and Shanti.

> ***Voices:*** *Growing up a Hindu in India, I found that pleasure and pilgrimage, religious rituals and daily life were intricately intertwined. My earliest memories are of sitting with the aged family cook, listening to tales from the* Rāmāyaṇa *and* Mahābhārata. *Listening spell-bound to tales of demons and* devas, *we absorbed the values of right and wrong, good and evil. Religion was always associated with joy and pleasure, never moralistic teaching. Every weekend we were taken to the beautiful sandstone Birla Mandir—cold marble below bare feet, the softness of the marigolds and rose petals in our hands, the smiling faces of Kṛishṇa, Śiva and Vishṇu, the harmonium and cymbals and the sheer faith of hundreds of devotees. Afterwards, there were joy rides in the temple complex, trinkets and holy pictures and a cold soda. For us, it was a spiritual Disney World.*

Hindus are not free of the crimes of abuse to women and children. There are thousands of reported cases each year of not just wife abuse, but of what are called dowry murders. These are cases where a wife is killed, frequently by burning to make it appear to be a kitchen accident, when she cannot procure more dowry. Children, too, are needing better protection in many Hindu communities, from physical battering, sexual abuse, forced labor, verbal badgering from parents and fellow students, and corporal punishment at home and in school. And the selective abortion of female fetuses is still practiced in cultures where male children are preferred for economic and cultural reasons. These problems seriously threaten the Hindu family in many nations and must be addressed in the decade ahead.

***Voices:** Where I grew up, mothers ruled the house, even though they did not go out in the olden days to earn. Sisters were respected and given gifts on at least two religious occasions. The rituals like Rāksha Bandhan and Bhau Bīj are woven around pure love between a brother and a sister and bonding of that relationship. In the former, the sister ties a specially made bracelet around her brother's wrist requesting him to protect her if need be, and in the latter, the sister does* ārati *(a worshipful expression of love and devotion through a tiny lighted* ghee *lamp) to her brother, wishing him long life and prosperity. The brother gives her gifts and sweets on both occasions. The Hindu religious principles emphasize that women should be respected. A Sanskrit saying goes, "Yātrā naryāstu pūjyante, ramante tatra devatah." It means that wherever the women are honored, those are the places where even the Gods rejoice.*

How is the Hindu concept of family experienced differently from that of other faiths? Only in the faiths of India does one encounter the tenet that we all experience a multitude of families in our journey toward God.. In birth after birth we evolve, our tradition assures. In family after family we grow and mature and learn. Thus, in the Hindu family we find that the past and the future are intricately bound together. How intricately? We know a Sri Lankan family who is certain that their daughter, now nine, is the father's deceased grandmother. In this community it is considered a very great blessing—especially if one has the privilege of being part of a fine, noble family—for a departed relative to be born again into its midst. There is a profound intuition that when relatives pass they will return, perhaps soon and perhaps in the very same home. So, everyone watches for the telltale signs. How wonderful, the family feels, to care for grandma as she once cared for us!

Thus, the spiritual insight into rebirth extends the family concept beyond the present, binding the present to the past, and promising further continuity with the future. Many Hindu families are aware of such relationships. Many others will consciously seek to be born into a particular family, knowing that life there will be fulfilling, secure and high-minded.

***Voices:** When a married daughter visits her parents' family, she is revered like a guest but showered with love like a daughter, with blessings and all the nice clothes as well as food the family can give. I had* *such a wonderful homecoming in India after I had lived for many years in the West. Such a homecoming of a few days is an emotionally gratifying, soul-satisfying event for the girl, who carries those fond memories for life.*

As an example of the ability of spiritual commitment to help families endure and do well, consider the experience of Saiva Siddhanta Church, our relatively small but widespread international Hindu fellowship. For every 500 families who are devout, practicing members of the fellowship, there have been only two divorces in the last forty years! In the US, the norm would have been forty percent, fully 200 fractured families. What kept those 198 families together when statistically they should have disintegrated? In my fifty years of ministry and counseling among Hindu families, I have concluded that it is their faith, their shared spiritual experience and goals, their ideals. Husbands and wives will stay together when they believe the rewards and human potentials are greater than if they split. And they will remain a kindred unit even more often when their joint or extended family is open to advice and counsel from one tradition, when they are firmly committed to one guru, one temple and one body of scripture.

Hinduism teaches a constellation of principles which, if followed by husband and wife, make the bold assertion that preserving the marriage and the integrity of the family holds rewards that far outweigh benefits they might expect from separation. We work with families on a daily basis, solving their problems, helping them to individually follow their path and to mutually work together. Hinduism teaches them the ideals of *dharma*, which includes duty, selflessness, virtue and faith. When *dharma* is the shared ideal of every family member—as opposed to self-fulfillment or social-economic objectives—it is easier to navigate troubled waters, easier to persist in seasons of loss or lack, in times of emotional or mental difficulty.

Voices: *Looking back to my early years, it was the scriptures that tied our family together. I would hear father and grandfather chanting the Vedic mantras together in the early hours of each day. Everyone I know held the highest esteem for the* Vedas, *the very voice of God, elders would say. I knew they were old, and everyone said they were profound. But it was not until I was in my teens that I really discov-*

ered the Upanishads. *Such beauty, such profundity, such humor and insight I had never before or since known. I would spend hours with the texts, talking with my parents and friends, wondering myself how these men, so many thousands of years ago, had gained all that wisdom—more, it seemed to me then, than people had today. Through the years I have seen so many families whose lives revolve around the sacred texts. While all honor the* Vedas, *for some the heart is moved by the* Gītā, *the epics, the* Tirumurai *or maybe their own family guru's writings composed only decades ago. Whatever texts they are, it's quite clear in my experience that sacred texts do much to bind a family together in thought.*

Then there is faith in *karma.* The Hindu family believes, in its heart, that even life's difficulties are part of God's purpose and the fruition of each member's past *karmas.* To go through things together is natural, expected, accepted. Breaking up, divorcing, separating—such reactions to stress don't resolve *karmas* that were brought into this life to go through. In fact, they make things worse, create new, unseemly *karmas* and thus further need for perhaps even more sorrowful births. The belief in *karma*—the law by which our thoughts, words and deeds reap their natural reactions—helps hold a family together, not unlike the crew of a storm-tossed ship would never think of jumping overboard when the going gets rough, but work together to weather the crisis, with their shared goal lying beyond the immediate difficulty.

Thus, difficult experiences can be serenely endured by the practicing Hindu. Knowing this in her heart, a Hindu wife in Kuala Lumpur can find solace in the midst of the death of a child. Knowing this in his heart, a Hindu father in Bangalore can sustain periods of privation and business failure. Each finds the strength to go on.

Voices: *There is a beautiful word in the Hindi language,* shukur, *which means acceptance. Sometimes it's very hard to accept the cards life deals one, yet the Hindu belief in the acceptance of God's will makes it possible to bear incredible hardships. A young friend of my husband went into a coma after going in for preventive surgery. They gave him too much chloroform, and he never came out of the coma. He was a young man, his children were young. In the beginning his wife was frantic, weeping all the time. Yet, her beliefs were solid as a* *rock within her, gradually calming her. It's now five years later, and she's picked up the pieces of her life. Yet she never forgets to have her* pūjās; *her husband's picture is always there in the ritual ceremonies. His presence is there in the family. She seems to know that the soul cannot die, that his spirit lives on. Every year on his death anniversary we all gather for the ritual ceremonies. Everybody feels the grief, and each religion teaches you to cope in a different way. Her belief in the undying soul gives her a little solace. She constantly has the prayers and the* satsaṅgas *at home, and they help her in the changing patterns of her life.*

There are many other ideals that help a family survive in Hinduism. An important one is that father and mother are the children's first *guru*, first teacher of things of the spirit. This brings a deep honoring to the parent-child relationship. Such a tie transcends the physical, emotional, intellectual relationship that is the sum of some family bonds. It brings an air of sacredness into the interactions, a deeper reverencing which powerfully connects a daughter or son to his mother and father. One sees this expressed so beautifully in the traditional family when young ones gently and lovingly touch the feet of their parents. They are worshiping the Divine in their parents and thus being prepared to see God in everyone.

In the strict Hindu family there is a clear and well-understood hierarchy, based fundamentally on age. Younger members are taught to respect and follow the directions from their elders, and to cherish and protect those younger than themselves. Even differences of a few months are respected. Many problems that could arise in less structured families—and do, as proven in the modern nuclear family—simply never come up. There is less vying for attention, less ego conflict, less confusion about everyone's role and place. With the lines of seniority known to all, regulations, changes and cooperative exchanges flow freely among family members.

Voices: *In the family life, today as well as in the times when Indian epics like* Mahābhārata *and* Rāmāyaṇa *were written, thousands of years ago, a Hindu was told, "Mātṛidevo bhava," "Pitṛidevo bhava" and "Āchāryadevo bhava." The Sanskrit dictums mean, "Be the one who respects his mother as God, his father as God and his guru or teacher as God." Such an ultimate reverence for the elders creates a* *profound, serene feeling and certainly prepares the mind to receive the good and loving advice from them in the proper spirit. Bowing down before the elders in respectful salutation and touching their feet is an exclusively Hindu custom. When such a deep respect is accorded to family members, no wonder the family bonds are strong and they remain unified.*

Daily worship in the home is a unique Hindu contribution to family sharing. Of course, faith is a shared experience in all religious households. But the Hindu takes it a step further, sanctifying the home itself with a beautiful shrine room—a kind of miniature temple right in the house. The father or oldest son is the family's liturgist, leading others in daily ritual. Others care for the sacred implements, gather fresh flowers for the morning rites and decorate for holy days or festivals. In Hindu culture, family and spirituality are intimately intertwined.

***Voices:** Every Hindu family in our village had a home shrine where the family members worship their Gods. Even the poorest set aside a place for this. Rituals are periodic celebrations which are religious and spiritual in character, and they address the inward feelings rather than outward. Such* pūjās *and rituals give an individual a chance to pause, look inward and concentrate on something more meaningful, more profound, than mere materialism and the daily drudgery of life. Worships and rejoicings in the name of God, fasting and observances of special days enable people to look beyond the day-to-day life to a larger scheme of things. In the best homes I know, the father performs the rites daily, and the family joins and assists. I guess it's like the old adage, "The family that prays together stays together." Even in the busy rat race of life in cosmopolitan cities like Mumbai or Los Angeles, there are many Hindus who perform at least a mini* pūjā *daily. They claim that even the small ritual of a few minutes a day makes them concentrate, feel elevated spiritually, brings their minds on an even keel, enabling them to perform better in their line of work.*

Another family tradition is the *kulaguru.* Though it is not required that every member of a Hindu family have the same *guru,* it often happens that way. This gives all members a shared spiritual point of reference, a voice whose wisdom will be sought in times of decision, difference or unclarity, a voice that will also be listened to, its advice followed. That means that there is a kind of outside counselor, a mediator to work out deadlocks, a referee to arbitrate and settle disputes. Thus, the family need never be stuck in some irresolvable impasse. The *kulaguru's* counsel can be trusted to transcend the personalities involved, to be impersonal and just. And that simple practice can bring a family through many a quandary.

> ***Voices:*** *The greatest beauty of Hinduism, for me at least, is that it's such an elastic religion. Thousands of years old, with scores of detailed rituals and* mantras *and texts, hundreds of holy days and fasts, countless Gods and Goddesses and saints, Hinduism still can be as young and uncomplicated as each individual wants it to be. It's really more a state of mind. You don't have to be a very ritualistic Hindu. Although having a* guru *or guide is the accepted way of reaching God, Hinduism allows you to follow your own path. You feel you can talk straight to God. When I go in the morning to drop my children to school, and there is no one in the car to hear me, I sing devotional songs at the top of my voice. At those moments, I feel I'm communicating straight to God. Many people feel it's essential to have a* guru *to show one the path to heaven, yet others feel they can deal directly with God, without any middlemen. It's very elastic. It's a well from which you can drink and replenish your creativity. It's a very loving relationship. One day if I don't light the incense, I feel God will understand. We do these rituals to please ourselves that we are serving God. Hinduism is a guiltless religion—God will forgive and He will understand because He knows what's in your heart. There is no fire and brimstone and no punishment. It's liquid love and forgiveness.*

Hindu heritage gives a strong definition to the growth and maturing of family members, through the application of the *āśramas.* Every member in a family is expected to spend the first twenty-four years or so in the *brahmacharya,* or student, stage. It's a time of learning, studying, serving and growing up. Then comes the stage of the *gṛihastha,* or householder, and with it marriage, children and social responsibilities. These stages are informally defined in nearly every culture, but in Hinduism the definitions are elaborately detailed beyond raising the family. Sometime around fifty, every member enters the *vānaprastha āśrama,* a stage of advisor and elder. By formalizing this stage, the Hindu family gives a place of prominence and usefulness to its senior citizens. They do not just retire, and they certainly are not sent off to a retirement home. Rather, their advice is sought, their years of experience drawn upon. Thus, Hinduism gives a place to those who have served the family in their youth but, with age, can no longer serve in that same way. They have a new place. Far from being a lesser function, it is a place of greater honor. This is one of the greatest gifts that the traditional Hindu family offers, thus averting one of the greatest tragedies: depriving elders of due recognition.

> ***Voices:*** *My mother-in-law, right up till she died in her seventies, was the head of the household. She could do anything with my children, and I wouldn't have the guts to tell her no. She would put* kohl, *mascara, adorning their eyes and oil in their hair and their eyes would be black and their hair greasy, but I wouldn't say anything to her. She would bribe the kids with candy, and they loved her for it. It's a loving relationship because you do something for someone and they do something for you. The blessings do come on you because she felt very wanted and happy. She taught me the sanctity of the family unit and respect for elders.*

Dowry is another threat to the Hindu family. Its economic and social costs are extraordinary, weighing down the wage-earner in a way hardly to be believed. Many Hindus have abandoned the practice of dowry on moral grounds, but the vast majority follow its well-worn ways. Take the case of Vasanti, a village girl in India. Her father, Ravi, told me of his lot—five daughters, all requiring huge dowries if they are to enjoy a good marriage, which roughly translates to buying a good husband. Even families that see the wrongfulness of the practice will seldom diminish demands for their sons, for they fear others in the community will presume something must be wrong with the boy if his price is nominal. Ravi tells of how he and his wife have scrimped and saved for nearly twenty-five years, gone without many things so that their daughters could have a good life. No vacations for them. No car. No new clothes not absolutely needed. Ravi works two jobs, and saves each month more than some of his associates make, for each of his five daughters will require over 50,000 rupees, more than a year's salary. Many Hindu families are bent and even broken by this social burden. Hindus reflecting on the future of the family tradition will be well advised to curb this onerous custom.

> ***Voices:** A daughter is pampered and protected, not necessarily spoiled, in a traditional Hindu family. She is married and sent to a suitable family with whatever gold jewelry and other assets her family can afford. In the old days, the dowry was not something to be forced, but was considered an honor to give. The Hindu rules of conduct also stated that women always deserved protection from men.* Manu Smṛiti, *an ancient treatise on religion and householder's duties, said, "Pita rakshati kaumare, bharta raskshati youvana, putraḥ rakshati varddhakye, na strī svatantryam arhati." "A woman is protected by father in childhood, her husband protects her in youth, and in old age she should be protected by her son. At no stage in life should a woman be left alone and destitute." She deserves protection by man at every stage in her life. When women are cared for, they can perform well their roles of creators, nourishers, educators of children and inspirers, so the society becomes happy.*

It is significant that Hindus, numbering over one billion today, constitute sixteen percent of the human race. One out of every six people on the planet is a Hindu. So, the ability of that large community to preserve its strengths, to pass on its values and cultural treasures, to protect its members and keep them well and fulfilled is important. Important does not suffice. Crucial, really. On the optimistic side, as much as eighty percent of Hindus live in rural India, in the 700,000 small villages which remain less affected by outside influences and thus retain the promise of carrying on the traditional ways, including language, religion and custom. As all the foregoing amply indicates, the Hindu concept of family is unique in many ways. The very definition, a rich one, is highly informative for those seeking to better comprehend the interactions of family members. Here's a detailed definition from *Dancing with Śiva, Hinduism's Contemporary Catechism:*

Joint family: *kuṭumba* or *kula.* The Hindu social unit consisting of several generations of kindred living together under the same roof or in a joining compound. Traditionally, joint families live in a large single home, but in modern times accommodations are often in individual, nuclear homes within a shared compound. The joint family includes the father and mother, sons, grandsons and great-grandsons with their spouses, as well as the daughters, granddaughters and great-granddaughters until they are married—thus often comprising several married couples and their children. The head of the joint family, called *kuṭumba mukhya* (also *mukhya* or *kartṛi*), is the father, supported by the mother, and in his absence, the elder son, guided by his mother and supported by his spouse. From an early age, the eldest son is given special training by his father to assume this future responsibility as head of the family. In the event of the father's death, sacred law does allow for the splitting of the family wealth between the sons. Division of family assets may also be necessary in cases where sons are involved in different professions and live in different towns, when there is an inability for all to get along under one roof, or when the family becomes unmanageably large. The main characteristics of the joint family are that its members 1) share a common residence, 2) partake of food prepared in the same kitchen, 3) hold their property in common and, 4) ideally, profess the same religion, sect and *sampradāya.* Each individual family of husband, wife and children is under the guidance of the head of the joint family. All work together unselfishly to further the common good. Each joint family extends out from its home to include a second level of connections as an "extended family."

Extended family: *bṛihatkuṭumba* or *mahākuṭumba.* One or more joint families plus their broader associations and affiliations. Unlike the joint family, whose members live in close proximity, the extended family is geographically widespread. The extended family is headed by the patriarch, called *bṛihatkuṭumba pramukha* (or *mukhya*), recognized as the leader by each joint family. He, in turn is under the guidance of the *kulaguru,* or family preceptor. It includes the following, in order of their precedence: priests of one's faith; elder men and women of the community; in-laws of married daughters; married daughters, granddaughters, great-granddaughters, and the spouses and children of these married girls; members of the staff and their families and those closely associated with the joint family business or home; maternal great-grandparents and grandparents, parents, uncles and their spouses, aunts and their spouses, children and grandchildren of these families; very close friends and their children; members of the community at large.

There is a more cosmic definition taught by every grandma and village elder, that in truth all of us on Earth are the creation of the One Great God; thus, in the broadest sense, we belong to a single family. *Vasudhaiva kuṭumbakam*—"The whole world is one family." That's not an innovative notion derived from New Age insights or Gaia ecology. It's been part of Indian folk culture for thousands of years.

Voices: I was always taught that we as Hindus must have a magnanimous attitude, that our Hindu religion visualizes the entire Earth as one family. But while looking at all human beings as one family, I also saw that elders deeply considered the smaller family unit, the dynamism of its members' relationships with one another, and the pivotal role the institution of family plays in building the society.

Leaving the womb, we enter another complex system of support, protection and nurturing. The family is an intricate web of relationships in which we grow from birth to maturity and old age, from ignorance to knowledge and from the cycles of death to immortality.

For World Peace, Stop the War in the Home

A talk given by Satguru Sivaya Subramuniyaswami to 1,200 delegates at the United Nations Millennium Peace Summit of Religious and Spiritual Leaders in New York, August 30, 2000. A few days earlier, on August 25, in the Dag Hammarskjöld Auditorium Gurudeva received the prestigious U Thant Peace Award.

I WAS ASKED BY THE UNITED NATIONS LEADERS HOW HUMANITY MIGHT BETTER RESOLVE THE CONFLICTS, HOSTILITIES AND VIOLENT HAPPENINGS THAT PLAGUE EVERY NATION. MY ANSWER WAS THAT WE MUST WORK AT THE SOURCE AND CAUSE, not with the symptoms. That is what we do in *ayurvedic* medicine—focus on the causes, on establishing the body's natural balance and health. That way we are not always working with illness and disease; we are spending time and resources instead to establish a healthy system that itself fights off sickness.

To stop the wars in the world, our best long-term solution is to stop the war in the home. It is here that hatred begins, that animosities with those who are different from us are nurtured, that battered children learn to solve their problems with violence. This is true of every religious community. Not one is exempt.

In Asia, in the United States and among Hindus all over the world, there's a war going on in every home. Few homes are exempt from the beating of children. This is a global problem, in all communities, but I believe that Hindus have the power to change it because our philosophy supports a better way. If we can end the war in our homes, then perhaps we can be an example to others and this will lead to ending war in the world. People will choose a different path.

In our homes when we strike our children, we teach everybody to beat everybody else, and the beating goes on, right on down the line, until they are a soldier or a gang member or rebel, and then they are fighting to kill. That's how all the religious wars have trained religious people to create the wars and to disturb the planet. The hitting and the hurting begin in the home. We should all be vowed to bring peace into the homes and stop the war within the home. Why? Because our neighborhoods and communities will not come up, the nation will not come up, the world will not come up until there is harmony within the home, until problems are solved before bedtime, until children are not abused and pushed down into fear, into a condition where they've lost all self-respect.

The children are amazingly intelligent these days, different than twenty or thirty years ago. These bright children are watching television. They see on TV that those people whom people like are loved and hugged, appreciated, lifted up, and nice things are said to them. They see on TV that other people whom people do not like, that they hate, are put down, told they're stupid, made to feel they're worthless and no good, they're hit and sometimes maimed or killed. Therefore, children will know with the first slap that they are hated, no longer wanted. Where are they to go? They can't, at a young age, go make a living. They can't run away from home, though some of them do and join gangs which will give them the only belonging, the only love and friendship that they have, to share their suffering with other people who have been suffering because of parental abuse, verbal abuse and physical abuse.

Sadly, in this day and age, beating the kids is just a way of life in many families. Nearly everyone was beaten a little as a child, so they beat their kids, and their kids will beat their kids, and those kids will beat their kids. Older brothers will beat younger brothers. Brothers will beat sisters. You can see what families are creating in this endless cycle of violence: little warriors. One day a war will come up, and it will be easy for a young person who has been beaten without mercy to pick up a gun and kill somebody without conscience, and even take pleasure in doing so.

I've had Hindus tell me, "Slapping or caning children to make them obey is just part of our culture." I don't think so. Hindu culture is a culture of kindness. Hindu culture teaches *ahiṁsā*, noninjury, physically, mentally and emotionally. It preaches against *hiṁsā*, hurtfulness. It may be British Christian culture—which for 150 years taught Hindus in India the Biblical adage, "Spare the rod and spoil the child"—but it's not Hindu culture to beat the light out of the eyes of children, to beat the trust out of them, to beat the intelligence out of them and force them to go along with everything in a mindless way and wind up doing a routine, uncreative job the rest of their life, then take their built-up anger out on their children and beat that generation down to nothingness. This is certainly not the culture of an intelligent future. It is a culture that will perpetuate every kind of hostility.

In some Asian countries, if children ask a question, they're answered with a slap across the face. How brutal can people be? These are mean people, vicious people. The working mother slaps her children at home when they add stress to her already stressed-out nerve system. Father has a tough day on the job and takes it out on his son's back or face with the hand, strap or cane. Does it give him a sadistic joy to hear young children cry in pain? Does it enhance his feeling of "I'm in charge here! You are not!"? How do I know all this is happening inside the Hindu home? Hotmail. Young kids are getting into Hotmail. They all have their own account. They all have their own computer, and they are writing to me, "Gurudeva! Gurudeva! My father beats me and I'm beaten in school and if I tell anybody I'm beaten in school my mother will strike me. At least three to five times a week, a knock on the head, a pinch, a cane across the back or the legs."

Is this the way of tomorrow? We hope not. But this is the way of today. It can be corrected by all of you going forth to bring peace within every family and every home, no matter what faith you belong to. If you know about the crime of a beating of a child or a wife, you are party to that crime unless you do something to protect that wife or to protect that child. Similarly, if you are driving with a friend in the car and he says, "Stop at this service station. I'm going into the convenience store." You stop and he goes into the convenience store, pulls out a gun, robs that store and jumps back into the car, you are an accomplice to the crime, whether you know it or not. You're an accomplice to the crime. All of a sudden, you become a criminal, unless you do something about it. That is taking on spiritual responsibility.

So, knowing that so much child abuse is happening behind a wall of silence, what do we do? Call one of our attorneys, call one of our missionary families and say, "Call the police. Have them watch this family very closely, to protect this child." We had one child put in a foster home and the father put in jail. He took the discipline a little too far. The child had burns all over his body, plus scars from earlier beatings. How do we know? Pictures were taken and sent to us by someone who cared enough not to ignore what was happening. In Canada, the teachers in school tell Asian kids, "If your parents hit you, you call this number." It happens to be 911. The police come to the house. Canadians want to stop the war in their homes.

In the past 85 years we've had two world wars and hundreds of smaller ones. Killers come from among those who have been beaten. The slap and pinch, the sting of the paddle, the lash of the strap, the blows of a cane must manifest through those who receive them into the lives of others. But there is a price to pay. The abuser one day becomes the abused. This is a law of life seen manifesting every day. It is called *karma.* Action gives an equal or more intense reaction, depending on the intent and the emotion behind it. Corporal punishment is arguably a prelude to gangs on the streets, those who will riot on call, and others who suffer in silence and hide behind a desk or in a routine profession, fearing reprimand and punishment, never talking back or offering an opinion.

We do know a few families who have never beaten their children or disciplined them physically in any way. We ask them "Why? "They say, "Because we love our children. We love them." "So, how do you train them; how do you discipline them?" "Well, we have them go into the shrine room and sit for ten minutes and think over what they did wrong, and they come back and we talk to them. We communicate. We encourage them to do better rather than making them feel worse." Then we ask, "What about TV? Aren't your kids watching TV all the time?" "No. We can't watch a lot of TV with children. Personal time with them is our family's way."

Holding the family together can be summed up in one word: *love.* Love is understanding. Love is acceptance. Love is making somebody feel good about his experience, whether the experience is a good one or not. Love is giving the assurance that there is no need to keep secrets, no matter what has happened. Love is wanting to be with members of the family. When harmony persists in the home, harmony abides in the community, and harmony exists in the country. When love and trust is in the family, love and trust extend to the local community, and if enough homes have this harmony among members, the entire country becomes stronger and more secure.

Sānanda Nartanam

सानन्द नर्तनम्

PART ONE

Dancing Joyously

Sarvatra Śivam Paśya
सर्वत्र शिवम् पश्य

See God Everywhere

He who knows God as the Life of life, the Eye of the eye, the Ear of the ear, the Mind of the mind, he indeed comprehends fully the Cause of all causes.

Śukla Yajur Veda, Bṛihadāraṇyaka Upanishad, 4.4.18. UPP, P. 179

Monday
LESSON 1
Awakening Comes Slowly

My *satguru*, Śiva Yogaswami, was a great *siddha*, a master and a knower of God. He would say, "Liberation is within you." He would order his seekers to "See God in everything. You are in God. God is within you. To realize the Supreme Being within you, you must have a strong body and a pure mind." He was a powerful mystic from Sri Lanka, near India—perhaps the greatest to live in the twentieth century. His words drove deeply into the hearts of all who heard them. "God is in everyone. See Him there. God is overwhelmingly present everywhere. Regard everything as a manifestation of God, and you will realize the Truth" were his words. Simple words for a simple truth, but very, very difficult to practice. ¶As we go on through life, we see only parts of life. We don't see the whole. We can't see the whole. Yogaswami said, "How can a part see the whole?" So, we live with a small part, our small part. We seek to avoid the painful areas and attract to us the joyous ones. Most people live in this duality life after life, bound in the forces of desire and the fulfillment of it. Occasionally a more mature soul breaks away from this cycle of desire-fulfillment-pleasure-loss-pain-suffering-and-joy and asks questions such as: "Who is God? Where is God? How can I come to know God?" ¶God has no names, but all names are the names of God. Whether you call Him this or that, He remains Who He is. But in our tradition we call God by the loving name Śiva, which is only one of His 1,008 traditional names. Supreme God Śiva is both within us and outside of us. Even desire, the fulfillment of desire, the joy, the pain, the sorrow, birth and death—this is all Śiva, nothing but Śiva. This is hard to believe for the unenlightened individual who cannot see how a good, kind and loving God could create pain and sorrow. Actually, we find that Śiva did not—not in the sense that is commonly thought. God gave the law of *karma*, decreeing that each energy sent into motion returns with equal force. ¶In looking closely at this natural law, we can see that we create our own joy, our own pain, our own sorrow and our own release from sorrow. Yet we could not even do this except for the power and existence of our loving Lord. It takes much meditation to find God Śiva in all things, through all things. In this striving—as in perfecting any art or science—regular daily disciplines must be faithfully adhered to. ¶Śiva is the immanent personal Lord, and He is

---

Against the San Francisco Bay, with its Golden Gate Bridge, a devotee practices seeing God in everyone. He understands that Lord Siva is living in people of all races, all colors, all cultures. All the chapter art that follows is by Indian artist Tiru A. Manivelu.

transcendent Reality. Śiva is a God of love, boundless love. He loves each and every one. Each soul is created by Him and guided by Him through life. God Śiva is everywhere. There is no place where Śiva is not. He is in you. He is in this temple. He is in the trees. He is in the sky, in the clouds, in the planets. He is the galaxies swirling in space and the space between galaxies, too. He is the universe. His cosmic dance of creation, preservation and dissolution is happening this very moment in every atom of the universe. God Śiva is, and is in all things. He permeates all things. He is immanent, with a beautiful form, a human-like form which can actually be seen and has been seen by many people in visions. He is also transcendent, beyond time, cause and space. ¶That is almost too much for the mind to comprehend, isn't it? Therefore, we have to meditate on these things. God Śiva is so close to us. Where does He live? In the Third World. And in this form He can talk and think and love and receive our prayers and guide our *karma.* He commands vast numbers of *devas* who go forth to do His will all over the world, all over the galaxy, throughout the universe. These are matters told to us by the *ṛishis;* and we have discovered them in our own meditations. So always worship this great God. Never fear Him. He is the Self of your self. He is closer than your own breath. His nature is love, and if you worship Him with devotion you will know love and be loving toward others. Devotees of God Śiva love everyone. ¶This is how God Śiva can be seen everywhere and in everyone. He is there as the Soul of each soul. You can open your inner eye and see Him in others, see Him in the world as the world. Little by little, discipline yourself to meditate at the same time each day. Meditate, discover the silent center of yourself, then go deep within, to the core of your real Being. Slowly the purity comes. Slowly the awakening comes.

Tuesday
LESSON 2
Spiritual Retreat

Does this seem too difficult? Can you just contemplate what it would take to seek the all-pervasive Śiva from hour to hour, throughout the day? One would have to be detached from all worldly responsibilities to a great extent in order to begin to bring this natural internal process through and into the external mind. The external mind is built up by an intellect formed from other people's knowledge and opinions. This borrowed knowledge shrouds the soul, and the natural, childlike intelligence often does not filter through. Therefore, a period of detachment and regular spiritual retreat or separation from the external world is necessary. ¶On a pilgrimage we strive to see God around us, to intuit

Him in the events that happen. During worship in the temple, we strive to feel Him, to experience Him more profoundly than during our normal activities. Eventually, as our spiritual efforts progress, we bring that same attention, that same one-pointedness, right into the everyday experiences that life presents to us, whether seemingly good or bad, whether causing pleasure or pain. This is the experience of the mature soul who performs regular *sādhana* after taking certain vows strong enough to cause a detachment of the intellect from seeing the external world as the absolute reality. All seekers hope for an occasional glimpse of Śiva during their yearly pilgrimage at some venerable temple. If they develop that little glimpse, it will grow. ¶Many have asked me whether everyone should worship Śiva both inside and out. Yes, that is the ideal according to our Śaiva Siddhānta philosophy, but which of these two comes more naturally depends on the nature of the disciple. The more introverted will meditate on Śiva within through their *yogas,* and the more extroverted will be inclined to worship in a temple or through music or religious service. The most awakened of seekers will do both with equal joy and ease. ¶God Śiva is within each and every soul. He is there as the unmanifest Reality, which we call Paraśiva. He is there as the pure light and consciousness that pervades every atom of the universe, which we call Satchidānanda. We also know that He is Creator of all that exists, and that He is His creation. All this we know. Yes, all this we know. Thus, we intellectually know that Śiva is within and without. This is yet to be experienced by the majority of people. ¶The nature of the worshiper develops through *sādhana* and *tapas,* performed either in this life or in previous lives. We must worship Śiva externally until compelled—as were the great *ṛishis* of yore—to sit down, to settle down, to turn within ourself, to stop talking, to stop thinking and thus to internalize our great energy of *bhakti,* devotion. This is how we evolve, how we progress along the path toward Śiva, diving deeper and deeper within. Everyone must worship Śiva externally prior to internalizing that worship fully and perfectly. We cannot internalize the worship that has not first been mastered externally. ¶When problems come in the family or workplace and emotions arise, it is only natural to forget Śiva. It's so much easier to be involved in twoness rather than oneness. It takes a lot of inner strength to remember Śiva all of the time, to keep the love for Śiva flowing. We forget. We get involved in ourselves and others. It is impossible when our ego is attacked or our feelings hurt. So it's easier, much easier, to forget Śiva and even regard Him as a God to be feared; whereas it is our own instinctive mind and our preprogrammed, nonreligious intellect that should be feared. That's the demon in our house, the mischief-maker who causes all the trouble. If you want to remember God, then first learn to forget yourself a little.

Wednesday
LESSON 3
By Experience We Evolve

A family provides toys for the children to make them happy. Śiva provides *karma* and *dharma* to all of us to make us happy, to bring us closer to Him. He created an expanding and contracting universe and eventually absorbs all in the great dissolution of the cosmos. He gave birth to all souls, our *ṛishi*-saints tell us; and we are evolving back into His image and likeness, they further explain. The toys of experience help us in our evolution, keeping us entertained so that we can learn and grow and experience our *karma, dharma* and other basic cosmic laws. Just as the children can laugh joyously as they play with their toys, or break them and cry or throw them at one another, hitting and hurting each other, we too can avoid duty and *dharma,* make *karma,* hurt ourselves and others, or help ourselves and others as we play with our own evolution, strengthening ourselves, learning and growing wise. ¶It is natural to forget about God, but there are many helpful ways that we can avoid distraction, that we can remember to keep seeing God Śiva everywhere. One of the practical ways to bring God Śiva into the midst of all this is to keep repeating His name. Do *japa* when you find yourself forgetting, when you just can't see God at all, let alone everywhere. Repeat "Aum Namaḥ Śivāya." When life becomes difficult or strained, say to yourself "Śiva Śiva" or "Aum Śivāya" or "Namaḥ Śivāya." Mentally put it all at His feet. See Him in everyone that you meet or confront, regardless of the circumstances. He is there as their life force, but you just need to quiet the mind to see. Smile when you feel unhappy with someone and say to yourself, "How nice to see you, Śiva, in this form." Animals, beggars, princes, politicians, friends and enemies, holy men, saints and sages are all Śiva to the soul that loves God. He smiles and thinks to himself, "How nice to see you, Śiva, in this, another of your many forms." ¶Nobody can think of Śiva in His formlessness. This, above all, has to be realized, and then the realizer has to realize that he has realized the Formless. The truth is that precious few will realize Paraśiva, though many can and will realize Satchidānanda, even in their later years or at the moment of death. The fullness of lives of experience experienced, the performance of prior goals perfected, would lead a soul to the burning desire to accomplish the ultimate goal. For each person on the planet, the immediate pattern is clear. Once it is fulfilled, the next step appears naturally. It is the same force of desire that accomplishes all of this. The desire of a mother to take care of her children and to be a good wife, the desire of the father to support his family, the desire of a scientist to discover, the desire of an athlete to excel, the desire of the *yogī* to merge in oneness with Śiva—it is the same force of desire, transmuted through the *chakras* as they awaken, as the soul evolves. It is that same desire that finally draws the seeker to know That which is timeless and formless, That which is spaceless and causeless. Be patient. It comes in the course of time to all. It comes. It will come. Be patient.

Thursday
LESSON 4
Knowing Self by Self

In the earlier stages, before *sādhana* is undertaken, the mind is agitated by current *karmas* and perhaps discouraged by its inability to know or to fulfill *dharma*. In this agitated state the world looks bleak and terrible, and it would be inconceivable to him for God to be any place but in the temple. "Certainly God could not reside within myself," the unenlightened concludes. ¶In the second stage, when the mind rests peacefully in the fulfillment of a life's pattern, *dharma*, when it has sufficient maturity to control and to dispatch past and current *karmas* through meditation, prayer and penance, then indeed God is seen as a helping hand within, but most potently felt within His temple. ¶In the third stage, the helping hand within becomes more than an aid to the troubled mind; it becomes pure consciousness itself. Rather than seeking God outside, God is enjoyed as a vital, integral dimension of the person, the Life of life, the power and radiant energy of the universe. The calm within is greater than the outside disturbance. In this stage of bliss-consciousness, it is clearly seen and exuberantly experienced that God is indeed within us. The experiencer's perceptions become acute, and in his daily life he becomes a witness, observing that others do not see God within themselves. He has a secret that he has discovered. God within becomes soul-realized as Truth-Knowledge-Bliss, Satchidānanda, the pervasive energy that glues all things together. Mind becomes serene, peace is seen to be everywhere, and the bliss so strong. A deeper inner eye opens at this stage, and it is truly perceived that this same presence of Śiva is in each and every living being, permeates every atom of the universe as the great, sustaining substratum of all that exists. Only when this is experienced can one truly say that God is within man and man is within God. ¶To know philosophy without experience is like going on a vacation to a distant and wonderful place by simply reading a book about the destination, hearing what others claim is to be enjoyed there. It is not true experience at all. The only spiritual experience is personal experience. My *satguru,* Siva Yogaswami, made it clear that "You will not attain *jñāna,* wisdom, even if you read a thousand scriptures. You must know your Self by yourself." ¶How can we with our finite mind come to understand Infinity, come to understand God? How can we intellectually encompass something as great as God? Our scriptures tell us that God Himself is Śaṅkara, the author of all knowledge, creator of the intellect. He is the great architect of the universe. Then if God created the intellect, how can the intellect understand Him? Well, it is possible. It has been done. The intellect has to expand, and awareness has to transcend the rational mind and see directly from superconscious knowing. That is why we worship Śiva in His highest form, symbolized by the Śivaliṅga, the simple elliptical stone. ¶It is good that you are trying to see Śiva everywhere. Keep trying. It will come. Who else can give your Self to you? The unfoldment of the Self within you is but Śiva. He can give you wealth. He can give you health. He can bestow everything that you would ever need or even desire. But to worship Him as formless, as we are doing tonight, carries the mind into infinity. Mind can only encompass what it identifies with. Mind cannot identify Truth in this subtle form which represents Śiva as beyond the mind—formless, timeless and spaceless. Yet, within you this very instant, only shrouded by your ignorance, only shrouded by the ego, which is the sense of personal identity and separation, is Śiva. He is there right now, not at some fictitious future time. Just get rid of the *māyā,* the *āṇava* and resolve the *karma,* and there He will be. The ego is the last thing to go. It is the last bond to break. ¶Once the bondage of personal ego is broken, it is seen that this mysterious God is all-pervading. He is what He has created. Think about that. It is very deep. Śiva pervades His creation constantly as ever-present Love and Light of the mind of everyone, as Intelligence and Being; and yet God also has a form. ¶In the subtle worlds, Śiva has the most beautiful form, not unlike a human form, but an absolutely perfect human form. He thinks. He talks. He walks. He makes decisions. We are fortunate to worship such a great God who pervades everything and yet transcends it, who is both form and beyond form, who is the Self within your very self at this very moment. So, all of you seekers of nondual Truth, you have a truly great path that offers God experience in form and beyond form. How fortunate you are!

Friday
LESSON 5
Working with Your Karma

Seekers more than often ask, "Why has Śiva given us *karma* to go through? Could He just have made us perfect from the beginning and avoided all the pain?" My answer is: accept your *karma* as your own, as a healing medicine and not a poison. As you go through your self-created experiences in daily life and seed *karmas* awaken, as your actions come back through your emotions, even in this life, not in a future one, resolve each and every experience so that you do not react and create new cycles to be lived through. Whether it is happy *karma,* sad *karma,* miserable *karma* or ecstatic *karma,* it is your *karma.* But it is not you, not the real you. It is the experience that you go through in order to evolve, in order to grow and to learn and to attain, eventually, wisdom. This is all Śiva's mysterious work, His way of bringing along devotees, His way to bring you close and closer to Himself. ¶The great Vedic *ṛishis* have explained that Śiva has created the body of the soul, permeated that body with His being, His essence. All souls are evolving back to His holy feet, and there are many lessons to be learned along the way. The lessons learned in the *karma* classroom are part of the process of evolution, the mechanism of evolution, the tool of evolution. Why did He do all of this? The *ṛishis* give no reason. They call it His dance. That is why we worship God Śiva as Naṭarāja, the King of Dance. Why does one dance? Because one is full of joy. One is full of life. Śiva is all life, God of life, God of death that brings new life, God of birth that brings through life. He is all life and He is everything. He danced with the *ṛishis.* He is dancing for you. You are dancing with Śiva. Every single atom in this room is dancing His dance. He is every part of you this very moment. By seeing Him, you see yourself. By drawing near to Him, you are drawing nearer to yourself. Our great *satguru,* Śiva Yogaswami, made a most perceptive remark. He said, "There is one thing only that God Śiva cannot do. He cannot separate Himself from me." He cannot separate Himself from you, because He permeates you. He is you. He created the soul, the *Vedas* and *Āgamas* tell us. He created your soul, and your soul is evolving, maturing through *karma,* through life, on its way back to Him. That is the goal of life, to know Śiva, to love Śiva and to find union in Him, to dance with Śiva, live with Śiva and merge with Śiva. This is what the oldest religion on the Earth teaches and believes. ¶Śiva is the God of love and nothing else but love. He fills this universe with love. He fills you with love. Śiva is fire. Śiva is earth. Śiva is air. Śiva is water. Śiva is ether. Śiva's cosmic energy permeates everything and gives light and life to your mind. Śiva is everywhere and all things. Śiva is your small, insignificant worry, the concern that you have been holding in your mind for so many years. See God Śiva everywhere and His life energy in all things. First we dance with Śiva. Then we live with Śiva. The end of the path is to merge with Śiva, the Self God within.

Saturday
LESSON 6
The Self God Within

The Self: you can't explain it. You can sense its existence through the refined state of your senses, but you cannot explain it. To know it, you have to experience it. And the best you can say about it is that it is the depth of your Being, the very core of you. It is you. ¶If you visualize above you nothing; below you nothing; to the right of you nothing; to the left of you nothing; in front of you nothing; in back of you nothing; and dissolve yourself into that nothingness, that would be the best way you could explain the realization of the Self. And yet that nothingness would not be the absence of something, like the nothingness inside an empty box, which would be like a void. That nothingness is the fullness of everything: the power, the sustaining power, of the existence of what appears to be everything. ¶After you realize the Self, you see the mind for what it is—a self-created principle. That is the mind ever creating itself. The mind is form ever creating form, preserving form, creating new forms and destroying old forms. That is the mind, the illusion, the great unreality, the part of you that in your thinking mind you dare to think is real. What gives the mind that power? Does the mind have power if it is unreal? What difference whether it has power or hasn't power, or the very words that I am saying when the Self exists because of itself? You could live in the dream and become disturbed by it. You can seek and desire with a burning desire to cognize reality and be blissful because of it. Man's destiny leads him back to himself. Man's destiny leads him into the cognition of his own Being; leads him further into the realization of his True Being. They say you must step onto the spiritual path to realize the Self. You only step on the spiritual path when you and you alone are ready, when what appears real to you loses its appearance of reality. Then and only then are you able to detach yourself enough to seek to find a new and more permanent reality. ¶Have you ever noticed that something you think is permanent, you and you alone give permanence to that thing through your protection of it? ¶Have you ever stopped to even think and get a clear intellectual concept that the Spirit within you is the only permanent thing? That everything else is changing? That everything else has a direct wire connecting it to the realms of joy and sorrow? That is the mind. ¶As the Self, your Effulgent Being, comes to life in you, joy and sorrow become a study to you. You do not have to think to tell yourself that each in its own place is unreal. You know from the innermost depths of your being that form itself is not real. ¶The subtlety of the joys that you experience as you come into your Effulgent Being cannot be described. They can only be projected to you if you are refined enough to pick up the subtlety of vibration. If you are in harmony enough, you can sense the great joy, the subtlety of the bliss that you will feel as you come closer and closer to your real Self. ¶If you strive to find the Self by using your mind, you will strive and strive in vain, because the mind cannot give you Truth; a lie cannot give you the truth. A lie can only entangle you in a web of deceit. But if you sensitize yourself, awaken your true, fine, beautiful qualities that all of you have, then you become a channel, a chalice in which your Effulgent Being will begin to shine. You will first think that a light is shining within you. You will seek to find that light. You will seek to hold it, like you cherish and hold a beautiful gem. You will later find that the light that you found within you is in every pore, every cell of your being. You will later find that that light permeates every atom of the universe. You will later find that you are that light and what it permeates is the unreal illusion created by the mind.

Sunday
LESSON 7
Every Temple Made of Brick

How strong you must be to find this Truth. You must become very, very strong. How do you become strong? Exercise. You must exercise every muscle and sinew of your nature by obeying the dictates of the law, of the spiritual laws. It will be very difficult. A weak muscle is very difficult to make strong, but if you exercise over a period of time and do what you should do, it will respond. Your nature will respond, too. But you must work at it. You must try. You must try. You must try very, very hard. Very diligently. How often? Ten minutes a day? No. Two hours a day? No. Twenty-four hours a day! Every day! You must try very, very hard. Preparing you for the realization of the Self is like tuning up a violin, tightening up each string so it harmonizes with every other string. The more sensitive you are to tone, the better you can tune a violin, and the better the violin is tuned, the better the music. The stronger you are in your nature, the more you can bring through your real nature; the more you can enjoy the bliss of your true being. It is well worth working for. It is well worth craving for. It is well worth denying yourself many,

many things for—to curb your nature. It is well worth struggling with your mind, to bring your mind under the dominion of your will. ¶Those of you who have experienced contemplation know the depth from which I am speaking. You have had a taste of your true Self. It has tasted like nothing that you have ever come in contact with before. It has filled and thrilled and permeated your whole being, even if you have only remained in that state of contemplation not longer than sixty seconds. Out of it you have gained a great knowing, a knowing that you could refer back to, a knowing that will bear the fruit of wisdom if you relate future life experiences to that knowing, a knowing greater than you could acquire at any university or institute of higher learning. Can you only try to gain a clear intellectual concept of realizing this Self that you felt permeating through you and through all form in your state of contemplation? That is your next step. ¶Those of you who are wrestling with the mind in your many endeavors to try to concentrate the mind, to try to meditate, to try to become quiet, to try to relax, keep trying. Every positive effort that you make is not in vain. Every single brick added to a temple made of brick brings that temple closer to completion. So keep trying and one day, all of a sudden, you will pierce the lower realms of your mind and enter into contemplation. Then you will be able to say: "Yes, I know, I have seen. Now I know fully the path that I am on." Keep trying. You have to start somewhere. ¶The Self you cannot speak of. You can only try to think about it, if you care to, in one way: feel your mind, body and emotions, and know that you are the Spirit permeating through mind, which is all form; body, which you inhabit; and emotions, which you either control or are controlled by. Think on that, ponder on that, and you will find you are the light within your eyes. You are the feel within your fingers. "You are more radiant than the sun, purer than the snow, more subtle than the ether." Keep trying. Each time you try you are one step closer to your true Effulgent Being.

Ahiṁsā-Satya
अहिंसा-सत्य

Noninjury and Truthfulness

Ahiṁsā is not causing pain to any living being at any time through the actions of one's mind, speech or body.

Atharva Veda, Śandilya Upanishad, 1.3. UPA, P. 173

Monday
LESSON 8
How to Live With Śiva

Religion teaches us how to become better people, how to live as spiritual beings on this Earth. This happens through living virtuously, following the natural and essential guidelines of *dharma.* For Hindus, these guidelines are recorded in the *yamas* and *niyamas,* ancient scriptural injunctions for all aspects of human thought, attitude and behavior. In Indian spiritual life, these Vedic restraints and observances are built into the character of children from a very early age. For adults who have been subjected to opposite behavioral patterns, these guidelines may seem to be like commandments. However, even they can, with great dedication and effort, remold their character and create the foundation necessary for a sustained spiritual life. Through following the *yamas* and *niyamas,* we cultivate our refined, spiritual being while keeping the instinctive nature in check. We lift ourself into the consciousness of the higher *chakras*—of love, compassion, intelligence and bliss—and naturally invoke the blessings of the divine *devas* and Mahādevas. ¶*Yama* means "reining in" or "control." The *yamas* include such injunctions as noninjury *(ahiṁsā),* nonstealing *(asteya)* and moderation in eating *(mitāhāra),* which harness the base, instinctive nature. *Niyama,* literally "unleashing," indicates the expression of refined, soul qualities through such disciplines as charity *(dāna),* contentment *(santosha)* and incantation *(japa).* ¶It is true that bliss comes from meditation, and it is true that higher consciousness is the heritage of all mankind. However, the ten restraints and their corresponding practices are necessary to maintain bliss consciousness, as well as all of the good feelings toward oneself and others attainable in any incarnation. These restraints and practices build character. Character is the foundation for spiritual unfoldment. ¶The fact is, the higher we go, the lower we can fall. The top *chakras* spin fast; the lowest one available to us spins even faster. The platform of character must be built within our lifestyle to maintain the total contentment needed to persevere on the path. These great *ṛishis* saw the frailty of human nature and gave these guidelines, or disciplines, to make it strong. They said, "Strive!" Let's strive to not hurt others, to be truthful and honor all the rest of the virtues they outlined. ¶The ten *yamas* are: 1) *ahiṁsā,* "noninjury," not harming others by thought, word or deed;

A boy has broken a clay flower vase and is hiding the mischief from his sister. Mother watches, hoping her son will learn the value of satya, *telling the truth. Inset: A man is beating a small boy, while an onlooker intervenes to enforce noninjury,* ahiṁsā.

2) *satya,* "truthfulness," refraining from lying and betraying promises; 3) *asteya,* "nonstealing," neither stealing nor coveting nor entering into debt; 4) *brahmacharya,* "divine conduct," controlling lust by remaining celibate when single, leading to faithfulness in marriage; 5) *kshamā,* "patience," restraining intolerance with people and impatience with circumstances; 6) *dhṛiti,* "steadfastness," overcoming nonperseverance, fear, indecision, inconstancy and changeableness; 7) *dayā,* "compassion," conquering callous, cruel and insensitive feelings toward all beings; 8) *ārjava,* "honesty, straightforwardness," renouncing deception and wrongdoing; 9) *mitāhāra,* "moderate appetite," neither eating too much nor consuming meat, fish, fowl or eggs; 10) *śaucha,* "purity," avoiding impurity in body, mind and speech.

Tuesday
LESSON 9
Twenty Disciplines

The *niyamas* are: 1) *hrī,* "remorse," being modest and showing shame for misdeeds; 2) *santosha,* "contentment," seeking joy and serenity in life; 3) *dāna,* "giving," tithing and giving generously without thought of reward; 4) *āstikya,* "faith," believing firmly in God, Gods, *guru* and the path to enlightenment; 5) Īśvarapūjana, "worship of the Lord," the cultivation of devotion through daily worship and meditation; 6) *siddhānta śravaṇa,* "scriptural listening," studying the teachings and listening to the wise of one's lineage; 7) *mati,* "cognition," developing a spiritual will and intellect with the *guru's* guidance; 8) *vrata,* "sacred vows," fulfilling religious vows, rules and observances faithfully; 9) *japa,* "recitation," chanting *mantras* daily; 10) *tapas,* "austerity," performing *sādhana,* penance, *tapas* and sacrifice. ¶In comparing the *yamas* to the *niyamas,* we find the restraint of noninjury, *ahiṁsā,* makes it possible to practice *hrī,* remorse. Truthfulness brings on the state of *santosha,* contentment. And the third *yama, asteya,* nonstealing, must be perfected before the third *niyama,* giving without any thought of reward, is even possible. Sexual purity brings faith in God, Gods and *guru. Kshamā,* patience, is the foundation for Īśvarapūjana, worship, as is *dhṛiti,* steadfastness, the foundation for *siddhānta śravana.* The *yama* of *dayā,* compassion, definitely brings *mati,* cognition. *Ārjava,* honesty—renouncing deception and all wrongdoing—is the foundation for *vrata,* taking sacred vows and faithfully fulfilling them. *Mitāhāra,* moderate appetite, is where *yoga* begins, and vegetarianism is essential before the practice of *japa,* recitation of holy *mantras,* can reap its true benefit in one's life. *Śaucha,* purity in body, mind and speech, is the foundation and the protection for all austerities. ¶The twenty restraints and observances are the first two of the eight limbs of *ashṭāṅga yoga,* constituting Hinduism's fundamental ethical code. Because it is brief, the entire code can be easily memorized and reviewed daily at the family meetings in each home. The *yamas* and *niyamas* are the essential foundation for all spiritual progress. They are cited in numerous scriptures, including the *Śāṇḍilya* and *Varāha Upanishads,* the *Haṭha Yoga Pradīpikā* by Gorakshanatha, the *Tirumantiram* of Rishi Tirumular and the *Yoga Sūtras* of Sage Patanjali. All of these ancient texts list ten *yamas* and ten *niyamas,* with the exception of Patanjali's classic work, which lists just five of each. Patanjali lists the *yamas* as: *ahiṁsā, satya, asteya, brahmacharya* and *aparigraha* (noncovetousness); and the *niyamas* as: *śaucha, santosha, tapas, svādhyāya* (self-reflection, scriptural study) and Īśvarapraṇidhāna (worship). ¶In the Hindu tradition, it is primarily the mother's job to build character within the children, and thereby to continually improve society. Mothers can study and teach these guidelines to uplift their children as well as themselves. Each discipline focuses on a different aspect of human nature, its strengths and weaknesses. Taken as a sum total, they encompass the whole of human experience and spirituality. You may do well in upholding some of these but not so well in others. That is to be expected. That defines the *sādhana,* therefore, to be perfected.

Wednesday
LESSON 10
Your Divine Chariot

The *yamas* and *niyamas* and their function in our life can be likened to a chariot pulled by ten horses. The passenger inside the chariot is your soul. The chariot itself represents your physical, astral and mental bodies. The driver of the chariot is your external ego, your personal will. The wheels are your divine energies. The *niyamas,* or spiritual practices, represent the spirited horses, named Hrī, Santosha, Dāna, Āstikya, Īśvarapūjana, Siddhānta Śravaṇa, Mati, Vrata, Japa, and Tapas. The *yamas,* or restraints, are the reins, called Ahiṁsā, Satya, Asteya, Brahmacharya, Kshamā, Dhṛiti, Dayā, Ārjava, Mitāhāra and Śaucha. By holding tight to the reins, the charioteer, your will, guides the strong horses so they can run forward swiftly and gallantly as a dynamic unit. So, as we restrain the lower, instinctive qualities through upholding the *yamas,* the soul moves forward to its destination in the state of *santosha. Santosha,* peace, is the eternal satisfaction of the soul. At the deepest level, the soul is always in the state of *santosha.* But outwardly, the propensity of the soul is to be clouded by lack of restraint of the instinctive nature, lack of restraint of the intellectual nature, lack of restraint of the emotional nature, lack of restraint of the physical body itself. Therefore, hold tight the reins. ¶It is important to realize that the *yamas,* restraints, are not out of the reach of the lowliest among us. No matter where we are in the scale of life, we all started from the beginning, at the bottom, didn't we? This is our philosophy. This is our religion. This is the evolution of the soul. We improve, life after life, and these guidelines, *yamas* and *niyamas,* restraints and practices, are gifts from our *ṛishis,* from God Śiva Himself through them, to allow us to judge ourself against these pillars of virtue as to how far we have progressed or strayed. In the early births, we are like children. We do not stray from anything. We run here and there and everywhere, disobey every rule, which when told of we cannot remember. We ignore any admonishment. As adolescents, we force our will on society, want to change it, because we don't like the hold it has on us. Wanting to express themselves in most creative ways, rebellious youths separate themselves from other people, children and the adults. They do make changes, but not always for the best. As an adult, we see both—the past and the impending future of old age—and, heads down, we are concerned with accumulating enough to see life through to its uncertain end. When the accumulations have become adequate, we will look back at the undisciplined children, the headstrong, unruly adolescents and the self-possessed, concentrated adults and try to motivate all three groups. In our great religion, the Sanātana Dharma, known today as Hinduism, twenty precepts, the *yamas* and *niyamas,* restraints and observances, are the guidelines we use to motivate these three groups. These are the guidelines they use to motivate themselves, for each group is mystically independent of the others; so it seems.

Thursday
LESSON 11
Ahiṁsā: Noninjury

The first *yama* is *ahiṁsā,* noninjury. To practice *ahiṁsā,* one has to practice *santosha,* contentment. The *sādhana* is to seek joy and serenity in life, remaining content with what one has, knows, is doing and those with whom he associates. Bear your *karma* cheerfully. Live within your situation contentedly. *Hiṁsā,* or injury, and the desire to harm, comes from discontent. ¶The *ṛishis* who revealed the principles of *dharma* or divine law in Hindu scripture knew full well the potential for human suffering and the path which could avert it. To them a one spiritual power flowed in and through all things in this universe, animate and inanimate, conferring existence by its presence. To them life was a coherent process leading all souls without exception to enlightenment, and no violence could be carried to the higher reaches of that ascent. These *ṛishis* were mystics whose revelation disclosed a cosmos in which all beings exist in interlaced dependence. The whole is contained in the part, and the part in the whole. Based on this cognition, they taught a philosophy of nondifference of self and other, asserting that in the final analysis we are not separate from the world and its manifest forms, nor from the Divine which shines forth in all things, all beings, all peoples. From this understanding of oneness arose the philosophical basis for the practice of noninjury and Hinduism's ancient commitment to it. ¶We all know that Hindus, who are one-sixth of the human race today, believe in the existence of God everywhere, as an all-pervasive, self-effulgent energy and consciousness. This basic belief creates the attitude of sublime tolerance and acceptance toward others. Even tolerance is insufficient to describe the compassion and reverence the Hindu holds for the intrinsic sacredness within all things. Therefore, the actions of all Hindus are rendered benign, or *ahiṁsā*. One would not want to hurt something which one revered. ¶On the other hand, when the fundamentalists of any religion teach an unrelenting duality based on good and evil, man and nature or God and Devil, this creates friends and enemies. This belief is a sacrilege to Hindus, because they know that the attitudes which are the by-product are totally dualistic, and for good to triumph over that which is alien or evil, it must kill out that which is considered to be evil. ¶The Hindu looks at nothing as intrinsically evil. To him the ground is sacred. The sky is sacred. The sun is sacred. His wife is a Goddess. Her husband is a God. Their children are *devas*. Their home is a shrine. Life is a pilgrimage to *mukti*, or liberation from rebirth, which once attained is the end to reincarnation in a physical body. When on a holy pilgrimage, one would not want to hurt anyone along the way, knowing full well the experiences on this path are of one's own creation, though maybe acted out through others.

Friday
LESSON 12
Noninjury for Renunciates

Ahiṁsā is the first and foremost virtue, presiding over truthfulness, nonstealing, sexual purity, patience, steadfastness, compassion, honesty and moderate appetite. The *brahmachārī* and *sannyāsin* must take *ahiṁsā*, noninjury, one step further. He has mutated himself, escalated himself, by stopping the abilities of being able to harm another by thought, word or deed, physically, mentally or emotionally. The one step further is that he must not harm his own self with his own thoughts, his own feelings, his own actions toward his own body, toward his own emotions, toward his own mind. This is very important to remember. And here, at this juncture, *ahiṁsā* has a tie with *satya,* truthfulness. The *sannyāsin* must be totally truthful to himself, to his *guru,* to the Gods and to Lord Śiva, who resides within him every minute of every hour of every day. But for him to truly know this and express it through his life and be a living religious example of the Sanātana Dharma, all tendencies toward *hiṁsā,* injuriousness, must always be definitely harnessed in chains of steel. The mystical reason is this. Because of the *brahmachārī's* or *sannyāsin's* spiritual power, he really has more ability to hurt someone than he or that person may know, and therefore his observance of noninjury is even more vital. Yes, this is true. A *brahmachārī* or *sannyāsin* who does not live the highest level of *ahiṁsā* is not a *brahmachārī.* ¶Words are expressions of thoughts, thoughts created from *prāṇa.* Words coupled with thoughts backed up by the transmuted *prāṇas,* or the accumulated bank account of energies held back within the *brahmachārī* and the *sannyāsin,* become powerful thoughts, and when expressed through words go deep into the mind, creating impressions, *saṁskāras,* that last a long time, maybe forever. It is truly unfortunate if a *brahmachārī* or *sannyāsin* loses control of himself and betrays *ahiṁsā* by becoming *hiṁsā,* an injurious person—unfortunate for those involved, but more unfortunate for himself. When we hurt another, we scar the inside of ourself; we clone the image. The scar would never leave the *sannyāsin* until it left the person that he hurt. This is because the *prāṇas,* the transmuted energies, give so much force to the thought. Thus the words penetrate to the very core of the being. Therefore, angry people should get married and should not practice *brahmacharya.*

Saturday
LESSON 13
Satya: Truthfulness

The second *yama* is *satya,* truthfulness. It seems that little children are naturally truthful, open and honest. Their lives are uncomplicated, and they have no secrets. National studies show that children, even at an early age, learn to lie from their parents. They are taught to keep family secrets, whom to like, whom to dislike, whom to hate and whom to love, right within the home itself. Their minds become complicated and their judgments of what to say and what not to say are often influenced by the possibility of a punishment, perhaps a beating. Therefore, to fully encompass *satya* and incorporate it in one's life as a teenager or an adult, it is quite necessary to dredge the subconscious mind and in some cases reject much of what mother or father, relatives and elders had placed into it at an early age. Only by rejecting the apparent opposites, likes and dislikes, hates and loves, can true truthfulness, which is a quality of the soul, burst forth again and be there in full force as it is within an innocent child. A child practices truthfulness without wisdom. Wisdom, which is the timely application of knowledge, guides truthfulness for the adult. To attain wisdom, the adult must be conversant with the soul nature. ¶What is it that keeps us from practicing truthfulness? Fear, mainly. Fear of discovery, fear of punishment or loss of status. This is the most honest untruthfulness. The next layer of untruthfulness would be the mischievous person willing to take a chance of not being caught and deliberately inventing stories about another, deliberately lying when the truth would do just as well. The third and worst layer is calculated deception and breaking of promises. ¶*Satya* is a restraint, and as one of the ten restraints it ranks in importance as number two. When we restrain our tendencies to deceive, to lie and break promises, our external life is uncomplicated, as is our subconscious mind. Honesty is the foundation of truth. It is ecologically, psychologically purifying. However, many people are not truthful with themselves, to themselves, let alone to others. And the calculated, subconscious built-in program of these clever, cunning, two-faced individuals keeps them in the inner worlds of darkness. To emerge from those worlds, the practice of truthfulness, *satya,* is in itself a healing and purifying *sādhana.* ¶What is breaking a promise? Breaking a promise is, for example, when someone confides in you, asks you to keep it to yourself and not to tell anyone, and then you tell. You have betrayed your promise. Confidences must be kept at all costs in the practice of *satya.* ¶There are certainly times when withholding the truth is permitted. The *Tirukural, Weaver's Wisdom,* explains that "Even falsehood is of the nature of truth if it renders good results, free from fault" (292). An astrologer, for instance, while reviewing a chart would refrain from telling of a heartbreak that might come to a person at a certain time in his life. This is wisdom. In fact, astrologers are admonished by their *gurus* to hold back information that might be harmful or deeply discouraging. A doctor might not tell his patient that he will die in three days when he sees the vital signs weakening. Instead, he may encourage positive thinking, give hope, knowing that life is eternal and that to invoke fear might create depression and hopelessness in the mind of the ill person. ¶When pure truthfulness would injure or cause harm, then the first *yama, ahiṁsā,* would come into effect. You would not want to harm that person, even with the truth. But we must not look at this verse from the *Tirukural* as giving permission for deception. The spirit of the verse is wisdom, good judgment, not the subterfuge of telling someone you are going to Mumbai when your actual destination is Kalikot. That is not truthful. It would be much better to avoid answering the question at all in some way if one wanted to conceal the destination of his journey. This would be wisdom. You would not complicate your own subconscious mind by telling an untruth, nor be labeled deceptive in the mind of the informed person when he eventually discovers the actual truth.

Sunday
LESSON 14
Honesty with Your Guru

Some people use the excuse of truthfulness to nag their spouse about what they don't like about him or her, or to gossip about other people's flaws. This is not the spirit of *satya.* We do not want to expose others' faults. Such confrontations could become argumentative and combative. No one knows one's faults better than oneself. But fear and weakness often prevail, while motivation and a clear plan to correct the situation are absent. Therefore, to give a clear plan, a positive outlook, a new way of thinking, diverts the attention of the individual and allows internal healing to take place. This is wisdom. This is *ahiṁsā,* noninjury. This is *satya,* truthfulness. The wise devotee is careful to never insult or humiliate others, even under the pretext of telling the truth, which is an excuse that people sometimes use to tell others what they don't like about them. Wise devotees realize that there is good and bad in everyone. There are emotional ups and downs, mental elations and depressions, encouragements and discouragements. Let's focus on the positive. This is *ahiṁsā* and *satya* working together. ¶The *brahmachārī* and the *sannyāsin* must be absolutely truthful with their *satguru.* They must be absolutely diplomatic, wise and always accentuate the good qualities within the *sannyāsin* and *brahmachārī* communities. The *guru* has the right to discuss, rebuke or discipline the uncomely qualities in raising up the *brahmachārī* and *sannyāsin.* Only he has this right, because it was given to him by the *brahmachārīs* and *sannyāsins* when they took him as their *satguru.* This means that *brahmachārīs* and *sannyāsins* cannot discipline one another, psychoanalyze and correct in the name of truthfulness, without violation of the number one *yama—ahiṁsā,* noninjury. ¶Mothers and fathers have rights with their own children, as do *gurus* with their *śishyas.* These rights are limited according to wisdom. They are not all-inclusive and should

Monday
LESSON 15
Asteya: Nonstealing

The third *yama* is *asteya,* neither stealing, nor coveting nor entering into debt. We all know what stealing is. But now let's define covetousness. It could well be defined as owning something mentally and emotionally but not actually owning it physically. This is not good. It puts a hidden psychological strain on all parties concerned and brings up the lower emotions from the *tala chakras.* It must be avoided at all cost. Coveting is desiring things that are not your own. Coveting leads to jealousy, and it leads to stealing. The first impulse toward stealing is coveting, wanting. If you can control the impulse to covet, then you will not steal. Coveting is mental stealing. ¶Of course, stealing must never ever happen. Even a penny, a peso, a rupee, a lira or a yen should not be misappropriated or stolen. Defaulting on debts is also a form of stealing. But avoiding debt in principle does not mean that one cannot buy things on credit or through other contractual arrangements. It does mean that payments must be made at the expected time, that credit be given in trust and be eliminated when the time has expired, that contracts be honored to the satisfaction of all parties concerned. Running one's affairs on other peoples' money must be restrained. To control this is the *sādhana* of *asteya. Brahmachārīs* and *sannyāsins,* of course, must scrupulously obey these restraints relating to debt, stealing and covetousness. These are certainly not in their code of living. ¶To perfect *asteya,* we must practice *dāna,* charity, the third *niyama;* we must take the *dāśama bhāga vrata,* promising to tithe, pay *dāśamāṁśa,* to our favorite religious organization and, on top of that, give creatively, without thought of reward. Stealing is selfishness. Giving is unselfishness. Any lapse of *asteya* is corrected by *dāna.* ¶It is important to realize that one cannot simply obey the *yamas* without actively practicing the *niyamas.* To restrain one's current tendencies successfully, each must be replaced by a positive observance. For each of the *yamas,* there is a positive replacement of doing something else. The *niyamas* must totally overshadow the qualities controlled by the *yamas* for the perfect person to emerge. It is also important to remember that doing what should not be done—and not doing what should be done—does have its consequences. These can be many, depending upon the evolution of the soul of each individual; but all such acts bring about

Two boys break the principle of asteya *by stealing a book while distracting a merchant. Insets:* kshamā *is shown by a mother's coping with her many duties : a brother protects his sister's purity,* brahmacharya, *from a rogue; workers display steadfast persistence,* dhṛiti, *in their craft.*

the lowering of consciousness into the instinctive nature, and inevitable suffering is the result. Each Hindu *guru* has his own ways of mitigating the negative *karmas* that result as a consequence of not living up to the high ideals of these precepts. But the world is also a *guru,* in a sense, and its devotees learn by their own mistakes, often repeating the same lessons many, many times.

Tuesday
LESSON 16
Debt, Gambling And Grief

I was asked, "Is borrowing money to finance one's business in accord with the *yama* of nonstealing? When can you use other peoples' money and when should you not?" When the creditors start calling you for their money back, sending demand notices indicating that they only extended you thirty days', sixty days' or ninety days' credit, then if you fail to pay, or pay only a quarter or half of it just to keep them at arm's length because you still need their money to keep doing what you are doing, this is a violation of this *yama.* ¶There are several kinds of debt that are disallowed by this *yama.* One is spending beyond your means and accumulating bills you can't pay. We are reminded of *Tirukural* verse 478 which says that the way to avoid poverty is to spend within your means: "A small income is no cause for failure, provided expenditures do not exceed it." We can see that false wealth, or the mere appearance of wealth, is using other peoples' money, either against their will or by paying a premium price for it. Many people today are addicted to abusing credit. It's like being addicted to the drug opium. People addicted to O.P.M.—other people's money—compulsively spend beyond their means. They don't even think twice about handing over their last credit card to pay for that $500 *sārī* after all the other credit cards have been "maxed out." When the bill arrives, it gets added to the stack of other bills that can't possibly be paid. ¶Another kind of debt is contracting resources beyond your ability to pay back the loan. This is depending on a frail, uncertain future. Opportunities may occur to pay the debt, but then again they may not. The desire was so great for the commodity which caused the debt that a chance was taken. Essentially, this is gambling with someone else's money; and it is no way to run one's life. ¶Gambling and speculation are also forms of entering into debt. Speculation could be a proper form of acquiring wealth if one has the wealth to maintain the same standard of living he is accustomed to even if the speculation failed. Much of business is speculation; and high-risk speculations do come along occasionally; but one should never risk more than one can afford to lose. ¶Gambling is different, because the games are fun, a means of entertainment and releasing stress; though even in the casinos one should not gamble more than he could afford to lose. However, unlike speculation, when one is in the excitement of gambling and begins to lose, the greed and desire to win it all back arises, and the flustered gambler may risk his and his family's wealth and well-being. Stress builds. The disastrous consequences of gambling were admonished in the oldest scripture, the *Ṛig Veda*, in the famous fourteen-verse "Gambler's Lament" (10.34. VE, P. 501). Verse ten summarizes: "Abandoned, the wife of the gambler grieves. Grieved, too, is his mother, as he wanders vaguely. Afraid and in debt, ever greedy for money, he steals in the night to the home of another." This is not fun; nor is it entertainment. ¶These are the grave concerns behind our *sūtra* that prohibits gambling for my *śishyas:* "Śiva's devotees are forbidden to indulge in gambling or games of chance with payment or risk, even through others or for employment. Gambling erodes society, assuring the loss of many for the gain of a few" *(sūtra* 76). Everyone really knows that the secret to winning at gambling is to own a casino. ¶Compulsive gambling and reckless, unfounded speculation are like stealing from your own family, risking the family wealth. More than that, it is stealing from yourself, because the remorse felt when an inevitable loss comes could cause a loss of faith in your abilities and your judgment. And if the loss affects the other members of the family, their estimation and respect and confidence in your good judgment goes way down. ¶Many people justify stealing by saying that life is unfair and therefore it's OK to take from the rich. They feel it's OK to steal from a rich corporation, for example: "They will never miss it, and we need it more." Financial speculation can easily slide into unfair maneuvering, where a person is actually stealing from a small or large company, thereby making it fail. The credibility of the person will go down, and businesses will beware of this speculative investor who would bring a company to ruin to fatten his own pockets. Entering into debt is a modern convenience and a modern temptation. But this convenience must be honored within the time allotted. If you are paying a higher interest rate because of late or partial payments, you have abused your credit and your creditors. ¶At the Global Forum for Human Survival in 1990 in Moscow, the participants began worrying about the kids, the next generation. "What are they going to think of us?" they asked. Is it fair to fulfill a need now, spoil the environment and hand the bill over to the next generation? No, it is not. This is another form of stealing. We can't say, "We have to have chlorofluorocarbons now, and the next generation has to face the consequences." The *yamas* and *niyamas* are thus not just a personal matter but also a national, communal and global matter. Yes, this takes *asteya* and all the restraints and observances to another dimension.

Wednesday
LESSON 17
Brahmacharya: Sexual Purity

Brahmacharya, sexual purity, is a very important restraint among the ancient Śaivite ethical principles known as *yamas* and *niyamas,* because it sets the pattern for one's entire life. Following this principle, the vital energies are used before marriage in study rather than in sexual fantasy, e-pornography, masturbation, necking, petting or sexual intercourse. After marriage, the vital energies are concentrated on business, livelihood, fulfilling one's duties, serving the community, improving oneself and one's family, and performing *sādhana.* For those who do not believe in God, Gods, *guru* or the path to enlightenment, this is a difficult restraint to fulfill, and such people tend to be promiscuous when single and therefore unfaithful in marriage. ¶The rewards for maintaining this restraint are many. Those who practice *brahmacharya* before marriage and apply its principles throughout married life are free from encumbrances—mentally, emotionally and physically. They get a good start on life, have long-lasting, mature family relationships, and their children are emotionally sound, mentally firm and physically strong. ¶Those who are promiscuous and unreligious are susceptible to impulses of anger, have undefined fears, experience jealousy and the other instinctive emotions. The doors of the higher world are open to them, but the doors of the lower world are also open. Even the virgin *brahmachārī* who believes firmly in God, Gods, *guru* and the path to enlightenment and has a strict family must be watched and carefully guided to maintain his *brahmacharya.* Without this careful attention, the virginity may easily be lost. ¶*Brahmacharya* for the monastic means complete sexual abstinence and is, of course, an understood requirement to maintain this position in life. This applies as well to any single individual who has taken the celibacy vow, known as *brahmacharya vrata.* If *brahmacharya* is compromised by the *brahmachārī,* he must face the consequences and reaffirm his original intent. Having lost faith in himself because of breaking his *vrata,* his self-confidence must be rebuilt. ¶It should be perfectly clear that it is totally unacceptable for men or women who have taken up the celibate monastic life to live a double standard and surround themselves with those of the opposite sex—be they fellow āśramites, personal aides, secretaries or close devotees—or with their former family. Nowadays there are pseudo-*sannyāsins* who are married and call themselves *swāmīs,* but, if pressed, they might admit that they are simply *yoga* teachers dressed in orange robes, bearing the title "*swāmī*" to attract the attention of the uninformed public for commercial reasons. ¶There is great power in the practice of *brahmacharya,* literally "Godly conduct." Containing the sacred fluids within the body builds up a bank account through the years that makes the realization of God on the path to enlightenment a reality within the life of the individual who is single. When *brahmacharya* is broken through sexual intercourse, this power goes away. It just goes away.

Thursday
LESSON 18
Brahmacharya In Family Life

The observance of *brahmacharya* is perhaps the most essential aspect of a sound, spiritual culture. This is why in Śaivism, boys and girls are taught the importance of remaining celibate until they are married. This creates healthy individuals, physically, emotionally and spiritually, generation after generation. There is a mystical reason. In virgin boys and girls, the psychic *nāḍīs,* the astral nerve currents that extend out into and through their aura, have small hooks at the end. When a boy and girl marry, the hooks straighten out and the *nāḍīs* are tied one to another, and they actually grow together. If the first sexual experience is premarital and virginity is broken, the hooks at the end of the *nāḍīs* also straighten out, but there is nothing to grow onto if the partners do not marry. Then, when either partner marries someone else, the relationship is never as close as when a virgin boy and girl marry, because their *nāḍīs* don't grow together in the same way. In cases such as this, they feel the need for intellectual stimuli and emotional stimuli to keep the marriage going. ¶Youth ask, "How should we regard members of the opposite sex?" Do not look at members of the opposite sex with any idea of sex or lust in mind. Do not indulge in admiring those of the opposite sex, or seeing one as more beautiful than another. Boys must foster the inner attitude that all young women are their sisters and all older women are their mother. Girls must foster the inner attitude that all young men are their brothers and all older men are their father. Do not attend movies that depict the base instincts of humans, nor read books or magazines of this nature. Above all, avoid pornography on the Internet, on TV and in any other media. ¶To be successful in *brahmacharya,* one naturally wants to avoid arousing the sex instincts. This is done by understanding and avoiding the eight successive phases: fantasy, glorification, flirtation, lustful glances, secret love talk, amorous longing, rendezvous and finally intercourse. Be very careful to mix only with good company—those who think and speak in a cultured way—so that the mind and emotions are not led astray and vital energies needed for study used up. Get plenty of physical exercise. This is very important, because exercise sublimates your instinctive drives and directs excess energy and the flow of blood into all parts of the body. ¶*Brahmacharya* means sexual continence, as was observed by Mahatma Gandhi in his later years and by other great souls throughout life. There is another form of sexual purity, though not truly *brahmacharya*, followed by faithful family people who have a normal sex life while raising a family. They are working toward the stage when they will take their *brahmacharya vrata* after sixty years of age. Thereafter they would live together as brother and sister, sleeping in separate bedrooms. During their married life, they control the forces of lust and regulate instinctive energies and thus prepare to take that *vrata.* But if they are unfaithful, flirtatious and loose in their thinking through life, they will not be inclined to take the *vrata* in later life. ¶Faithfulness in marriage means fidelity and much more. It includes mental faithfulness, non-flirtatiousness and modesty toward the opposite sex. A married man, for instance, should not hire a secretary who is more magnetic or more beautiful than his wife. Metaphysically, in the perfect family relationship, man and wife are, in a sense, creating a one nervous system for their joint spiritual progress, and all of their *nāḍīs* are growing together over the years. If they break that faithfulness, they break the psychic, soul connections that are developing for their personal inner achievements. If one or the other of the partners does have an affair, this creates a psychic tug and pull on the nerve system of both spouses that will continue until the affair ends and long afterwards. Therefore, the principle of the containment of the sexual force and mental and emotional impulses is the spirit of *brahmacharya,* both for the single and married person.

Friday
LESSON 19
Rules for Serious People

For virtuous individuals who marry, their experiences with their partner are, again, free from lustful fantasies; and emotional involvement is only with their spouse. Yes, a normal sex life should be had between husband and wife, and no one else should be included in either one's mind or emotions. Never hugging, touching another's spouse or exciting the emotions; always dressing modestly, not in a sexually arousing way; not viewing sexually oriented or pornographic videos; not telling dirty jokes—all of these simple customs are traditional ways of upholding sexual purity. The *yama* of *brahmacharya* works in concert with *asteya,* nonstealing. Stealing or coveting another's spouse, even mentally, creates a force that, once generated, is difficult to stop. ¶In this day and age, when promiscuity is a way of life, there is great strength in married couples' understanding and applying the principles of sexual purity. If they obey these principles and are on the path of enlightenment, they will again become celibate later in life, as they were when they were young. These principles persist through life, and when their children are raised and the forces naturally become quiet, around age sixty, husband and wife take the *brahmacharya vrata,* live in separate rooms and prepare themselves for greater spiritual experiences. ¶Married persons uphold sexual purity by observing the eightfold celibacy toward everyone but their spouse. These are ideals for serious, spiritual people. For those who have nothing to do with spirituality, these laws are meaningless. We are assuming a situation of a couple where everything they do and all that happens in their life is oriented toward spiritual life and spiritual goals and, therefore, these principles do apply. For sexual purity, individuals must believe firmly in the path to enlightenment. They must have faith in higher powers than themselves. Without this, sexual purity is nearly impossible. ¶One of the fastest ways to destroy the stability of families and societies is through promiscuity, mental and/or physical, and the best way to maintain stability is through self-control. The world today has become increasingly unstable because of the mental, physical, emotional license that people have given to themselves. The generation that follows an era of promiscuity has a dearth of examples to follow and are even more unstable than their parents were when they began their promiscuous living. Stability for human society is based on morality, and morality is based on harnessing and controlling sexuality. The principles of *brahmacharya* should be learned well before puberty, so that the sexual feelings the young person then begins to experience are free of mental fantasies and emotional involvement. Once established in a young person, this control is expected to be carried out all through life. When a virgin boy and girl marry, they transfer the love they have for their parents to one another. The boy's attachment to his mother is transferred to his wife, and the girl's attachment to her father is transferred to her husband. She now becomes the mother. He now becomes the father. This does not mean they love their parents any less. This is why the parents have to be in good shape, to create the next generation of stable families. This is their *dharmic* duty. If they don't do it, they create all kinds of uncomely *karmas* for themselves to be faced at a later time.

Saturday
LESSON 20
Kshamā: Patience

The fifth *yama*, patience, or *kshamā*, is as essential to the spiritual path as the spiritual path is to itself. Impatience is a sign of desirousness to fulfill unfulfilled desires, having no time for any interruptions or delays from anything that seems irrelevant to what one really wants to accomplish. ¶We must restrain our desires by regulating our life with daily worship and meditation. Daily worship and meditation are difficult to accomplish without a break in continuity. However, impatience and frustration come automatically in continuity, day after day, often at the same time—being impatient before breakfast because it is not served on time, feeling intolerant and abusive with children because they are not behaving as adults, and on and on. Everything has its timing and its regularity in life. Focusing on living in the eternity of the moment overcomes impatience. It produces the feeling that one has nothing to do, no future to work toward and no past to rely on. This excellent spiritual practice can be performed now and again during the day by anyone. ¶Patience is having the power of acceptance, accepting people, accepting events as they are happening. One of the great spiritual powers that people can have is to accept things as they are. That forestalls impatience and intolerance. Acceptance is developed in a person by understanding the law of *karma* and in seeing God Śiva and His work everywhere, accepting the perfection of the timing of the creation, preservation and absorption of the entire universe. Acceptance does not mean being resigned to one's situation and avoiding challenges. We know that we ourselves created our own situation, our own challenges, in a former time by sending forth our energies, thoughts, words and deeds. As these energies, on their cycle-back, manifest through people, happenings and circumstances, we must patiently deal with the situation, not fight it or try to avoid it or be discouraged because of it. This is *kshamā* in the raw. This is pure *kshamā*. Patience cannot be acquired in depth in any other way. This is why meditation upon the truths of the Sanātana Dharma is so important. ¶It is also extremely important to maintain patience with oneself—especially with oneself. Many people are masters of the façade of being patient with others but take their frustrations out on themselves. This can be corrected and must be corrected for spiritual unfoldment to continue through an unbroken routine of daily worship and meditation and a yearly routine of attending festivals and of pilgrimage, *tīrthayatra.* ¶Most people today are intolerant with one another and impatient with their circumstances. This breeds an irreverent attitude. Nothing is sacred to them, nothing holy. But through daily exercising anger, malice and the other lower emotions, they do, without knowing, invoke the demonic forces of the Narakaloka. Then they must suffer the backlash: have nightmares, confusions, separations and even perform heinous acts. Let all people of the world restrain themselves and be patient through the practice of daily worship and meditation, which retroactively invokes the divine forces from the Devaloka. May a great peace pervade the planet as the well-earned result of these practices. ¶The next time you find yourself becoming impatient, just stop for a moment and remember that you are on the upward path, now facing a rare opportunity to take one more step upward by overcoming these feelings, putting all that you have previously learned into practice. One does not progress on the spiritual path by words, ideas or unused knowledge. Memorized precepts, *ślokas,* all the shoulds and should-nots, are good, but unless used they will not propel you one inch further than you already are. It is putting what you have learned into practice in these moments of experiencing impatience and controlling it through command of your spiritual will, that moves you forward. These steps forward can never be retracted. When a test comes, prevail. ¶*Sādhakas* and *sannyāsins* must be perfect in *kshamā,* forbearing with people and patient under all circumstances, as they have harnessed their *karmas* of this life and the lives before, compressed them to be experienced in this one lifetime. There is no cause for them, if they are to succeed, to harbor intolerance or experience any kind of impatience with people or circumstances. Their instinctive, intellectual nature should be caught up in daily devotion, unreserved worship, meditation and deep self-inquiry. Therefore, the practice, *niyama,* that mitigates intolerance is devotion, Īśvarapūjana, cultivating devotion through daily worship and meditation.

Sunday
LESSON 21
Dhṛiti: Steadfastness

The sixth *yama* is *dhṛiti,* steadfastness. To be steadfast, you have to use your willpower. Willpower is developed easily in a person who has an adequate memory and good reasoning faculties. To be steadfast as we go through life, we must have a purpose, a plan, persistence and push. Then nothing is impossible within the circumference of our *prārabdha karmas.* ¶It is impossible to be steadfast if we are not obeying the other restraints that the *ṛishis* of the Himalayas laid down for us as the fruits of their wisdom. All of these restraints build character, and *dhṛiti,* steadfastness, rests on the foundation of good character. Character—the ability to "act with care"—is built slowly, over time, with the help of relatives, preceptors and good-hearted friends. Observe those who are steadfast. You will learn from them. Observe those who are not, and they, too, will teach you. They will teach what you should not do. To be indecisive and changeable is not how we should be on the path to enlightenment, nor to be successful in any other pursuit. Nonperseverance and fear must be overcome, and much effort is required to accomplish this. Daily *sādhana,* preferably under a *guru's* guidance, is suggested here to develop a spiritual will and intellect. ¶In the *Śāndilya Upanishad* (UPM, P. 173-174), *dhṛiti* has been described as preserving firmness of mind during the period of gain or loss of relatives. This implies that during times of sorrow, difficult *karmas,* loss and temptation, when in mental pain and anguish, feeling alone and neglected, we can persevere, be decisive and bring forth the *dhṛiti* strength within us and thus prevail. One translator of the *Varuha Upanishad* used the word *courage* to translate *dhṛiti.* Courageous and fearless people who are just and honest prevail over all *karmas*—benevolent, terrible and confused. This virtue is much like the monk's vow of humility, part of which is enduring hardship with equanimity, ease of mind, which means not panicking. The *Tirukural* reminds us, "It is the nature of asceticism to patiently endure hardship and to not harm living creatures" (261). And we can say that *dhṛiti* itself is a "hard ship"—a ship that can endure and persevere on its course even when tossed about on the waves of a turbulent sea. ¶Some might wonder why it is good to passively endure hardship. To persevere through hardship one must understand, as all Hindus do, that any hardship coming to us we ourselves participated in setting into motion in the past. To endure hardship and rise above it in consciousness is to overcome that *karma* forever. To resent hardship, to fight it, is to have it return later at a most inconvenient time. ¶An essential part of steadfastness is overcoming changeableness. Changeableness means indecision, not being decisive, changing one's mind after making a deliberate, positive decision. Changing one's mind can be a positive thing, but making a firm, well-considered decision and not following it through would gain one the reputation of not being dependable, even of being weak-minded. No one wants a reputation like this. ¶How can we discriminate between this and the strength of a person who changes his or her mind in wisdom

routine job. ¶We recently heard of a Western science lab study that fed two groups of rats different portions of food. Those who were allowed to have any amount of food they could eat lived a normal rat life span. Those who were given half that much lived twice as long. This so impressed the scientists that they immediately dropped their own calorie input and lost many pounds, realizing that a long, healthy life could be attained by not eating so much. ¶People on this planet are divided in two groups, as delineated by states of consciousness. The most obvious group is those ruled by lower consciousness, which proliferates deceit and dishonesty and the confusion in life that these bring, along with fear, anger, jealousy and the subsequent remorseful emotions that follow. On the purer side are those in higher consciousness, ruled by the powers of reason and memory, willpower, good judgment, universal love, compassion and more. A vegetarian diet helps to open the inner man to the outer person and brings forth higher consciousness. Eating meat, fish, fowl and eggs opens the doors to lower consciousness. It's as simple as that. A vegetarian diet creates the right chemistry for spiritual life. Other diets create a different chemistry, which affects your endocrine glands and your entire system all day long. A vegetarian diet helps your system all day long. Food is chemistry, and chemistry affects consciousness; and if our goal is higher consciousness, we have to provide the chemistry that evokes it.

Saturday
LESSON 27
Take Charge Of Your Body

There is a wonderful breathing exercise you can perform to aid the digestion and elimination of food by stimulating the internal fire. Breathe in through your nose a normal breath, and out through your nose very fast while pulling the stomach in. Then relax your stomach and again breathe in naturally and then out quickly by pulling the stomach in to force the air out of the lungs. Do this for one minute, then rest for one minute, then do it again. Then rest for a minute and do it again. About three repetitions is generally enough to conquer indigestion or constipation. This *prāṇāyāma* amplifies the heat of the body and stimulates the fire that digests food and eliminates waste. It is especially good for those who are rather sedentary and do a lot of intellectual work, whose energies are in the intellect and may not be addressing their digestive needs adequately. ¶Take charge of your own body and see that it is working right, is healthy and you are eating right. If you do overindulge, then compensate by fasting occasionally and performing physical disciplines. Most people have certain cravings and desires which they permit themselves to indulge in, whether it be sweets or rich, exotic foods or overly spiced foods. Discovering and moderating such personal preferences and desires is part of the spiritual path. If you find you overindulge in jelly beans, cashew nuts, licorice, chocolate, varieties of soft drinks or exotic imported coffee, moderate those appetites. Then you are controlling the entire desire nature of the instinctive mind in the process. That is a central process of spiritual unfoldment—to control and moderate such desires. ¶The *ṛishis* of yore taught us to restrain desire. They used the words *restrain* and *moderate* rather than *suppress* or *eliminate.* We must remember that to restrain and moderate desire allows the energy which is restrained and moderated to enliven higher *chakras,* giving rise to creativity and intuition that will actually better mankind, one's own household and the surrounding community. ¶The *ṛishis* have given us great knowledge to help us know what to do. Study your body and your diet and find out what works for you. Find out what foods give you indigestion and stop eating those things. But remember that eating right, in itself, is not spiritual life. In the early stages seekers often become obsessed with finding the perfect diet. That is a stage they have to go through in learning. They have to find out what is right for them. But it should balance out to a simple routine of eating to live, not living to eat.

Sunday
LESSON 28
Reasons for Vegetarianism

Vegetarianism has for thousands of years been a principle of health and environmental ethics throughout India. Though Muslim and Christian colonization radically undermined and eroded this ideal, it remains to this day a cardinal ethic of Hindu thought and practice. A subtle sense of guilt persists among Hindus who eat meat, and there exists an ongoing controversy on this issue. The Sanskrit for vegetarianism is *śākāhāra,* and one following a vegetarian diet is a *śākāhārī.* The term for meat-eating is *mānsāhāra,* and the meat-eater is called *mānsāhārī. Āhāra* means "food" or "diet," *śāka* means "vegetable," and *mānsa* means "meat" or "flesh." ¶Amazingly, I have heard people define *vegetarian* as a diet which excludes the meat of animals but does permit fish and eggs. But what really is vegetarianism? It is living only on foods produced by plants, with the addition of dairy products. Vegetarian foods include grains, fruits, vegetables, legumes, milk, yogurt, cheese and butter. The strictest vegetarians, known as vegans, exclude all dairy products. Natural, fresh foods, locally grown without insecticides or chemical fertilizers are preferred. A vegetarian diet does not include meat, fish, shellfish, fowl or eggs. For good health, even certain vegetarian foods are minimized: frozen and canned foods, highly processed foods, such as white rice, white sugar and white flour; and "junk" foods and beverages—those with abundant chemical additives, such as artificial sweeteners, colorings, flavorings and preservatives. ¶In the past fifty years millions of meat-eaters have made the decision to stop eating the flesh of other creatures. There are five major motivations for such a decision. 1) Many become vegetarian purely to uphold *dharma*, as the first duty to God and God's creation as defined by Vedic scripture. 2) Some abjure meat-eating because of the *karmic* consequences, knowing that by involving oneself, even indirectly, in the cycle of inflicting injury, pain and death by eating other creatures, one must in the future experience in equal measure the suffering caused. 3) Spiritual consciousness is another reason. Food is the source of the body's chemistry, and what we ingest affects our consciousness, emotions and experiential patterns. If one wants to live in higher consciousness, in peace and happiness and love for all creatures, then he cannot eat meat, fish, shellfish, fowl or eggs. By ingesting the grosser chemistries of animal foods, one introduces into the body and mind anger, jealousy, fear, anxiety, suspicion and a terrible fear of death, all of which are locked into the flesh of butchered creatures. 4) Medical studies prove that a vegetarian diet is easier to digest, provides a wider range of nutrients and imposes fewer burdens and impurities on the body. Vegetarians are less susceptible to all the major diseases that afflict contemporary humanity, and thus live longer, healthier, more productive lives. They have fewer physical complaints, less frequent visits to the doctor, fewer dental problems and smaller medical bills. Their immune system is stronger, their bodies purer and more refined, and their skin clearer, more supple and smooth. 5) Finally, there is the ecological reason. Planet Earth is suffering. In large measure, the escalating loss of species, destruction of ancient rainforests to create pasture lands for livestock, loss of topsoil and the consequent increase of water impurities and air pollution have all been traced to the single fact of meat in the human diet. No single decision that we can make as individuals or as a race can have such a dramatic effect on the improvement of our planetary ecology as the decision to not eat meat. Many conscious of the need to save the planet for future generations have made this decision for this reason and this reason alone.

Śaucha-Hrī
शौच-ह्री

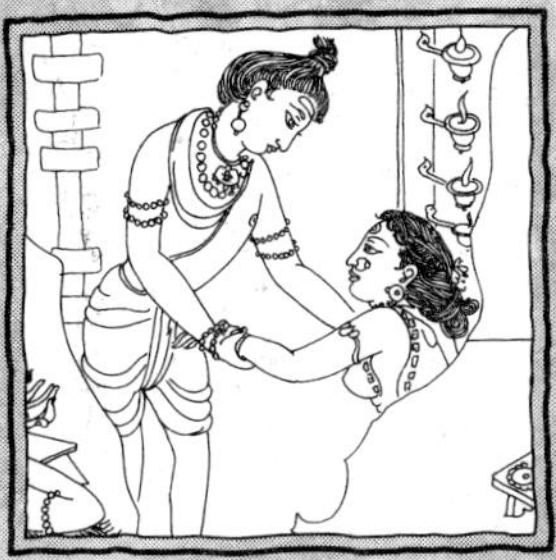

Purity and Remorse

That disciple is considered to be pure, capable and eligible for receiving the Śiva initiation who never feels unhappy or annoyed, who is nonviolent, merciful, ever vigilant, egoless, wise, devoid of jealousy, sweet-tongued, simple-hearted, soft-spoken, pious, modest, decisive, neat and clean, humble, righteous and devoted to Śiva.

Chandrajñāna Āgama, Kriyāpāda, 2.78-81. BO CJ P. 22

THEATRE
A
WINE SHOP
MANI

Monday
LESSON 29
Śaucha: Purity

Purity, *śaucha,* number ten of the *yamas,* is the outcome of restraining ourselves in all the other nine. Purity is the natural heritage of men and women disciplined in mind and body, who think before they speak, speaking only that which is true, kind, helpful and necessary. People whose thoughts are pure—and this means being in line with the *yamas* and *niyamas*—and whose bodies are free from incompatible alien obstructions, are naturally happy, content and ready to perform *japa. Japa yoga* lifts the spiritual energies and annihilates pride and arrogance by awakening within the superconscious areas of the mind an extraterrestrial intelligence, far surpassing the ordinary intellect one would encounter in the schools and universities of the present day. To be pure in mind means to have a bright, luminous aura filled with the pastel hues of the primary and secondary colors under every circumstance and life situation. Those who practice this restraint have realized that thoughts create and manifest into situations, actual physical happenings. Therefore, they are careful what they think and to whom they direct their thoughts. ¶A clean personal environment, wearing clean clothes, bathing often, keeping the room spotless where you meditate, breathing clean air, letting fresh air pass through your house, is all very important in the fulfillment of purity. *Śaucha* also includes partaking of clean food, which ideally is freshly picked food, cooked within minutes of the picking. There are creative forces, preservation forces and forces of dissolution. The preservation force is in the continued growing of a fruit or a leafy vegetable. It reaches its normal size and if not picked remains on the plant and is preserved by the life of that plant. As soon as it is picked, the force of dissolution, *mumia,* sets in. Therefore, the food should be cooked and eaten as soon after picking as possible, before the *mumia* force gets strong. *Mumia,* as it causes the breakdown of the cells, is an impure force. When we constantly eat food that is on the breakdown, the body is sluggish, the mind is sluggish and the tongue is loose, and we say things we don't mean. Many unhappy, depressed situations result from people eating a predominance of frozen foods, processed foods, canned foods, convenience foods, which are all in the process of *mumia.* ¶Clean clothing is very important. One feels invigorated and happy wearing clean clothing. Even hanging

Tears on the boy's face show his remorse, hrī, *at having kicked a soccer ball into a neighbor's home. Inset: A man has encountered his friend at an X-rated theater and is warning him to follow the ways of* śaucha, *and not get ensnared in pornography and low-minded sensual life.*

clothing out in the sunlight for five minutes a day cleanses and refreshes it. An incredible amount of body waste is eliminated through the skin and absorbed by the clothing we wear. It is commonly thought that clothing does not need to be cleaned unless it has been dirtied or soiled with mud, dirt or stains. Very little concern is given to the body odors and wastes that are exuded through the pores, then caught and held by the fabric. Small wonder it's so refreshing to put on clean clothing. The sun and fresh air can eliminate much of the body waste and freshen up any garment.

Tuesday
LESSON 30
Keeping Pure Surroundings

Cleaning the house is an act of purifying one's immediate environment. Each piece of furniture, as well as the doorways and the walls, catches and holds the emanations of the human aura of each individual in the home, as well as each of its visitors. This residue must be wiped away through dusting and cleaning. This regular attentiveness keeps each room sparkling clean and actinic. Unless this is done, the rooms of the home become overpowering to the consciousness of the individuals who live within them as their auras pick up the old accumulated feelings of days gone by. Small wonder that a dirty room can depress you, and one freshly cleaned can invigorate. ¶In these years, when both mother and father work in the outside world, the house is often simply where they sleep and eat. But if a home receives all of the daily attentions of cleaning it sparkly bright, both astrally and physically, it becomes a welcoming place and not an empty shell. The *devas* can live within a home that is clean and well regulated, where the routine of breakfast, lunch and dinner is upheld, where early morning devotionals are performed and respected, a home which the family lives together within, eats together within, talks together within, worships together within. Such a home is the abode of the *devas.* Other kinds of homes are the abodes of *asuric* forces and disincarnate entities bound to Earth by lower desires. ¶It is very important that the *saṁskāras* are performed properly within a *śaucha* abode, particularly the *antyeshṭi,* or funeral, ceremonies so as to restore purity in the home after a death. Birth and death require the family to observe a moratorium of at least thirty-one days during which they do not enter the temple or the shrine room. Such obligatory ritual customs are important to follow for those wishing to restrain their desires and perfect *śaucha* in body, mind and speech, keeping good company, keeping the mind pure and avoiding impure thoughts. ¶Purity and impurity can be discerned in the human aura. We see purity in the brilliancy of the aura of one who is restraining and disciplining the lower instinctive nature, as outlined in these *yamas* and *niyamas*. His aura is bright with white rays from his soul lightening up the various hues and colors of his moods and emotions. Impure people have black shading in the colors of their aura as they go through their moods and emotions. Black in the aura is from the lower worlds, the worlds of darkness, of the *tala chakras* below the *mūlādhāra.*

Wednesday
LESSON 31
Wholesome Company

It is unfortunate that at this time in the Kali Yuga there are more people on the Earth in important positions who have risen into physical birth from the Narakaloka, the world of darkness, than have descended from the Devaloka, the world of light. Therefore, they are strong as they band together in anger, corruption, deceit and contempt for the Devaloka people, who live in the *chakras* above the *mūlādhāra.* It is important for the Devaloka people to ferret out who is good company and who is not. They should not presume that they can effect any sustainable changes in the Narakaloka people. And they need to know that the *asuric* people, bound in anger, greed, jealousy, contempt, covetousness and lust, can make and sustain a difference within the *devonic* people, bringing them down into their world, torturing and tormenting them with their callous, cruel and insensitive feelings. To sustain *śaucha,* it is important to surround oneself with good, *devonic* company, to have the discrimination to know one type of person from another. Too many foolish, sensitive souls, thinking their spirituality could lift a soul from the world of darkness, have walked in where even the Mahādevas do not tread and the *devas* fear to tread, only to find themselves caught in that very world, through the deceit and conniving of the cleverly cunning. Let's not be foolish. Let's discriminate between higher consciousness and lower consciousness. Higher-consciousness people should surround themselves with higher-consciousness people to fulfill *śaucha.* ¶Changing to a purer life can be so simple. You don't have to give up anything. Just learn to like things that are better. That is the spirit of purity. When you give up something because you think you should give it up, that creates strain. Instead, search for a better life; search for *śaucha.* From *tamasic* eating we go to *rajasic* eating, and because *sattvic* food tastes better and makes us feel better, we also leave much of the *rajasic* food behind. Are not all persons on this planet driven by desire? Yes, indeed. Then let's redirect desire and let our desires perfect us. Let us learn to desire the more tasty, *sattvic* foods, the more sublime sounds, the most perfect things we can see, more than the gross, exciting and reprehensible, the desires for which will fade away when we attach ourselves to something better. Let our desires perfect us. The ultra-democratic dream of life, liberty and the pursuit of happiness we can use as a New-Age goal and pursue the happiness of something better than what we are doing now that is bad for us. Let's go forward with the spirit of moving onward. ¶A devotee told me, "I gave up coffee because coffee is a stimulant and a depressant. I stopped eating meat because meat is a cholesterol-creating killer and forest decimator." Another approach would be to give up coffee because you have found a beverage that is better. Test all beverages. Some have found that coffee gives you indigestion and green tea helps you digest your food, especially oily foods and foods that remain in your stomach undigested through the night. It also tastes good. Others have found that freshly picked, nutritious vegetables, especially when cooked within minutes of the picking, give more life and energy than eating dead meat that has been refrigerated or preserved. Still others have found that if you kill an animal and eat it fresh, it has more nutritive value than killing it, refrigerating it, preserving it, then cooking it to death again! ¶Be mature about it when you give something up. The immature spiritual person will want everyone else to give it up, too. The spiritually mature person quietly surrenders it because it is simply his personal choice and then goes on with his life. The spiritually immature person will make a big issue of giving anything up and want everyone to know about it.

Thursday
LESSON 32
Hrī: Remorse And Modesty

Hrī, the first of the ten *niyamas,* or practices, is remorse: being modest and showing shame for misdeeds, seeking the *guru's* grace to be released from sorrows through the understanding that he gives, based on the ancient *sampradāya,* doctrinal lineage, he preaches. Remorse could be the most misunderstood and difficult to practice of all of the *niyamas,* because we don't have very many role models today for modesty or remorse. In fact, the role for imitation in today's world is just the opposite. This is reflected in television, on film, in novels, magazines, newspapers and all other kinds of media. In today's world, brash, presumptuous, prideful—that's how one must be. That's the role model we see everywhere. In today's world, arrogant—that's how one must be. That's the role model we see everywhere. Therefore, to be remorseful or even to show modesty would be a sign of weakness to one's peers, family and friends. ¶Modesty is portrayed in the media as a trait of people that are gauche, inhibited, undeveloped emotionally or not well educated. And remorse is portrayed in the world media as a characteristic of one who "doesn't have his act together," is unable to rationalize away wrongdoings, or who is not clever enough to find a scapegoat to pin the blame on. Though modesty and remorse are the natural qualities of the soul, when the soul does exhibit these qualities, there is a natural tendency to suppress them. ¶But let's look on the brighter side. There is an old saying, "Some people teach us what to do, and other people teach us what not to do." The modern media, at least most of it, is teaching us what not to do. Its behavior is based on other kinds of philosophy—secular humanism, materialism, existentialism, crime and punishment, terrorism—in its effort to report and record the stories of the day. Sometimes we can learn quite a lot by seeing the opposite of what we want to learn. The proud and arrogant people portrayed on TV nearly always have their fall. This is always portrayed extremely well and is very entertaining. In their heart of hearts, people really do not admire the prideful person or his display of arrogance, so they take joy in seeing him get his just due. People, in their heart of hearts, do admire the modest person, the truthful person, the patient person, the steadfast person, the compassionate person who shows contentment and the fullness of well-being on his face and in his behavioral patterns. ¶We Hindus who understand these things know that *hrī*, remorse, is to be practiced at every opportunity. One of the most acceptable ways to practice *hrī*, even in today's society, is to say in a heartfelt way, "I'm sorry." Everyone will accept this. Even the most despicable, prideful, arrogant, self-centered person will melt just a little under the two magic words "I'm sorry." ¶When apologizing, explain to the person you hurt or wronged how you have realized that there was a better way and ask for his forgiveness. If the person is too proud or arrogant to forgive, you have done your part and can go your way. The burden of the quandary you have put him into now lies solely with him. He will think about it, justify how and why and what he should not forgive until the offense melts from his mind and his heart softens. It takes as much time for a hardened heart to soften as it does for a piece of ice to melt in a refrigerator. Even when it does, his pride may never let him give you the satisfaction of knowing he has forgiven you. But you can tell. Watch for softening in the eyes when you meet, a less rigid mouth and the tendency to suppress a wholesome smile.

Friday
LESSON 33
Body Language And Conscience

There is another way to show remorse for misdeeds. That is by performing *seva,* religious service, for persons you have wronged. Give them gifts, cook them food. Some people are unreachable by words, too remote for an apology, which might even lead to an argument, and then the wrong would perpetuate itself. Be extra polite to such people. Hold the door open as they walk through. Never miss an opportunity to be kind and serve. Say kind words about them behind their back. The praise must be true and timely. Mere flattery would be unacceptable. This kind of silent behavior shows repentance, shows remorse, shows that you have reconsidered your actions and found that they need improvement, and the improvement is shown by your actions now and into the future. ¶Often people think that showing shame and modesty and remorse for misdeeds is simply hanging your head. Well, really, anyone can do this, but it's not genuine if the head is not pulled down by the tightening of the strings of the heart, if shame is not felt so deeply that one cannot look another in the eye. When the hanging of the head is genuine, everyone will know it and seek to lift you up out of the predicament. But just to hang your head for a while and think you're going to get away with it in today's world, no. In today's world, people are a little too perceptive, and will not admire you, as they will suspect pretense. ¶There is an analogy in the Śaivite tradition that compares the unfolding soul to wheat. When young and growing, the stalks of wheat stand tall and proud, but when mature their heads bend low under the weight of the grains they yield. Similarly, man is self-assertive, arrogant and vain only in the early stages of his spiritual growth. As he matures and yields the harvest of divine knowledge, he too bends his head. Body language has to truly be the language of the body. It's a dead giveaway. Body language is the language of the mind being expressed through the body. Let there be no doubt about this. To cry, expressing remorse—the crying should not be forced. Many people can cry on cue. We must not think that the soul of the observer is not perceptive enough to know the difference between real tears and a glandular disturbance causing watering of the eyes. ¶*Hrī* is regret that one has done things against the *dharma,* or against conscience. There are three kinds of conscience—one built on right knowledge, one built on semi-right knowledge and one built on wrong knowledge. The soul has to work through these three gridworks within the subconscious mind to give its message. Those who have been raised with the idea that an injustice should be settled by giving back another injustice might actually feel a little guilty when they fail to do this. Those who are in a quandary of what to do, what is right and what is wrong, remain in confusion because they have only semi-right knowledge in their subconscious mind. ¶We cannot confuse guilt and its messages with the message that comes from the soul. Guilt is the message of the instinctive mind, the *chakras* below the *mūlādhāra*. Many people who live in the lower worlds of darkness feel guilty and satisfy that guilt through retaliation. This is the eye for an eye-for-an-eye, tooth-for-a-tooth approach. This is not right conscience; it is not the soul speaking. This is not higher consciousness, and it is certainly not the inner being of light looking out of the windows of the *chakras* above the *mūlādhāra*. Why, even domesticated animals feel guilty. It is a quality of the instinctive mind. ¶True conscience is of the soul, an impulse rushing through a mind that has been impregnated with right knowledge, *Vedic*, *Āgamic* knowledge, or the knowledge that is found in these *yamas* and *niyamas*, restraints and practices. When the true knowledge of *karma* is understood, reincarnation, *saṁsāra* and *Vedic dharma*, then true remorse is felt, which is a corrective mechanism of the soul. This remorse immediately imprints upon the lower mind the right knowledge of the *dharma*—how, where and why the person has strayed and the methodology of getting quickly and happily back to the path and proceeding onward. There is no guilt felt here, but there is a sense of spiritual responsibility, and a driving urge to bring *dharma*, the sense of spiritual duty, more fully into one's life, thus filling up the lack that the misdeeds manifested through adhering to these twenty restraints and practices and the *Vedic* path of *dharma*, which is already known within the bedrock of right knowledge, firmly planted within the inner mind of the individual.

Saturday
LESSON 34
Compensating For Misdeeds

The soul's response to wrong action comes of its own force, unbidden, when the person is a free soul, not bound by many materialistic duties—even while doing selfless service—which can temporarily veil and hold back the spontaneous actions of the soul if done for the expectant praise that may follow. The held-back, spontaneous action of the soul would, therefore, burst forth during personal times of *sādhana*, meditation or temple worship. The bursting forth would be totally unbidden, and resolutions would follow in the wake. For those immersed in heavy *prārabdha karmas*, going through a period of their life cycle when difficult *karmic* patterns are manifesting, it will be found that the soul's spontaneity is triple-veiled even though the subconscious mind is impregnated with right knowledge. To gain absolution and release, to gain peace of mind, one should perform pilgrimage, spiritual retreat, the practice of *mauna,* recitation of *mantras* through *japa,* deep meditation and, best of all, the *vāsanā daha tantra.* These practices will temporarily pierce the veils of *māyā* and let the light shine in, bringing understanding, solutions and direction for future behavior. ¶Having hurt another through wrongdoing, one has to pay back in proportion to the injury, not a rupee less and not a rupee more. The moment the healing is complete, the scar will mysteriously vanish. This is the law. It is a mystical law. And while there are any remaining scars, which are memories impregnated with emotion, much work has to be done. Each one must find a way to be nice if he has been not nice, say kind words if previous words have been unkind, issue forth good feelings if the feelings previously exuded were nasty, inharmonious and unacceptable. Just as a responsible doctor or nurse must bring the healing to culmination, so the wrongdoer must deal with his wrongdoing, his crime against *dharma,* his crime against right knowledge, *Vedic-Āgamic* precepts, his crime against the *yamas* and *niyamas,* restraints and practices, which are in themselves right knowledge—a digest of the *Vedas,* we might say. He must deal with his wrongdoings, his errors, within himself until rightness, *santosha,* returns. ¶There are no magic formulas. Each one must find his own way to heal himself and others until the troublesome situation disappears from his own memory. This is why the practice called *vāsanā daha tantra,* writing down memories and burning them in a fire to release the emotion from the deep subconscious, has proven to be a solution uncomparable to any other. Only in this way will he know that, by whatever method he has applied, he has healed the one he wronged. True forgiveness is the greatest eraser, the greatest harmonizer. It is this process of misdeeds against *dharma,* followed by shame and remorse, as people interrelate with one another, that moves them forward in their evolution toward their ultimate goal of *mukti.* ¶The Japanese, unlike most of the rest of the world, have a great sense of loss of face, and a Japanese businessman will resign if he has shamed his family or his country. This is *hrī* and is very much ingrained in the Japanese society, which is based on Buddhist precepts. Buddhism itself is the outgrowth into the family community from a vast monastic order; whereas Hinduism is a conglomerate of many smaller religions, some of which are not outgrowths of a monastic community. Therefore, *hrī* is an integral part of the culture of

Japan. They have maintained this and other cultural precepts, as the Buddhist monastic orders are still influential throughout Asia. ¶A materialist who loses face smiles and simply puts on another mask and continues as if nothing had ever happened. The saying goes, "Change your image and get on with life." No shame, repentance or reconciliation is shown by such people, as is so often portrayed on American television, and much worse, as it actually happens all the time in public life.

Sunday
LESSON 35
Humility, Shame And Shyness

The Hindu monastic has special disciplines in regard to remorse. If he doesn't, he is an impostor. If he is seen struggling to observe it and unable to accomplish it all the time, he is still a good monastic. If he shows no remorse, modesty or shame for misdeeds for long periods of time, even though he continues apparently in the performance of no misdeeds, the abbot of the monastery would know that he is suppressing many things, living a personal life, avoiding confrontation and obscuring that which is obvious to himself with a smile and the words, "Yes, everything is all right with me. The meditations are going fine. I get along beautifully with all of my brothers." You would know that this is a "mission impossible," and that it is time to effect certain tests to break up the nest of the enjoyable routine and of keeping out of everybody's way, of not participating creatively in the entire community, but just doing one's job and keeping out of trouble. The test would bring him out in the open, into counseling sessions, so that he himself would see that his clever pride had led him to a spiritual standstill. A monastery is no place to settle down and live. It is a place to be on one's toes and advance. One must always live as if on the eve of one's departure. ¶Another side of *hrī* is being bashful, shy, unpretentious. The undeveloped person and the fully developed, wise person may develop the same qualities of being bashful, shy, unpretentious, cautious. In the former, these qualities are the products of ignorance produced by underexposure, and in the latter, they are the products of the wisdom or cleverness produced by overexposure. Genuine modesty and unpretentiousness are not what actors on the stage would portray, they are qualities that one cannot act out, qualities of the soul. ¶Shyness used to be thought of as a feminine quality, but not anymore, since the equality of men and women has been announced as the way that men and women should be. Both genders should be aggressive, forceful, to meet and deal with situations on equal terms. This is seen today in the West, in the East, in the North and the South. This is a façade which covers the soul, producing stress in both men and women. A basically shy man or woman, feeling he or she has to be aggressive, works his or her way into a stressful condition. I long ago found that stress in itself is a byproduct of not being secure in what one is doing. But this is the world today, at this time in the Kali Yuga. If everything that is happening were reasonable and could be easily understood, it certainly wouldn't be the Kali Yuga. ¶If people are taught and believe that their spiritual pursuits are foremost, then, yes, they should be actively aggressive—but as actively passive and modest as well, because of their spiritual pursuits. Obviously, if they are performing *sādhanas*, they will intuitively know the proper timing for each action. Remorse, or modesty, certainly does not mean one must divorce oneself from the ability to move the forces of the external world, or be a wimpy kind of impotent person. It does mean that there is a way of being remorseful, showing shame, being humble, of resolving situations when they do go wrong so that you can truly "get on with life" and not be bound by emotionally saturated memories of the past. Those who are bound by the past constantly remember the past and relive the emotions connected with it. Those who are free from the past remember the future and move the forces of all three worlds for a better life for themselves and for all mankind. This is the potent Vedic *hrī*. This is true remorse, humility and modesty. This is *hrī*, which is not a weakness but a spiritual strength. And all this is made practical and permanent by subconscious journaling, *vāsanā daha tantra*, which releases creative energy and does not inhibit it.

Santosha-Dāna

सन्तोष-दान

Contentment And Giving

The liberal man is he who gives to the beggar
who wanders in search of food, lean and forlorn;
the one who helps the passerby, when asked,
makes of this same a friend for days to come.

Ṛig Veda 10.117.3. VE, P. 850

Monday
LESSON 36
Santosha: Contentment

Contentment, *santosha,* is the second *niyama.* How do we practice contentment? Simply do not harm others by thought, word or deed. As a practitioner of *ahiṁsā,* noninjury, you can sleep contentedly at night and experience *santosha* then and through the day. Contentment is a quality that everyone wants, and buys things to obtain—"Oh, if I only had my house redecorated, I would be content." "A new wardrobe would content me, give me joy and serenity." "To be content, I must have a vacation and get away from it all. There I can live the serene life and have joyous experiences." ¶The *dharmic* way is to look within and bring out the latent contentment that is already there by doing nothing to inhibit its natural expression, as *santosha,* the mood of the soul, permeates out through every cell of the physical body. Contentment is one of the most difficult qualities to obtain, and is well summed up within our food blessing *mantra,* from the *Śukla Yajur Veda, Īsa Upanishad* invocation, "That is fullness. Creation is fullness. From that fullness flows this world's fullness. This fullness issues from that fullness, yet that fullness remains full." This joy we seek is the joy of fullness, lacking nothing. ¶Life is meant to be lived joyously. There is in much of the world the belief that life is a burden, a feeling of penitence, that it is good to suffer, good for the soul. In fact, spiritual life is not that way at all. The existentialist would have you believe that depression, rage, fear and anguish are the foremost qualities of the human temper and expression. The communists used to have us believe that joy and serenity as the outgrowth of religion are just an opiate of the people, a narcotic of unreality. The Semitic religions of the Near East would have us believe that suffering is good for the soul, and there is not much you can do about it. The Śaivite Hindu perspective is that contentment is a reflection of centeredness, and discontentment is a reflection of externalized consciousness and ramified desire. ¶Maintaining joy and serenity in life means being content with your surroundings, be they meager or lavish. Be content with your money, be it a small amount or a large amount. Be content with your health. Bear up under ailments and be thankful that they are not worse than they are. Protect your health if it is good. It is a valuable treasure. Be content with your friends. Be loyal to those who are your long-time, trusted companions.

Santosha, *contentment, is shown by three generations living at home, enjoying one another, happy and fulfilled in their simple life. Inset: A well-to-do woman takes joy in giving clothing to her poorer neighbors in a selfless act of* dāna.

Basically, contentment, *santosha,* is freedom from desire gained by redirecting the forces of desire and making a beautiful life within what one already has in life. ¶The rich seeking more riches are not content. The famous seeking more fame are not content. The learned seeking more knowledge are not content. Being content with what you have does not mean you cannot discriminate and seek to progress in life. It doesn't mean you should not use your willpower and fulfill your plans. ¶It does mean you should not become upset while you are striving toward your goals, frustrated or unhappy if you do not get what you want. The best striving is to keep pushing along the natural unfoldment of positive trends and events in your life, your family life and your business. Contentment is working within your means with what is available to you, living within your income, being grateful for what you have, and not unhappy over what you lack. ¶There are many frustrated souls on the path who torment themselves no end and walk around with long faces because they estimate they are not unfolding spiritually fast enough. They have set goals of Self Realization for themselves far beyond their abilities to immediately obtain. If people say, "I am not going to do anything that will not make me peaceful or that will threaten my peace of mind," how will they get anywhere? That is not the idea of *santosha.* True *santosha* is seeing all-pervasiveness of the one divine power everywhere. The light within the eyes of each person is that divine power. With this in mind, you can go anywhere and do anything. Contentment is there, inside you, and needs to be brought out. It is a spiritual power. So, yes, do what makes you content. But know that contentment really transcends worrying about the challenges that face you. *Santosha* is being peaceful in any situation. The stronger you are in *santosha,* the greater the challenges you can face and still remain quiet on the inside, peaceful and content, poised like a hummingbird hovering over a flower.

Tuesday
LESSON 37
Keeping Peace In the Home

Santosha is the goal; *dharma,* good conduct, remains the director of how you should act and respond to fulfill your *karma.* This goal is attainable by following the ten Vedic restraints: not harming others by thought, word or deed, refraining from lying, not entering into debt, being tolerant with people and circumstance, overcoming changeableness and indecision, not being callous, cruel or insensitive to other people's feelings. Above all, never practice deception. Don't eat too much. Maintain a vegetarian diet for purity and clarity of mind. Watch carefully what you think and how you express it through words. All of these restraints must be captured and practiced within the lifestyle before the natural contentment, the *santosha,* the pure, serene nature of the soul can shine forth. Therefore, the practice to attain *santosha* is to fulfill the *yamas.* Proceed with confidence; failure is an impossibility. ¶I was asked by a cyberspace cadet among our Internet congregation, "Where do we let off steam? Mom works, dad works, the kids are in school, and when everyone comes home, everyone lets off a little steam, and everyone understands." My answer is don't let off steam in the home. The home is a sanctuary of the entire family. It should have an even higher standard of propriety than the office, the factory or the corporate workplace. When we start being too casual at home and letting off steam, we say things that perhaps we shouldn't. We may think the rest of the family understands, but they don't. Feelings get hurt. We break up the vibration of the home. Young people also let off steam in school, thus inhibiting their own education. They behave in a way in the classroom that they would not in a corporate office, and who is hurt but themselves? It's amazing how quickly people shape up their behavior when they sign a contract, when they get a job in a corporate office. They read the manual, they obey it and they are nice to everyone. This is the way it should be within the home. The home should be maintained at a higher standard than the corporate office. ¶The wonderful thing about Hinduism is that we don't let off steam at home; we let our emotions pour out within the Hindu temple. The Hindu temple is the place where we can relate to the Gods and the Goddesses and express ourselves within ourselves. It's just between ourselves and the Deity. In a Hindu temple there may be, all at the same time, a woman worshiper crying in a corner, not far away a young couple laughing among themselves with their children, and nearby someone else arguing with the Gods. The Hindu temple allows the individual to let off steam, but it is a controlled situation, controlled by the *pūjās,* the ceremony, the priesthood. ¶So as to not make more *karma* in this life by saying things we don't mean, having inflections in our voice that are hurtful to others, we must control the home, control ourselves in the workplace, keep the home at a higher vibration of culture and protocol than the workplace, and include the temple in our lives as a place to release our emotions and regain our composure. ¶It is making a lot of really bad *karma* that will come back in its stronger reaction later on in life for someone, the husband or wife or teenager, to upset the vibration of the home because of stress at school or in the workplace. It is counterproductive to work all day in a nice office, control the emotions and be productive, and then go home and upset the vibration within the home. After all, why is someone working? It's to create the home. Why is someone going to school? It's to eventually create a home. It is counterproductive to destroy that which one works all day to create. That's why I advise the professional mother, the professional father, the professional son and the professional daughter to use in the home the same good manners that are learned in the workplace, and build the vibration of the home even stronger than the vibration of the workplace, so that there is something inviting to come home to. ¶We have seen so many times, professionals, men and women, behave exquisitely in the workplace, but not so exquisitely at home, upset the home vibration, eventually destroying the home, breaking up the home. And we have seen, through the years, a very unhappy person in retirement, a very bitter person in retirement. No one wants him around, no one wants to have him in their home. Therefore, he winds up in some nursing home, and he dies forgotten. ¶The Sanātana Dharma and Śaiva Samayam must be alive in the home, must be alive in the office, must be alive in the temple, for us to have a full life. Where, then, do we vent our emotions, where do we let off steam, if not in our own home? The answer is, within the temple.

Wednesday
LESSON 38
Dāna: Giving

Giving, *dāna,* is the third great religious practice, or *niyama.* It is important to remember that giving freely of one's goods in fulfilling needs, making someone happy or putting a smile on his face, mitigates selfishness, greed, avarice and hoarding. But the most important factor is "without thought of reward." The reward of joy and the fullness you feel is immediate as the gift passes from your two hands into the outstretched hands of the receiver. *Dāna* is often translated as "charity." But charity in modern context is a special kind of giving by those who have to those who have not. This is not the true spirit of *dāna.* The word *fulfillment* might describe *dāna* better. The fulfillment of giving that wells up within the giver as the gift is being prepared and as the gift is being presented and released, the fulfillment of the expectancy of the receiver or the surprise of the receiver, and the fullness that exists afterwards are all a part of *dāna.* ¶*Daśamāṁśa,* tithing, too, is a worthy form of *dāna*—giving God's money to a religious institution to fulfill with it God's work. One who is really fulfilling *dāna* gives *daśamāṁśa,* never goes to visit a friend or relative with empty hands, gives freely to relatives, children, friends, neighbors and business associates, all without thought of reward. The devotee who practices *dāna* knows fully that "you cannot give anything away." The law of *karma* will return it to you full measure at an appropriate and most needed time. The freer the gift is given, the faster it will return. ¶What is the proportionate giving after *daśamāṁśa*, ten percent, has been deducted? It would be another two to five percent of one's gross income, which would be equally divided between cash and kind if someone wanted to discipline his *dāna* to that extent. That would be fifteen percent, approximately one sixth, which is the *makimai* established in South India by the Chettiar community around the Palani Temple and now practiced by the Malaka Chettiars of Malaysia. ¶If one were to take a hard look at the true spirit of *dāna* in today's society, the rich giving to religious institutions for a tax deduction are certainly giving with a thought of reward. Therefore, giving after the tax deductions are received and with no material benefits or rewards of any kind other than the fulfillment of giving is considered by the wise to be a true expression of *dāna*. Making something with one's own hands, giving in kind, is also a true expression of *dāna*. Giving a gift begrudgingly in return for another gift is, of course, mere barter. Many families barter their way through life in this way, thinking they are giving. But such gifts are cold, the fulfillment is empty, and the law of *karma* pays discounted returns.

Thursday
LESSON 39
Hospitality And Fullness

Hospitality is a vital part of fulfilling *dāna*. When guests come, they must be given hospitality, at least a mat to sit on and a glass of water to drink. These are obligatory gifts. You must never leave your guest standing, and you must never leave your guest thirsty. If a guest were to smell even one whiff from the kitchen of the scented curries of a meal being prepared, he must be asked four times to stay for the meal. He will politely refuse three times and accept on the fourth invitation. This is also an obligatory giving, for the guest is treated as God. God Śiva's veiling grace hides Śiva as He dresses in many costumes. He is a dancer, you know, and dancers wear many costumes. He will come as a guest to your home, unrecognizable. You might think it is your dear friend from a far-off place. That, too, is Śiva in another costume, and you must treat that guest as Śiva. Giving to Śiva Śiva's own creation in your mind brings the highest rewards through the law of *karma*. ¶Even if you think you are giving creatively, generously, looking for no rewards, but you are giving for a purpose, that *karma* will still pay you back with full interest and dividends. This is a positive use of the law of *karma.* It pays higher interest than any bank. This is not a selfish form of giving. It is the giving of the wise, because you know the law of *karma,* because you know the Sanātana Dharma—the divine, eternal laws. If you see a need that you can fill and have the impulse to give but recoil from giving, later, when you are in need, there will be someone who has the impulse to give to you but will recoil from giving. The wheels of *karma* grind slowly but exceedingly well the grains of actions, be they in thought, emotion or those of a physical nature. So, one can be quite selfish and greedy about wanting to practice *dāna* to accumulate the *puṇya* for the balance of this life, the life in-between lives, in the astral world, and for a good birth in the next incarnation. The practice of *dāna* is an investment in a better life, an investment that pays great dividends. ¶We are not limited by our poverty or wealth in practicing giving. No matter how poor you are, you can still practice it. You can give according to your means, your inspiration, your ability. When the fullness has reached its peak within you while preparing the gift, be it arranging a bouquet of freshly picked flowers, a tray of fruit, counting out coins, sorting a pile of bills or putting zeros on a check that you're writing, then you know that the gift is within your means. Gifts within your means and from your heart are the proper gifts.

Friday
LESSON 40
The Selfish And Miserly

The virtue of *dāna* deals with the pragmatic physical transference of cash or kind. It is the foundation and the life blood of any other form of religious giving, such as giving of one's time. Many people rationalize, "I'll give my time to the temple. I'll wash the pots, scrub the floor and tidy up. But I can't afford to give of my limited wealth proportionate to what would be total fulfillment of giving." Basically, they have nothing better to do with their time, and to ease their own conscience, they volunteer a little work. There is no merit, no *puṇya,* in this, only demerit, *pāpa.* No, it's just the other way around. One who has perfected *dāna* in cash and in kind and is satisfied within this practice, this *niyama,* will then be able and willing to give of his time, to tithe ten percent of his time, and then give time over and above that to religious and other worthy causes. Shall we say that the perfection of *dāna* precedes *seva,* service? ¶What can be said of someone who is all wrapped up in his personal self: concealing his personal ego with a pleasant smile, gentle deeds, soft words, but who just takes care of "number one"? For instance, if living with ten people, he will cook for himself and not cook for the others. He gets situations confused, entertains mental arguments within himself and is always worried about the progress in his religious life. We would say he is still trying to work on the restraints—compassion, patience, sexual purity, moderate appetite—and has not yet arrived at number three on the chart of the practices called *niyamas.* Modern psychology would categorize him as self-centered, selfish, egotistical. To overcome this selfishness, assuming he gets the restraints in order, doing things for others would be the practice, seeing that everyone is fed first before he eats, helping out in every way he can, performing anonymous acts of kindness at every opportunity. ¶In an orthodox Hindu home, the traditional wife will follow the practice of arising in the morning before her husband, preparing his hot meal, serving him and eating only after he is finished; preparing his lunch, serving him and eating after he is finished; preparing his dinner, serving him and eating after he is finished, even if he returns home late. Giving to her husband is her fulfillment, three times a day. This is built into Hindu society, into Śaivite culture. ¶Wives should be allowed by their husbands to perform giving outside the home, too, but many are not. All too often, they are held down, embarrassed and treated almost like domestic slaves—given no money, given no things to give, disallowed to practice *dāna,* to tithe and give creatively without thought of reward. Such domineering, miserly and ignorant males will get their just due in the courts of *karma* at the moment of death and shortly after. The divine law is that the wife's *śakti* power, once released, makes her husband magnetic and successful in his worldly affairs, and their wealth accumulates. He knows from tradition that to release this *śakti* he must always fulfill all of the needs of his beloved wife and give her generously everything she wants.

Saturday
LESSON 41
Many Ways Of Giving

There are so many ways of giving. Arising before the Sun comes up, greeting and giving *namaskāra* to the Sun is a part of Śaivite culture. *Dāna* is built into all aspects of Hindu life—giving to the holy man, giving to the astrologer, giving to the teacher, giving *dakshiṇā* to a *swāmī* or a *satguru* for his support, over and above all giving to his institution, over and above *daśamāṁśa,* over and above giving to the temple. If the *satguru* has satisfied you with the fullness of his presence, you must satisfy yourself in equal fullness in giving back. You can be happily fat as these two fullnesses merge within you. By giving to the *satguru,* you give him the satisfaction of giving to another, for he has no needs except the need to practice *dāna.* ¶Great souls have always taught that, among all the forms of giving, imparting the spiritual teachings is the highest. You can give money or food and provide for the physical aspects of the being, but if you can find a way to give the *dharma*, the illumined wisdom of the traditions of the Sanātana Dharma, then you are giving to the spirit of the person, to the soul. Many Hindus buy religious literature to give away, because *jñāna dāna*, giving wisdom, is the highest giving. Several groups in Malaysia and Mauritius gave away over 70,000 pieces of literature in a twenty-month period. Another group in the United States gave away 300,000 pieces of literature in the same period. Many pieces of that literature changed the lives of individuals and brought them into a great fullness of soul satisfaction. An electric-shock blessing would go out from them at the peak of their fulfillment and fill the hearts of all the givers. Giving through education is a glorious fulfillment for the giver, as well as for the receiver. ¶Wealthy men in India will feed twenty thousand people in the hopes that one enlightened soul who was truly hungry at that time might partake of this *dāna* and the *śakti* that arises within him at the peak of his satisfaction will prepare for the giver a better birth in his next life. This is the great spirit of *anna yajñā*, feeding the masses. ¶Along with the gift comes a portion of the *karma* of the giver. There was an astrologer who when given more than his due for a *jyotisha* consultation would always give the excess to a nearby temple, as he did not want to assume any additional *karma* by receiving more than the worth of his predictions. Another wise person said, "I don't do the *antyeshṭi saṁskāra*, funeral rites, because I can't receive the *dāna* coming from that source of sadness. It would affect my family." Giving is also a way of balancing *karma*, of expressing gratitude for blessings received. A devotee explained, "I cannot leave the temple without giving to the *huṇḍi*, offering box, according to the fullness I have received as fullness from the temple." A gourmet once said, "I cannot leave the restaurant until I give gratuity to the waiter equaling the satisfaction I felt from the service he gave." This is *dāna*, this is giving, in a different form. ¶Children should be taught giving at a very young age. They don't yet have the ten restraints, the *yamas*, to worry about. They have not been corrupted by the impact of their own *prārabdha karmas*. Little children, even babies, can be taught *dāna*—giving to the temple, to holy ones, to one another, to their parents. They can be taught worship, recitation and, of course, contentment—told how beautiful they are when they are quiet and experiencing the joy of serenity. Institutions should also give, according to their means, to other institutions.

Monday
LESSON 43
Āstikya: Faith

Faith, *āstikya*, is the fourth *niyama*. Faith is a substance, a collection of molecules, mind molecules, emotion molecules—and some are even physical—collected together, charged with the energies of the Divine and the anxieties of the undivine, made into an astral form of shape, color and sound. Being a creation built up over time, faith can just as readily be destroyed, as the following phrases indicate: crisis of faith, loss of faith, dark night of the soul, and just plain confused disappointment leading to depression. Because of faith, groups of people are drawn together, cling together, remain together, intermarry and give birth, raising their children together in the substance of faith that their collective group is subconsciously committed to uphold. ¶Anyone can strengthen another's faith through encouragement, personal example, good natured humoring, praise, flattery, adulation, or take it away by the opposite methods. Many people with more faith than intellect are pawns in the hands of those who hold great faith, or of those who have little faith, or of those who have no faith at all. Therefore, we can see that a clear intellectual understanding of the philosophy is the bedrock to sustaining faith. Faith is on many levels and of many facets. We have faith in a person, a family, a system of government, science, astronomy, astrology. Faith in philosophy, religion, is the most tenuous and delicate kind and, we must say, the most rewarding of all faiths, because once it is sustained in unbroken continuity, the pure soul of the individual begins to shine forth. ¶Faith has eyes. It has three eyes. The seer who is looking at the world from the perspective of monistic Śaiva Siddhānta and sees clearly the final conclusions for all mankind has faith in his perception, because what he sees and has seen becomes stronger in his mind as the years go by. We have the faith of those who have two eyes upraised. They look at the seer as Dakshiṇāmūrti, God Himself, and gain strength from His every word. There is also the faith of those who have two eyes lowered. They are reading the scriptures, the teachings of all the seers, and building the aura of faith within their inner psyche. Then there are those who have faith with their eyes closed, blind faith. They know not, read not and are not thinking, but are entranced by the spiritual leader in whom they have faith as a personality. They are nodding their head up and down on

---

Hands held above her head during a pūjā, *a devotee venerates Lord Gaṇeśa in an act of* Īśvarapūjana, *worship. Inset: A man's car has stalled on the tracks just as a train approaches. He keeps his faith,* āstikya, *despite the ordeal, and Śiva is nearby to guide him to safety.*

his every word and when questioned are not able to adequately explain even one or two of his profound thoughts. ¶And then we have the others, who make up much of the world population today. They are also with eyes closed, but with heads down, shaking left and right, left and right. They see mostly the darker side of life. They are those who have no faith at all or suffer a semi-permanent loss of faith, who are disappointed in people, governments, systems, philosophies, religions. Their leaders they condemn. This is a sorry lot. Their home is the halls of depression, discouragement and confusion. Their upliftment is jealousy and anger.

Tuesday
LESSON 44
Faith Is on Many Levels

Faith extends to another level, too, of pleasure for the sake of pleasure. Here we have the jet-set, the hedonists, the sensualists, the pornographers and their customers. All these groups have developed their own individual mindset and mix and interrelate among themselves, as the astral molecules of this amorphous substance of thought, emotion and belief that we call faith creates their attitudes toward the world, other people and their possessions. ¶The Hindu, therefore, is admonished by the *sapta ṛishis* themselves to believe firmly in God, Gods, *guru* and the path to enlightenment, lest he stray from the path of *dharma*—for faith is a powerful force. It can be given; it can be taken away. It is a national force, a community force, a group force, a family force. And it is more than that, as far as the Sanātana Dharma is concerned, which can be translated as the "eternal faith," the most strengthening and illuminating of all, for it gives courage to all to apply these twenty *yamas* and *niyamas*, which represent the final conclusions of the deepest deliverers of eternal wisdom who ever resided on this planet. ¶Some people have faith only when things are going right and lose faith when things go wrong. These are the ones who are looking up at their leaders, whom they really do not know, who are looking up at the scriptures, which they really do not understand. Because their eyes are closed, they are seeking to be sustained and constantly uplifted by others. "Do my *sādhana* for me" is their plea. And when some inconsistency arises or some expectation, unbeknownst to their leader and maybe never even recorded in the scriptures, does not manifest, a crisis of faith occurs. Then, more than often, they are off to another leader, another philosophy, to inevitably repeat the same experience. Devotees of this kind, who are called "groupies" in rock and roll, go from group to group, teacher to teacher, philosophy to philosophy. Fortunately for them, the rent is not expensive, the *bhajanas* are long and the food is good. The only embarrassing situation, which has to be manipulated, is the tactic of leaving one group without totally closing the door, and manipulatively opening the door of another group. ¶When that uplifted face with eyes closed has the spiritual experience of the eyes opening, the third eye flashing, he or she would have then found at last his or her *sampradāya,* traditional lineage of verbal teaching, and now be on the unshakable path. The molecules of faith have been converted and secured. They shall never turn back, because they have seen through the third eye the beginning and ending of the path, the traditional lineage ordained to carry them forth generation after generation. These souls become the articulate ones, masters of the philosophy. Their faith is so strong, they can share their molecules with others and mold others' faith molecules into traditional standards of the whys and wherefores that we all need on this planet, of how we should believe and think, where we go when we die, and all the eternal truths of the ultimate attainments of mankind.

Wednesday
LESSON 45
Stages of Evolution

Faith is the intellect of the soul at its various stages of unfoldment. The soul comes forth from Lord Śiva as an embryo and progresses through three stages *(avasthā)* of existence: *kevala avasthā, sakala avasthā* and *śuddha avasthā.* During *kevala avasthā,* the soul is likened to a seed hidden in the ground or a spark of the Divine hidden in a cloud of unknowing called *āṇava,* the primal fetter of individuality, the first aspect of Lord Śiva's concealing grace, *tirodhāna śakti. Sakala avasthā,* the next stage in the soul's journey, is the period of bodily existence, the cyclic evolution through transmigration from body to body, under the additional powers of *māyā* and *karma,* the second and third aspects of the Lord's concealing grace. ¶The journey through *sakala avasthā* is also in three stages. The first is called *irul pāda,* "stage of darkness," where the soul's impetus is toward *pāśa-jñānam,* knowledge and experience of the world. The next period is *marul pāda,* "stage of confusion," where the soul begins to take account of its situation and finds itself caught between the world and God, not knowing which way to turn. This is called *paśu-jñānam,* the soul seeking to know its true nature. The last period is *arul pāda,* "stage of grace," when the soul yearns for the grace of God. Now it has begun its true religious evolution with the constant aid of the Lord. ¶For the soul in darkness, *irul,* faith is primitive, illogical. In its childlike endeavors it clings to this faith. There is no intellect present in this young soul, only primitive faith and instinctive mind and body. But it is this faith in the unseen, the unknown, the words of the elders and its ability to adjust to community without ruffling everyone's feathers that matures the soul to the next *pāda*—*marul,* wherein faith becomes faith in oneself, close friends and associates, faith in one's intellectual remembrance of the opinions of others, even if they are wrong. ¶It is not very quickly that the soul gets out of this syndrome, because it is here that the *karmas* are made that bind the soul, surround the soul, the *karmas* of ignorance which must be gone through for the wisdom to emerge. Someone who is wise got that way by facing up to all the increments of ignorance. The *marul pāda* is very binding and tenacious, tenaciously binding. But as the external shell of *āṇava* is being built, the soul exercises itself in its own endeavor to break through. Its "still small voice" falls on deaf ears. ¶*Yoga* brings the soul into its next experiential pattern. The soul comes to find that if he performs good and virtuous deeds, life always seems to take a positive turn. Whereas in negative, unvirtuous acts he slowly becomes lost in a foreboding abyss of confusion. Thus, in faith, he turns toward the good and holy. A balance emerges in his life, called *iruvinaioppu.* ¶Whether he is conscious of it or not, he is bringing the three *malas*—*āṇava, karma* and *māyā*—under control. *Māyā* is less and less an enchanting temptress. *Karma* no longer controls his state of mind, tormenting him through battering experiences. And *āṇava,* his self-centered nature, is easing its hold, allowing him to feel a more universal compassion in life. This grows into a state called *malaparipakam,* the ripening of the *malas.* ¶This will allow, at the right moment in his life, *arul* to set in. This is known as the descent of grace, *śaktinipāta.* The internal descent is recognized as a tremendous yearning for Śiva. More and more, he wants to devote himself to all that is spiritual and holy. The outer descent of grace is the appearance of a *satguru.* There is no question as to who he is, for he sheds the same clear, spiritual vibration as that unknown something the soul feels emanating from his deepest self. It is when the soul has reached *malaparipakam* that the Lord's *tirodhāna* function, His concealing grace, has accomplished its work and gives way to *anugraha,* revealing grace, and the descent of grace, *śaktinipāta,* occurs. ¶At this stage, knowledge comes unbidden. Insights into human affairs are mere readings of past experiences, for those experiences that are being explained to others were actually lived through by the person himself. This is no mystery. It is the threshold of *śuddha avasthā.* Lord Śiva is at the top, Lord Gaṇeśa is at the bottom, and Lord Murugan is in the heart of it, in the center.

Thursday
LESSON 46
Faith in Tradition

The intellect in its capacity to contain truth is a very limited tool, while faith is a very broad, accommodating and embracing faculty. The mystery of life and beyond life, of Śiva, is really better understood through faith than through intellectual reasoning. The intellect is a memory/reason conglomerate from the lower *nāḍī/chakra* complex. Its refined ability to juggle information around is uncanny in some instances. Nevertheless, the intellect is built upon what we hear and remember, what we experience and remember, what we explain to others who are refined or gross in reasoning faculties. What we remember of it all and the portions that have been forgotten may be greatly beneficial to those listening, or it may be confusing, but it is certainly not Truth with a capital "T." ¶There are two kinds of faith. The first kind is faith in those masters, adepts, *yogīs* and *ṛishis* who have had similar experiences and have spoken about them in similar ways, unedited by the ignorant. We, therefore, can have faith that some Truth was revealed from within themselves, from some deep, inner or higher source. The second aspect of faith is in one's own spiritual, unsought-for, unbidden flashes of intuition, revelations or visions, which one remembers even stronger as the months go by, more vividly than something read from a book, seen on television or heard from a friend or a philosopher. These personal revelations create a new, superconscious intellect when verified by what *yogīs* and *ṛishis* and the *sādhus* have seen and heard and whose explanations centuries have preserved. These are the old souls of the *śuddha avasthā,* being educated from within out, building a new intellect from superconscious insights. Their faith is unshakable, undaunted, for it is themself. It is just who they are at this stage of the evolution, the maturation, of their soul in the *śuddha avasthā.* ¶One of the aspects of faith is the acceptance of tradition rather than the questioning or doubting of traditions. Another is trust in the process of spiritual unfoldment, so that when one is going through an experience, one always believes that the process is happening, instead of thinking that today's negative experience is outside the process. However, it is not possible for souls in the *irul pāda,* stage of darkness, to trust in the process of anything except their need for food, a few bodily comforts and their gaining the abilities to adjust transparently into a community without committing too many crimes for which they would be severely punished. They gain their lessons through the action-and-painful-reaction ways. ¶It is difficult and nearly impossible for those in the *marul pāda*, stage of confusion, to have faith in the process of spiritual unfoldment and trust in tradition, because they are developing their personal ego, manufacturing *karmas*, good, bad and mixed, to sustain their physical existence for hundreds of lives. They will listen to sermons with a deaf ear and, after they are over, enjoy the food and the idle chatter the most. They will read books on philosophy and rationalize their teachings as relevant only to the past. The great knowledge of the past tradition, even the wisdom their grandparents might hold, is an encroachment on their proud sovereignty. ¶It is only when the soul reaches the maturity to enter the *arul pāda*, the stage of grace, that the ability will come from within to lean on the past and on tradition, perform the present *sādhanas*, live within *dharma* and carve a future for themselves and others by bringing the best of the past, which is tradition, forward into the future. This transition is a happy one. Truth now has a capital "T" and is always told. The restraints, the *yamas*, truly have been perfected and are a vital part of the DNA system of individual living beings. Now, as he enters the *arul pāda*, the *niyamas*, spiritual practices, stand out strongly in his mind. ¶The Sanskrit word *āstikya* means "that which is," or "that which exists." Thus, for Hindus *faith* means believing in what is. *Āstikya* refers to one who believes in what is, one who is pious and faithful. We can see that these two words, *faith* and *āstikya*, are similar in nature. Faith is the spiritual-intellectual mind, developed through many superconscious insights blended together through cognition, not through reason. The insights do not have to be remembered, because they are firmly impressed as *saṁskāras* within the inner mind. ¶There is an old saying favored by practical, experiential intellectuals, "Seeing is believing." A more profound adage is "Believing is seeing." The scientists and the educators of today live in the *marul pāda.* They see with their two eyes and pass judgments based on what they currently believe. The *ṛishis* of the past and the *ṛishis* of the now and those yet to come in the future also are seers. There is a thin thread through the history of China, Japan, India, England and all of Europe, Africa, the Americas, Polynesia and all the countries of the world connecting seers and what they have seen. This seeing is not with the two eyes. It is with the third eye, the eye of the soul. One cannot erase through argument or coercion that which has been seen. The seer relates his seeing to the soul of the one who hears. This is *sampradāya.* This is *guru-śishya* transference. This is Truth. This is *śuddha.* This is the end of this *upadeśa.*

Friday
LESSON 47
Īśvarapūjana: Worship

Worship, Īśvarapūjana, is the fifth *niyama.* Let us declare, in the last analysis, that human life is either worship or warship, higher nature or lower nature. We need say no more. But we will. The brief explanation for Īśvarapūjana is to cultivate devotion through daily worship and meditation. The soul's evolution from its conception is based solely on Īśvarapūjana, the return to the source. In the *irul pāda,* the stage of darkness, its return to the source is more imminent than actual. The burning desire is there, driven by the instinctive feelings and emotions of living within the seven *chakras* below the *mūlādhāra.* There is a natural seeking on the way up. People here will worship almost anything to get out of this predicament. Bound in blind faith, with the absence of a coherent intellect guided by reason, and the absence of a matured intellect developed by superconscious experience, they struggle out of their shell of ignorance, through worship, to a better life. The small thread of intuition keeps assuring them it is there, within their reach if they but strive. They call God, they fear God, seek to be close to Him and see Him as oh-so-far away. ¶When they are matured and stepping into adolescence in the *marul pāda,* where confusion prevails, worship and the trappings and traditions that go with it seem to be primitive, unreasonable and can all well be dispensed with. It is here that a young lady looks into the mirror and says, "What a fine person! I am more beautiful than all the other girls I know." A young man may likewise be conceited about his looks or physique. Worship still exists, but is tied closely to narcissism. It is only in the stage of grace, *arul,* and on its doorstep that true worship arises, which is invoking and opening up to the great beings, God, Gods and *devas,* in order to commune with them. ¶Faith, *āstikya,* creates the attitudes for the action of worship. We can see that from the soul's conception to its fullness of maturity into the final merger with God Śiva Himself, worship, communication, looking up, blending with, is truly monistic Śaiva Siddhānta, the final conclusions for all mankind. We can conclude that in Sanātana Dharma faith is in What Is, and in the Abrahamic religions faith is in What Is Yet to Be. ¶Worship could be defined as communication on a very high level: a truly sophisticated form of "channeling," as New-Age people might say; clairvoyant or clairaudient experience, as mystics would describe it; or heart-felt love interchanged between Deity and devotee, as the ordinary person would describe it. Worship for the Hindu is on many levels and of many kinds. In the home, children worship their father and mother as God and Goddess because they love them. The husband worships his wife as a Goddess. The wife worships her husband as a God. In the shrine room, the entire family together worships images of Gods, Goddesses and saints, beseeching them as their dear friends. The family goes to the temple daily, or at least once a week, attends seasonal festivals and takes a far-off pilgrimage once a year. Worship is the binding force that keeps the Hindu family together. On a deeper level, external worship is internalized, worshiping God within through meditation and contemplation. This form of worship leads into *yoga* and profound mystical experiences.

Saturday
LESSON 48
Rites of Worship

Many people are afraid to do *pūjā,* specific, traditional rites of worship, because they feel they don't have enough training or don't understand the mystical principles behind it well enough. To this concern I would say that the priesthood in Hinduism is sincere, devout and dedicated. Most Hindus depend on the priests to perform the *pūjās* and sacraments for them, or to train them to perform home *pūjā* and give them permission to do so through initiation, called *dīkshā.* However, simple *pūjās* may be performed by anyone wishing to invoke grace from God, Mahādevas and *devas.* ¶Love and dedication and the outpouring from the highest *chakras* of spiritual energies of the lay devotee are often greater than any professional priest could summon within himself. Devotees of this caliber have come up in Hindu society throughout the ages with natural powers to invoke the Gods and manifest in the lives of temple devotees many wondrous miracles. ¶There is also an informal order of priests called *paṇḍara,* which is essentially the self-appointed priest who is accepted by the community to perform *pūjās* at a sacred tree, a simple shrine or an abandoned temple. He may start with the *mantra Aum* and learn a few more *mantras* as he goes along. His efficaciousness can equal that of the most advanced Sanskrit *śāstrī,* performing in the grandest temple. Mothers, daughters, aunts, fathers, sons, uncles, all may perform *pūjā* within their own home, and do, as the Hindu home is considered to be nothing less than an extension of the nearby temple. In the Hindu religion, unlike the Western religions, there is no one who stands between man and God. ¶Years ago, in the late 1950s, I taught beginning seekers how to offer the minimal, simplest form of *pūjā* at a simple altar with fresh water, flowers, a small candle, incense, a bell and a stone. This brings together the four elements, earth, air, fire and water—and your own mind is *ākāśa,* the fifth element. The liturgy is simply chanting "Aum." This is the generic *pūjā* which anyone can do before proper initiation comes from the right sources. People of any religion can perform Hindu *pūjā* in this way. ¶All Hindus have guardian *devas* who live on the astral plane and guide, guard and protect their lives. The great Mahādevas in the temple that the devotees frequent send their *deva* ambassadors into the homes to live with the devotees. A room is set aside for these permanent unseen guests, a room that the whole family can enter and sit in and commune inwardly with these refined beings who are dedicated to protecting the family generation after generation. Some of them are their own ancestors. A token shrine in a bedroom or a closet or a niche in a kitchen is not enough to attract these Divinities. One would not host an honored guest in one's closet or have him or her sleep in the kitchen and expect the guest to feel welcome, appreciated, loved. All Hindus are taught from childhood that the guest is God, and they treat any guest royally who comes to visit. Hindus also treat God as God and *devas* as Gods when they come to live permanently in the home. ¶But liberal sects of Hinduism teach that God and *devas* are only figments of one's imagination. These sects are responsible for producing a more materialistic and superficial group of followers. Not so the deep, mystical Hindu, who dedicates his home to God and sets a room aside for God. To him and the family, they are moving into God's house and living with God. Materialistic, superficial Hindus feel that God *might* be living, sometimes, maybe, in their house. Their homes are fraught with confusion, deceptive dealings, back-biting, anger, even rage, and their marriages nowadays often end in divorce. ¶They and all those who live in the lower nature are restricted from performing *pūjā*, because when and if they do *pūjā*, the invocation calls up the demons rather than calling down the *devas*. The *asuric* beings invoked into the home by angry people, and into the temple by angry priests, or by contentious, argumentative, sometimes rageful boards of directors, take great satisfaction in creating more confusion and escalating simple misunderstandings into arguments leading to angry words, hurt feelings and more. With this in mind, once anger is experienced, thirty-one days should pass to close the door on the *chakras* below the *mūlādhāra* before *pūjā* may again be performed by that individual. Simple waving of incense before the icons is permissible, but not the passing of flames, ringing of bells or the chanting of any *mantra*, other than the simple recitation of *Aum*.

Sunday
LESSON 49
Living in God's Home

The ideal of Īśvarapūjana, worship, is to always be living with God, living with Śiva, in God's house, which is also your house, and regularly going to God's temple. This lays the foundation for finding God within. How can someone find God within if he doesn't live in God's house as a companion to God in his daily life? The answer is obvious. It would only be a theoretical pretense, based mainly on egoism. If one really believes that God is in his house, what kinds of attitudes does this create? First of all, since family life is based around food, the family would feed God in His own room at least three times a day, place the food lovingly before His picture, leave, close the door and let God and His *devas* eat in peace. God and the *devas* do enjoy the food, but they do so by absorbing the *prāṇas,* the energies, of the food. When the meal is over, and after the family has eaten, God's plates are picked up, too. What is left on God's plate is eaten as *prasāda,* as a blessing. God should be served as much as the hungriest member of the family, not just a token amount. Of course, God, Gods and the *devas* do not always remain in the shrine room. They wander freely throughout the house, listening to and observing the entire family, guests and friends. Since the family is living in God's house, and God is not living in *their* house, the voice of God is easily heard as their conscience. ¶When we are living in God's house, it is easy to see God as pure energy and life within every living form, the trees, the flowers, the plants, the fire, the Earth, humans, animals and all creatures. When we see this life, which is manifest most in living beings, we are seeing God Śiva. Many families are too selfish to set aside a room for God. Though they have their personal libraries, rumpus rooms, two living rooms, multiple bedrooms, their superficial religion borders on a new Indian religion. Their shrine is a closet, or pictures of God and Goddesses on the vanity mirror of their dressing table. The results of such worship are nil, and their life reflects the chaos that we see in the world today. ¶The psychology and the decision and the religion is, "Do we live with God, or does God occasionally visit us?" Who is the authority in the home, an unreligious, ignorant, domineering elder? Or is it God Śiva Himself, or Lord Murugan or Lord Gaṇeśa, whom the entire family, including elders, bow down to because they have resigned themselves to the fact that they are living in the *āśrama* of Mahādevas? This is religion. This is Īśvarapūjana. ¶It is often said that worship is not only a performance at a certain time of day in a certain place, but a state of being in which every act, morning to night, is done in Śiva consciousness, in which life becomes an offering to God. Then we can begin to see Śiva in everyone we meet. When we try, just try—and we don't have to be successful all the time—to separate the life of the individual from his personality, immediately we are in higher consciousness and can reflect contentment and faith, compassion, steadfastness and all the higher qualities, which is sometimes not possible to do if we are only looking at the external person. This practice, of Īśvarapūjana *sādhana*, can be performed all through the day and even in one's dreams at night. ¶Meditation, too, in the Hindu way is based on worship. It is true that Hindus do teach meditation techniques to those who have Western backgrounds as a mind-manipulative experience. However, a Hindu adept, *ṛishi* or *jñānī*, even an experienced elder, knows that meditation is a natural outgrowth of the *charyā, kriyā* and *yoga* paths. It is based on a religious foundation, as trigonometry is based on geometry, algebra and arithmetic. ¶If you are worshiping properly, if you take worship to its pinnacle, you are in perfect meditation. We have seen many devotees going through the form of worship with no communication with the God they are worshiping or even the stone that the God uses as a temporary body. They don't even have a smile on their face. They are going through the motions because they have been taught that meditation is the ultimate, and worship can be dispensed with after a certain time. Small wonder that when they are in meditation, their minds are confused and subconscious overloads harass them. Breathing is irregular, and if made regular has to be forced. Their materialistic outlook on life—of seeing God everywhere, yet not in those places they rationalize God can never possibly be—contradicts their professed dedication to the Hindu way of life. ¶Yes, truly, worship unreservedly. Perfect this. Then, after initiation, internalize that worship through *yoga* practices given by a *satguru.* Through that same internal worship, unreservedly, you will eventually attain the highest goal. These are the Śaiva Siddhānta conclusions of the seven *ṛishis* who live within the *sahasrāra chakra* of all souls.

and to go through many tests. And this is why one must choose one's *guru* wisely and be ready for such an event in one's life. ¶*Sampradāya* actually means an orally transmitted tradition, unwritten and unrecorded in any other way. True, *satgurus* of *sampradāyas* do write books nowadays, make tape recordings, videos and correspond. This is mini-*sampradāya*, the bud of a flower before opening, the shell of an egg before the bird hatches and flies off, the cocoon before the butterfly emerges. This is mini-*sampradāya*—just a taste, but it does lay a foundation within the *śishya's* mind of who the *guru* is, what he thinks, what he represents, the beginning and ending of his path, the *sampradāya* he represents, carries forth and is bound to carry forth to the next generation, the next and the next. But really potent *sampradāya* is listening, actually listening, to the *guru's* words, his explanations. It stimulates thought. Once-remembered words take on new meanings. Old knowledge is burnt out and replaced with new. This is *sampradāya.* ¶Are you ready for a *satguru?* Perhaps not. When you are ready, and he comes into your life through a dream, a vision or a personal meeting, the process begins. The devotee takes one step toward the *guru*—a simple meeting, a simple dream. The *guru* is bound to take nine steps toward the devotee, not ten, not eleven or twelve, only nine, and then wait for the devotee to take one more step. Then another nine ensue. This is the dance. This is *sampradāya.* ¶When a spiritual experience comes, a real awakening of light, a flash of realization, a knowing that has never been seen in print, or if it had been is long-since forgotten, it gives great courage to the devotee to find that it had already been experienced and written about by others within his chosen *sampradāya.* ¶If all the temples were destroyed, the *gurus* would come forth and rebuild them. If all the scriptures were destroyed, the *ṛishis* would reincarnate and rewrite them. If all the *gurus, swāmīs, ṛishis, sādhus,* saints and sages were systematically destroyed, they would take births here and there around the globe and continue as if nothing had ever happened. So secure is the Eternal Truth on the planet, so unshakable, that it forges ahead undaunted through the mouths of many. It forges ahead undaunted through the temples' open doors. It forges ahead undaunted in scriptures now lodged in nearly every library in the world. It forges ahead undaunted, mystically hidden from the unworthy, revealed only to the worthy, who restrain themselves by observing some or all of the *yamas* and who practice a few *niyamas.* ¶Coming under a *satguru* of one lineage, all scripture, temple and home tradition may be taken away from the eyes of the experience of the newly accepted devotee. In another tradition, scripture may be taken away and temple worship allowed to remain, so that only the words of the *guru* are heard. In still another tradition, the temple, the scripture and the voice of the *guru* are always there—but traditionally only the scripture which has the approval of the *satguru* and is totally in accord with his principles, practices and the underlying philosophy of the *sampradāya.*

Wednesday
LESSON 52
One Focus Per Lifetime

Life is long; there are apparently many years ahead. But time is short. One never knows when he is going to die. The purpose of *sampradāya* is to restrict and narrow down, to reach out to an attainable goal. We must not consider our life and expected longevity as giving us the time and permission to do investigative comparisons of one *sampradāya* to another. This may be done before making up one's mind to follow a traditional verbal lineage. After that, pursuing other paths, even in passing, would be totally unacceptable. ¶But it is also totally unacceptable to assume the attitude of denigration of other paths, or to assume the attitude that "our way is the only way." There are fourteen currents in the spine. Each one is a valid way to escalate consciousness into the *chakra* at the top of the skull and beyond. And at every point in time, there is a living *guru,* possessing a physical body, ordained to control one or more of these *nāḍīs,* currents, within the spine. All are valid paths. One should not present itself as superseding another. Let here be no mistake about this. ¶The *yamas* and *niyamas* are the core of Hindu disciplines and restraints for individuals, groups, communities and nations. In fact, they outline various stages of the path in the development of the soul, leading out of the *marul pāda* into the *arul pāda,* from confusion into grace, leading to the feet of the *satguru,* as the last five practices indicate—*siddhānta śravaṇa, mati, vrata, japa* and *tapas.* ¶Since the *sampradāyas* are all based on Hinduism, which is based on the *Vedas,* any teacher of Indian spirituality who rejects the *Vedas* is therefore not a Hindu and should not be considered as such. Anybody in his right mind will be able to accept the last section of the *Vedas,* the *Upanishads,* and see the truth therein. One at least has to accept that as the basis of *siddhānta śravaṇa.* If even that is rejected, we must consider the teacher a promulgator of a new Indian religion, neo-American religion, neo-European religion, neo-New-Age religion, nonreligion, neo-*sannyāsī* religion, or some other "neo-ism" or "neo-ology." This is not *sampradāya.* This is not *siddhānta śravaṇa.* This is what we speak against. These are not the eternal paths. Why? Because they have not been tried and tested. They are not based on traditional lineages; nor have they survived the ravages of time, changing societies, wars, famine and the infiltration of ignorance. ¶For *sādhakas, yogīs, swāmīs* and mendicants who have freed themselves from the world, permanently or for a period of time according to their vows, these *yamas* and *niyamas* are not only restraints and practices, but mandatory controls. They are not only practices, but obligatory disciplines, and once performed with this belief and attitude, they will surely lead the mendicant to his chosen goal, which can only be the height that his *prārabdha karmas* in this life permit, unless those *karmas* are burned out under extreme *tapas* under the guidance of a *satguru.* ¶Some might still wonder, why limit oneself to listening to scripture of one particular lineage, especially if it has been practically memorized? The answer is that what has been learned must be experienced personally, and experience comes in many depths. This is the purpose of disregarding or rejecting all other *sampradāyas,* -ism's, -ologies and sects, or denominations, and of limiting scriptural listening to just one *sampradāya,* so that each subtle increment of the divine truths amplified within it is realized through personal experience. This and only this—experience, realization, illumination—can be carried on to the next birth. What one has merely memorized is not transforming and is forgotten perhaps shortly after death. Let there be no mistake that *siddhānta śravaṇa,* scriptural listening, is the only way; and when the seeker is ready, the *guru* will appear and enter his life.

Thursday
LESSON 53
Mati: Cognition

Cognition, *mati,* is the seventh *niyama.* Cognition means understanding; but deeper than understanding, it is seeing through to the other side of the results that a thought, a word or an action would have in the future, before the thought, word or action has culminated. *Mati* is the development of a spiritual will and intellect through the grace of a *satguru,* an enlightened master. *Mati* can only come this way. It is a transference of divine energies from the *satguru* to the *śishya,* building a purified intellect honed down by the *guru* for the *śishya,* and a spiritual will developed by the *śishya* by following the religious *sādhanas* the *guru* has laid down until the desired results are attained to the *guru's* satisfaction. *Sādhana* is always done under a *guru's* direction. This is the worthy *sādhana* that bears fruit. ¶*Mati,* cognition, on a higher level is the awakening of the third eye, looking out through the heart *chakra,* seeing through the *māyā,* the interacting creation, preservation and dissolution of the molecules of matter. *Mati* is all this and more, for within each one who is guided by the *guru's* presence lies the ability to see not only with the two eyes but with all three simultaneously. The spiritual intellect described herein is none other than wisdom, or a "wise dome," if you will. Wisdom is the timely application of knowledge, not merely the opinions of others, but knowledge gained through deep observation. ¶The *guru's* guidance is supreme in the life of the dedicated devotee who is open for training. The verbal lineages of the many *sampradāyas* have withstood the tests of time, turmoil, decay and ravage of external hostility. The *sampradāyas* that have sustained man and lifted him above the substratum of ignorance are actually great nerve currents within the spine of the awakened *satguru* himself. To go further on the path of *yoga,* one will encounter within his own spine—within one of the fourteen *nāḍīs* within it—a *satguru,* a *guru* who preaches Truth. He will meet this *guru* in a dream or in his physical body, and through the *guru's* grace and guidance will be allowed to continue the upward climb. These fourteen currents, at every point in time on the surface of the Earth, have a *satguru* attached to them, ready and waiting to open the portals of the beyond into the higher *chakras,* the throat, the third eye and the cranium. ¶To say, "I have awakened my throat *chakra,*" "I now live in my third eye" or "I am developing my *sahasrāra chakra,*" without being able to admit to being under a *guru,* a *satguru* who knows and is personally directing the devotee, is foolishness, a matter of imagination. It is in the heart *chakra,* the *chakra* of cognition, that seekers see through the veils of ignorance, illusion, *māyā's* interacting preservation, creation and destruction, and gain a unity with and love for the universe—all those within it, creatures, peoples and all the various forms—feeling themselves a part of it. ¶Here, on this threshold of the *anāhata chakra,* there are two choices. One is following the *sampradāya* of a *satguru* for the next upward climb into the *viśuddha, ājñā* and *sahasrāra.* The other is remaining *guru*-less, becoming one's own *guru,* and possibly delving into various forms of psychism, astrology, some forms of modern science, psychic crime-detection, tarot cards, pendulums, crystal gazing, psychic healing, past-life reading or fortunetelling. These psychic abilities, when developed, can be an impediment, a deterrent, a barrier, a Berlin Wall to future spiritual development. They develop the *āṇava,* the ego, and are the first renunciations the *satguru* would ask a devotee to make prior to being accepted. ¶Coming under a *satguru,* one performs according to the *guru's* direction with full faith and confidence. This is why scriptures say a *guru* must be carefully chosen, and when one is found, to follow him with all your heart, to obey and fulfill his every instruction better than he would have expected you to, and most importantly, even better than you would have expected of yourself. ¶Psychic abilities are not in themselves deterrents on the path. They are permitted to develop later, after Paraśiva, *nirvikalpa samādhi,* has been attained and fully established within the individual. But this, too, would be under the *guru's* grace and guidance, for these abilities are looked at as tools to fulfill certain works assigned by the *guru* to the devotee to fulfill until the end of the life of the physical body. ¶It is the personal ego, the *āṇava,* that is developed through the practice of palmistry, astrology, tarot cards, fortunetelling, past-life reading, crystal gazing, crystal healing, *prāṇa* transference, etc., etc., etc. This personal ego enhancement is a gift from those who are healed, who are helped, who are encouraged and who are in awe of the psychic power awakened in the heart *chakra* of this most perfect person of the higher consciousness who doesn't anger, display fear or exhibit any lower qualities.

Friday
LESSON 54
Untying The Bonds

The three *malas* that bind us are: *māyā,* the ever-perpetuating dance of creation, preservation and dissolution; *karma* (our *prārabdha karma,* brought with us to face in this life, along with the *karma* we are creating now and will create in the future); and *āṇava,* the ego, ignorance or sense of separateness. *Māyā* can be understood, seen through and adjusted to through the heart-*chakra* powers of cognition, contentment and compassion. *Karmas* can be harnessed through regular forms of disciplinary practices of body, mind and emotions, and the understanding of the law of *karma* itself as a force that is sent out through thought, feeling and action and most often returns to us through other peoples' thought, feeling and action. But it is the *āṇava mala,* the *mala* of personal ego, that is the binding chain which cannot be so easily dealt with. It is the last to go. It is only at the point of death, before the greatest *mahāsamādhi* of the greatest *ṛishi,* that the *āṇava mala* chain is finally broken. ¶If we compare this *āṇava mala,* personal ego, to an actual *mālā,* a string of *rudrāksha* beads, the purpose on the path at this stage, of *mati,* is to begin eliminating the beads, making the chain shorter and shorter. The *mālā* should be getting shorter and shorter rather than our adding beads to it so that it gets longer and longer. A warning: if the *āṇava mala*—symbolically a garland of *rudrāksha* beads—has thirty-six beads and it steadily grows to 1,008 because of practices and the adulation connected with them within the psychic realms of the pseudoscience of parapsychology—such as bending spoons, telepathy, channeling and ectoplasmic manifestations—this 1,008 strand of *rudrāksha* beads could become so heavy, so dangerous to the wearer, that eventually he would trip and fall on his nose. The wise say, "Pride goes before a fall." And the still wiser know that "spiritual pride is the most difficult pride to deal with, to eliminate, to rise above in a lifetime." The spiritually proud never open themselves to a *satguru*. The mystically humble do. ¶*Mati* has also been interpreted as "good intellect, acute intelligence, a mind directed toward right knowledge, or Vedic knowledge." Good intellect, in the context of a Hindu seer, would be right knowledge based on *siddhānta śravaṇa,* scriptural study. Acute intelligence, of course, means "see-through" or panoramic intelligence which cognizes the entire picture rather than only being aware of one of its parts. "A mind directed toward right knowledge or Vedic knowledge" refers to the intellect developed through *siddhānta śravaṇa.* The study of the *Vedas* and other scriptures purifies the intellect, as belief creates attitude, and attitude creates action. An intellect based on truths of the Sanātana Dharma is intelligent to the divine laws of the universe and harnessed into fulfilling them as a part of it. To this end, all the *prārabdha karmas* of this life and the action-reaction conglomerates formed in this life are directed. The intellect, like the emotions, is a force, disciplined or undisciplined, propelled by right knowledge or wrong knowledge. It, of itself, processes, logically or illogically, both kinds of knowledge or their mix. What harnesses the intellect is *siddhānta śravaṇa,* study of the teachings and listening to the wise of an established, traditional lineage that has stood the test of time, ravage and all attempts at conversion. ¶The intellect is a neutral tool which can be used for bad or for good purposes. But unlike the emotions, which are warm, and also neutral, the intellect is cold. It is the fire of the *kuṇḍalinī* force—impregnating the intellect, purifying it, burning out the ignorance of wrong concepts, thought forms, beliefs, connected attitudes, causing an aversion to certain actions—that forges the purified intellect and spiritual will of cognition, known as *mati. Mati,* in summary, is the harnessing of the intellect by the soul to live a spiritual life.

Saturday
LESSON 55
Purifying The Intellect

There are many things which have their claim on people's minds. For many it is the physical body. The hypochondriac thinks about it all the time. Then there is the employer who has bought the intellect of the employee. The emotions consume the intellect with hurt feelings and the rhetorical questions that ensue, elated feelings and the continued praise that is expected. And then there is television, the modern *viśvaguru* that guides the intellect into confusion. As a dream leads only to waking up, television leads only to turning it off. Yes, there are many things that claim the intellect, many more than we have spoken about already. ¶The intellect is guided by the physical; the intellect is guided by the emotions, by other people, and by mechanical devices. And the intellect is guided by the intellect itself, like a computer processing and reprocessing knowledge without really understanding any of it. It is at the stage when anger has subsided, jealousy is unacceptable behavior and fear is a distant feeling, when memory is intact, the processes of reason are working well, the willpower is strong and the integrity is stable, when one is looking out from the *anāhata chakra* window of consciousness, when instinctive-intellectual thought meets the superconscious of the *purusha*, the soul, that the inner person lays claim on the outer person. ¶There is a struggle, to be sure, as the "I Am" struggles to take over the "was then." It's simple. The last *mala*, the *āṇava* "*mālā*," has to start losing its beads. The personal ego must go for universal cosmic identity, Satchidānanda, to be maintained. This, then, is the platform of the throat *chakra*, the *viśuddha chakra*, of a true, all-pervasive, never-relenting spiritual identity. Here *guru* and *śishya* live in oneness in divine communication. Even if never a word is spoken, the understanding in the devotee begins to grow and grow and grow. ¶Some people think of the intellect as informing the superconscious or soul nature, instructing or educating it. Some people even think that they can command the Gods to do their bidding. These are the people that also think that their wife is a slave, that children are their servants, and who cleverly deceive their employers and governments through learned arts of deception. ¶These are the prototypes of the well-developed ignorant person, even though he might feign humility and proclaim religiousness. It is the religion that he professes, if he keeps doing so, that will pull him out of this darkness. When the first beam of light comes through the *mūlādhāra chakra*, he will start instructing his own soul as to what it should do for him, yet he still habitually dominates his wife, inhibiting her own feelings as a woman, and his children, inhibiting their feelings in experiencing themselves being young. ¶But the soul responds in a curious way, unlike the wife and children, or the employer and government who have been deceived through his wrong dealings. The soul responds by creating a pin which pricks his conscience, and this gnawing, antagonistic force within him he seeks to get rid of. He hides himself in jealousy, in the *sutala chakra,* until this becomes unacceptable. The confusion of the *talātala chakra* is no longer his pleasure. He can't hide there. So, he hides himself in anger and resentment—a cozy place within the *vitala chakra*—until this becomes unbearable. Then he hides himself in fear, in the *atala chakra,* fear of his own *purusha,* his own soul, his own psyche, his own seeing, until this becomes intolerable. Then he hides himself in memory and reason, and the being puts down its roots. The change in this individual can only be seen by the mellowness within his eyes and a newborn wisdom that is slowly developing in his conversations among those who knew him before.

Sunday
LESSON 56
Transmuting Willpower

Willpower is a *prāṇic* force which exudes out of the *maṇipūra chakra.* This energy, when directed downward, can be used up through excessive reason, excessive memorization, fear and amplification of fears, anger, the perpetuation of resentment without resolution, amplified by instinctive jealousies, all of which eventually dissipate the semi-divine energy of willpower and eventually close the *maṇipūra chakra.* But when this same energy of willpower is upwardly directed, it pulls memory into a purified memory, making it forget what has to be forgotten, namely wrong knowledge, and remember what has to be remembered—*siddhānta,* the final conclusions of the *ṛishis* who live within the *sahasrāra chakra,* the *siddhas* who are contacted through great *tapas.* ¶There is no reason to believe that developing and unfolding the ten petals of the *maṇipūra chakra* comes easily. To develop an indomitable will capable of the accomplishments needed as a prerequisite to make the upward climb to the *anāhata, viśuddha, ājñā* and *sahasrāra chakras,* and to sustain the benign attitudes of humility, is certainly not an easy task. But it comes naturally to one who has attained such in prior lifetimes, an older soul, I would say. Fulfilling each task one has begun, putting the cap back on the toothpaste tube after squeezing the toothpaste on the brush, the little things, and perfecting the *yamas* and the *niyamas,* especially contentment, austerity, giving, faith and regular worship, builds this indomitable will. These are mini-*sādhanas* one can perform on his own without the guidance of a *guru.* Yes, it is the little things that build the indomitable will that dominates the external intellect, its memory and reason abilities, and the instinctive impulses of fear, anger and jealousy. Doing this is just becoming a good person. ¶Willpower is the muscle of the mind. We lift weights, exercise, run a mile, all to develop the muscles of the physical body. The more we perform these practices, the more muscular we become. The process of strain reshapes the cellular properties and the structure of the muscles. Intermittent rest allows them to build up double. Strong muscles appear on the body as a result. The *maṇipūra chakra* is the sun center of the physical body and of the astral body, the place where all nerve currents of these two bodies meet and merge. It emanates the power of life. It is the seat of fire, the *agni homa.* It is the bridge between the ultimate illumination and a prolonged, ongoing, intellectual processing of ideas, coupled with instinctive willfulness. Let there be no mistake, we must get beyond that by transmuting this tool, willpower, into *mati,* cognition, where its energies are usable yet benign. Therefore, the more you use your personal, individual willpower in your religious service, in your business life, your personal life, your home life, your temple life, in fulfilling all the *yamas* and *niyamas,* the more willpower you have. It is an accumulative, ever-growing bank account. ¶Of course, you can lose some of it through lapses into fear, anger and jealousy, just as in an economic depression one loses money. But you can also court an inflation by seeking higher consciousness in the *viśuddha chakra* of divine love through the *anāhata chakra* of direct cognition, through understanding the oneness of a well-ordered, just universe, both inner and outer.

this should be minimized so that your focus and concentration is upon what you were initiated into, because you are expected to advance on the path of that particular lineage. ¶There are certain simple vows in Hinduism which are easy to take and often are taken, such as, "If I'm successful in this business dealing, I will give twenty percent of the profits to my temple." Or, "If my spouse comes back to me, I shall always obey the *strī dharma* principles (or *purusha dharma*), be dedicated and devoted always." "If my dear mother, who is so devoted to my children, lives through her cancer operation (and Lord Gaṇeśa, the doctors have said the chances are not good), you will see me at the temple every Friday without fail. This is my *vrata,* Lord Gaṇeśa, and I say no more." We take vows to change our ways, vows to meditate daily, vows to desist from lying, vows to not eat meat, vows to remain celibate, vows to obey the *guru* and his tradition, vows to follow these *yamas* and *niyamas.* ¶Perhaps the most obvious and important vow, which can be taken most readily and renewed once a year on a day which you consider your most sacred day—such as Śivarātri, Gaṇeśa Chatūrthi, Skanda Shashṭhī or Dīpāvalī—is the *yama* and *niyama vrata.* These twenty restraints and practices are easy to memorize. Commit them to memory. The *vrata* should go like this: "O Lord Gaṇeśa, open the portals of my wisdom that I might take this *vrata* with open heart and clear mind. O Lord Murugan, give me the will, fortitude and renewed strength every step of the way to fulfill the *vrata* that I am taking. O Lord Śiva, forgive me if I fail, for these twenty restraints and practices are truly beyond my ability to perfectly uphold. So, this first year, Lord Śiva, I vow to fulfill these lofty ideals, to the best of my ability, at least fifty percent. I know I am weak. You know I am weak. I know you will make me strong. I know that you are drawing me ever patiently toward your holy feet. But, Lord Śiva, next year I will faithfully renew this *vrata,* this sacred vow, to these rules, these observances. And if I have succeeded in fulfilling my meager fifty percent according to my conscience, that shall increase my dedication and devotion to you, Lord Śiva, and I shall determine to fulfill the *yamas* and *niyamas* in my life and soul seventy-five percent or more."

Wednesday
LESSON 59
Success And Failure

Many people feel that when they don't fulfill their *vrata* they have failed. One practical example to the contrary is Mahatma Gandhi, who took a vow to be celibate but broke it many times, yet continued the effort and ultimately conquered his instinctive nature. In taking a *vrata,* at the moment it is heard by priests, elders and all community members, when one hears oneself taking it, and all three worlds rejoice, a balanced scale has been created. Success is on one side, failure on the other. One or the other will win out. This is where the unreserved worship of Lord Murugan will help overbalance the scale on the success side. But if the scale teeters and wavers, the blessings and knowledge of the elders of the community should be sought: the mothers and fathers, the old aunties and uncles, the priests, the *pandits* and sages, the *ṛishis* and *gurus*. This and this alone will steady the balance. But if actual failure occurs, Lord Gaṇeśa Himself will catch the fall in His four arms and trunk. He will hold the devotee from going into the abyss of remorse of the darkness of the lower worlds. He will speak softly into the right ear and encourage that the *vrata* be immediately renewed, lest time elapse and the *asura* of depression take over mind, body and emotion. Yes, the only failure is that experienced by the one who quits, gives up, turns his back on the path and walks the other way, into the realms of darkness, beyond even the reach of the Gods. As Tiruvalluvar said, it is better to strive to fulfill great aspirations, even if you fail, than to achieve minor goals in life. Yes, this is very true. ¶On the everyday level there are *vratas* or contracts made with people of the outside world whom you don't even know. Buy a piece of property, and once you sign the contract you are bound to fulfill it. But a religious *vrata* is a contract between yourself, the religious community, the *devas* and the Gods and your *guru*, if you have one, all of whom know that human failure is a part of life; but striving is the fulfillment of life, and practice is the strengthening effect that the exercise of the human and spiritual will have over the baser elements. ¶Vows before the community, such as those of marriage and celibacy and other vows where community support is needed, are very important. Other, more personal vows are taken before the community, a temple priest, *pandit*, elder, *swāmī*, *guru*, or *satguru* if help is needed to strengthen the individual's ability to fulfill them. For a certain type of person, a vow before Lord Gaṇeśa, Lord Murugan, Lord Śiva or all three is enough for him to gain strength and fulfill it. A vow is never only to oneself. This is important to remember. A vow is always to God, Gods and *guru*, community and respected elders. ¶One cannot make one's vow privately, to one's own individual *āṇava*, external personal ego, thinking that no one is listening. This would be more of a promise to oneself, like a New Year's resolution, a change in attitude based on a new belief, all of which has nothing to do with the *yamas* and *niyamas* or religion. ¶In speaking about the *yama* and *niyama vrata,* there is no difference in how the family person upholds it and the celibate monastic upholds it. The families are in their home, the monks are in their *maṭha,* monastery. In regards to the *vrata* of sexual purity, for example, the family man vows to be faithful to his wife and to treat all other women as either a mother or sister and to have no sexual thoughts, feelings or fantasies toward them. *Sadhākas, yogīs* and *swāmīs* vow to look at all women as their mothers or sisters, and God Śiva and their *guru* as their mother and father. There is no difference.

Thursday
LESSON 60
Japa: Recitation

Now we shall focus on *japa,* recitation of holy *mantras,* the ninth *niyama.* Here again, a *guru* is essential, unless only the simplest of *mantras* are recited. The simplest of *mantras* is Aum, pronounced "AA, OO, MMM." The AA balances the physical forces when pronounced separately from the OO and the MMM, as the OO balances the astral and mental bodies. The MMM brings the spiritual body into the foreground. And when pronounced all together, AA-OO-MMM, all three bodies are harmonized. *Aum* is a safe *mantra* which may be performed without a *guru's* guidance by anyone of any religious background living on this planet, as it is the primal sound of the universe itself. All sounds blended together make the sound "Aum." The overtone of the sounds of an entire city would be "Aum." In short, it harmonizes, purifies and uplifts the devotee. ¶One might ask why a *guru* is important to perform such a simple task as *japa.* It is the *śakti* of the *guru,* of the Gods and the *devas* that give power to the *mantra.* Two people, a civilian and a policeman, could say to a third person, "Stop in the name of the law." The third person would only obey one of them. The one who had no authority would not be listened to. In this example, the policeman had been initiated and had full authority. Therefore, his *mantra,* "Stop in the name of the law," seven words, had the desired effect. The person who had not been initiated said the same words, but nobody paid any attention to him. Now, this does not mean one can choose a *guru,* study with the *guru,* become accepted by the *guru,* feign humility, do all the right things and say all the right words, become initiated, receive the *mantra* and then be off into some kind of other activities or opt for a more liberal path. The *guru's* disdain would diminish if not cancel the benefits of the initiation, which obviously had been deceptively achieved. This is why *siddhānta śravana* (choosing your path carefully) and *mati* (choosing your *guru* carefully, being loyal to the *sampradāya,* to your *guru* and his successor or successors and training your children to be loyal to the *sampradāya)* are the foundation of character that the first fifteen restraints and practices are supposed to produce. ¶*Mantra* initiation is *guru dīkshā*. Traditionally, the family *guru* would give *mantra dīkshā* to the mother and the father and then to the young people, making the *guru* part of the family itself. There is no way that *mantras* can be sold and be effective. There is no way that the *dīkshā* of *mantra* initiation, which permits *japa,* could be effective for someone who was not striving to fulfill the first seventeen of the *yamas* and *niyamas.* Any wise *guru* would test the devotee on these before granting initiation. There is no way a *mantra* can be learned from a book and be effective. Therefore, approach the *guru* cautiously and with a full heart. When asked if you are restraining yourself according to the ten *yamas,* know that perfection is not expected, but effort is. And if you are practicing the first seven *niyamas,* know that perfection is not expected here either, but regular attentiveness to them is. You, the *guru,* your family and your friends will all know when you are on the threshold of *mantra dīkshā,* which when performed by an established *guru* is called *guru dīkshā.*

Friday
LESSON 61
Tapas: Austerity

The tenth and final *niyama* is austerity, performing *sādhana,* penance, *tapas* and sacrifice. All religions of the world have their forms of austerity, conditions which one has to live up to—or which individuals are unable to live up to who are too lazy or too dull-minded to understand; and Hinduism is no exception. Our austerities start within the home in the form of daily *sādhana.* This is obligatory and includes *pūjā,* scriptural reading and chanting of holy *mantras.* This personal vigil takes about half an hour or more. Other *sādhanas* include pilgrimage to a far-off sacred place once a year, visiting a temple once a week, preferably on Friday or Monday, attending festivals and fulfilling *saṁskāras,* rites of passage, for the children especially, but all the family members as well. To atone for misdeeds, penance is obligatory. We must quickly mitigate future effects of the causes we have set into action. This is done through such acts as performing 108 prostrations before the God in the temple. ¶*Tapas* is even more austere. It may come early in a lifetime or later in life, unbidden or provoked by *rāja yoga* practices. It is the fire that straightens the twisted life and mind of an individual, bringing him into pure being, giving a new start in life, awakening higher consciousness and a cosmic relationship with God and the Gods, friends, relatives and casual acquaintances. *Tapas* in Hinduism is sought for, feared, suffered through and loved. Its pain is greater than the pains of parturition, but in the aftermath is quickly forgotten, as the soul, in childlike purity, shines forth in the joys of rebirth that follow in the new life. ¶ *Tapas* is walking through fire, being scorched, burnt to a crisp, crawling out the other side unburnt, without scars, with no pain. *Tapas* is walking through the rain, completely drenched, and when the storm stops, not being wet. *Tapas* is living in a hurricane, tossed about on a churning ocean in a small boat, and when the storm subsides, being landed on a peaceful beach unharmed but purified. *Tapas* is a mind in turmoil, insane unto its very self. A psychic surgery is being performed by the Gods themselves. When the operation is over, the patient has been cut loose of the dross of all past lives. *Tapas* is a landslide of mud, a psychic earthquake, coming upon the head and consuming the body of its victim, smothering him in the dross of his misdeeds, beneath which he is unable to breathe, see, speak or hear. He awakens from this hideous dream resting on a mat in a garden hut, smelling sweet jasmine, seeing pictures of Gods and *devas* adorning the mud walls and hearing the sound of a flute coming from a distant source. ¶Truly, *tapas* in its fullest form is sought for only by the renunciate under the guidance of a *satguru*, but this madness often comes unbidden to anyone on this planet whose dross of misdeeds spills over. The only difference for the Hindu is that he knows what is happening and how it is to be handled; or at least the *gurus* know, the *swāmīs* know, the elders know, the astrologers know. This knowledge is built into the Hindu mind flow as grout is built into a stone wall.

Saturday
LESSON 62
A Lesson In Sacrifice

Sacrifice may be the least-practiced austerity, and the most important. It is the act of giving up to a greater power a cherished possession (be it money, time, intelligence or a physical object) to manifest a greater good. There are many ways to teach sacrifice. My *satguru* taught sacrifice by cooking a great feast for several hundred people, which took all day to prepare. Their mouths were watering. They had not eaten all day, so as to prepare their bodies to receive this *prasāda* from the *satguru*. The meal was scheduled to be served at high noon. But Satguru Yogaswami kept delaying, saying, "We have not yet reached the auspicious moment. Let us sing some more *bhajanas* and *Natchintanai*. Be patient." At about 3PM, he said, "Before we can partake of our *prasāda*, I shall ask eleven strong men here to dig a deep, square hole in the ground." They stepped forward and he indicated the spot where they should dig. Shovels were obtained from homes nearby, and the digging commenced. All waited patiently for his will to be fulfilled, the stomachs growling, the mouths watering at the luscious fragrances of the hot curries, the *rasam* and the freshly-boiled rice, five sweet-smelling curries, mango chutneys, *dal*, yogurt and delicious sweet *payasam*. It was a real feast. ¶Finally, just before dusk, the pit was completed, and the great saint indicated that it was time to serve the food. "Come, children, surround this pit," he said. Two or three hundred people stepped forward and surrounded the ten-by-ten-foot hole. Women and children were sitting in the front and the men standing in the back, all wondering what he was going to say and hoping he would not delay any longer with the feast. He said, "Now we shall serve our *prasāda*." He called forward two of the huskiest of the eleven men, the strongest and biggest, and commanded, "Serve the rice. Bring the entire pot." It was a huge brass pot containing nearly 400 pounds of rice. By this time, many had left, as they had been cooking all morning and singing all afternoon. Only the most devout had remained to see the outcome. When the day began, 1,000 had come. The preparations were for a very big crowd. ¶Now he said, "Pour the rice in the middle of the pit." Banana leaves had been laid carefully at the bottom of the pit to form a giant serving plate. The crowd was aghast. "Pour it into the pit?" "Don't hesitate," he commanded. Though stunned, the men obeyed Yogaswami without question, dropping the huge mass of steaming rice onto the middle of the banana leaves. He told one man, "Bring the eggplant curry!" To another he said, "Go get the potato curry! We must make this a full and auspicious offering." ¶As all the curries were neatly placed around the rice, everyone was wondering, "Are we to all eat together out of the pit? Is this what the *guru* has in mind?" Then the *kulambu* sauce was poured over the middle of the rice. Five pounds of salt was added on the side. Sweet mango and ginger chutneys were placed in the proper way. One by one, each of the luscious preparations was placed in the pit, much to the dismay of those gathered.

Sunday
LESSON 63
Giving Back to Mother Earth

After all the food had been served, the *satguru* stood up and declared, "People, all of you, participate. Come forward." They immediately thought, finishing his sentence in their minds, "to eat together this luscious meal you have been waiting for all day as a family of *śishyas*." But he had something else in mind, and directed, "Pick up the eleven shovels, shovel some dirt over this delicious meal and then pass your shovel on to the next person. We have fed our Mother Earth, who has given so generously of her abundance all these many years to this large Śaivite community. Now we are sacrificing our *prasāda* as a precious, heartfelt gift. Mother Earth is hungry. She gets little back; we take all. Let this be a symbol to the world and to each of us that we must sacrifice what we want most." ¶In this way, our *satguru*, Śiva Yogaswami, began the first Earth worship ceremony in northern Sri Lanka. He taught a lesson of *tapas* and sacrifice, of fasting and giving, and giving and fasting. By now the hour was late, very late. After touching his feet and receiving the mark of Śiva from him in the form of *vibhūti*, holy ash, on their forehead, the devotees returned to their homes. It was too late to cook a hot meal, lest the neighbors smell the smoke and know that mischief was afoot. We are sure that a few, if not many, satisfied themselves with a few ripe bananas, while pondering the singular lesson the *satguru* had taught. ¶Let's worship the Earth. It is a being—intelligent and always giving. Our physical bodies are sustained by her abundance. When her abundance is withdrawn, our physical bodies are no more. The ecology of this planet is an intricate intelligence. Through sacrifice, which results in *tapas* and *sādhana*, we nurture Mother Earth's goodwill, friendliness and sustenance. Instill in yourself appreciation, recognition. We should not take advantage of all of this generosity, as a predator does of those he preys upon. ¶Yes, austerities are a vital part of all sects of Hinduism. They are a call of the soul to bring the outer person into the perfection that the soul is now, has always been and will always be. Austerities should be assigned by a *guru*, a *swāmī* or a qualified elder of the community. One should submit to wise guidance, because these *sādhanas*, penances, *tapas* and sacrifices lift our consciousness so that we can deal with, learn to live with, the perfection of the self-luminous, radiant, eternal being of the soul within. Austerity is the powerful bath of fire and bright rays of showering light that washes the soul clean of the dross of its many past lives, and of the current life, which have held it in the bondage of ignorance, misgiving, unforgivingness and the self-perpetuating ignorance of the truths of the Sanātana Dharma. "As the intense fire of the furnace refines gold to brilliance, so does the burning suffering of austerity purify the soul to resplendence" (*Weaver's Wisdom/Tirukural*, 267).

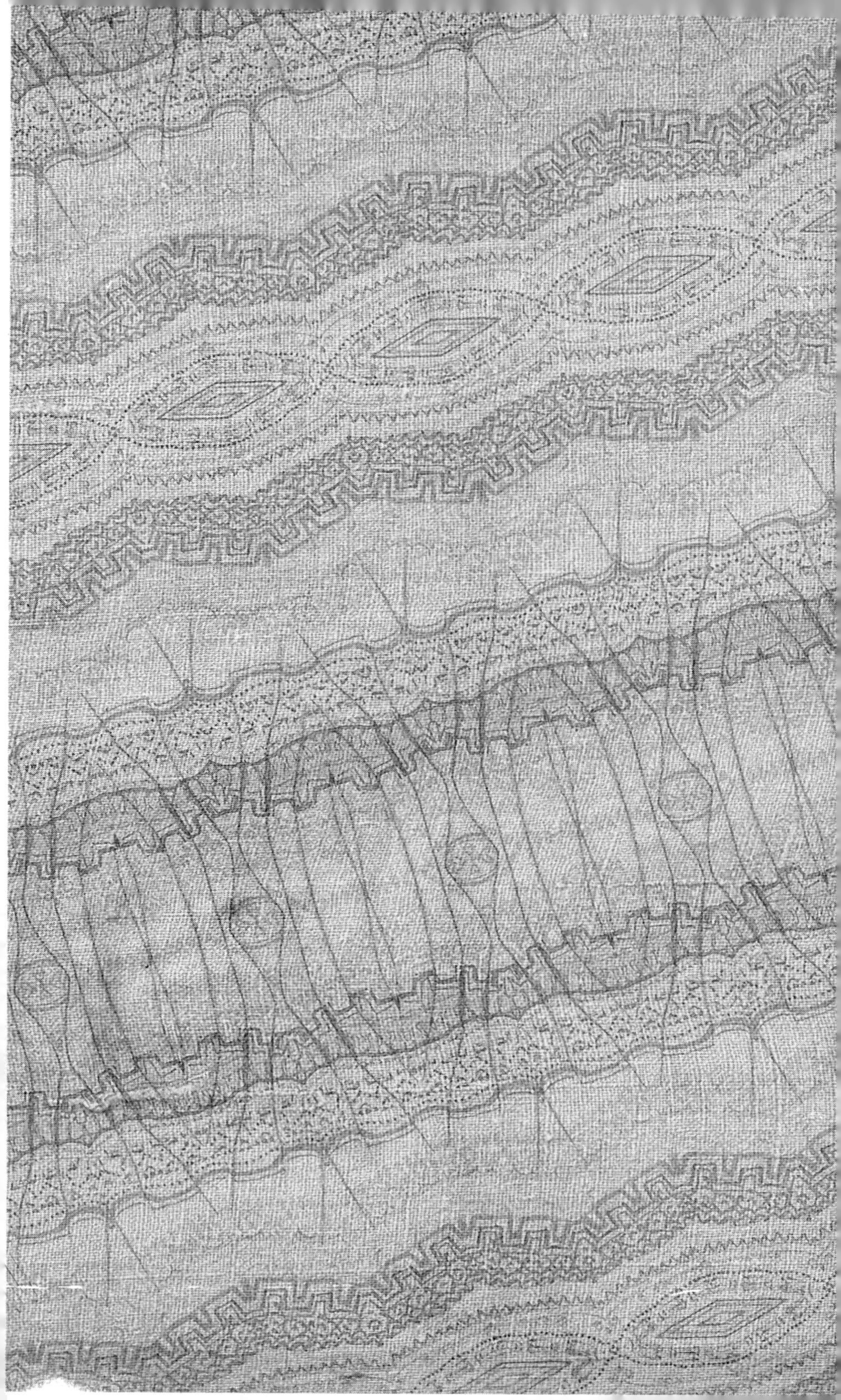

Brahmacharyam Pātivratyam cha
ब्रह्मचर्यम् पातिव्रत्यम् च

Celibacy and Fidelity

The *brahmachārī* moves, strengthening both the worlds. In him the *devas* meet in concord; he upholds Earth and Heaven.

Atharva Veda 11.5.1. AVG, P. 55

Monday
LESSON 64
The Power Of Purity

Every culture acknowledges the power of relationships between men and women and seeks to direct it toward the highest good, both for individuals and for society. The masculine and feminine forces, partly sexual but more broadly *tantric*, can either create or destroy, bring peace or contention, foster happiness or misery, depending on how consciously they are understood and utilized. ¶Hindu ideals of manhood and womanhood and their interaction are among the most subtle, insightful and graceful in all the world. When followed, these principles strengthen man and woman, sustain a joyous and balanced marriage, stabilize the family and assist husband and wife in their mutual spiritual and worldly goals. Of course, such high ideals are rarely followed to perfection. But the soul's inner perfection is naturally revealed in the attempt. ¶What is religious life? It is the balance of two forces, the odic force and the actinic force. In married life this means that there is a prevailing harmony between the man and the woman. This guides and governs the inner currents of the children up until the age of twenty-five. For the single person living a celibate life and performing *sādhana,* this means balancing those same forces—the masculine/aggressive force and the feminine/passive force—within himself or herself. ¶*Brahmacharya,* the *yoga* of celibacy, is a traditional practice in Śaivite Hinduism. It allows the adolescent or young adult to use his vital energies to prepare for a rewarding life, to develop his mind and talents for his chosen vocation. The first of the four stages, or *āśramas,* of life is actually called the *brahmacharya āśrama.* Love, including sex, is one of the legitimate four goals of life, according to our religion. Sex is not bad. Its place, however, is properly within the confines of a sanctified marriage. Nor are sex drives unnatural. The goal of the *brahmachārī* and *brahmachāriṇī* is not to become fearful of sex, but to understand sex and the sexual impulses in a balanced way. During the time of *brahmacharya,* the goal is to control the sex urges and transmute those vital energies into the brain to gain a great mental and spiritual strength. Yes, this vital life force must be focused on studies and spiritual pursuits. *Brahmacharya* maintained until marriage, and faithfulness thereafter, helps enable the devotee to merit a good wife or husband, a happy, stable marriage and secure, well-adjusted children. ¶The spiritual

Deep in an Indian forest a couple enjoy a private moment, their love and faithfulness to one another framed by the private, protected and pristine forest. Among a lasting marriage's strengths are togetherness, dedication, mutual respect, honesty and shared spiritual goals.

value of celibacy has long been understood in the Hindu tradition. Most religions also provide a tradition of monastic life in which young men take lifetime vows of celibacy. Many of our greatest spiritual lights were celibate throughout their entire life, including Śiva Yogaswami, Sankara and Swami Vivekananda. Others, such as Buddha, Gandhi and Aurobindo, became celibate after a period of marriage. For the individual preparing for monastic life, *brahmacharya* is essential in harnessing and transmuting the powerful sexual life energies into spiritual and religious concerns.

Tuesday
LESSON 65
Psychic Tubes

It is said that when man first killed a kinsman, great strength came into the nerve system of the animal body of all upon this planet. Normal seasonal cycles of mating turned into promiscuity. The population increased and is increasing even now with this intensification of *kuṇḍalinī* fire through the sexual nature of men and women. ¶Through the ancient traditions of Śaivite monasticism, the inner laws of *brahmacharya* have been preserved down through the centuries to help guide humanity through the Kali Yuga. This knowledge records the methods of how to preserve the vital energy within the body of men and women so that Śaivism, the remembrance of Śiva and His crystal clear *śakti,* can be passed through the darkness of the Kali Yuga in unbroken continuity. For only through the power of the *tapas* of *brahmacharya* can His *śakti* be passed on from one to another until the individual's *śakti* finally accrues enough intensity so that the *brahmachārī* becomes as Lord Śiva Himself. ¶It is when fear pervades a country or the planet that the impulses of the animal nerve system cause desires for mating to intensify for the prolongation of the species. During intercourse, the astral bodies of the man and woman merge together, and conception may occur, as a person in the Devaloka gains a body from the woman to enter this world. The connection formed between a man and a woman during intercourse makes a psychic, astral, umbilical-cord-like tube in the lower astral-plane world which lasts for twelve years or more. Providing no other connection with the same or other individual occurred in the meantime, the tube would slowly wear away during the ensuing years. This is provided that, at the same time, *sādhana* or *tapas* is performed and regular pilgrimages and visits to Śaivite temples are made. ¶*Brahmacharya* is holding the power of the Divine within the core of the individual spine so that, as Lord Śiva sends His power through the five great winds of the astral body within the physical body, the winds adjust among themselves and emanate a *śakti* strong enough to adjust the five great psychic fluids within everyone around. This power of *brahmacharya* is accrued and disseminated through sublimation, then transmutation, of the sexual force. Transmutation occurs automatically through regular daily *sādhana,* the rigors of positive living and adherence to the ceremonial customs of our religion. Ideally, *brahmacharya* begins at puberty for virgins and continues on until marriage. Otherwise, *brahmacharya sādhana* begins after the last sexual encounter with a member of the opposite sex has occurred and when a conscious decision is made to begin the practice of *brahmacharya.* ¶While "in the process" of *brahmacharya,* those who have had sexual encounters with one or more members of the opposite sex experience times of trial. Great temptation may occur on the physical plane as the astral matter of the animal nerve system and systems of fluids and odors that attract the opposite sex store up in great abundance. This creates a magnetism which attracts those of the opposite sex. Especially attracted will be those of a similar nature and deportment as those of past encounters. ¶Each person is born in a full state of *brahmacharya.* Upon reaching puberty, those boys and girls who remain virgins maintain the inherent state of *brahmacharya.* They are able to ward off, and may not even notice, many emotional and sexual temptations that would be troublesome to the nonvirgin. This is because the psychic shield surrounding the virgin's aura has never been penetrated. They are the ones "who walk in the rain without getting wet, sit long in the sun without getting burned." They are the ones for whom reading about worldly experiences nurtures only their curiosity, whereas had they established psychic tubular connections with a member of the opposite sex, the reading would nurture a much deeper sexual desire. It is the virgins performing *brahmacharya sādhana* since puberty who can, if they persist, live in "Brahm," or God consciousness, most of the time, even without performing intense *sādhanas.* This is because they have never consciously entered into worldly consciousness. Instead they look out into it as if through a veil.

Wednesday
LESSON 66
Astral Magnetism

The force of *kuṇḍalinī* flows as a river through men and women. Sexual intercourse gives that river an outlet, creates a channel, a psychic-astral tube between their *mūlādhāra chakras.* After the first intercourse, awareness is turned outward into the external world and the man or woman is more vulnerable to the forces of desire. The ramification of the intellect can now be experienced more than ever before. If the force is contained within the marriage covenant, with blessings from the Devaloka and Śivaloka, rays similar to the astral tube established between the couple are established between each of them through the higher *chakras* with the Mahādevas and their *devas.* A holy state of matrimony has been entered into. *Dancing with Śiva, Hinduism's Contemporary Catechism* states: "When a young virgin man and woman marry and share physical intimacy with each other, their union is very strong and their marriage stable. This is due to the subtle, psychic forces of the human nerve system. Their psychic forces, or *nāḍīs,* grow together, and they form a one body and a one mind. This is the truest marriage and the strongest, seldom ending in separation or divorce. Conversely, if the man or woman has had intercourse before the marriage, the emotional/psychic closeness of the marriage will suffer, and this in proportion to the extent of promiscuity." ¶The higher rays and lower astral-psychic tubes that are created between husband and wife can contain the forces of desire within them. They also control the instinctive curiosities of the intellect, allowing its full power to manifest and create a productive and abundant life for the family which has continuity and consistency. A life of *dharma* can be lived. ¶The release of the sacred seed into the woman during sexual intercourse establishes, through the first *chakra,* a connecting psychic astral tube which can be clearly seen on the astral plane. It is through this psychic tube that desires, feelings and even telepathic messages can be passed from one to another. This connecting tube is generally about six inches in diameter. ¶Nowadays, because of promiscuity, masses of people are connected one to another in this way. A great bed of astral matter envelops them as they go from one partner to another. This causes the forces of intense fear to persist. From an inner perspective, their soul bodies are obscured by this astral matter, and it is most difficult for those living in the Devaloka to contact anyone on the Earth plane who is thus involved. Such individuals must fend for themselves, with little or no protection from the Devaloka or the Śivaloka, as do the animals, who do not have benefit of the intellect to guide their actions. ¶Any two people touching in other ways—kissing, embracing—also establishes a temporary connecting link of astral matter which penetrates their auras and completely covers their forms. This is sometimes called the great magnetism, for it appears in the Second World as a psychic mass connecting the two of them as wide as the length of their bodies. This astral matter is created from the diverse expulsion of emotional energies, blending their auras together. The psychic connection is magnetic enough to repeatedly pull them back together or cause emotional pain if they are separated. But unless the encounter is repeated, the astral matter will wear away in three or four days, a month at the most. In this way, touching or caressing someone causes an abundant release of magnetic force to occur.

Thursday
LESSON 67
The Path To Perfection

It is the *brahmachārī's* duty to be the channel of the three worlds. In this way he can help stabilize humanity through the Kali Yuga so that the forces of promiscuous desire do not blot out our culture, creativity and all connection with the Śivaloka. This is why the *sādhana* of *brahmacharya* is so extremely important for each unmarried Śaivite to understand and observe. ¶As a *brahmachārī* or *brahmachāriṇī*, you must endeavor to hold the force of the Śivaloka and the Devaloka in line with the higher forces of the Bhūloka, the Earth plane. This happens naturally through the transmutation process and living a contemplative life. Regular personal *sādhana* and noninvolvement in the emotional nature of others is the practice to be observed. ¶A great aid to the accomplishment of this is to invoke Lord Śiva daily. Then the higher *chakras* open within your psychic body. Peace of mind comes unbidden, and bliss flows forth from your aura for all to feel. Regular *pūjā* invoking the assistance of Lord Murugan will also greatly aid in a premature banishing of connections with the external world and in severing the tubular connections with inhabitants in it. When Lord Murugan is reached through your *pūjā*, He will also give wisdom and the divine understanding of the transmutation process. ¶An occasional loss of the reproductive fluids does not "break" or interrupt *brahmacharya sādhana*, though this should be avoided and is minimal when the *brahmacharya sādhana* takes hold. If one does have a "wet dream," this should not cause undue concern. Rather, this should be regarded as simply the natural release of excess energy, of which the vitality, or *prāṇa*, goes up into the higher *chakras* as the physical fluid goes out. This does not happen during masturbation. ¶Those who have resolved to follow the path of *brahmacharya*, but are troubled by sexual fantasies and nightly encounters during their dream state, should not despair. These are simply indications that their creative energies are not being used to capacity. The *brahmachārī* or *brahmachāriṇī* should simultaneously resolve to work more diligently in guiding the flow of thought through the day. They should work harder, mentally and physically, get up early in the morning and do *sādhana*, go to bed early and seek the more refined areas of consciousness during the dream states. How can you seek these more refined areas during sleep? This is done through chanting and meditating before going to sleep, and through praying for guidance from Lord Gaṇeśa. ¶There is a simple remedy or penance, self imposed, that we recommend for one who indulges briefly in a sexual fantasy: to have just rice and dal for lunch, rather than a full meal. If he indulges longer in such fantasies, he fasts for that meal with his empty plate before him to remind him of the need to control his inner forces. The instinctive mind will eventually get the idea that if you persist in these visualizations in moments of careless fascination you don't get to eat. And what's more important?

Friday
LESSON 68
Psychic Ties With Parents

It is only sexual intercourse between a man and a woman that breaks *brahmacharya sādhana*, causing an astral umbilical-like psychic cord about six to twelve inches wide to form in the inner ether between them. It is within this psychic tube that the forces of energy and desire flow from one to another. These are the same forces between mother and father which culminate in the birth of a child and surround and protect him or her through earthly consciousness until age twenty-five. The psychic connection between mother and father emotionally stabilizes all children of the family. But if there are other tubes involved due to pre-marital promiscuity, or new ones being created with members of the opposite sex outside of the marriage, the children suffer emotionally while growing up. The unleashed forces of instinctiveness may often cause them to be disturbed or frustrated. ¶As a child grows to maturity, he gradually detaches himself, year by year, from the connection between his father and mother. The detachment is complete by the age of twenty-five. But if the son, or daughter, develops a psychic, astral tube with a member of the opposite sex before this age, he disconnects from his father and mother immediately at that point. From that time onward he no longer relates to them in the same way as he once did. Through the sexual act, he now has "left home" and entered the world. The mother and father can feel the difference, and so can the son. ¶Virgins also have strong temptations with the opposite sex from time to time, especially if they meet former spouses from past lives. Unless a strict understanding of *brahmacharya* is observed, these encounters with past-life lovers may move their fluids and emotions to the point of intercourse. All parents should explain to their children at an early age the importance of remaining virgin until married. They must be taught that the elations and the depressions that follow from disciplining oneself are a part of life on this planet. They can be gently but firmly taught the practice of mentally and physically "walking away" from temptation. ¶Learning to walk away from a situation in dignity is more effective than almost anything else in protecting the *brahmachārī* and the *brahmachāriṇī* from the overpowering temptation to allow their sacred power to flow out to those of the opposite sex. Walking away from temptation, mentally, emotionally and physically, is so easy to remember, so easy to practice. Teach it to the children. Practice it yourself. And through the grace of Lord Śiva a new generation of knowledgeable people will walk the path to His holy feet.

Saturday
LESSON 69
Redirecting Sexual Desire

Brahmacharya literally means Godly conduct, which in practice and by tradition means celibacy, complete abstinence from sexual relations. *Brahmacharya* is practiced traditionally by: 1) monastics; 2) young persons living at home with parents prior to entering marriage or a monastery; 3) single persons living alone in the world; and 4) married couples who observe celibacy in later life, generally after age sixty. In our traditional and strict organization, the formal title *brahmachārī* (or *brahmachāriṇī*) is used only by single men (or women) who have taken lifetime vows of celibacy under the auspices of our Śaivite Hindu Church. ¶To aid in fulfilling the principles of purity, the devotee commencing this discipline is encouraged to take a vow of celibacy and purity, known as *brahmacharya vrata.* In fulfillment of this solemn oath, the individual vows to value and protect purity in thought, word and deed, and chastity in body, and to sublimate and transmute the sexual energies and the instinctive impulses of anger, jealousy, greed, fear, hatred and selfishness. In our Hindu Church, all young persons take such a pledge and promise to remain virgin until such time as they are married, preferably to another Śaivite Hindu by arrangement of the parents of both families and with the blessings of the *satguru.* The sacred cord is worn around the waist to betoken this solemn oath. The formal study of the Śaivite religious teachings is begun under an authorized catalyst and with the supervision of parents. The parents share in his oath and accept full responsibility to see that it is fulfilled. As the fourth *yama,* or restraint, *brahmacharya* is emulated in married life in the sense of fidelity, confining all sexual thoughts and expressions to one's spouse. ¶*Brahmacharya* is transmutation—the changing of a grosser form or force into a finer one. It can be likened to the boiling of water into steam to give a greater power. As the fluids are reabsorbed by the bloodstream, the actinic force of them feeds each of the seven *chakras* in turn. The *Tirumantiram* states, "If the sacred seed is retained, the body's life does not ebb, and great strength, energy, intelligence and alertness are attained" (1948). Transmutation of the sacred fluids does not mean to suppress, repress or inhibit. ¶Just lift your arm. It took energy to lift it. If you were tired, it took even more energy than usual. This energy does not come from a power plant outside you. It comes from within you, of course. Your stamina, the actinic glow in your eyes, the radiance of your personality—these are all manifestations of energy, of your creative life force. And so are the male and female reproductive fluids. They comprise aggressive and passive forces drawn from the *piṅgalā* and the *iḍā* currents within the soul body. They are sparked with pure spiritual force from the door of Brahman, at the core of the *sahasrāra chakra.* When correctly channeled, the subtler forms of this creative energy are the essence of artistic, intellectual and spiritual expression. Those who practice transmutation awaken many latent talents from within. It becomes second nature for them to create and express, being in tune with the essence of creative energy.

Sunday
LESSON 70
Inner-Plane Education

The goal of perfect *brahmacharya* is the continual rechanneling of sexual desire. This is also the practice, for one does not suddenly reach a point where desire goes away. Desire is life. Desire can be directed according to the personal will. Living life according to basic spiritual principles is your *sādhana.* Through *sādhana* you can gain mastery over all the forces of your mind and body. As man leaves his instinctive-intellectual nature and unfolds spiritually, the forces of that nature must be brought under his conscious control. ¶We hope that you have been able to set aside half an hour a day, or at least fifteen minutes, for the study of these lessons. If not, don't be discouraged. Keep trying. If nothing more, please try to read a little from your daily lesson each night before you retire to sleep. These holy teachings will then draw you naturally into the more spiritual areas of the Devaloka while you sleep. Many inner-plane people are there to help you. You are not alone in your study and desire for spiritual unfoldment. It is known by all mystically minded people that "As we think, so we become." Thinking of the great Mahādevas and Deities of high evolution stimulates our own evolution. Our spiritual unfoldment is hastened. ¶Each night you are taught many wonderful things on the inner plane during sleep. You may not realize this upon awakening or even remember what you have learned. This is because the astral brain functions at a much higher rate of vibration than the physical brain. Most nights, you probably spend several hours learning from *gurus* and guides in Śaivite schools within the spiritual areas of the Devaloka, the astral world. Sometimes dozens, even hundreds, of devotees with similar interests gather together to learn. They are all in their astral bodies, on the astral plane, while their physical bodies are asleep. When one is firm in the practice of *brahmacharya,* it is possible to remain for long periods of time in inner-plane schools and absorb much more of the teaching being given there. Those who are not strong in *brahmacharya* are often seen appearing and then disappearing from among the group as they are drawn back to their physical bodies by emotions and desires. ¶Remember, your own soul knows the reasons why you were born in this life. It knows what you need to accomplish in this birth. As a soul, you know what obstacles and challenges you need to face and overcome to grow stronger and conquer past *karmic* patterns through fulfilling your chosen *dharma.* These and other matters are examined by you and your teachers in the Devaloka schools while your physical body sleeps. The more fully established you are in *bramacharya,* the more religious you become and the more able to face the world with a positive mental attitude.

Śārīrika Mānasika Rāgātmaka Āhāra
शारीरिक मानसिक रागात्मक आहार

Physical, Mental, Emotional Foods

When nourishment is pure, nature is pure. When nature is pure, memory becomes firm. When memory remains firm, there is release from all knots of the heart.

Sāma Veda, Çhāndogya Upanishad, 7.26.2. UPR, P. 489.

Kg 6$
Kg 6$
Kg 8$
Kg 5$
Kg 7$
Kg 6$
Kg 9$
Kg 9$
Kg 7$
Kg 8$
Kg 9$
Kg 5$
Kg 6$
$ 12-00
2 Kg.
RATE $6.
MOBILE SH

Monday
LESSON 71
Examining Your Total Diet

Each day that we live, we are striving for the middle path, the balanced life, the existence which finds its strength beyond joy and sorrow, beyond pleasure and pain, beyond light and darkness. But in order to arrive at this state of contemplative awareness, we must begin at the beginning, and this week our study is diet: physical, mental and emotional foods. According to the ancient science of *āyurveda,* nature is a primordial force of life composed in three modes, qualities or principles of manifestation called *guṇas,* meaning "strands" or "qualities." The three *guṇas* are: *sattva,* "beingness;" *rajas,* "dynamism;" and *tamas,* "darkness." *Sattva* is tranquil energy, *rajas* is active energy and *tamas* is energy that is inert. The nature of *sattva* is quiescent, rarefied, translucent, pervasive. The nature of *rajas* is movement, action, emotion. The nature of *tamas* is inertia, denseness, contraction, resistance and dissolution. The *tamasic* tendency is descending, odic and instinctive. The *rajasic* tendency is expanding, actinodic, intellectual. The *sattvic* tendency is ascending, actinic, superconscious. The three *guṇas* are not separate entities, but varied dimensions or frequencies of the single, essential life force. ¶The food we eat has one or more of these qualities of energy and affects our mind, body and emotions accordingly. Hence, what we eat is important. *Sattvic* food is especially good for a contemplative life. ¶*Tamasic* foods include heavy meats, and foods that are spoiled, treated, processed or refined to the point where the natural values are no longer present. *Tamasic* foods make the mind dull; they tend to build up the basic odic energies of the body and the instinctive subconscious mind. *Tamasic* foods also imbue the astral body with heavy, odic force. ¶*Rajasic* foods include hot or spicy foods, spices and stimulants. These increase the odic heat of the physical and astral bodies and stimulate physical and mental activity. *Sattvic* foods include whole grains and legumes and fresh fruits and vegetables that grow above the ground. These foods help refine the astral and physical bodies, allowing the actinic, superconscious flow to permeate and invigorate the entire being. ¶People who are unfolding on the *yoga* path manifest the *sattvic* nature. Their path is one of peace and serenity. The *rajasic* nature is restless and manifests itself in physical and intellectual activities. It is predominant in the spirit of nationalism, sports and busi-

At a roadside market in India a typical merchant is selling fresh fruits, vegetables and grains from a simple cart. He stocks no preserved or packaged foods, but provides only fresh, wholesome fare which he gets that same day from farmers tending fields nearby.

ness competition, law enforcement and armed forces and other forms of aggressive activity. The *tamasic* nature is dull, fearful and heavy. It is the instinctive mind in its negative state and leads to laziness, habitual living, physical and mental inertia. As it is by cultivating the *rajasic* nature that *tamas* is overcome, so it is by evolving into the pure *sattvic* nature that the continual ramification of *rajas* is transcended. It is important to maintain a balance of our several natures, but to attain toward the expression of the *rajasic* and *sattvic* natures in as great a degree as possible. ¶As you examine a menu closely, you will find that you may allow your inner guidance to tell you what is most appropriate to eat. The desire body of the conscious mind may want one type of food, but the inner body of the subsuperconscious may realize another is better for you. It is up to you to make the decision that will allow a creative balance in your diet. This awakens the inner willpower, that strength from within that gives the capacity for discrimination.

Tuesday
LESSON 72
Moderation Is The Keynote

I call our diet "nutrition for meditation." We watch what we eat. Each type of food taken into the body tends to make us aware in one or another area of the nerve system. When we eat gross food, we become aware in the gross area of the nerve system, and less aware in the refined area of the nerve system. When we eat refined foods, such as fruit and vegetables that grow above the ground and absorb sunlight, this then makes us aware in the refined areas of the nerve system. When we are aware in the gross areas of the nerve system, over time the cells of the physical body begin to reflect this and cause the body to become gross in appearance. When we are aware in the refined areas of the inner nerve system predominantly—the psychic nerve system, the superconscious nerve system—the cells of the body also respond and we begin to look more refined. Therefore, *āyurvedic* nutrition for meditation and the practice of *haṭha yoga āsanas* are an aid in refining the physical body by allowing awareness to travel through the perceptive areas of the nerve system that are inner, refined and blissful. ¶However, we do not want to put too much emphasis on the consciousness of food, lest our entire nature become wrapped up in our stomach, and our subconscious and its astral body constantly involved in eating. To allow this would not only be detrimental to our own diet, but it would be an unnecessary disturbance as well to those about us, since we would be held in a strange emotional mold. ¶In deciding what foods you will buy and eat, listen to the voice of your intuition, which knows best what your current physical body needs are. It is possible that your forces might become too *sattvic,* too delicately refined, for the kind of activity and responsibilities you are engaged in. If this is the case, perhaps you should have a little *rajasic* food for balance. Likewise, you may become overstimulated from time to time through eating spicy foods, or foods with too high a concentration of sugar. In this case, you may need more fruits in your diet to raise the vibratory rate of your physical and astral bodies. Should your inner consciousness tell you that you are too *rajasic,* refrain from eating *tamasic* foods, those with lower rates of vibration. Eat more of the foods that grow naturally above the ground. ¶Of course, we have an emotional diet as well. Emotion is a condition or color of the mind. Emotions will always be with us as long as we have a physical body, but there is a difference between having emotion and being emotional. We have to balance our emotional activity. Our entertainment, our cultural pursuits, our social activities should be balanced and blended with everything else that we are doing. It would be a good idea to plan an entire month's emotional diet along with your physical diet. Decide ahead of time what music you wish to hear, what plays, movies or concerts to attend. Think of your reading, the people you plan to be with, the traveling that may be involved. Make a list of those things which you conceive to be beneficial to your emotional diet, but proceed along the middle path, not too much to one side, not too much to the other. Look for a balanced emotional color in your life.

Wednesday
LESSON 73
Choosing Your Mental Diet

Have you ever given thought to the diet of your mind? Of course, our physical diet and our emotional diet are also diets of the mind, because they affect our consciousness. But let's now consider the intellectual processes. How much information, how many facts is it necessary and healthy for us to ingest in a single day? It's a good idea for a devotee to budget his reading, to choose and discriminate what he wants to make a part of himself through the process of mental digestion. We have to discriminate to the nth degree whether or not we will have the time and the capacity to digest everything that we desire to place in our minds. For instance, quickly reading an article in a newspaper might stir your mind and emotions. If it is not properly digested, it could conceivably upset your whole day. In the realm of intellect, the commonsense rule "Don't eat when you are already full" also applies. ¶You may read a book of philosophy, and if you have time to digest it, well and good, but many people don't and suffer from philosophical indigestion. They have read so many things and only digested a small part of what has passed through the window of the mind. Then again, it is one thing to digest something, and it is still another to assimilate it and make it a part of you, for when it becomes fully a part of you, you have a hunger and room for something more. ¶Many people come to lectures and then tune themselves out and simply benefit from the vibration created by the teacher and others in the room. They tune themselves out so that what is said is not absorbed consciously, but rather subconsciously. This is a good method for those who are still digesting material received from previous lectures. Another practice that makes for a very good mental indigestion pill is that of opening a spiritual book and allowing your eye to fall upon a random sentence on the page. Often you will find it will accent ideas that you are currently concerned with. ¶Just as you would participate in a seminar, gaining from the interpersonal relationships, so can you learn from the intrapersonal relationship established between your perceptive state of mind and the conscious and subconscious states of mind. When you awaken to the point where your inner mind teaches your personality, you are involving yourself in the "innerversity" of your own being. But this will not occur until you have balanced your physical and emotional bodies to the point where they are functioning at a slightly higher rate of vibration. ¶Add to your contemplative lifestyle a hobby or craft. Working creatively with your hands, taking physical substance and turning it into something different, new and beautiful is important in remolding the subconscious mind. It is also symbolic. You are remolding something on the physical plane and by doing so educating yourself in the process of changing the appearance of a physical structure, thus making it easier to change the more subtle mental and emotional structures within your own subconscious mind. Energy, willpower and concentrated awareness are needed for both types of accomplishments—hard work, concentration and concerted effort to produce an effective and useful change in either the physical substance or the mental substance.

Thursday
LESSON 74
Balance and Discrimination

Observe your life objectively for a minute and decide how much of a working balance actually exists between your physical, emotional, mental and actinic aspects. Know that you have the power to begin to readjust this balance if you find you are taking in too much "food" at one time or another. Apply the concept of diet to all the areas of your life.

Every experience that we ingest is going to produce its own reaction. In surveying our own internal balance of *tamasic, rajasic* and *sattvic* tendencies, we need to apply the power of discrimination so that everything we take into our mind and body can be easily and harmoniously digested and assimilated. Life becomes more beautiful in this way, and we become the master of our forces, because we have given the guiding power of our lives to actinic will. But no diet is of much value to anyone unless it can be consistently applied through the power of decision. ¶Life becomes overly complicated, a series of self-created and unnecessary involvements, when we live too much in the *tamasic* and *rajasic* natures. It is necessary to slow down the activity of everyday life by entering into *sattvic* awareness as a matter of practice. Life is tiring and overactive in the conscious, physical plane when it is not balanced and tempered by the *sattvic* nature. The greater the *sattvic* activity, the greater the activity of the spiritual being that man is. ¶Here is an internal concentration exercise. Allow the activity of your brain to relax. Let the muscles of your body relax. Let your eyes relax and easily shut. Visualize in your mind's eye a menu with three panels. On the left panel of the menu are all the prepared and cooked foods of the *tamasic* nature, which are instinctive, heavy and often indigestible. These are the foods which would satisfy the purely instinctive man. In the middle panel are the *rajasic* foods, such as spices, garlic and onions, which provide physical energy and stimulation. On the right panel of the menu are the *sattvic* foods, such as fruits, vegetables, grains and nuts, which calm, balance and prepare the body to hold the actinic vibration of a higher consciousness. Let's examine the three parts of this menu and see where our consciousness is guided from within. ¶Let us visualize another menu now—which is the menu of our emotional diet. On the left panel are the instinctive, sensual pleasures of the moment and the more raucous forms of entertainment. On the middle panel are the routine emotional experiences of everyday life with family, friends and work associates. On the right panel are high cultural and artistic expressions. Fill in your own list of specifics and see where your consciousness leads you. ¶Visualize now another menu in three panels. On the left side of this menu are books, magazines, newspapers or websites that lead us into our *tamasic*, instinctive nature, be they novels, stories, articles or Hollywood exposes. On the middle panel are those intellectual studies, items of current interests and news which stimulate our *rajasic* mind and therefore require the close use of discrimination. At certain times, some of these readings might offer just the required understanding and intellectual clarity to elucidate important areas of your conscious-mind existence. ¶On the right side of this menu are the *sattvic* writings and studies, the scriptures of East and West, the great philosophical ideas of Socrates or Emerson, the dissertations of Plotinus or Kant, the sayings of Lao-tzu and Confucius, Tiruvalluvar or the *Upanishads,* Adi Sankara, Ramakrishna or Gibran. Compose your own list and then balance out your mental diet by studying this menu from your inner consciousness.

Friday
LESSON 75
Diet and Consciousness

It is wise to have a free mind, a clear, serene and relaxed attitude toward life before partaking of food. That is why people on the inner path traditionally meditate for a moment, chant a *mantra* or say a prayer before a meal. A simple practice is to intone "Aum." This harmonizes the inner bodies with the external bodies and frees awareness from entangled areas. If you find yourself in a situation where you cannot chant Aum aloud, then chant it mentally. Take several seconds before you begin your meal to recenter yourself in this way. You will find that your food profits you very well. There are many traditional Hindu *āyurvedic* guidelines for eating. A few rules that we have found especially important include giving thanks in a sacred prayer before meals; eating in a settled atmosphere, never when upset, always sitting down and only when hungry; avoiding ice-cold food and drink; not talking while chewing; eating at a moderate pace and never between meals; sipping warm water with meals; eating freshly cooked foods whenever possible; minimizing raw vegetables; avoiding white flour and refined sugar; not cooking with honey; drinking milk separately from meals; including a balance of protein and carbohydrates in all meals; cooking with *ghee* or olive oil only; experiencing all six tastes at least at the main meal (sweet, sour, pungent, astringent, bitter and salty); not overeating, leaving one-third to one-quarter of the stomach empty to aid digestion; and sitting quietly for a few minutes after meals. I might add that ginger root is a magical potion. Our *āyurvedic* doctor has taught us, and experience confirms, that fresh ginger can settle your stomach, relieve a headache, help you sleep if you are restless and keep the *agni,* fires of digestion, strong, especially while traveling. Grate two inches of fresh ginger, then hold the mash in your hand, add slowly an ounce of warm water and squeeze the juice into a glass. Repeat three times. Drink this extract fifteen or twenty minutes before meals. It is also quite necessary to drink at least eight glasses of water each day. Inadequate water intake results in dehydration, giving rise to many common ailments. ¶Let us realize this law in our consciousness: we don't want to place anything into our physical, emotional or mental being that cannot be digested, assimilated and used to the best advantage in giving birth to our highest consciousness. Let every second be a second of discrimination. Let every minute be a minute of realization. Let every hour be an hour of fulfillment. Let every day be a day of blessing, and every week a week of joy. Then, in a month's time, look at the foundation that you have laid for those who will follow you. Let the past fade into the dream that it is. It is only experience, to be understood as such in the "now." In keeping life simple through our powers of discrimination, we give our greatest gift to community, loved ones, country and the world, because we are beginning to vibrate in the superconscious realms of the mind. Your very presence is a blessing when you live in the eternal now, in full command of your life's diet through the process of discrimination.

Saturday
LESSON 76
Restraining Television

Television provides so much of the mental diet of so many people today that it deserves special attention, lest it become a deterrent to a balanced, contemplative life. Television at its best is the extension of storytelling. We used to sit around and tell stories. The best storyteller, who could paint pictures in people's minds, was the most popular person in town. Television is also the extension of the little theater, and as soon as it became popular, the little theater groups all over the country became unemployed. It is the extension of the stand-up comedian, of vaudeville, drama, opera, ballet, all of which have suffered since television has become a popular mode of entertainment. In every country, at every point in time, humans have sat down and been entertained, and entertainers have stood up and entertained them. ¶Today, television has become an instrument to convey knowledge and bring the world together, set new standards of living, language, styles of dress and hair, ways of walking, ways of standing, attitudes about people, ethics, morality, political systems, religions and all sorts of other things, from ecology to pornography. This vast facility unifies the thinking—and thus the actions—of the peoples of the world. Today, at the flick of a finger with the magic wand, one can change the mental flow and emotional experience of everyone watching for the entire evening. ¶Śaivites know that our *karmas* are forces we send out from ourselves—creative forces, preserving forces, destroying forces, and a mixture of either two or the three—and they usually come back to us through other people or groups of people. Television has afforded us the ability to work through our *karmas* more quickly than we could in the agricultural age. On TV, the "other people" who play our past experiences back to us, for us to understand in hindsight, are actors and actresses, newscasters and the people in the news they broadcast. Śaivites know nothing can happen, physically, mentally or emotionally, but that it is seeded in our *prārabdha karmas,* the action-reaction patterns brought with us to this birth. Therefore, on the positive side, we look at television as a tool for *karmic* cleansing. ¶Śaivites know that the object of life is to go through our experiences joyously and kindly, always forgiving and compassionately understanding, thus avoiding making unseemly *kriyamāna karmas* in the current life which, if enough were accumulated and added to the *karmas* we did not bring into this life, would bring us back into another birth, and the process would start all over again. The great boon that television has given humanity, which is especially appreciated by Śaivites, is that we can soften our *prārabdha karmas* very quickly by analyzing, forgiving and compassionately understanding the happenings on the screen, as our past is portrayed before us, and as we work with our nerve system, which laughs and cries, resents, reacts to and avoids experiences on the TV. ¶Television can be very entertaining and helpful, or it can be insidiously detrimental, depending on how it is used. Therefore, fortify your mind with a thorough understanding of what you are watching. Television works on the subconscious mind. This is an area of the mind which we are not usually conscious of when it is functioning, but it is functioning nevertheless, constantly, twenty-four hours a day. Television works strongly on the subconscious minds of children. If they watch TV for long periods of time, they begin to think exactly as the programmers want them to think. Responsible parents have to choose just what goes into their children's minds, as well as into their own minds. It is advisable to prerecord the shows you wish to watch, avoiding sexual scenes, obscene language and excessive violence; and even then be ready to fast-forward through inappropriate scenes that are found today even on PG-rated programs.

Sunday
LESSON 77
Insights from Astrology

Astrology explores the stars and planets as they move in the heavens and their subtle effects on our physical, mental and emotional condition, mapping the ebb and flow of our *karma.* Astrology plays a very important part in every Hindu's life. An established family is not complete without their master of *jyotisha.* Guided by the stars from birth to death, devout Hindus choose a *śubha muhūrta,* auspicious time, for every important experience of life. Astrology has been computerized through the efforts of brilliant *jyotisha śāstris* of both the East and West. In our *āśrama,* we use *jyotisha* quite a lot to determine the best times to travel, meditate, begin new projects or just rest and let a harsh time pass. Experience assures us that astrology is a reliable tool for maintaining a balanced life and flowing with the forces of nature. ¶We take a metaphysical approach to the "good" or "bad" news or predictions that astrology brings from time to time. When unfavorable times arise which have to be lived through, as they all too frequently do, we do not carp or cringe, but look at these as most excellent periods for meditation and *sādhana* rather than worldly activities. Just the reverse is true for the positive periods. However, spiritual progress can be made during both kinds of periods. Both negative and positive times are, in fact, positive when used wisely. A competent *jyotisha śāstrī* is of help in forecasting the future, as to when propitious times will come along when advancements can be made. A positive mental attitude should be held during all the ups and downs that are predicted to happen. Be as the traveler in a 747 jet, flying high over the cities, rather than a pedestrian wandering the streets below. ¶For raising offspring, an astrological forecast can be of the utmost help. A baby predicted to have a fiery temper should be raised to always be kind and considerate of others' feelings, taught to never argue with others. Of course, good examples must be set early on by parents. This will soften the inclination toward temper tantrums. Fighting the child's natural impulses will just amplify them. A child of an independent nature should be taught early on to care for himself in all respects so that in the life ahead he will benefit society and bring honor to the family. So much can be gained by reading the chart when approached with the attitude that all that is in it is helpful and necessary to know, even if it seems to be bad news. Difficulties need not be bad news if they are approached as opportunities to grow in facing them. ¶We have for years in our monasteries lived by the Hindu calendar and system of time divisions known as Lahiri Ayanāṁśa Pañchānga. All *pūrṇimā, amavāsya* and *ashṭami* days (full moon, new moon and the eighth day of the fortnight) are days of retreat. They are our weekends. To be in harmony with the universe, at least our little galaxy, it is important to observe these days for happy, healthy, productive living.

Rāsāyanika Avyavasthā
रासायनिक अव्यवस्था

Chemical Chaos

If I totter along, O wielder of thunder, like a
puffed-up wineskin, forgive, Lord, have mercy!
If by ill chance in the dullness of my wits I went
straying, O Holy One, forgive, Lord, have mercy!

Ṛig Veda 7.89.2-3. VE, P. 517

Monday
LESSON 78
Chemical Consciousness

In the early '60s I became conscious that more and more of the people who came to me for counseling wanted to talk over aspects of their experience in higher states of the mind, states of the mind that had been opened through psychedelic experience. Their interest was in relating these experiences to *yoga* and the consciousness attained through meditation. These people were highly enthusiastic about their new world, for it seemed like sort of a canned meditation, something they could get very quickly without entering into the sometimes tedious *yoga* training that may take years to open the individual to the within of himself. People all over the nation now are becoming awakened to the world within. ¶Around the same time, we had a seminar in San Diego attended by many seekers and LSD users. It seemed to us that the LSD people are almost like a new race, a race of people that have been reborn in bodies that already existed. Those who use psychedelics are different in many respects from those who have had no psychedelic experience. Their feelings are different. Their relationships are different. They are closer to some people, but at the same time they have created a gap between themselves and society. It is a gap of loneliness, because the breach between the inner consciousness and the external world has become so great that they have only themselves to depend upon. The degree of success of this dependence is another story, which brings us into the subject of *yoga.* We cannot say that the psychedelic experience in itself is either good or bad. It is enough to say that it is an experience that has occurred to thousands of people. ¶These ideas I am sharing with you are not so much for the psychedelic people as for those who have not had the psychedelic experience. I do not encourage you to go through it. Rather, I would encourage you to continue with the slower process of *yoga.* But I want to awaken you to the fact that there is this new group of people living with us. Their approach to life is entirely different from the one which you may have. Their perception generally is entirely different. Some of these people can look into your mind and even read your thoughts. Those who have not had psychedelic experiences will have to learn to adjust to the psychedelic consciousness. Likewise, those who use these drugs, if they ever stop, will have to learn to adjust their thinking again to the normal conscious-

---

At the end of the day, two businessmen discuss matters of mutual interest while enjoying a glass of wine. They know the wisdom of indulging in beer and wine in moderation and avoiding the harder liquors and all drugs of abuse.

plane way of doing things. ¶I believe that the gap which has been created between "turned on people" and "turned off people" can best be bridged through meditation, gaining control of the mind so that the individual can become master of himself. When you become master of yourself, you truly stand alone in completeness, not in loneliness. In doing so, you are able to bring forth knowledge and wisdom from yourself through the process of meditation, through being able to sit down and think through a problem, ultimately seeing it in full, superconscious perspective and bring forth an answer, a workable answer filled with life. Meditation is a dynamic process. It is much more than just sitting around and waiting. It creates a highly individualistic type of mind.

Tuesday
LESSON 79
Young and Old Souls

There are young souls in this world, and there are old souls. The young soul shows you how you can't do something. The old soul shows you how you can. But a young soul can evolve in this very life in the same way that a weak, skinny man can go to a gym and become a husky bundle of muscle. ¶Spiritual unfoldment and the growth and development of the subtle nerve system are the same thing. Most of us are familiar with the structure of the body's muscles, but how many of you are familiar with your nerve fibers? The life force flows through you along these nerve channels in a degree directly proportionate to the condition of your mind. We call this actinic force or cosmic force. This actinic force flowing out into the muscle and skin structure produces *prāṇa*, or magnetism. The magnetic force in nature we call odic force. Have you ever had somebody suddenly call you up and say, "Come on, let's go to a party," when you feel tired and lacking in energy, and suddenly your nervous system floods a new force through you, rejuvenating your magnetic response? This is an involuntary response, a subsuperconscious release of actinic force. ¶The nervous system in a young soul is, shall we say, immature. The many, many incarnational experiences of the old soul have instilled in the subtle nervous system a strength of fiber, a spiritual maturation. Therefore, the older soul entering into meditation can sustain the force and unfoldment that one meditation carries over into another. This process is a steady building, an opening up, until finally, in a contemplative moment of cosmic consciousness, one opens to Self Realization, beyond the experience of the mind, and is able to sustain it because the nerve structure is very powerful. ¶So, this is the unfortunate aspect of psychedelic experience as I see it. It is especially damaging to the young soul and leads the older soul off track. If the individual taking LSD or some other psychotropic drug is an old soul, it has perhaps awakened him so that he is able to face the new situation of his consciousness with intelligence. But the reaction inhibits further spiritual unfoldments because lower *chakras* are wrenched open, causing severe mood swings. In the case of the young soul, he has not yet developed the nerve fiber to adjust to the awakening, to the intensity of the psychedelic experience, and his mind very often "turns off." ¶I have interviewed seekers who have had a few psychedelic experiences and have come through them more vibrant, more alive, and more ready to face the challenges of a new world. I have met others who only stand and look at you blankly, who have lost their desire, even their self-respect. They have lost, shall we say, the structure through which their mind force previously flowed, and it has not been replaced. ¶What happens to a Hindu *yogī* when he enters a superconscious state of bliss in which his mind opens up, turns to light, and he sees the world revolving below the state of his suspended consciousness? He has arrived at this state through many years of practice in concentration, meditation and contemplation, many years of building strong nerve fiber. But in a momentary high on LSD or any other powerful psychedelic, such as mushrooms, peyote, ecstasy or DMT, the nerve structure is strained, in a sense which we can best describe as abnormal, to allow the individual to reach this exalted consciousness. Coming out of it, the result is often a kind of shock in which the person has a great difficulty in readjusting to any kind of normal routine. Because these drugs are illegal, the consciousness of fear also has been awakened within the seeker. Fear is the first step down into the lower worlds of darkness. The next is anger.

Wednesday
LESSON 80
Maintaining Control

I don't want to see a nationwide or worldwide movement built around a little bit of "acid." I don't want to see this, because of the young souls for whom this would be devastating. Some young souls who have been opened up without preparation stumble into psychic ability. They may read thought forms, see auras or travel astrally. In *yoga* we would say that this path of psychism must be avoided until you have attained Self Realization. This is because in opening up the mind to higher forces and beautiful experiences, we also open ourselves up to the unpleasant experiences of the shadow world of the *chakras* below the *mūlādhāra* center at the base of the spine, areas of consciousness which we cannot control without preparation and training. In *yoga*, the *guru* knows how to protect his students in the opening-up process by closing off the lower realms as the higher ones open. He knows how to do this, but it is a steady training and does require time. I have met people who have had the psychedelic experience who but cannot walk down the street past certain houses because they have become so sensitive to the contention, the negative force field, emitted from a certain home. Some of these people are opened up to the more subtle forces of the lower mind. ¶The old soul, in wisdom, enters into the experience of meditation. Here he learns to control the lower forces even while he is awakening the higher forces. Therefore he can sustain himself in a higher state of consciousness. He has the strength of nerve fiber to do it. ¶So, I am asking the leaders of the LSD movement, the psychedelic movement, to stop it, for the sake of protecting souls on the path against the too abrupt awakening, against being opened up to obsession or possession. Most people who take drugs are followers. They're not leaders, they're followers. A leader takes a stand. A leader stands for what he believes and believes what he stands for. We need to train our children to be leaders and to stand up against that which they know is wrong and dangerous. ¶When a person is opened up, in a somewhat defenseless position, as in an LSD experience, he can be possessed or obsessed by an accumulation of thought power and impelled to do things that he would otherwise have no intention of doing, simply because his nervous system has become sensitive and open to the lower mind forces of hate, greed, mistrust, fear and malice that ooze out of some people who have no control. ¶If you have not been opened up in this manner, if you are just going along in an ordinary state of consciousness, you might feel, "I don't like so-and-so and I won't see him anymore," and you place a mental barrier between yourself and this person. You are able to shut your mental door against people whose vibration does not blend with yours. But a prematurely opened soul cannot do this. He remains open to all influences. Therefore, I plead to the innate intelligence of the intellectuals and the old souls who can appreciate what is happening, to stop the indiscriminate use of dangerous drugs, to bring this movement to a halt.

Thursday
LESSON 81
Tapping the Superconscious

The youngsters in their late teens and early twenties who are going into LSD and other drugs are going to meet their *karma* in an unnatural sequence. The upset of their nervous system, if it continues, will be drastic and will even affect others' personal lives, whether they have had LSD or not. I have traveled through India and the Orient where there are no laws against narcotics, and the people who live on narcotics there are absolutely deplorable. They have no spiritual impetus. They just sit and say, "Well, if I have food, that's fine. If not, then I'll probably die. So, let's see, if I reincarnate, where would I like to go?" Whereas when the spiritual force, the actinic force, floods through your nervous system, permeating you with magnetism, and you see the light of your mind, you don't have time for rationalizations like that. ¶When we are dealing with the nervous system, we are talking about three states of mind at the same time. The conscious, subconscious and superconscious all exist, alive and vibrant, within you at this moment. You could be "turned on" superconsciously without drugs at any instant. It is all there waiting for you. Your brain is basically an acid structure. When you learn to concentrate your mind, to concentrate the thinking force, you are turning on the "acid" of your brain. LSD is an acid, too, but it can do nothing for you that you cannot do for yourself. When you learn the subtle arts of meditation, you will learn how to tap into your spiritual force, your always-existing actinic power which transmits its energy through body and mind into the magnetic currents. This magnetic force can be stimulated also through food, through breathing or through the quality of thought. ¶Now is a marvelous time for people to tap their latent potential to unfold these higher states of consciousness. All of the activity and discussion of outer space contributes to this unfoldment, too, because every time you mentally project yourself with a rocket or a spaceship, your consciousness touches back on the Earth again, having undergone a definite change. ¶What is going to be the reaction over a period of time to the psychedelic movement? Meditating *yogīs* have found that even in the integrated process of meditation, one's *karma* is intensified, and experiences come to you thick and fast to work through. Under LSD and similar drugs, the wheels are spinning faster and faster until some drug takers will be spinning in consciousness completely away from any kind of stable living. I believe that with the continued use of LSD, the forces will slip over to the other side, past the point of no return. The spiritual unfoldment of the human soul can no more profitably be forced than can the growth of a plant in a hot house. *Yoga* is the path of control. If you go at it through *yoga*, you will be so much better off, and through your new radiant energy you will be able to help so many people.

Friday
LESSON 82
The Power Of Decision

Many are the *karmic* consequences of using, selling and encouraging others to use illegal drugs, such as marijuana, cocaine, heroin, methamphetamines, barbiturates and psychedelics like LSD and mushrooms. The *karmic* chain works like this. Suppose someone sold drugs to another and that person overdosed and killed himself. The *karma* would be murder. Maybe the law wouldn't call it murder, but the *karma* would be murder. This means that the person who sold the drugs would be killed in his next life. One act creates another act and that act comes back on those who helped create it. Similarly, if movie actors cause others to hurt themselves or kill another person, commit robbery, anything like that, because of what they're acting out, that *karma* comes back on them, as well as the director, as well as the writer. It's pretty messy business to fool around with the law of *karma.* ¶I tell young people who are tempted to use drugs that the power of decision is a very great power. Very few people know how to use this power, but everybody has the power of decision. It takes a little bit of willpower, it takes a little bit of research, and we are going to give you some ammunition to help you make the decision to be free from drugs. ¶The consequences of illegal drug use are that the drug user becomes a criminal. His home or car can be confiscated under drug assets seizure laws. His parents' home or car can be seized. He can be arrested for driving under the influence of controlled substances. People may steal drugs from him, putting him and his family in danger. Eventually, he can't earn enough to buy the drugs he needs. He can't even steal enough. He has to deal, to sell drugs, to support the habit. And to deal, he must recruit new users. Drugs make him meet people he would never meet otherwise, not-so-good people—sellers, dealers, junkies. It puts him into a lower realm of life. He may become violent. He has to get a gun to protect himself. More danger follows. The government has to deal with him, as he has become a criminal. It's very expensive for society. He can't behave normally. He does harm to his body. He does harm to his mind. He becomes paranoid, always looking over his shoulder, fearful that bad things are going to happen. As a student, he can't study well anymore, and he probably won't graduate—he gets no education, therefore no career and no steady job. He does things he never thought he would do: rob, steal, lie, forge, pull away from and humiliate his parents, pull away from his teachers, create abnormal relationships with friends, girlfriends, boyfriends, ruin his reputation, even go into prostitution. ¶I warn youths, you might think it won't happen to you. Well, everybody who takes drugs says, "That won't happen to me. I can handle it." Every junkie on the street has said that at one time or another. Why do we have groups talking about how to handle drugs and drug rehabilitation centers, which are very expensive for states, counties and private organizations to run? Because you cannot handle it. No one can handle it. It all starts with that first puff of a joint, the first time you cross the line into what's not legal. One drug leads to the next, which leads to the next and the next. It's the Narakaloka, active every day in the lives of the people on this planet who use illegal substances. So don't get started. ¶Drugs may seem like an escape from the problems of life, but it is not a solution to them. In Hindu, Jain and Buddhist thinking, all this adds up to bad *karma,* then a bad birth. You can't escape from *karma.* It will always catch up with you—if not in this life then in the next. But we can't just say no because somebody has told us to say no. We need to meditate, we need to think upon the consequences, of what will happen to us, of using these terribly dangerous, illegal substances. ¶Talk to young people in your community. Tell them, "Think about it. Only you can make the decision. No one else can make it for you." You can't convince a young person here on the island of Kauai to surf on a fifty foot wave. Youths also don't drive a hundred miles an hour down the winding mountain road from Kokee. Why? Because they know the consequence. They are well educated. They know the consequence and, be they 12 years old, 16 years old, 20 years old, 24 years old, they make the proper decisions about such things. ¶The issue is training people to make the proper decisions so that they are law-abiding citizens because they have decided to be law-abiding citizens, so that they do not take drugs, because they do not want to alter their mind, because they do not want to lose their standing in the community, because they do not want to lose the functioning of their physical body. The power of decision is a great power to pass on to the next generation.

Saturday
LESSON 83
Alcohol in Moderation

Alcohol is a very misunderstood substance. Its original use in many cultures was limited to the priesthood, to enliven consciousness by restricting the activities of the conscious mind, so that the superconscious knowledge within the individual can flow freely, uninhibited by daily thought and concerns. In Japan, *sake,* a rice wine, is considered the potion of the poets and is served in Buddhist and Shinto monasteries to enhance the spiritual nature and diminish worldly attachments. The drinking of sake goes along with certain other practices of controlling the mind, based on a well-understood philosophy. In other cultures—Aztec, Mayan, Hindu, Christian and Jewish—wine is considered a holy sacrament. ¶Beer is a lesser potion, a drink for the common man, and does not fall into this category. Both beer and wine are produced from natural ingredients and through natural fermentation processes, whereas hard liquors are distilled. Another important difference is the concentration of alcohol. In beer the alcohol content is from 3 to 8 percent, and in wine from 9 to 18 percent, compared to hard liquors which are from 25 to nearly 100 percent. The latter our scriptures admonish us to not imbibe. ¶Man's religious traditions provide different answers to the consumption of alcohol. The Muslim faith considers it the mother of all evils, the most basic of human sins. The Jews, Christians and others consider it acceptable in moderation, and, in fact, provide wine as sacraments in their places of worship. In Asian societies, propaganda against alcohol is severe, primarily directed toward hard liquors, meaning those of high alcohol content, which tend to quickly craze the mind, punish the body and let loose the lower emotions. These include distilled home brews, such as arrack, bathtub gin, homemade rum and vodka. ¶In Hinduism there are traditions that are strictly abstemious, and there are traditions that are open to the use of alcohol. Especially the Śaivas and Śāktas are more lenient in this matter and have no objection to the moderate, wise use of alcohol. In North India, for example, it is traditional in certain orders for Śaiva *sannyāsins* to drink alcohol. This is the tradition that our particular *paramparā* has adopted and it is the custom that we follow today. If you are in a tradition which has a heritage of complete abstention, then you should follow it. If you are in a tradition which does not look down on drinking wines or beers, then you should feel free to follow that tradition. ¶Hindus of the Jaffna community explain that hard liquor, known as *kal* in Tamil, are the intoxicants prohibited in the *Tirukural* and *Tirumantiram* and which are to be totally abstained from, and that beer and wine, including honey wine, are referred to in the *Vedas* and *āyurveda* texts as beneficial for spiritual and religious life under the restraint of *mitāhāra.*

Sunday
LESSON 84
Alcohol in Śaiva Tradition

The time periods allotted for drinking wine and beer should be during a meal (lunch or dinner), or to relax after the day's *dharmic* duties are fulfilled. Obviously, one should not drink during the work day, in the office, during *pūjā* or in the early morning hours. ¶Of course, this hardly need be said, but drinking and driving don't mix. This extends also to other potentially dangerous activities. One would never drink while on the job, especially using industrial equipment, such as saws and drills, as alcohol slows down the reactions of the physical body and the conscious mind. While enjoying a glass or two of wine, one should be in good company. Drinking should bring up the higher nature, of creativity, good ideas, conversation, philosophy, intuitive solutions to the problems of the world, healthy encounters of all kinds. One should not drink when depressed, troubled or with a group that enters into confrontation, argument, contention and criticism, personal, mental and emotional abuse. Therefore, we emphasize good company, good conversation, creativity, relaxation, toward the advancement of humanity and of spirituality. That is what these two substances, wine and beer, have been created on Earth by Lord Śiva Himself to produce. Of course, imbibing even wine and beer falls under the restraint of *mitāhāra*. To overindulge would be unacceptable. ¶One should not drink alone, not even a glass of wine or beer at a solitary dinner. All the social harnesses are absent when you drink in isolation. Then it becomes a subconscious instead of a subsuperconscious experience. Additionally, there are those who by their constitution or genetics cannot drink even moderately without catastrophic effects: physiological, psychological, sociological difficulties. Even a single beer can provoke extreme responses. When these reactions come, they suffer physically, their families suffer, their professions suffer, their spiritual unfoldment suffers. Therefore, these individuals must, under all circumstances, completely avoid alcohol for a healthy, happy life. Statistically it is estimated that some seven percent of people are in this category. A clear indication that an individual falls into this category is that his friends don't want to drink with him because it inevitably becomes an unpleasant event for all. Friends and associates are duty-bound to monitor and sanction him. In such cases insisting on moderation is not sufficient. Total abstinence must be required. ¶In a similar vein, I am often asked about tobacco. My answer is, do you want to live a happy, healthy, productive and long life, or do you want to die early and suffer all the diseases that have been documented that smoking, the world's worst health hazard, can bring up in your body to destroy it? If the answer is "I don't mind dying early and I'm looking forward to all the diseases that are promised," then go ahead and smoke. I should say here that not one of my sincere devotees smokes.

Sādhanā
साधना

Discipline for Self-Transformation

Find a quiet retreat for the practice of *yoga*, sheltered from the wind, level and clean, free from rubbish, smoldering fires and ugliness, and where the sound of waters and the beauty of the place help thought and contemplation.

Kṛishṇa Yajur Veda, Śvetāśvatara Upanishad, 2.10. UPM, P. 88

Śiva
Śiva

Monday
LESSON 85
Sādhana and The Five Duties

When we study and practice our religion, we are not necessarily performing deep *sādhana.* We are simply dispatching our religious duties. These duties are concisely outlined in the *pañcha nitya karmas,* the five minimal religious obligations of Hindus. The first duty is *dharma,* proper conduct, living one's life according to the teachings of the *Tirukural* and atoning for misconduct. The second duty is *upāsana,* worship, performing a personal vigil each day, preferably before dawn, including a *pūjā,* followed by the performance of *japa,* scriptural study, and meditation. The third duty is *utsava,* holy days, observing each Friday (or Monday) as a holy day, as well as the major festival days through the year. On the weekly holy day, one cleans and decorates the home altar, attends the nearby temple and observes a fast. The fourth duty of all Hindus is *tirthayātrā,* pilgrimage. At least once each year, a pilgrimage is made to a Hindu temple away from one's local area. Fifth is *saṁskāras,* the observance of traditional rites of passage, including *nāmakaraṇa,* name-giving; *vivāha,* marriage; and *antyeshṭi,* funeral rites. ¶Another vital aspect of Hindu duty is service. The *Vedas* remind us, "When a man is born, whoever he may be, there is born simultaneously a debt to the Gods, to the sages, to the ancestors and to men" (*Śukla Yajur Veda, SB* 1.7.2.1. VE, P. 393). Service to the community includes helping the poor, caring for the aged, supporting religious institutions, building schools and upholding the lofty principle of *ahiṁsā* in raising one's children. Hinduism is a general and free-flowing, relaxed religion, experienced in the temple, in the *āśramas,* the *aadheenams,* at festivals, on pilgrimage and in the home. ¶The performance of personal *sādhana,* discipline for self-transformation, is one step deeper in making religion real in one's life. Through *sādhana* we learn to control the energies of the body and nerve system, and we experience that through the control of the breath the mind becomes peaceful. *Sādhana* is practiced in the home, in the forest, by a flowing river, under a favorite tree, in the temple, in *gurukulas* or wherever a pure, serene atmosphere can be found. A *vrata,* vow, is often taken before serious *sādhana* is begun. The *vrata* is a personal pledge between oneself, one's *guru* and the angelic beings of the inner worlds to perform the disciplines regularly, conscientiously, at the same time each day.

A Malaysian, whose home is near the Petronas Towers in Kuala Lumpur, has just concluded his morning Gaṇeśa pūjā *and is reading from* Merging with Śiva. *Angelic beings,* devas, *bless his striving by showering baskets of flowers on him in the inner worlds.*

Tuesday
LESSON 86
Establishing Your Sādhana

Many of you here today have studied with me for some time and understand how a good religious life can be lived in this technological age. You have learned how to pass the knowledge of Śaiva Dharma on to the next generation, the next and the next. But you may not yet feel fully confident to teach Śaiva Dharma outside your home and immediate family. All of you are preparing yourselves to be teachers of Śaiva Dharma, so that the Śaivite who has not had the benefits of knowing a lot about his religion may know more, so that the Hindu who does not have the benefit of knowing whether he is a Śaivite, a Vaishṇavite, a Śakta or a Smārta may learn the difference and then fully practice one of these four great religions of our heritage. In order to teach with confidence, you must train yourselves. Since this is an inner teaching, you must train yourselves inwardly through the regular daily practice of *sādhana.* ¶Who sets the course of *sādhana?* The course of *sādhana* can be set by an elder of the Hindu community. It can also be set by one's *satguru.* Your mother and father, who are your first *gurus,* can also set the course of *sādhana* for their children. Or, it can be set by yourself, from a book. There are many fine books available, outlining the basics of *yoga, sādhana* and meditation. ¶Where does *sādhana* begin? It begins within the home, and it begins within you. This is ancient wisdom recognized not only in India, but among many great civilizations of history. Thus upon the wall of a famous ancient Greek temple and oracular center at Delphi was inscribed "Know thyself." The religion of the Greeks, which was in many respects not unlike Hinduism, is long since gone, but remaining temple ruins testify to its magnificence. By disciplining your mind, body and emotions through *sādhana,* you come more and more into the inner knowing of yourself. ¶You will first discover that when the breath is regulated, it is impossible for the thinking mind to run wild, and when the breath is slightly held, it is impossible for more than one thought to remain vibrating in the mind at a time. You will experience that when the nerve currents are quieted through diaphragmatic breathing, it is impossible to be frustrated, and it is possible to absorb within yourself, into the great halls of inner learning, into the great vacuum within you, all of your problems, troubles and fears, without having to psychoanalyze them. ¶Through the regular practice of scriptural study, which is a vital part of your daily *sādhana* vigil, you will soon find that it is possible to touch into your subsuperconscious mind and complement that study with your own inner knowing. After you are well established in your *sādhana,* you will enjoy a greater ability to discipline your body, your breath, your nerve system and your mind. ¶We first have to learn that in order to control the breath, we have to study and understand the breath, the lungs, how the body is constructed and how the *prāṇas* move through it. This enables us to understand the subtle system within the body that controls the thinking mind. Then we are ready to study the mind in its totality.

Wednesday
LESSON 87
The Five States of Mind

In *Merging with Śiva* we embarked on a great study of the mind in its totality. Here we shall review the five states of mind. The conscious mind is our external mind. The subconscious mind contains our memory patterns and all impressions of the past. The sub of the subconscious mind holds the seeds of *karmas* that are not yet manifest. The subsuperconscious mind works through the subconscious mind, and intuition flows daily as a result. Creativity is there at your bidding. Your superconscious mind is where intuitive flashes occur. The accomplished mystic can consciously be in one country or another instantaneously, according to his will, once he has, through the grace of Lord Śiva, attained a full inner knowing of how to remain in Satchidānanda, the superconscious mind, consciously, without the other states interfering. ¶Yes, *sādhana* begins in the home, and it begins with you. It must be practiced regularly, at the same time each day—not two hours one day, one hour the next and then forgetting about it for three or four days because you are too busy with external affairs, but every day, at the same time. Meeting this appointment with yourself is in itself a *sādhana.* In the technological age nearly everyone finds it difficult to set one hour aside in which to perform *sādhana.* This is why in your *sādhana vrata* you promise to dedicate only one half hour a day. In the agricultural era, it was easy to find time to perform *sādhana* two to three hours a day. Why? The demands of external life were not as great as they are now, in the technological age. Half an hour a day, therefore, is the amount of time we dedicate for our *sādhana.* ¶*Brahmachārīs* and *brahmachāriṇīs,* celibate men and women, in their respective *gurukulas* dedicate their time to the performance of *sādhana.* They rise together early in the morning, perform their *sādhana* as a group, and then are off to their daily work. The regular practice of *sādhana,* they have found, enables them to get along admirably well with one another because of their newly acquired abilities of absorbing their difficulties, thus avoiding argument and confrontation. In these *gurukulas,* found worldwide, various kinds of *sādhanas* are performed, such as scriptural study, chanting the names of the Lord on the *japa* beads, group chanting of *bhajanas*, the singing of *Devarams* and the *yogic* concentration of holding the mind fixed on one point and bringing it back to that one point each time it wanders. The more disciplined *gurukulas* religiously administrate group *sādhana* at the same time each day, every day without fail. Daily life revolves around this period of *sādhana*, just as in a religious Śaivite home life revolves around the shrine room and each one's daily personal vigil. ¶Ask yourself what you put first in your daily life. Do your emotions come first? Does your intellect come first? Do your instinctive impulses come first? Does your striving to overcome worries and fears and doubt come first inside of you? Does your creativity, your love for all humanity, your search for God and peace within yourself come first inside of you? What are your priorities? The *pañcha nitya karmas* outline our basic religious priorities. Your inner priorities in implementing these five duties must be just as well defined, and you must define them for yourself and therefore, come to better "Know thyself."

Thursday
LESSON 88
Questions and Challenges

When you first begin your daily *sādhana*, it is likely to begin in an awkward way, and you may come to know yourself in a way that you don't want to know yourself. Don't be discouraged when the mind runs wild as you sit quietly and are unable to control it. Don't be discouraged if you find that you are unable to even choose a time to sit quietly for one half hour on a regular daily basis. If you persist, soon all this will be overcome and a firmness of mind will be felt, for it is through the regular practice of *sādhana* that the mind becomes firm and the intellect pure. It is through the regular practice of concentration that awareness detaches itself from the external mind and hovers within, internalizing the knowledge of the physical body, the breath and the emotions. Concentration of the forces of the body, mind and emotions brings us automatically into meditation, *dhyāna*, and into deeper internalized awareness. ¶The spiritual practice should be reasonable, should not take up too much time, and should be done at the same time every day. Often seekers who become associated with Hindu *sādhana* go to extremes and proceed with great vigor in an effort to attain results immediately. Sitting two or three hours a day, they wear themselves out and then stop. Here's a formula for beginners: Monday, Tuesday, Wednesday, Thursday, Friday, twenty minutes to a half an hour of *sādhana* at the same time every day; Saturday and Sunday, no *sādhana.* ¶The keys are moderation and consistency. Consistency is the key to the conquest of *karma.* If you go to extremes or are sporadic in your *sādhana,* you can easily slide backwards. What happens when you slide backwards? You become fearful, you become angry, you become jealous, you become confused. What happens when you move forward? You become brave, you become calm, you become self-confident and your mind is clear. ¶It is often feared that meditation and religious devotion cause a withdrawal from the world. The practice of *sādhana* I have described does not detach you from or make you indifferent to the world. Rather, it brings up a strength within you, a *śakti,* enabling you to move the forces of the world in a positive way. What is meant by "moving the forces of the world"? That means fulfilling realistic goals that you set for yourself. That means performing your job as an employer or as an employee in the most excellent way possible. That means stretching your mind and emotions and endurance to the limit and therefore getting stronger and stronger day by day. You are involved in the world, and the world is in a technological age. ¶The *sādhana* that you perform will make your mind steady and your will strong so that you can move the forces of the physical world with love and understanding, rather than through anger, hatred, antagonism, cunning, jealousy and greed. Daily *sādhana* performed in the right way will help you overcome these instinctive barriers to peace of mind and the fullness of being. If you have children, the rewards of your *sādhana* will help you educate your children properly in fine schools and universities and see that all of their physical needs are met through the flow of material abundance that automatically comes as you progress in your inner life. ¶Through daily *sādhana* we shall come to know the body, we shall come to know the emotions, we shall come to know the nerve system, we shall come to know the breath and we shall come to know the mind in its totality. Each one of you will soon be able to mentally pick up all of the dross of your subconscious, throw it within, into the great cavity of inner knowing at the feet of the Gods, there to be absorbed, dissolved and disappear. All this and more can be unfolded from within each one of you through your daily practice of *sādhana.* *Sādhana* is one of the great boons given to us in our religion.

Friday
LESSON 89
Guardian Angels

When the *devas* within your home see you performing your *sādhana* each day, they give you psychic protection. They hover around you and keep away the extraneous thought forms that come from the homes of your neighbors or close friends and relatives. They all mentally chant "Aum Namaḥ Śivāya," keeping the vibration of the home alive with high thoughts and *mantras* so that the atmosphere is scintillating, creating for you a proper environment to delve within yourself. The fact that the devonic world is involved is one more good reason why you must choose a specific time for *sādhana* and religiously keep to that time each day, for you not only have an appointment with yourself but with the *devas* as well. ¶By performing the *pañcha nitya karmas,* living the *yamas* and *niyamas* to the best of your ability and performing your daily *sādhana,* your religion becomes closer and closer to you in your heart. You will soon begin to find that God Śiva is within you as well as within the temple, because you become quiet enough to know this and experience that Lord Śiva's superconscious mind is identical to yours; there is no difference in Satchidānanda. From this state, you will experience the conscious mind as "the watcher" and experience its subconscious as the storehouse of intellectual and emotional memory patterns. In daily life you will begin to experience the creativity of the subsuperconscious mind, as the forces of the First World are motivated through love as you fulfill your chosen *dharma* in living with Śiva. ¶Thus our religion is an experiential religion, from its beginning stages to the most advanced. You have already encountered the magic of the temple, and you have had uplifting experiences within your home shrine. Now, as you perform your *sādhana,* you will enjoy spiritual experiences within yourself on the path of self-transformation. ¶It is up to you to put your religion into practice. Feel the power of the Gods in the *pūjā.* If you don't feel them, if you are just going through ritual and don't feel anything, you are not awake. Get the most out of every experience that the temple offers, the *guru* offers, the *devas* offer, that your life's experiences, which you were born to live through, offer. In doing so, slowly the *kuṇḍalinī* begins to loosen and imperceptibly rise into its *yoga.* That's what does the *yoga;* it's the *kuṇḍalinī* seeking its source, like the tree growing, always reaching up to the Sun. ¶It is up to you to make the teachings a part of your life by working to understand each new concept as you persist in your daily religious practices. As a result, you will be able to brave the forces of the external world without being disturbed by them and fulfill your *dharma* in whatever walk of life you have chosen. Because your daily *sādhana* has regulated your nerve system, the quality of your work in the world will improve, and your mood in performing it will be confident and serene. ¶When your *sādhana* takes hold, you may experience a profound calmness within yourself. This calmness that you experience as a result of your meditation is called Satchidānanda, the natural state of the mind. To arrive at that state, the instinctive energies have been lifted to the heart *chakra* and beyond, and the mind has become absolutely quiet. This is because you are not using your memory faculty. You are not using your reason faculty. You are not trying to move the forces of the world with your willpower faculty. You are simply resting within yourself. Therefore, if you are ever bothered by the external part of you, simply return to this inner, peaceful state as often as you can. You might call it your "home base." From here you can have a clear perception of how you should behave in the external world, a clear perception of your future and a clear perception of the path ahead. This is a superconscious state, meaning "beyond normal consciousness." So, simply deepen this inner state by being aware that you are aware.

Saturday
LESSON 90
Control of The Prāṇas

A great flow of *prāṇa* is beginning to occur among the families of our congregation worldwide because each one has decided to discipline himself or herself and the children to perform *sādhana*. That brings the *prāṇa* under control. If the *prāṇa* is not under the control of the individual, it is controlled by other individuals. The negative control of *prāṇa* is a control, and positive control of *prāṇa* is a control. That's why we say, "Seek good company," because if you can't control your *prāṇa*, other people who do control their *prāṇas* can help you. The group helps the individual and the individual helps the group. If you mix with bad company, then the *prāṇas* begin to get disturbed. Once that happens, your energies are like a team of horses out of control. It takes a lot of skill and strength on the part of the individual to get those *prāṇas* back under control. ¶The control of *prāṇa* is equally important on the inner planes. When you leave the physical body, you are in your astral body, your subtle body. It is not made of flesh and bones like your physical body—as the Buddhists say, "thirty-two kinds of dirt wrapped up in skin." The astral body is made of *prāṇa*. It floats. It can fly. It's guided by your mind, which is composed of more rarefied *prāṇa*, actinic energy. Wherever you want to go, you'll be there immediately. And, of course, you do this in your sleep, in your dreams and after death. Many of you have had astral experiences and can testify how quickly you can move here and there when your astral body is detached from the physical body. However, if you don't have control of your *prāṇa*, you don't have control of your astral body. Then where do you go when you drop off your physical body at death? You are magnetized to desires, uncontrollably magnetized to fulfilling unfulfilled desires. You are magnetized to groups of people who are fulfilling similar unfulfilled desires, and generally your consciousness goes down into lower *chakras*. Only in controlling your astral body do you have conscious control of your soul body, which is, of course, living within the astral body and resonating to the energy of the higher *chakras*. ¶My *satguru*, Siva Yogaswami, spoke of Śaivism as the *sādhana mārga*, "the path of striving," explaining that it is a religion not only to be studied but also to be lived. "See God everywhere. This is practice. First do it intellectually. Then you will know it." He taught that much knowledge comes through learning to interpret and understand the experiences of life. To avoid the *sādhana mārga* is to avoid understanding the challenges of life. We must not fail to realize that each challenge is brought to us by our own actions of the past. Yes, our actions in the past have generated our life's experiences today. All Hindus accept *karma* and reincarnation intellectually, but the concepts are not active in their lives until they accept the responsibilities of their own actions and the experiences that follow. In doing so, no blame can fall upon another. It is all our own doing. This is the *sādhana mārga*—the path to perfection. ¶The *sādhana mārga* leads us into the *yoga pāda* quite naturally. But people don't study *yoga*. They are not taught *yoga*. They are taught *sādhana*, and if they don't perform it themselves—and no one can do it for them—they will never have a grip strong enough over their instinctive mind and intellectual mind to come onto the *yoga mārga*, no matter how much they know about *yoga*. So, we don't learn *yoga*. We mature into it. We don't learn meditation. We awaken into it. You can teach meditation, you can teach *yoga*, but it's all just words unless the individual is mature and awake on the inside. ¶To be awake on the inside means waking up early in the morning. You woke up early this morning. That may have been difficult. But you got the body up, you got the emotions up, you got the mind up, and your instinctive mind did not want to do all that. Did it? No! Spiritual life is a twenty-four-hour-a-day vigil, as all my close devotees are realizing who have taken the *vrata* of 365 Nandinātha Sūtras. It means going to bed at night early so you can get up in the morning early. It means studying the teachings before you go to bed so that you can go into the inner planes in absolute control. It means in the morning reading from my trilogy, *Dancing with Śiva, Living with Śiva* and *Merging with Śiva,* to prepare yourself to face the day, to be a strong person and move the forces of the world.

Sunday
LESSON 91
Sādhana and Life's Stages

Devotees who are doing *sādhana* and who are in the *gṛihastha āśrama,* between age twenty-four and forty-eight, should move the forces of the world rightly, dynamically, intelligently, quickly and make something of their lives. Such devotees should not be stimulated by competition. In today's world most people have to be stimulated by competition to produce anything worthwhile, even if that means hurting other people. They have to be stimulated by conflict to produce anything worthy of producing in the world, and that hurts other people. They have to be stimulated by their home's breaking up, and that hurts other people. And they have to be stimulated by all kinds of other lower emotions to be able to get enough energy to move the forces of the world to do something, whether it be good or bad. Those who perform *sādhana* draw on the forces of the soul to move the forces of the world and make a difference. ¶It is during the latter stages of life that family devotees have the opportunity to intensify their *sādhana* and give back to society of their experience, their knowledge and their wisdom gained through the first two *āśramas.* The *vānaprastha āśrama,* age forty-eight to seventy-two, is a very important stage of life, because that is the time when you can inspire excellence in the *brahmacharya* students and in the families, to see that their life goes along as it should, according to the *Nandinātha Sūtras,* which have the entire ideal life pattern embedded within them. Later, the *sannyāsa āśrama,* beginning at seventy-two, is the time to enjoy and deepen whatever realizations you have had along the way. We are all human beings, and every one of us—including the *sapta ṛishis,* seven great sages who help guide the course of mankind from the inner planes—is duty-bound to help everyone else. That is the duty. It must be performed by everyone. If you want to help somebody else, perform regular *sādhana.* ¶Traditionally, a Hindu home should be a reflection of the monastery that the family is attached to, with a regular routine for the mother, the father, the sons, the daughters, so that everyone is fulfilling their rigorous duties and *sādhanas* to the very best of their ability. We had a seventeen-year-old youth here as a guest in our monastery from one of our families in

Malaysia that performs *sādhana.* That *sādhana* enabled him to come here to perform *sādhana.* If his parents had not been performing *sādhana* in their home regularly, he would not have been inclined to come here and perform a more strenuous *sādhana* with us. ¶I was asked recently what to do about all the things that you cannot avoid listening to and seeing on the TV and news and reading about—atrocities, crime, murders, poverty, unfairness—which may tend to disturb one's *sādhana.* To perform good *sādhana,* we have to have a good philosophical foundation, which is found in *Dancing with Siva, Living with Siva* and *Merging with Siva—The Master Course* trilogy. A good philosophical foundation allows us to understand why we have the highest and the lowest human expressions here on planet Earth. Philosophers and mystics have for centuries said, "Only on planet Earth in a physical body can you realize the Self, because only here, in this world, do you have all twenty-one *chakras* functioning." You need the lowest in order to realize the highest. Some people are born peaceful because of merits attained in past lives. They are born helpful, and they are the uplifters of mankind. Others are born angry, scheming, conniving, resentful, and they are the doubters, the detractors, of mankind. But all have an equal place here on planet Earth. All are going through a similar evolution up the spinal column to the top of the head, through the door of Brahman and finally out. ¶From the Western religionist's point of view, God is doing it all. He is punishing mankind. He is helping mankind. And many Hindus who were raised in Christian schools hold that perspective. But from the perspective of Sanātana Dharma, the oldest religion in the world, we do it all. By our *karmas* we are creating our future this very moment. So, as you proceed in your *sādhana,* disconnect from the lower and proceed into the higher. As a family person, it is your *dharma* to serve society, uplift mankind and help relieve human suffering within your sphere of influence. But do not try to fix, or even entertain the desire to fix, that which you cannot fix, which is the *karma,* the action and reaction, of individuals who are going through the lower phases of life and must experience what they are experiencing and which you read about and hear about daily in newspapers, on TV and on the Internet.

Dhyānī

ध्यानी

The Meditator

One should meditate on his own *guru,* his tradition and God Śaṅkara after bathing and assuming a suitable sitting posture in a sanctified place. He should purify the five elements of his body with deep concentration.

Chandrajñāna Āgama, Kriyāpāda, 8.52-53. CJ P. 80

Monday
LESSON 92
Turning Inward

Meditation is a long journey, a pilgrimage into the mind itself. Generally we become aware that there is such a thing as meditation after the material world has lost its attraction to us and previous desires no longer bind us to patterns of fear, greed, attachment and ramification. We then seek through philosophy and religion to answer the questions, "Who am I? Where did I come from? Where am I going?" We ask others. We read books. We ponder and wonder. We pray. We even doubt for a while that there is a Truth to be realized, or that we, with all our seeming imperfection, can realize it if it does exist. Oddly enough, this is the beginning of the meditator's journey on the path, for we must empty ourselves fully before the pure, superconscious energies can flow freely through us. Once this state of emptiness and genuine searching is reached, we soon recognize the futile attempt to find Truth on the outside. We vividly begin to know, from the depth of ourselves, a knowing we could not explain or justify. We simply know that Reality, or the Self God, resides within, and we must go within ourselves to realize it. Of itself, that knowing is not enough. Even great efforts to meditate and vast storehouses of spiritual knowledge are not enough. Many have tried to find the Truth this way. The Truth is deeper and is discovered by the resolute devotee who dedicates his life to the search, who lives a balanced life according to the *yamas* and *niyamas*, the Vedic spiritual laws, who willingly undergoes change, who finds and obeys a spiritual teacher, or *satguru*, and who learns precisely the disciplined art of meditation. This, then, outlines the destination of the meditator's journey and his means of travel. ¶One of the first steps is to convince the subconscious mind that meditation is good for us. We may want to meditate consciously, yet maintain fears or doubts about meditation. Somewhere along the way, a long series of events occurred and, upon reaction to them, awareness became externalized. We became geared to the materialistic concepts of the external world. As we begin to feel that urgency to get back within, the old patterns of thought and emotion, cause and effect, naturally repeat themselves. For a while, the contents of the subconscious may conflict with our concepts of what it is like to fully live spiritually. Our habits will be undisciplined, our willpower ineffective. Quite often the subconscious seems almost like

---

Śiva's blessings pour from His coiled hair upon two men. One is an advaitin, *meditating on a mountain. The other is a* siddhāntin, *finding Divine Grace through devotional surrender in a modern temple. Both the* bhakta *and the* yogī *receive Śiva's Love in full measure.*

another person, because it is always doing something unanticipated. ¶In these early stages, we must mold the areas that are different into a new lifestyle so that there will be nothing in the subconscious that opposes what is in the conscious or superconscious mind. Only when all three of these areas of consciousness act in harmony can meditation be truly attained and sustained. For us to be afraid of the subconscious is unwise, for it then holds a dominant position in our life. The subconscious is nothing more than the accumulation of vibratory rates of experience encountered by awareness when it was externalized, a storehouse containing the past.

Tuesday
LESSON 93
Remolding the Subconscious

Externalization of awareness results in one layer upon another layer of misunderstanding void of an inner point of reference. We have to reprogram the subconscious to change it, and not worry over the old impressions. We have to make this change in a very dynamic way by always remaining positive. You have heard many people say, "It can't be done," and then go right ahead and prove it by failing. ¶Never use the word *can't,* as it becomes very restrictive to the subconscious. If often used, it becomes almost an incantation. This is not good. As soon as we say, "I can't," all positive doors subconsciously close for us. The flow of pure life force is diminished, the subconscious is confused and we know we are going to fail, so we don't even try. The solution to subconscious confusion is to set a goal for ourselves in the external world and to have a positive plan incorporating meditation daily as a lifestyle within that goal. Through this positive initiative and daily effort in meditation, awareness is centered within. We learn how to disentangle and unexternalize awareness. ¶As soon as strong initiative is taken to change our nature toward refinement, a new inner process begins to take place. The forces of positive accomplishment from each of our past lives begin to manifest in this one. The high points of a past life, when something great has happened, become strung together. These merits or good deeds are vibrations in the ether substance of our memory patterns, because each one of us, right now, is a sum total of all previous experience. All of the distractions of the external area of the mind begin to fade, and positive meditation becomes easily attainable. It is not difficult to move our individual awareness quickly within when distractions occur. ¶This new pattern of setting goals and meeting them strengthens the will. One such goal is to perform *sādhana* every day without fail during a morning vigil period of worship, *japa,* scriptural study and meditation. Daily meditation has to become part of our lifestyle, not just a new something we do or study about. It must become a definite part of us. We have to live to meditate. This is the only way to reach the eventual goal on the path—the realization of the all-pervasive Śivam. Deep meditation takes the power of our spiritual will, which is cultivated through doing everything we do to perfection, through meeting the challenges of our goals, and through its constant expression as we seek to do more than we think we can each day. So, set your spiritual goals according to where you are on the path. Set goals for deeper, more superconscious meditation, for a change of your personality or outer nature, for better service to your fellow man, and for a totally religious lifestyle. ¶Goals are generally not used in spiritual life, because the inner mechanism of goal setting is not clearly understood. Dynamic, successful people who go into business for themselves have to have a positive, aggressive plan and keep their lives in a good routine to achieve success. The most prominent among them begin and end each day at a certain time in order to sustain the pressure of the business world. We can and should approach the practice of meditation in a similar way. Like the businessman, we want to succeed in our quest, the only difference being the choice of an inner goal as opposed to the choice of an outer goal, the fulfillment of which entangles us and further externalizes awareness.

Wednesday
LESSON 94
Setting Inner Goals

If we plan our meditation goals unrealistically, we create unnecessary problems. For example, it might be unrealistic to say, "I am going to realize the all-pervasive Sivam in two months." The seeker setting this goal for himself may be far too externalized to face the resultant reaction in the short period of two months. Ten years, however, may be a more realistic goal for him, providing time is spent regularly every day in meditation as he directs awareness in and in and in, day after day after day, until all of the forces of the nerve currents of the inner body begin to respond. ¶As they respond, something new happens. He gains firm confidence in his own abilities to fulfill positive goals by using his willpower. As each inner goal is established then met, the pattern of his life is changed and refined. The conscious mind, the subconscious mind and the superconscious areas of the mind come together, and a spiritual dynamic occurs. All aspects of his nature work together to strengthen and deepen his meditations. Doubts and fears loosen their hold on him, allowing awareness to penetrate to the core of mind substance. The mind becomes quiet enough to turn back upon itself. ¶In the early stages of meditation, it's very difficult to sit without moving, because that has not been part of our lifestyle. The subconscious mind has never been programmed to contentedly sit quietly. We didn't see our families doing that. Perhaps we haven't seen anybody doing that. No example has been set. Therefore, we have to be patient with ourselves and not sit for too long in the beginning. Start by sitting for ten minutes without moving. In a few weeks extend it to twenty minutes, then a half hour. Thus we avoid being fanatical and allow the subconscious to make its necessary adjustments. ¶These adjustments are physical as well as emotional and intellectual. The nerve currents rearrange themselves so that prolonged stillness and absence of external activity is comfortable. Similarly, the philosophy of the path of enlightenment fully penetrates every layer of the subconscious, adjusting previous erroneous concepts of ourselves and enabling us to consciously intuit various philosophical areas and know them to be right and true from our personal experience of superconsciousness. This, then, may take a few years. ¶If we plant a tree, we have to wait for it to grow and mature before we enjoy its shade. So it is in meditation. We make our plans for beginning the practices of meditation, then give ourselves enough time, several years, to fully adjust and remold the subconscious mind. Living as we do in the externalized culture of the West, we are conditioned to be in a hurry to get everything. When we try to internalize awareness too quickly through various intense and sometimes fanatical ways, we reap the reaction. Meditation goes fine for a brief span, but then externalizes again according to the programming of our family and culture. ¶To permanently alter these patterns, we have to work gently to develop a new lifestyle for the totality of our being—physically, emotionally, intellectually and spiritually. This we do a little at a time. Wisdom tells us that it cannot be done all at once. We have to be patient with ourselves. If we are impatient on the path, failure is in view. We are going to fail, because instant spiritual unfoldment is a fairy tale concept. It is far better that we recognize that there will be difficult challenges as the subconscious looms up, with all of its conflicts and confusions, heavy and strong. When it does, we must face them calmly, through spiritual journaling, *vāsanā daha tantra.* If our eventual goal is clearly in mind and we have a positive step-by-step plan on how to reach that goal, then we won't get excited when something goes wrong, because we view our mental and emotional storms in their proper and temporary perspective.

Thursday
LESSON 95
Dealing With Doubt

Not only does the subconscious create barriers in our own minds, it also draws to us the doubts and worries of other people for us to face and resolve. There is such a vast warehouse of negative conditioning against meditation that it is almost useless to begin if we believe any of it at all. We have all heard a few of the fears: "Something terrible must have happened to you as a child if you want to go into that." "You don't love me anymore. That's why you meditate—you're withdrawing." "You're just afraid of society and responsibility. It's an escape from the real world that you can't cope with." "You're going to be poor if you meditate. Everyone who meditates is broke, you know." And so it goes, on and on. ¶We do have to answer these objections for the subconscious and thus settle all doubts within ourselves. Of course, the results of meditation will themselves convince the subconscious of the benefit of inner *sādhana* as we bring forth perceptive insights, renewed energy, a happy and balanced life and spiritual attainment. Negative conditioning breaks down as we prove to ourselves according to our own experience that it was wrong. Such conditioning is inhibiting to some and has to be corrected. To counteract it, we can ask ourselves, "Why? What is it all about? How did I attract these problems? Do I still have such doubts in my subconscious, consciously unknown?" We can further ask, "Who has done the conditioning? What was their life like? Were they happy people?" Finally, from our own positive efforts to cognize, we actually remold the subconscious, erase false concepts and become free. ¶The mind in its apparently endless confusion and desires leads us by novelty from one thing to the next. The reaction to this causes the miseries of the world, and miseries of the world happen inside of people. But occasionally we have to call a halt to the whole thing and get into ourselves. That's the process of meditation. It's an art. It's a faculty we have within ourselves which, when developed, gives a balance and a sense to life. And everyone, whether they know it or not, is searching, trying to find out what life is all about. ¶So many people tell me, "Oh, I would like to study *yoga*, but I just don't have the time," "I can't get quiet enough," or "The kids make too much noise," or some excuse like that. They don't realize that you don't become quiet automatically. Becoming quiet is a systematic process. You become quiet systematically. It might take you two weeks of practice before you can sit down and feel that you've made any progress at all, or even feel like sitting down and trying to become quiet. But it's one of those things you eventually have to do. You get up and cook breakfast because you have to eat. You are hungry. And when you become hungry enough to get quiet within yourself, you will do so automatically. You will want to. And then what happens? You will sit down, and your mind will race. Say, "Mind, stop!" and see how fast you can make your mind stop and become quiet. Say, "Emotions, you are mind-controlled," and see how quiet you become.

Friday
LESSON 96
The Right Conditions

We now come to the practical aspects of meditation. In the beginning, it is best to find a suitable room that is dedicated solely to meditation. If you were a carpenter, you would get a shop for that purpose. You have a room for eating, a room for sleeping. Now you need a separate room just for the purpose of meditation. When you find it, wash the walls and ceiling, wash the windows. Prepare a small altar if you like, bringing together the elements of earth, air, fire and water. Establish a time for your meditations and meet those times strictly. There will be days when you just don't feel like meditating. Good. Those are often the best days, the times when we make strong inner strides. The finest times to meditate are six in the morning, twelve noon, six in the evening, and twelve midnight. All four of these times could be used, or just choose one. The period of meditation should be from ten minutes to one-half hour to begin with. ¶By sitting up straight, with the spine erect, we transmute the energies of the physical body. Posture is important, especially as meditation deepens and lengthens. With the spine erect and the head balanced at the top of the spine, the life force is quickened and intensified as energies flood freely through the nerve system. In a position such as this, we cannot become worried, fretful, depressed or sleepy during our meditation. But if we slump the shoulders forward, we short-circuit the life energies. In a position such as this, it is easy to become depressed, to have mental arguments with oneself or another, or to experience unhappiness. So, learn to sit dynamically, relaxed and yet poised. The full-lotus position, with the right foot resting on the left thigh and the left foot above, resting on the right thigh, is the most stable posture to assume, hands resting in the lap, right hand on top, with both thumbs touching. ¶The first observation you may have when thus seated for meditation is that thoughts are racing through the mind substance. You may become aware of many, many thoughts. Also the breath may be irregular. Therefore, the next step is to transmute the energies from the intellectual area of the mind through proper breathing, in just the same way that proper attitude, preparation and posture transmuted the physical-instinctive energies. Through regulation of the breath, thoughts are stilled and awareness moves into an area of the mind which does not think, but conceives and intuits. ¶There are vast and powerful systems of breathing that can stimulate the mind, sometimes to excess. Deep meditation requires only that the breath be systematically slowed or lengthened. This happens naturally as we go within, but can be encouraged by a method of breathing called *kalībasa* in Shūm, my language of meditation. During *kalībasa,* the breath is counted, nine counts as we inhale, hold one count, nine counts as we exhale, hold one count. The length of the beats, or the rhythm of the breath, will slow as the meditation is sustained, until we are counting to the beat of the heart, *hṛidaya spaṇḍa prāṇāyāma.* This exercise allows awareness to flow into an area of the mind that is intensely alive, peaceful, blissful and conceives the totality of a concept rather than thinking out the various parts.

Saturday
LESSON 97
Control Of Breath

Control of the breath, to be learned properly, might take months or even years. That's all right. If you were learning to play a musical instrument, it would take months or even years to perfect the basic principles of making chords and putting chords together into a melody. There is no hurry. Hurry is the age we want to bypass when we meditate. The control of the breath is exactly the same as the control of awareness, so it is good to be patient in the early stages and perfect each element of practice. ¶As we learn to breathe rhythmically and from the diaphragm, we also release tensions in the solar plexus. We learn to be spontaneous and free on the inside, and life force runs through us in an uninhibited way. We achieve and learn to maintain contentment, *santosha.* All of these things come through the simple techniques we practice while in meditation. But the practice of meditation is not the end. It is the total being of man that is the end to be sought for—the well-rounded, content, spontaneous being that is totally free. ¶After you have quieted the body, and the breath is flowing regularly, close your eyes. Close your ears and shut off the external sense perceptions. As long as you are aware of sights and sounds on the outside, you are not concentrated. It is a fallacy to think you have to find a totally silent place before you can go within. When your senses are stilled, you don't hear any sounds. You're in a state of silence. You don't hear a car that passes, you don't hear a bird that sings, because your awareness has shifted to different perceptions. It helps, but it's not necessary, to have a totally silent place. This is not always possible, so it is best not to depend on outer silence. We must discover silence within ourselves. When you are reading a book that is extremely interesting, you are not hearing noises around you. You should be at least that interested in your meditations. ¶Having thus quieted the outer forces, we are prepared to meditate. Just sitting is not enough. To meditate for even ten or fifteen minutes takes as much energy as one would use in running around a city block three times. A powerful meditation fills and thrills us with an abundance of energy to be used creatively in the external world during the activities of daily life. Great effort is required to make inner strides. We must strive very, very hard and meet each inner challenge.

Sunday
LESSON 98
Four Steps To Meditation

When we go into meditation, what do we meditate upon? What do we think about during meditation? Usually the sincere devotee will have a *guru*, or spiritual guide, and follow his instructions. He may have a *mantra*, or mystic sound, which he concentrates upon, or a particular technique or attitude he is perfecting. If he has no *guru* or specific instructions, then here is a *rāja yoga* exercise that can enhance inner life, making it tangibly real and opening inner doors of the mind. Use it to begin each meditation for the rest of your life. Simply sit, quiet the mind, and feel the warmth of the body. Feel the natural warmth in the feet, in the legs, in the head, in the neck, in the hands and face. Simply sit and be aware of that warmth. Feel the glow of the body. This is very easy, because the physical body is what many of us are most aware of. Take five, ten or fifteen minutes to do this. There is no hurry. Once you can feel this warmth that is created by the life force as it flows in and through the body's cells, once you can feel this all over the body at the same time, go within to the next step. ¶The second step is to feel the nerve currents of the body. There are thousands of miles of nerve currents in each of us. Don't try to feel them all at once. Start with the little ones, with the feeling of the hands, thumbs touching, resting on your lap. Now feel the life force going through these nerves, energizing the body. Try to sense the even more subtle nerves that extend out and around the body about three or four feet. This may take a long time. When you have located some of these nerves, feel the energy within them. Tune into the currents of life force as they flow through these nerves. This is a subtle feeling, and most likely awareness will wander into some other area of the mind. When this happens, gently bring it back to your point of concentration, to feeling the nerves within the body and the energy within the nerves. ¶The third step takes us deeper inside, as we become dynamically aware in the spine. Feel the power within the spine, the powerhouse of energy that feeds out to the external nerves and muscles. Visualize the spine in your mind's eye. See it as a hollow tube or channel through which life energies flow. Feel it with your inner feelings. It's there, subtle and silent, yet totally intense. It is a simple feeling. We can all feel it easily. As you feel this hollow spine filled with energy, realize that you are more that energy than you are the physical body through which it flows, more that pure energy than the emotions, than the thought force. Identify yourself with this energy and begin to live your true spiritual heritage on this Earth. As you dive deeper into that energy, you will find that this great power, your sense of awareness and your willpower are all one and the same thing. ¶The fourth step comes as we plunge awareness into the essence, the center of this energy in the head and spine. This requires great discipline and exacting control to bring awareness to the point of being aware of itself. This state of being totally aware that we are aware is called *kaīf.* It is pure awareness, not aware of any object, feeling or thought. Go into the physical forces that flood, day and night, through the spine and body. Then go into the energy of that, deeper into the vast inner space of that, into the essence of that, into the that of that, and into the that of that. As you sit in this state, new energies will flood the body, flowing out through the nerve system, out into the exterior world. The nature becomes very refined in meditating in this way. Once you are thus centered within yourself, you are ready to pursue a meditation, a *mantra* or a deep philosophical question.

Dhyāna Vighnāḥ

ध्यानविघ्नाः

Obstacles to Meditation

Born along and defiled by the stream of qualities, unsteady, wavering, bewildered, full of desire, distracted, one goes on into the state of self-conceit. In thinking, 'This is I' and 'That is mine' one binds himself with himself, as does a bird with a snare.

Kṛishṇa Yajur Veda, Maitrī Upanishad, 3.2. UPH, P. 418

MARVEL

Monday
LESSON 99
Taming Distraction

Throughout your inner investigations in meditation, cling to the philosophical principle that the mind doesn't move. Thoughts are stationary within the mind, and only awareness moves. It flows from one thought to another, as the free citizen of the world travels through each country, each city, not attaching himself anywhere. When you are able, through practice, to sit for twenty minutes without moving even one finger, your superconscious mind can begin to express itself. It can even reprogram your subconscious and change past patterns of existence. That is one of the wonderful things about inner life. That's why it's inner life—it happens from the inside. ¶If you just sit and breathe, the inner nerve system of the body of your psyche, your soul, begins to work on the subconscious, to mold it like clay. Awareness is loosened from limited concepts and made free to move vibrantly and buoyantly into the inner depths where peace and bliss remain undisturbed for centuries. However, if you move even a finger, you externalize the entire nervous system. Like shifting gears from high to low, you change the intensity of awareness, and the outer nerve system then is active. Superconscious programming ceases, awareness returns to the body and the senses, and the external mind takes over. By sitting still again at this point, it is just a matter of a few minutes for the forces to quiet and awareness to soar in and in once again. Sitting quietly in this state, you will feel when the superconscious nerve system begins to work in the physical body. You may feel an entirely different flow through your muscles, your bones and your cells. Let it happen. ¶As you sit to meditate, awareness may wander into past memories or future happenings. It may be distracted by the senses, by a sound or by a feeling of discomfort in the body. This is natural in the early stages. Gently bring awareness back to your point of concentration. Don't criticize awareness for wandering, for that is yet another distraction. Distractions will disappear if you become intensely interested and involved in your meditation. In such a state you won't even feel the physical body. You have gone to a movie, read a book or sat working on a project on your computer that was so engrossing you only later discovered your foot had fallen asleep for a half hour because it was in an awkward position. Similarly, once we are totally conscious on the inside, we will never

---

Seated by a river in the yogic pose, a seeker tries to meditate. As he quiets his mind, obstacles arise from within. He thinks of this morning's patient. He feels hungry. He recalls a moment of anger and dwells on money worries and recalls past bouts with alcohol.

be distracted by the physical body or the outside. ¶If distractions keep coming up in meditation over a long period of time, then perhaps you are not ready to meditate. There has to be a point where distractions stop. Until then you are hooked very strongly into the instinctive or intellectual area of the mind, and the whole idea of meditation won't inspire you very much. Therefore, you need something to spur you on inwardly. In Hinduism when this occurs, the grace of the *satguru* is sought. By going to your *guru* openly, you receive *darśana,* a little extra power that moves awareness permanently out of the areas of distraction. You are then able to sit in inner areas for long periods of time. Distractions become fewer and fewer, for he has wrenched you out of the instinctive and intellectual areas and changed the energy flow within your body. ¶After the meditation is over, work to refine every attribute of your nature. Learn to work and work joyfully, for all work is good. Learn to be happy by seeking happiness, not from others but from the depths of the soul itself. In your daily life, observe the play of the forces as they manifest between people and people, and people and their things. Don't avoid the forces of the world, for the meditator lives fearlessly, shying away from nothing. The "out there" and the within are his playground, his kingdom. He becomes vibrant and confident in himself. He learns to lean on his own spine and not on any other person, teacher, book, organization or system. Answers begin to become real and vibrant, hooked onto the end of every question. His body radiates new grace and strength. His mind, disciplined and uncluttered, becomes one-pointedly agile. His relationships take on new, profound meanings. His emotions are stabilized and reflect his newfound tranquillity. These and many more are the dynamic rewards of the sincere aspirant who searches within through meditation.

Tuesday
LESSON 100
Sleep and Dreaming

Get into the habit of meditating before sleep each night. If you catch yourself dropping off to sleep while sitting for meditation, know that your meditation is over. The best thing to do is to deliberately go to sleep, because the spiritual power is gone and has to be invoked or opened up again. After getting ready for bed, sit in the lotus position and have a dynamic meditation for as long as you can. When you feel drowsy, you may deliberately put your body to sleep in this way. Mentally say to yourself, "*Praṇa* in the left leg, flow, go to sleep. *Prāṇa* in the right leg, flow, go to sleep. *Prāṇa* in the left arm, flow, go to sleep. *Prāṇa* in the right arm, flow, go to sleep. Torso *prāṇa*, flow, go to sleep. Head filled with inner light, go to sleep." The first thing you know, it's morning. ¶The whole dream and sleep world is very interesting. Often we go into inner planes of consciousness at night. How do you know if you have been in meditation all through the night, studying at the inner-plane school in higher states of mind? You will wake up all of a sudden with no interim period of sleepiness. You wake up invigorated. There you are, as if you came out of nowhere back into external consciousness. Otherwise, you wake up through the subconscious dream world. You feel a little off-key, and you know that you have been in the dream or astral world or the realms of intellectual aggressiveness much of the night. Striving *yoga* students do go into inner-plane meditation schools for short periods of time during their sleeping hours. This occurs when the mind is a well-trained mind, a keen mind, a crystal-clear mind. ¶Perhaps by this time you have seen the clear white light, or less intense inner light, and you have seen how crystal clear and sharp it is. Each thought, each feeling, each action has to be crystal clear and sharp to maintain and bring through a balance of your consciousness to the external world. When this happens, you have control over these states of consciousness, so much so that you are your own catalyst, and you can slide into higher states and out to external states of consciousness without being disturbed by one or the other. ¶When we act and react in daily affairs, we dream at night. We are living in the external or the aggressive magnetic force, called *piṅgalā*. Thus, we dream in pictures. Should a *yogī* live in the passive force, the magnetic indrawn force, called *iḍā*, he feels and emotes on the astral plane. He would have a fretful, eventful night, an emotional night. He would not dream in pictures as much as he would in feeling. When one is living in the pure spiritual force, *sushumṇā*, the primary life force, he flows from sleep into meditation. The meditator should strive to put his body to sleep consciously and deliberately, after balancing the external and internal magnetic forces. So, whether he is lying down in his body or sitting in the lotus posture, he is in deep meditation, going to schools of learning and schools of spiritual unfoldment within his own mind. In the morning, many of my students remember inner-plane class activities which occurred during the night, not as a dream but as their own experience. So, you can meditate while you sleep, but don't sleep while you are meditating!

Wednesday
LESSON 101
Clearing the Subconscious

After you have practiced meditation for some time, your inner vision will become keen and clear. For a while there may be the feeling of arrival, that you have at last conquered life's cycles, that you are pure now and free at last. But soon, layer by layer, your past will begin to unfold itself to you as your subconscious mind shows you in vivid, pictorial form all the vibratory rates you have put into it in this life. Like a tape recorder, it begins to play back the patterns and vibrations of previous cause and effect. ¶Since some of these memories and actions may not have been complimentary, you may try to avoid looking at them. The more you avoid facing them, the more apparent they will become. You might think that everyone is seeing them, but they are not. This natural phase of spiritual unfoldment can be a pitfall, for these associations and attachments of the past seem temporarily attractive as they pass before the mind's eye. Old desires, old friends, old and comfortable habits you thought were gone now come up to tempt awareness, to pull it back into a seemingly desirable past. This event should not be taken too seriously. It is natural and necessary, but you must avoid a fear of the process, which, in order to stop the unpleasant feedback, often brings people to stop their efforts at meditation. This is not the time to stop meditating. Nor is it the time to avoid the past. It is the time to fully review each year of your life that led you to where you are now. ¶As you remain inwardly poised, watching the images of life but remaining detached, they gradually fade away, leaving awareness free to dive ever deeper into superconscious realms. This sometimes intense experience brings you into renewed desire to live the kind of life that does not produce distorted images. You become religious and consciously shape up your lifestyle according to the *yamas* and *niyamas*, so that the reverberation of each action is positive in the subconscious. You have seen the uncomplimentary results of living according to the moods and emotions of the instinctive mind and the senses, and that experience has taught a great lesson. In reviewing life according to this new guideline, you may change your profession, your address, your diet and values. You will undoubtedly find new friends, for it is essential to associate with people that are of good character. Choose your friends carefully, but don't get too closely attached. People clinging to people is one of the biggest deterrents to the life of meditation. ¶Generally as soon as someone gets on the path and starts meditating, he wants to tell everyone else how to do it even before he has learned himself. This socializing never produces inner results. Keep your meditation abilities and activities to yourself. Don't talk about inner things with anyone but your *guru*. When it comes others' time to turn within, they will do so naturally, just as you did. That is the law.

Thursday
LESSON 102
Conflicts with Other People

Good interpersonal relationships help the meditator a great deal, and meditation helps keep those relations harmonious. When we get along nicely with others, meditation becomes easy. If we have problems with other people, if we argue or disagree mentally and verbally, we must work exceedingly diligently in order to regain the subtlety of meditation. Poor interpersonal relationships are one of the biggest barriers, for they antagonize awareness, causing it to flow through the instinctive and intellectual forces. This puts stress and strain on the nerve system and closes inner doors to superconsciousness. ¶If we cannot get along with our fellow man whom we watch closely, observing the expressions on his face and the inflections of his voice, how will we ever get along with the forces of the subconscious, which we cannot see, or the refined superconscious areas of the inner mind, when we face them in meditation? Obviously, we must conquer and harmonize all our relationships—not by working to change the other person, but by working with that other person within ourself, for we are only seeing in him what is in us. He becomes a mirror. We cannot allow the unraveling of the relationship by attempted outer manipulation, discussion or analysis to become a barrier to deeper meditation. Instead, we must internalize everything that needs change, work within ourselves and leave other people out of it. This helps to smooth interpersonal relationships, and as these relationships improve, so does our ability to meditate. ¶Our nerve system is just like a harp. It can be played by other people. They can cause many tones to be heard in our nerve system. All styles of music can be played on a harp, but no matter what kind of music is played, the harp remains the same. People can do all sorts of things to our nervous system, and make patterns of tone and color appear. This does not hurt the nervous system. It, like the harp, remains the same. The same nervous system can be played by our superconscious or by our passions. We can experience beautiful knowledge from within, which is the outgrowth of good meditation abilities, or experience a mental argument with another person. All tones are played at different times through the same nervous system. We want our nervous system to be played from the inside out through the beautiful rhythm of superconsciousness. This is bliss. We do not want to allow other people to affect our nerve system in a negative way, only in a positive way. That is why it is imperative for those on the path to be in good company.

Friday
LESSON 103
The Journey Within

Beginning to meditate can be likened to starting a long journey. The destination and the means of travel must be known before setting out. Meditation is an art, a definite art, and well worth working for to become accomplished. Meditation is not easy, and yet it is not difficult. It only takes persistence, working day after day to learn to control and train the outer as well as the subtle, inner forces. We must realize that meditation is the disciplined art of tuning into the deepest and most subtle spiritual energies. It's not a fad. It's not a novelty. It's not something you do because your next-door neighbor does. It is sacred, the most sacred thing you can do on this planet, and it must be approached with great depth and sincerity. At these moments, we are seeking God, Truth, and actually controlling the forces of life and consciousness as we fulfill the very evolutionary purpose of life—the realization of the Self God. Unless we approach meditation in humility and wonder, we will not reach our goal in this life. ¶Now we are in a new age. Everything is changing. Everything is different. We must believe that we can change by using our powers of meditation, for we are here, on the surface of this Earth, to value and fulfill our existence. Value yourself and your fellow man. Say to yourself again and again, "I am the most wonderful person in the whole world!" Then ask yourself, "Why? Because of my unruly subconscious? Not necessarily. Because of what I know intellectually? Not so. I am the most wonderful person in the world because of the great spiritual force that flows through my spine, head and body, and the energy within that, and the That within that." ¶Know full well that you can realize the very essence of this energy in this life. Feel the spine and the power within it that gives independence, enthusiasm and control. Then say to yourself, over and over, "I am a wonderful person," until you can fully and unreservedly believe it. Lean on your own spine. Depending on the greatness within is the keynote of this new age. Get your willpower going. If you find an unruly part of your nature, reprogram it, little by little, using the *yamas* and *niyamas* as your guideline. Live a dynamic, God-like life every day. Dance with Śiva, live with Śiva and merge with Śiva. Get into this area of the mind called meditation. Make it a fundamental part of your life, and all forms of creativity, success and greatness will find expression in your life. Everyone is on this planet for one purpose. That purpose will be known to you through your powers of meditation, through seeing and then finally realizing your Self at the very core of the universe itself.

Saturday
LESSON 104
Inspiration Unbridled

I would like to tell you about one of my students and his experience with the discovery of the superconscious state of the mind. When I first met him, this young man told me that he wanted to be a composer, to write music. He wanted to compose more than anything else in the world. He had just graduated from a university with a degree in music, and he had learned all the accepted, intellectual rules for the composition of music. But he wasn't entirely satisfied with being told how to compose according to certain mechanical laws. He wanted his music to flow through him without a thought. One day I said to him, "Sit over here at the piano and get in touch with your superconscious through diaphragmatic breathing. Now, find a chord with your right hand. Write it down. You are a composer aren't you? You are a composer now, not fifty years from now. The superconscious mind that you are contacting works in the eternity of the moment, not tomorrow. Subconscious is yesterday, superconscious is immediate, now." So he wrote down the chord that his fingers found. "Now write another chord," I said, "and then another and then another." ¶We finished a page of music with the right-hand staff, and I asked him, "What about the left hand? You don't have a complete piece of music with only the top bars filled in. "Well," he said, "I would have to work out the left hand according to what I have already written with the right hand." "No you don't," I replied, "Let the superconscious work it out for you. Make your first chord with your left hand now, without referring to what your right hand has done." He exclaimed that the sound of the two hands together might be terrible, but I insisted that he continue writing the chords with the left hand until the entire page was finished for both hands. When I asked him to play what he had written, he laughed and put his hands over his ears but obliged, "All right, if you insist...." "I do," I said. He played what he had written. It was a difficult piece of music, but there was no discord whatsoever. I congratulated him, "Now you are a composer. You created that piece superconsciously, without consciously knowing how you put the tones together. But you had sufficient faith in yourself to do it. In the same way, you must always depend upon yourself in the eternity of the moment to be able to accomplish whatever you set out to do." ¶The next day, he was right on time for his appointment, and he wanted me to help him compose from his superconscious again. "No," I said, "I am not going to be a composing machine for you; you will have to find your inspiration from within. It is time you put your *yoga* laws into practice now and attain concentration and meditation." He tried and he tried, but somehow his subconscious kept getting in the way. It told him he wasn't a composer anymore. Then I realized that his present conditions were a little too easy, and he was finding too much security in the conscious mind. Since his next step was to stabilize himself as a composer and find the ability at will to create inspirationally, I sent him on a very difficult mission: to resolve the negative *karmas* in his subconscious that were blocking his superconsciousness. As his major tool, I gave him the *mahā vāsanā daha tantra.* I told him that he could not come back until he fulfilled all the conditions of the mission and began to compose again as he wished. He was reluctant, because he would have to leave all of his current friends for a time. But being a sincere and determined student, he went out and successfully fulfilled his mission. In the process, he had to suffer through all of the things in his subconscious mind that had been bothering him since he was a small boy. In doing so, he lifted many of the blocks that had been a part of his subconscious for years, until one day his higher faculties completely opened to him, and music poured through him almost as fast as he could write it down.

Sunday
LESSON 105
Exercising Concentration

There are many faculties of the superconscious mind just waiting to be tapped by you. Only by tapping into and opening your superconscious, creative powers will you ever come to know and realize your real Self. It is not difficult, but in order to open the higher or inner consciousness, you have to gain a perfect control of the thinking faculties of your mind. ¶Concentration has to be practiced and perfected before meditation can begin. If you find that you are sitting and trying not to fall asleep for a half hour, you have only accomplished sitting and trying not to go to asleep for half an hour—and perhaps refraining from scratching your nose when it begins to itch. But that cannot be called meditation. Meditation is a transforming state of mind, really. A person once said to me, "Well, I concentrate my mind by reading a book, and when I'm reading, I don't hear a thing." This is not concentration, but attention, the first step to concentration. Concentration is thinking about one definite thing for a given length of time until you begin to understand what you are thinking about. What should we concentrate upon? Start with any solid object. Take your watch, for instance. Think about your watch. Think about the crystal. Think about the hands. Let your mind direct itself toward the mechanism of your watch, and then observe how your mind, after a few moments, begins to wander and play tricks on you. You may start thinking about alarm clocks or a noise in the street. ¶Each time your concentration period is broken by a distraction, you must start all over again. Breathe deeply and coordinate all the energies of your body so that you are not distracted by an itch or a noise. Direct your awareness once again to your watch. Before you know it, you will be thinking about a movie you saw four weeks ago and living through all the fantasies of it again without realizing that ten minutes of your time has gone by. Be careful and gentle with your awareness, however. Bring it back to the object of your concentration in a firm, relaxed manner and say to yourself, "I am the master of my thought." Eventually, your awareness will begin to do just what you want it to. ¶Once you are able to direct your awareness, without wavering, upon one object, you will begin to understand what you are concentrating upon, and you will find that this state of understanding is the beginning of your meditation. You are more alive in this state than you were in the noisy condition of your mind before you began to concentrate, and you come forth from your meditation a little wiser than you were before you went in. ¶The next state of consciousness, which is attained when meditation has been perfected, is contemplation. In the contemplative state of awareness you will feel the essence of all life pouring and radiating through your body and through the object you have been meditating upon. When contemplation is sustained, the final step is *samādhi,* and that is finding or becoming your true Self, which is beyond all conditions of your mind, all phases of consciousness. Only after you have attained *samādhi* can you answer the question "Who am I?" from your own experience. Only then will you know that you are all-pervasive, and finally, in the deepest *samādhi,* that you are causeless, timeless, spaceless and that you have been able to realize this through a balance of your awakened inner and outer consciousness, a bringing together of the forces of your mind in *yoga,* or union.

Saṅkalpa Śakti Vardhanam

संकल्पशक्तिवर्धनम्

Harnessing Willpower

O All-Knowing God, that powerful strength with which sacrifice endows you, the strength of the sun, the strength of the elephant, King among men—may the two Spirits, garlanded with lotus, vouchsafe that to me! Behold the elephant, best of all creatures to mount and to ride! I anoint myself with his share of strength, with his elephant splendor!

Atharva Veda 3.22.4; 6. VE, P. 344

Monday
LESSON 106
Awareness, Will And Life Force

The primal life force ever resident within the body, emotions and mind of man is, when used or allowed to function, what I term willpower. Now we can see that the ever-present persistence of life force gives an overabundance of willpower and with it the ability to direct it from deep within. This ability to direct the willpower is the *jñāna*, the wisdom we seek. We have but two choices: to gain *jñāna* through learning the tried-and-tested, set patterns for living and conducting ourself or, through assuming a relaxed approach of ignorance, be guided by the "good" and "bad" and mixed emotional forces of the wills of others. Therefore, the devotee seeks to gain the conscious control of his own willpower, to awaken knowledge of the primal force through the direct experience of it, and to claim conscious control of his own individual awareness. ¶Thus we can begin to see that our individual awareness, willpower and the primal life force deep within body, emotion and mind are, in fact, one and the same—that willpower, individual awareness and life force, their habits and usages, are but various aspects. ¶You will notice that, through our study together, these three aspects are referred to time and time again, individually as well as collectively. However, in the study of *yoga* it is important to keep in mind the totality of their sameness in order to fully identify your personal and continued experience of yourself as a being with unlimited will, constantly and fully aware of the primal life force flowing through body and emotions, as you, awareness, travel through the mind. This is the goal of the *jñānī*, the one who has attained to wisdom, to the acquisition of divine knowledge and the personal experience of what he has learned. ¶A child in his early years becoming acquainted with living with his family on this planet will show tendencies toward a quiet, peaceful will or a provocative willfulness. The wise parent teaches the culture and etiquette of the household and the community at large, ever endeavoring to bring forth the inner knowledge within the child as to the wise use of his willpower, guiding him carefully away from impulsive, willful behavior so that, little by little, he becomes responsible for the action he causes, as well as its reactions. The unwise parent with no particular cultural heritage, completely vulnerable to his own instinctive impulses, overlooks this area of childhood training. Therefore, impulsive

Enlightenment takes enormous willpower. A yogī *has moved into a forest among the animals. Living simply, intent on realizing Paraśiva, Absolute Reality, he ardently performs his inner disciplines, balancing the* iḍā *and* piṅgalā *energies, symbolized by the sun and moon.*

willfulness bursts forth from within the children, cultivating abilities to hurt themselves as well as others, and to upset the home, with no particular remedy in view. ¶This of course is the opposite to what we have in mind to obtain for ourselves. It is the attainment of that ever-collected mastery over our faculties through holding our inner perspective of them that keeps a heavy reign over the aspect of awareness called willpower, maintaining an even balance between the emotional-instinctive, the intellectual and the spiritual aspects of our being. It is through the study of *rāja yoga*, while always holding a silent overview as to what you are learning and how it relates to your particular life patterns, that you will come to know that an inner change is taking place. Harness the powers of your will in the ways indicated. The reward is simultaneous with the effort employed. The results are immediate.

Tuesday
LESSON 107
Inner and Outer Willpower

There are basically two aspects to the force of willpower. One controls our external life in the world and with those about us. The other controls our internal life, strivings and personal spiritual disciplines, or *sādhanas*. The externalized individual, who throws his force totally into the outer aspect of willpower, inwardly suffers nervousness, confusion and the lack of self-mastery. The devotee who throws his force totally into the inner aspect of willpower suffers total withdrawal from being able to face and cope with the forces of the world at large. ¶It is the total willpower, through both these two aspects of will, the inner and the outer, that the devotee seeks to develop within himself, with an emphasis on the internalized, spiritual processes of his being, for he full well knows that only in this way is he able to serve effectively in the world without being of the world in any way. ¶Willpower developed in this way brings forth the complete being of man to the foreground of himself. He no longer feels he has to sit and meditate to leave one area of the mind, through detaching himself from that area because of his sense of dislike of it, in order to go into another more desirable area. His free flow of awareness from the inner to the outer is but a short distance, so to speak, when the fulfillment of his *sādhana* has equalized the forces of the totality of his willpower. ¶Only the more evolved souls, through acute perceptions, can understand these analogies without confusing them into prior conceptions they may have had about the force of will. We must always try to grasp the totality of what is being said, from the overview, rather than endeavor to hassle with one individual concept or another. It is only through *sādhana* performed regularly over a long period of time that any of this knowledge becomes experiential reality in one's life. The first *sādhana,* therefore, is to always hold the overview and cling in your memory to the intuitive flashes that come as a result. These intuitive flashes come from deep within and are the only thing that should be remembered, for this is your *jñāna,* your insightfulness, your own wisdom, breaking through. ¶It is only when one identifies his willpower as separate and a tool unto itself that he is able to move into the next phase, of discerning the difference between the primal life force within him and what it manifests. Then he can separate awareness from these manifestations, for he has gained the intuitive knowledge that he is the all-pervading life force in the universe. Once awareness has attained individuality and the devotee becomes the onlooker rather than identifying with what he looks upon, then he becomes full of the substance of the totality of the primal force which he experiences as willpower and is able to use this willpower in his daily life, which he experiences as awareness flowing through the mind. This shows the evolution of this awakening on the inner path.

Wednesday
LESSON 108
Harnessing Willpower

In the beginning stages on the path, you will surely experience your mind wandering. This is what "the mind wandering" means, that awareness is totally identified with everything that it is aware of. This gives us the sense, the feeling, that we are the mind, or that we are the emotions or the body. And so, when you are sitting for meditation, myriad thoughts bounce through the brain, and it becomes difficult to even concentrate upon what is supposed to be meditated upon—in some cases, even to remember what it was. That is why the *sādhana* of the practices of *yoga* given in *Merging with Śiva* must be mastered to some extent in order to gain enough control over the willpower and subtle sense organs to cause the meditation to become introverted rather than extroverted. ¶The grace of the *guru* can cause this to happen, because he stabilizes the willpower, the awareness, within his disciple, as a harmonious father and mother stabilize the home for their offspring. If one has no *guru,* or has one and is only a part-time disciple whose *guru* is a picture on the wall, then he must struggle in his efforts as an orphan in the institution of external life. I feel some of the basic tools to struggle along with are clearly explained in this book, and every effort made toward the Divinity of oneself only serves to bring forth blessings, which may not immediately be seen, but will manifest in years to come. ¶It is the regular practice of *sādhana* that really counts, for the habit patterns of the subconscious mind must be gently guided into new channels of expression. It is only when this begins to occur that some results will be visibly seen. ¶Willpower is first identified through the processes of self-control when the devotee finds himself impelled by instinctive impulses into directions that he has long since passed through and experienced. Thus, self-control, of the appetite, the fantasies, the reactions, is diligently sought for through performance of his *sādhana*—chanting on the beads, performing regulated religious routine and ritual during the day and various other more personal disciplines given to him by his *satguru*. It is not without great effort that this control of the little "self" is attained. ¶The next challenge then is the use of the willpower to control the intellect. A precisely controlled intellect pierces deeply beyond the veil of words into the threshold of spiritual experience. The noble devotee uses his willpower to discriminate philosophically as to the nature of his quest. It is the elimination of words and thoughts, which are the intellect, that is his goal. He already has a great deal of self-discipline through having conquered, somewhat, the emotions and passionate instincts of his past. Now comes the more advanced practice of *prāṇāyāma*, the control of breath and inner direction of *prāṇa* in transmutation toward the highest goal, of realization of the Self, that he hopes one day to attain.

Thursday
LESSON 109
Merging into The Self God

When one looks at the Earth and the Sun, one thinks more of the Earth than of the Sun, which is so far away. Traveling through space toward the Sun, the Earth fades into a distant speck and one contemplates the Sun as it looms larger and larger as he draws nearer and nearer. There is no intellect here, you see, for the intellect is connected to the Earth in its exterior ramifications of worldliness. The devotee's path is to merge into the Sun. The devotee's path is to merge—in the totality of his awareness, willpower and life force—into the Self, God, Śiva. Śiva is the ancient name of the Self, God. Mystically, *Śi* is the Absolute state. *Va* is the All-Pervading Self flowing through the mind. It is only when the devotee, through *yoga* disciplines under the direction of his *satguru*, traverses the thought strata of his mind that he begins to experience what he has been learning philosophically. Then the Sun, his Śiva, the Self God, blooms paramount before his vision. Earthiness, worldliness, humanness, instinctiveness fade into a speck within his memory patterns; and like the astronaut hurtling through space toward the Sun, awe-struck as to the impending annihilation of the remnants of his identity, the devotee piercing his inner depths awes at the magnificence of Śiva. ¶This then brings willpower into its crowned usage. The transmuted force of the divine will of the devotee compellingly guides the last remnants of intellect and passions, and in total surrender, when confronted to respond, he voices, "I know not. Śiva's will be done." The will of Śiva—the totality of all force that is active, quiescent force and nonforce as found in *Śi* and *Va*—begins to take over the *dharma* and the *karma* and floods through the being of the devotee on the threshold of Reality. And so, while in a dual state of assuming some personal identity, he states, "Śiva's will be done," as his new and most refined *sādhana* of giving up the last of personal worldliness to the perfect timing of the infinite conglomerate of force and nonforce within him. This he says as a *mantra* unto himself when he sees and hears in the external world. But when eyes and ears are closed, through the transmuted power of his will he merges into the *samādhi* of *Va* and *Śi* and *Śi* and *Va*, experiencing Reality as himself and himself as Reality.

Friday
LESSON 110
The Two Great Transmutations

It is important to gain an intellectual concept of what it is like to experience through a prolonged term the deep, inner will of Śiva—for, granted, we are always experiencing something. Therefore, it is easy to categorize in one of three departments just where the impulses are coming from that cause our motivations. Number one: the instinctive impulses are from us and from others, and mainly concern our body and baser emotions. These are easy to distinguish, as these impulses provide most of the daily activities. Number two: the impulse to speak and to think, begun through one's own efforts or those of another. This is generally based on recurring knowledge accumulated in the past, churned up through present observations and conjecture about the future. This is also easy to distinguish, as these impulses generally fill any gaps that the instinctive impulses have made in a typical day. We can easily see that unless some break occurs, there is absolutely no room for number three, which is simply for Śiva's will to occur. ¶Therefore, the process is one of breaking up the patterns of instinct and intellect, separating the impulses of them both, through regular and regulated periods of *sādhana* and meditation, so that the divine will, spiritual energy and infinite awareness can filter in and cause a new intellect to form. Beginning the *sādhana*, and the continued practice, is the first sign that Śiva's will is being done in the aspirant's life. New energy abides within him because of the transmutation from the base to the Divine. New knowledge comes forth from within him as he builds upon it through remembering his accumulated inner experiences as if they occurred but a moment ago. ¶Should you wish to separate number one from number two and experience the dominance of number three, Śiva's will, simply begin to say to yourself, "Śiva's will be done," throughout each day as the occasions arise. Be careful to categorize each impulse, so that it is clear to your intellect which category you are aware in, just as by being more aware of the Sun than the Earth you begin to forget the Earth and come to know the Sun. Śiva's will is being done always. By being more aware of the inner processes and impulses of willpower than the outer configurations of other people, their thoughts and feelings, you will soon live in the world contentedly and come to know the Śi, the Absolute Self beyond all form, time and causation, and the Va, the All-Pervading Self, as actinic energy permeating all form, and you will rest blissfully in this new knowledge on your new intellectual threshold. "Śiva's will be done"—the first *sādhana* on the path. "Śiva's will be done"—the last *sādhana* on the path, after all others have been perfected.

Saturday
LESSON 111
Conscious Comprehension

You have, of course, comprehended something at one time or another. You have a certain power of comprehension latent within yourself, the power to grasp, to encompass with the mind. It is an all-knowing state. In spiritual unfoldment, thinking is not enough. You have to comprehend the *yoga* path and the steps on the path. You have to comprehend your own nature. That is why in the study of *yoga* we work to clear the subconscious mind as one of the first steps. Then you can comprehend the subconscious state of your own mind. When the subconscious is comprehended, it no longer holds power over you. It does not have the ability to influence your life by itself. Many people think they comprehend things which they do not comprehend at all. Others do comprehend, but they do not maintain a consciousness of their power of comprehension, or a consciousness of what they have comprehended. By not doing so, they become vulnerable again to the instinctive states of the mind. By holding a consciousness of comprehension, on the other hand, the higher states of mind, the realms of intuition and perception, remain open while living in the everyday world, even while facing some of the reactions of the subconscious. ¶There is a story told about a great spiritual teacher, a *satguru,* who lived in India many years ago. In his small group of disciples, two were in perfect harmony with the mind of their *gurujī.* They could easily comprehend everything that he had to say. The *yoga* master used to send them on long trips, traveling all over India doing good for other people. When they returned, they found they were able to grasp and master even deeper actinic controls and laws and powers. The continuity of consciousness does not stop. In other words, the continuity of spiritual unfoldment for the *chelas* did not stop in the *satguru's* absence. ¶However, other disciples who were not in absolute actinic harmony with their teacher, even when they were with him, found that when they were away from him for a few hours they would quickly lose their comprehension of the spiritual path and teachings that were quite natural to them while they were in the radiance of his vibrations. ¶Have you ever been with someone and found yourself able to understand things of a deeper nature better in his presence than when you are away from him? His actinic vibration opened your actinic force field, harmonizing and quieting your odic forces. Such people unfold in you a certain power of comprehension. But unless it opens up your own actinic force field permanently, the power is really temporary, and when you are away from the vibration, it closes up again. Just so, the students who were in harmony with their Indian *satguru* traveled all through India maintaining their consciousness of comprehension. They were in full control of that power, for a *jñāna yoga* master, or *satguru*, can effect a permanent actinic awakening for his *chelas.*

Sunday
LESSON 112
Continuity of Consciousness

Students functioning odically and out of actinic harmony with their *satguru* found that they did not have control of the actinic power and had difficulty in maintaining the continuity of consciousness of the *yoga* path and its teachings. Something went wrong. In realizing this, these students wondered what they could do to regain and maintain this awakening. They knew the laws of the disciplines, the practices. They entered into concentration and meditation, and yet they were not able to maintain their power. They discovered that it was the law of actinic harmony in effect between themselves and their *satguru* that maintained them as actinic force channels through a deeper state of comprehension. By working with the law of harmonious flow of actinic forces, they would have been able to enter into complete harmony with all states of their own mind and those of their *satguru,* whether or not they were in his presence. ¶This particular *yoga* master had gained a cumulative power of actinic force within himself through his *yoga* unfoldment, enabling him to hold the vibration of comprehension for his students. Because his actinic *yoga* students were in harmony with him, they were tuned into his actinic force reservoir. The odic *yoga* students analyzed themselves and found that much of the time they were not in harmony with the *satguru*, that they were mentally criticizing him on worldly matters or debating with him in a way which they did not think would make much difference. And they did not use their actinic power to resolve these differences. In discovering this, they went to the *guru* and said, "We have realized something about the necessity of being in harmony with you." The *guru* said, "Yes, you have realized your own actinic force, and now I am going to start testing you." In his testing he showed them consciously that they had been attached to their personalities and had not been able to attain any realization at all, because of this attachment. ¶There are some people who go after a job with the idea of working for advancement. But after they are settled into the routine for awhile, they begin to lose their impetus, their self-reliance. They begin to feel, "Oh, it's too much trouble; there are too many blocks in the way." In their mind they keep working for promotion, but never really get around to doing anything to advance themselves. These *yoga* students were in the same predicament. They had started their *yoga* training, and then became settled and comfortable in it. They began to lose their impetus for unfoldment subconsciously. In other words, they began to live instinctively, using only the odic force. ¶To demonstrate the difference between the use of odic and actinic forces, this Indian *satguru* began to test his students, asking them to do different tasks. He would start them on one thing, and when they were in the middle of it and personally attached to the doing, he would ask them to do something different. The students found it very hard to drop one thing and go into another because, involving themselves in odic power, they had become egotistically attached to what they were doing, instead of just enjoying the action. When the *guru* showed them how they were more interested in and attached to material things than to awakening an actinic cognition and comprehension of the truths within themselves, they were able at that time to comprehend what he was saying. But the comprehension was projected to them from the *guru*, maintained by his own actinic vibration at the moment of their harmony. They had yet to awaken this ability on their own. ¶It is the actinic continuity of comprehension that is the important ability to be awakened and maintained in this study. For instance, if you comprehend formlessness, and then you find that you comprehend the form of a particular experience, you have to maintain that comprehension while you are going through your everyday-world experiences in the external mind. In other words, you must become conscious of having actinically comprehended something that is out of the realms of the lower states of consciousness. ¶By holding your mind to one particular physical object and seeing how long you can maintain this one-pointedness, you are mastering the art of concentration, controlling the odic forces. You will discover the consciousness of comprehension that encompasses an entire principle, and eventually all the great *yogic* laws of life. Comprehension is superconsciousness, the actinic force flowing through the mind; and maintaining the consciousness of comprehension is having conscious control of the superconscious mind.

Ānanda Jīvanam

आनन्दजीवनम्

Life Is Meant To Be Lived Joyously

Instill in us a wholesome, happy mind, with goodwill and understanding. Then shall we ever delight in your friendship like cows who gladly rejoice in meadows green. This is my joyful message.

Ṛig Veda 10.25.1. VE, P. 302

Monday
LESSON 113
Living In Spirit

Stress is a consequence of the technological age, and these days everybody is talking about stress. Stress and strains of a fast-paced and demanding modern age affect every organ of the body. A calm mind, a peaceful mind, is needed to encompass changing times. Times are changing very rapidly. To cope with these changes, we have to rely on ourselves to keep a balance of physical, mental, emotional and spiritual life. Our religion has ways to combat stress and the diseases it causes, ways to avoid the mental anguish which this fast-paced world brings about. These pressures did not exist in the agricultural age. Things were more relaxed then. All we had to do was plant our crops and wait for the harvest. Plant and wait. Plant and wait. And in-between there was plenty of time for religious activities. ¶But life in the technological age is a life of constant work, constant activity, all of the time. So, we tend to set religion aside just when we need it the most. We have to rely on our religion to keep a balance in our life. It is a proven fact that religious people can cope with stress and strain better than nonreligious people. The answer to stress is not to take a pill to be able to relax. The answer is not to give up the temple, not to give up the culture, not to give up the scriptures which put everything into perspective, not to give up the art of meditation and the practices of *yoga.* ¶Spiritual things you must understand with your heart, with your feeling. Feeling and thinking, working together, give you that deep understanding that you need to cognize the wisdom of the spirit. All you can do in living your life every day is to make today just a little bit better than yesterday was. You will then have confidence in yourself, so that tomorrow will be all right, too, and you won't fear the tomorrows. Why? Because in striving to make today the perfect day of your lifetime, you bring through your spirit. You allow the spirit, God, to permeate through all layers of your mind. ¶At our sunrise pilgrimage this morning to the top of Mount Tamalpais we had over thirty devotees. It was a beautiful, inspiring time. Let me explain to you just a little bit what we were researching together on the mountaintop. Your thoughts sometimes literally flood your body or flow through your body. Sometimes you find your thoughts spinning and jumping from here to there. You don't know where they come from, and they confuse you as they flow

---

Two devotees are take great joy in celebrating a village festival. Adorned with rudrāksha *beads, they walk bare-chested past homes with quaint tile roofs and elaborate pillars, one sounding a silver-inlaid conch and the other playing the traditional South Indian* mṛidaṅga *drum.*

through your body or your brain. Just as thought can flow through the body, so can spirit, or God, flow through the intuitive, the intellectual and the instinctive mind. When your thoughts flow through the body, your body becomes either dejected and heavy, or light and happy, depending upon the nature of your thinking. Affirmations can help you to improve the patterns of your thought and feeling. You have to repeat certain affirmations for certain lengths of time to produce a certain result. Every word—and the meaning of each word if you know the meaning—has a certain vibration. As a thought goes into motion, it permeates your nervous system and gives you a particular feeling. Just as your thoughts and your words can make your body feel a certain way, in the very same way the spirit, or God, flowing through the mind, can illumine and does illumine the mind and purify it. ¶In facing your past, if your past is not exactly what you would like to look at, and you look at it and still react to it, you will create today as a day much worse than yesterday. You will not be living the spiritual life. But if you seek first the spirit within you each day, and make the day a little bit better than yesterday, you flood the spiritual being of you, the real you, through the mind. And you wipe away and clarify much of the past and bring much understanding through your mind. ¶What is responsible for negative reactions of the subconscious mind? Simply the transgressions that you have caused against the natural laws of the mind, that's all. If you transgress the laws of the physical body, eat the wrong things, behave in the wrong way, your physical body will suffer because of it. If you transgress the natural laws of the mind, hurt another instead of help another, discourage instead of encourage another person, then your mind will suffer. A part of the mind goes out of control, and that is called being emotional. The emotions are a part of the mind out of control. They gain a momentum of their own and eventually take over the entire mind. But when the will of the spirit comes up and controls the emotional nature, the emotions subside for a period of time until they gain momentum again. This goes on sometimes all through life.

Tuesday
LESSON 114
Are You Ready?

When you control your emotions, you are bringing through your spiritual being. It is only your spiritual being, your soul in action, bringing through the spirit, or bringing through God, that can control the mind. When you are living in an emotional state, you are only experiencing the mind temporarily out of control. And like anything that gains its own momentum, even if you do not control it, it will subside automatically after a period of time until it builds up again. This is all caused by subtle transgressions of natural laws of the mind, in this life and in previous lives. ¶There are many subtle laws. For instance, if you are planning to do something for someone and then you decide for some reason that you won't, all of the spiritual power that you had previously brought through from your spiritual being will be coagulated and blocked by your hesitation. Then tomorrow will not be as good as today was. It will be worse. ¶To keep your spirit flowing, always allow yourself to be in the line of understanding. In other words, do not allow misunderstanding to arise in your mind. Should misunderstanding arise, sit down, be quiet and do not get up until you understand the problem. You might have to sit for an hour. Instinctively your animal nature will not allow you to do that, but if you use willpower and persist, tomorrow will be a perfect day. Now, this is easy to talk about, and also easy to understand, but it takes a very discerning mind, utilizing the power of discrimination, to master these laws of the mind. ¶Train your mind to awaken the spiritual being. This is as difficult to do as it is to train a person to dance or to swim, or to accomplish any athletic feat requiring a highly trained body. You have to always be the master, and be attentive to your goals in life. ¶What is your goal in this life? Is your goal to sit and wallow in the emotions? Is it to memorize a lot of things that different people have said so you can quote from them? Or is your goal in life to find first your Infinite Being within yourself? If you could only once gain just a glimmer of your true Being—the spiritual Being flowing through the mind which you always thought was you. Instead, you have things that you have to do that you haven't done, things that you will do, and things that you will not do, things that you haven't made up your mind to do as yet and things you thought you would like to do but decided you wouldn't do. All of this is going on as a process within yourself, and it keeps you nicely confused. ¶A confused mind creates the form to which you give a name, and you become Mr. or Mrs. Somebody from Somewhere. You go along like that for years and years until all of a sudden you drop dead and give up the physical body. Then what happens? What happens to this mind that is so concerned about "What will my friends think?" All of these various concepts that make up your personality, when you lay down your physical body and die, just what happens to them? Are you ready for that experience of death? You should always be ready, especially nowadays when the opportunities are so great. Always be ready, spiritually ready. ¶Are you spiritually ready?

Have you done your duty to your family? Have you done your duty to your temple? Have you done your duty to yourself? Or do you shirk some of your responsibilities? It's not up to your *swāmī* to know all those things about you. Somebody once said, "Well, Gurudeva just knows everything about me." What good does that do? It's up to you to take a running total on yourself, daily, through feeling. You can't do it through thought; you'll get all mixed up. Are you ready to become a spirit, a spiritual being, an illumined mind, at the moment of death? Or at the moment of death are you ready to become a completely confused, congested mass of gaseous matter, which is what a confused mind looks like? These are vital religious questions that the individual must face and find the answers to.

Wednesday
LESSON 115
You Must Purify Yourself

Ask yourself, "Have I followed all the good advice given me?" You come to hear my *upadeśa*. Your coming is the asking for advice. You get advice, and many of you ignore it and you have your own opinion. If you have your own opinion, why come? Opinions are just of the instinctive and intellectual mind. Most opinions are only moldy concepts! You come to have your opinions changed. You come to have them changed from within you through your own spiritual insight. But if you come with the armor of your opinions, then you are very foolish. You might as well stay home and live with your opinions, because there will be no spiritual progress or unfoldment for you for many, many years, maybe many lives. ¶Ask yourself these vital questions. What are you going to do with the past that keeps bothering you and sometimes makes today a hell on Earth for you? It is really easy to transcend this state of mind. Just remember and try to understand that the spirit within you flows through you, flows through the mind, like water flows through the Earth. If you build barriers, then you fight your own spiritual Being flowing through you. You develop qualities of jealousy, hatred, anger, revenge, and malice. Negative qualities are just congested masses of mind-stuff that are temporary and do not allow the spirit to flow through. If you have negative qualities as boulders in your mind, the spirit cannot flow through you; but as it tries to flow through, it will automatically set a part of your mind out of control, and you will be emotional. You can't help it. ¶So, you must purify yourself. You purify yourself by being kind to others, being generous until it hurts, being benevolent, being ready to serve at all times until you are strained in serving. Put a smile on the faces of other people. Gain your happiness and your positive states of mind by making other people happy.

Negative people are always worried about themselves. Positive people are concerned with the happiness of others. Be strong enough to understand, and do not allow yourself to sleep at night until you have understood the problems of the day. If you go to sleep with problems on your mind, you will go into a confused state of mind, and you will toss around and later say, "That is just the dream world" or "I had a nightmare." All you did was lose your consciousness in a troubled subconscious state. But if you practice *yoga*, and you sit and master each problem before falling asleep, even if it takes you several hours, you will gain enough rest for the next day, for you will have made this day a perfect day. ¶If you refuse to do what you should do when you have the chance to do it, what hope is there for anybody else who does not even know what he should do? If you resist a spiritual life, possibly the responsibility for others falls on your shoulders, because everything starts with the one and multiplies into the many. It behooves you to understand very acutely and discriminatingly these basic principles and immediately put them into action in your life. Seize every spiritual opportunity you have to advance your soul, because when you do, the reaction is glorious on you. But when you resent and when you fight within yourself, the reaction is disastrous unto yourself, because you lose the battle when you begin to fight your own inner Self. You win the battle when you begin to express yourself spiritually, when you begin to live with Śiva.

Thursday
LESSON 116
Daily Mental Maintenance

Shall we all close our eyes for just a moment and think and feel what living with Śiva really means? When you are tired of playing in the emotions, that will indicate that your soul is ready to take over and control the lower states of mind. Śiva is always within you, always there. Through silence, quieting your mind, you can become That which you truly are and shine out through that which you thought you were. Your experience will have a healing effect upon the mind and burn away the past. Intensify the spirit within you and heal any wounds that the mind may have. As Mother Nature heals the body, so does Śiva, the Self, heal the mind. Give yourself in to the real you. Turn your mind inward. Turn your will inward and live that glorious spiritual life and be ready as a spiritual being to meet the experience of death. ¶Morning *pūjās* are excellent opportunities for you to practice self-discipline, to offer yourself opportunities to change, to alter the habit patterns that have been built into your mind during the year. In these early morning meditations, you may learn to cease criticizing yourself and begin having a greater understanding of yourself. When you learn to stop criticizing yourself, you are able to appreciate the many experiences that you have been through during the year, rather than regretting them. Regret possibly is an experience more harmful than the experience you have been regretting. Some people actually live by a righteous code of ethics which offers a justification for constantly hurting themselves through regret, guilt or related emotions. Through your meditation you will appreciate your experiences for what they are—good or difficult. Simply make a resolution not to repeat the difficult ones and have faith enough to correct what your experiences have caused in the world as a result of your going through them. The first step in learning to rejuvenate your mind is being able to look objectively at your experiences. You will find this difficult to do, because you are so closely associated and identified with your mind. The mind claims you, and therefore you think that your experiences are the real you, but they are not. ¶After your morning *pūjā*, take five minutes to write down on a piece of paper those things which disturb you. Write concisely and honestly, without reason or justification, what is burdening your subconscious mind. In doing so, you will release yourself from the reactions to those experiences. Burn the paper in a fireplace or garbage can (not in your shrine room), and realize that the experience is complete, finished, except for the wisdom which you have now derived from it. You will find that this practice, known in Sanskrit as *vāsanā daha tantra*, does much to make your subconscious transparent and give you a greater power and control over your mind. Making the subconscious mind transparent is a basic religious practice. Only when this is first done is it possible to make progress in seeking God. Try now to find Śiva within you, the permanent Reality that never changes. ¶Sri Ramakrishna, the great Indian saint, compared the mind's turning inward, seeking to connect itself to God, with the image of a little boy holding on to a rope tied to a post. The little boy swings on the rope and it winds him around and around the post. Then he swings the other way, still holding on to the rope, and the rope wraps him around the post again. The little boy represents man simply having fun and enjoying the experiences of life. He is perfectly safe as long as he holds on to the rope and the rope is connected to the post, for the post is God, and That doesn't move. The little boy we would call mind. The rope connecting mind to God is the soul, the indomitable will. And so, Sri Ramakrishna went on to say, if man turns his mind inward and keeps his mind looking within, he will see the reality of Spirit and the transient nature of all of the mind's activity. He may live in and enjoy the activity of the mind and never be hurt or harmed so long as he holds on to that rope, maintains his inward vision constantly and holds himself connected to the permanence of his own Being.

Friday
LESSON 117
To Realize the Spirit Within

When you have nothing in your subconscious that particularly bothers you, it is easy to turn the mind inward. But if you are bothered or disturbed, the subconscious acts as a barrier and makes it difficult to turn within. When you try to do so, up from the subconscious come all the remnants of the experiences which you hold on to through regret. If this is the case, you will have one more experience to go through before your mind does turn within. You will have to experience the understanding of all your experiences—not through analysis, not through, reason (although the "whys" may come to you intuitively), but through the higher experience of pure understanding. You will find it is possible to have an understanding of yourself without going through the process of analysis. ¶A disturbed mind which is not permeated with Śivaness is strong in a negative sense, strong in that it will keep you from the realization of God. When the mind is disturbed, it is outwardly strong. The mind that is not disturbed is inwardly strong. Your inner strength is always more dependable than your outward display of strength. When you have gained your inner strength, you will be able to sit in meditation for at least a half hour every day and practice being the guardian of every thought and the ruler of every feeling within your body. If you do this, you will realize That which is the center of your Being. You will be uplifted, elevated, through the purification that you have brought to your mind. ¶Hold your consciousness high, keep your mind alive and alert so that your soul is alive and alert. You have heard me say many times, "Observation is the first awakening of the soul." If your observation is intense and accurate, your mind is not bothered and you are not regretting things that have happened to you in the past. But people who have poor observation often do hold on to their regrets, and they rationalize most of what happens to them, putting the blame for their own experiences on someone else. It is so much easier to close the door on these reactions and live more like on a spring day rather than in the dead of winter. Life is meant to be lived joyously. The awakened soul is a joyous soul with a positive mind. The practice of observation will bring you closer and closer to this state of consciousness. ¶If you feel that your observation is not keen, begin observing things more closely. Observe the different colors in a store window. Study the shadows and the shades of color in one tree. Listen to the sounds of the city. How many can you distinguish? What do they mean to you? If your observation is already good, you can participate more fully in life and find yourself living above the dreary happenings of the day. ¶Recognizing that all experience is but a fading dream, you are closer to the permanence within you that never changes. You can sense it. It is God. It is Śiva. It has never changed. It will never change. You have all felt this permanence at one time or another, but then perhaps you find that you lose this feeling, this consciousness, and you drift out into the mind and find yourself thinking again that the mind is real. But then, maybe tomorrow, you will face it again. And as soon as you have found it, you leave it again, for the mind cannot bear the intensity of God, and you forget all about it. But then, a little later, you face that permanence within you yet again. And little by little you find that you are turning inward, opening up the inner channels more and more each day, making a greater and greater contact with God by turning within, drawing yourself ever closer to the pole at the center, the core of your Being. You will go through many different tests to prove your own realization to yourself. Face each test graciously. Welcome each test, and welcome each temptation that shows you the strength of your will over the chaotic senses. You have only to quiet all things of the mind to realize your identity with the eternity of God Śiva, the spirit, the Eternal Self within you.

Saturday
LESSON 118
Overlapping Reactions

When you die, you are freed from your senses. While you are living, you are caught up in your senses and reacting to memories of things you wish you had or had not done. Many people live in a constant state of overlapping reactions. They try to find peace of mind on the outside, externally. Reactions are caused by what we have placed in the subconscious mind that we have not fully understood. Reactions are packed away in the subconscious mind, influencing our everyday life, attracting our successes and failures to us. We keep meeting blocks because of our reactions in the subconscious mind that we set up in the past. Overcome these reactions, and opportunities will open up and we will begin to succeed. Reaction is a natural thing, either positive or negative. If we are reacting in a negative way, that is because of lack of understanding; if in a positive way, that gives us more understanding, and we become our own teacher or psychologist. ¶If you do not understand your reaction to something, wait until it subsides emotionally, so you will not be upset, then try to understand it by writing about it in a quiet moment. Then burn the paper in an inauspicious fire, such as in a garbage can. This *vāsanā daha tantric* process releases or detaches the emotion from the memory. This means that the memory of the experience no longer harbors the emotion that was previously attached to it and vibrating twenty-four hours a day. You will still have the memory, but without a reaction or emotional charge attached to it. ¶There are many individuals who get their security from their reactions, who make themselves disappointed and keep themselves in a constant state of emotional vibration. Peace of mind is not a blank state. It is not having emotion attached to the memory patterns within the subconscious. These memory patterns, once freed from emotion, remain at peace, and then pure contentment resides through the entire mind. A negative reaction can be likened to a fog over the city. You cannot see clearly because of the fog. ¶When we react to something, how long does it take before it subsides? How can we guide our lives so as to have only positive reactions? We have to awaken a certain control over our nature. We have to anticipate what is going to happen to us. Whether we admit it or not, we attract everything that happens to us. What we react to, and what we have reacted to in the past, we will create in our future. If we face experience with understanding, we will free ourselves from recreating past unpleasant experiences. Experience is man's greatest chain. It holds him in a certain pattern. The chains of experience get stronger and stronger until man enters spiritual life through the realms of understanding. Every man must decide whether he wants to be caged in by experience or be freed by understanding the cause of the experience. ¶A negative reaction may have been set up in the mind many years ago. How long does it take to subside? In a person with some understanding, the initial reaction will subside in a few hours, but it takes five to seven days before it subsides enough for him to get a complete understanding. The average man reacts to something every day. That's what makes him average. A reaction today, another one tomorrow, another one the day after tomorrow, then those reactions are overlapping. To stop these overlapping reactions, we have to sit down and face everything that we have created for ourselves in the past and control our circumstances until the reaction subsides. ¶Be on your guard. Control your circumstances and your life. Guard your weak points with understanding, and don't allow yourself to be put into a position where you will react. Then you can become fully conscious of what is within you and within your fellow man.

Sunday
LESSON 119
How to Face Yourself

Life must become positive. In reactions, man is not his best friend. He is seeking outside for something to quiet his nature. He is carrying his reactions with him, keeping old habit patterns going. For a person to renovate his subconscious mind, he must be willing to move out for awhile, redesign, rebuild, redecorate, then move back in. This is a form of spiritual discipline. Overlapping reactions are dangerous. Living in overlapping reactions and understanding nothing of how to get along without them, because of no discrimination, makes man give up. ¶Overcoming reaction is easy. You can wipe it out of your life and realize the benefit of having done so. Sit down and think. Look at your life. Look at the tendencies within your nature which created your habit patterns and which formed your subconscious mind and gave it the foundation for many more of the same old situations. The tendencies will be greater in each succeeding situation unless you apply the brakes of understanding. If you sit down and realize the law of cause and effect and live according to the basic laws of life, you will overcome the reactions within you. You will be able to overcome old reactions by understanding them. More realization will burst forth from within you, and you will live a more spiritual life. You can either walk through a city full of fog, or climb above it. ¶Thinking and believing clearly are only possible when a man knows that he knows. When you realize something, you only know of your realization after you have realized it, not before. Realization is your teacher. Realize something every day, or something will block the subconscious mind. The reactionary nature must subside. Its death gives birth to a greater understanding. If you can live for three weeks without reacting to anything, you will attain a realization. ¶If you simply remember this without practicing it, you will not be helping yourself or anyone else. But if you take the law and put it into practice, you will be doing something for yourself and your fellow man, because you will realize a greater spiritual power, a greater humility, and be the person you should be. Then don't react again. Discriminate as to each move you make, each word you say, and decide whether there will be a reaction. If you can see ahead that you will not react, proceed. Dictate to yourself, face yourself, face your mistakes and don't make them again. Breaking spiritual laws creates reactions in the subconscious, and man loses spiritual power. We can find actual peace of mind in a certain place, right here and now, within ourselves, when we overcome reactions. ¶Let us look within and see if we are reacting to anything right now, holding any resentment, holding any fear. Let us know that that is just a gauge of experience of the instinctive nature. Loosen it and let it go. Mentally look ahead to the future and know that everything we do and say will have a reaction. Let us give birth to good, positive, controlled reactions, and be sure that if they overlap, they are transparent—that they create a light growing brighter. Overlapping negative reactions bring darkness, depression, and make man nervous. ¶We have been delving into our consciousness. If you have understood all this about your reactions, your subconscious mind has been impressed. Look into your mirror. Your reflection is your subconscious mind objectified. Find out what is holding you back. Face yourself and find out what is keeping you from expressing the great things which are within you here and now. After all, life is meant to be lived joyously.

Prāyaśchitta Śakti
प्रायश्चित्तशक्ति

The Power Of Penance

Vāsanā is divided into two, the pure and the impure. If thou art led by the pure *vāsanās,* thou shalt thereby soon reach by degrees My Seat. But should the old, impure *vāsanās* land thee in danger, they should be overcome through various efforts.

Śukla Yajur Veda, Mukti Upanishad, 2. UPA P. 7

Monday
LESSON 120
Means of Atonement

Vitalized by *bhakti's* grace, a devotee's conscience is aroused, bringing the desire to confess, repent and make up for misdeeds. Through divine sight, the soul perceives unwise actions, performed when in the lower nature, as a hindrance to spiritual progress. *Tantras* are many to release the soul from these burdensome bonds. Penance well performed propels the soul into its natural state of bliss. ¶*Chakras* look like lotus flowers. There are four petals on the *mūlādhāra chakra,* which is situated at the base of the spine. These petals unfold one after another as a person's consciousness emerges upward from jealousy, anger and fear into memory, reason and willpower. Only then awakens the consciousness of religiousness and the ability to admit the existence of God and angelic beings. This new humility causes the devotee to admit that grace is needed to progress on the spiritual path and resolve unwholesome *karmas* of the past, to admit that wisdom is needed to avoid making new unwholesome *karmas* in the future. The four petals of the *mūlādhāra* can be described as unrestrained remorse, confession, repentance and reconciliation. ¶All help is given by the divine *devas* to those who admit their mistakes and are seen performing a sincere penance. These *devas* that oversee those in a penitent state of mind are similar to doctors and nurses gathered to help their patient become well again. The angelic helpers surround their "patient," assisting in the relief of mental and emotional illness caused by transgression of *dharma* and the guilt that follows. When the penitent is undergoing penance, it is a form of *tapas,* described by some as psychic surgery performed by the *devas* working together to bring the soul from darkness into light. It truly is a happy event, but only long after it is over. ¶When penance is given, it must be fulfilled, especially when requested. Otherwise, the life of the penitent is vulnerable to the company of *asuras.* Penance is given after a certain degree of remorse is shown and the urgency is felt by the devotee to rid his mind of the plaguing matter. Admitting a transgression, I have discovered, is often preceded by one of three forms of denial: casual denial, soft denial or hard denial. Say a boy steals some candy from a store. Casual denial is making little of the matter, "Big deal! Why is everyone so upset?" Soft denial is rationalizing, "Yes, I took the candy, so what? It was only two dollars' worth!"

The Hindu practice of penance is called prāyaśchitta. *A wrongdoing has brought great suffering to a devotee. He confesses it to his* satguru. *After performing* kavadi, *carrying a special arch with milk attached in small pots to a Murugan shrine, he gains* karmic *release.*

Hard denial is to say, "I didn't do it. They have me mixed up with another boy!" ¶We all know the refined, uplifting feeling of *bhakti.* Every religious person in the world has experienced this at one time or another. It is the total surrendering of oneself to God and the Gods. As the soul emerges out of the lower aspects of the instinctive mind, the *mūlādhāra chakra* begins to unfold because of the *bhakti* that has been awakened through daily worship and *sādhana.* Admission and honest confession then bring up repentant feelings through the subsuperconscious mind quite unbidden. When this happens within the devotee, it is truly a boon, marking progress on the spiritual path. Confession, the voice of the soul, can now be heard. As the intellect clears, the honest truths of experience, formerly hidden to oneself as well as to others, are revealed. The soul, the conscience, emerges in all honesty and remorsefully confesses the burdens it has been carrying. Yes, confession is truly the voice of the soul. Nothing is hidden to oneself when *dharma* supersedes *adharma.*

Tuesday
LESSON 121
Confession And Penance

As a mature being in the higher nature, above the *mūlādhāra chakra,* ever seeking higher plateaus through *sādhana,* the Śaivite seeks peace whenever the mind is troubled. How does such a Śaivite confess? How does one tell of the reactions to misdeeds performed in all innocence when but a child in the lower consciousness, living in the lower nature, below the *mūlādhāra chakra?* How and whom does one tell of misdeeds performed during a lapse of conscience, even when living a life of *dharma?* A Śaivite confesses to God Śiva, the Gods or his *guru.* To confess to God Śiva, go to His temple and mentally, psychically place your burden at the holy feet of the *mūrti* in the sanctum sanctorum. To confess to Gods Murugan or Gaṇeśa, go to their temple and place your confession at their holy feet. Or go to your *satguru* and tell him of your inner plight, holding nothing back. This is how a Śaivite confesses inner burdens as he emerges out of the instinctive mind of the lower nature into the purified intellect of the higher nature. ¶Yes, reconciliation is food for the soul. After the soul has unburdened itself of the dross of the lower mind through honest confession, a resolution must be made not to reenter the lower states or rekindle the flames of the *chakras* below the *mūlādhāra.* To achieve reconciliation by apology for hurts caused another, or to atone by performing acts of penance if a long time has passed since the apology could have been made and received, is truly food for the soul. ¶There are many forms of penance, *prāyaśchitta,* such as 1,008 prostrations before Gods Gaṇeśa,

Murugan or Supreme God Śiva, apologizing and showing shame for misdeeds; performing *japa* slowly 1,008 times on the holy *rudrāksha* beads; giving of 108 handmade gifts to the temple; performing manual chores at the temple for 108 hours, such as cleaning, making garlands or arranging flowers; bringing offerings of cooked food; performing *kavadi* with miniature spears inserted in the flesh; making a pilgrimage by prostrating the body's length again and again, or rolling around a temple. All these and more are major means of atonement after each individual confession has been made. ¶The keynote in serious cases is asking one's *satguru* to give a specific penance once the problem has been revealed. Once the *satguru* is asked for penance, the penance must be performed exactly according to his instruction. It should be done with full energy and without delay. Deliberate delay or refusal to perform the penance shows the devotee has rejected the assistance of the *satguru*. Further advice and guidance will not be forthcoming until the instruction has been fulfilled. Therefore, a devotee in such a condition does not approach the *satguru*. He may, however, beseech the *guru's* assistance and continued guidance if he is in the process of fulfilling the penance over a period of time.

Wednesday
LESSON 122
The Esoterics Of Penance

The inner process of relieving unwanted *karmic* burdens occurs in this order: remorse and shame; confession (of which apology is one form); repentance; and finally reconciliation, which is making the situation right, so that good feelings abide all around. Therefore, each individual admission of a subconscious burden too heavy to carry must have its own reconciliation to clear the inner aura of negative *saṁskāras* and *vāsanās* and replenish the inner bodies for the struggle the devotee will have to endure in unwinding from the coils of the lower, instinctive mind which block the intellect and obscure spiritual values. When no longer protected by its ignorance, the soul longs for release and cries out for solace. *Prāyaśchitta,* penance, is then the solution to dissolve the agony and bring *śānti.* ¶The *guru* has to know the devotee and his family *karma* over a long period of time before *prāyaśchitta* is given. Otherwise, it may have the wrong effect. Penance is for religious people, people who practice daily, know the philosophy and have a spiritual head of their family, people who genuinely want to reach a state of purity and grace. It is not for nonreligious people. Just as in the Catholic Church, penance, to be most effective, is given to you by the spiritual preceptor. It is not a "do-it-yourself," New-Age kind of thing. Those who try to do it alone may overdo it. It takes a certain amount of talking and counseling to gain an understanding of what is involved. Before undertaking any of the physical *prāyaśchittas,* I have devotees do the *mahā vāsanā daha tantra*—"great purification of the subconscious by fire"—writing down and then burning ten pages of memories, called *saṁskāras,* good and bad, for each year of their life to the present day. ¶Anything can be written down that concerns you: friends, home, family, relatives, sports, TV shows, vacations, work, pastimes, indulgences, anything that is in your mind. This may automatically clear up events of the past. The idea is to remove the emotions from the experience and bring yourself to the eternal now. Forgetting the past, concern yourself with the now, move with life day to day and create a glorious future for yourself and others. Also, I've experienced that sometimes just making the confession to the *satguru* is a sufficient *prāyaśchitta* and nothing else is necessary. What the troubled conscience thought was bad may not have been bad at all, just normal happenings, but the conscience suffers until that fact is known. ¶It is important to note that the *vāsanā daha tantra* must be done by hand, with pen and paper. Various devotees have tried it on the computer and found it not effective. Writing is uniquely effective because in the process the *prāṇa* from the memory flows from your subconscious through your hand, through the pen and is embedded in the paper, bringing the memory out in the open to be understood, defused and released when the paper is burned. Some devotees have also tried sitting and pondering the past, meditating on it and even visualizing themselves writing down their recollections and burning them. This often does more harm than good, as it only stirs up the past.

Thursday
LESSON 123
Suitable Prescriptions

Anger, I have observed, is the most difficult fault for people to overcome, because it comes in so many different forms: pouting, long silences, shouting, yelling, swearing and more. Psychotherapist Ron Potter-Efron says in his book, *Angry All the Time,* that there are eight rungs of anger on the "violence ladder:" sneaky anger, the cold shoulder, blaming and shaming, swearing, screaming and yelling, demands and threats, chasing and holding, partly controlled violence, and blind rage. Some people are just angry all the time because they live in the lower nature, constantly engaged in mental criticism and arguments. Anger can eventually be controlled by putting a sum of money—five dollars, for example—in a jar each time one becomes angry and then donating that money to an orphanage. It soon gets too expensive to get angry. However, for devotees who are wealthy, that doesn't work. For them, I've found the penance of fasting for the next meal after they get angry works. ¶The "flower penance" has proven useful especially to young people who have been beaten and abused by their parents. They put up a picture of the person who beat them—father, mother or teacher—and every day for thirty-one days place a flower in front of the picture. While doing so, they sincerely forgive the person in heart and mind. Some are able to see the experience as their own *karma.* They forgive their parents and experience a great deal of freedom. Others have so much hatred and resentment toward their parents that they can't do it at all. This penance has also worked for those who have a mental conflict with their employer. There is a severe penance, too, for one who beats his children. It involves private self-punishment and giving public lectures against corporal punishment, as well as teaching classes on Positive Discipline to the public many times throughout the years. ¶For wife-beating, adultery and various collections of smaller transgressions, I advise the traditional, age-old penance of *kavadi,* putting small spears in the body, at least fifteen, and circumambulating the temple many times during a temple festival with the supervision of trained priests. Wife-beating and adultery are very serious matters; they break up homes astrally and often physically and create for the perpetrators a rotten birth in the next life. To atone for all that is very difficult. ¶Without resolve and remorse, no penance will work. People have an internal ego and an external ego, and for many, one is quite different from the other. For instance, someone may be smiling and joking all the time, but inside himself be angry and critical of those around him, though he lets no one see that he is. There are also those who are smiling and sociable on the outside but crying on the inside over hurts and memories of things that have happened in the past. The *mahā vāsanā daha tantra*—writing down and burning all the emotion out of the memories of the past, the hurts of the past, the good things and the bad things that have happened to us since birth—harmonizes the internal and external ego so that we are the same person on the inside as on the outside. When we write down our hurts and fears and misunderstandings, as well as all the happy times, our loves and losses, our joys and sorrows—and then crumple up the paper, light it with a flame and watch it burn, thinking of it as the garbage of yesterday—we detach the emotion from the memories. Almost magically, the emotion that had held the memory vibrating within the subconscious mind, perhaps for years, goes away in the flame. There is nothing left but the quiet memory. As a result, finally the soul begins to shine forth within the person as the memory patterns of the deep past no longer bind awareness. The inner and outer become one and the same. ¶It is very easy to read the external personality of an individual by listening to what he says, looking at what he does and observing his various forms of communication. The internal personality of the person can be read by observing body language, facial expressions, movements of the eyes, movements of the feet and hands, the way a person walks, the hesitancy before he answers a question. All of this shows the workings of the internal ego, which generally blocks the natural joyousness of the soul. So, the first step in spiritual unfoldment is for the individual to harmonize the internal and the external ego so that he is a complete, integrated person twenty-four hours a day, and nothing is hidden, even to himself.

Friday
LESSON 124
Releasing The Past

The older we get, the more memories we have, and those memories contain emotion—both positive emotion and negative emotion. Emotion takes many forms. We can have happy emotions, we can have sad emotions, we can have emotions of depression, we can have emotions of elation, we can have emotions of discouragement, we can have emotions of encouragement. As you go over your life, reliving it year by year, writing it all down from year one to the present, ten pages per year, you are the author of your own script. You are the star upon the stage of your own life. You may run into happy emotion, discouraging emotion, encouraging emotion. It's good to get rid of it all. If you uncover a period of your life that makes you depressed, then you have been carrying that depression around with you for many, many years. Reliving the depression and the unhappy feelings as you write about the experiences in detail and burn the paper unwinds and releases the *prāṇic* emotional energy from each memory. You especially want to deal with the traumatic areas of the inner mind and release the discouragement, the regret, the depression, the loss of faith in humanity, the loss of faith in yourself and all those negative emotions that you've been carrying for so many years. They will go away like paper dragons. They will disappear. ¶You have three kinds of *prāṇa* inside of you: spiritual, intellectual and instinctive. When you think, you make or cause a motion in that *prāṇa* and create a form of *prāṇa*. You speak, laugh, cry, think and interact with others; all this is the use and movement of one kind of *prāṇa* or another, or a mixture of the three. In the inner mind, the subconscious *prāṇic* forms have a color and a corresponding sound when they vibrate with emotion, not unlike a Technicolor production. The purpose of this ancient *tantra* is to remove the color/sound from the memory pattern so that the memory would appear as a black-and-white silent movie when revisited, without the vivid, vibrating emotion. Your life, in moving and creating with the *prāṇa* inside of you, can be like writing on water. An experience happens and it just goes away, without residue, without attachment, without lingering emotion. Or your life can be like carving in stone; each experience remains with you, embedded in memory by the impact of emotion. As you look back through the pages of your life, you want to melt the stone, break it up and make it go away. That's the whole idea, regardless of what the motion is of the mind. The stones in your past are generally the surprise things that come along in life. Living a routine life—you go to work and you come home, and one day is pretty much the same as another—does not produce memories with emotions so much. But then you come to a major change, such as moving to a new home, or some new person coming into your life. That makes a big impact, and you have to deal with it. Like many people, you may deal with these things by packing them away: "I don't want to think about that anymore." "I don't like that person" or, "I like that person," but you are married so you can't like him or her too much; so you just pack it away and try not to think about it anymore. Those are some of the things you want to dig up and discharge, to break up the patterns. ¶Each of us has a story. You are the major actor on the stage of your life, playing the script that you wrote. You are the director and you are the lighting engineer, the stage manager, costume designer and make-up artist. When a particular experience or pattern of experience is repeated over a long period, it creates in the sub of the subconscious mind a latent tendency or propensity in that same direction. This is a *vāsanā,* which may be positive, *śubha,* or negative, *aśubha.* A negative *vāsanā* is like a subconscious motor that makes you do things you later wish you had not done. A positive *vāsanā* brings success and good fortune. Through the *vāsanā daha tantra,* we withdraw the energy from the memories, and in so doing weaken, even destroy, the pathways or *vāsanās* that led us to the experiences that created the negative memories and leave in place the pure, positive *vāsanās* that will continue to create a positive future.

Saturday
LESSON 125
Spiritual Journaling

The *mahā vāsanā daha tantra,* a once in a lifetime experience, is the practice of writing down ten pages of memories on lettersize lined paper (about ten words per line, twenty-eight lines, totaling 250-280 words per page) for each year of your life to date and burning them in an ordinary, nonauspicious fire. To begin, put together a collection of ten blank pages for each year of your life. Each page must be carefully marked with the page number, the year and your age at that time. Then set aside at least fifty pages for each of the other four parts of this *tantra.* As you proceed in your journaling, you will find it necessary from time to time to backtrack or jump ahead to a year when memories pop up related to a certain period. In other words, it's okay to write about years out of order, especially when old memories arise naturally, but do so on the designated pages. This is the reason for numbering each page in the way suggested above. Each time a page on one of the years has been completed, it must be immediately burned. ¶After your journaling of ten pages per year is complete, there are five more steps, making six in all. Step two, the "spot check," is to scan back through the years of your life and see if there are memories you missed in your previous journaling. These, of course, would be the happy and unhappy experiences, and anything else that comes to mind. The mere remembrance of an experience coming unbidden proves there is still color/sound emotion attached to it. Pay close attention to times when you did not apply the eternal laws of *karma,* reincarnation and the acknowledgment that Śiva is everywhere and in all things. Note the times when you blamed others for what happened to you, when you did not acknowledge all happenings in life as your own creations accomplished in one life or another in the past. Be honest here. It is important to acknowledge when we do and do not put Sanātana Dharma into action in our lives. Be honest; no one is looking. You are the actor on the stage of your own experience, having written the script yourself. Write down those experiences and burn them up as garbage. ¶Step three is the "people check"—to write about each person who had an influence in your life, including family, friends, neighbors, teachers, co-workers and casual acquaintances. Write about your interaction with them, happy times, misunderstandings, upsets and apologies. Ask for forgiveness, forgive and give best wishes for a long life and positive future. Call each face before you and write a letter expressing appreciation, dismay, hatred, anguish, misunderstanding. Get it all out. Don't hold anything back. No one will read it. It is a letter you do not mail, e-mail or leave lying around. Just burn it as garbage. The effect of the "people check" is to harmonize the *prāṇas* that flow from one to another. We are all connected, for we are a one human race. Those we know and whose faces and names we can remember are the closest, whether they be friends or enemies. Sometimes enemies are closer, because they are thought about more than friends. During the "people check," bring up the love, the forgiveness, the acceptance that whatever happened in the relationship was part of the birth *karmas*, the *prārabdha karmas*, of each of you. Once the letter or series of letters has been written, the memories fade into the silent, colorless past. Then you should truly be able to bring up each face in your mind and mentally say the six magic words, the magic *mantra*, "I love you. You love me."

Sunday
LESSON 126
Three More Steps to Clarity

Step four is "sex check"—to go over any past sexual experiences, including visual images such as pornography in adult movies, on the Internet, television or in magazines, dreams and fantasies. This is quite an obsession for some people, often called an addiction. Also be sure to write about youthful experimentation and, yes, masturbation and the thoughts before, during and afterwards. Include sexual repressions, regrets that you have had throughout your life up to the present day, especially any that are currently bothering you, then write them down and burn the emotion out of the memories as the garbage of the mind. This area is very important, as repeated experiences that have produced guilt or ended in sadness, and those that no one knows about but you and your partner—and happy, satisfying, longing-to-be-repeated experiences—do leave colorful memories. Some are brightly colored and sing happy songs in the memory patterns, while others are bathed in darkness and resound with dull tones. Both need to be reduced to black-and-white pictures. The modern notion of "Let's put this behind us and go on with life" is held hostage here as color/sounds pile up in the inner aura and inhibit creativity, productivity, energy flows and even health. The "sex check" should be written in many pages of explicit detail, including letters to the partner or partners, which are not saved or mailed, of course, but immediately burned. Be open and honest with yourself; you may be writing the best porno novel of all times. Include on your last page of "sex check" some new resolves for the future in regard to sexual matters. ¶Step five, the "teacher check," is to write about your relationship with your *satguru*, teachers, mentors or advisors, including your first meetings, initiations, encounters, instructions and any misunderstandings, large or small. Again, letters may be written, descriptions in detail, about whatever need be said. Of course, the person's face and name should always be present in your mind when writing, as if a conversation were being held. Appreciation can be shown that was never shown, misunderstandings settled and hurts on both sides healed. As you complete each writing session, burn the pages as garbage. ¶The sixth stage is the "penance check." Penance, *prāyaśchitta,* is of three kinds: mental, emotional and physical. In completing parts one through five of this *tantra,* you have completed the mental and emotional *prāyaśchitta.* Now we must deal with the physical in a different way. There will be a few emotional memories that writing will never cause to go away, such as not paying full taxes several years ago, stealing something, killing birds or animals for sport, or beating children, wives or husbands. These and other transgressions require resolution through actually physically doing something to mitigate these *karmas* made in this life. You can not write them away. Should there be in your life any of these kinds of experiences that require a physical *prāyaśchitta,* tell your spiritual teacher about them, and if ordained to do so, he or she will give you a penance to perform to put to rest those specific *karmas.* If I, or a *satguru* successor of my lineage, happen to be your *satguru,* write a letter of rededication and mail or e-mail it to prayas@hindu.org before beginning this sixth and final stage of the *mahā vāsanā daha tantra.* ¶After these six steps of the *mahā vāsanā daha tantra* have been completed, rejoice. Now you are ready to begin the serious practice of traditional meditation, as you dance with Śiva, live with Śiva and merge with Śiva. ¶The *mahā vāsanā daha tantra* is a once-in-a-lifetime experience. Thereafter, you continue your subconscious spiritual journaling, *vāsanā daha tantra,* when needed to maintain the clarity and inner freedom that you have achieved. I encourage everyone to write at least ten pages at the end of every year about the just-completed year in the same way, ten pages for the year, followed by the other steps, including the sixth one. This annual journaling is called the *vatsarika vāsanā daha tantra.* ¶Those who have performed and continue to perform this lifetime, yearly and when-needed *sādhana* have testified to remarkable transformations. They find that they are free of burdens, clear of mind, joyously alive in the eternal now, eager to serve and able to enjoy sublime, penetrating meditations. Unlike before, their past is now small and their future, once limited, looms large and inviting. They enjoy new-found harmony with family and friends. They find it easy and natural to fulfill the Hindu restraints and observances, the *yamas* and *niyamas*. Why? They are not burdened by *vāsanās* created by past experiences that have not been understood, resolved and released. ¶Of course, at the time of death it is the memories of all the emotional happenings that pop up before one's inner vision, and which have the power to bring you back in a future birth to be faced. Those that have been resolved and released in understanding are no longer strong in the mind. So, you are effecting a near-death experience, in a sense, upon yourself by doing this *tantra*, because you are putting to rest the memories of the past that you might not otherwise face until you actually die. This doesn't mean that you forget your past. It just isn't bothersome to you anymore. It seems almost as though it all happened to someone else.

When the soul gradually reduces and then stops altogether its participation in darkness and inauspicious powers, the Friend of the World, God, reveals to the soul the limitless character of its knowledge and activity. *Mṛigendra Āgama, Jñāna Pāda* 5.A1. MA, P. 138

O God, grant us of boons the best: a mind to think and a smiling love, increase of wealth, a healthy body, speech that is winsome and days that are fair. *Ṛig Veda* 2.21.6. VE, P. 191

O self-luminous Divine, remove the veil of ignorance from before me, that I may behold your light. Reveal to me the spirit of the scriptures. May the truth of the scriptures be ever present to me. May I seek day and night to realize what I learn from the sages.
Rig Veda, Aitareya Upanishad, Invocation. UPR, P. 95

O earthen vessel, strengthen me. May all beings regard me with friendly eyes! May I look upon all creatures with friendly eyes! With a friend's eye may we regard each other! *Śukla Yajur Veda* 36.18. VE, P. 342

There are five great sacrifices, namely, the great ritual services: the sacrifice to all beings, sacrifice to men, sacrifice to the ancestors, sacrifice to the Gods, sacrifice to Brahman.
Śukla Yajur Veda, Śatapatha Brāhmaṇa 11.5.6.1. VE, P. 394

The world of Brahman belongs only to those who find it by the practice of chastity and the study of Brahman. For them there is freedom in all the worlds. Sāma Veda, Çhāndogya Upanishad 8.4.3. VE, P. 638

What people call salvation is really continence, for through continence man is freed from ignorance. And what is known as the vow of silence, that too is really continence. For a man through continence realizes the Self and lives in quiet contemplation.
Sāma Veda, Çhāndogya Upanishad 8.5.1. UPP, P. 123

Maintaining the austerity of silence, facing east or north, having full control over the system of inhalation and exhalation and the air of *prāṇa*, he should recite the Pañchākshara hymn and meditate.
Chandrajñāna Āgama, Kriyāpāda 8.54-55 CJ, P. 80

O Agni, since we are kindling the fire of the Spirit through *tapas*, may we be dear to the *Veda*, long-lived and bright in intellect.

Atharva Veda 7.61.1. BO HV, P. 71

Like butter hidden in milk, true knowledge dwells in all that lives; ever with mind as the churning rod, everyone should churn it out in himself. Using the whirling rope of knowledge, one should obtain, like fire by friction, that partless, stainless silence; "I am Brahman," as it's said.

Atharva Veda, Brāhmabindu Upanishad 20–21. UPB, P. 690

Say not, "This poor man's hunger is a heaven-sent doom." To the well-fed, too, comes death in many forms. Yet the wealth of the generous giver never dwindles, while he who refuses to give will evoke no pity.

Ṛig Veda 10.117. 1. VE, P. 850

In vain the foolish man accumulates food. I tell you, truly, it will be his downfall! He gathers to himself neither friend nor comrade. Alone he eats; alone he sits in sin. The ploughshare cleaving the soil helps satisfy hunger. The traveler, using his legs, achieves his goal. The priest who speaks surpasses the one who is silent. The friend who gives is better than the miser. *Ṛig Veda* 10.117. 6–7. VE, P. 851

Against fear, against anger, against sloth, against too much waking, too much sleeping, against too much eating, not eating, a *yogin* shall always be on his guard. *Atharva Veda, Amṛitabindu Upanishad* 27. UPB, P. 696

Lightness, healthiness, steadiness, clearness of complexion, pleasantness of voice, sweetness of odor, and slight excretions—these, they say, are the first results of the progress of *yoga*.

Kṛishṇa Yajur Veda, Śvetāsvatara Upanishad 2.13. UPR, P. 723

The word Nāmaḥ should be put first, then the word Śivāya. This is called the knowledge of Pañchākshara, the greatest among the hymns of the scriptures. In short, the wisdom of Pañchākshara is the matrix of all *śabda* (word). This wisdom, which emanated from the mouth of Śiva, expresses the very nature of Śiva Himself.

Chandrajñāna Āgama, Kriyāpāda 8. 5-6 CJ, P. 72-73

Dhārmika Jīvanam

धार्मिक जीवनम्

PART TWO

Living Dharmically

Yaḥ Karaḥ Dolāṁ Chālayati, Saḥ Eva Jagat Pālayati

यः करः दोलां चालयति । सः एव जगत् पालयति

The Hand that Rocks the Cradle Rules the World

May there be the woman at home with husband and children. May there be born to the worshiper heroic youths with the will to victory, the best of chariot-fighters, fit to shine in assemblies.

Yajur Veda 22.22. HV, P. 161

Monday
LESSON 127
Women's Liberation

Anbe Sivamayam Satyame Parasivam! "God Śiva is Immanent Love and Transcendent Reality!" This morning we are going to talk about a vast subject, one that is important to every Hindu family: *strī dharma,* the *dharma* of the Hindu wife and mother. In Sanskrit *strī* means "woman." *Dharma* is a rich word which encompasses many meanings: the path to God Śiva, piety, goodness, duty, obligation and more. *Strī dharma* is the woman's natural path, while *purusha dharma,* we can say, is the man's. ¶There is much controversy about the role of the woman in society these days. In the West, a strong women's liberation movement has been at work for many years, and now there has arisen an equally vigorous opposition which defends traditional values. The struggle for women's liberation has affected women the world over—in India, Iran, Europe, Japan and elsewhere. In North America, I began a campaign informally called the Hindu Women's Liberation Movement. It is not what you might expect. Its purpose is to liberate our Hindu women from the liberators, to save them from worldliness and to allow them to fulfill their natural *dharma* as mother and wife. ¶For a religious woman, being liberated starts with resigning from her job and coming home. Once she is home, she is liberated and liberated and liberated. Working in the world keeps her in the outer dimensions of consciousness, while being at home allows her to live in the depth of her being. I have seen this work many times. There are so many distractions and influences in the world today that divert women away from being a wife and mother. In the West a woman is a wife first and a mother second, but in the East her traditional duties as a mother are foremost. She is trained from early childhood in the arts of homemaking, trained by her mother who was trained in exactly the same way by her mother, and so on right down through history. It's an old pattern. ¶The Hindu woman is looked upon as most precious. Two thousand years ago Saint Tiruvalluvar observed: "What does a man lack if his wife is worthy? And what does he possess if she is lacking worth?" (*Tirukural* 53) There is more respect in the East for women and for their role in society. Here in the West, the woman is not fully appreciated. Her contribution is underrated and misunderstood. In fact, this is one of the reasons she seeks fulfillment and recognition in other spheres,

---

An infant rests safely in an Indian-style wooden cradle, swinging on ropes suspended from above. His mother's hand rocks him to sleep. Loving maternal hands around the world, in every culture, quietly mold the future of the human race.

because Western society has become oblivious of her unique and vital role. Abused by neglect and disregard, she seeks other avenues where she may be appreciated, recognized and rewarded.

Tuesday
LESSON 128
Masculine And Feminine

Don't forget that in the East the ties of the extended family are traditionally very close. Women live in a community, surrounded by younger and older women, often living in the same house. They enjoy a rewarding life which includes helping the younger ones and being helped by those who are more mature. Several generations work together in sharing the joys as well as the burdens of household culture. It is different in the West. Women here usually do not have the advantages of close association with other family members. Naturally, they become a little lonely, especially if they do not have a religious community of friends. They get lonely and want to get out in the world and enjoy life a little. This is another reason women leave the home. It is very unfortunate. ¶In the East there is a better balance of the masculine and feminine forces. In the West the masculine is too strong, too dominant. The feminine energies need to be allowed greater expression. But that does not mean women should start doing what men do. No. That only confuses the forces more. A better balance must be found. In Asia the woman is protected. She is like a precious gem. You don't leave it unattended. You protect it, you guard it well because you don't wish to lose it. Hindu women are guarded well. They are not allowed to become worldly. They are not exposed to the looks and thoughts of a base public, nor must they surrender their modesty to contend in the tough world of business affairs. She can be perfectly feminine, expressing her natural qualities of gentleness, intuitiveness, love and modesty. The home and family are the entire focus of a Hindu woman's life. ¶Many of you here this morning are too young to know that this was also the prevalent pattern in America up to World War II, which started in 1939. Before World War II, Western women were very much reserved in public appearances and were nearly always chaperoned. It was that war that broke down the ancient roles of men and women. The men were taken away from industry by the army, and women were forced out of the home into the factories and businesses so that production could continue. Earlier they had been protected, seldom seen unaccompanied in public. Throughout history, women had been the caretakers of the home and the defenders of virtue. They valued their purity, their chastity, and were virgins when they married. Many people don't know that the old values were upheld quite strictly until 1940 or so. Then the Second World War broke up the family and disturbed the balance between men and women. For the first time, women were seen alone in public. For the first time, they left the home and competed with men for their jobs.

Wednesday
LESSON 129
Society in Transition

I speak often of the change humanity is going through in moving out of the agricultural era and into the technological age. This change has affected the *dharma* of the woman and the *dharma* of the man in an interesting way. During the tens of thousands of years of the agricultural age, families lived and labored mostly on farms or in craft guilds. The entire family worked on the farm. The men all worked in the fields; the women and children mostly worked in the home. Children were a great asset. More children meant more help, a bigger farm, more wealth. There were many chores that a young boy or girl could do. When harvest time came, everyone joined in. It was a one team, and everyone contributed. When the crop was sold, that was the income for a combined effort from all members—men, women and even children. In a very real sense, everyone was earning the money, everyone was economically important. ¶With the onset of the technological era, only the man of the house earns the family income. Everyone else spends it. The husband goes to work in a factory or large company office while his wife and children stay at home. There is not much they can do to help him during the day with his work. His work and his wife's are not as closely related as in the old days. He is the provider, the producer now; she and the children are consumers. Because the children cannot help much, they have become more of an economic liability than an asset. This, coupled with the population problems on the Earth, devalues the economic importance of the woman's traditional role as wife and mother. Whereas raising children and taking care of the farmhouse used to be a woman's direct and vital contribution toward the family's livelihood and even the survival of the human race, today it is not. Whereas they used to be partners in a family farm business, today he does all the earning and she feels like a dependent. The answer is not to have women join their men in the factories and corporations. The answer is to bring traditional religious values into the technological era, to find a new balance of *karma* that allows for the fulfillment of both the man's and the woman's *dharma*. ¶When young couples marry, I help them write down their vows to one another. He must promise to support her, to protect her, to give her a full and rewarding life. She must promise to care for him, to manage the home, to maintain the home shrine and to raise fine children. I ask them each to respect the other's realm, to never mentally criticize the other and to make religion the central focus of their life together. I ask the young bride to stay at home, to be a little shy of involvement in the world. I instruct the young husband to provide for her, throughout her life, all that she needs and all that she wants.

Thursday
LESSON 130
Working in The World

A mother's place is within the home and not out in the world working. When she is in the home all day, she brings love and security to the children, sensitivity and stability to the husband. By raising her children, she changes the course of history. How does she do that? She raises strong children, good and intelligent children. They will grow up to be the great men and women in the community, the leaders of the nation. They will be the worthy farmers, artists, businessmen, the teachers, the doctors, the lawyers, the architects, the presidents and, most importantly, the spiritual leaders. They will be the good mothers, the homemakers and child-raisers, scientists and inventors, pioneers and poets, artists and sculptors and creators in all dimensions of life. It is such men and women who change the course of human history. This is the great power held by the mother and by no one else: to properly mold the mind and character of her children. And she trains her daughters to do the same by example and gentle guidance. ¶Of course, she also holds the opposite power, expressed through neglect, to allow her children to grow up on their own, on the streets where they will learn a base life. Such children will as surely change society and human history, but negatively. They will be the common men and women, or fall into mental and emotional abysses, there to express the instinctive nature and become the exemplars of violence and lust, of dependence and crime. The very direction of mankind is right there in the early years, to be turned toward a great potential through love and attentiveness or allowed to decay through neglect. The mother is the child's first *guru,* and she alone can shape the mind in those impressionable years. So, you can all see the truth in the old saying: "The hand that rocks the cradle rules the world." ¶Take the case of a mother who is at home every day, morning and night, attending to her children. As she rocks the cradle, her love and energy radiate out to the infant, who then feels a natural peacefulness and security. She has time for the child, time to sing sweet lullabies and console when the tears come, time to teach about people, about the world, about the little things in growing up, time to cuddle for no reason except to express her love. On the other hand, the working mother has no time to do extra things. When the infant cries, she may, out of her own frustrations of the day, become impatient and scold him, demanding that he keep quiet. "I told you to be quiet!" she shouts. The infant doesn't even understand the language yet. You can imagine this helpless child's feelings as he receives an emotional blast of anger and frustration directed toward his gentle form. Where is he to turn? He cannot find refuge even in his mother's arms. ¶What will the next generation be like if all the children are raised under such circumstances? Will it be strong and self-assured? Will it radiate kindness to others, never having had kindness given to it? Will it be patient and understanding? No. It is a proven fact that most prison inmates were seriously neglected or beaten as children. It is also a proven fact that nearly all parents who mistreat their children were themselves mistreated by their parents. Unless mothers care for and love their children, society will inherit an entire generation of frustrated adults who were once frustrated children. These will later be the people who rule the world. Then what happens? They in turn raise their children in the same manner, for that is the only example of parenthood they have. They will think that neglect is natural, that children can get along on their own from an early age or be raised by a governess or nurse or at a day-care center. It's a circle: a childhood of neglect produces a bitter adult life; a childhood of love and trust produces a loving and happy adult life.

Friday
LESSON 131
The Psychic Force Field

We learn so many important things from the mother. This learning is not just from the things she explains to us, but from the way she lives her life. If she is patient, we learn patience. If she is angry and unhappy, then we learn to be angry and unhappy. How wonderful it is for a mother to be in the home and give her children the great gifts of life by her example. She can teach them so many things, bring them into profound understandings about the world around them and offer them basic values and points of view that will sustain them throughout their life. Her gift of love is directly to the child, but indirectly it is a gift to all of humanity, isn't it? A child does not learn much from the father until he is older, perhaps eight or nine, or ten years of age. ¶We have a book in our library which describes a plan made by the Christians to destroy Hinduism in Sri Lanka and India. One of their major tactics is to get the Hindu women out of their homes and working in the world. They knew that the spiritual force within the home is created by the unworldly woman. They knew that a secure woman makes for a secure home and family, a secure husband and a secure religion. They knew that the Hindu woman is the key to the perpetuation of Hinduism, as long as she is in the home. If the woman is in the home, if she is happy and content and the children are nurtured and raised properly, then the astral beings around the home will be *devonic*, friendly and beneficial. But if she is out of the home and the husband is out of the home, the protective force-field around the home disintegrates, allowing all kinds of astral *asuric* beings to enter. Such a neglected home becomes inhabited by base, *asuric* beings on the lower astral plane. You cannot see these beings, but they are there, and you can sense their presence. Things just don't feel right in a home inhabited by negative forces. You have the desire to leave such a home as soon as you enter it. The children absorb these vibrations, these feelings. Children are open and psychically sensitive to such influences, with little means of self-protection. They will become disturbed, and no one will know the reason why. They will be crying and even screaming. They will be constantly disobedient. Why should they become disobedient? Because there is no positive, protective force field of religion established and upheld by the mother. This leaves the inner force field vulnerable to negative and confusing forces of all kinds, especially in modern, overpopulated cities where destructive psychic influences are so strong. These negative vibrations are penetrating the inner atmosphere of the home, and the children are psychic enough to pick them up and suffer.

Saturday
LESSON 132
People Caring For People

Religion begins in the home under the mother's influence and instruction. The mother goes to the temple to get strong. That is the reason Hindus live near a temple. They go to the temple to draw strength from the *śakti* of the Deity, and they return to the home where they maintain a similar vibration in which to raise the next generation to be staunch and wonderfully productive citizens of the world, to bring peace on Earth, to keep peace on Earth. There is an ancient South Indian proverb which says one should not live in a city which has no temple. ¶If a child is screaming in its cradle, and the babysitter is yelling at him and couldn't care less about his feelings, and the mother is out working, that child is not a candidate for keeping peace on Earth. That child is going to keep things confused, as they are today. So, it's all in the hands of the mother; it's not in the hands of the father. Religion and the future of society lie solely in the hands of the mother. It is in the hands of the father to allow or not to allow the mother to be under another man's mind out in the world. ¶Just as World War II took women out of the home, so did another change affect mankind. When the automobile came along, people forgot about breeding, because it replaced the horse, which they cared for and learned to mate with other horses to strengthen the genetics. The automobile did one terrible thing: it made people forget how to breed and how to take care of one another. When people kept horses, horses were a part of the family. People had to care for their horses, and in the process learned to care for one another. People also had to breed their horses, and in that process learned about the value of intelligent breeding. In those days you often heard of the "well-bred" person. You don't hear of the well-bred person anymore. Although among biologists there is much talk about heredity, ordinary people no longer consider that humans, too, are involved in the natural process of breeding. They have become forgetful of these important laws, and this has led to lack of forethought and discipline, to bodies indiscriminately procreating more bodies. Who is living in them nobody quite knows, and too many simply don't care. That's what we as a society forgot when the automobile replaced the horse. When you had a horse, you had to feed and water it. You had to train it, you had to harness it, curry it, stable it and breed it. In breeding, you had to choose a stud for your mare or find a suitable mare for your stallion. The qualities of both the sire and the dam were closely observed, and the resultant combination of genetics was consciously planned. It was therefore natural for people in those days to seek proper mates for their children, and the results were the vital, creative and industrious children of the children. As a civilization, we are slowly forgetting such basic things, being more and more careless about our children's future, about their lives and their mates.

Sunday
LESSON 133
The Impact Of Television

Television has not helped society to raise its children. In fact, it has virtually stopped the proper education of the child in those communities where it is watched for hours each day. Instead of developing an active curiosity by adventuring for hours through a forest or climbing a tree, instead of discovering the wonders of nature and art, music, literature and conversation, instead of becoming involved in sports and hobbies, children are mentally carried along by television stories through positive and negative states of mind. They become uncreative, passive, inactive, never learning to use their own minds. Admittedly, not all television is negative. Some of it can be quite educational; but hours and hours each day of passive absorption is not good for a child's mental and emotional development. Children need to be active, to involve themselves in a wide variety of experiences. ¶If the mother is there, she can intelligently guide their television, being careful that they do not get in the habit of watching it for hours on end, and watching that bold sex, casual and brute violence, raw language and other bad influences are not a daily experience. When the program is over, she can send them out to play. Or, better still, she can take a few minutes to explain how what they just saw on TV relates, or often does not relate, to real life. Of course, if she is gone, they will watch anything and everything. For the young, television is one of the most senseless pastimes there is, carrying the mind further and further away from the true Self. ¶I think you will all agree that our values, the values found in the holy *Vedas, Tirukural* and other sacred scriptures, are rarely found on television. Instead, TV, at this time in our history, gives our children a brutal, romantic and unbalanced view of life which distorts in their minds how life really is. These are very serious issues. It is the mother who protects her children from negative influences, guiding their young minds into positive channels of expression. ¶Take the case of a farmer who raises livestock, who milks cows and goats. He works hard. He gets up early and takes care of his animals. He cannot succeed if he is also working part-time in the grocery store downtown. Those animals need attention. There is no sensible man who would run a farm, with cows and goats and chickens, and not be there to take care of them, because those animals need a lot of help. He stays there and takes care of his business. He is a farmer and that is his duty, and he knows it. ¶Well, what's more important than the child? He needs twenty-four-hour-a-day care. He is learning to walk, to speak, to learn, to think. He falls down and needs consoling. He catches the flu and needs to be nursed back to health. It is the mother's duty to provide that care. No one else is going to do it for her. No one else can do it for her. She brought that soul into a physical body, and she must prepare that child for a positive and rewarding life. ¶If the farmer neglects his animals, he creates a serious *karma.* The animals suffer. The farm suffers. The community suffers when the farm fails, and the man himself suffers. There is a grave *karma,* too, for the woman who neglects her *strī dharma,* who goes out into the world and does not nurture the physical, emotional, intellectual and spiritual needs of her children. She knows this within herself, but she may be influenced by ill-advised people, or by a mass movement that tells her that she has only one life to live and that she cannot find fulfillment in the home, but must express herself, venture out, seek her own path, her own fortune. You have all heard these ideas. I tell you that they are wrong. They spell the disillusionment of the mother who heeds them, then the disintegration of the family that is sacrificed by her absence. Finally, they result in her own unhappiness as she despairs at the loss suffered by her family and herself.

Strī Śakti, Strī Dhāma
स्त्रीशक्ति स्त्रीधाम

Her Power, Her Domain

Be a queen to thy father-in-law, a queen to thy mother-in-law, a queen to thy husband's sisters, and a queen to thy husband's brothers.

Ṛig Veda 10.85.46. HV, P. 139

Monday
LESSON 134
Sanctity of The Home

From the point of view of the Second World, or astral plane, the home is the family temple, and the wife and mother is in charge of that spiritual environment. The husband can come into that sanctum sanctorum but should not bring the world into it. He will naturally find a refuge in the home if she is doing her duty. He will be able to regain his peace of mind there, renew himself for the next day in the stressful situations that the outside world is full of. In this technological age a man needs this refuge. He needs that inner balance in his life. When he comes home, she greets him at the entrance and performs a rite of purification and welcome, offering *āratī* to cleanse his aura. This and other customs protect the sanctity of the home. When he enters that sanctuary and she is in her soul body and the child is in its soul body, then he becomes consciously conscious in his soul body, called *ānandamaya kośa* in Sanskrit. He leaves the conscious mind, which is a limited, external state of mind and not a balanced state of mind. He enters the intuitive mind. He gets immediate and intuitive answers to his worldly problems. ¶How can he not be successful in his *purusha dharma* in the outside world when he has the backing of a good wife? She is naturally perceptive, naturally intuitive. She balances out his intellect, softens the impact of the forces which dash against his nervous system from morning to night. Encouragement and love naturally radiate out from her as she fulfills her *strī dharma.* Without these balancing elements in his life, a man becomes too externalized, too instinctive. ¶If a woman is working, she cannot provide this balance. She has to start thinking and acting like a man. She has to become a little tougher, create a protective shell around her emotions. Then the home loses its balance of the masculine and the feminine forces. Take for example the situation in which the wife rushes home from work fifteen minutes before the husband. She's upset after an especially hard day at work. The children come over from Grandmother's house or she tells the babysitter to go home. She scurries to prepare something for dinner before he comes home, then rushes to get herself looking halfway decent. Emotionally upset, she tries to calm herself, tries to relax and regain her composure. Her astral body is upset. The children's astral bodies are upset. The husband enters this agitated environment—already upset by

---

A mother sings a traditional lullaby as her child plays with a small Earth, signifying the global impact all mothers of the world have by passing along religious culture and values to their children. She is raising him near the Nallur Murugan Temple in Jaffna, Sri Lanka.

being in the world—and he becomes more disturbed. He was looking forward to a quiet evening. But is he going to get it? No. He begins to feel neglected, disappointed, and that leads him to become distraught, to say angry words that make everything even worse. The *prāṇic* forces are spinning out of control. It seems like a totally impossible situation for both of them. Furthermore, it's not going to get better, but exceedingly worse, as the days wear on.

Tuesday
LESSON 135
The Wife's Special Power

The situation I have just described is one of the main reasons that marriages today have become less stable, that so many married couples—sixty to seventy percent, I'm told—are experiencing difficulties and breaking up. But couples never get married with the intent of breaking up. Never. The *praṇic* forces do it. You put two magnets together one way and they attract one another. Turn one around, and they repel each other. The same force that brought the people together, when it is not handled right, makes them pull apart and hate each other. They can't see eye to eye. Then to make up, they go out to dinner to talk it over—in another frustrating, *asuric* situation, as far out in the world as they can get—to try to make up. When that doesn't help, they come home still frustrated. If they went to the nearby temple and worshiped the family Deity together, that would help. They would return home in a different state of mind and discover that their vibration had changed. Why does it help to go to the temple? Because the God is in the temple, the Deity is there to adjust the forces of the inner nerve system, to actually change the forces of mind and emotion. ¶In the home, the mother is likened to the Śakti Deity. She is the power, the very soul of the home. None other. So she has to be there. She has to be treated sensitively and kindly, and with respect. She has to be given all the things she needs and everything she wants so she will release her *śakti* power to support her husband, so that he is successful in all his manly endeavors. When she is hurt, depressed, frustrated or disappointed, she automatically withdraws that power, compromising his success in the outside world along with it. People will draw away from him. His job, business or creative abilities will suffer. This is her great *siddhi,* her inborn power, which Hindu women know so well. ¶It is the man's duty, his *purusha dharma,* to provide for her and for the children. The husband should provide her with all the fine things, with a good house which she then makes into a home, with adornments, gold and jewels and clothes, gold hanging down until her ears hurt, more bracelets, more things to keep her in the home so she is feeling secure and happy. In return she provides a refuge, a serene corner of the world where he can escape from the pressures of daily life, where he can regain his inner perspective, perform his religious *sādhana* and meditations, then enjoy his family. Thus, she brings happiness and peace of mind to her family, to the community and to the world.

Wednesday
LESSON 136
The Home As a Temple

This working together of the home and the temple brings up the culture and the religion within the family. The family goes to the temple; the temple blesses the family's next project. The mother returns home. She keeps an oil lamp burning in the shrine room on the altar to bring the *śakti* power of the God and *devas* into their home. This is only one of the beautiful practices of her religious *strī dharma,* so sensitive and so vital to the furtherance of the family and its faith. All this happens because her astral body is not fretted by the stresses and strains of a worldly life, not polluted by the lustful thoughts of other men directed toward her, causing her to live in the emotional astral body to ward them off, or be tempted by them. She is not living in the emotional astral body. She is living in her peaceful soul body of love, fulfilling her *dharma* and radiating the soulful presence called *sannidhyā.* She was born to be a woman, and that's how a woman should behave. ¶If she does not do her *dharmic* duty—this means the duty of birth—then she accrues bad *karma.* Every time she leaves the home to go out to work, she is making *kukarma.* Yes, she is. That negative *karma* will have its affect on her astral body and on her husband's astral body and on the astral bodies of their children, causing them to become insecure. ¶The Judaic-Christian-Islamic idea of just one life, after which you either go to heaven or to hell gives the impression that time is running out. Some even think "you have to get everything out of this life, because when you're gone, you're gone, so grab all the gusto that you can." This has given the modern Western woman the idea that she is not getting everything she should, and therefore the man's world looks doubly attractive, because she is just passing through and will never come back. So, living a man's life is very, very attractive. She doesn't want to stay home all the time and not see anything, not meet anybody, go through the boredom of raising a family, taking care of the children. She wants to be out with life, functioning in a man's world, because she is told that she is missing something. Therefore, you can understand her desire to get out and work, start seeing and experiencing life and mixing with people, meeting new people. ¶The traditional Hindu woman, however, does not look at life like that. She knows that she was born this time in a woman's body—this soul has taken an incarnation for a time in a woman's body—to perform a *dharma,* to perform a duty, for the evolution of the soul. The duty is to be a mother to her children, wife to her husband, to strengthen the home and the family, which are the linchpin of society. She knows that the rewards are greater for her in the home. She knows that all she is missing is a man's strenuous work and responsibility, that her *strī dharma* is equally as great as a man's *purusha dharma,* even though they are quite different by nature. Because she knows these things, she fulfills her *dharma* joyously.

Thursday
LESSON 137
Mother in The Home

Now, a woman may wonder, "If I don't work, how are we going to pay the bills?" The stated reason that most women work is economic. The economy of the world is becoming more and more difficult, and the first answer to money problems, especially in the West, where the family unit is not too strong these days, is to have the wife go to work. This is an unhappy solution. Much too often the sacrifices are greater than the rewards. It is a false economy. Many times I have told young wives to stay home with their children. They worry. Their husbands worry. But with the wife at home, working to strengthen her husband, he soon becomes confident, creative, energetic and that makes him prosperous. He is reinspired and always finds a way to make ends meet. ¶As long as the mother is home, everything is fine. There is security. Without this security, a family begins to disintegrate. Just think how insecure a child is without its mother. When the mother is there, security reigns in the home. As long as the mother is home, doing whatever she naturally does as a mother—she doesn't even have to read a book about how to do it—the husband has to support the home; he feels bound to support the home. Of course, religion must be the basis of the home to make it all work. When women leave the home to work in the world, they sacrifice the depth of their religion. Their religious life then simply becomes a social affair. This is true of both Eastern and Western religions. As long as the mother is home, the celestial *devas* are there, hovering in and around the home. ¶How many of you here this morning were raised with your mother staying at home? Well, then you know what I mean. Now, what if she wasn't at home when you were a child? You had to fix your own snack in an empty house. You didn't feel much cared for. You were alone in an empty house, perhaps frightened, and you went around seeing if someone was hiding in the closet. You didn't feel that motherly, protective feeling. ¶When mother finally does come home, she has other things on her mind. She is tired. She has worked hard, and now she has to work even more. She is not thinking about the helpless kid who can't take care of himself. She may get home and think to herself, "I just can't forget about that good-looking man I met at the office. I even see him in my dreams. I have a husband and I shouldn't be thinking about such things, but…" And on and on and on. Arguments begin to happen for the first time in the home. What do you do? You worry for awhile. You cry a little. As soon as you can, you start fending for yourself. You work out ways to take care of yourself, or even to get away from the unhappy situation as soon as you can. You end up out on your own in the world at a young age, before you are mature enough to cope with it.

Friday
LESSON 138
A Feminine Incarnation

The Hindu woman knows that she is born in a woman's body to fulfill a woman's *dharma,* to perform her duty and not to emulate the men. The duty is to be a mother to her children and a wife to her husband, whom she looks to as her lord. She performs that duty willingly, as does the man perform his duty which arises out of being born in a man's body. The Hindu woman is trained to perform her *strī dharma* from the time she is a little girl. She finds ways to express her natural creativity within the home itself. She may write poetry or become an artist. Perhaps she has a special talent for sewing or embroidery or gardening or music. She can learn to loom cloth and make the family's clothing. If needed, she can use her skills to supplement the family income without leaving the home. There are so many ways for a Hindu wife and mother to fully use her creative energies, including being creative enough to never let her life become boring. It is her special blessing that she is free to pursue her religion fully, to study the scriptures, to sing *bhajana* and keep her own spiritual life strong inside. ¶Then there is the situation in which the wife is working for her husband in the home. This is not ideal, but it is far better than having her out away from her husband, under another man's mind. At least the family is working together toward a single goal, and the mother is there to care for the child and answer questions. Of course, if working in the home does not allow for closeness of mother and children, then it is to be avoided—if, for instance, the work is so demanding that the mother is never free to play with the young ones or is so pressured by her other duties that she becomes tense and upset. Otherwise, it is a positive situation. From the child's point of view, mother is home. She is there to answer questions, to make a *dosai* or say, "Go make yourself a nice *dosai* and I will help you." She is there with a kiss and a band aid for a scratch. She is there to explain why the grass is green, to tell a story, to teach a simple lesson in why things are the way they are. Mother is home, and that is very important for a young child. Yes, her *prāṇa* in the house makes the house a home. ¶We are nowadays witnessing a big wave of change rushing to the shores of Hinduism in Colombo, Chennai, Mumbai, New Delhi, Kuala Lumpur, New York, Durban and London. I have seen it coming. Hindu women no longer feel they have to adhere to the old traditions. They are changing traditions. They adopt new ways these days. Now a Hindu woman can go out and work, especially if she lives in the city, and she is encouraged by family and friends to do so. She can neglect her family, and that is deemed all right, too. She doesn't have to fulfill her *strī dharma*. Staying home is old-fashioned, they say. I have been told that eighty percent of all Hindu women living in the West work in the world. Eighty percent! Apparently those who have worked for the demise of Hinduism have done their work quite well. Still, I am not worried. I know the nature of waves, and this one will ebb as soon as it reaches the height of its power, replaced by the greater power of returning to tradition.

Saturday
LESSON 139
Why Respect Tradition?

Let's look at the word *tradition*. Webster defines *tradition* as "a story, belief, custom or proverb handed down from generation to generation, a long-established custom or practice that has the effect of an unwritten law." We all know human nature, because we are people living on this planet. We are fickle; we are changeable. We are always curious to try new things. Change is a wonderful part of life, within certain bounds. We do not want to be too restrictive, yet we do want to be strict. Be strict without being restrictive, and life will be balanced between discipline and freedom. This has always been the Asian way. Take a look back into history, back to the time of Saint Tiruvalluvar, who lived 2,200 years ago. He would not have written the *Tirukural* if people were perfect, if they were, as a whole, strong, steady and self-disciplined. He wrote those sparkling gems of wisdom and advice for fickle, changeable people, so that they could keep their minds controlled and their lives in line with the basic principles of *dharma* for men and women clearly set forth in the *Vedas* six to eight thousand years ago. ¶Tradition adapts itself to culture and climate. The Hindu women raised in Western countries will not be able to follow all the traditions of the East. But they have to fulfill enough of those traditions to fulfill their *strī dharma.* And, of course, they will have to adjust slowly. ¶Scriptural advice is just as pertinent today, thousands of years later. Why? Because people are human, because they are little different today than they were then. Societies change, knowledge changes, language changes. But people do not change all that much. That is exactly the reason that traditions do not change much or change very slowly. They still apply. They are still valid. They are the wisdom of hundreds of generations assembled together. The wise always follow the ways of wisdom, always follow tradition. Does that mean they cannot be inventive? No. Does that mean they cannot use their mind and will to advance themselves and humanity? No. Does that mean they must avoid being creative, original, individualistic? No. It simply means that they express these fine qualities within the context of religious tradition, thus enhancing tradition instead of destroying it. Tradition, with its spoken and unspoken ways, is far too precious to throw out or tear down. The unwritten laws and customs of tradition are what has developed and proved out to be best for the peoples on this planet for centuries. We cannot casually change tradition. It takes centuries to build a tradition. We cannot sit at a meeting and arbitrate a change like that. ¶Take all of this that has been said into your meditations. Think deeply about the natural balance of masculine and feminine energies in the world and within yourselves. You will discover a new appreciation for the woman's role and for the traditions which allow her to fulfill it.

Sunday
LESSON 140
A Personal Testimony

By way of illustration I will ask you now to read a fine message we received from a Śaivite lady in Sri Lanka who follows beautifully the spirit of *strī dharma.* ¶"I am a Hindu wife and take pride and pleasure in being one. I am a graduate of the London University and was a teacher in a girls' school before I got married in 1969. I belong to an orthodox Śaivite Hindu family, and when I reached age twenty-six my parents proposed a marriage. My future husband, too, hailed from an orthodox Śaivite family and was thirty years of age. After our parents discussed and decided upon details, an opportunity was afforded to us to meet. The venue was a Gaṇeśa temple, and the time was 7AM. As each of us stepped into the temple from different directions almost simultaneously, the temple bells started ringing to herald the 7:00 *pūjā.* 'A good omen,' both of us thought independently. After the *pūjā* was over, we were introduced to each other by my mother. Out of inborn shyness and a certain amount of fear of meeting a stranger, I was hardly able to look up and even see the color of the man who was going to be the lord of my life. I heard him talk and even noticed him gazing meaningfully at me all the time. The 'confrontation' lasted about ten minutes, and we parted. Each of us approved the selection so carefully made by our parents and, to make a long story short, our marriage was solemnized in due course. ¶"From the date of marriage, I resigned my job as teacher because my duties as a housewife appeared more onerous and more responsible. My husband earned enough to maintain a family, and we started setting up a home of our own. I brought in some money by way of a dowry, and this helped us to furnish our home with all essential requirements. We loved each other very much and lived like Śiva and Śakti. The most important corner of our house is the shrine room where our day-to-day life starts every morning. ¶"I get up from bed at 5AM every day. After a wash, I enter the shrine room and clean up the place. Remnants of flowers from the previous day's *pūjā* are removed, the brass lamps and vessels are polished, water is sprinkled on the floor and the place kept ready for the day's *pūjā*, performed by my husband. Then the kitchen is swept and the pots and pans washed. Water is kept on the gas to boil, and I go for a bath. Returning from the bath, I do a short prayer and pick flowers for my husband's *pūjā*. By now it is 6AM—the time my husband awakens. I go to the bedroom and wait there ready to greet him for the day. He looks upon me as the Lakshmī of the home, and it pleases him a lot to wake in my presence—all gleaming with holy ash and *kumkum pottu* on my forehead. As soon as he gets up, he goes out for a half-hour walk and is back home by 6:30. A cup of coffee is now ready for him. He takes this and, after five minutes' rest, enjoys a fine bath. He then makes the necessary preparations for the *pūjā*. I could do this myself, but my husband feels these preparations are also a part of the *pūjā*. Sharp at 7AM, the *pūjā* starts. I join him and so do our children (we now have two boys and a girl). It is a pleasure to watch my husband at *pūjā*, which he does very piously and meticulously. At 7:30 we come out of the shrine room for our breakfast. I personally serve my lord and the children meals prepared by my own hands and then get the two elder children ready for school. By 8:30 all the three are out of the house on their respective missions. I then clean up the house, put my little three-year-old son to sleep and by 9:30 I am back in the kitchen preparing lunch.

¶"In the evening I am dressed up and ready for an outing with my husband and children. Almost every day he takes us out, but occasionally he comes home tired and prefers to remain indoors. At 6PM I start cooking the dinner and at 7:00 we have a joint prayer in the shrine room. Dinner at 7:30, then a little bit of reading, listening to the radio, some chit chat and off to bed by 9:30. This has been my routine for the last eleven years, and I have enjoyed every minute of it. ¶"In the house, I give first place to my husband. It has never been my custom to find fault with him for anything. He understands me so much and so well that he is always kind, loving, gentle and compassionate towards me. I reciprocate these a hundredfold, and we get on very well. My husband is the secretary of a religious organization, and I give him every help and encouragement in his work. My household duties keep me fully occupied, and so I don't engage myself in other activities. I respect my husband's leadership in the home, and so life goes on smoothly."

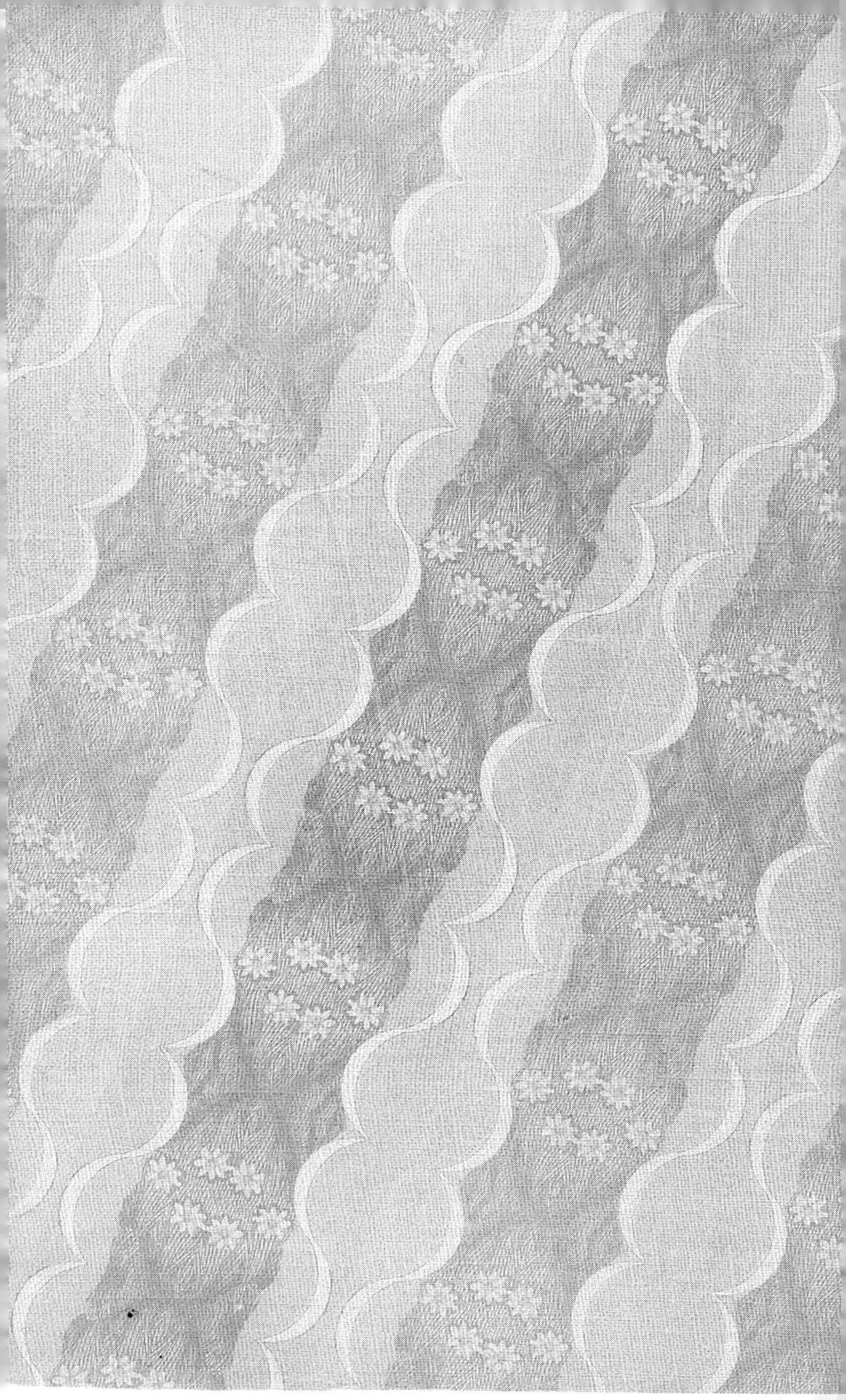

Vivāha, Gṛihastha Dharma

विवाह गृहस्थधर्म

Marriage and Family Life

Have your eating and drinking in common. I bind you together. Assemble for worship of the Lord, like spokes around a hub. Of one mind and one purpose I make you, following one leader. Be like the Gods, ever deathless! Never stop loving!

Atharva Veda 3.30.6-7. VE

Monday
LESSON 141
The Ideals Of Marriage

Marriage is an institution, a business, a spiritual partnership, a furtherance of humanity and a contract—a three-level contract involving body, mind and emotion. Marriage is a necessary commitment not only for the continuation of the human race but also for the furtherance of each individual soul's spiritual unfoldment. The interaction on all levels between the couple, and later their children, molds the good, bad and confused *karmas* into new dimensions. Śaivite marriages involve not only the bride and groom but also their parents, their priest, *guru*, astrologer, relatives on both sides and the entire community. The feeling of responsibility to the community is ever present. The community's feeling of responsibility to make each of its marriages work out well is also always present. ¶Why are Śaivite marriages different from other kinds of marriages? It is because of the ever-abiding belief in the ever-present oneness of God Śiva within each one. God Śiva is within you, and you are within God Śiva. God Śiva is the Life of our lives. This and more the Śaivite saints sang. To forget that Śiva is within the wife, to forget that Śiva is within the husband is to forget Śaivism itself. This basic Śaivite belief lays the psychological foundation for the husband to see the wife as a Goddess and the wife to see the husband as a God. All other behavior comes out of this belief. Belief creates attitudes, and attitudes create actions. ¶The knowing that each one has come into life to work out certain *karmas* they brought with them in this birth, and that *karmas* are generally worked out through other people, gives a challenge and a goal—to resolve these *karmas* and receive the reward of *mukti*, freedom from rebirth. Because of this belief, this understanding, the husband and wife blend their energies more constructively. Their attitudes are naturally more generous, forgiving and understanding, their actions and interactions more harmonious and mutually supportive. A woman gives her *prāṇa*, spiritual energy, to her husband, making him strong. Children give their *prāṇa* to their parents, because to them the parents are Śiva-Śakti, the first *guru*. The wife, always attending to her husband's needs, sets the pattern for the children. By focusing her energies within her family, she builds up a great spiritual vibration in the home. In fulfilling his *purusha dharma*, the husband gives his *prāṇa*, love and loyalty to his family, and

---

A bride and groom, one an Indian, the other of Oriental descent, are living in Hawaii, where volcanos are still active. They offer flower garlands to one another on the day of their wedding, as God Śiva, in the Third World, cradles them mercifully in His hands.

he benefits the community through his service. He never, ever raises his voice in the home; nor does he show anger in any way. He is the model for the entire family. When his sons come of age, they join their *prāṇas* with his, and as a result, the family, the community and the country flourish. ¶Believing in reincarnation, the parents know that their relatives—and they themselves—will be born back into their family again and again to work out their unfinished *karmas.* A Śaivite home is a *karmic* factory, a recycling of souls, a mill that grinds exceedingly fine the seed *karmas* of this and past lives.

Tuesday
LESSON 142
Mysticism In the Home

The Śaivite Hindu lifestyle is very special, very binding, strengthened by: the *pañcha nitya karmas;* the Monday family home evening and the daily family meetings; the knowing that each child is and has been totally a part of the family, maybe for hundreds of years; the knowing that there is *karma* to be worked out within the family—feelings of happiness, unhappiness and misunderstandings, all to be resolved; and the knowing that there is a purpose for them all being together and that they may all be together until *mukti,* liberation from the cycle of rebirth. All this and more distinguishes the Śaivite family from all other families on the planet. ¶It is on the astral plane, the inner world of this world, that twenty-four-hour life takes place. Beings there do not have to sleep. The positive activity of the astral world within the house or the apartment transforms it into a home, or if negative into a hotel room. To stabilize this astral activity and make sure it is positive, the home *pūjā* is performed by every Śaivite family daily. Scriptures are read, the *yamas* and *niyamas* are fulfilled and all difficulties, large and small, are resolved before sleep. Divine ancestral *devas* are coaxed to live in the home, as well as *devas* from nearby temples where the family frequently worships. This magic makes the home into a spiritual abode, not unlike a temple itself. ¶Children are always treated with great respect and awe in a true Śaivite home, for one does not always know who these young ones were in past lives. They may be incarnations of a grandmother, grandfather, aunt or uncle, dearly beloved mother, sister, brother, respected father, distant related *yogī* or *ṛishi.* Who are they? What is their destiny to fulfill in this life? ¶The answers lie in the voice of the universe, the mystical Śaivite astrological system laid down by the *ṛishis* of yore. The family's astrologer carefully explains the nature of each child, and how it will develop, flourish and unfold year after year. This gives the parents knowledge and hope, courage and understanding, tolerance and forgiveness, and all the other fine qualities that all Śaivites want to cultivate within themselves. In raising the children and simultaneously realizing that each is a part of Śiva's well-ordered universe and has entered the family with his or her own *prārabdha karmas* to be lived out, the parents are neither excited nor dismayed when the predicted characteristics begin to manifest within the child. Yes, the Śaivite home is a factory, an intricate mechanism manufacturing spiritual unfoldment for every member of the family.

Wednesday
LESSON 143
Bringing Up Children

Many families look at their children as intruders, as strangers. Śaivites don't. There is great power and wisdom in the knowledge of astrology in bringing the necessary information to the parents to know the nature of their new arrival. Non-Hindu families generally do not have this kind of insight into the nature and future of their offspring and are generally at a loss to understand or know how to deal with patterns and developments as they arise. ¶Hindu parents view each child as an adult in a very young body, growing up into the fulfillment of its potential. Using the knowledge gained through astrology, they work to strengthen the strong character traits and never aggravate the weaker or antagonistic ones. This is to say that should the child have a propensity toward anger, jealousy and argumentativeness, and another propensity toward generosity, creativity and acquisition of knowledge, the wise parents will, of course, never argue with the child, because they do not want to awaken and strengthen this quality; they would carefully refrain from angering the child and quickly quell the anger when it flares up. In order to avoid strengthening the tendency toward jealousy, they would seek to secure the child's relationship with friends and things so that he never felt unloved or disadvantaged. They would praise his creativity, generosity and acquisition of knowledge. For all this he would be rewarded with kind words and gifts, because once these tendencies are strengthened, the negative ones will fall aside. ¶This example is given to explain the way in which mother and father must work together to formulate patterns of positive discipline that they will understand and implement in the same way, so as to bring out the best qualities within the child. When these best qualities are brought up and become a part of the child's daily life, the worse qualities will naturally be subdued by the best qualities. It is an interactive mechanism within the child himself that brings him closer to perfection. Non-Śaivite families often bring up the worst within their child, and the child has to, for his own salvation, leave home to be with people of a higher nature, a more expanded consciousness, who will strengthen his finer qualities, or be drawn to those of a lower nature, who will strengthen his lesser qualities. Everyone is on the path to perfection, and they are instinctively and superconsciously seeking out those who are capable and able to help them progress. Śaivites want this to happen within the home itself, and hence welcome the involvement of the *guru*, the *swāmīs* and the entire community. ¶Because people are human, differences arise. If everyone were the same, humanity would be called a herd, with the instinctive nature the predominant functioning intelligence. But humans are not a herd; they are individuals, each and every one of them. Each has a destiny and on the path to fulfill that destiny must go through an intricate series of unique experiences. Śaivites appreciate the differences. If any sameness exists, it is because of the shared understanding of the Śaiva Dharma and each one's ability to live up to it in his own way, helped or restricted by his *prārabdha karmas*. In our own Śaivite organization—a worldwide family it has been called—a pilgrim can visit a mission in Canada, California, Malaysia, Singapore, Mauritius or India, and experience his brothers and sisters, fathers and mothers, aunts and uncles. This worldwide extended family exists because of their shared, basic Śaiva beliefs and attitudes, and their striving to live up to the culture and *sādhanas* in their own way, only being helped or inhibited by their *prārabdha karmas*.

Thursday
LESSON 144
The Roles of Man and Wife

Is there anything unique in the Śaivite marriage that helps in dealing with the roles that men and women traditionally play? Are women always to be meek and dependent and men aggressive and in charge? Sometimes an aggressive woman marries a passive man. How does Śaivism deal with this?" This totally depends on the education of both the husband and the wife. This has been my experience. When the modernization of education occurred, which taught people how to live in the world, run a business or work for someone else, family life began to evolve out of the village consciousness and into the technological age. In this change, traditional roles also changed. ¶Today there are five basic patterns of marriage. In an agricultural community, women take care of the house, and men take care of the farm, the business and industry; or in some other societies where women are stronger, they work side-by-side with the men. There, for a man to have his wife work side-by-side with him in the field is a sign of status, better meals for the family and more attention to himself. Also we must understand that in these marriages both husband and wife share a similar educational level, a similar understanding of how the world works. This is the first and oldest pattern. ¶However, as society changes because of technology and industrialization, people change and their relationships change. I have found that a Western-educated man who marries an Eastern village-educated girl will always be head of the house, and she will allow this. Basically, she does not understand the ways of urban life. This is the second type of marriage. The educated man marrying an uneducated girl will not expect her to understand what he is thinking about or feeling. And she would probably not understand even if he explained it all to her. She would naturally be submissive; he would be aggressive. ¶It has been my experience that it works exactly the same the other way around in cases where the woman is more highly educated than the man. The intellectually educated lady marrying an uneducated man would most likely be the principal wage-earner, and he would be submissive. She will naturally make the major decisions about how to spend her money. He will naturally concur. Or, they will fight. This third, more difficult, relationship will demand a leader and a follower, especially if she earns more money than he and has more job security and greater benefits, such as medical insurance and retirement. ¶The second and third types of marriage share a common factor. A village girl has no way of earning her own living, should her husband die or leave her, and would have no recourse but to return to her family, unless he left her a substantial bequest or alimony. A nonprofessional village man would have no other recourse than to seek his own level of income should his educated wife die or leave him without providing a generous support or inheritance.

Friday
LESSON 145
Special Types Of Marriage

The fourth type of marriage, like the first, is between those of similar educational backgrounds. Here, though, each is sophisticated, has professional skills and could be a wage-earner in his or her own right. Within these marriages, even though the skills may not be used, they are a potential source of income and security. This fourth rule book, which has been written more recently by the actions and experiences of various couples and the societies in which they live, is most important to elaborate on. Two fairly equally educated people should work in unanimous agreement, in partnership, in all things regarding raising of the children and management of the home. ¶The first three rule books are fairly well set, and society understands them. They have been functioning for hundreds and thousands of years. In the fourth type of marriage, men and women meet in equality through intelligence developed and cultivated through Western education, Western experience and the equal ability to be wage earners. The intellect, intelligence, has no sex; it is equal. To apply agricultural village traditions to these marriages would be to foster contention, misunderstanding and feelings of rejection, leading to possible separation. Two potential wage earners living together must themselves reach consensus on every issue. ¶The fifth type of marriage is more religious, more spiritual. Here the couple has blended together for the purpose of fulfilling religious aspirations, for ministry, producing sons for the monastery or future priests and *pandits.* These lofty marriages have definite *guru* involvement and *swāmī* involvement. The couple is intent on practicing *yoga* and serving their religion selflessly as missionaries, exemplars and teachers. My Saiva Siddhanta Church encourages each couple to write a two-part marriage contract. Part one is the mutual agreement, laying out the overall purpose of the marriage and the aspirations and goals that the union hopes to fulfill. The other part is a statement of the duties and responsibilities of each of the partners. This semi-corporate approach has proven successful in stabilizing many marriages, as each partner clearly understands his or her role. ¶Any couple following any of the other four types of marriage could move to the fifth at the right time. They would ultimately take the *brahmacharya vrata,* later in life, after a decision was made to have no more children, and then live together as brother and sister. This is traditional within Śaivite culture and consistent with community expectations.

Saturday
LESSON 146
Marital Harmony

One might ask about the traditional role of the husband as *guru* of the wife, whether he should give in equally to her views when difficulties arise or expect most of the compromise to come from her. In the ideal of the husband's being the *guru* in the family, the word *guru* simply means teacher. So, to be a *guru* in the household means that he is a very religious, knowledgeable, understanding, humble husband who is kind, honest and respected in the community as an exemplar. Otherwise, the ideal of family guru does not apply, and more of a partnership arrangement between spouses is the default in today's world. ¶People are held in bondage in many ways—physical bondage, emotional bondage, intellectual bondage. In India's Hinduism, unfortunately, as in many other societies on the Earth, disproportionate numbers of women are still not educated, while the men more often are. Therefore, the woman is held in intellectual bondage, sometimes not even being able to count to a hundred and only being able to, and expected to, gossip in the marketplace and bargain for food. Naturally she would follow the religion of her husband. Naturally she would also depend on him fully for guidance in all other matters, financial and otherwise. ¶But times have now changed, and many Hindu women have been educated and can formulate their own opinions through the reasoning processes of their own minds, talk intelligently among themselves and arrive at pragmatic conclusions. The *guru*-disciple relationship does not exist in marriages of this kind. She does not need to learn anything from her husband. In most cases she has sufficient skills to be financially independent. Therefore, the relationship is not that of a *guru* and student, but is more like a business partnership, the fourth type of marriage. ¶Their business is birthing children and raising them to be good citizens, maintaining a harmonious home by reconciling differences before sleep, even if they are reconciled a few hours after dawn, maintaining the family budget, paying all of the bills on time, saving for their children's higher level of education, seeing to the children's being settled in a life of their own, paying off the mortgage on the house, preparing for retirement, seeing to the spiritual upliftment of the community by contributing to the local temple society, maintaining a shrine room in their home, and hiring a local priest to perform house ceremonies and certain *saṁskāras* within the home. To fulfill all of this, a fair, professional attitude toward one another must be maintained. ¶Professional people in large corporations do not argue endlessly before reconciliation, nor do they undermine each other, lest they soon find themselves looking for another place of employment. Divorce in this modern time is like being dismissed, fired, and then the search is on for another partner with whom the same unresolved *karma* will finally mature. This is because we are born with certain *prārabdha karmas* to be lived through, if not with one person, then with a surrogate. The way to avoid creating new *kriyamāna karmas* is to face up to the *karmas* with the first spouse rather than with a second, third or fourth, which would create a *kukarma*, or bad *karma*, mess along the way to be later cleaned up, if not in this life, then hopefully in the next life. ¶It is said that the wife should see the husband as Śiva and he should see her as Śakti, which is often misconstrued as putting him in a superior position. The only up-down situation is the educated husband married to an illiterate wife, yet even here the relationship should be one of love and mutual respect. Śiva and Śakti are totally and equally interrelated as far as Śaiva Siddhānta philosophy is concerned, and cannot exist without one another. Therefore, is the husband Śiva, and is she Śakti? It's a yes and no answer. In Śaiva Siddhānta, Śiva and Śakti are two aspects of a one Being, Śiva being the unmanifest Absolute and Śakti being the manifest Divinity. ¶If the wife is as capable as the husband in the external world and the intellectual world, emotional world and physical world, there is no up-down relationship between them, and they are Śiva and Śakti, absolutely equal. The old system of male dominance originated in early human societies when physical strength—for war, hunting and heavy muscular effort—was a prime survival factor. It was perpetuated as the way of life in villages of preindustrial India, Europe and early America, where the man received the education and the woman, as a rule, did not. To apply this system in today's sophisticated technological societies would be to plant the seedlings of the destruction of the marriage.

Sunday
LESSON 147
Commitment To Harmony

Traditionally, every Hindu family should have a family *kulaguru,* a preceptor who knows the flow of *karma* within all the family connections and the birth *dharma* of the family itself. To be without a *kulaguru* is likened to a child being without its parents. ¶One of the greatest disruptive forces in a marriage is the amateur psychiatrist or psychologist practicing on his or her spouse. This tactic for solving problems is totally unacceptable. Such efforts, however well-intended, to straighten out a spouse through subconscious analysis are antagonizing, disruptive and hurtful emotionally and mentally. All these psychiatric games are based on the principle, "Something is wrong with you, and I'm going to straighten it out. Come to me. I have all the solutions." Śaivism is different. It is based on the principle that you are perfect. The only problem is that you don't know it. Let's talk ourselves into our own perfection through reading scripture, praying, doing Śivathondu together, doing *japa* together, to lift our consciousness into the perfection that is always there. ¶If your spouse is trying to hurt you, protect yourself in the Sanātana Dharma as your first line of defense. Recognizing that this is your *karma,* fulfill your *dharma* fully, be it *strī dharma* or *purusha dharma,* the best you understand it. The *Vedas* assure us that truth always wins over evil (*Muṇḍaka Upanishad* 3.1.6). It is the wife's duty to uplift the husband, the husband's duty to uplift the wife. A husband bent on hurting his wife could not outlast—his hurtfulness could not survive—the wife's chanting "Aum, Aum, Aum" all day long and placing spiritual vibrations into his food. In this way, good overcomes evil, *ahiṁsā* overcomes *hiṁsā*, *dharma* overcomes *adharma*. This is why we are born on this planet, to evolve through such challenges. We are here for no other reason. But should the husband ever become physically violent, the wife should take the children and run to safety. She should stay in a safe place until he has undergone counseling, made amends to her and to the congregation, asked the family *guru* to prescribe a penance and fully performed that penance. ¶When families who are trying to meditate and unfold spiritually go through times of internal or external violence they should not practice *rāja yoga* or other forms of meditation. This will only aggravate and worsen the situation. *Yoga* practices are not for them. What they should do is Śivathondu, or *karma yoga*, *bhakti yoga* and simple *japa yoga*. That is all. If a disharmonious situation comes up between husband and wife, they must resolve it before they go to bed, even if they must stay up all night into the light of day. ¶Sleep puts the problem to rest over a period of two or three nights, and it will eventually fade into the memory patterns of forgetfulness over a longer period of time. Having sex does not solve the problem. It puts the problem into seed, into the memory patterns of current forgetfulness, and these will definitely materialize at another time. Sex and sleep are not solutions to marital disputes. One is immediate postponement and the other is a slower postponement. To resolve a conflict between husband and wife, lest it affect the lives of the children by being postponed into forgetfulness, it must be done before sleep. There is no other way. This is the way husbands and wives catalyze their spiritual unfoldment on the path and develop themselves. Another reason sex is not a solution to disharmony is that babies that are conceived in a union that is supposed to settle a squabble are more often than not invoked from the Narakaloka. Such children might harass the family for the rest of their lives.

Kuṭumba Maitrī

कुटुम्बमैत्री

Family Togetherness

May you two, waking up in your pleasant chamber, both filled with laughter and cheer, and enjoying mightily, having good sons, a good home, and good cattle, pass the shining mornings.

Atharva Veda 14.2.43. HV, P. 141

Monday
LESSON 148
What Is a Real Family?

How to strengthen family ties is a very important question these days. It is said that Jawaharlal Nehru was instrumental in breaking up the extended family structure in his attempt to industrialize India. After that, once tightly-knit families really suffered as age-old family ties became loosened. The wealth of extended families dispersed in many directions as nuclear families formed and money was unnecessarily spent to maintain the ever-increasing needs of a multiplicity of households. ¶Let's explore what a family actually is. People seem to have forgotten. In America before the First World War there were wonderful, well-established and large joint families, with twenty, thirty or more people all living as one unit, often in one home. Everyone had chores. And they all knew their place within the family structure. They loved and cared for each other, and mother was always in the home. We may be a long time in rebuilding family togetherness to the point where the extended family is back in vogue, but meanwhile we are still faced with maintaining family unity. Hindus around the world are working hard to rediscover their roots and strengthen family values. Our staff of HINDUISM TODAY had many inspiring interviews with bright young Asian Hindus in America who are working in their communities to make a difference and reestablish the old culture of caring for one another. We congratulate them and welcome their efforts, for they are the leaders of tomorrow. ¶I tell parents who seek my advice that one way to keep a family together is to show all members that you want to be with them, that you need them in your life. Not: "Get out of my life, you are bothering me. I have other things to do. I have goals in life that don't include you." This hurtful attitude is based on the belief that when children reach age eighteen they should leave home and support themselves. In the West, this pattern is the result of two world wars, when every able-bodied young man left home to join the armed forces. This callousness on the part of parents leads to alienation from their children, who then begin leading independent lives. That leads to the first step in leaving home: keeping secrets from the parents. ¶With each secret kept, a small distance is created. A large distance is created when five or ten secrets accumulate and deception becomes a habit. When too many secrets mount up, parents and their children don't talk

---

Here's a mom who made a decision to stay at home to raise her family in Sydney, Australia, known for its modern Opera House. Raising children well requires constant attention, nurturing and positive discipline that only a loving, full-time mom can provide.

to each other much anymore. Why do secrets create a distance? Because every secret must be protected. This requires cleverness, sneaking around to keep the matter hidden, even lying. Secrets give rise to angry outbursts to keep others away, such as, "I'm insulted that you would even suspect me of that!" Arguments erupt that go unresolved, and an impenetrable barrier is established. ¶Mom and Dad are heard confiding to one another, "They're so different now. I can't reach them anymore." Of course, the children have been taught to be cautious, in a sense forced into keeping secrets, lest unloving parents curse them or physically punish them without mercy for transgressions large and small. Many are afraid of the wrath of mothers and fathers who rule their families by fear. In today's world it is so easy to leave home. It is so easy for the family to break up. It's even expected. Husbands' and wives' keeping secrets, similarly, creates a distance between them. The final divorce decree started with the first secret. ¶In an ideal family, children should be able to tell their mother and father anything and everything. The parents should want to understand and realize that if they don't understand but misunderstand, they participate in the break-up of their own family. Of course, it might be hard for them to deal with certain experiences their children are having, but all they have to do is look back at their own life, actions and private thoughts to know that their children are living out the same fantasies. The children repeat the still-active *karmas* of their parents. Children are born into families with *karmic* patterns that are compatible with their own. I can predict what young people are going to do in their future, and the temptations that will come up, if I know the *karmic* patterns of their parents. With this knowledge, it is easy to guide them through life, helping them avoid temptations and unwholesome experiences that their parents lived through. All of these experiences are set into motion by the individual himself, by his own past actions.

Tuesday
LESSON 149
The Magic Of Love

Every experience, no matter how difficult or embarrassing, is a good experience, providing the lesson to be learned is extracted from it. Experiences that are unresolved and repressed can be very burdensome for the individual. Living Śaiva Dharma makes us our own psychologist, psychiatrist, counselor and problem-solver. This is because one slowly becomes the watcher of his mind thinking, the watcher of his emotions feeling, acting and reacting. ¶Holding the family together can be summed up in one word: *love.* Love is understanding. Love is acceptance. Love is making somebody feel good about his experience, whether the experience is a good one or not. Love is giving the assurance that there is no need to keep secrets, no matter what has happened. Love is wanting to be with members of the family. A father who is eager to hold his family together rushes home from work. He doesn't think to himself, "Why should I go home to all their problems when I can continue working at the clinic for awhile longer." Loving parents, father or mother, want to be with their children, and they let them know this in so many ways. They face up to problems with love, trust and understanding. They know that problems are only problems because of lack of understanding. They also know, through living Śaiva Dharma, that love and trust bring understanding and acceptance of the lessons of the experiences, which are natural manifestations of individual birth *karmas* and collective family *karmas.* This approach keeps the family strong and cohesive. In a home where *dharma* is lived, no one has a private life. No one has a secret life. ¶When harmony persists in the home, harmony permeates the community, and harmony permeates the country. When love and trust prevail in the family, love and trust extend to the local community, and the country becomes stronger and more secure. Making strong distinctions between good and bad does not help youths understand their desires and temptations. The only path through their lives is one experience after another. They evolve into better people through understanding their experiences. ¶Children and young adults who have been holding secrets and now feel that it is time to become close to their family again should tell their parents they want to be completely open and disclose what they have been hiding. Then give parents a few days to adjust and prepare to listen. Once reconciliation takes place, hugging and talking will begin again, and the warm, loving feeling of family will take over the home. Something magical happens when secrets are brought out in the open among loved ones. Many youths have told me that when secrets were divulged, their parents were surprisingly understanding. Secrets are psychic burdens, and releasing them, youths tell me, gives a great sense of upliftment, like a balloon dropping its counterweight and soaring skyward. They feel instantly closer to their parents, free of guilt, happier, less stressful, no longer defensive and more interested in helping others. ¶One of the biggest areas of secrecy is sex. It is important that parents give their children an education in sexual behavior early on. This will also bring and keep the family togetherness. Many parents find it difficult to talk about sex, pornography, drugs and the various other kinds of temptations the world offers today. If this is the case in your home, it is best to seek community or professional help. Not talking leaves children unprepared. Parents force their children into secrecy by showing that these are areas that cannot or will not be faced in the light of day. All begin wishing that conditions will improve, but they never do. ¶We can now see that the first secret is the crucial issue, for it leads to many, many more, be it on the part of children keeping secrets from their parents, wives from husbands, husbands from wives, students from *guru,* and on and on. The solution is to follow the *yamas* and *niyamas,* the dos and do nots of Hindu Dharma. These are the natural laws of Sanātana Dharma. These are the human ethics that hold families together, marriages together, communities together, countries together. These eternal Vedic precepts are for everyone, no matter who they are.

Wednesday
LESSON 150
What Makes a House a Home?

What is it that makes a house a home? A home is a place of companionship with people in it who love each other, who are harmonious and closer inside with one another than they are outside with associates in the workplace or with classmates at school. A home is a place that's so magnetic that it's difficult to leave. In a home there is love, kindness, sharing and appreciation, and the inhabitants help one another. It's a place of selflessness and togetherness, where everybody has time for everybody else. In a home, the guests are treated like Deities or *devas* coming to the temple. That is the spirit of hospitality in the Hindu framework. It is the same spirit of sublime energy flowing to the guest that also flows within the household. And a righteous household that worships every morning together as one family is like a temple. That's a home, and everything else is just a house or a hotel lobby. ¶If you were to look at a harmonious home with your astral vision, you would see the three primary colors—pale pink, pale blue, pale yellow—and white, all intermingling in a big *prāṇic* force field. Moving over to another house, you might see a congestion of various colors, with dark and light shades and strange astral forms, and you would know that house was not much different from a hotel lobby. ¶I was once asked about the desperately poor, homeless families living on the street in America and what can be done for them, when so many other families have large, luxurious homes. I, too, have seen families on the street. But if they live together, if they sleep together, if they talk together, if they eat together, they are a family, even if they are destitute.

Such a family is at home wherever they are. You don't need a roof to make a family. You don't need a roof to make a home. The truly homeless are some of the rich people who build multi-million-dollar houses and are too busy to really live in them. The truly homeless are those who have turned their home into a hotel lobby. The husband works. The wife works. The children are delinquent. There's no companionship. They don't talk together every day. They don't eat together every day. They rarely see each other. The truly homeless people are those with babysitters, caretakers, gardeners and maids, but who don't spend quality time with the family in their house. Babysitters often abuse their children. Parents are unaware, too busy making money outside the home that they don't live in. This is another way of looking at the rich and the homeless. Who is to be pitied? ¶Control of the computer and the Internet is also important to make a house into a home. If the computer is on all the time, the house turns into an office, even if everyone is at home. Many homes these days are just offices. Human communication has stopped. The computer eats up the time that one should be giving to others within the home. Using the computer moderately gives us time for gentleness, play and communication, not with a screen, but with a human being. And that is the vibration needed in a home.

Thursday
LESSON 151
Discouraged Families

There are too many dysfunctional families in the world today. What is a dysfunctional family? A dysfunctional family is a discouraged family, a family that has no home. True, they may have a million-dollar house, but it would take a lot of constant, magnetic love and kinship to turn that house into a home. Many million-dollar homes are just houses, totally impersonal. ¶The guests are not God in those homes; guests are seen as business potentials and social obligations. The father works late in his profession so he can avoid his wife and family. When he comes home, he sits down in front of the television while eating his dinner. The kids are running here and there; the mother comes home tired from her equally demanding profession and begins yelling at them. Verbal abuse becomes a way of life. The youngsters come and go unchaperoned. Nobody knows what anybody else is doing. Girls are getting pregnant out of wedlock. Boys are swearing, getting involved in gangs and experimenting with drugs. That is the hotel lobby home of a definitely dysfunctional family, a discouraged family. ¶No wonder that in discouraged families teens want to leave home as quickly as possible—as soon they're able to get a job and rent an apartment. That is not quality living, is it? Sorry to say, but most dual-professionals' homes, where husband and wife both have high-paying jobs, are more like a hotel lobby with a snack bar than like a home with a hearth, which is home with a heart. Think about your home. Is the guest God? Is your house a home? What kind of astral vibration does it actually have? Be honest with yourself. Evaluate! ¶The astral *prāṇas* or energies radiating out from the hotel lobby kind of home make the occupants frustrated people. They make people around them uncomfortable, because they live in an uncomfortable place. Yes, the *prāṇas* that emanate from an empty house make one an empty person. All Hindus in the world should reverse this situation for a stable, well-adjusted community for the new and coming generations of Hindus in the West, as well as in the East. This is the next step which those of the diaspora have to heartfully take. It is only intelligence that can reverse a negative situation and turn it into a positive, encouraging situation. ¶It is important for the mother to be mother, and for the father to allow her to be mother, so that together they can nurture the astral atmosphere within the house and make it vibrate with spiritual energies into a real home. To make the house into a home is the next step. You will know if it is a home when you want to hurry back to it. You won't want to stay away too long, and you will find it difficult to leave. That's because you enjoy the vibration that you have created from your soul body. And your focus for whatever you are doing will be exquisite. It won't get divided. ¶It is a slow process for a mother and a father to turn a house into a home. They have to be spiritually present in the home. The auras of the mother and father and each of the children have to permeate the walls of the house. The Gods and guardian *devas* and ancestors have to be worshiped and invoked in the home. That turns a house into a really *prāṇically* viable home, building up the vibration so that you never want to leave.

Friday
LESSON 152
What Is Real Prosperity?

A spiritual vibration in the home can be initiated or renewed by having a priest come and perform a purification ceremony. That makes the *prāṇas* flow correctly in the home, which when carried out to the community make you a full person. Another key is to have Monday evenings at home. Monday home evening is practiced by many religions, including the Hindus. On Monday evening, Śiva's day, the family members get together, prepare a wonderful meal, play games together and verbally appreciate one another's good qualities. It's an evening when the television is not turned on. They don't solve any problems on that day. They just love each other, and everybody has a voice, from the littlest child to the oldest senior. It's a family togetherness, one day a week when everyone will look forward to having mom and dad at home. That doesn't mean it will be on Tuesday or any other day if Monday is missed. Family home evening is always on Monday, and everyone's life has to adjust to that. ¶Many families find even this is impossible because of their careers. Nowadays people think that they have to have two incomes, three incomes, to be comfortably well off. Money is gained and lost, sometimes rather quickly. As quickly gained, often as quickly lost. But what is wealth? Wealth is a diamond with many facets. One facet of wealth is money, but it is not the only one. A happy family that enjoys each other—that is a great wealth. Doing things together and enjoying doing things together is another great wealth. Rushing home to be with one another—if you can create that in your family, you are wealthy. Wealth is growing your own food, making your own furniture, sewing your own clothing, picking oranges off the tree the family planted together several years ago. Another great wealth is living within your income. Even multi-millionaires are poor if they do not live within their income and always worry about debts, payments and responsibilities. They often are very lonely people, because in all their efforts to gain those millions, they have had to sacrifice their family, their children and their own happiness. Many content themselves with building big multi-million dollar mansions—but to benefit whom? A gardener? Maybe a cook, a maid or two who get to live there all the time while the owners are traveling around the world, coming home late and leaving early. That's not wealth. That's also not wisdom. That's a good way to die young. ¶To have a maid take care of the children while the parents both work and come home late is not a substitute for a mother; nor are grandparents, though they may be a better choice. A surrogate mother cannot replace a real mother and a real father for children growing up, because children model themselves more than you know upon what they see adults do, what they hear adults say to each other, what they feel adults are feeling. That shapes who they are and what they are going to do in their future. There is no substitute for a real mom and a real dad in a real home with a vibration of a family, the vibration of loving and the vibration of sharing. A mother's place is in the home ¶What is a mother? A mother is a person who loves her children, who is calm, serene, doesn't become angry, doesn't become frustrated with children, realizing that a child goes through many stages of development. One must not expect a child to behave like an adult or expect too much of a child too early. A mother knows of all this intuitively; but for her intuitive mind to work, she has to be free from the worries of the outside world, of bills and bill collectors, of travel, of TV and various other concerns, so that she can raise up the next generation strong enough to meet the challenges of the impending new age of peace and prosperity for all mankind. ¶Now, if mothers beat their children, the children will beat other kids, and later on in life they will become warriors and fight all through life, emotionally, mentally, because they're taught right in the home that solutions are reached through violent means. We don't want that. That won't bring in the New Age. That is bringing back the Old Age. Those methods of raising children have to go. A mother must be a real mother. For many, it's not a popular idea for a mother to stay at home. During the Second World War in the United States, mothers left their homes and never went back, because they were needed in airplane factories and shipyards, as the men were all off to war. But before the Second World War and before the First World War, mothers remained home. Juvenile delinquency was not a phrase in anyone's vocabulary. If a teenager made some mischief, the family was held responsible by the community. Such things were regulated in those days, but went out of balance when mother left home and never went back.

Saturday
LESSON 153
Mothers-In-Law

When devotees speak with me of their experiences with family togetherness, the mother-in-law is a common concern. Mothers-in-law on both sides are often even the cause of separation or divorce. They often have the attitude, "This girl is not good enough for my son," or "This boy is not good enough for my daughter." That constant harassment—emotional harassment, mental harassment and even physical harassment—can cause the couple to separate, just for their own peace of mind. When we are asked to ascertain astrological compatibility for marriage, we not only check the compatibility between the boy and the girl, but also between the girl and the boy's mother. ¶It is important to be aware that all mothers-in-law of the world—and every daughter may eventually be one—have their own insecurities in giving sons and daughters over to a spouse they don't know deeply. Social security and pension plans are relatively new, and only exist in certain parts of the world. In the absence of these, worries about the future naturally arise. Every society has evolved solutions to the in-law issue, mothers-in-law, fathers-in law, but in today's world it's even more difficult. Young people need to be aware of their needs, their feelings, their insecurities, and have compassion when behavioral patterns that are the by-products of insecurity show themselves, such as being overly dominant, proud, extremely critical and unrelenting. In America there is a sad saying, "Old and gray and in the way." The solution used all too often is to put bothersome elders away in nursing homes, rest homes or "paradise retreats." ¶The major focus of the problem is the authority of the mother-in-law and her occasional abuses. But consider also that in modern cultures the authority of elders is all too frequently usurped by both the son and the daughter-in-law, who then wield the power and make life-and-death decisions about their parents. The tables are turned. This causes an even greater instability. One has to ask which is the preferable culture—to allow the elderly to remain in charge of their lives and have a strong say and respect in the family or to deny their contribution and condemn them to a life of helplessness and dependence, which is what happens all too frequently in the West. Obviously, a harmonious balance is needed. ¶First of all, I suggest that the myth that mothers-in-law are unable to adjust or learn anything new should be thrown out. Second, I hold the husband, the mother-in-law's son, totally responsible for bringing about harmony in the home so that his wife is happy and not at odds with his mother, and that his mother does not make his wife miserable. As in all family conflicts, each incident must be resolved before sleep. Issues or problems can be put on an agenda, as described in our system of positive discipline, and brought up in a calm manner at the daily family meeting, just as is done nowadays by children in many school classrooms. ¶Anyone, including mothers-in-law, can change if they want to. A problem mom is a discouraged mom, just as a problem child is a discouraged child. A young bride told me her mother-in-law was totally transformed when she changed her attitude toward her, when she began to consider what it would be like to be in her place and looked for ways to win her love and trust. Without a single confrontation, a single harsh word, their relationship improved and they actually began enjoying each other and working together with enthusiasm.

Sunday
LESSON 154
Striving for Teamwork

The mother-in-law has much to offer. A strong, kindly mother-in-law will see that divorce does not happen for her son by helping to hold the family together. A strong, loving mother-in-law will see that an untrained wife becomes trained in various household skills and the human arts of nurturing and education. A strong, understanding mother-in-law will care for the children and give occasional rest and freedom to the busy young homemaker. The mother-in-law is a precious artifact. Whatever her qualities are, likeable or unlikeable, they are also the qualities of the son, since she raised him. She is a library of useful knowledge for the young bride. If the young homemaker takes the attitude that she is in school and the mother-in-law is her teacher, and adopts that relationship, then it will be a positive learning experience for the daughter-in-law, and she will become a better, more accomplished, more refined person as positive qualities awaken in her. The mother-in law teaches the ins and outs of the whole family, and if there are dozens of members of the extended family, there is a lot to share and know. She should listen carefully. ¶Many families are not patient and persistent enough to bring about harmony in the home. Often they resort to splitting apart. When the mother-in-law living with her son and daughter-in-law is not kindly, loving or understanding, one common solution that works when the going gets tough for the bride is for the son to get an apartment for himself and his wife next door to his mother and father's home, or at least not too far away. After the first baby is born, mom-in-law may soften. ¶Another solution is a condominium with members of the extended family living in separate apartments in the same building. This happens in many parts of the world where ancestral compounds provide closeness, but also separateness. Within this independence enjoyed by each nuclear family, there is yet a valuable dependence on the extended family as a support in marriage, crises, births and deaths. Here, without too strict a rein, the elderly mother may reign supreme. Honor her, respect her when she visits and realize that each in turn may be a mother-in-law or father-in-law one day. Thus we set a new *karmic* pattern in families where Eastern values and those of the West merge for a happy elderly experience among Hindus in today's world. With this in mind, shall our motto now be "Old and gray and here to stay"? ¶Still, we must admit that to move across town to avoid the mother-in-law is to cause new *karmas* to be worked out in a future birth. To conquer the home situation in love and trust leads us to deepen our religious commitments through *sādhana*, to quell the flames of fight within us. When this is done, a better person emerges. The family *dharma* is a very important part of Hinduism today. We must reaffirm that we are born into a family to merge our *prārabdha karmas* with those of others and endeavor to work them out with all family members. ¶It is best to take a positive attitude. Mothers-in-law are not going to go away. They have always been with us; they will always be with us. Many, if not most, are not going to adjust to being retrained. Most will have a hard time accepting suggestions or hearing about a better way of doing things. They are who they are. If the wife receives pleasure from her husband, simultaneously she can bless his mother for bringing him into a physical body. Let's be kindly. Let's be tolerant. Let's be accepting. Let's be nice to the aged. Let's work out issues at the daily family meeting as they come up. If all else fails and the situation becomes unbearable, let's get an apartment a few minutes away, and treat Mom as an honored guest when she comes to visit, which will probably be twice a day.

Yuva Vivāha Prajñā

युवविवाहप्रज्ञा

The Wisdom of Early Marriage

Unite, O Lord, this couple like a pair of lovebirds. May they be surrounded by children, living both long and happily.

Atharva Veda 14.2.64. BO VE, P. 259

Monday
LESSON 155
Traditions of Early Marriage

We are now entering the dawning of a new age in which everyone is becoming more and more conscious of life and the inner laws of life in their investigation of the inner man. Child marriage is one of the most interesting and least understood practices of ancient India, which has a very real basis in spiritual law. I thought you would be interested this morning to hear of some of the intricacies of this ancient custom. ¶For many thousands of years, India has practiced early marriage in a variety of forms, making the Indian home through the centuries strong and stable, losing much of its power and stability only in more recent times as some of the ancient practices such as early marriage have begun to fall away from common use. But still, in thousands of homes throughout Asia today, families practice the betrothal of their children no later than the age of puberty. Such a practice is continued in many homes surrounding our *āśrama* in the northern part of Sri Lanka. In a typical home, the father and mother begin to take a great interest in finding the proper mate for the child when he or she arrives at the age of six or seven years. In the most traditional communities, many matches are proposed when a boy is five and six years of age to a girl who is just born, because the family wants a happy life with the other family and it seeks to protect the youthful life of the children who are raised together with this vision in mind. Such matches are fulfilled in holy matrimony at age sixteen or later. The principle of such a match is considered to be much the same as the grafting of one kind of an apple tree upon another kind of apple tree, producing a tree which will then bear different kinds of apples. The children are matched by their parents according to an intricate system of character delineation which allows the parents to know the respective basic tendencies of their children. ¶Sometimes a betrothal is made several years before the marriage takes place. In such cases, the little boy or the little girl is told, perhaps at the age of six or seven, who will one day be his wife or her husband. From that day on, the child's mind is constantly directed towards the person he or she will one day marry. The father talks about it, the mother talks about it, the older brothers and sisters are constantly filling the child's mind with thoughts of the husband- or wife-to-be; and the betrothed child begins to anticipate the approaching

Lord Murugan blesses a Śaivite home where a couple dances playfully with their children. When two virgins marry young, they grow especially close and are themselves youthful as their children arrive, making for a close-knit family.

marriage as a sacred and permanent lifetime contract. From the moment of decision, the parents and relatives in both families are quite happy and content with the arrangement, and eventually it is sanctified with the aid of the temple priest. Generally it is when the two children reach their mid-teens that they become actually married. Then the little girl packs her bag and is taken to the house of the boy, where she lives with him, but just like any one of the rest of the family. ¶In some cases in India, prior to the marriage ceremony, the bride and groom may not even have met; but as soon as they begin to live together, they come to know one another slowly in the security of his family's home. Gradually, their minds, which have long been directed toward one another, come together in a natural and harmonious way. When they begin living together, the emotions of each blend one with another, and this is really the marriage of the emotions. First occurs the marriage of the soul. Then the two minds become married. Then the emotions become married or interblended. Finally, the physical consummation of the marriage takes place when both bodies are mature enough for this to happen. The physical bodies continue to grow, and the marriage is a continuing growing together of the physical bodies, emotional bodies and mental bodies, just as you would mold together two pieces of clay until finally you could not tell where one began and the other stopped. Ideally such a marriage is as perfect and complete as the harmonious grafting of one limb upon another.

Tuesday
LESSON 156
Marriages Of the Spirit

Now, you might ask, suppose a young married couple find that they don't like one another. Suppose they are not suited to one another? Well, they are, assuming the match was carefully determined according to the basic tendencies in the nature of each child, according to harmonious and compatible character delineations and not as a forced marriage. The two children, being of the same basic tree, actually grow together in growing up together. This is an ancient ideal among Hindus and other peoples. Though it is not widely practiced in today's world, it may be in the future when society regains the inner understanding that dispels the misconceptions surrounding the subject. ¶One of the most compelling aspects of a compatible child marriage is that divorce never even enters into the consciousness of these husbands or wives. In such a relationship, to think of divorce would be like thinking of cutting off your arm. You don't even consider cutting off your own arm to solve a problem. Nor do children who have grown up together in marriage consider divorcing each other. They have their children at an early age, and they grow up with their own children, so the whole family is closely knit. ¶The success of a good early marriage is due to the fact that it is a marriage of the spirit. It is not simply an emotional, impulsive pairing or a sexual mating. When the family elders, the mothers and fathers, consult with the family *jyotisha śāstrī* and make the betrothal at the very early age of perhaps seven, the destinies of the children are fully directed in the mind of each member of the family. There is no doubt, uncertainty or suspense. ¶We might think that children should not have their lives determined for them in this way by other people, that they should be given free will to make their own mistakes, to find their own happiness. But think for a minute, how much free will do we really have in our Western culture? Without even knowing it, we buy what manufacturers and advertisers determine we should buy, our minds are filled with what the media presents to us, and we date and marry those we contact by chance circumstance. Our existence in all ways is dependent upon our surroundings more than we would like to admit. ¶Now, I am only giving you one view of early marriage. You will have to arrive at your own conclusion on this subject. Certainly, there are abuses of the practice of arranged marriage in general. For instance, in response to such abuse, in 1999 England passed a law forbidding forced marriages of young girls. ¶The responsibility for the marriage of youths lies with the parents, just as they were responsible for their children's conception. After both families have agreed upon the betrothal, it is the duty of the parents in each family to thoughtfully direct the minds of the children toward one another. The parents and all the elders of the family watch carefully to see that the children do not form any other romantic alliances. They may have other close friends, but first and foremost in the mind of each is the husband- or wife-to-be. In this way, a slow amalgamation of the souls of the two children is made; and looking within, it is possible to see the process of interweaving which takes place on the higher planes of consciousness.

Wednesday
LESSON 157
Advantages of Early Marriage

I have observed that children born in such early marriages are spiritually inclined. They are religious and intuitive by nature. Intellectual education does not concern them too much. Nor are they concerned with the worldly pursuits of Western people who are suffering, basically, from frustrated sex emotion, or of those unhappy, incomplete people of the West who live in the frustrations of intellectual ramification and who arrive at the end of their lives and suddenly ask themselves, "Who am I, where did I come from and where am I going?" for unless they have a particularly strong memory, most of their study will have left them. Just as the memory of each detail of your yesterday has flowed through you, so does intellectual knowing eventually flow through the life of the person who contains it, as a thing of only temporary value. ¶The custom of early marriage in Asia does not stop with the marriage ceremony. The mothers and fathers enter into an unwritten contract together to support the son and the daughter and set aside a certain amount of money for them, so that they can eventually have their own house. The boy usually follows along the line of business of his father, and in this way, spiritually, socially, culturally and economically, the youthful husband and wife are taken care of until the young man is old enough to assume his full family responsibilities. If the young man exhibits special aptitude that might warrant it, and if the parents are sufficiently well off, perhaps they will send him to the university. If not, he follows happily and usually successfully in his father's trade. The result of such stable early marriage is to give the nation a solidarity and to bring forth, as well, spiritually strong children. ¶You may enter a home in which such marriages have taken place and find ten people living in the same small area so harmoniously and so well adjusted that you would hardly know that more than one or two are living there. Very large families may live in close contact with each other, and because they are so well adjusted and have such inner respect for each other, there is no contention, no feeling of being crowded. This inner respect for the moods and feelings of another is only possible because the soul qualities are awakened at an early age in the children. Without all of this, we would not, in all wisdom, recommend such early marriage.

Thursday
LESSON 158
Drawbacks of Late Marriages

The further a culture strays from the basic laws of early marriage, the more difficulty do its people have mentally and emotionally, and the more difficult it is for them to awaken spiritually. They have to struggle to internalize and utilize the laws of willpower, concentration and meditation; whereas in a spiritually adjusted Asian home, inner knowledge and inner peace are more or less second nature. ¶Now let us consider marriage the way we know it today in the West. Boys and girls grow up and may not enter into marriage until eighteen, twenty, twenty-five, thirty or later. Along the way they enter into various relationships, and each time they wonder, "Is this the right one?" They compare one experience with another, and each experience they have in this line makes them more unsure of themselves than the last. When marriage finally does happen, instead of the wife going to the husband's home and looking to him completely for her security, she goes to him with reservation. ¶Prior to many Western marriages, the years of looking around, wondering, investigating, experimenting and dating only build up an unnatural conscience, because during the crucial, early years, the young men and women are going against the natural inclinations of their own soul, and the resulting states of uneasy conscience only make them insecure. The man who does marry with a foundation of such insecurity can no longer depend fully upon himself, and he finds himself depending upon his wife. She, in turn, is only half depending upon him. They are like two rickety posts leaning up against each other. Jar them a little bit, and they both fall down. By contrast, a well-raised man who marries early develops, with the support of his family, a natural reliance upon his own inner being, and the wife depends upon her husband. ¶Perhaps you wonder what this force is that amalgamates a husband and wife at their early age. It is an inner force of the nervous system. Perhaps you are somewhat familiar with the central nervous system and the sympathetic nervous system. The arms and legs could be likened to the gross projections of our nervous system which can be seen with the two eyes. But there is also a subtle projection of man's nervous system composed of millions of tiny nerve currents which radiate out from his body and which form an aura about him. When you are close to someone, it is through this subtle nerve force of the aura that you can feel how that person feels. ¶Before a young boy or girl reaches puberty, the nervous system is pure and strong and vital in its growth, providing the child is not beaten or abused and lives in a harmonious home. If you could see psychically the subtle nervous system that permeates the physical body and extends beyond it, you would find that it has little hooks at the end of the nerve force. In an early marriage, these little hooks come together, connecting the boy and the girl like interlocking fingers, and thus the subtle nervous system of each grows together. ¶The soul brings the boy and girl together, the mind brings them together, and finally the nervous system in this manner binds them closer and closer together in an actual amalgamation. Once the subtle forces are completely intertwined, they cannot be torn apart. This is why children scheduled for an early marriage are watched very closely, because until the marriage actually takes place, the power to properly amalgamate the subtle forces and projections of this nervous system may be lost. This virginal power may be dissipated in an instant, never to be regained until a new birth. The children are watched so that they do not have any sexual experience with another of the opposite sex before their intended marriage. If they do, the pristine amalgamating power of the subtle nervous system is lost; and though they could still come together in marriage, there would not be the same binding force to hold their lives together. Thus, early marriage as described above is the ideal only when both boy and girl are virgins.

Friday
LESSON 159
Marriages and Social Problems

When a marriage takes place after the boy or girl have already dissipated their sex energy in one way or another, the main force that holds the two together is one which the woman emanates from within herself in order to stabilize her own security. This is a psychic force which projects subconsciously from her solar plexus. To psychic vision, this force looks like a long, translucent white rope, about six inches in diameter and up to fifty yards in length, which is manifested by the woman's desire for security and is sent out from herself to "hook" onto the frame of a man and wind round and round his spinal column, thus binding him to her, even at times against his conscious will. This is why you find so many weakened men over whom women have gained an inner, psychic control, holding them in lower states of consciousness. Some mothers exert this kind of control over their sons, too, from time to time, when they do not have their husbands. When a man feels "edgy" and "peculiar" without knowing why, he may well be under the psychic domination of a woman. ¶When this is the only binding force of a marriage, it is not a marriage at all. Women are inwardly very unhappy in using this force, because it leads them into a lower, instinctive plane of consciousness as well. Until they renounce the use of it, they are never able to contact the faculties of their own soul or to find the Divinity within. Until a man frees himself from these psychic forces, he can never realize freedom within himself or realize his true Divinity. Yet this is the basis upon which our new culture, or nonculture, in the West has formed. ¶Even in Asia today, which is now tending toward later marriage, the boys and girls are making up their own minds about marriage. But basically they aren't making up their own minds at all. Instead of the soul forming the marriage, it is done the other way around. First the body makes the marriage, then the emotions make the marriage, then the couple become intellectual partners in marriage and spend all their time and energy trying to see eye to eye on many subjects which they can't see eye to eye on. When the intellect makes such a marriage, it never becomes a spiritual marriage. It can't be, because the power of the spirit, which was not harnessed in chastity at an early age, is gone. As man loses the power of a spiritual marriage, his life depends more and more upon his instinctive nature, upon his instinctive drives, and fulfilling his instinctive drives becomes popular, becomes the cultural way of life, the social custom. ¶The news media are now making us aware of the terrible social problems being created by the tradition of late marriage in America. Child marriage is not considered modern, and yet each day the percentage of children engaging in intercourse, and of teen pregnancy out of wedlock, is increasing, especially with the help of the Internet's pornographic enticements. Hotmail is not only e-mail! What proper guidance, what *dharmic* fulfillment, is given to the Western, and now Eastern, boy and girl at the age of puberty? Very little, very little. ¶In 1962 someone gave me an article telling about the many families in the United States who were considering entering their children into early marriage with the consent and support of the two families through a legal contract and agreement. Even in our own state of Hawaii, the law sets the age of consent for intercourse, and hence marriage, at a youthful fourteen. This is a basic social issue for us to think about and consider. If you know two people who were married at an early age without prior sexual experience, compare their lives with a couple who married later in life after many affairs and experiences. Early marriage has long been practiced by many cultures and civilizations of the world, including the early Jews, Christians and Muslims. Such practices are not thought out intellectually but are arrived at through observation and the intuitive knowing of the tremendous forces in the instinctive nature of man.

Saturday
LESSON 160
Growing Up Together

Now let us suppose that a young boy and girl are pushed, even forced, into marriage together who are not astrologically, intellectually and spiritually compatible. That would be like trying to graft a pine tree upon an apple tree, which just would not work. The chemistry of the inner forces of this boy and the girl simply would not mix, and naturally the marriage would not be a happy one. This is often the case when two different types of people, who are basically not suited to one another, marry at a later age and thus do not have the chance to grow and mature together. In this case, they are only "glued" together, and when the circumstances of their companionship become too intense, the glue melts and they fall apart. ¶This indicates why we see so little of early match-making for youths today. There is simply not sufficient knowledge widespread in our society to make proper matches between children. This sophisticated knowledge must be present in both families. Furthermore, both must necessarily be mature and traditional religious families. Similarly, where there is no proper experience in grafting, trees never get grafted. ¶Among my initiates, we arrange marriages at a slightly later age, such as twenty-one for the boy and seventeen for the girl, and we always require the blending of the two families as a one family and the unequivocal consent of the young man and woman, as well as a written agreement between the couple. There is a lot to be said for marriages that are arranged at these formative ages, because after age twenty-five, personal patterns are already set, and it is more difficult for anyone to adjust to a marriage partner and be guided by community elders. ¶Years ago in the West, before the two World Wars, it was looked down upon, even unheard of, if there was not at least a three- to five-year difference between the groom and the bride. And to keep genetics strong, cousins never, ever married. The boy was always older, of course. It has been my observation that there is more strain and misunderstanding in marriages when the woman is of the same age or older than the man. When younger, he may feel like a boy, and she like a mother. Whenever the husband is older, his masculinity and sense of protective caring is stimulated, as his wife is younger than he and therefore depends upon him, as eventually do the children. ¶In today's world the new trend is to marry when the professions are well established and earning power is up—enough to support a nuclear family. But what about the children? The generation gap is humongous, or at least very big, for them. The mom who marries as a child herself, around sixteen or even earlier and having a baby ten months later, would be only about sixteen or seventeen years older than her first child. By the time she and her husband are fortyish and in the stressful throes of male and female menopause (yes, men go through it, too), their children will be in their early twenties and totally able to help handle their parents' traumas. ¶Compare this to a young woman of twenty-five marrying a man who is thirty or older. Mom will be fortyish and dad, too, when the children are in puberty. Hot flashes for mom, while dad is wondering whatever happened to his youth and resisting having an affair. In the midst of all this, the children are demanding their freedom as they experience their own budding powers of procreation. Under these circumstances, the emotional ups and downs in the home can be almost unbearable for everyone, including the neighbors, who sometimes have to listen to loud, high-pitched voices and banging of doors. ¶Many nuclear families blow up because of the simultaneous release of the biological forces of bodily change experienced by both generations, which inevitably happens in families who marry late in life—father going through middle age crisis while his teenage son is coping with "testosterone poisoning," mother going through menopause while her adolescent daughter is transforming into an estrogen-powered woman. Of course, the generation gap of twenty-five to thirty years or more between mom and dad and their offspring also contributes to deeper misunderstandings. ¶What price profession, a well-established financial plan and enough income to maintain a nuclear family? The divorce lawyers get their share, and so do the marriage counselors and psychiatrists—and, oh yes, the doctors, the druggists and the hospitals all take a cut. So, there is a lot to be said, in contemporary Hindu families, for marriage beginning around sixteen for girls and twenty for boys. By this age such children are practically young adults, which even present-day laws recognize.

Sunday
LESSON 161
Not Growing Up Together

One suggestion is for marriageable youth to give up those summer vacations and study around the year to get through school and into a profession so they can wed and establish a family while they are still young, rather than delaying the completion of education and the time of marriage. ¶Can you tell this to the young people of today? No. They will say, "We will deal with it when it happens." To delay marriage until age thirty or later and go into a situation with no plan of how to deal with the problems when they come up is flying blind, isn't it? We don't even buy our automobiles like that. Will youth listen to such advice from elders? No, not any more. "It's not cool," they say. Well, it won't be cool when emotions get hot and the family has to live through the seven teenage years of puberty simultaneously with the five or more fortyish years of menopause. Think about it. ¶Here's a story: Little Jyoti got interested in sailing when his father purchased a boat. Dad was reliving his youth, but had no time to take Jyoti out on a sail, except once, and that was the time they nearly capsized. Dad was forty-seven, and Jyoti was seventeen. There were thirty years between them. Imagine! It certainly didn't used to be that way, but it is now. All their lives the father and the son lived in different universes, seldom communicating. Even when they thought they communicated, they didn't. The distance between the ages of Jyoti and his parents contributed to the breakup of the family. ¶Jyoti went to live with mom after the divorce. They were all happier, now that the fights about the cost of the boat were over. Mom thought the money spent on the boat would be better spent on a new wing built on their house for her mother, who was getting old. Now mom and Jyoti live in her mother's house, which is big enough for all three of them. Jyoti and dad have finally become friends. Dad sees Jyoti whenever he comes over. Jyoti does not visit dad's place too often and only when dad's "significant other" is at work and it's dad's day off. It's all too true that this story is the tale of many families in today's world. ¶Another story: Rani's mom was married at seventeen to a boy who was twenty. They were both virgins and grew together as they discovered each other physically, emotionally, intellectually and spiritually. Then came little Rani, then Kumar and then Krishna. Mom, dad and the kids were all children together, and they are still together. Mom stays home. She has never held a job. Dad makes enough for the whole family; they live simply. Mom is always there for her family, laughing and smiling. She is rarely tired and never stressed out. Dad has mutual-interest projects going in the attic, the basement and the garage for the two boys. Mom is teaching her daughter how to sew, cook, sing and serve. Mom, dad, Rani and the boys enjoy each other because they are not so far apart in age. Are those days gone? Are there going to be no more happy times when the entire family enjoys each other without too much distance between their age and interests? Dad doesn't have to worry about giving quality time to his family. He is there with them—there for them—and so is mom. They have no marriage counseling bills to pay; no problems, really. ¶The moral to these stories is simple. There is a wisdom in the old ways of marrying early, which is exactly what happened in tribes and cultures for thousands of years prior to World Wars I and II. That is the natural way, the way that avoids frustration and promiscuity, marriage failure and unhappy families.

Ādhunika Vivāha Ghaṭaka

आधुनिकविवाहघटक

Modern Matchmakers

May the suitor, O Agni, win our friendship by choosing this maiden and bringing us good luck. Liked by the wooers, lovely in assemblies, may she have good fortune with her husband.

Atharva Veda 2.36.1. HV, P. 123

GOOD
DATA
DEL
OFF
M+
M-
MR
Mc
EXP
7
8
9
4
5
6
C
1
2
3

Monday
LESSON 162
Arranged Marriages

Marriage is a union not only of a boy and girl, but of their families as well. Not leaving such crucial matters to chance, all family members participate in finding the most suitable spouse for the son or daughter and thereafter commit hearts and minds to assist in times of need. Marriage is a sacred covenant which all relatives take up the responsibility to care for and protect. It is one of the most sacred events of life. Through the *homa* rite at the marriage ceremony, the priest invokes the Gods. The elders, the priests, the Gods, the *devas,* the planets and even cows witness the couple vow themselves to holy, harmonious matrimony for the rest of their lives. Thus, divorce or annulment are considered out of the question. The *Ṛig Veda* intones: "United your resolve, united your hearts, may your spirits be one, that you may long together dwell in unity and concord" (10.191.4. VE, P. 863). ¶While not all marriages must be arranged, there is wisdom in arranged marriages, which have always been an important part of Hindu culture. Their success lies in the families' judgment to base the union on pragmatic matters which will outlast the sweetest infatuation and endure through the years. Compatibility of culture and education is also taken into consideration. A spouse is generally sought from within the same religious community. The man and woman should at least be of the same religious sect for long life and a happy marriage. This may not seem important if both are not religiously active, but conditions will tend to change in future years, especially after children are born, and the disparity can lead to separation and divorce. Most families begin early in finding the proper mate for their children among families they know and esteem for the kinship bonds the marriage would bring. Those involved ponder whether the two families can blend into a one family harmoniously with benefits to both. Stability is enhanced if the groom has completed his education, established earnings in a profession and is at least three years older than the bride.

Tuesday
LESSON 163
Seeking the Best Match

In arranging a marriage, the families consult astrologers regularly until a match is found. Sometimes the boy and girl are allowed to get to know each other long before they are aware that a marriage is being arranged for them. Of course, if they do not get along well, the matter is

---

With temple spires on the horizon, a modern matchmaker in Bali uses a computer to assess the astrological compatibility of a young couple considering marriage. Hindus know that harmony of the two natures is one key to a successful marriage.

dropped and the search is on again. If one match is not agreeable, another is sought. The inner-world *devas* also help to arrange the best matches. Most traditional astrologers have one or more *devas* assisting them to provide knowledge from the *ākāśic* records and insight into the planetary powers that impel *karmas.* ¶Astrological compatibility is also sought for and acquired between the girl and her prospective mother-in-law. The results are taken especially seriously if they will be living in the same home, because in this case the bride will be under the guidance of the mother-in-law and may spend more time with her than with her own husband. In marrying the son, she becomes the daughter of his mother. ¶Once a potential spouse is selected, discreet, informal inquiries are made by a relative or friend. If the response is encouraging, the girl's father meets with and presents a proposal to the boy's father. In some communities it is the boy's father who presents the proposal. In these modern times, with the worldwide diaspora of Hindus from India and other countries, the fathers must take an aggressive role in helping their sons and daughters become well settled in life. If fathers do not fulfill this obligation, it becomes the duty of the mothers. This pattern differs from the tradition of well-settled village communities where only the father of the girl makes the overtures. In today's widely dispersed global Hindu village, it becomes everyone's duty to help in the task of matchmaking for the next generation. ¶Once the union has been tentatively agreed upon, the families gather at the girl's home to get further acquainted and allow them to meet and discuss their potential life together. Of course, mutual attraction and full consent of the couple are crucial. After all the input from the community is in place, it is the couple themselves who must make the final decision whether to spend their life together, based on their own personal sensibilities and judgments. They do have the right to say no. In recent years, we have found that an excellent way for a young prospective couple to gradually get to know each other before committing to marriage is through correspondence by e-mail over a period of several months. The first and the last important factor for a good match is that the boy and girl must be happy and comfortable in each other's company.

Wednesday
LESSON 164
Pledges and Blessings

Love marriages that are not arranged by the parents are also fully acceptable if the astrology is excellent, the parents on both sides agree and the young lady and the young man are of the same religious denomination. Of course, these ideals cannot always be met, and if not, more support will be needed from family and friends to make the marriage a success. ¶Before the wedding, the bride and groom each writes out a covenant by hand, pledging loyalty to one another and formalizing their promises, ideals, expectations and love. The couple share and discuss these documents together, read them carefully and make necessary revisions until 100 percent agreement is achieved. Like a ship's chart, these detailed vows can be referred to if the relationship gets off course. Each of the two families makes a written pledge as well, signed by the mother and father of the groom and the mother and father of the bride, stating what they promise to do and give toward supporting this marriage in the areas of *artha, kāma, dharma* and *moksha.* Also most welcome are written testimonies in support of the marriage from grandfathers, grandmothers, uncles and aunts, sisters and brothers, as well as from other members of the religious community. This is also a time when anyone among family and friends may, in deepest confidence, even anonymously, share with the family preceptor any obstacles to this marriage that should be known and understood. A full, honest disclosure of the boy's life and the girl's life, including sexual experiences, should be made to both families and to the *kulaguru.* ¶From the time of inquiry into a match, several months should be allowed for the *jyotisha āchāryas* and *śāstrīs* to assess compatibility. The whole process of arranging a proper match for a son or daughter often takes two or more years. There should never be a sense of urgency for this or any other lifetime commitment. As Jnanaguru Siva Yogaswami so wisely said, "No hurry. No worry. No sorry." Nor should the arrangements ever be forced on the boy or girl. They remain free to cancel the process at any time if the match does not seem suitable to them. ¶When all agreements have been reached, the boy's mother adorns her new daughter with a gold necklace. Generous gifts are exchanged between the members of both families to bind the two families together in love and loyalty. Rejoicing begins with the formal engagement party, when the boy and girl exchange gifts, such as engagement rings. Later, they read their pledges to each other in the presence of elders. All arrangements and ceremonies culminate on the wedding day, when members of both families join to wish the couple a righteous, prosperous, happy life leading to the ultimate goal of enlightenment. During weddings or related ceremonies, the vegetarian diet should in no way be compromised. Meat and other nonvegetarian foods should not be served, even to please guests of other religions or communities. All Hindus attending should be requested to dress in formal Hindu attire.

Thursday
LESSON 165
Supporting The Marriage

Once a marriage has occurred, both families are relied upon to hold it together through the years. It is the duty especially of the husband's parents to support and make the marriage work and to offer a home to their new daughter. But it is unacceptable in modern Hindu society, and especially in our fellowship, to follow the oppressive tradition in which the girl becomes the total charge of the boy's family and is seldom allowed to see her family of birth. It is the duty of the bride's parents to monitor her protection and observe the couple's abilities to dwell in unity and concord, while allowing them freedom to work things out together in their new home. ¶If she is abused physically, they must open their doors to receive her back, to be sheltered, comforted and consoled. It then becomes their duty and that of all *śishyas* in the community to try to patch things up, restore harmony and obtain trustworthy promises from the husband that this will never happen again. The bride should receive no blame for her husband's violence, for it is he who has broken his promise to adore her and protect her from harm. ¶The blending of the two families as a one family gives both the son and daughter two families to support them in good times and bad. It is the responsibility of both families to work toward assuring an endearingly enduring marriage, as well as to guide the raising of the progeny, so that they may become good, productive, *dharma*-aware citizens, contributing to society at large. If the two families fail in this mutual effort, society fails. ¶To build solid marriages, some Hindu institutions provide a family evening for fellowship and discussion with a trained counselor. Once a year during the holy time of Pañcha Gaṇapati, the couple take out their marriage agreement and together study where they have been lax or derelict. They trace back in their minds to incidents that are still vibrating as negative *saṁskāras*, and apologize humbly and seek forgiveness and total resolution. They renew their commitment to each other. This is a wonderful key for setting the tone for the coming year—of harmony and peace, which leads to abundance and happiness. We call this *anāhaṭa yoga*, cleansing the heart *chakra*, bringing up that true love for one another. It is the process of bringing up all those things that were not settled before going to sleep, to retrieve those seeds before they get ploughed under and produce another crop of sorrow in the coming years. It is bringing up little things that each one said or did that hurt the other and were not resolved. It is bringing up incidents of anger, any physical violence, which should never be but may have been. It is time to extend apologies, talk with your *kulaguru,* and make promises and New Year's resolutions to set the course of the future on the path of *dharma,* which is based on *ahiṁsā.*

Friday
LESSON 166
Cross-National Marriages

Many are the cross-national marriages happening today, marriages between members of different nations, religions, cultures or races. Times have changed. It is communication that has done it. With no communication, there is no change. When information flows freely, independent thinking is the result, and change is inevitable. Yes, inevitable, and that is what we are seeing today. The younger generation are thinking for themselves, no longer relying on elders to advise. This is unfortunate, for now they will have to learn from their own mistakes. What a way to learn! But this is what is happening, and it is happening faster than we would like to see. Much faster. ¶Any kind of marriage can survive if true love is there as its glue. True love is the kind of love that gives the couple the ability to give and take from each other without serious conflict, to go through the ups and downs together in trust, to support each other without fail and to reign as benign king and queen strong enough to bind all members of the family together. Even the *ṛishis* said that when true love is there, any kind of astrology is good and the marriage will be lasting. Love overrides all bad influences and softens incompatibilities. Love is the sum of the law. But how would a young couple know if theirs is true love or magnetic love? By giving the love a test. That is how. Test it with time. Magnetic love weakens and all but disappears over time. True love grows stronger, much stronger, with time. True love mellows through the years. ¶Cross-national marriages are essential to the Hindu thought that *avant-garde* thinkers are sharing today, "All the world is one family," *Vasudhaiva kuṭumbakam.* Citizens of the world bound in love can survive the torrents of the upheavals that naturally come as lives are lived through together and individuals grow ever closer and closer in body, mind and spirit. ¶Every marriage needs a support of some kind or another built into it. True love is the best support of all, but support from the parents on both sides is a necessary help, too, especially for couples who were drawn together only by magnetism. It is when the magnetic love fades away, and all that's left are the children, that support from parents and friends is essential for the marriage to last without violent outbursts of released stress which was once undying passion. ¶Shall we have a look into the future? Since cross-national marriages have happened, are happening, and will continue to happen, there must be some sensible way for them to happen without undue strain on the families of the couple. Wisdom is supposed to fix things, heal conditions, and settle problems. But first we have to admit that there is a problem. And, yes, cross-national marriages are a problem to many people of the old school. The old school only became old just ten years ago. Before then it was a school sharing standards of how things should be to maintain a growing and stable society.

Saturday
LESSON 167
When It's Too Late to Say No

When an Asian girl marries a black boy, should she be banished from the kingdom? Yes, according to the old school, the old standard. No, according to the new school, the new standard. The banishment method of parental punishment is outdated and bizarre today. Today's girls think. They understand. They do not intend to be the ill-treated servants of the mother-in-law. The days of Cinderella have long since passed when the mean old stepmother made her cringe beneath her wrath. Boys, too, think for themselves. They read, they listen and evaluate. Theirs is an ever-changing world ahead. They are busy preparing for it. But then along comes love, of one kind or another, to complicate their lives. ¶When Karen falls in love with Shan and elopes to his country, go visit them and bring her home in your heart. "I love you, therefore, I love whom you love." That should be the attitude. When Kumar announces his undying love for Carmen, his lover from Mexico, and informs you that her father has a place for him as senior partner in his business, accept it. Enjoy Mexico City. It is a great place, because Kumar and Carmen are there. ¶Yes, hands across the ocean are loving hands. Hands across the ocean are binding continents to continents, businesses to businesses. This and more is what all Hindu elders are seeing happening around them today. Today's world is a happening world. Cross-national marriages are inevitable as the peoples of the world become more and more a global village. This is the real, earthy expression of our belief in one God and one world, The soul has nothing to do with nationalism, social restrictions, ethnic taboos or restrictive, prejudicial upbringing. Two souls joining in *dharmic* matrimony transcend all such boundaries. ¶My advice has always been that families should arrange marriages for their children. That's part of their *purusha* and *strī dharma*. This is a process they should begin early on. But if they don't do that, obviously their young people will start arranging their own marriages. And very often when they do arrange a marriage for themselves, the family objects. They have no right to object, because they didn't perform their duty in the first place. ¶The dilemma is that matches are not being arranged, and yet parents also want strict control over their youth, and youths are going to find partners, one way or another. Girls especially should be chaperoned. It's very easy in today's world to meet the wrong kind of people. As one solution, though not the ideal, I recommend in such cases that mature young ladies double-date and chaperone each other. Then they can talk together about the young men they are dating, and bypass the families who've neglected their duties, and arrange a good marriage for themselves that will be lasting, and in the future raise the next generation by doing their duty by arranging a marriage according to tradition for their own children early on. ¶We cannot stand in front of progress, lest we get run over by it. But we can sit by the side of progress and guide it so it doesn't run off the track. This cannot be done when we break off communications and refuse to talk to the youth when they don't obey the old standard. It is communication that is catalyzing the changes in the first place, so we all must guide the young by keeping the channels of communication open. Don't let them go. Go with them. Love them and gently guide them.

Sunday
LESSON 168
Interfaith Marriages

I tell young ladies, if you are planning on getting married, do not do what the average mother might tell you, "Get the husband under your thumb right at the beginning. Otherwise you might have a terrible time, because it's harder to do it later on." Don't do that. Go into your marriage for better or for worse and live up to your vow. Be to your husband like melted butter is on toast; it is absorbed. Be one. You will have a very happy old age. ¶It might be rough at the start, but don't hold divorce over his head to force him into various preconceived ideas that your girlfriend has put into your mind, as so many do, or that you've seen on television or in the movies. You have seen the results that Hollywood marriages have played upon the lives of those who have had them as they have gotten older through the years. They are not happy people, though they are advertised as glamorously as they make their living. That is not the way. The way is, when you take your vow, think about it first, and then stick to it for better or for worse. ¶I tell young men, Gentlemen, if you are thinking about getting married, do not marry a young lady who won't be one with you in your religion, who will not be willing to stay at home and take care of and raise your family, one who doesn't respect you as a man and starts, right off the bat, by telling you what to do. Don't do that, because if you do you will be miserable and you will lose your manhood and be nothing but a puppet on the strings of your wife. And you will both be unhappy, but she especially, in older age. Rather, choose a girl who will blend with you for better or for worse. And whether you are successful or not, she will be happy to eat what you eat and go where you go. A Roman ideal pronounced by the bride at weddings was "Where you are, there I will be." It might be difficult in the beginning years, but it will be much better later. ¶A seeker wrote to me saying, "I'm in love with a Christian girl but she wants me to give up my religion and accept Jesus Christ. How can I explain to her that Hinduism is my path and I want to stay with it, but I love her very much? What should I do, Gurudeva?" I responded that you have to think of the children and how you want to raise them. Obviously you want to raise them to be good Hindu children. Since there is very little connection between Hinduism and Christianity—because Christianity does not accept *karma* or reincarnation, the existence of an all-pervasive God or our temples and ceremonies—there will be serious problems. If she remains a Christian and you remain a Hindu, the children are going to be very confused. If your beloved doesn't want to go along with you intellectually and spiritually, maybe your love is only physical; that is called carnal love—love of the flesh. That is a very limited type of love, and it is not long lasting. Don't be guided by your carnal, instinctive emotions. Be guided by your spiritual intellect, or by my good advice. Go shopping. Find a good Hindu girl, or let your parents find one for you, so you can raise a good new generation of high souls. ¶I've seen many cases of Hindus marrying outside of their own religion, and I've seen the young couple be very happy for a while. But after the children come and the sensuality of the marriage has cooled off, then there arises a tension between the husband and wife. Generally one becomes more religious than the other. The non-Hindu spouse argues, "You should be religious in my religion," and the Hindu insists, "You should be religious in my religion." The victims of this conflict, which generally goes on throughout life, are the children. It is a couple's shared allegiance to a religious tradition that is the most important common ground.

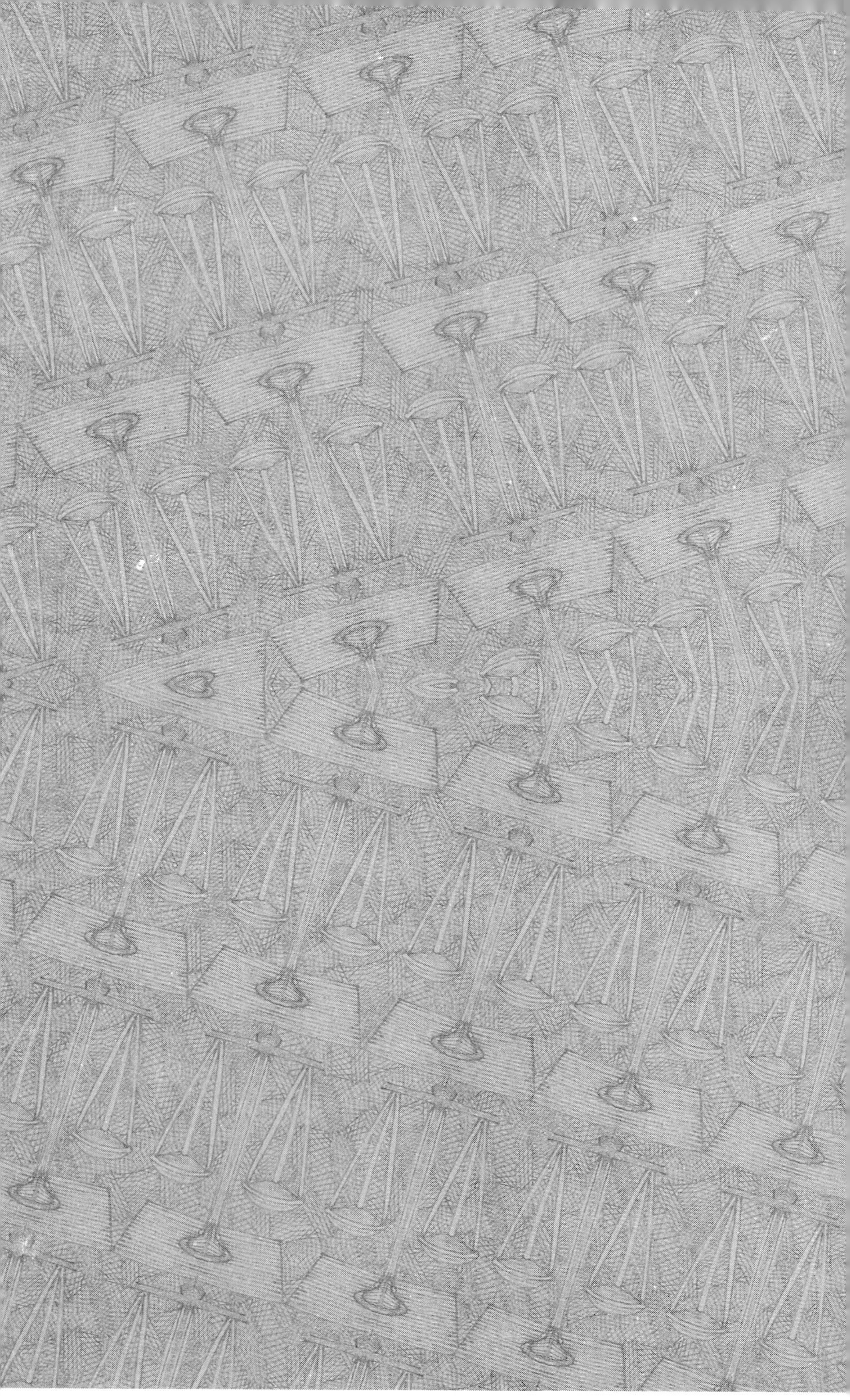

Vivāha Vicçhedaḥ Pīḍanam cha

विवाहविच्छेदः पीडनम् च

Divorce and Abuse

Dwell in this home; never be parted! Enjoy the full duration of your days, with sons and grandsons playing to the end, rejoicing in your home to your heart's content.

Ṛig Veda 10.85.42. VE, P. 256

Monday
LESSON 169
Marriage Is Forever

There is a breakdown that has been under way among Hindus for some time all over the world. Complaints as well as suggestions come in daily to my publisher's desk. These are some of the typical problems: mothers are no longer teaching righteousness, Vedic Dharma, worship and *pūjā* to their children, for fear their little ones won't fit into the alien cultures in which they are living. That's one. Fathers are no longer taking their sons into the family business or profession, but giving them choices of their own, for fear of being regarded as the "dominant" parent figure and not fitting in with the society in which they are living. That's another. There are more. ¶Children are orphaned in their own homes because the minds of both mother and father are in the work-a-day world in which the children play no part. Kids content themselves within the *asuric* realms of video arcades and TV. Families have given up *dharma* and even the hope of *moksha,* liberation from rebirth. Instead, they are immersed in the insatiable search for *artha* (wealth) and *kāma* (enjoyment) and the many other magnetic pulls, so that they, too, are able to blend into modern society. ¶Hindu people, we are told in many e-mails, have almost all become passive followers, with few active leaders among them. No one wants to stand out over another, lest he be harshly criticized and put down. Many moderners fear openly affirming the *dharma* if it conflicts with modern society. Society as we know it today is the doctrine of materialism governed by anarchy. Lay down a rule, and someone will break it, no matter what it is. Are we in the Kali Yuga? ¶There is one institution that there is still hope in saving. It has been cherished in scripture, in living cultures, in all the major religions for thousands of years. It is the precious institution of marriage. It is the binding, contractual agreement between a man and woman who have come together to take on the responsibility of birthing, raising and educating a new generation. How are we going to have a brave new world, a new world order, a new age, based on anarchy within the family itself? Yet, here, too, Hindus are taking their examples from those who do not understand or observe *dharma*; they are seeing divorce as a solution instead of a problem. ¶When the institution of marriage breaks down, everyone suffers. We see this happening all around us. A husband and wife bound by holy sacraments are

---

Divorce is a growing problem today. Here a judge guides the proceedings of a family that is breaking up, listening to allegations of the husband and wife. The real victim here is the boy, who cries as he realizes he will no longer live together with his mother and father.

psychically attached to each other. To separate for a month, a week or even for a day can be painful on the part of one or both. They reach out to one another during the time of physical absence in dreams and longing. How painful then is their permanent separation? How much anguish does it bring to their beloved children, whose wounds never really heal? And how is it that only the priest, a person who invokes God and the Gods, can sanctify a marriage, and that a court judge, a man of the world, can cancel that divine contractual agreement? Impossible. Only in the Kali Yuga. ¶A long and joyous life is theirs who remain firmly on the faultless path of the control of the five senses. There are still a few elders left today who speak out, whether listened to or not. Their fire of righteous indignation, their love for *dharma,* is making an impression upon the younger generation and their parents alike. We appeal to these elders to take courage and proclaim the ancient values, whether their children and grandchildren listen to them or not. Some part of them will be hearing. Preach the *dharma.* There is little to lose and much to gain. We appeal to elders to speak against divorce, to patiently work to harmonize matrimonial tensions and diffuse difficult family situations.

Tuesday
LESSON 170
Drawbacks Of Divorce

Divorce only begins new problems. Is a divorce similar to going out of business? Or bankruptcy? Yes, because in both cases everyone is the loser. The employees are losers, the children are losers, the suppliers are losers; everyone is a loser, and everyone takes sides. In the case of the failing business, the employees take sides, the partnership breaks up, the partners take sides, and their friends take sides. In case of a marriage, the friends of a husband take his side, the friends of a wife take her side, and there is a permanent division. Sometimes the courts take the side of the children, and the children are divided. It is the breakdown of the community, it is the breakdown of society, and it is the creation of a lot of *kukarma* that has to be worked out in this or probably in a future life. There's another great loss in the case of a marriage that breaks up or a business that breaks up, and the loss is trust in the individuals concerned. They lose their ability to trust each other, to trust themselves; and, of course, no one trusts them. ¶Couples have been taught to look to psychiatrists, psychologists, family counselors and attorneys for solutions to marital problems. But who can give better solutions than our qualified elders who know the *karmas,* who know the *adharma* involved in divorce? Their experience has great value. Find a *swāmī, sādhu, guru,* a *jyotisha śāstrī,* someone who can help tighten the bonds of family love and trust and make this person an integral part of your family. Every family needs its spiritual preceptor to strengthen the support group, who in turn hold the family together when hard times come. The plea is to hang on to one thing: the family life. Marriage is forever. ¶Indian culture has within it all the solutions to maintain proper relationships of a man being manly and a woman being womanly. Today men are confronted by women who have, often out of necessity, nurtured their masculine qualities. Naturally, such couples will fight, compete and suffer. In my life-long ministry, those who are not getting along well in marriage come occasionally for advice. We work it out according to ancient *śāstric* principles that transcend the immediate problems. Marriage is like a voyage by ship. Sometimes the going is easy and sunny, and sometimes there is bad weather to endure. But at all times it's advisable to stay with the ship and not jump overboard. My experience is that the bad *karmas,* or *kukarmas,* as well as harsh astrology and difficult attitudes, are always finally overcome, so long as no one gives up the hope and the effort. The marriage continues. The word *divorce* is never uttered or seen as a solution in the hundreds of extended families who look to me as preceptor. ¶Those who don't take such advice are overwhelmed by the tugs and pulls of *prāṇic* forces between them stimulated by hatred and confusion, tears, remorse, unresolvable misunderstandings which have gone on unattended for fifteen or twenty years. Couples who did not listen to my advice to not end their marriage ten years ago still speak to me today of their separation as though it all happened a week ago. They admit that divorce was no solution, only a postponement of problems that still linger, which could have been solved and still have to be. Those who have gone through the experience know that divorce and remarriage is just trading one set of problems for another. We have seen that divorcees remarry others with the same traits, temperament, faults, failings and even looks as their previous spouse. No one, however clever they may be, can run away from their birth *karmas.* No, divorce is no solution. Separation, though better, is still not the solution. Both are only the beginning of new problems.

Wednesday
LESSON 171
Unofficial Divorce

In Hinduism marriage is still highly respected, and so divorce is a sign of failure, because life is a spiritual journey and failing to fulfill that journey is a weakness. In a sense, it is a crime against one's own *karma* and *dharma* in this life. It is like saying, "I can't do what I came here to do." Divorce brings loss of social position and respect in the community. By getting divorced, one betrays a sacred covenant, a betrayal that weakens the whole of society. ¶There is divorce, and there is divorce. I have observed through the years that a modern form of Hindu divorce has become a part of Indian culture. It is a clever way to not hurt the feelings of elders, parents and relatives, or to avoid incurring the community stigma of divorce. A modern form of Hindu divorce, it seems, has cleverly been conceived in the following way. The husband is under great stress, a stress that is not natural for a human being, a stress based on living up to materialistic expectations. He comes home psychically wounded, tired, worried. If things do not go well at home, he may verbally or even physically abuse his wife and family, blaming her for everything bad that happens to him. Sensing his failure to cope with all of this, he secretly wishes he did not have to face his weakness. ¶He learns from compatriots that the Big Solution to the marriage problem is to get away from the wife and the kids. He is advised to accept a job in another part of the world, knowing that his association with his family will become distant and tenuous, and he will no longer have to confront his wife, who has become his conscience. He knows he will hardly have to speak with her, rarely visit her and will be able to avoid, most of the time, the challenges the marriage has brought to him which he is unwittingly unable or unwilling to resolve. He knows, too, that he won't have to face the community's disdain that a formal divorce would bring, and that he can avoid the financial pains of alimony. ¶After reorganizing his professional life, the husband takes a job in a far-off land. He returns home for brief periods and only occasionally, thus effecting a separation without the expensive inconvenience and social stigma of formal divorce proceedings. He assures everyone, mostly himself, that this is the right thing to do, since he is making more money. Of course, money will never make up for his absence, never buy the children their childhood back. Lacking in fatherly guidance, the children are running wild, turning promiscuous, later to repeat the example of neglect that dad is teaching them. No one wins. ¶Husband and wife should always be together. If there is an unavoidable separation, he should call her daily, ask how her day was, inquire about the children. After all, it is the harmonizing of their *prāṇas* that will create through their children a brave new world, a new world order and a new age.

Thursday
LESSON 172
Whom to Hold Responsible?

HINDUISM TODAY ran a quiz about divorce on the women's page. The subject struck a nerve among readers. Here's a question that a young Hindu asked about coping with divorce. ¶Question: My mother and father got a divorce, and I really resent it. It happened seven years ago when I was sixteen, and almost every day I regret what I missed by not having my mom and dad together in a loving home. How can I deal with the resentment, Gurudeva? ¶Answer: It's not easy experiencing the separation and divorce of one's mom and dad, at any age—six, sixteen or thirty-one. There is a feeling of emptiness; something is lost, never to be regained. The feelings and thoughts of blame grow, they do not diminish, as the years go by. But look at it this way. Any marriage, yours maybe, needs a loving, strong support group that wants to help the young couple, or the older couple, work out their problems rather than avoid them through separation and finally divorce. Basically, when there are children involved as a result of a marriage, there really is no divorce—only separation. Every marriage is truly irrevocable, carved in the *ākāśic* records when the first child's umbilical cord is cut. Thereafter, there can be no separation without a great deal of pain and unforeseen *karmic* repercussions. ¶Upon whom should the children put the blame? Put it where it truly belongs. Put it on the support groups—the mothers, the grandmothers, the grandfathers, the aunts, the uncles, the cousins, the next-door neighbors, the business partners and friends of the family. Everyone in the community shares the tragedy of the home's breaking up—the members of the temple society, the marriage counselor, psychiatrist, psychologist, the hairdresser, the gym instructor and the attorney were all responsible to become part of the solution rather than part of the dissolution of the marriage. Put the blame on them, not on your mom and dad. ¶An extended family that loves one another and looks out for the good of all, a religious group of loving souls who pride themselves on low percentage of divorce in their community or congregation—these and more are all the people who can or should see the tension growing between husband and wife and who have the ability to diffuse it at the early stages. Don't blame your mother and father. If blame is to be cast, blame all those people that surrounded your family who were not alert enough, good souls that they may be, to help diffuse the tension between your parents. ¶Obviously, the support group has failed their marriage. You must admit that failure, lest it drag you down to its own depth. Be part of the solution. Don't perpetuate the problem. Don't make them feel guilty. For your own peace of mind, transfer the blame, the hurt feelings, the pain and resentment over to the relatives, the community and national value system. Become an agent of goodwill. Have kind words to say about dad to mom and kind words to say about mom to dad. Resist the impulse to criticize one to the other and cause an even greater separation within the family. They are not to blame. Society is. ¶If you take sides, you are creating bad *karma, kukarma,* for yourself, to be faced later. So treat each one the same. Don't make deals, don't deceive them or keep secrets from them, lest you psychically alienate yourself from the home. Maybe, just maybe, you can help them to understand and reconcile their differences if you follow this advice. Maybe, just maybe, time and the forces of nature will all come to your aid, and your parents will remarry and you will all become a family again. Don't perpetuate the problem. Be part of the solution. Work with it. You, their child, may be their very best hope.

Friday
LESSON 173
Support at Crucial Times

When the tensions of the burdens of life begin to build, if friends, relatives and community begin to pull away rather than come forward to help, mom and dad are rendered helpless, absolutely helpless. Certain crises are predictable in the course of a marriage. When the first child is born, everything changes. This is the first crisis in their life. He lost his sweetheart and lover when she gave birth to her first child and became a mother. She lost her lover, too, when he became a father. Their roles first began to change during the time of her pregnancy. He had to watch very closely his thoughts toward other women, while feeling neglect because she was thinking about their baby soon to be born more than she was thinking about him. She used to think only of him. ¶Moving into another home is another crisis time. It's easy for dad because he is involved in new employment and new friends, but hard for mom because she has to adjust to the change of her entire environment. Is this a time for her to be emotionally upset? Yes it is. ¶At middle age, around forty, mom goes through menopause—another big crisis. Dad doesn't admit it—no man ever does—but he goes through a corresponding change at that time, too. At that time they both begin to think how it would have been if they had married somebody else. Dad, maybe, especially is ready for one last fling. They both have a desire to return to the surroundings of their youth. This is another intense crisis time. If dad reaches fortyish first and mom later, then they experience two crisis times instead of one. When their daughter entered puberty, another crisis time occurred for the family. They didn't know what she was going to do next, and they often blamed themselves and each other for her erratic and sometimes erotic behavior. Another crisis time. ¶Grandma, Grandpa, great aunts and uncles, the neighbor next door, even the deliveryman, can help in times of crisis. The temple community, the church congregation, the priest, the minister, friends, Rotary Club members, executive at the office, if they don't help, are all negligent. We can blame them for the failure. Don't blame mom and dad. They are helpless. Do we blame somebody who is sick for being ill? Of course not. Do we blame a person who is emotionally distraught for being emotionally distraught? Of course not. We try to understand. We try to help. If the help is offered or is not offered, we blame those who do not help. ¶Therefore, I tell troubled youth, for your own peace of mind, dear child, love your mother and your father. Keep them as one in your mind. Don't separate them in your mind. You yourself are the greatest marriage counselor. It is only you who at this juncture can become a binding force for the family. Rise above the accepted standards of the nonculture of today, which advise divorce to solve the problem. Remember, don't take sides.

Saturday
LESSON 174
The Dreadful First Slap

Though divorce is not an acceptable solution to family problems according to Hindu Dharma, there is one regrettable exception to maintaining a divine union, and that is in the case of domestic violence. We've encountered much talk lately in *Time, Newsweek, Hinduism Today* and on TV about the taboo subjects of wife beating, date rape and even sexual abuse of children. Things once not even whispered about behind closed doors are now out in the open. No more secrets. ¶Of course, domestic violence never was much of a secret, for all those involved knew: husbands and wives, their friends, the kids, close relatives and neighbors. Knew but said nothing. If the neighbors are making too much noise at a party, no one hesitates to complain. But if that same neighbor is beating his wife and she is screaming and crying, nothing is done. No knock on the door. No call to authorities. We never allow a fist fight in a public place, but we do permit, by our silence, such heinous violence in the home. ¶In the spirit of standing for *ahiṁsā* and not permitting violence, when you see a man slapping his wife or a parent hitting his child, call the police! Don't protect the wrongdoer. Don't be a party to the crime by remaining passive. Don't think that no *karma* is attached to inaction. It is no longer acceptable to turn up the TV to drown out the screams and sobs of a wife being beaten. ¶Recently, the California case of O.J. Simpson released an immense outpouring of sympathy for abused women. It took a world-famous athlete to bring forward an infamous worldly behavior. It is an admirable trait that an uncensored press can come forward to awaken a nation's conscience. In a way, the images and stories that are appearing are not unlike Indian epics or Greek stage plays that seek to establish morals by depicting tragic happenings, or Italian operas which conceal morals in melodrama. All in all, the world has not changed that much. ¶As hard as it is to discuss wife abuse and why it happens, people are discussing it openly and without shame. We see graphic, real-life pictures of this violence and battered wives speaking out in magazines and on television. The big question is, will it ever end? Maybe not, but we can end the cultural sanction of the sport where father and mother watch their son slap down his wife and then drag her across the room by her hair. ¶A man who strikes his wife in an effort to make her cower, to control her, actually karmically does the opposite. His brutality turns against him, becomes his disadvantage. Her love and dependence weaken, and her psychic bonds to him unravel. After that, she has the spiritual upper hand, is more free from him than ever, less under his control than before that first slap. Yes, it all begins with the first slap. ¶It does not matter as much when they fight with words—the name-calling, insinuations, insults and arguments. That's all part of the play of married life and may be fairly intense when their astrological compatibility is not as perfect as it might be. But that first slap changes everything! It is that first slap that brings dire *kukarma*, that degrades and demeans, that makes her his enemy and not his friend. This is not acceptable. Kids cannot accept it. Wives will never forgive it. Families should not endure it, even to defend beloved sons. It is not less violent just because it happens behind closed doors, just because we know the people so well. All who know of this crime and who do not speak up for *dharma,* for *ahiṁsā,* are accomplices. Like a thief or rapist, they are enemies of a stable society.

Sunday
LESSON 175
What Can Be Done?

"What can I do about domestic violence?" you may ask. You can refuse to remain silent. You can object, as I did recently upon finding in my own community three cases of wife abuse. Imagine, if devotees performing *sādhana* can succumb, how easy it must be for others. There is help available. Peer pressure, elders, police, counselors and shelters are there, and much more. It's like the olden days when people first started objecting to slavery. Everyone knew in their heart it was wrong, but no one dared go against the conventional wisdom that it was "necessary." Finally, mankind came to its senses and stopped it. It was no longer acceptable. In that same way, we are now coming to our senses about spouse abuse and child abuse. ¶What is the difference between beating a woman and raping her? Not much, really. Violent harm is done. Her body has been violated, moved by his body against her will. A sin has been committed, equally as psychologically serious. *Kukarma* for the man, bad consequences, results from that first slap. *Prāyaśchitta,* penance, must be performed to mitigate the backlash of his actions, lest they seriously affect his next birth. ¶The first push, bruised wrist, pinch without mercy, slap or bleeding lip tells her nerve system that "this is no place for me to be." Her fear takes over, and the process of breaking up the family nest begins. His future is jeopardized as she instinctively withdraws her *śakti.* Perhaps he struck her to show that he's the boss and that she cannot control him. But, in fact, he thereby appointed her as another boss that may well torment his consciousness the rest of his life and bring to him sorrows to equal her own, now or in his next birth. ¶Of course, it is the birth *dharma* of Hindu elders to rule society with a firm hand and demand of their younger male generation that they never defile themselves by giving that first slap. When a domestic situation is brought before me that involves violence, my immediate response is to advise the wife to run for safety. Unless counseling, if ever accepted, brings about an actual change in the offender, and there are actual apologies, remorse and genuine efforts to mend ways and transform that are acceptable to relatives and the congregation at large, I know it is my responsibility to step in and advise separation. Yes, this may lead to divorce, unless, of course, a deeply sincere correction has taken place and a new marriage covenant has been written by the couple. Continued physical violence is the singular justification for divorce in modern Hindu culture—a regrettable exception to the lifelong covenant of marriage. This is comparable to an abortion performed to save the life of the mother, which is *dharmically* permissible because it is an even worse *kukarma* for a child to kill his mother. All concerned will accept the wisdom of these exceptions, both of which save the life of the mother.

Bāla Poshaṇam
बालपोषणम्

Bringing Up Children

I will utter a prayer for such concord among family members as binds together the Gods, among whom is no hatred. Be courteous, planning and working in harness together. Approach, conversing pleasantly, like-minded, united.

Atharva Veda 3.30.4-5. VE

Monday
LESSON 176
Be Patient And Caring

There is an old saying: "If you can't beat them, join them," and this is wise in certain respects. We are thinking of the young adults who will not follow the traditional family patterns of their well-raised Hindu parents. Admittedly, they can be made to fear their parents and be forced to obey for a time. The problem with such an approach is that it usually ends up with the sons or daughters losing respect for them and leaving home as soon as they are able. Often parents take the authoritarian approach, not realizing there are alternatives, well-proven techniques of a more positive discipline. In actual practice, it is more useful to work with children little by little as they grow and mature. They can be reasoned with and will be very open if the parents show a definite interest in their cross-cultural way of life and their natural inclinations, one of which is to keep in with their peers. To lament the modern young adult's behavior, to merely criticize it, is not going to help, and may cause, in the case of sensitive children, irreparable damage. ¶My advice to parents has always been to stay close to their children, but at the same time give them some space to grow and mature in today's world. Today's world is not all that bad. But children must be taught how to live in it—what to be wary of, whom to trust, whom to befriend and marry, how to proceed in business, social life, education, career upscaling, religious life and on into the raising of their own family. So, keep the communication lines open. ¶True, today's world has its challenges, its temptations and definite drawbacks, but it is today's world and the world of tomorrow. We can't ignore that fact. We cannot recreate yesterday's world or wish for the return of olden days. We have to move forward and teach the children to move the forces of the outside world for a better world in the tomorrows that are to come. So, be wise and pass your deeply profound Hindu culture and wisdom along to the children so they can make proper decisions for themselves. This is what they will do anyway, make their own decisions, so they might as well be trained early on how to do it right. Who better to teach them this than their own parents? True, times have changed, and things may never be as they were, but the religious and cultural traditions of the former generation are still valid and must be passed on gently yet firmly to the modern children, educated to think for themselves rather

Three generations in a modern Hindu home—with television and computers. Yet they find time for closeness and sharing. Mother is decorating her daughter's hair. Grandfather helps the son with his homework. Grandma is playing with the baby.

than simply carry out orders from elders. Don't close the doors on them. This will not help society or the family unit. Nor will it fulfill the *dharma* of parenthood. ¶Parents of all ages and all cultures have always worried about their teenagers, so take heart. Don't give up on them. They are the future. Some must learn by their own mistakes, while others, more sensitive, thoughtful and loving, who are polite enough to at least listen, can learn by the mistakes and successes of their parents. So, communicate your wisdom to them; whether they listen or not makes no difference for the time being. Your message, given with conviction but without anger or resentment, sinks deep into their subconscious mind, making a positive *saṁskāra.* To accomplish this best, give it just before bedtime, when they are more open and less defensive. It will be their last thought before sleep. Don't rant and rail during the day. That will simply sow the seeds of long-lasting animosity and create division within the family. At night before sleep—this is the key to getting your message through. Also, before sleep, all differences must be resolved, lest they become unwanted *vāsanās* to be worked through later in this life or the next.

Tuesday
LESSON 177
Training in Energy Use

Another way to communicate is when mom serves her children meals. While they are eating their favorite food served by their favorite person, she gently speaks some loving advice for their deportment, or a gentle correction, in the right ear, not the left. These timely suggestions, well implanted at that very human psychological moment, are absorbed in the subconscious as the meal digests. Five decades ago in Sri Lanka, I learned of this shrewd Hindu ingenuity by which women have been known to turn an election by whispering in their husband's ear whom he should vote for, just as he is putting into his mouth his favorite morsels of food. This wisdom is one of the positive laws behind Nandinātha Sūtra 99, which requires the wife to serve her husband food, enjoying her own meal only after he and the children have been well satisfied. Politicking? Well, yes! of the highest womanly order. She has her ways. Yes, the clever wife is indeed the queen of her castle. The *ṛishis* tell us there are eighty-four ways a woman can influence her man and keep him on—or lead him off—the path of *dharma.* Some call these wiles; others know them as the feminine *siddhis.* ¶It is the parents' duty to provide a sound education in the use and misuse of the life forces, the sexual energies, and teach their children how to control them as they grow into adulthood. Only in this way will they have the knowledge required to face the challenges of their own instinctive/intellectual nature. ¶There are two main areas that parents can feel free to speak about with their boys and girls as they are growing up from a very young age. These are *prāṇa* and the *chakras*. Once your children have a clear idea of what *prāṇa* actually is and what the *chakras* actually are, they will be confident in lifting up the sexual *prāṇas* into the higher *chakras* when puberty is upon them. ¶You who are parents know that this *prāṇa* will increase within your physical body until you are about forty years of age. After that, the *prāṇa* increases in power within the mental body until you are about the age of seventy. Then the *prāṇa* continues to increase within the spiritual body of the soul. Carefully explain time and time again to your children that it is up to them to control their *prāṇa*, their life force, which is the total energy of their body. Until forty years of age, this is done through education, exercise and hard work. After forty until seventy, this is done through study, caring for those younger than themselves, community service and additional education. After seventy this is done through worship, *sādhana*, *tapas* and deep meditation. ¶When explaining the *chakras* to your children, refer to these force centers as lovely flowers within them that need to be fed by their vital energies. Teach them to breathe deeply and lift the sexual energy from the lower *chakras* to the higher ones and hold it there, as if to feed and water these flowers. Teach them that *chakras* are also rooms of consciousness, and the energy we put into the *chakras* awakens this consciousness and makes us very alert and intelligent. ¶In other words, as soon as your children can understand, you can begin teaching them about their energies. In this way, you give them the tools to handle their sexual nature so that their forces do not run away with their mind during puberty. In this way, you will open channels to talk freely with them about sex when the time comes. Many parents give absolutely no guidance in this area to their children, who then have to learn from other children or from the Internet, alone in a room, about this natural function of their life. So, be a wise parent and begin early. Remember, there are only two basic areas to cover: *prāṇa* and *chakras*. Your own intuition will guide you as to how to proceed.

Wednesday
LESSON 178
Be Firm But Kind

Children respond well to correction, discipline, talking and explaining, and being treated like the intelligent beings that they are. Many parents these days are afraid of their children and dance around them, as if they were things to be avoided. They bribe them with toys and sweets, bow before their every whim and appoint them, by default, the head of the house. Truly, children these days like to be told what to do, but also to be told the reasons why. ¶The "Obey me because I said so" stance will not work anymore for the Western-educated child. What will work is, "Obey me because this is what our family needs and wants you to do, because we love you and want you to remain a member of this family, and these are the reasons why...." This approach even a truant kid will accept, because he or she still needs to eat, still wants a roof over head, clothes to wear and, in the future, maybe a paid-for education. Less obstinate children will conform because they love their family and intuitively know how to fit in when they are urged to and have been given clear directions, explanations and expectations. Yes, there are children in the Western world who do not throw temper tantrums at home, who are still nice to their elders, who will turn off the TV when asked and even show appreciation for all that their parents have done for them. ¶Who are the mentors of the home, the kids or the parents? Children raised on bribery or raised in fear will in their future bribe others, subjugate others by instilling fear of their wrath and unruly ways. If you are ambivalent and insecure, your children will not listen to you. This may be embarrassing, but nonetheless true. It is not necessary to let your children go headlong into Western ways. It is not necessary or even helpful to leave them alone to find their own values in life, from the streets, from peers, from people more confused than they are. What is most helpful is for you to share with them the Eternal Path, with all of its values, all of its insight into humanity and Divinity. What is most helpful is for you to spend lots of time with your children. Many parents these days minimize the hours they spend with their kids and don't even have time for an in-depth conversation anymore. Just "Hello" and "Good-bye" and "Why did you get a low grade on your report card?" Kids need more, more of you, more of your time, more direction and more guidance. Don't be afraid to give to them what they need most—all of you, not just a token part. Teach them traditional religious and cultural values at an early age. Don't be afraid that they will be different from the other children. They are already different. They are Hindus, inheritors of India's fountainhead of mystery and Truth. ¶An all-pervasive mental disease has come to the planet. It started in the West and is spreading worldwide. It is the modern way that parents talk to their children, by stating a question when actually giving direction or instruction, such as, "Why don't we all get in the car now?" "Why don't you put on your coat?" "Don't you think it's time for you children to turn off the TV and go to bed?" These kinds of phrases are used in the family homes and in offices throughout the modern world. Children given the choice "Why don't you?" before the instruction of what to do are disadvantaged. They are forced to make a yes-or-no decision before complying with the request, and sometimes it might be "no." When undecided, children comply reluctantly. Giving these kinds of choices to young people, which is being done today even at the five-year-old level and younger, is a new way of raising them which puts parents at a disadvantage. They become beholden to their child's every mood, thought and preference.

Thursday
LESSON 179
The "Why Don't You" Approach

It does not take long for even very young children raised in the "why don't you" method to catch on and understand that they are permitted, indeed expected, to make a personal choice in all that happens in family life. An aggressive few of these children will take over the home and begin giving orders to the parents, unkindly, abusively. Most often, when choices are given, they take the opposite point of view. When you ask a child, "Why don't we turn off the TV?" he may answer, "No, I'm not turning off the television, because the program I'm watching has not ended yet." When you suggest, "Shall we all get into the car?" he will respond, "I am not getting in the car. You all go. I'm staying home." If you then force him to change his decision after asking him to make a choice, you are considered unreasonable. When this happens, respect is lost and is hard to regain. ¶Is the child being disobedient? Well, yes! And well, no. Yes, by responding in opposition to the expected answers, and no because the question itself invites them to decide, and one possible response is to refuse. Such questions from adults tell the child that each one in the household is an independent entity, free to go his or her own way. The child is being taught how to do this by the parents themselves, by the way they phrase their directions. Some parents want their kids out of the home, on their own, supporting themselves. Others don't. ¶There are only two ways: teach dependence or teach independence. Independence should be taught when the child has become an adult and is educated well enough to make it on his own, not before. Then he is responsible and will do right by his parents when they are older, because he understands *dharma*, duty, because he depended upon and flourished under their direction, their love and their wisdom for oh-so-many years. Don't let them leave home too early and then continue to learn by their own mistakes. What a sad and often painful way to learn. Don't let them face up to this. Protect them while you can. Simply don't give choices. They will never notice the change in your approach and will appreciate the security of positive direction: "Let's all get into the car. Come along." "It is time now to turn off the TV. We are all going to bed." Keep affirming that "Our family is a team. We move together. We are loyal to each other and tell each other everything, keeping no secrets. We will always stay together and care for one another." This should come up at every opportunity, at least three times a week. ¶What is the binding force that keeps youths in the home? Love. If you love your children completely, they won't want to leave. You won't be able to force them out of the house, even if you try. You are bound together by bands of steel made of love. Within this loving relationship, you can guide them and watch over them and help them to live a good life without getting into trouble. Three hugs a day keeps trouble away. How can you apparently practice Hindu *bhakti,* which is love of God, Gods and *guru,* and not have enough love in your heart for your son or daughter to make them want to be close to you? If you don't love your children, they will find someone else to love them.

Friday
LESSON 180
Financial Independence

In summary, Hindu parents should make decisions for their children and refrain from giving them choices until they are educated and about to leave the home. Offering children freedom with money has similar problems. By giving adolescents financial independence too soon, parents breach the protective atmosphere of the home and invite exploration of who knows what in the world. It begins with an allowance that they can squander any way they want. They soon learn that by putting heavy demands upon parents they can get more. Then parents add gifts for good behavior, a form of bribery not recommended. In training adolescents, any money they handle should be accounted for and the change returned to and counted by the caring parents. This teaches honesty, accuracy and cooperation with the core group, the parents. ¶Many times I have seen an allowance lead to a desire for a summer job or to work after school, more independence, more time away from home and family. The summer job taxes the child when he or she should be playing, resting, going to school or doing wholesome extracurricular reading. The early-morning paper route or the job after school takes precious time away from education. Adolescents should not be allowed to handle their own money or to earn an income until their high school education is nearly complete. Then any money earned, the full amount, should be given to the parents, and all spending money accounted for. This will mold the young adult into a frugal, income-producing person. ¶One choice young people can and must participate in is their profession. A *jyotisha śāstrī,* Vedic astrologer, will help in this. In principle, the *karma* of the child is to accept the profession of the parent. He had a choice and could have been born into another family. He chose you. So, don't compromise him or her, and be sure that you have unanimous agreement with all members of the family when the choice of profession or occupation is made. The ideal, of course, is for the children to work in the family business and develop the wealth that can be passed along to others in the family, generation after generation. This is the way Hinduism has persisted through trial and tribulation, siege and battle, oppression and subjugation for the past 10,000 years. Let's not allow it to stop now. It is all up to you, the mom and dad, and how you phrase your direction, how you discipline with love and patience as their growing-up process continues. Raise your children right, and you will be rewarded by the justly fair law of *karma* when you are on the other side of life, about to experience *moksha.* Don't raise your children correctly, and you will be born again into an unwholesome, *adharmic* household and learn by feeling how they felt under your neglect.

Saturday
LESSON 181
Responsible Chaperoning

I described the importance of chaperoning in Nandinātha Sūtra 149: "Śiva's followers accept the serious responsibility of guiding the private and social life of their children. They chaperone and monitor friendships to help ensure that young ones grow up safe and celibate." An Indian lady once told me what she considered to be her most important duty in life: that she would never, ever let her daughter out of her sight until she was married and well settled. Someone asked, "Don't you trust her?" The lady's answer was, "No." ¶Why do *swāmīs* of traditional orders like ours go out only in pairs? Is it because we don't trust them? We trust the soul and we trust them individually, but we don't trust worldly people they might encounter who would love nothing more than to deter them from their *dharma.* We follow the ancient traditions so that problems don't arise. ¶Many parents are faced with the dilemma of sending children off to college for a higher education at the risk of their exposure to undesirable influences. I tell my devotees, if you want your son and daughter to attend the university, you should, if at all possible, move into a home near that campus so you can be close to them and keep them from getting into trouble, share meals with them, monitor their friendships. You will be investing a lot of money to put them through school, and if you are not there, you will be investing a lot of worry. ¶If sending them to a far-off school is unavoidable, and you cannot move to a home nearby, remind them to at least perform simple *pūjā* every day and tune into a picture of you, and of the family *guru* and the Gods of our beautiful religion. The object of going to college, you can explain, is to learn what they need to learn and come out the other side as a professional, able to make their way in the world. So, explain to them that they are not going to college to make friends, to join sororities or fraternities, or to get sidetracked in any way by the temptations of the world as it is today. Encourage them to treat everyone the same, with a happy smile, to not take sides, to not like one person more than another. ¶There is a wonderful lady from the Tamilian community who sent her two sons off to the University of California, and every day, to stay close, she cooked a meal for them, packaged that meal and sent it by courier to their apartment 400 miles away. Another pattern that has worked in our congregation is for young people to marry and then, as a married couple, move near a university for the husband to attend school. Then he is naturally chaperoned by his wife as they grow up together. ¶Many children don't follow their parents' religion, don't want to be sheltered or restricted and want to leave home in their teens and go off on their own. I say that if you have really made the religious teachings a part of your life, you will naturally be able to convince your family and friends of those wonderful truths. Your youth will see the wisdom of not going out without a chaperone, be it an adult or a trusted peer. If you can't convince your family of the teachings, that shows that they are just intellectual thoughts that in practice don't mean anything to you. ¶I watch for those in my international congregation who can do this, who are deeply involved, active and committed members who can bring others along the path that they themselves have trod. And I watch for those, indifferent and apathetic, who can't and are just hanging on because of the social benefits or the mystique.

Sunday
LESSON 182
Our Young Missionaries

All of the young people here today, each and every one of you, must be proud that you are living the Śaiva Dharma. You must be proud to be Śaivites, proud that you know this great God personally. Now, this is not an egotistical kind of pride which sets you apart from everyone. It is a pride of humility which makes you very compassionate toward all.

Stand strong for Śaivism. It is your duty to help spread the Śaiva Dharma throughout the world, to let each one hear about Śiva, about the great Mahādeva Gaṇeśa, about the great Mahādeva Murugan. Let them accept or reject, as they choose, but first they must hear your message. You are all the young missionaries of our religion, the young missionaries of Śaivite Hinduism. You must study this religion most diligently. Study hard so that you can turn the minds of others toward goodness, toward selflessness, toward Godliness. You must study very, very hard, very diligently, committing the Śaiva Dharma to memory so that when you are asked questions about your religion you have a ready and convincing answer and can give forth that answer with confidence. You must be strong, for there are many more temptations in the world today than when your parents and grandparents were raised. Those who are young nowadays face far more temptations than ever before, especially from the Western world. ¶Proceed with confidence and with courage, and your life will be a strength to others who are waiting and longing for your message. I ask each of you young adults and children here tonight to grow up tall and proud of our Śaivite religion. How do you do this? Through discipline and obedience. Nothing was ever accomplished on this Earth without these two qualities. Be self-disciplined, cultivate self-control. Obey your *gurus.* Obey your mothers. Obey your fathers. Obey your elders. Obey your Śaivite teachers. Don't be influenced by Western ways. Western ways are based on a Christian belief structure. If you do all of this, you will become the leaders of the Śaivite Hindu temple tradition. ¶Religious learning is the greatest learning, the only permanent learning. All else is transitory and changing. Religion is the knowledge of the soul. God Śiva created your soul. Your mother and father created your body, brought you into this world. But you create your own experiences in this life from the sum total of experiences in your past lives. You came to this Earth for one purpose: to learn of your religion. You are on this Earth for the evolution of your soul. You are not here to earn money. You are not here to gratify yourself through excesses. You are not here to fight with each other. You are not here to accumulate material conveniences. You are here to learn of and then to fulfill your religion. It is knowledge of religion in your life that makes the soul evolve. So, learn your religion fully, properly, intelligently, and it will guide you through this life into a better birth or on into *moksha,* liberation from earthly existence.

Saprema Vyavahāraḥ

सप्रेमव्यवहारः

Positive Discipline

Disputes, worldly associations and quarrels should be avoided. Not even spiritual disputations should be indulged in, whether good or bad. Jealousy, slander, pomp, passion, envy, love, anger, fear and misery should all disappear gradually and entirely.

Devākālottara Āgama, Jñāna Pāda, 77-78. RM, P. 116

Monday
LESSON 183
The Bane Of Battering

The whole world is reevaluating how we treat women, children, the aged and infirm. Ways of behaving toward our fellow human beings that were normal and acceptable a hundred years ago are no longer acceptable. We now comprehend, as never before, the tragedy of a battered wife or an abused infant. Shamefully, we do not always live up to the Hindu ideal in these areas. ¶What is that ideal? It is this: Never injure others. Hindu children are always treated with great respect and awe, for one does not always know who they are. They may be incarnations of a grandmother, grandfather, aunt or uncle, dearly beloved mother, sister, brother, respected father, a *yogī* or *ṛishi* returned to flesh to help mankind spiritually. We must ask, "Who are these souls? What is their destiny in this life? How can I help?" ¶Parents love their children, or at least they should, and the principle of *ahiṁsā,* nonviolence and nonhurtfulness—physically, mentally or emotionally—does apply in the parent-child relationship, as well as in the husband-wife relationship. Children must be nurtured prenatally without being hurt in the process. Children must be allowed to develop physically, emotionally and mentally without being hurt in the process. We know they are sometimes mischievous and can get on your nerves, but the religious parents who are avowed to *ahiṁsā* are in truth more mature than their children and are able to handle situations as they come up without recourse to pinching, hitting or verbal abuse. Only in an *ahiṁsā* home can we bring children from one stage of physical, emotional, mental growth to another and still nurture spiritual qualities. ¶To hurt a child in any way is to drive that child into fear and cause the development of anger and resentment at an early age. Parents are supposed to lift their offspring into the higher nature, of love, forgiveness, friendliness and security, not to drive them into the lower nature, of hate, mistrust, resentment, offishness and insecurity. Obedience through fear is not a desirable obedience. ¶Psychologically, parents breed guilt by telling their children they sacrificed everything for them, gave them so much, saying, "Look what we are getting in return. You are worthless and ungrateful." Guilty people are not creative, often not reasonable and are lacking willpower, for their inspiration has been destroyed. Their self-image is at the bottom of the bottom, like rust on the soul. "I'm

---

Two Hindus from different cultures are raising a child in Chicago, famed for its elevated trains. Mother is placing holy ash on the infant's forehead for protection and blessings. They have vowed to raise the child using the principles of positive discipline.

nobody, I'm nothing. She is right. I don't appreciate anything, I'm worthless." These are the thoughts of those who live in this state of mind. True, this is the Kali Yuga in which mothers give birth and then destroy their young. They do it through beating them when they are young and later through defamation of character through cutting insults to keep them "in their place." ¶Conformity through threats does not build a loving family or a strong society. To bribe children into submission with sweets or promises that are never meant to be fulfilled is to engender in them an eventual mistrust of their parents and foster rebelliousness coupled with selfish expectations about life. To anger a child at an early age is to place him on the path of retribution toward others later in life. To strike or pinch a child may seem expedient in the confusion of the moment. It may provide a short-term solution. But never forget the long-term *karmic* price that must be paid. The "I own you, you owe me" attitude is no longer acceptable, and is being replaced by "I love you, you love me," in the homes of righteous Hindu families who realize that the hurtful methods do not bring positive results.

Tuesday
LESSON 184
The Sad Truth Of Hurtfulness

I have been asked, "Should parents never spank a child?" Of course, one should never spank children, ever. Those who are spanked are taught to later punish their children, and this is a vicious cycle. Have you ever seen an animal in its natural habitat abuse its offspring? Does a lion cause blood to flow from its cub, a bird brutally peck its own chick, a cow trample its calf, a whale beach a disobedient calf? How about a dolphin, a dog, a butterfly, a cat? It is only humans who become angered by and hurtfully, sometimes lethally, aggressive toward their offspring. ¶The wife-husband relationship is where it all begins. The mother and father are *karmically* responsible for the tenor of society that follows them. An *ahiṁsā* couple produces the protectors of the race. *Hiṁsā*, hurtful, couples produce the destroyers of the race. They are a shame upon humanity. It's as simple as that. It's so crucial that it needs to be said more than once. "*Hiṁsā*, hurtful, couples produce the destroyers of the race. They are a shame upon humanity." ¶A five-foot-ten-inch adult beating on a tiny child—what cowardliness. A muscular man slapping a woman who cannot fight back. What cowardliness! Yet another kind of cowardliness belongs to those who stand by, doing nothing to stop known instances of harm and injury in their community. Such crimes, even if the law does not punish, earn a lifetime of imprisonment in the criminal's *karma*, because they always know that they watched or knew and said nothing. This sin earns lifetime imprisonment in their own mind. Beating a child destroys his or her faith. It destroys faith in humanity and therefore in religion and in God. If their father and mother beat them, whom are they going to trust throughout their whole life? Child beating is very destructive. ¶Innocent children who see their father beating their mother or their mother spitefully scratching their father's body after she emotionally shattered his manhood by provocative insinuations, threats and tongue lashing have at those very moments been given permission to do the same. Of course, we can excuse all of this as being simply *karma*—the *karma* of the parents as taught by their parents and the *karma* of the children born into the family who abuses them. But the divine law of *karma* cannot be used as permission or an opportunity to be hurtful. Simply speaking, if hurtfulness has been done to you, this does not give you permission to perform the same act upon another. It is *dharma* that controls *karma*. It is not the other way around. In Hinduism, the parents are to be the spiritual leaders of their children, not the mental, emotional and physical abusers of their children. ¶Those sensitive children who see their mother and father working out their differences in mature discussion or in the shrine room through prayer and meditation are at that moment given permission to do the same in their own life when they are older. They become the elite of society, the pillars of strength to the community during times of stress and hardship. These children, when older, will surely uphold the principles of *dharma* and will not succumb to the temptations of the lower mind.

Wednesday
LESSON 185
Instilling No Fear

There is no greater good than a child. Children are entrusted to their parents to be loved, guided and protected, for they are the future of the future. However, children can be a challenge to raise up into good citizenship. There are many positive ways to guide them, such as hugging, kindness, time spent explaining, giving wise direction and setting the example of what you want them to become. Most children were adults not so many years ago, in previous births. The mind they worked to develop through the great school of experience is still there, as are the results of their accomplishments and failures. They have been reborn to continue to know, to understand and to improve themselves and the community they are born into. Parents can help or inhibit this process of evolution. They have a choice. ¶There are six *chakras*, or centers of consciousness, above the *mūlādhāra chakra,* which is the center of memory, at the base of the spine. Above the *mūlādhāra* lies the *chakra* of reason. Above that is willpower. There are seven *chakras* below the *mūlādhāra,* the first being fear, below it anger and below that jealousy. The choice of each individual parent is to discipline the child to advance him or her upward into reason, willpower, profound understanding and divine love, or downward into fear, anger, distrust, jealousy and selfishness—personal preservation without regard for the welfare of others. ¶Children have an abundance of energy, and sometimes it can make them rather wild, and this can be extreme if they are consuming too much sugar. How should this be controlled by the parents? When children run around excitedly, refer to their energy as Śiva's *prāṇa* within them. Congratulate them each time they exercise control over it, but don't punish them when they don't. Instead, explain that it is important that they learn to control and use their energies in positive ways. Have them sit with you and breathe deeply. Teach them to feel energy. Go into the shrine room and sit with them until their *prāṇas* become quiet, and then help them observe the difference. To hit them or to yell at them when they are rowdy is only sending more aggravated *prāṇa* into them from you. Another technique is to withdraw your *prāṇa* from them and tell them you are retiring to another room until they calm down. ¶Beating, spanking, pinching, slapping children and inflicting upon their astral bodies the vibration of angry words are all sinfully destructive to their spiritual unfoldment and their future. Parents who thus force their child to fear and hate them have lost their chance to make him or her a better person by talking, because they have closed the child's ears. Those who beat or pinch or hurt or slap or whip their children are the enemies to religion, because they are pushing the next generation into lower consciousness. Is that religious society? No! Such behavior is not even common in the animal kingdom. It's below the animal kingdom. But that is what we face in the world today. That helps explain why there are so many problems in this modern age. ¶Sadly, in this day and age, beating the kids is just a way of life in many families. Nearly everyone was beaten as a child, so they beat their kids, and their kids will beat their kids, and those kids will beat their kids. Older brothers will beat younger brothers. Brothers will beat sisters. You can see what families are creating in this endless cycle of violence: little warriors. One day a war will come up, and it will be easy for a young person who has been beaten without mercy to pick up a gun and kill somebody without

culture of an intelligent future. ¶Nor is an overly permissive approach. A senior *sādhu* from the Swaminarayan Fellowship's 654-member order of *sādhus*, who visited us recently echoed our thoughts on child-beating and emphasized the need for firm, even stern, correction and teaching right from wrong. "Parents these days fail to impart what is good and what is not good," he said. "As a result, a very crude society is being developed." ¶I advise parents: if you are guilty of beating your children, apologize to them, show remorse and perform the child-beating penance, *bāla tāḍayati prāyaśchitta,* to atone. Gain their friendship back, open their heart and never hit them again. Open channels of communication, show affection. Even if you never beat your children, be alert in your community to those who do and bring them to your understanding that a happy, secure family is free from violence.

Friday
LESSON 187
Penance and Reconciliation

Those who have been physically abused are as much in need of penance to mitigate the experience as are those who abused them. The penance, or *prāyaśchitta,* for abusees is called the flower penance, or *pūshpa prāyaśchitta.* It has been successfully performed by many children and adults to mitigate the hate, fear, resentment and dislike toward the parents, teachers or other adults who beat them, by hitting, pinching, slapping, caning, spanking or other methods of corporal punishment. This penance is very simple to perform, but often very difficult to carry out. Each person—child or adult—who has been beaten at any time, no matter how long ago, is enjoined to put up in the shrine room a picture of the person or persons by whom they were beaten, be it a father, mother or teacher. Then, every day for thirty-one consecutive days, without missing a single day, he or she must place a flower in front of each picture, and sincerely forgive the person in heart and mind. If no picture is available, then some symbol or possession can be substituted, or even a paper with his or her name written on it. ¶When it becomes difficult to offer the flower of forgiveness, because hurtful memories come up from the subconscious mind, the abused individual must perform the *vāsanā daha tantra,* writing down the hurtful memories and burning the paper in a trash can. This *tantra* releases the deep emotions within the individual who finds that he or she does not like or deeply resents the parent or other relative, school teacher or principal. After writing about these experiences, expressing in words the emotions felt on many pieces of paper, the area of the subconscious mind holding the suppressed anger and resentment gradually disappears as the papers are seen burning to ashes in a garbage can. ¶Upon recognizing and admitting their fear or hatred of their abuser, they must deal with the pangs of pain that arise each day by mystically turning the slap, beating or spanking into a beautiful flow of *prāṇa* by placing a flower before the picture with a heart full of love. Each day while performing the "flowers of forgiveness *prāyaśchitta*," the individual should mentally approach the tormentor—the person or persons who beat him or her—and say, "I forgive you. I don't hold anything against you, for I know that you gave back to me the *karma* that I set in motion by committing similar misdeeds at a prior time." If possible, this act of verbal forgiveness should be done in person at least once during the thirty-one days, ideally face to face, but at least by phone, if the person is still on this Earth plane. ¶Of course, for most it's much easier to pass on the slap or beating to someone else. Parents often hit their own child, or abuse another person in order to "get it out of their system." That slap has to go someplace, and turning it into a flower is very, very difficult. This *prāyaśchitta* brings up all those awful memories. This discipline brings up all the pain. It brings all the injustice to the surface of the mind. Nevertheless, this *tantra,* or method, has been a great help to many. It is difficult to forgive, and some had to work very diligently within themselves to face up to being able to place that little flower lovingly before the picture of a parent or a teacher. Many have tried and failed again and again when deep-seated resentment emerged, but finally succeeded in true forgiveness, whose byproduct is forgetfulness. They all feel so much better today. Now they are responsive, creative and happy inside. Yes, hitting people is wrong—and children are people, too.

Saturday
LESSON 188
In Defense Of Battering!

There is an old saying in Tamil that is often recited before or after slapping or beating a child: அடியும் உதையும் உதவுவது போல் அண்ணன் தம்பி உதவ மாட்டார். *Adium uthaium uthavu vathu pol annan thambi uthava maddar.* It means, "Even the help of one's younger and older brothers cannot compare to the benefit of being kicked and beaten." It seems this proverb, printed in certain school books, is taught to students. ¶This makes me ask the Hindu community worldwide: What fearful expectations are we nurturing in young minds by repeating such a cruel, stupid edict? Study until midnight to avoid a plastic rod across the back? Obey the teacher or get hit with a strap or cane, then slapped in the face at home for getting beaten in school? Are there more *ślokas* promoting *hiṁsā,* violence, in the home, more guidelines for corporal punishment? Is it our intention to pass this despicable attitude from generation to generation? Unfortunately it seems to be so. My young Asian monks can recite the above verse from childhood memories. Parents seeking to defend corporal punishment of children will also quote a saying from *Manu Dharma Śāstra* (7.198), "*Sama, dana, bheda, daṇḍa,*" which means "using kind words (or negotiation), bribery, sowing dissension, and punishment (or striking)." These are the four successive steps in achieving success against an enemy of the realm. It is advice for kings, not parents. I, for one, hope the rules will change in this nuclear-family age, for there are more seeming reasons to hit and fewer places where a beaten child can find solace and love, without the presence of grandma, auntie and others. ¶The working mother slaps her children at home because they add stress to her already stressed-out nerve system. Father has a tough day on the job and takes it out on his son's back or face with the hand, strap or cane. Does it give a sadistic joy to hear young children cry in pain and humiliation? Does it enhance the feeling of "I'm in charge here; you are not!"? ¶In the past century we've had two world wars and hundreds of smaller ones. Killers come from among those who have been beaten. The slap and pinch, the sting of the paddle, the lash of the strap, the blows of a cane must manifest through those who receive them into the lives of others. But there is a price to pay. The abuser one day becomes the abused. This is a law of life seen manifesting every day. It is called *karma.* Action gives an equal or more intense reaction, depending on the intent and the emotion behind it. Corporal punishment is arguably a prelude to gangs on the streets, those who will riot on call, and others who suffer in silence and hide behind a desk or in a routine profession, fearing reprimand and punishment, never talking back or offering an opinion.

Sunday
LESSON 189
Time Out And Time In

Is there a covert consciousness that accounts for the fact that for forty-eight years, until early 1996, I didn't even know that children of my international congregation were being beaten? Perhaps. Hindus know it's wrong in their heart of hearts, but are blindly obeying the cultural attitude expressed in this *hiṁsā,* violent, senseless proverb, and thoughtlessly reacting to their own stress and anger. They don't even look for a better way. Well, there is a better way. ¶It has been over fifty years since my ministry started, way back in 1949. Now, in its maturity, there are uncounted encounters to rely upon, much experience to guide the fellowship and much energy to march into the future of futures. Among the concerns, one has become crucial to parents, who ask, "Are there better ways to raise our children? We are entirely dedicated to *ahiṁsā*, noninjury, physically, emotionally and mentally. But how is this lofty ideal possible to follow when troubled by emotions that are too easily released by taking them out, in the fire of the moment, on those we love? How can misdeeds that happen in the home be absolved, and examples set that prevent their repetition generation after generation?" ¶For parents seeking effective nonviolent alternatives, they are readily available today in excellent books. One strategy educators recommend is called time out, one minute for each year of the child's age; hence ten minutes for a ten-year-old. This tells the child that if he doesn't behave in a reasonable way, he will be separated from other people. Time out, sitting quietly in a room, works best in conjunction with its opposite, time in. Time in is quality time spent with the child in an activity he enjoys, and just being together. Time in includes letting children share their feelings, positive or negative, with parents lending a receptive, understanding ear. ¶There are new methods and new principles, such as in Nandinātha Sūtra 138: "Śiva's followers never govern youth through fear. They are forbidden to spank or hit them, use harsh or angry words, neglect or abuse them. They know you can't make children do better by making them feel worse." This goes along with the innovative approach being taken by psychologists, sociologists and educators, in consideration of the turmoil that engulfs today's world. The truth is being accepted that methods that rely on what experts call "punishment power"—scolding, taking away privileges, spanking—do not elicit more desirable behavior in children or adults. Rather, they produce hostility, resentment and the desire for retaliation. In communities around the world, our family missionaries are conducting study groups on Dr. Jane Nelsen's *Positive Discipline* as a public service to help parents raise their children without violence.

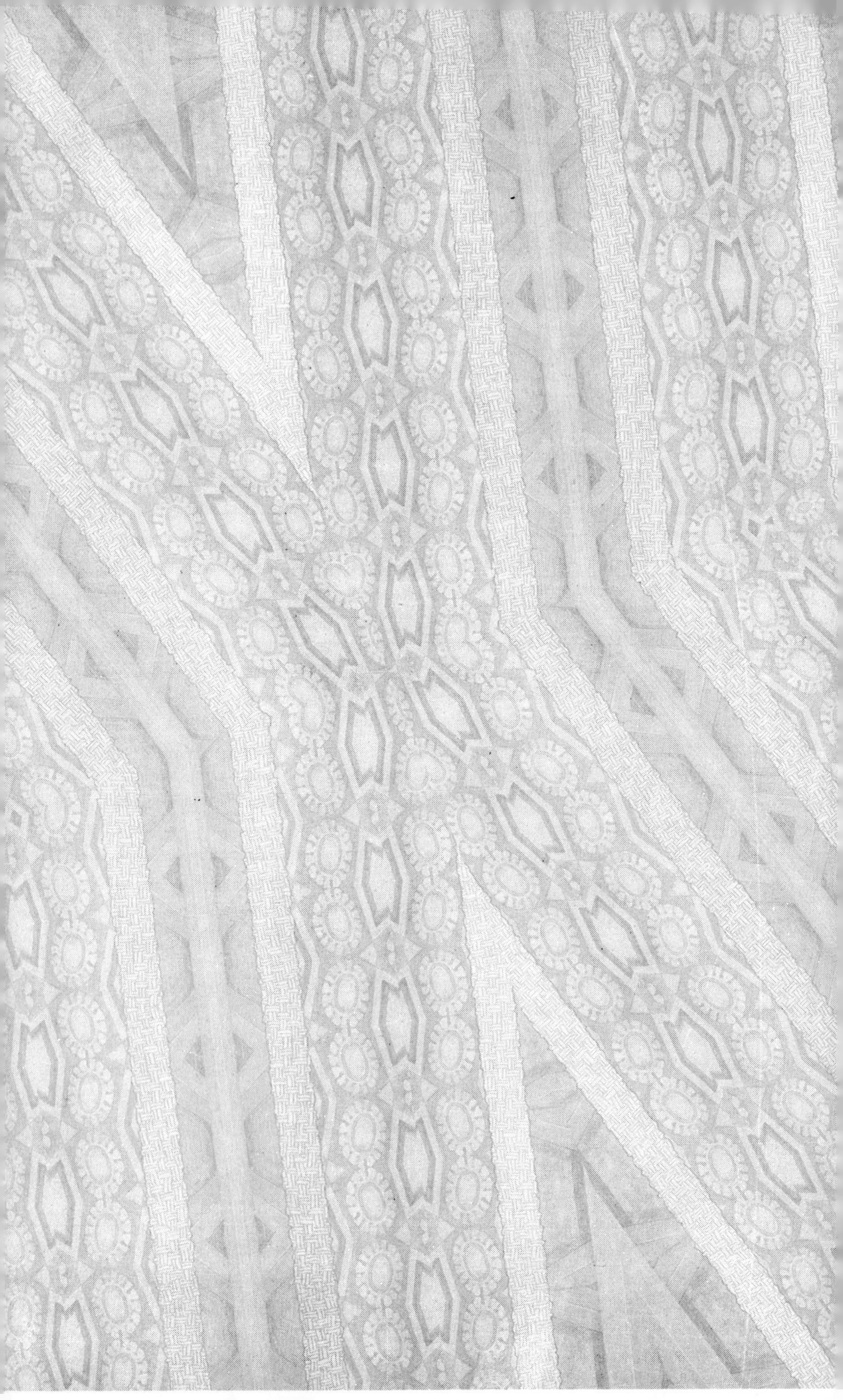

Yuva Kleśa

युवक्लेश

Teenage Trials

Be one to whom the mother is a God. Be one to whom the father is a God. Be one to whom the teacher is a God. Be one to whom the guest is a God.

Kṛishṇa Yajur Veda, Taittirīya Upanishad 1.11.2. UPR, P. 537-8

MASTER

Monday
LESSON 190
Keep Teaching, Keep Loving

The more things change, the more they stay the same, it seems. Children are perfect *devas* until puberty, when so many changes come, when *prārabdha karmas*—the results of past actions they bring with them to live through in this birth—begin to manifest and the growing-up process intensifies. Is there a set way, a rule book, for raising Hindu children in our contemporary society? I think not. But the basic principles of Hinduism have not failed. No, not at all. Teach the young adults to look ahead mentally into the future before making a decision, and to base their decisions for life on the value judgments of Sanātana Dharma as well explained in *Dancing with Śiva, Hinduism's Contemporary Catechism,* here in *Living with Śiva, Hinduism's Contemporary Culture* and in *Merging with Śiva, Hinduism's Contemporary Metaphysics.* This Master Course trilogy is all that's needed for a fine future for young adults. What are these values? Peace; harmony within the home; tolerance for others; appreciation of the wisdom of those who have gone before us and of those who are older; purity of thought, word and deed; chastity until marriage; and, above all, cooperation and patience in choosing the right partner in life, for marriage is actually the joining of two families. ¶Marriage is not merely an individual decision between two people who are sexually attracted to each other. No, not at all. A marriage, to be successful, needs the support both of the young man's family and the young lady's. The days are going away very fast when, through the dowry system, the girl buys herself a husband or the boy commands a price to take her into his home as a servant girl for his mother. ¶All this should be explained time and time again to children who are growing up with mixed values. After all, they spend more time with their peers than they do with their parents in today's world! This means that the parents have to actively teach them as well, and talk and talk and talk on well-rehearsed subjects to keep their children in the home, out of harm's way and guided into a substantial, happy marriage in which the bride and the groom's parents get along famously. It is a circle of love when two families marry along with their children. ¶These matters must be discussed when children are young, before puberty. Give many examples from your life and the successful lives of others they and you know. Later, when they reach the stage

---

A group of teens gather to talk and share, not far from the Seattle Space Needle in Washington state. Positive peer groups are essential to young men and women, taking them through the difficult teenage years protected and unscathed.

of puberty, watch out, for they may reject everything they have heard. But the knowledge is in there, deeply buried in their subconscious mind, just waiting to burst out when the right moment comes. So, even when they are not inclined to listen or discuss, you can know they are hearing. And you can be sure they are listening when you gossip about someone who is experiencing a similar problem they are facing—a high school senior you read of in the paper who is in dire circumstances, or a story with a moral that you have creatively thought up to put across the point that you are trying to make. Yes, they are listening, because who is it on planet Earth that does not just really, really love to hear a good story. Your well-placed parable will lift up the *vāsanās* you implanted early on.

Tuesday
LESSON 191
Tapas of the The Teen Years

When your adolescents make the decision that you want them to make, never, ever say, "I told you so." Just bow your head and say, "Darling, you are making a wise decision." Believe it or not, when they are not listening and you are talking, they are hearing, and what you are saying is going deep into their subconscious state of mind, which never sleeps. So, be tactful in what you say, and say it always with a smile and plenty of healthy *āyurvedic* sweets (not made with white sugar, but with jaggery or honey, or raw sugar if these are not available). We don't want tooth decay and diabetic conditions from highly processed white sugar. It is too expensive and time-consuming to treat these home-created ailments. Don't you agree? Good health—mental and physical—begins or ends in the home. ¶Teenagers are suffering the pangs of sex, desire and distrust, independence and all sorts of other things. They are as if sick during this time. In Moscow one cold 1990 winter, astrophysicist Carl Sagan once told me they are poisoned by their own hormones. This is nothing new. Over two thousand years ago, the Greek philosopher Plato lamented, "What is happening to our young people? They disrespect their elders. They disobey their parents. They riot in the street, inflamed with wild notions. Their morals are decaying. What is to become of them?" Not much has changed, has it? So, be the mother, father, nurse, and doctor. Talk together and work out a strategy for the seven years from age thirteen to nineteen. It will be over in only seven years. Does this seem like a long haul? Does getting through it seem like an impossible dream? It surely does, but teenage trials are a natural part of the extended family, the joint family, the nuclear family and even of the no-family-at-all. Most of all, realize that you will surely win out if you persist in love and understanding. Before long, they will be raising their children in the very same way and loving you for how you had the patience, willpower, forbearance and love—mainly love—to see them through. Proceed with confidence. Get a strategy, a battle plan, if it's all that bad. Stand up straight, be willing to take insult, disobedience and be shamed in the very home in which you have raised them. Similarly, a nurse does not pay all that much attention to the ranting and raving of a patient who is delirious. Reason does not rank that high as a quality for the teenager. But to tell them that would be to alienate them, for in their view they are so, so much more intelligent than you are in the ways of the world. And that may well be true, as they, we must never forget, spend more time with their peers than at home. You, the parents, bear the handicap of this and must in all fairness compensate. ¶When you have successfully performed your seven-year *tapas* of bearing up under the pain of the teenage trials, truly you will enjoy great satisfaction and be able to sit back and smile. Remember and be assured that it won't last forever. It truly won't. Have compassion and give some leniency, for during this time they are all mixed up inside; they are, they surely are. They are facing an uncertain future in an unsure world, becoming adults, keeping in with their peers, keeping in with their parents, facing marriage, job, career and community expectations. No wonder so many kill themselves because their parents just did not understand and were not there for them at a time when they truly, truly needed them. Such a death of a child is on the heads of the parents. Don't let this happen in your family. Please don't. Be a mom. Be a dad. Be a nurse. Be a doctor. And, most of all, be a friend—their friend, their closest friend—during this tumultuous, turbulent, troublesome time called teenage.

Wednesday
LESSON 192
A Story of Heartbreak

Here is a letter a discouraged Malaysian Hindu girl wrote to her parents just before she attempted to end her life at age eighteen. One of the main reasons she cited for this attempt was too much pressure coming from her parents. It was published in the Malaysia edition of HINDUISM TODAY. ¶"Dear Mom and Dad: You'll never understand why I did this. Never. In your opinion, you always did what was best for me. You always knew what was best for me. You always believed I was your naive, irresponsible little girl who always needed your hand to hold on to. You thought it was necessary to use the sharp edge of your tongue to keep me on the right track. ¶"But that was the biggest problem—you were the ones who chose that track for me. I never had any say in my own life. Did you realize that that right track became a psychological prison for me? That your leading hand became a set of chains for me? That the sharp side of your tongue got to be a barbed wire that was continuously lashing out at me? No, you never did. ¶"You have said many things to me when you were angry, and you always excused yourself by saying that you weren't in your senses when you said them. But did you realize how much those things could have hurt me? No. You never even thought about it. How about if I called you a b . . . . when I was angry? Would you excuse that with the same reasoning? I think not. ¶"Didn't you ever stop to think that maybe I should have some say in what I wanted to do with my life? You decided which college would be the right one for me to attend and what academic field I should go into. The college, of course, had to be the most prestigious and elite one, so you could brag to your friends about it. You never thought that maybe I wanted something more than school and books, but that was never important to you. You only wanted me to achieve academically so your friends would be duly impressed. That was the same reason that you wanted me to become a doctor. I didn't want anything to do with it. ¶"You never realized that maybe I had wanted a social life, to make real friends for once in my life. When I told you that, you scoffed at me and told me that we Indians were so much superior that we didn't need to deal with them. There was never anything in my life that you let me have any control over. When I finally met someone who meant something to me, you two couldn't handle the fact that maybe someday I would learn to control my own life and rid myself of your manipulations. So, then you decided who it was that I was going to see and who it was that I didn't. You forced me to break the first real relationship that I ever had in my life. I was constantly harassed by you about him. You told me that I was disgracing the family name. '...what would everyone say?' You destroyed everything for me. This 'relationship' between us is nothing but a farce. And there is no reason to continue it. I have searched for some way to escape you, but I have come up empty handed. And now, unable to do anything else, I want you to understand the meaning of 'empty handed.' Always remember that you can only control someone for so long. Now you must live with this guilt. I hope you will never be able to forgive yourself." ¶Isn't that sad? Yes, very sad. Fortunately, the young woman lived through this ordeal. In contacting the editors, knowing her letter would strike a chord in many youth, she cautioned that she now knows suicide is not the way out. She firmly believes that all things, no matter how bad they seem at the time, can be lived through. She allowed the publication of this very personal letter in the hope that her battle with suicide would help others—parents and children—deal better with problems before they reach hopelessness.

Thursday
LESSON 193
Keep the Doors Open

Many parents hesitate teaching Hinduism to their children as they do not want to make them different than their school chums. But it is only a "storybook Hinduism" that would do that. We do not need stories these days that were created for a society that no longer exists. We do need the philosophical, metaphysical and psychological Truths which are as eternal as space, time and gravity. These should be well implanted into their minds. One is never too young or too old to learn the Eternal Truths that never fail. World thinking is built on only a few Truths and more than a few false concepts. Never give up on your young adults, whatever the problems that arise. They will be just fine with you, their parents, by their side all along the way. ¶Yes, your children need both of you as friends, someone to come home to when the going gets rough, someone who accepts and loves and, in heartfelt tolerance, tries to understand. It is possible, you know, to close the door on them in your hearts and minds, especially when they are not obeying. Remember that there are others out there who will take them in and may lead them even further astray. Be a friend. Don't force them out of your hearts and minds. Always keep the doors of a compassionate heart, loving arms and an understanding mind open. Listen to their problems and come forward for their needs, even when you may not agree with them or approve of what they are going through. Remember, three hugs a day keeps trouble away. This is modern Hindu Dharma. This is ancient Hindu Dharma. This is living Śiva's contemporary culture. ¶Young people have to prove for themselves the basic principles of Sanātana Dharma. Some go at it in a straightforward way and others go about it in a roundabout way, trying to disprove everything, and therefore proving it. What is the straightforward way? Accepting it as it is and trying to prove it also by relating it to your own life experience. We should not be discouraged with young people if we find they reach a certain age and pull away a little bit. They can come to understand the law of *karma* by going through a few experiences and finding out how they themselves created those experiences. They have to have those basic realizations in this life if they didn't have them in a previous life. If they had these basic realizations in a previous life very, very strongly, their confidence in the teachings would be very strong. Those things carry over from life to life, and in the end the soul builds on them. ¶The new breed of *swāmīs* that have come up in the past three decades relate well to the young adults who were born as Hindus but raised as modern youth with little knowledge of their hereditary religion. These *swāmīs* know the problems, the pitfalls and some of the solutions. They, too, were raised "modern" and by their own conviction learned Eternal Truths and now preach them with a vigor and practical clarity that is unsurpassed. Introduce your young adult to them, and he or she will find an understanding friend and religious mentor. ¶When we are young, the old ways can seem stiff, old-fashioned or just plain silly. Help your young adult see into the reasons and discover the meaning in our culture, philosophy and religion. Then the Sanātana Dharma will belong to them, too, never to be lost, but to be preserved and passed along to their children when the time comes and the cycle begins again.

Friday
LESSON 194
Education And Career

Many youth are pushed into professions by their family, even if they are not suited to that profession. They graduate and ask themselves, "What do I do next? Do I get a job near my family home? Do I go to a far-off country and seek employment?" Family pressure is on, and comments, sometimes hurtful, are made to motivate the youth. But in today's world youth have to think on their feet, take their life into their own hands and make their own goals for their future, especially if they have been abused by senseless beatings from angry parents whose cruel hearts drive them from their home. ¶The long-term goals of education and career should be planned out ahead of graduation. Ideally the planning takes place with the family, but only if it is a cooperative, reasonable family that has enough love to foresee their youth fulfilling happy lives with productive futures. As we saw earlier, too harsh an upbringing can lead to their taking their life with their own hands. ¶In the United States before the First and Second World Wars, people were committed—committed to their family, to their community, to their country, to the growth of the nation and to their business. Everyone knew what they were going to do with the rest of their life by the time they were eighteen or nineteen years of age. They went forward and lived out their life as planned. When I was seventeen, I knew what I would be doing right now. That is commitment, clarity of mind, the ability to see a direct path into the future and then to have the character and the willpower to live to make that path manifest. Society was stable, society was strong, and there were simpler problems. ¶After the First World War and Second World War, the family unit began to break up, and people were no longer committed. The word of the times was not *commitment,* but one that also started with a "c." It was *choices.* "I'll make a choice and see where it leads me. Then I will make another choice and see where that leads." People didn't stick with one occupation and perfect it. They dabbled half-heartedly at ten occupations which they didn't perfect, and the quality of work suffered as a result. The opportunities of choice were so grand. Parents would encourage their children "Make your own choice of what you are going to do with your life. We just want you to be happy." The same child was not allowed to make his own choice about what clothes to wear or what foods to eat. But he was allowed to make the really important choices, including: "What are you going to do with your entire life?" and "Whom are you going to marry?" Of course, to buy a car he was taught by his parents to read *Consumer Reports* and pick just the right one. But he could take up any career and marry anyone he wanted to, just on a whim and fancy.

Saturday
LESSON 195
So Many Choices

Society drastically changed after the two world wars, and the country's crime rate went up. Mental institutions became overpopulated, hospitals overcrowded. People who have no commitment to family, friends, community and religion end up making the wrong choices in life. And today we have a new group called the New Age which, ironically, is totally committed to being uncommitted. ¶Many people are not committed to anything. They take a vow, they take a pledge, but it doesn't mean anything. Even a marriage vow or pledge doesn't mean anything anymore. But that is not religion. That may be secular humanism. That may be existentialism. That may be just a big nothingism; but it is not religion. Religion is the acceptance of spiritual laws that guide our life. We have to make decisions and make commitments, and live up to those commitments so that we can look in the mirror every morning and say, "You did a good job with yesterday. Now what about today?" This is the ethic we need to instill in teenagers. Then the strength of the soul comes forward. When the strength of the soul comes forward, it permeates the intellectual mind. Creativity comes forth. New, inspiring, insightful thoughts that you didn't even know you were able to think come into your mind from your superconscious, and many wonderful things begin to manifest in your life. ¶Nowadays the mind seems to be confused for young people and older people alike. There is too much television, too much surfing, too much input, and not enough planning, not enough talking, not enough camaraderie to sit down and plan out what you are going to do this year, next year, the year after and the year after that. But that's how you keep your *karma* under control: short-term goals and long-term goals planned out according to Śaiva Dharma. ¶Families have been asking me about careers for their maturing youth. What courses should they pursue in college? Higher education should prepare a youth for what he is going to do in life. This applies to women as well. That is why we are educated, to prepare ourselves for our future. There is no other point of being educated but for that. If a young lady is going to be a homemaker, it would be wise to be educated to be a homemaker. Many women these days are married and can't cook, don't know how to put on a band-aid, don't know how to take care of the children when they come, because they've never been educated to be a wife. Women who foresee another kind of life for themselves should choose an education that will prepare them for that. It is also wise these days for a woman who is a homemaker to have an education in a profession, such as nursing, that she can fall back on in case misfortune befalls the family, a death or a divorce, so she can get a job to support the children and herself. Education is for the future career, whether it be a homemaking career or another kind of career. That is the purpose of it. There is much education now available that is just general education. It goes on and on and on. You go in wanting to know, and you come out confused at the end of it. We see this happening all the time. This type of education should definitely be avoided. ¶It is through prenatal experience and influence during year one, year two, year three, year four, year five, that a youth is absorbing the knowledge from the cells of his father's body into his, from the emotions of the father into his, from the mind of his father into his. If the child is a girl, she learns mostly from her mother. These vibrations, in the very same way, enter her inner psyche. Thus children establish the foundation on which they will later build their adulthood. They are their father's and mother's children. It was no accident that they incarnated into their family. They had a choice before they were born. Every family is an expression of such choices.

Sunday
LESSON 196
The Family Profession

Nowadays many people believe that somehow it was an accident that one was born in a family of a certain profession and that the youth deserves a so-called better profession than that of the parents. But the traditional wisdom is that a person is born into a family to fulfill the profession of that family, and ideally to stay within that family business. Being raised in the family business, the person learns from a young age, even prenatally. Going into another profession, he leaves the family *dharma* and goes into worldly *adharma.* It then takes two or three generations to establish a new family *dharma* in that profession. ¶Now, of course, if the father and mother do not have a formal profession or business when their offspring are babies, from prenatal to six, whatever they are doing is absorbed and becomes the children's habit pattern of how they should live their lives on Earth. In such conditions, the chances for the son or daughter to follow the father's or mother's footsteps in a formal profession at a later age, such as at puberty, lessens because the children have already been programmed, from ages one to six, to live from day to day without a goal, without strong material security, without a profession, as their mother and father did, as casual, temporary employees or students, often unemployed or seeking employment. ¶Obviously, there is no greater boon to a youth than to enter the family business or profession, that is, provided this is his inclination as well. Occasionally, however, there comes into a family a child who is to become a leader in another field, not a follower of the family profession. Perhaps he shows special aptitude as a religious leader, a *swāmī,* a community leader, a politician, a social organizer, an activist, an investigative genius, a scientist or a scholar. Such a child will identify himself at an early age and must be especially carefully nurtured, for he was born with a mission. ¶Then there are others who will shy away from the family profession, whatever the rationale. There are many reasons that youth reject the family profession, but the point is that it is the duty of the family to make that profession available to them, knowing this can stabilize them throughout life. Therefore, we should encourage the traditional family ideal in any case, at any age. There is great mental, emotional and physical security for the son or the daughter to follow the family vocation. Such children have observed their parents, learned from them, slowly become partners with them in life. It is not always wise to allow your children to make the decision of what they want to do, allowing them to leave the home and make a stranger wealthy in another profession because of their service to him. Lovingly encourage them to do what you do and to become an extension of yourself. The ideas of "do your own thing," "satisfy your own desires," "wander into a career," "move from one career to another midway in life" are modern *adharmic* concepts. It may work out, but there is a fifty percent chance of failure and crippling debt. Then, too, the family has lost a great asset. The children have lost half their family connection, as they no longer have a shared interest in what mom and dad are doing, and vice versa. And the stranger, way out there, benefits. A family should not end at the puberty of its children, who then go off into other spheres of interest. It should continue and mature into father-and-son corporations, father-and-daughter corporations, with mother and father, sons and daughters all sharing the same interests, all working to increase the family assets. ¶The *dharma* of the householder is to build up wealth and knowledge, and to pass these on to the children, generation after generation. If they are in the jewelry profession, the wealth should go to the jewelers of the next generation, not to the musicians or computer programmers. Family wealth equals community wealth. Community wealth equals national wealth. National wealth equals global abundance. Hindu elders say that by following the occupation of the father and mother one will never go hungry, even if the occupation is a meager one. This is what I learned in Jaffna, Sri Lanka, at an early age. One might not become rich, but security is virtually assured. ¶So, don't be afraid to bring your sons and daughters into the family business deliberately. Get them interested. Get them working with you. Your business or occupation is what feeds them. Naturally they should be interested in it. The simple answer for modern Hindu families following the traditional *gṛihastha dharma* is to form a family corporation and bring sons and daughters at an early age into what mom and dad are doing. Educate them in the family occupation from age six to thirteen and then engage them as partners all through life. What better partners could one have? Who would be more honest and loyal than your own children? Need we say more? You have caught the idea.

you realized?" "Well, that I shouldn't get angry." "Do you still get angry?" "Uh-huh, yes, sometimes." Those people haven't been with Gurudeva at all! They've just been hanging around. Because the results of everything we have been teaching have not taken hold. Results have to manifest in the lives of each of you. Otherwise, you're just bodies, sitting there listening to me talk, living your own private life, living a double standard. Just bodies. So, there can be a lack of sincerity. I want my *śishyas* to do a job, do it right, and be on to the next one, not this insincerity of playing with me, playing with my mind. I don't like that. ¶You can't *work* at correcting something. You either do it or you don't do it. You don't work at not falling off a cliff, a big precipice that drops off a hundred feet. You just don't step forward; that's what you don't do! When you come to the point where you hear about the Self, and you get interested in the Self, you're at a point where you can break the cycle of certain *karmas* through *sādhana*. You're either going to do it or you're going to think, "Oh, that's kind of silly, you know. It's really nice to listen to Gurudeva, but to actually take these teachings seriously and make changes in my life, well...ho hum." That kind of attitude, that kind of ho-hum, lazy attitude, also results in making new *karmas*, because others look at you as an example and take up your example. It's living a double life that I am talking about. It depends on the strength of the person's soul whether he actually makes some definite changes in his character or not.

Wednesday
LESSON 199
Verbal Abuse Of Children

It's one thing to hurt yourself through swearing, but it's a double hurt of yourself if you hurt another person. We wrote quite extensively on the widespread problem of corporal punishment and child abuse last year in HINDUISM TODAY. We explained that those who abuse their children, their spouse—even husbands get abused and hit and scratched—are hurting themselves five to ten times worse than if they simply hit themselves once instead of hitting their child. We find that in some homes the advice to stop was taken very seriously. Scaring children by threatening them has also ceased, at least in the homes that I am aware of in the broad Hindu community. But verbal abuse of children has increased, calling children bad names in order to put them down, expressing anger by viciously badgering them: "You're stupid!" "You're worthless!" There's a long list that apparently nearly every mother and every father has memorized. It goes on and on and on, this constant downgrading and demeaning, expressed in the name of discipline, starting at five or six years of age and continuing until youths are old enough to leave home on their own. ¶The verbally abused child's self-image is terrible, but the pain and humiliation is locked away in his subconscious. He covers it up and forgets it, but it continues festering there, and one day bursts forth. If he is a kind-hearted child, he will protect his own children in the future from verbal abuse. If he is a mean-spirited child, he will release what his parents put upon him and into his mind, all of that hatred, upon his children. So, the verbal abuse continues generation after generation. Its pain and hurt long outlast that of a slap or a beating. ¶In some parts of the Hindu community we hear a lot about curses. The more intellectual, Western-educated Hindu doesn't believe in curses at all. But what is a curse? A curse is negative energy gathered together and pointed at someone you don't like. Those priests who are able to conjure up a curse—and are often paid for it—take careful precautions to protect themselves from being cursed by their own curse! Sometimes that protection doesn't work, and they become ill, occasionally even die, or become tremendously confused as long as the curse is working. ¶To freely hurl mental harassment and abuse at a child who can't talk back—lest he be slapped down, dragged across the floor and slammed against the wall—is cursing the child as well as oneself. It is also cursing the home, as well as the entire family, because this tremendous force of negative, angry energy that has been suppressed leaches out and fills the room and the entire house. Call a child one bad name and you are calling yourself ten bad names. And that goes into your subconscious mind, because the perpetrator of the crime also hears what he has said. ¶Many people verbally abuse children in order to motivate them, to make them courageous, to make them stand up straight, to make them do better in school. Any psychiatrist or psychologist will tell you that to tell a child he's stupid is no motivation to do better in school! To tell him that he's a pig, he's a dog—and then there are the four-letter words, the "f" word and the "b" word—is no motivation whatsoever. But the children have to take it, because they are dependent for housing, clothing and food. The verbal abuse goes into their subconscious mind. But it goes double, triple, quadruple into the subconscious mind of the mother—and the father also if he hears the mother cursing the kid—and on and on until finally the whole family has cursed itself, become filled with the hatred, the scorn and the filthy meanings of the words they have spoken to one another a thousand times. ¶Will that family be successful? Never. Will that family enjoy vacations?

No way. Will they be totally frustrated on the inside? Yes. Will disease come to that family? Of course! They are creating disease by the disease they are putting into their own subconscious mind, and the harm to the astral body will eventually affect the physical body.

Thursday
LESSON 200
Making Up For Abuse

Of course, parents who curse their children can't hug them, can't show the same love for them. That would be counterproductive! In fact, many families think it's weakening to the child to hug a child and to show love or to congratulate the child. Thus we have whole societies and entire countries that hold themselves down, generation after generation and do not flourish, and therefore are held down by other communities who are doing the same thing, and that are held down by other communities. ¶What is the *prāyaśchitta,* what is the penance, for foul or abusive language—for language that hurts? If you call a child stupid, or call him a little bastard, counteract it by telling him he is intelligent, wanted in the family, loved. Counteract the abuse by saying five good words for every bad word. Otherwise, the parents will have a bad birth. What is a bad birth? Being born diseased. A bad birth is being born without parents. A bad birth is being born in a land that has no room for children. There are lots of suffering kids these days who abused their children in a past life without mercy, taking out their frustrations on them. Which is worse, beating the child physically or berating him with words? The pain of the beating will go away, even the memory, somehow. But the words will ring deep in the mind of the child throughout his lifetime. ¶Now, if the child performs certain *sādhanas* and is able to forgive the family for the verbal beatings, what then happens? It breaks the curse. Then what happens? The whole force of that curse goes back on the mother and the father. The child walks away free, healed, and his parents take the impact of their impropriety. They take the impact of their bad words. To young people who are cursed by your families, I say take your life in your own hands and plan for your own future. After all, why would parents curse and call bad words and put down a child but to control him, use him as a meal ticket, social security, make him so afraid that he can't talk to them! ¶In many homes parents are not beating their children anymore, but they still raise their hand in the threat to hit them! The child knows that if he persists, he's going to get it right in the head. Physical threats and verbal abuse turn a child into a person who is weak, discouraged, without courage—without courage enough to have a conversation with his mother, without courage enough to have a conversation with his father, without courage enough to have a conversation with himself, to develop any initiative, to stand on his own two feet, to be a leader. If your kids cannot or will not talk to you and have a conversation with you, you have probably hurt those kids and scared those kids so much that they don't want to be hurt by you anymore. It's as simple as that. ¶There are awful stories we hear about slavery, how slaves were brought to America, Europe and all over the world, beaten and whipped to bring them down to abject servitude so they wouldn't cause any problems lest they be beaten without mercy for the slightest thing—beaten even if they did nothing wrong, just to keep them in their place. That's what verbal beating does, too. It keeps kids "in their place" so they become useless slaves in the family, earning money to give to parents who still curse them, and then feigning love toward the parents lest they get more verbal abuse. We see this happening all the time. I hear and receive by e-mail desperate testimonies from children and young adults on how they have been abused, physically and with words, in their own home. From the many experiences I know about, I can assure you that words can hurt a child as much or more than a bamboo switch, a belt or a fist.

Friday
LESSON 201
Advice for Abused Youth

We want to talk to the next generation that's coming up. Fourteen-year-olds, eighteen-year-olds, twenty-year-olds, stand on your own two feet! Make your decisions according to *dharma*. What is the book of *dharma? Weaver's Wisdom,* the famous *Tirukural.* It gives you all the tools you need to live a very good life. If your parents are verbally abusing you, don't let their words affect you. Try to have compassion by appreciating what led them to the point where they could say these cruel things to you; but realize that they can offer you nothing but more abuse, because they are in the process of cursing themselves. The message is to "stand on your own two feet, take your life in your own hands, claim your independence," once you realize that life at home is not going to get any better. ¶In certain shops in Asian cities, parents can buy bamboo switches, belts and other instruments of torture made just for punishing kids. Few realize that their mean words can cause just as much hurt, if not more. Parents have developed long lists of words used to demean and belittle. It has become an unspoken rulebook of how to bring their child down to feeling like he's a big nothing, willing to do anything you say, because he inwardly begs: "Don't hurt me anymore. Don't hit me with your words.

Don't hurt me with your long silences and by turning your head away from me. Don't hurt me that way anymore. I'll do anything. I'll get a dumb job and work at it fourteen hours a day to give you some money, to pay you for not hurting me anymore." That's what we have in the Hindu community around the world. And that's what we don't want to have in the Hindu community around the world. ¶What can a child of eight, ten or twelve do who is being verbally and physically beaten at home and in school? Nothing. It's a sad situation. I've received lists of abuses from children of that age, just exactly what their mothers have said and what their fathers have said. It's a tremendous pain in their mind. We've given young people the *prāyaśchitta,* the remedy, of putting a flower in front of their parents' picture for thirty-one days. Most can't do it. They just can't do it. We ask them to say each day, "I forgive you for playing my *karma* back to me," but they just can't do it. The hate, the mistrust, the disappointment, the hurt, is so great, they've been put down so low, that they just cannot do it. ¶My counsel to Hindu families is: Stop the physical abuse. Stop the verbal abuse. Stop the war in the home. Use positive discipline. Praise your children. Discover the good things that they do and tell them how well they have done. Celebrate their Divinity. Enjoy them and enjoy good times with them. This is the family tradition and the ideal of Sanātana Dharma, the Hindu Dharma of the past, before the Church of England reigned over India for 150 years and changed education to their way of thinking, making beating a must in schools and homes in accordance with the many biblical verses that highly recommend "not to spare the rod," and the theological rationale to "beat the devil out of them." Hindus of today's world have begun working together to stop the abuse, passing and enforcing laws to bring us back to the true meaning of *discipline,* which is to teach, train and patiently guide. We must remember that *ahiṁsā,* nonhurting, physically, mentally or emotionally, is the bedrock of Sanātana Dharma. ¶My advice to verbally abusive parents: stop tearing them down by telling them they're stupid, that they're too small, too fat, too lazy, too ugly or too naughty. If you constantly tell a child he is naughty, he will become naughtier. If you constantly tell a child he's nice, he will be nicer. It just works like that. All the psychiatrists agree with this approach, to be sure, as do mothers and fathers who really love their children and take an interest in their children.

Saturday
LESSON 202
Backbiting And Gossip

There are two very great religious laws, and you have heard me talk about them before, and if you follow them and obey them, you will have the spiritual protection of your own intuitive mind. Your intuitive mind will be available to you all of the time. ¶One of these great laws is the law of *daśamāṁśa,* tithing, and the other great law is *śaucha kriyā,* doing good. Now, what is doing good? Doing good is controlling your mind, really, because when the mind is out of control or when you allow it to be out of control, you are really under the control of the instinctive mind of other people. You are more or less like a puppet in their hands. Therefore, we teach, "Think before you speak, and speak only that which is true, kind, helpful and necessary." This is very, very difficult for most people to do. If you carry each thought on the tip of your tongue, quite often it won't be your thought at all. It may be what is seething in the instinctive mind of people around you. That's what makes for backbiting and gossip. Like those who swear, those who gossip do not think. They pick up the low, seething vibrations of the instinctive mind of everyone around and, like stovepipes, emanate the smoke of the fire that is burning or smoldering or fuming or raging underneath. Many undeveloped people believe and repeat the last thing they hear spoken by someone they consider higher than themselves. They gossip freely, hurt freely and are often the pawns of strong-minded, unscrupulous individuals who use their ignorance and weakness to further their own selfish ends. ¶Do you know what gossiping is like? It's like scratching an itch. Something is antagonizing your mind, so you gossip, and you go on and on and on until somebody changes the subject for you, or until somebody does something else that you can gossip about. Shall we say that backbiting and hurtful gossip are the dissipation of the creative, spiritual force? That's all they are, dissipation of your great, God-given inner power. Anyone will tell you that to dissipate your energy is bad for you, but you do that when you gossip. By doing that, you are only the chimney, the dirty smokestack, of the seething instinctive mind, the ugly state of mind, of other people. You are not in control of your own mind. Have I painted a picture that is bad enough, hideous enough, gruesome enough, for you all to stop gossiping and control your mind a little bit? Gossip invokes the *asuric* beings on the lower astral plane and makes new *karmas* for the gossiper, who will be gossiped about in the future when the *karmas* return. ¶Let's paint another picture. When you defile others, mentally and verbally, through backbiting gossip about the happenings in their lives, you are hurting them. You are actually making it difficult for them to succeed, to even persist where they are. They sense, they feel, the ugliness that you are projecting toward them. Many women gossip about their husbands over the telephone to other women while their husbands are at work. How can the husband be successful with the wife's mind, in which he presumably trusts, working and plotting against him in such a chaotic condition? Gossip and backbiting, like verbal abuse, hurt another. You know what happens according to spiritual law when you hurt another. You are only hurting yourself in the future. Of course, you don't meet the hurt right away, but in a few months you will find that it will come to you. You are hurting yourself in the future if you hurt another in the present. ¶It takes great sincerity in life to control the mind. And the power to be sincere is based on honesty. Honesty, *ārjava*, gives a great boon to you. It gives you stability. It makes you strong. It makes every atom in your being vibrate with an inner power. It gives you perspective; it gives you the eye to justice. But you must first be honest with yourself. Then the next time you see something happening in the life of another person that you would just love to sit down and gossip about, stop the menacing wheel of your mind and think about the experience and feelings the other person is going through.

Sunday
LESSON 203
Thoughts Have Power

Each thought and each word has a form, an etheric form. That is why when a room is happy and you walk into it, you feel joyous. When a house is sad and you walk into it, you can sense that misery, for every thought you think and every word you speak takes form and shape in the ether. ¶*Prāṇa* is mental energy. When you use mental energy, you make mental creations. When you use physical energy, you can create physically. With your hands, you can build a house, you can cook a dinner; you can do many things with your physical energy and your physical body. With your mind, through the use of *prāṇa,* you can also create for yourself. How many understand the meaning of the words *prāṇa* and *mental energy?* You would be surprised at the power that you have in your mind as an individual. ¶Every positive thought that you have manifests in a subtle world and remains there for the length of time that it took you to generate it. Everything that you make with your physical energy on the physical plane will remain on the physical plane in physical form according to the time and effort that you took to generate it. If you have done a very fine job, it may remain over a hundred years. If you didn't put much effort into it, it will not remain long on the physical plane. ¶Let's think about the mental world for a moment. Suppose you are generating a thought for something good to happen, a positive circumstance you want to come your way. You concentrate upon it, and you generate it and you make the picture just the way you want to see it. Then you are happy and joyous. You feel as if it has already happened. Now suppose you drop into a lower state of consciousness. You begin to gossip. You use foul language and backbite. You lose control of your mind. You don't put your intuitive mind first. You put the instinctive mind first and begin to think: "Oh, that can't possibly happen because of this..." or "I can't possibly do this because of that...." You are building a negative pattern of fear, worry and doubt that covers up the beautiful picture and snuffs it out. Then, when it does not manifest, you say: "My prayers were not answered. God was too busy helping somebody else. He couldn't help me." But you were the creator. You preserved it on the mental plane for as long as you could, and without knowing it you destroyed it before it manifested physically. That is one way you can go on through life, as so many, many Hindus do—blaming others for their own self-created failures. ¶Do you know what all of that is? Confusion of the mind! So, we have two alternatives: confusion or control. And we have all the spiritual laws to follow that help you control your mind. When the external mind is controlled, then the spirit or inner being, the Reality of you, can shine forth. Shall we say that a confused mind is like a cloud the sun cannot shine through? A controlled mind is like clear ether which the radiance of the sun can shine through.

know where the money came from, then tactfully find out in some way. How does the donor earn his living? Did the money come from performing abortions, from gambling, accepting bribes, *adharmic* law practices or shady business dealings? Is it being given to ease the conscience? ¶Even today's election candidates examine the source of donations exceeding US$10,000—investigating how the donor lives and how the money was gotten—then either receive the gift wholeheartedly or turn it back. When the source is secret, the source of gain is suspect. When the source is freely divulged, it is freed from such apprehension. In the Devaloka, there are *devas*, angels, who monitor carefully, twenty-four hours a day, the sources of gain leading to wealth, because the *prāṇic* bonds are heavy for the wrongdoer and his accomplices. ¶Imagine, for instance, an arms dealer who buys his merchandise surreptitiously and then sells it, secretly or in a store—shotguns and pistols, machine guns, grenades and missiles, instruments of torture and death. Money from this enterprise invested in a religious institution or educational institution or anything that is doing good for people will eventually turn that institution sour, just like pouring vinegar into milk. ¶The spiritual leader's duty is to turn his or her back to such a panderer of bad money and show him the door, just as an honest politician would turn back election donations coming from a subversive source, gained by hurtful practices, lest he suffer the censure of his constituency at a later time, which he hopes to avoid to hold his office. A politician has to protect his reputation. The spiritual leader will intuitively refuse bad money. He doesn't need money. When money comes, he does things. If it doesn't come, he also does things, but in a different way, perhaps on a smaller scale. ¶In Reno, Nevada, for many years the gambling casinos gave college scholarships to students at high schools. Then there came a time of conscience among educators when they could no longer accept these scholarships earned from gambling to send children forward into higher studies. They did not feel in their heart, mind and soul that it was right. Drawing from their example, we extend the boundaries of religion to education and to the human conscience of right conduct on this Earth. ¶Humans haven't changed that much. Over 2,200 years ago, Saint Tiruvalluvar wrote in his *Tirukural*, perhaps the world's greatest ethical scripture, still sworn on in Indian courts of law in Tamil Nadu: "A fortune amassed by fraud may appear to prosper but will all too soon perish altogether. Wealth acquired without compassion and love is to be cast off, not embraced. Protecting the country by wrongly garnered wealth is like preserving water in an unbaked clay pot" (283, 755, 660).

Wednesday
LESSON 206
Three Kinds Of Bribery

Let me tell you a true story. A young man is riding his motor scooter in busy Kuala Lumpur. His tail light is out and he knows it. Hearing a siren behind him, he slows and is pulled over by a motorcycle policeman. In Malay, the officer informs him of the infraction, and pulls out his ticket book, then indicates through well-known gestures that a small bribe would take care of the matter. Heart pounding, palms sweating, the boy musters up his courage and says, "Officer, are you asking me to bribe you? I'm not paying you anything. What is your badge number? Take me to your superior!" Visibly shaken and seeing that the youth is no easy mark, the policeman spins around, mounts his bike and speeds away. There was a bad feeling about this real-life incident. The cop knew he was committing a crime. The youth was tempted to become the accomplice, but resisted, sidestepping for the moment one of society's most sinister problems. ¶Yes, briber and bribed are bound together in their dishonest, dark deed. Reluctance, resignation, efficiency, disdain—none of these sentiments relieve a person from the guilt, the ever-accumulating *kukarma,* the bad *karma,* of the crime. There are three kinds of bribery. The first is the most common—withholding services one has been paid to perform until that additional, secret compensation is paid. The second kind is a little more subtle. Favors—contracts, concessions, legal immunity, etc.—are given to those who pay a bribe in cash or kind. The briber offers money, saying, "I am giving you this money, and this is what you can do for me," and if the party accepts it, that is what he must do. It's a purchase of secret, unauthorized use of influence, position or authority. The third form of bribery, even more subtle, is to provide a paid service and then exact an additional reward. This is, however, the most easily detected of all, because when asked for further service, it will be delayed or denied—that is, if the gift expected after the first service was performed was not given or was not large enough. ¶*Bribe* comes from an Old French word, meaning a morsel of bread given to a beggar. Says *Webster's Dictionary,* a bribe is "1) anything, especially money, given or promised to induce a person to do something illegal or wrong; 2) anything given or promised to induce a person to do something against his or her wishes." Bribery money when received, in cash or kind, is bad money, because it is wrongly gotten—in whatever of the three ways—by psychological force, the arousal of greed or by devious coercion. ¶In many countries, bribery has become a way of life. Bribes are demanded, and usually paid, for most anything, from getting a contract signed to buying a train ticket. A prominent politician in India told me he finds it impossible, simply impossible, to get anything done without it. Most, but not everyone, would agree. A successful, sophisticated Bangalore businesswoman, now in her forties, swears she has never, ever paid a bribe in her entire life.

Thursday
LESSON 207
Bribery Is Corruption

Spiritual people and institutions sometimes feel compelled to accept or pay bribes because the alternative is so frustrating or because their sense of mission is so strong, and they want it to go forward at all costs. Still, it must be remembered that it is not only what you do that is important, but how you do it. Bad money cannot be purified by spending it on good projects. Rather, bad money sours and fails them. ¶In our spiritual fellowship, we have a rule that we do not engage in bribery, even when it means great sacrifice. In our efforts to carve a granite temple in Bangalore to be shipped to Hawaii—for which we established a village of a hundred workers and their families—we have been called upon time and time again to hand over a bribe. Yes, even a giant project can be hampered by a small bribe. We had to ask ourselves, shall we pay the petty pittance to keep the electricity on and the phones working? It was hard sometimes not to submit, but now it is well known that we don't pay, and the bribe takers no longer ask. One previous bribe seeker actually apologized for his earlier demands. ¶By neither accepting nor paying bribes, my devotees are telling the community that bribery is unacceptable and ultimately unnecessary. If enough people follow this principle in any society, then bribery will go away. If enough people do not, then bribery becomes the accepted way of doing business, and everyone will accept bribes as a source of additional income, and pay bribes as a means of getting things done. The acceptance of a bribe is an affirmation of the practice. Every time a family, an individual, a community, a nation disavows or rejects the practice of bribery, then bribery is diminished. To walk away from a bribe, to reject a bribe or to refuse to pay is to fulfill Hindu Dharma. ¶Where does bribery begin? The same place as everything else—at home, often at a young age. Mothers bribe their children to behave and earn good grades. Fathers bribe youths to marry according to their race and financial position. Dowry, we could say, is another form of bribery. If it's not given, the marriage does not take place. If it were really a gift, that would not be the case. Those who take bribes and pay bribes raise a corrupt family. ¶Mercy, through personal *prāyaśchitta,* sincere penance, can help relieve the bad *karma,* but that, too, is all for naught unless one stops the practice. The power of decision rests on the character of each person in the family. If that power is used rightly, the *kukarmas* clear. If not, the family and all members go down and down and down, for bribery is stealing and being stolen from. It is similar to walking into someone's house late at night, opening their cash box and taking money. Bribery has the same emotional and psychological impact. He who pays a bribe is an accomplice to the person who demands it. He who accepts a bribe proffered to buy his favors is likewise bound to his crafty benefactor. There are two criminals in each case, he who accepts and he who pays. Inwardly, *karmically,* astrally, they are bound together as one. Those who pay bribes for the sake of efficiency or accept gifts without examining the intent may deem themselves innocent, but they are not. *Karmic* law spares no one.

Friday
LESSON 208
Steps Against Bribery

Bribery breeds an educated criminal generation. It blocks the free flow of business. Bribery disrupts positive projects. Bribery diverts creative energies to worries about who, if not paid, will disrupt the progress, cut the phone lines, turn off the electric power or otherwise cause delay after delay after delay. Bribery is devastating to a nation's economy. No one knows how much anything really costs; and since it is illegal money, black money, the recipients don't pay taxes on it. Two sets of books have to be kept. Honest companies are put out of business by dishonest competitors who give and accept bribes. ¶What can be done about bribery? On the governmental level, there are instructive examples from recent history. Twenty years ago in America, undercover FBI agents approached various politicians and offered them bribes to help a fictitious Arab company gain American business. A few politicians accepted the bribes and quickly found themselves jailed. Every politician got the message. A few years ago, New Orleans hired a new police chief to reform its notoriously corrupt police force. First he demanded and got the officers' pay doubled. Then he arrested, prosecuted and fired the next sixty-five officers caught taking bribes. The rest, it's said, no longer risk their now well-paying careers for bribe money. ¶Internationally, only the United States has a law preventing its companies from bribing foreign officials. As far as we know, other countries—including all of Europe—have refused to pass similar statutes on the excuse that it would put their business communities at a disadvantage. In fact, the bribes so paid are even tax-deductible. Yet, the same companies' paying a bribe in their own country can result in prosecution. One organization, Transparency International in Berlin, is attempting to end this global double standard which makes it so difficult for individual countries to root out the scourge of bribery. ¶From a psychological point of view, bribery is a criminal consciousness of deceit, cheating, on the darker side of life. Guilt is always involved, secrecy, fear of being caught for extorting funds, fear of what might happen if bribes are not paid and worry over obligations incurred by accepting bribes. Such surreptitious dealings create an erosion of trust in society. ¶Bribery is basically stealing through intimidation. The able-bodied beggar demanding alms on the street is no different from the able-bodied businessman who withholds his services. The beggar shirks his legitimate work, and the businessman uses his position to exact payments not due. Both reap bad *karma* that will reflect on every generation in the future and a few in the past.

Saturday
LESSON 209
Bribery and Tipping

A healthy society is based on honesty, openness, love, trust and goodwill. It is at the grass roots level, in the home, in schools, in the marketplace, office and factory, that bribery should first be stopped. Hindu Dharma is the law enforcer. Simply don't bribe. It really is OK not to bribe. More and more, not bribing is becoming acceptable behavior. It is difficult to step back from this practice, but you can live your whole life and not pay a one rupee bribe, even in a place where everyone pays bribes. ¶One might wonder if tipping is a form of bribery. It is legal in nearly every country to tip a waiter, busboy, carhop, valet, cab driver, maitre d', and no one has ever been arrested and prosecuted for giving such a gratuity. True, a tip is expected, but services can't be withheld if it is not given, lest the individual lose his or her job. Giving tips, or gratuities, is not bribery when it is the custom for paying waiters in restaurants, bell boys in hotels and valets who will get your car from the parking lot and drive it up to the door. Tips are expected, and because they are receiving tips, their salary from the hotel or restaurant is often very low. The giving of gratuities is an accepted custom. But the employees would be bound by the hotel or restaurant to perform the same service even if tips were not forthcoming. This is not to be extended to areas where this custom does not exist, such as to paid government servants who have a salary much higher than those who live by being tipped. ¶Similarly, the giving of gifts on auspicious occasions to anyone who has been of service is spreading goodwill, but is not expected and is completely voluntary. The service would not diminish if the gifts were not given. Our giving gifts to the *śilpis* several times a year at our temple worksite in Bangalore is an example. Even if we did not honor our carvers by a gift, they would still have to do their work up to specifications. This is the pure vibration we want to work into Iraivan Temple—the vibration of *dharma*, not the vibration of giving something to someone for fear they will in the future withhold their services or do us some harm. ¶There are many other wrongs, too, such as prostitution, paying for sex—that's sex without love, which is lust—that create *kukarmas*, that are also against the law. Then, we might ask, why don't some countries in which bribery and prostitution have become part of the national culture make these practices legal, at least to protect the lawmakers, who would then pass legislation to control them? ¶There is small time bribery and big time bribery. In the Western world, bribery is big time. It's at the top, involving millions of dollars. We've seen cases where a senator will put his family, his reputation or his life in jeopardy by accepting a $10,000 bribe—which is about seven percent of his yearly salary—and lose his office, lose his reputation. In India, bribery comes down to a few pennies to facilitate the little chores of life. We have heard of unspoken rules in different parts of India as to how bribery should be done if you want to get anything done, even buying a train ticket. ¶Why is it that people are willing to live in fear of being found out? Why is it that politicians who accept great bribes often finally bribe their way out of the situation with those who brought about their indictment? And why are they caught, but maybe to siphon off some of the wealth that they had garnered from bribery, which could be quite lucrative for law-enforcement people? Even after their punishment, those who have become wealthy through receiving bribes often maintain a higher standard of living than they would have before they mastered the art of bribery.

Sunday
LESSON 210
Bribery in The Home

Then there is bribery of children: "I'll give you a sweet if you do what I want you to do. I'll take the sweet away if you don't." Some call this discipline, but true discipline is training and teaching, learning to uphold a known rule. Anything else is punishment, which closes the lines of communication between the elder and the child. The child has to be clearly taught what the rules are and who is in charge. The child has to know what he is going to get and not get, according to his or her misdeeds. But to bribe the child who has not been educated in this way, to awaken his desire for something and not give it to him, that is a form of corruption. The child will carry that out into the community. He will not be a good citizen, and his *kukarma* will reflect upon the family and several generations back and several generations in the future. The blame is upon the father and the mother, because children follow the example of the parents. Bribing and beating go hand in hand. When it becomes a way of life, children are bribed to behave, to get good grades, to go to bed on time. ¶There is still another, even more insidious, form of bribery that happens within the home. This is emotional bribery: "I shall be unhappy unless you please me," "I shall be happy to include you in my will if you do what I want, but if you don't, you're out of my will." That is bribery. It inhibits the freedom of the individual. "Marry this girl and you will please your family. After all we have done for you, you have to marry the way we want you to marry, and you have to give up the girl you really, really love." Even if the boy has been having an affair with that girl, even if she is pregnant, his family will bribe him to marry someone else by threatening exclusion from the family, disrespect and the ruin of his name in the community. Oh, that is a favorite form of bribery: "I shall blacken your name in the community, make up stories about your character. I shall ruin your reputation. Your name will look like mud in the minds of an ever-increasing group of people unless you buckle down and do what we say." That is a form of intimidation or blackmail that is used quite often in today's world. Blackmail is a kind of reverse bribery. While a briber demands money to do something for you, a blackmailer demands money to not do something against you. The blackmailer says, "Give me what I want or I'll expose the secrets I know about you." This demand for hush money is an ominous form of reverse bribery, but bribery nonetheless. There is serious *karma* involved in all forms of bribery, which are part of the negative culture which tears down a nation, which tears down a community, which tears down a family, which the younger generation, hopefully, will not put up with.

Saṅgaṇaka Yantra
संगणकयन्त्र

What about Computers?

With earnest effort hold the senses in check. Controlling the breath, regulate the vital activities. As a charioteer holds back his restive horses, so does a persevering aspirant restrain his mind.

Kṛishṇa Yajur Veda, Śvetāśvatara Upanishad, 2.9. UPP, P. 192

They played soldier in the streets, like the big boys, and when they grew up, moved on to real guns. Toy imports from Europe supplied the need, and soon many homes had a toy gun collection. ¶When the Sinhalese army moved through Tamil homes looking for hidden weapons, they were sometimes fooled by the realistic plastic guns. This caused them so much trouble, they took to beating the men of households that had toy guns. Soon the toys became less popular. The world of toys and the world of real war are not always separated. ¶Technology today, especially computer technology, the Internet, can enhance everything you want to do. It is not unlike the *ākāśic* memory banks of the inner world. Tuning in to the Internet, you can find out almost anything you want to know within a split second. We are communicating electronically and instantaneously with *āśramas* in the Himalayas and the jungles of South America. It used to take a letter one month to arrive, and we would sometimes wait two to three months to get a reply, if any ever came. Now we are communicating with Rishikesh, high in the Himalayas, and receiving e-mail back within a day, sometimes within minutes. The e-media has enhanced communication tremendously. ¶It has also enhanced pornography. It has enhanced terrorism. It will enhance anything that you want. It is up to you and your powers of decision to decide what you want to put into your subconscious mind and live with, perhaps for the rest of your life. We are not in the agricultural era anymore. We are in the technological age. We are in the communication age. It's the age of the mind, where the mind is in technology, working through technology. We can't change that. It's not going to go away. It is up to each individual to decide within himself how he wants to use the technology available to him. ¶The computer is just like the mind. It has memory, a certain amount of reasoning ability, a certain motivation. But it doesn't have the controls that you, as a human, are able to exert within yourself, such as willpower and the power of *viveka*, discrimination, which is so central to our religious tenets. Therefore, ask yourself, what is spirituality to you? What is important to you? What do you want to impress in your inner mind to perhaps manifest in this or your next life? You can use these tools to enhance what is important to you, and thereby benefit not only your own life but the lives of others.

Friday
LESSON 215
The Web's Vast Potential

http://www.hinduismtoday.com/ No, that's not a typographical error or a foreign language. It's HINDUISM TODAY'S World Wide Web address. If you have access to a computer, you can read our Hindu family magazine from any of Earth's hundreds of millions of Internet nodes, for free. True, you would not get all those wonderful photos or art, but the text is there for anyone searching the net for *dharma*. Years ago, before the Internet really took off, I meditated on what it would mean for Sanātana Dharma and could see a time when Hindus would all be connected on the Internet. An *āśrama* in Fiji could download explanations for *saṁskāras*. A *yoga* society in Orissa would be able to locate graphical information about *chakras* for a public slide show. A pilgrim could call up a home page with all the sacred sites, temples, *tīrthas* and *āśramas* his family can visit on their way back to Bhārat, complete with maps, train schedules and cost of A/C rooms. I saw more, much more. A *pañchāngam*, sacred Hindu calendar, we all use together, would be available, listing the holy days and festivals. I noted that our own timeline of Hindu history, from *Hinduism's Contemporary Catechism*, was already on the Net. It has stirred historians to write us many letters and discuss the new way India's history is being understood. Even now you can access it and search for when Ramakrishna was born, when the *Vedas* were written down or when South Indian Chola kings set sail for Indonesia. ¶I foresaw interactive courses. A teacher in South Africa could download wonderful resources to enrich the lessons she prepares for her students—photos, maps, Vedic verses, illustrations and sounds, all the things that interest children. How about an encyclopedia of Hinduism online? How about a library of *dharma* graphics which anyone could log onto, find that perfect piece of art for illustrating a brochure, download it and never leave their desk? The possibilities are endless. ¶Say your daughter just had a new baby and you want a special name. What to do? Search for Hindu names on the Net, through thousands of names on numerous sites, for the perfect name, with the meaning and the right pronunciation. Need a good time to start a business, sign an important contract or leave on a trip? Just call up the WWW home page on astrology for a computer analysis of the auspicious moment.

Saturday
LESSON 216
Hinduism On the Net

The World Wide Web is difficult to say fast, all those w's one after another. It comes out "wurlwyewep." The pros just call it the Web. But what is it? I have been learning a little about the Web. It took me a while to get the Internet connection on my Power Macintosh working right, and the monks had to install some special software for me. But soon I was out there on the Infobahn, in the slow lane. I found that the Web is the first user-friendly, interactive global information medium. It extends any individual's reach, facilitating everything from the sharing of information to finding it. Soon, we hope, all the religionists of the Global Forum for Human Survival and Parliament of World Religions will communicate their thoughts, programs and knowledge on the Web. I remember when in Moscow and Rio de Janiero, at Global Forum gatherings of political and religious leaders, the former US Vice President Al Gore unveiled his vision to expand the Internet, previously only available to the government and universities, into an Information Highway to tie the world together. Congratulations, Mr. Gore. Just three years later your vision of a digital superhighway adds four new users every minute, and we are among them. ¶From HINDUISM TODAY's home page, by a click of a button you can bring up a page that allows you to write an instant, postage-free letter to the editor. Another click sends you into the vastness of cyberspace. It's that easy, and easy to get lost, too. Give it a try. They say the Web has changed things completely. The old Internet was OK for physicists, but it was an unfriendly, type-only, black-and-white technical world. The Web added images, color, a variety of typefaces, pictures, designs, animation and buttons that lead to the next destination. Now it's everybody's tool. Click on a button and go to a home page of Vedic verses in Bangalore. Click a button there about astrology and suddenly you're in San Francisco or browsing a London database on *āyurveda.* Click again and you're reading a page on Sanskrit studies in Durban. It's called hyperlinking. I learned how to make bookmarks yesterday—links to connections you have made, kept by a program in case you want to return but don't recall the address. Just click and you're there again. Easy. Another nice thing is the Web is so democratic. Whether you are Birla Pvt. Ltd., IBM or Mrs. Bhatt, a poetess from Pune, everyone is equal on the Web. ¶Electronic mail is like having the post office in your house. Messages come and go through the phone lines and can be read almost immediately anywhere in the world. Our institutions use the Web to connect the missions we oversee in several countries. We put new information on the home page in Hawaii, and members in Mauritius, India, Malaysia, Singapore, Sri Lanka or Germany can access it instantly. Not only that, it's nearly free. Most of those big fax and phone bills are gone. Hindu institutions are working hard to upgrade to the Web, driven by an amazing group of Hindu engineers who have become a driving force in the Internet world. These cyberspace networks are all interconnected, but totally disorganized and decentralized, just like Hinduism, so everyone will feel at home there! Let's meet on the "wurlw-yewep" and share our experience, vision and tools. ¶The editor of a Jain magazine in London once asked, "Gurudeva, how do you feel about using all this modern technology to promote religion?" I said, we marvel at our ancient handwritten scriptures. The stylus and the *olai* leaf were modern technology at one point in time, the pen and paper at another, as was the old typewriter at yet another point in time. Now we have computers and the Internet—modern technology capable of bringing the spiritual beings and all religious people of the world closely together wherever they live. This one thing the typewriter could not do, the pen and paper could not do, the stylus and *olai* leaf did not do.

Sunday
LESSON 217
Harnessing Technology

Building up the spiritual vibration in the home requires a control of the computers. Here at our Śaivite Hindu monastery in Hawaii, all of the monastics have a computer. When they take their vows, they are given their robes, their beads, their staff of *tapas* and their Macintosh! This enables us to serve the very best that we can from our tiny little island. At this *āśrama* we look at our technology as our tools. We control these tools. They do not control us. We use these tools to enhance our religious work, to amplify the Sanātana Dharma and bring it out into the Western world and throughout the world through written publications and on the Internet. Our tools do not dominate our life. We turn them on at a certain time. We turn them off at a certain time. At twelve noon they are turned off and not turned on again until 3:00PM. At 6:30PM, they're turned off again and not turned on until after worship and intense guided meditation the next morning. On retreat days—two days each week—we don't use them at all, except possibly for an hour on rare occasions and only for very important things. What does this do? It allows everyone to talk with everyone else, to communicate, to share, to appreciate each other, to work together for the good of all. It allows us to live a balanced life, a human life in which the spirit within us can shine through and we have time to enjoy the sunset on our 459-acre spiritual sanctuary on the Garden Island of Kauai, to listen to the song of a bird, to meditate and enjoy the company of one another, even in this technological age. ¶Perhaps the most prevalent electronic media is television. A family watching television together is a togetherness, provided the program is a wholesome choice that everyone enjoys. You can laugh and talk together and discuss what you watched afterwards. But there should be an afterwards and a before. That balances the mesmerizing capacity of television. Television shouldn't consume all of the family's time. Before the TV is turned on in the evening, the family should sit together, talk about the day, acknowledge or praise each other and mutually decide what will be viewed. Afterwards, some time should be taken to discuss what was watched and to explain it to the children, especially if they are young, allowing them to partake of the wisdom of the parents. Especially if they see a program you don't approve of, sit them down afterwards and talk it over with them, discuss the values portrayed in relation to our Śaivite values. Let them be aware of other points of view. This is your duty. ¶Treat the television like you would going to a movie: the whole family gets in the car as if they are going to a big event. They drive to the movie house, buy the tickets, some popcorn and soda, have a wonderful time and come home and enjoy one another's company. ¶Children should not be allowed to watch TV constantly, but made to live a balanced life that includes exercise, games and outdoor activities. Some children can and do watch TV for many hours each day, filling their minds with all kinds of ideas and neglecting their studies. It is up to the parents to set wise rules for TV and to enforce those rules for the benefit of the child's mind. One such wise rule is to limit daily watching to one or two hours. ¶Use television if you wish, but use it wisely and you will avoid these problems. Learn to control television. Realize that it is a great instrument for entertainment, but a dangerous instrument if it overcomes you, if it fills up your subconscious mind, if it brings alien thoughts into your home and upsets your family. ¶While TV has enormous negative potential, music does as well. The type of music played in the home and the message it delivers is crucial. Ideally, it should be beautiful Hindu music played on traditional instruments by Śaiva souls. Great care should be exercised to exclude the crass music and lyrics of lower consciousness. Whatever you listen to brings you into one state of consciousness or another.

Vyabhichāra, Lampaṭatva

व्यभिचार लम्पटत्व

Adultery and Pornography

Sin of the mind, depart far away! Why do you utter improper suggestions? Depart from this place! I do not want you! Go to the trees and the forests! My mind will remain here along with our homes and our cattle.

Atharva Veda 6.45.1. VE, P. 489

Monday
LESSON 218
Controlling The Forces

There are three kinds of adultery: physical (the worst); emotional (very distressing); and mental (the secret kind). Physical adultery breaks up marriages, destroys homes and creates distraught children. Even if it is forgiven and the couple reunites, it is not forgotten. There is always wondering, "Will it happen again? Did it happen last night?" Emotional adultery is quite common. In the workaday world, husbands often become more attached to their female employees and associates than to their wives. Working wives become more emotionally attached to their boss and fellow workers than to their husbands. It is understandable. After all, she spends more waking hours with men at work than with her husband. ¶I was asked, "How should a Hindu man relate to women in the workplace and maintain his religious life?" Very carefully, very carefully. It's important that you remember that you have a path to follow and you are in the workplace to do your job, be friendly to everyone equally, not having favorites nor any likes or dislikes. Behavior should be professional. Professional behavior is detached behavior yet friendly behavior. The *Tirukural* reminds us, "The chivalry that does not look upon another's wife is not mere virtue—it is saintly conduct" (148). ¶Mental adultery—that's the secret culprit. Who knows what anyone is thinking? But the feeling is one of drifting away into a fantasy world, of deciding to become or not become emotionally or physically involved with someone other than one's spouse. ¶But most devastating, most insidiously devastating, is mental adultery through pornography. The visualizations, the fantasies, the changes in sexual habits it produces and the secrecy all bundled into one creates a distance between spouses, unless of course they are enjoying the same pornographic episodes. A verse in the *Atharva Veda* implores, "Sin of the mind, depart far away! Why do you utter improper suggestions? Depart from this place! I do not want you! Go to the trees and the forests! My mind will remain here along with our homes and our cattle" (6.45.1. VE, P. 489). It is hard to believe such verses were composed thousands of years ago. Human problems haven't changed that much, have they? ¶The Sanātana Dharma is the oldest religion in the world. Therefore, its followers are the oldest people in the world, having fully explored sex (the *Kāma Sūtra* is the oldest known erotic text) and learned how to

---

We are in Singapore, as the lion monument shows, where a wife has just come from her garden with a basket of vegetables. Returning earlier than expected, she is hurt and shocked to see a strange woman leaving her house and her husband waving good-bye to his mistress.

control it; established a system of sanctified marriages and found out how to keep interpersonal relations going unhindered. India's culture spread all through Asia, and because of it one rarely sees any affection shown in public—kissing, hugging, hand-holding, touching or feeling. One might wonder how such a large population can be accounted for! ¶Hindus know that the sexual force is an energy, either under control or out of control. When controlled, it creates peace, well-being and health and provides a mental, emotional, physical balance. When out of control, just the opposite is the case: confusion, secrecy, stress, fear of discovery, lingering guilt, which creates misunderstandings and unresolvable situations.

Tuesday
LESSON 219
The Psychic Ties of Intimacy

Adultery is in the news today, not only in national but also international scandals. Television plots give permission for "sneaking around." It is not uncommon, and many don't give it a thought, for husbands to visit "ladies of pleasure" and pay for their services during their wife's monthly retreat or many months of pregnancy—and, of course, on business trips. Yes, those business trips! ¶The South Indian ethical masterpiece, *Tirukural,* advises, "Among those who stand outside virtue, there is no greater fool than he who stands with a lustful heart outside another's gate. Hatred, sin, fear and disgrace—these four will never abandon one who commits adultery" (142, 146). ¶The adulteress has a *karma* to bear that affects many generations of her relatives and friends, for she is psychically connected to every man with whom she has had intercourse. A mystic could see a fog-like psychic tube connecting their astral bodies that will not disintegrate for many years. The adulteress may have many of these tubes, especially if she is a woman for hire. A man is connected in the same way to all women he has been with. It is through these psychic tubes, which are like the umbilical cord connecting a baby to its mother, that the energies flow, and the *karmas* as well—good, bad and mixed. ¶A husband and wife who were both virgins at marriage have only a singular psychic tube through which energies pass between them. If their relationship is pure and they are intellectually and emotionally compatible, they automatically control their *karmas* of *dharma, artha, kāma* and *moksha*: Their children are lovingly raised, because they are never entangled in family feuding. There is no fight involved, because no intruder has established a new psychic umbilical cord with either spouse, which would cause disruption between them and impending havoc to the children. ¶Once an astral-psychic tube is established between a man and a woman through sexual encounters, it becomes a telepathic channel, conveying thoughts, feelings and emotions. This is an important connection for married couples, tying them intimately together. Those who are married and stay faithful to their life companions know that it is possible to feel the spouse's moods and emotions and even read his or her thoughts, all of which are conveyed through this psychic laser beam or subtle astral *prāṇic* channel. For those who have had sexual encounters with several of the opposite sex, the psychic connections become confusing. Small wonder they experience stress of which the cause eludes even the best psychiatrists. It would be like watching four, five or more TV programs at the same time, all day long and especially during the night.

Wednesday
LESSON 220
The Costs Of Adultery

Now imagine a married woman working with men in a hospital or an engineering firm and a husband working as a computer programmer among women. Each is attracted to someone of the opposite sex, maybe because of *karmas* from a past life. Their emotional *prāṇas* move out of their bodies and connect with their workmates. Compatibility is established. Talking and laughing together become easy. When the "big happening" happens, as affairs so often do, the physical-mental-emotional-*prāṇic* exchange of energies forms an astral tube *(nāḍī)* which connects the two for a period of at least twelve years. ¶Through this *nāḍī*, the information conveyed is as subtle as: she sneezes and he coughs; he gets angry and she becomes pensive and sulks for no reason. Certainly no high-minded telepathic communication is happening as it maybe once did when the *prāṇas* were just forming a connection. Now, because they are psychically attached and pulling on each other in their secret affair, they become antagonistic toward each other. That's why they say sexual intercourse outside wedlock ruins a relationship. They still have to work in the same office together and attend the same meetings, which were quite different when the flirting first began. Then when one, or both, turns a roving eye toward someone else, a feeling of jealousy comes up, and rejection. A good TV script, perhaps, but a disaster in real life. ¶Now let's think of the adulterer's wife, at home doing her daily chores, taking care of the children. How does she begin to feel? She becomes listless, uninspired, as he draws on her energies to feed the adulteress. The home becomes an empty place. She and the children are alone in a barracks, between walls that do not hold in love and compassion and kindness. ¶Indeed, adultery is one of the great wreckers of human relationships.

Don't dismiss it as irrelevant on the spiritual path, the path to liberation, or at least to getting a better birth in the next life. What is the healing when adultery has happened? It is necessary to perform some kind of penance that will sever the psychic tubes: maybe walking on fire or sleeping on a bed of nails for three days and nights, or performing *kavadi* with fifteen spears pierced through the flesh—three well-known public penances. One of Hinduism's ancient lawbooks, the *Manu Dharma Śāstra*, prescribes intense fasting, which in modern times would be fifteen to thirty-one days, under professional care. In the absence of true reconciliation, the best resolution is to live with the spouse like brother and sister under vows of celibacy. Those who don't do something to mitigate the *kukarmas* and break the astral ties of adultery will suffer through the lives of their children, who will follow the patterns that they secretly set. ¶Adultery can be stopped on the mental plane. In fact, if it is not stopped there, watch out. It can be stopped on the emotional plane. Husbands, beware of secretaries more beautiful than your wife. Wives, beware of employers who may be more exciting than your husband. Pornography adulterers, you *can* turn off that computer and stop the pornography on the mental plane. ¶Finally, beware of the siren, the professional seducer, who is there, always there, when the wife is incapacitated or when the husband is on a business trip. They appear in many forms. There is always a price to pay. They may break up the marriage. Children may lose their mother or father. Guilt supersedes and far outlasts all temporary pleasure. Fidelity and infidelity are part of the human experience. The choice is yours which part of the human experience you want to experience.

Thursday
LESSON 221
The Abyss of Pornography

Live and learn, live and learn. We learn something every day, and it is not always what we want to learn. Sometimes it is good for us to know, and other times not so good. It is difficult for us to speak of certain subjects. They are too sensitive, taboo, delicate and private, and so we avoid them. But it is necessary to understand and cope with these matters; and if father and grandmother are not speaking about them, then others must. Pornography is one. Not that it is bad in the sinful sense. Hinduism is too tolerant of sexuality to make such pronouncements. We can say it is neither good nor bad, but we can also say it does place big obstacles in relationships, including unexplainable misunderstandings leading to arguments. And it certainly can and does interfere with serious spiritual effort and progress. Those on the path of *sādhana* are admonished not to indulge in graphic, explicit sexual imagery, and if they are involved already, to give it up, just give it up. The porno path is a downhill path to be avoided. It is ever enticing but never fulfilling. I recently was told that pornography is addictive. I always understood that alcohol, tobacco and certain drugs are addictive, but to find out that pornography is addictive, that was something new for me. ¶Veterans on the porno path say it is more fun, more stimulating, more exciting and more satisfying than the wife waiting in the other room. This lonely life of low self-esteem centered around pornography slowly becomes habitual, an addiction that is difficult to overcome. Looking at the results in a porno addict's life, we can see that sex on the Internet is engrossing, all consuming. They become reclusive, tight lipped, secretive, drawing away from humanity. After a *cybersex* session and expenditure of energies, the voyeur becomes sharp, even demanding, with his wife and the children. Guilt manifests in numerous ways. It has been my observation that addicts develop chronic lower back problems that cannot be cured by chiropractors or even be rightly diagnosed. When the lust, which is sex without love, takes over, the lower nature is unnaturally stimulated, not unlike a plague that has fallen upon us. I am told that one-third of those who use the Internet do so to view pornography, have phone sex and visit lewd chat rooms. "What is this world coming to?" elders exclaim. Well, *cybersex* has arrived for adults, young adults, children and, yes, some elders, too. ¶An even more serious problem is with sons and daughters who become addicted to this kind of vicarious stimulation. Most parents in the modern Hindu community work and get two paychecks every payday. They have little or no time at all to give to their children. The duty of watching after the children is often delegated to a baby-sitter, and the older children baby-sit when they are able. What goes on behind those closed doors, when the shades are down and the computer is on, nobody knows, and nobody is telling. "Don't ask, don't tell" seems to be the policy in most homes. Pornography is a secret thing, but all that is seen is carried forward in the mind as vivid images and then recreated in dreams and daytime fantasies long after the computer has been turned off.

Friday
LESSON 222
Seductive Fantasies

During this past year, I have been delving into the lives of those among my international congregation who are addicted to blue movies, Internet sex sites and all the artificial modern means of stimulation. To say the least, interesting discoveries were made. The most hurtful of them all is a mature and sexually experienced man, accustomed to pornography, marrying an innocent virgin girl who absolutely cannot perform the way he expects and who is then humiliated, beaten or burned, divorced and traded in for another. This crisis is often blamed on dowry. Or it's claimed she really wasn't a virgin, so he had to send her back to her family. One would only know the truth about his actions from an unabashed and totally honest confession by the young man. There is much to be said for early marriage, before the boy is exposed to the sexual fantasy world and all its temptations, before he develops habit patterns that absolutely cannot be broken by the seven matrimonial steps around the sacred fire. Parents should question their children's personal life before arranging a marriage. ¶Psychologically, pornography is closely linked to adultery. Maybe the other woman is not warm flesh and bones, but she is an unforgettable, reoccurring image within his mind, taking up the mental real estate. She appears quite alive in his dreams—more beautiful, more accomplished, more seductive, more enchanting, more alluring than his wife. ¶Dad never shares his pornographic books, magazines or World Wide Web addresses with his teenager, and neither does mom. But the children are allowed to become addicted on their own, with free, unchaperoned time at the keyboard. Does this make any sense to you? It certainly doesn't make sense to me.

Saturday
LESSON 223
Breaking the Addiction

I was told, and didn't want to hear it, that pornography is here and there and everywhere on the Internet. Its advocates rationalize that it helps boys and girls establish their sexual identity even at a very young age. That, to say the least, is a very much debatable point. It robs them of their innocence, their childhood. That is for sure. Men and women, men and men, women with women, *trois, quatre, cinq,* how to kiss and how to do many other things—it's all there. Question: do you know what your children are doing at home when you are both at work or out receiving an award for some social outreach beyond your family? Are they surfing porno sites on the Web? Even in the highly ethical families of my international congregation, this is sometimes happening. ¶In the old days, pornography was available in the big cities only. Separate areas with sex shops and prostitutes were called red light districts, areas decent people would never be seen in, and this alone kept pornography under control. During the First World War, soldiers were made to feel at home with posters of pin-up girls. These were girls in bathing suits, well covered up by today's standards, but healthily endowed. In America before the turn of the century, the skirts did not show the ankles. Then they did. A big uproar! Moralists said showing ankles made women more sexually attractive to the men. Then up and up went the skirts, to way above the knees. Have you ever looked at knees? Some say they are the ugliest part of the human body. ¶I could go on and on. My job as *satguru* to so many souls in many countries is to break up addictions. It's a dirty job, but somebody has to do it. The phenomenon of porno addiction was very new to me, and we needed a *prāyaśchitta*, penance. So, we asked Sri Sri Sri Pramukhswami's senior *sādhus* the remedy to be used. His Swaminarayan Fellowship is one of the strictest orders in the world, if not the strictest. They said to look at a girl and follow her movement for five seconds as she walks would require a fast for twenty-four hours. This is a self-imposed penance among their 654 *sādhus* which can be applied to pornography. They well know, as our wise scriptures say, that sex manifests in eight levels, each one leading to the next: fantasy, glorification, flirtation, lustful glances, secret love talk, amorous longing, rendezvous and intercourse. So if the brothers see someone not eating breakfast, lunch and dinner for one or two days, they know he is trying to get control of the sexual forces and transmute them into tireless creativity.

Sunday
LESSON 224
Regaining Perspective

When your husband seems distant, preoccupied, not at home even when he is there, sits pensively in his shrine room, won't eat his dinner, breakfast or lunch for several days while consuming a *sattvic* diet of fruit and yogurt, do not live under the illusion that he is going to become a *sādhu*. He may just be trying to break the cycle of his addiction to pornographic viewing, thinking and dreaming. Know that he still loves you, and never, ever question him about his self-imposed *sādhana*. Rather, choose the best of fruits. And if you find all those unspeakable pictures in the garbage can, along with a couple of X-rated videos and CDs, don't throw your findings up in his face, even if you are perturbed and angry with him. That might become his excuse to again pursue his addiction and perverse enjoyment, possibly without you in his life. ¶Pornography is not only on the Internet. In hotels, we are told, four- and five-star, there are channels on cable TV that guests buy to watch hard- and soft-core pornography. Is this fun for the whole family? No, it is not. The cable channels on regular TV also bring all this into every home. It even flows through the telephone. Watch the bills. They might be telling a story of buying fantasy sex. ¶It may be argued that Hindus invented pornography, considering the compromising images carved in certain ancient temples. But this is out in the open. The whole family can stand and see—the six-year-old, the ten-year-old, mom and dad. Recently the Spice Girls, a famous band from the UK known for their sassy, sexy ways, planned to perform in front of India's Khajuraho Temple, known for its erotic imagery. Hindu activists responded that this was unthinkable because "Eroticism without spirituality is nothing but pornography." ¶Defenders of free expression say pornography is a disease-free diversion. There is no danger of venereal disease. We might agree, but must say that the consequences mentally are even more devastating, bringing "dis-ease" that no doctor can cure, for which there are no quick remedies, no drugs. Enough said. A word to the wise is sufficient, but a thousand to the fool is not quite enough.

Janma, Bhrūṇahatyā, Ātmahatyā

जन्म भ्रूणहत्या आत्महत्या

Birth, Abortion And Suicide

A slayer of an embryo is
like the slayer of a priest.

Kṛishṇa Yajur Veda 6.5.10

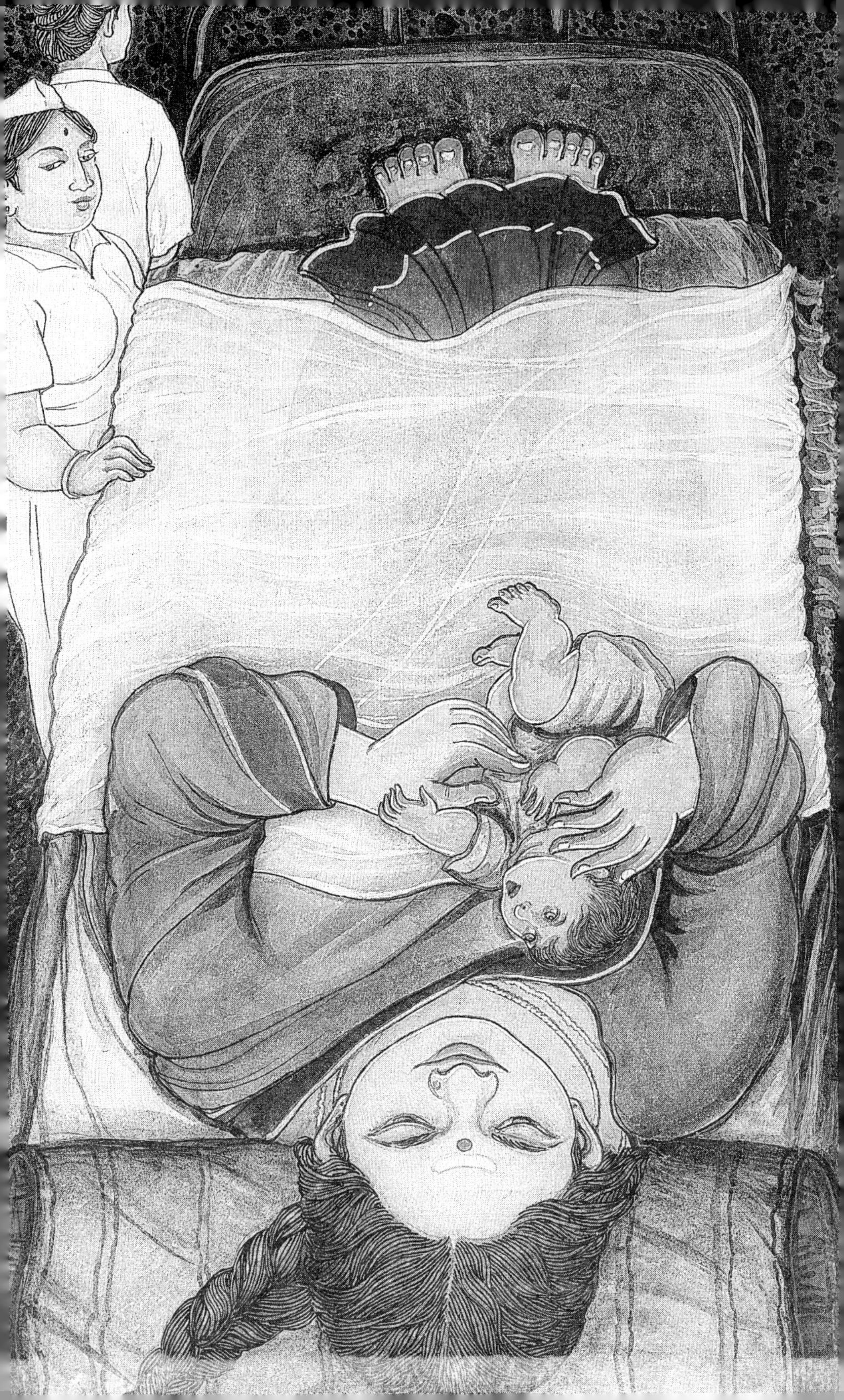

Monday
LESSON 225
Conception And Birth

I am often asked, "What is the point at which a soul enters into a new incarnation?" Many advanced souls choose their parents long before conception, electing to live in their homes, especially if the parents worship. Especially if they were relatives in a past life, they want to be born back into those families to work out their *karmas*. Therefore, a soul may become connected with his mother-to-be long before conception. An unreligious couple that does not seek the inner forces at the moment of conception or slightly before, depending on wherever they are—in a hospital or hotel—may attract and draw into the process of incarnation anybody who is magnetized to them. I call this "potluck off the astral plane," even the lower astral. Someone could die in a hospital and, in a motel three blocks down the street, be immediately conceived. If the husband and wife had been fighting and arguing, this could magnetize a child that would not help the family, but instead would disrupt the household. The difference between the two situations is that one family is thinking of the Divine at the time of conception and the other is living an ordinary life with no contact with the inner, spiritual forces. ¶In either case, when the fetus starts to move in the womb, the soul simultaneously enters and occupies physical life, fully incarnates, or enters flesh. That's when the soul is totally "hooked in," around three or four months. It's there before, hovering near the mother, but not fully connected. The 2,200-year-old *Tirumantiram* of Rishi Tirumular tells us in verses 453-455 that from the moment of conception a soul is associated with the growing physical form of the infant. He says that at the instant of conception, as vital fluids are released and flow from both parents, the embryo is formed; the twenty-five *tattvas* rush in and lie concealed within its third eye, *ājñā chakra*. At this point, life begins. For nine months, the embryo, then fetus, develops physically, and the soul that will inhabit the physical form gradually awakens to First-World embodied consciousness, becoming more or less fully conscious of its new physical form at birth. ¶It is good to understand that the soul exists in the macrocosm within the microcosm. It has no need of traveling to or from; it is where its awareness is. Outward forms, even physical bodies, do not depend on the soul's awareness being present constantly, just as you are not dead when you

---

A mother cradles her newborn infant moments after birth, holding her child close to her breast with two midwives nearby. Hindu religious ethics hold that all life is sacred, and therefore Hindu scriptures stand opposed to abortion.

are asleep. As you might say, "I was not in my body," after you find yourself day dreaming, in the same sense, the soul is not constantly in the infant body while it is growing in the womb. ¶The life of the body is odic, and it runs on by itself. The spiritual energies and presence of the soul dominating the physical, emotional and mental elements is what makes us human. As Rishi Tirumular says, the moment life departs the body, the cherished friend becomes merely a bad smell. The soul's association with the body—the "nine-holed bag of skin"—is life. It begins at conception and continues until the moment of death. In summary, the soul is psychically connected and increasingly aware of its physical body in the womb throughout the pregnancy, just as the soul is connected with the physical body outside the womb until the moment of death. ¶At the time of birth, the previous astral body is still there. The new astral body grows within the child, and the old astral body is eventually sloughed off. It's not immediate. Like moving into a new house, it takes time to get settled. A newborn baby sometimes looks like an old person right from the beginning. This is because it has an old astral body. As the child gains its new identity, a new astral body is formed from the *iḍā* of the mother and the *piṅgalā* of the father, and that development is enhanced by harmony between the parents. It is a slow transition. ¶Just as the former physical body finally disintegrates, its old astral body does also. It takes time for these things to happen. For older souls it takes a shorter time. Still, it's a gradual transition. As one astral body develops, the other goes. Once in Virginia City I inwardly saw a young girl running around dressed in the old Western style clothing as an adult, and I knew that this was her old astral body. A child may be able to remember who he was in his last life until the old astral body dissipates.

Tuesday
LESSON 226
When Does Life Begin?

The question of when human life begins is often asked with the modern-day controversy over abortion in mind. In speaking of this delicate subject with my devotees, I have explained that conceiving a child is like planting a seed in the ground. Although you may not see anything for a while, there are life forces building which will one day appear before your physical eyes, emerging out of the microcosm into the macrocosm, or First World. If you interrupt or cut off that process, for whatever reason, the consequences fall to you, according to the law of *karma* propounded by our Śaiva faith. ¶Abortion is definitely a concern, not only to wives and daughters but to husbands as well. The aborted child, if allowed to live, may have become the husband's heir, a preeminent member of society, and tenderly cared for him and his wife in their elder years. But they will never know and will always wonder, wonder. ¶Abortion is a concern all over India, where it is legal. Doctors there and elsewhere have developed an inexpensive version of the French "abortion pill." Many see this as a blessing for India's population problem and a safer alternative to the thousands of surgical abortions performed each month, from which many women die or suffer infections. It is perhaps a good time to reflect on another side of this issue, on the *karma* and on *dharma*. ¶Wives often please their husbands by aborting an unwanted girl—which she is blamed for, when, in fact, it is the male sperm that determines the child's gender—but secretly wonder, "Who is she? Who was she in her past life? Will she find another womb to incarnate through? Would she perhaps have become a Florence Nightingale, Madame Curie or Anandamayi Ma, a saint like Auvaiyar or Mirabai?" The subliminal subjective sadness that abortion brings, with all the "maybes" that lie unanswered, in itself is a sign from the soul that abortion is wrong; a new bad *karma*, a *kukarmaphala*, has been created. It did not have to be, but it was. After all, the still, small voice of the soul sometimes speaks loudly when a wrong is committed, and doesn't stop talking until a counterbalancing *puṇya*, merit, is achieved and solace sought for.

Wednesday
LESSON 227
Atonement For Abortion

Built within the great Hindu religion is the process of atonement. What is the *prāyaśchitta*, the penance, to be done to atone for abortion? One that works very well in this modern age is to adopt a child, raise it with tender loving care, believing this soul is akin to the aborted soul who sought to take refuge within one's family. This, then, atones. Mahatma Gandhi utilized this principle when one day he counseled a Hindu man who said he had slain a Muslim in revenge for his son's killing at the Muslim's hands. He was deeply troubled about his crime. Gandhi advised him to adopt and raise a Muslim boy as penance for the deed. ¶One becomes his own psychiatrist by utilizing the psychology that when something has gone wrong, it has to be fixed. Why would it have to be resolved? Because the persons involved don't feel good about the action, or *karma*. Resolution is not only mending and healing, it is eradicating the memory of the event—not actually a total forgetfulness, but the emotions that come up with the memory are eradicated. This can be done in various ways. Write to the person who was aborted and burn the letter in a fire. Explain how sorry you are, how miserable you are feeling, and attest that you will never do it again. This is a great way to unload a subconscious mind that is filled with guilt. ¶Accepting reincarnation, *punarjanma,* we acknowledge souls existing in subtle form in astral bodies waiting to incarnate through a womb. When that womb is disturbed, this is recorded as a sense of eviction for the conscious fetus; and it has similar empty effects on the potential mother's life and all those connected to her in the family. It is a *kukarma* that affects all, is felt by all and must be paid for by all. ¶So, we can see the consequences. This does not mean that anyone is cursed or that there is any "mortal sin" involved. Hinduism is a free-flowing religion. It threatens no everlasting hell; it preaches no mortal sin, as a transgression that, if unexpiated in this one and only life, would deprive the soul from closeness to God for eternity. Hinduism accepts life the way it is, even its flaws and frailties. It teaches us the right path but knows we may not always follow that path and thus gives the remedies to correct whatever bothers us at every stage of the great journey to *moksha,* liberation from rebirth. ¶Abortion brings with it a *karmic* force of destruction that will come back on the mother and father who set it in motion. They may be denied a dwelling. They may be denied a noble child. They may beget a child who will persecute them all the days of their life. The parents, the abortionist and the nurses will suffer difficulties in attaining another birth, perhaps by experiencing as many abortions as they participated in while on Earth. The price is high for abortion, much higher and more costly than giving birth, raising and educating the child and establishing him or her in life. ¶Life must go on. It is said that children often bring great fortune to their parents. They pay their own way. Nevertheless, abortions do happen, have happened and will happen in the future. Men and women who have participated, and their doctors and nurses, are involved in the deep *kukarmic* consequences. The action's reaction, which is *karma,* must be resolved in some way for a peace of mind, a quiescent state, to persist. The Hindu religion forbids abortion because of the laws of personal *dharma,* social *dharma* and *ahiṁsā*—noninjury to any living creature, physically, mentally or emotionally.

Thursday
LESSON 228
Difficult Issues

The Sanātana Dharma states that abortion is sanctioned only if the life of the mother would be lost by the birth of the child. Hindu scripture speaks strongly against the deliberate attempt to kill a embryo/fetus, telling us life starts at conception, when the astral body of the newborn child-to-be in the Antarloka is hovering over the bodies of the mother and father. The *Kaushītaki Upanishad* (3.1) counts abortion among such heinous sins as killing one's parents. The *Atharva Veda* (6.113.2) lists the fetus slayer, *brūnaghni*, among the greatest of sinners. ¶Our research among scholars and *swāmīs* tells us there is nothing within Hinduism that opposes contraceptives or birth-control methods. However, if conception occurs, the man and woman have already taken on the *karmic* responsibility. It is *dharma's* path to then open the doors of their hearts to receive the incarnating soul. A miscarriage is something different—an unintentional action of nature, shall we say. Try again and the same soul may come through. ¶What about rape, incest, adultery or premarital pregnancies? Mothers are the life-givers of the planet. Even in these most terrible conditions, scripture gives no permission to injure, and certainly not to kill. However, it would be a sin upon the child to be born and kill his mother in the process. This is why abortion to save the life of the mother is the one and only exception which tradition allows. Yet, even that exception must not be resorted to lightly by some clever doctor or a husband falsely saying, "She might die," or "My wife's life is in peril," or by a devious wife herself claiming, "I am going to die if I don't abort this child." It must be an honest and competent diagnosis, not for the sake of money, not for the sake of saving face in the community, not for the sake of repudiating an infant girl. It must be an honest diagnosis made by compassionate, *dharmic* doctors. ¶The central principles at work here are: *ahiṁsā*, noninjury; the energy of God everywhere; the action of the law of *karma;* the strict rules of *dharma* defined in our holy scriptures; and the belief in reincarnation. These five make a Hindu a Hindu and make not committing abortion an obvious decision.

Friday
LESSON 229
Questions On Suicide

Another very serious issue faced today in every society is suicide. The percentages are too high to ignore the problem that exists in far too many Hindu communities. Well, we can advise, as many elders do: "Don't kill yourself." After all, they became elders by avoiding such extreme solutions. But do those who are all wrought up with emotion and confusion listen to such advice? No. Many die needlessly at their own hand. How selfish. How sad. But it is happening every day. Suicide does not solve problems. It only magnifies future problems in the Antarloka—the subtle, nonphysical astral world we live in before we incarnate—and in the next life. Suicide only accelerates the intensity of *karma*, bringing a series of immediate lesser births and requiring several lives for the soul to return to the evolutionary point that existed at the moment of suicide, at which time the still existing *karmic* entanglement that brought on the death must again be faced and resolved. Thus turns the slow wheel of *saṁsāra.* To gain a fine birth, one must live according to the natural laws of *dharma* and live out the *karma* in this life positively and fully. ¶Suicide is termed *prāṇatyāga* in Sanskrit, "abandoning life force." It is intentionally ending one's own life through poisoning, drowning, burning, stabbing, jumping, shooting, etc. Suicide has traditionally been prohibited in Hindu scripture because, being an abrupt escape from life, it creates unseemly *karma* to be faced in the future. ¶However, in cases of terminal disease or great disability, religious self-willed death through fasting, *prāyopaveśa,* is sometimes permitted. Hinduism is not absolutely black and white in this matter. Rather, it takes into account the broader picture. How will this affect the soul? How will it affect humanity? How will it affect one's future incarnations? All that must be taken into account if a wise and compassionate, right decision is to be made on so serious a matter. ¶There are very few extraordinary situations in which self-willed death is permitted. It is not enough that we are unhappy, disappointed, going through a temporary anguish, such as loss of loved ones, a physical injury, a financial loss or the failure to pass an exam and the fear of an angry thrashing from parents when they find out. That is called life. It is not enough that we are filled with sorrow. None of these reasons is enough to justify suicide, and thus it is in such cases an ignoble act. It is not necessarily even enough we are suffering a serious, terminal illness, one of the thousands that beset human beings on this planet.

Saturday
LESSON 230
Expiring By Fasting

In their love, their wisdom of the meaning and purpose of life, the *ṛishis,* the divine lawmakers, provided an alternative for extraordinary human suffering. They knew that excruciating suffering with no possible end in view is not conducive to spiritual progress and that it is best to have a fully conscious death in a joyous, religious mood, meditating or listening to scripture and sacred songs to the Gods. So, the Vedic *ṛishis* gave, in rare circumstances, the anguished embodied soul a way to systematically, nobly and acceptably, even to loved ones, release itself from embodiment through fasting. They knew, too, that life is more than a body, that the soul is immortal, that a proper exit can, in fact, be elevating. Death for Hindus is a most exalted human experience, a grand and important departure, *mahāprasthāna.* ¶The person making such a decision declares it publicly, which allows for community regulation and distinguishes the act from suicide committed privately in traumatic emotional states of anguish and despair. Ancient lawgivers cited various stipulations: inability to perform normal bodily purification; death appears imminent or the condition is so bad that life's pleasures are nil; and such extraordinary action must be done under community regulation. ¶The gradual nature of *prāyopaveśa* is a key factor distinguishing it from sudden suicide, *svadehaghata,* for it allows time for the individual to settle all differences with others, to ponder life and draw close to God, even to change his mind and resume eating, as well as for loved ones to oversee his gradual exit from the physical world. One begins this highly ritualized practice by obtaining forgiveness and giving forgiveness. Next a formal vow, *mahāvrata maraṇa,* "great vow of death," is taken before one's *guru,* following a full discussion of all *karmas* of this life, especially confessing one's wrongdoings fully and openly. Thereafter, attention is focused on scripture and the *guru's* noble teachings. Meditation on the innermost, immortal Self becomes the full focus as one gradually abstains from food. At the very end, as the soul releases itself from the body, the sacred *mantra* is repeated as instructed by the preceptor. ¶To leave the body in the right frame of mind, in the right consciousness, through the highest possible *chakra,* is a key to spiritual progress. The seers did not want unrelenting pain and hopelessness to be the only possibilities facing a soul whose body was failing, whose only experience was pain without reprieve. So they prescribed a kindly way, a reasonable way, especially for the pain-riddled, disabled elderly and the terminally diseased, to choose a righteous release. What wonderful wisdom. No killer drugs. No violence. No involvement of another human being, with all the *karmic* entanglements that inevitably produces. No life-support systems. No loss of the family wealth for prolonged health care or into the hands of unscrupulous doctors. No lapsing into unconscious coma. No loss of dignity. No unbearable anguish. And no sudden or impulsive decision—instead, a quiet, slow, natural exit from the body, coupled with spiritual practices, with *mantras* and *tantras,* with scriptural readings, deep meditation, reflection and listening to favorite religious songs, with joyous release, with all affairs settled, with full self-awareness and with recognition and support from friends and relations. But don't try it unless you meet up to the qualifications and, above all, have community support.

Sunday
LESSON 231
Thirty-One-Day Retreats

From our cyberspace congregation through the Internet came a question about the thirty-one-day period of seclusion that a family observes following a death or a birth in the family. The traditional practice is to not go to the temple, to not visit *swāmīs* and *gurus,* and to put white cloth over the Deities in the shrine room. An understanding of the esoterics behind traditions is very important in order to fulfill them. When someone is born or dies, a door, to either the higher or lower inner worlds, is opened for all who share a psychic bond, depending on where the soul has come from or has gone. For thirty-one days a psychic passageway of vulnerability persists, which is particularly magnetic in instances of death. "Still," the devotee asked, "isn't a birth especially a happy, sacred event? If so, why can't we go into the shrine room? Why can't we go into the temple?" ¶Yes, birth is a very sacred and happy event for the entire family and should be regarded as such. However, it is also a very inner time for the family. Inner worship, meditation, singing songs, doing *japa* are totally acceptable. A primary reason behind this tradition is to protect the health and well-being of the newborn. Secondly, it is observed so that the baby can become adjusted to the big experience of birth, which is a tremendous experience for the soul, to come into a physical body. During this first month, the astral body of the child is getting accustomed to its tiny new physical body and is experiencing leaving that body and reentering that body. This is an important time of astral, physical adjustment for the newly born. Often when a baby is crying uncontrollably, we can assume that the astral body is out of the physical body, trying to reenter. Also, to bring a newborn child during his first month to a temple would be unwise, as everyone would crowd around, relatives and strangers and friends, breathing into his face, and the baby could contract a disease. Thirty-one days is given to keep the child protected from disease and allow him or her full entrance into the physical body. ¶The observance of the thirty-one day period immediately after a death in the family is the same traditional practice: closing up the shrine room, putting white cloth over all the Deity pictures and refraining from visiting temples, and from approaching *swāmīs* or other holy persons. Cases of a birth and a death are mystically very similar, in that the door of the inner world is open. We want to help that door close, not keep it open by worshiping in the shrine or going to the temple. Spiritual practice is curtailed to avoid the pitfalls that could result in inadvertently drawing forth the energies

lives of promising people and encourage them to greater heights. This is the time also to perform *sādhana* and intense *tapas*. This is where the *yoga mārga* naturally comes in a lifetime. The physical forces are fading, the muscular structure diminishing. Great spiritual progress in burning out the last *prārabdha karmas*, even those that did not manifest in this life, can be accomplished at this time. If retirement is thought of, it should be at eighty-one, eighty-two, eighty-three, eighty-four, around that time. This should be the slowing-down period, yet still being active in the mental, emotional, sociological, political, ecological arenas. Here, now, is a time to practice *haṭha yoga* and pay close attention to *āyurveda*. ¶There is another forty years before the natural life span of 120 is reached, plenty of time to fulfill the Sanātana Dharma, to get out there and give of the wisdom that has been accumulated through the past eighty years. This is the real fulfillment of a life well lived. Or if your life was not well lived, you can teach people, from experience, what they should not do, and explain if they don't follow that advice, things won't work out right. If you did do what you should, you can teach people that you did and how it worked out well. Nine times nine is eighty-one; eight and one are nine. This is the beginning of the final cycle toward the fulfillment of the Sanātana Dharma—toward *mukti*.

Thursday
LESSON 235
Mentalities On Aging

Society in the Western world has no tolerance for the aged, only for the young. Therefore, the aged and the aging must look out for themselves and guide society into a new and mature outlook as to their value to society as senior citizens within society. In the Western world, the elderly are not respected. They are shoved aside, considered useless, as they interfere with the pursuit of the life and liberty of the younger people by giving advice and direction based on their experience. That's why Western people have to learn by their own experiences, because they have relegated the older generation to obscurity. It has become part of the culture. Not so in Asia. In Asian cultures traditionally the aged are venerated more and more each year for their knowledge, their guidance, their wisdom, their compassion, their existence. So much are they venerated in life, that when they have given up their Earth suit they are still venerated and invoked for their guidance, because of their accumulated wisdom and their new-found powers in the inner world, so that the family, which makes up society, moves forward uninterrupted by chaos or contention, wars and famine. These ancestors in the inner world guide and correct and hopefully are born again into the same family as a fresh, knowledgeable influence. This is how Asian families progress as institutions from one stage of development to another because of ancestor worship. ¶It might not surprise you to hear this, but everyone is getting older. A three-year-old will soon be a six-year-old; a twelve-year-old will soon be eighteen. There is a great difference between the eighteen-year-old and the six-year-old, and it all happened in twelve years. Society and parents are adjusted to the differences between a six-year-old and an eighteen-year-old. But Western society, and even modern Asian society, is dearth in adjustments to understand the differences between the forty-year-old and the eighty-year-old, their needs, their wants and their desires. ¶Western psychology says the older you get, the less planning you should do for the future; you should make short-term plans. This philosophy does not take into account that no one is ever too young to die, no matter how long-term his plans have been. "Agedness" is a state of consciousness of settling down, giving up and having nothing ahead in the future more than six months or one year. At seventy-five, I myself have a ten-year plan. I'm going to have another ten-year plan, then another one and still another one. Life is willpower. Life is not only physical. Death can be foreseen as an astrological time of trauma, and if given into, hey, you lose your Earth suit—no doubt about it! But if anticipated and known about, that and other lows in the cycles of the energies of life can be overcome with a strong mind and indomitable will, both of which never age, never weaken and are constantly, day by day, month by month, year by year, accumulating in strength and power. ¶Anyone who passively gives in to old age simply does not understand the process. He looks at his physical body and it looks different. But the twenty-year old looks different than he did when he was ten, and that was only ten years ago, and he is happy to look different. If the twenty-year-old is aloof from the world, having fun, and is frivolous and absents himself from the responsibility of the reality of the material world, he is forgiven, coached along. If the seventy-year-old were to be frivolous and absent himself from the realities of the world, he'd be dubbed senile. That would be the end of him.

Friday
LESSON 236
Fears and Preparations

Society does not adequately explain the transitions that one goes through in life. Children are smart at the age of four, five or ten, and should be told what will happen through their whole life, as a picture book. When they are going through adolescence, the changes they experience should be explained to them. When they are forty and are experiencing the withdrawal of the vitality of the physical forces into a keenness of mind and shorter-term physical goals, this should also be explained. Before fifty your goals are simply for the future, not knowing what that is. When the forces turn around at fifty, you start to withdraw. The body does not throw off the toxins like it used to. It does not heal itself like it used to. It does not regenerate itself like it used to. Then at sixty the forces tend to even out. Two things people are often worried about and need to firm their minds against are the youthful fear "Who is going to take care of me?" and the aged fear "Who is going to take care of me?" These fears are very similar. ¶The truth is, if you are not driven to fulfill *dharma*, you get old. You get old attitudes. You get set in your ways—bigoted, opinionated, communal, divisive. You seek division rather than amalgamation, become racist, basically self-centered and old by clinging onto your old ideas and not keeping up with the changing times. And, having perfected grossness and subtlety of selfishness, you become ignorantly dominant as an elder, manipulating sons, daughters and relatives for travel, comforts and other kinds of considerations. This is not the Sanātana Dharma. This is the "*asanātana dharma*" of the lower nature. Elders beware! You cannot hide behind your old age. The mind does not get old. Nor do the emotions. The astral body does not deteriorate. Neither does the body of the *purusha*, the soul. It is only the physical body that is slowly dissolving into the essences from which it came. ¶It is well known that even certain advanced souls on the planet may do well when they are young but at their still unperfected stage of evolution have the propensity of deterioration in spirit, mind, emotions as the body sinks, through age, into the substances from which it is created. This is not Sanātana Dharma as emulated by spiritual, devotional, happy, religious men and women who have experienced the frailties of the physique and added greater zeal, power and joy to the now dominant energies of the intellect and the soul. Let there be no mistake that admittance to old age is to admit failure on the path to enlightenment. Admittance to old age is to invoke another birth. Admittance to old age means being set in one's ways, not wanting to be interfered with by the young, unable to learn anything more or new, holding an inflexibility that cannot be challenged. ¶In the West, growing old is something people take for granted, something they do not look forward to, and yet it happens. And since it does happen and they don't look forward to it, they try to squeeze everything out of what presents itself to them. In the East they look at growing old in a different way, more in the line of becoming full, becoming mature, becoming satisfied. ¶But very few people become satisfied in the West. They are too self-centered. And the balance between husband and wife is reversed. The woman is trying to live the part of a man, and the poor man, he doesn't have a chance. Consequently, old age sets in very quickly, and nothing is left to do but sit and grumble about the instinctive nature: "She didn't bring my food in on time" "Somebody made a noise and I couldn't sleep" and all the various things that people, as they get older and older, find to complain about. There is nothing profound, which is too bad, because each and every one has profundity within them.

Saturday
LESSON 237
Growing Old Gracefully

A short while ago I had the privilege of visiting a rest home for elderly ladies. Being experienced in looking at people and discerning the type of lives they had lived, seeing these ladies who sat grumbling, I could see the types of lives they lived in their marriages. I would say that all but two in the entire group had hung divorce over their husband's head all through life. That is how they got their way: "If you don't give me what I want, I will divorce you!" But there were two souls sitting there who were also suffering, but they were happy. They had an inner joy. The conditions weren't too good—they never are in such places—but these two souls sat happily observing, and I could see that they were understanding what they observed. That is the secret of growing old, being able to understand what you observe. ¶To grow old gracefully—and to get away from the habit of just growing old naturally and thus physically and emotionally losing the spirit entirely—you have to plan ahead. You have to know where you are going. Everyone who goes on in life is going to get old, believe it or not. But we can pass through those years beautifully, providing the balance is right. You get that right balance by following good advice and conquering the mistakes that you have made in the past and making them right. ¶When we are selfish, self-centered and flare up and lose control of ourselves, we are like animals. When we reflect understanding, have control of ourselves and use our will to conquer our lower nature, we are using the Godly part of our mind. That's why I say people do just exactly what they want to do. It is either the spiritual being that is stronger, or the animal within them that is stronger. If they control the animal nature, then what happens? The spiritual being automatically takes over. ¶If they live according to the rules of the animal nature, then what happens? They snuff out the spirit, they snuff out life, and they decay. Decay immediately sets in. It is terrible to think about, but that's the rule. That's what happens. That's why we have basic laws and basic principles to live by. If we live by them, automatically good things will happen. You don't even have to wish or hope. Good things will just automatically come along. And if you don't live by the laws, automatically things that aren't too palatable present themselves before you, and you get entangled in them quite automatically. ¶So, let's think about the years to come. Let's see if we are laying the foundation for our mature years to rot away, or to become beautiful and content and happy with ourselves. Look into your home right now. Look at your life. What are you doing now? What have you done? What are you going to do? Do you have a foundation for a future that is real and permanent and full and joyous and happy? Or is your life like a child's sandbox? These are the things we have to face as we look ahead to our own advanced age. ¶So, don't come to me this morning and say, "You gave a very nice *upadeśa,* Gurudeva. I really got so much out of it." Rather, come back in ten years and let me see by your radiant face how much you got out of it. That will make me happy. Let me see by your tomorrows and how you meet challenges—when various things come up that you should do and you are given advice on what to do—how you face them, how polite you are, how kindly you are, how understanding you are. That will show your sincerity, your reality, your character as individuals.

Sunday
LESSON 238
Real Security Lies Within

It is a fast-moving age. Many people are now either on tranquilizers, alcohol, anti-depressants, nicotine, stimulants or high-powered vitamins of one kind or another to stabilize their emotions enough to get by, just to get by, to get through all the various things that present themselves that they can't cope with due to the rickety foundations that they have in their home. What they really want and need is to get within, to get quiet enough to get an answer within themselves that will give them a little security. But there is no narcotic, no stimulant, no tranquilizer, no high-powered vitamin that is going to take you within. The only way is to sit down and become quiet, and not throw your energy into concentrating on how you are going to out-do or out-smart somebody else, get a little bit better control over your husband's finances or anything like that. That is not going to do it. That will bring sure misery, a fine hell on Earth, really. That's where the only hell is anyway. No, the way to true security is getting in touch with the divine spirit within you. ¶Try to feel it permeating you. Find out what life is. You are going to give up this physical body someday. Find out what's going to happen to you when you die. You can find out. Find out whether you are immortal or not. You will be able to go within yourself and find that out if you become quiet enough. Then you will not fear death. Then you will be somebody within yourself. A great new life force will permeate you. At first you won't know where it comes from or where it's going, but it will be there, and you won't have to try to be positive or think positively or make affirmations about this and that. You will be Mr. or Mrs. Positive. That is spiritual life. ¶There comes a time when you have to buckle down and do the right thing, because we are all faced with growing old. Growing old can be decay or it can be full, joyous and beautiful. Think about that. Where are you headed? Are you headed for decay and misery, to drop back into the animal mind and complain about how little the five senses have to offer when you get old? Are you headed for complaints, suffering over old memories that pop up through the subconscious mind that you no longer have the will to even try to penetrate and understand but still have to live with? Or are you going to become full and beautiful by adjusting your life right now so that you will have an alive, alert mind to the end? The choice is yours. You must start now. ¶Aging is inevitable. The years go by. They go by so quickly, we hardly notice them. We can go on in our old habit patterns, becoming stronger and stronger in the negative ones; and the positive ones eventually will turn to negative ones, too. That's a certainty of evolution we don't want to look forward to. But there is another way. Become a spiritual being. That is your goal, your liberation, for as the years go by you can live in heaven, or you can live in your own self-created hell, and you don't want to do that. Think about it and create a heaven right now by living with Śiva.

Atimṛityu, Sūkshmadeha Jīvanam

अतिमृत्यु सूक्ष्मदेहजीवनम्

Beyond Death, Astral Life

Just as a caterpillar, having reached the end of a blade of grass and approaching another one collects itself, even so this *ātman*, having discarded the body and overcome ignorance, approaching another one collects itself. That to which the heart is attached, toward this the subtle body moves together with its action which still adheres. Attaining the goal of whatever actions he performed here on Earth, he goes once more from that world to this world of action.

Śukla Yajur Veda, Bṛihadāraṇyaka Upanishad, 4.4.3&6 VE, P. 759

Monday
LESSON 239
The Doorway Called Death

There is a lot to be said about death and reincarnation. Most people are afraid of death because it is the most dramatic experience that has happened to them during a lifetime, as it put a stop to a lot of aggressive *prāṇa* going out through a physical body. At transition, this *prāṇa* has to contract immediately and go to seed. What is death? The realization is that nobody dies. You can't say a human dies because he must now live in his astral body rather than his physical body. We live in our astral body twenty-four hours a day and in our physical body only sixteen hours a day. That means for eight hours each day we are already "dead." When the soul departs the physical body at death, one chapter of life has ended and another chapter of life has begun. It is a total continuum, except that after departing the physical body the being is full-time awake, because on the astral plane we don't have to sleep. ¶There are helpers in the inner world who assist those who have departed their physical sheath through their new adjustments, as well as assist with preparations for their reentry into flesh—reincarnation. These helpers are well trained, efficient, courteous and kindly. They are similar to those found performing the same services in this physical world, the doctors, nurses, psychologists, religious workers—aiding souls as they enter or exit the earth plane. In the physical world, hospitals now even help you to die. Or accidents may occur or old age simply comes. In any case, the assistance is there through the medical profession, the mortuaries and so forth to care for the dying and take care of the remains. These are all well-trained, kindly people doing their jobs. The soul meets them again at birth when reentering the flesh, in the hospital and in the home. It is the loving care of such workers that assists the mother through the many years ahead until the child is fully grown. ¶A doctor or nurse will perform the same professional duties when disembodied, continuing along, doing the same kind of things they did during their last physical life. The process of reincarnation is a revolving cycle. Those who abide permanently in their astral body are not alone. They are with other people, some who remain on the astral plane permanently, some who are just visiting. It is a fuller life, not lesser. People die on the astral plane, too. When they take a birth, their old astral body has to be disposed of. Those on the astral

---

A husband applies holy ash to his wife's forehead at the moment of her Great Departure. In her astral body, she consciously leaves the physical body through a high chakra*—shown by a ray of light—and is being received by her guardian* devas *in the higher astral world.*

plane have to "die" there to come here, and later they have to "die" here to go there. ¶The mind does not need a physical body to function properly. Nor do the emotions. Nor does the soul. A disembodied person is totally functional in every respect. Suppose a seamstress dies. On the astral plane, she may keep making dresses, but with a difference: she would now have all the fabric she ever wanted. But she would probably continue this same activity. She would not become a carpenter. However, it is not possible to experience the *karmas* of this physical world in the inner worlds. For this, a physical body is needed. When the time comes for acquiring and entering a physical body, proper parents must be chosen, an environment and country. This can be time-consuming and is sometimes disappointing on the occasion of miscarriage or abortion. But negatives aside, when the first cry and mother's gentle hug is experienced, this is reincarnation.

Tuesday
LESSON 240
Mourning and Fear of Death

People wonder about their past lives, but it doesn't really matter who you were in your past lives. It is the cumulative creation of what you've done in the past which has manifested in what you are in this life that should concern you. Knowing how these things are going to manifest in the future is a forewarning that can improve the quality of the next life. Therefore, though possible, it is irrelevant to know what nationality, station in life or occupation one was in the past. What is relevant is the knowledge of accumulated deeds of all the past lives, especially those that will manifest in this life. ¶People who don't truly understand reincarnation fear death. Fear of the unknown is part of the human psyche. To understand reincarnation, you have to understand and accept the existence of the astral body and have an intuitive knowledge of the soul. Then you understand that reincarnation is as natural as a child becoming a teenager and a teenager becoming a young adult. Reincarnation records are kept in the *sahasrāra chakra* of every individual. They are readable by inner-plane helpers and by trained psychics. The *sahasrāra chakra* is in the *ākāśa*. Every soul is packing his dossier right along with him. ¶Devotees ask, "When someone dies, what should be the attitude of loved ones?" Because the fear of death is so much a part of social consciousness today, as ignorance prevails in these matters, sorrow rather than joy is often experienced. In not understanding life in its fullness, many cannot help but misunderstand death. The attitude should be one of joy based on beliefs that come from the knowledge of *karma* and *saṁsāra*. Experience of joy and a total release of the loved one would come from a pure understanding of the processes of life. ¶A better word than *death* is *transition,* passing into a new form of life—life into life. It is similar to moving to a new country, having completed all of one's tasks. Death is a closing of the door on deeds well done, on all beneficial *karmas. Karmas* performed in ignorance will be faced at a later time. Death is also the opening of a new door to a place where the good and the bad, the happy and the sad experiences are forgotten. Should we not be cheerful and joyous that our loved one has earned a new start, having completed another step on the path? ¶Inordinate grief, sorrow and loss are felt by those who do not understand the Sanātana Dharma. They are dwelling in the world of darkness. Those who live in the worlds of light understand intuitively. They are happy that the person's *karmic* cycle has ended. You have to realize that the person who is dying is going on a joyous journey, and he knows it. He is still going to see his loved ones who are still connected to their physical bodies when they sleep at night, and he is not losing anybody. So, one or two close loved ones in the vicinity at the time of death is enough consolation. Even if no one is with him, he is fine. He is going on a journey. He has the fullness of everything. Why should you mourn for the person who is, at the death experience, having the highest moment of his life? ¶Mourning at death, for example, is not a part of the Chinese culture. They send money and paper houses and write letters to the departed through the fire ceremony. Morbid mourning is not a part of every culture, as it is among those heavily influenced by Christian beliefs. We must remember that Hindus are often so influenced. Dying is not a super traumatic experience anymore, as people move around the world so much, wives are working and families are not that close. But the fact is that the departed person does not go away, has two bodies besides the physical—astral and soul—and is always there, existent. Whether he is living in his astral body, his *purusha* body or is in San Francisco or Paris, he is always there.

Wednesday
LESSON 241
Ancestor Worship

Ancestor worship is a form of communicating with departed ancestors, seeking to be guided by their advice because they have a broader vision, a superconscious vision. They are not bothered by the mundane affairs of eating and sleeping and family intrigues. They know how to bring the collective family along to its next phase of development. They will eventually, of course, seek to reincarnate in the same family to work out their *prārabdha karmas.* One reason for the Hindu *śrāddha* ceremonies is to help the departed soul be reborn in the same family. Similarly, we would want our monks to come back to the same monastery and keep coming back until they fulfilled their highest aspirations. The Hindu wants to be born back into the same family, even in the same house, and families want to bring relatives back as well, so the *karmas* can be worked out consistently, lifetime after lifetime. This is one reason that on the *nakshatra* of the death, certain rites are performed to court the departed person back. ¶In many Hindu traditions, after the death of a loved one, *śrāddha* ceremonies are performed on the death anniversary for twelve years. Therefore, each family that shares in ancestral worship or ancestral communication is, in a sense, a tribal group within a sectarian portion of the religion. Who better would know the solutions within a family than someone who has lived in it? If the ancestor has already reincarnated, the whole family would intuitively know it. Then they would seek advice from another ancestor, perhaps through a psychic channeler. If an ancestor reincarnated outside the family, they would also be told. Those who practice ancestor worship generally seek for channelers outside their community, from those who don't know their family. ¶In the fifty years of our Śaiva Church, we have documented birth to death to birth again within the lives of our devotees and close initiates. A continuum of birth to death to birth to death, a continuum of *karmas* in unbroken continuity—that makes up a spiritual, alive religious organization. ¶The greater the maturity of your soul, the longer you can stay in the inner planes. Some world-of-darkness people come back immediately. They die in one end of the hospital and are born in the other end. The average person would usually reincarnate somewhere within the twelve-year cycle. If the family realizes the person is coming back and prays for that to happen, he or she would have to come back within twelve years. Once they realized the person is back, they would stop doing the ceremony and be off doing other things. ¶At this time in the Kali Yuga, the races of the world are relocating to improve genetics and to recreate families with better genes by intermarrying between races and in different localities. It is a time of breaking up, a time of destruction. But the new race coming out of this into a good genetic body will be the industrious spiritual leaders for a better world which will recreate itself around them.

Thursday
LESSON 242
Life in the Inner Worlds

The world is quite blissful from the perspective of someone who has reached a high stage of maturity, and life on the inner planes for him is even more blissful. This is because all of the lower *chakras,* the instinctive and lower natures, are totally inoperable. So, it is a wonderful, self-perpetuating time, a time of rest and healing, of meeting others known on the Earth who have experienced the same level of bliss. For some it may be a time of communicating with those on the Earth, learning how to channel messages to them. This sojourn in the in-between is similar to sleep, which is an earned time of rest for the physical body. After death is a cosmic sleep for all the inner bodies. ¶Even someone who has committed the most heinous sins and played the part of the destructive element of Śiva's great dance would, after death, experience the Narakaloka only for a limited period, until he again enters flesh and continues his mischief or repents, performs *sādhanas* and lifts himself up into the Devaloka. However, by no means should death necessarily be taken as a form of liberation from rebirth. It is for the vast majority an in-between period of preparation for the next life, a time to gain faith and strength to face the impact of the already-developed good, bad and mixed *karmas* of previous lives. ¶Within the inner worlds, there are realms far more subtle than the astral plane. Advanced souls residing on the astral plane are able to access those higher worlds at will, there to learn from and receive blessings from *ṛishis* and great *devas.* For most, in order to do this, the astral body would not "die," but simply be left behind temporarily. Similarly, here on the physical plane, you can go into meditation and get "beamed up" into the higher world in your *purusha* body. Your physical body and astral body are temporarily left behind. However, there are beings in the inner world who reside fully in these higher planes in their mental body, having dropped off their lower astral body long ago. But the law is that after death you won't be able to go any higher in the inner worlds than the level you had attained in a physical birth, because it is only in physical birth that all twenty-one *chakras* are available. In physical birth, the lowest ones become attainable, and the highest become attainable as well. Whatever your attainment on Earth is, you carry that with you into the astral worlds unchanged. Whatever your accomplishments are of living in the gamut of the *chakras,* lower or higher, you can't go lower and you can't go higher in the inner planes. That is why you need a physical birth. ¶I was once asked about *ātura sannyāsa,* renouncing the world at the moment of death? Personally, I think that is like icing a stale cake. People do it, it is possible, and it may quiet a person's mind if he wanted to do that, but it does not mean a lot. Perhaps he will be a *sannyāsin* in his next life, but maybe he will not. If you are going to be a *sannyāsin*, you have to try to live the life. ¶Occasionally a great soul will know before his grand departure, his death, that he will not be reincarnating again. In this case the astral body has to be totally absorbed by the causal body while he is alive in his physical body. That means all the lower *chakras* have to be closed off. When this has occurred, the soul body takes over the physical body and there is very little astral body present, just a shell. Eliminating the astral body and the *chakras* it is attached to is accomplished through *yoga* and *tapas* in a physical birth. This is a process that goes on in the First World. To fulfill these various laws relating to the *chakras* and the soul's unfoldment, it is very important that we have a physical planet at a certain distance from a sun, with edible vegetation, fertile soil, breathable atmosphere, a benign climate and gravity, all suitable for human life. You have seven *chakras* below the *mūlādhāra* in the world of darkness. Through *dharma* and following the principles of Śaivism, they are to be slowly closed off and systematically put to rest. The nature of the *chakras* is what makes one individual different from another, other than the personal vibratory rate.

Friday
LESSON 243
Creating on The Astral Plane

The astral plane is within this world as its etheric counterpart, and when you drop off the physical body, you are in it. You are in it now but are not aware of it as yet. It is a world just like this one. You can travel from country to country on the astral plane. While I was studying in Sri Lanka in 1948, my teacher living in America used to come and visit me in the astral body. When I returned to America, people from Sri Lanka used to come on the astral plane and visit me in America, and I would see them in their astral bodies. While I was in Sri Lanka, I introduced a *yogī* from the Himalayas to my teacher in America, and they met on the astral plane. The next day, the *yogī* came back and described my teacher perfectly and told me of their conversation. After I returned to America, one day my teacher asked, "Who was that *yogī* that I met on the astral plane?" and then described him perfectly, and told of the same conversation as well. ¶If we did not use the astral body on a daily basis, we could not move the physical body. It is not the physical body that moves; it is the astral body that moves within it. When we step out of the physical body in the astral body, we cannot move the physical body until we get back inside it. While conscious in the astral body, we are more on the astral plane than on the physical plane. Only when the astral body and the physical body are connected do we seem to be in a physical world. ¶Because the astral plane is of a higher rate of vibration, or a more intense rate of vibration, *prāṇa* flows within it a little freer and faster. We have everything there that we have on the physical plane. However, things there are manifested by the mind quickly, whereas on the physical plane they are created more slowly. This is because the physical body needs the *mūlādhāra chakra* in order to function, and this brings us into a different dimension of time. The first *chakra* is not so dominant on the astral plane. Therefore, we are in reason and in will. If we want to build a house, we just think about it, and a house becomes constructed within a matter of minutes; whereas it takes a matter of months on the physical plane. ¶On the astral plane, we see other people—other people that have died and do not have a physical body and people that do have a physical body but have just left it for a time. They have left their physical body sleeping and they are traveling on the astral plane. Therefore, it is a more populated plane than this Earth, but there is more room in it, being of a lighter substance. Then, too, uninhabited land on Earth and the oceans are used on the astral plane. ¶Why do we sleep? The mental body, which we dream in, is within the astral body and functions through the astral brain of that body. Through certain hours of the day during the waking state, the astral body uses the physical body, and the mental body works through the astral-body brain and the brain of the physical body. There is also another body to be considered, and that is the soul body. This body is what we touch into at least once through the sleeping state, and that gives not only a release of the *karmas,* often *karmas* that have been concluded, but also a new flush of energy into the astral, mental and physical bodies. So, we touch into the Divine through sleep. We must remember that the astral body doesn't need sleep; nor would the physical body need as much sleep if the Divine hookup were always perpetuating or flooding through the energy. ¶It is a twenty-four-hour cycle of consciousness. Our individual awareness simply moves from physical consciousness into mental, emotional or astral body consciousness, or soul consciousness in the case of deep sleep, where nothing is ever remembered. People wonder why they don't recall their dreams. It is as difficult to recall a dream that happened last night as it is to recall what you were thinking about between 12 noon and

4PM three days ago. Now, should the dream last night have been a fantastic departure from your personal reality, you would recall it. If your thoughts three days ago between 12 noon and 4PM were a fantastic departure from your personal reality, you would certainly recall that. It is the process of recall that is being challenged, not the connection between the sleep state and the waking state. ¶We do not usually remember our astral experiences, because the astral brain and the physical brain are of two different rates of vibration. Therefore, when we return to the physical body after being in the astral body during sleep, any knowledge that we have gained on the astral plane begins to seep through into the physical plane during a period of four days afterwards. This knowledge accumulates, and we call it an inner knowing. Ideas seem to come to us from within, but actually we did learn and discuss them previously on the astral plane.

Saturday
LESSON 244
Awareness, The Traveler

Reading and analyzing dreams from the *shūmīf* perspective, of awareness flowing through the mind—the inner mind being stationary, and awareness being a mercury-like substance that is aware in various states—will keep the aspirant emotionally and intellectually detached from areas of consciousness, or mind, which he becomes conscious in as he travels here, there and everywhere, as he does through the day. We therefore know that we need not be emotionally or mentally attached within our dreams to everything that happens. In the very same way we are not mentally and emotionally attached to even two-thirds of what we see and experience in our waking state on television or when we are walking about in public. Therefore, the *shūmīf* perspective, once it is well set within the subconscious, aids in understanding dream consciousness juxtaposed to waking consciousness and seeing them as one and the same. Pure awareness, *nīf,* never sleeps. This mercury, mirror-like substance travels here and there, guided by the will of the perceiver. It is the venerable eye of the *purusha.* It is constantly aware, from the moment of the creation of the soul; and at the soul's final merger into Śiva it experiences super, super, super, superconscious totality. Most people who meditate do not enter the astral plane during sleep. When they sleep at night, they go deeper within than the astral, into superconsciousness, in the beautiful body of the soul. There they communicate with other people who are also in their body of the soul. ¶On the astral plane, talking is done through thoughts. It is the world of thought. On the inner plane of the soul, intelligence is transferred from one to another through light vibrations. This is a beautiful form of communication. The body of the soul can also appear on the astral plane and communicate with those who are functioning in their astral bodies, even though the body of the soul is a more refined body. It is these two bodies that are predominantly used on the astral plane. The intellectual body is used primarily through the day when we are awake, as is the physical body. Man carries his intellect into the astral as well. ¶Modern man does not use his physical body as much as his ancestors used to. He sits and walks and occasionally exercises, and that is about all. That is why much of his energy has been transmuted into the intellect. Our astral body, body of the soul and intellectual body all are very definite forms in the inner ether. They are used most by the evolved, educated, modern man. To understand these bodies, we have to forget the way we usually think about things and think about them differently, from a new perspective. Then insights are gained. ¶Some people do at times see what we call ghosts and wonder what they are. They are astral beings without a physical body. Only rarely are they able to have any effect on anything in our world and are generally harmless. A ghost is a person, a soul just like all of us, that has lived in a human body and died, and is now in the part of the astral plane called the Pretaloka. ¶The word *ghost* generally has unfavorable connotations attached to it, such as scary, haunting, perhaps even fear, for most people do not fully understand what a ghost is. From the ghost's point of view, he feels very much alive, living in the inner world which this outer world mirrors. Ghosts, more often than not, see us, but we don't see them, except very rarely, and they feel hurt when not included in family gatherings, and sad at being mourned for. Often the realization that they have "departed" comes to them slowly, but comes especially when they find they can now walk through closed doors, even walls. ¶There are certain astrological times, such as Halloween, when ghosts are most easily seen. I was in Singapore on one of those days when all the Chinese people were in the street sending prayers through fires to the inner world. The prayers were printed and purchased and then burned in piles on nearly every street. The astral doubles of the prayers were collected by astral helpers trained for the job, then given to the departed relatives to be read by them. When we asked about the event, we were told that this was the time of year when ghosts make their visitations. And, actually, in the early morning, upon awakening in our hotel, the *maṭhavāsis* and myself saw ghosts walk through the walls, stare at us in our beds, then pass on through a wall into another room to investigate the other guests. This was a shared experience, for we all saw the same ghosts. We talked about it at breakfast. Some found it a little bit scary, as the astral beings were all draped in white, which was, of course, their *prāṇic* body covering their astral body. They looked white because they still maintained an odic body made of ectoplasmic substance.

Sunday
LESSON 245
Possession and Mediumship

Ghosts are mysterious, unknown and not understood by most people and therefore feared. They usually stay close to a familiar place in the physical world and are occasionally seen or felt by people who knew them, especially if they have just recently passed on. At the time of passing, their astral body hovers over their physical body until they become aware that they have died. Inner-world helpers eventually explain to them the facts of death and take them deeper into the Devaloka to do what they have to do to prepare for another physical birth. In unusual cases, the astral person remains in a favorite area of the physical world for an extended length of time, making his presence felt by people in the Bhūloka. This is what is meant by the word *haunting.* ¶On rare occasions, we may experience one or more ghosts in our presence. When this happens, we must project love, while visualizing pink and light blue. This will help them, and they will eventually realize that all is well with the life they left, and be able to continue their evolution, released from the static state they have been experiencing. This is the great *siddhi* of love. Everyone has this power. Few use it. ¶In one sense, we could say that the *devas* of the Devaloka are also ghosts, for they are discarnate entities, too, the difference being that they are helping the Gods of our religion and are fully functioning at their duties in-between physical births, completely aware of who and what they are. The places they inhabit most frequently are the hundreds of thousands of great temples of our religion, the homes of the Gods. ¶When an Earth-bound soul claims a body of a physical person, this is known as possession. In most cases, that soul is very upset at not having a physical body, because he has things to do, desires. Such a soul finds somebody who is susceptible, who is on drugs or half out of his body for some reason, takes over that body and uses it for a while to satisfy his desires. In Asia they have dances, songs and temple rituals, and in America they have electrical shock treatment, to get rid of the unwanted astral entity. It's the same primitive process, called exorcism. ¶Mediumship is another matter. There is no conflict. It is communication by arrangement and can be accomplished on many different levels. One

Dhairyapūrvakam Vilayanam

धैर्यपूर्वकं विलयनम्

PART THREE

Merging Courageously

Hindu Dharma Sukhāni

हिन्दुधर्मसुखानि

The Joys of Hinduism

All the Gods in the heaven of Brahman adore in contemplation their Infinite Spirit Supreme. This is why they have all joy, and all the worlds and all desires. And the man who on this Earth finds and knows *atman*, his own Self, has all his holy desires and all the worlds and all joy.

Sāma Veda, Çhāndogya Upanishad 8.12.6. UPM, P. 126

Monday
LESSON 246
Knowledge of Reincarnation

Tonight we want to speak on the joys and happiness found in Hinduism, our ancient religion which brings forth the wonderful feelings of a belief in the cosmic processes of reincarnation coupled with knowledge of the laws of *karma* and the wisdom of *dharma* in which everyone has his rightful place and purpose in life. It brings the broad-mindedness of total acceptance of all other religions as expressions of the One God's creation, the blessing of a complete devotional path revolving around powerful temples, the fulfillment of a profound mystical teaching founded on *yoga* and brought forth by the seers and saints and *gurus*, and so much more. Our religion is so strong, so rich and varied that very few can claim to understand it in its completeness. It is immense, an immense religion, so immense that we have difficulty sometimes explaining it to those who hold to a simpler doctrine, especially if they have been subjected to erroneous concepts about our religion promulgated by invaders and missionaries of a score of alien religions. It is time that the world knew of the greatness of Hinduism, knew it as it is. Of course, we cannot explain it in an evening. My *satguru*, the great Siva Yogaswami of Columbuthurai, would say, "The time is short and the subject is vast." But we can have a look at some of the aspects of Hinduism that bring such joys and happiness to over a billion devotees around the world. ¶Each Hindu's belief in reincarnation is so strong that it totally eliminates the fear and dread of death. No true Hindu really fears death; nor does he look forward to it. The word *death* in the vocabulary of the Hindu holds a different meaning. He does not take death to be the end of existence; nor does he look upon life as a singular opportunity to be followed by eternal heavenly existence for those souls who do well, and by unending hell for those who do not. Death for the Hindu is merely transition, simultaneously an end and a new beginning. Over two thousand years ago, Saint Tiruvalluvar wrote, "Death is like falling asleep, and birth is like awakening from that sleep" (*Tirukural* 339). In one of the ancient languages of our religion, the physical body had a name which literally meant "that which is always dropping off." ¶The Hindu's knowledge of reincarnation gives him the hope of attaining a future birth and in that birth making further progress toward the perfection that he intuitively

A Hindu youth spreads his arms joyously, knowing that his religion provides for his every need, every resource for a rich, rewarding spiritual life. Lord Śiva, with the Ganges flowing from his hair and wearing traditional gold bracelets, cradles the devotee in His interlaced hands.

knows is his *ātman,* his soul. He is working in this life to gain enough good merit, enough *puṇya,* to deserve welcome into a fine religious family as a good soul that will not upset the family but add to its love and harmony and productivity. That is one aim ever on the mind of the devout Hindu, to live well that he may live even more perfectly in a future life on this planet. That is our aim; and our other beliefs, our accumulated knowledge and the many facets of our religion, give us the strength and the wisdom to believe in such a far-reaching way, to look beyond the immediate day-to-day concerns into our ultimate objective, which is realization and liberation, *moksha.* ¶Nor is this belief in the cycles of earthly existence, in reincarnation, merely a belief. It is a certain knowledge for those who have had even a tiny glimpse into their origins, to the point of remembering another life or just intuiting that the soul did not come into existence just before one's birth. The Hindu believes that the soul undertakes many sojourns on the planet. We see the wisdom in this cycle of birth, death and rebirth.

Tuesday
LESSON 247
Karma Is Always Just

We see reincarnation as an explanation for many of the apparent inequalities observed in life. Thus we understand the fairness even in a bad birth, say a birth as a cripple or a child who dies in infancy. To the Hindu this is not an accident, but is a natural event brought forth by the soul itself through the *karma* of unseemly acts and desires in a previous life. To the Hindu there is not one force in the universe at work to make all things good and an opposing force trying to destroy the soul. No. All is God's work. All *karma* is natural and worthy of the soul to which it comes. ¶The Hindu knows that it is the younger souls who lack understanding, who cannot live in harmony with others and who shun the higher forms of culture and faith. Rather than inheriting eternal suffering for their acts, they earn instead another opportunity for experience, for learning, for evolving. The ideas of sin and evil are different in Hinduism from the concepts held by Abrahamic religions. If there is such a thing as sin to the Hindu, it is the breaking of the natural laws, a lapse in the patterns of *karma* and *dharma,* and that transgression brings its own punishment in the form of an additional *karma* created to then be worked out. Thus the Hindu does not live in fear of sin or under the notion of original sin. We do not look upon humanity as inherently sinful, but inherently perfect and striving to unfold that perfection from within. The Hindu knows that we will have as many opportunities as needed to refine and evolve our nature—a thousand lives or more if needed. We don't have to think that we only have a single chance, a one life in which everything must be accomplished and all desires must be fulfilled. Therefore, we are not in a hurry. We are patient. We exhibit more patience with circumstances than do those who believe in a one life, and we are more forgiving of ourselves when we fall short. Thus it is that Hinduism offers a great joy to its followers—a blessing of fearlessness in the face of death, an assurance of the continuation of consciousness after physical death, another assurance that each soul creates its own *karma* and that such *karma* is just and right, even when it seems that some people are less fortunate than others and that fate has unfairly given all the advantages to a few. All these things are bestowed on Hindus simply because they understand the doctrine of reincarnation. ¶Hinduism is a hopeful and comforting religion. Hope for a future life makes this life worthwhile, joyous, contented and happy, because the Hindu can live and deal with current problems, knowing that they are transitory problems, that they will not last forever; nor will they affect us forever. They are problems; we cannot deny that. But they are problems to be worked out with a positive attitude and a high energy and a helping hand from our Gods.

Wednesday
LESSON 248
The World as Our Teacher

The Hindu also wants to improve conditions in the world, in the physical world. We do not look upon all that happens to us as unreal. That is a misconception. It is real. Life is real. It is through life that we progress. Life is the means provided by the Primordial God for finding Reality. True, it is *māyā*. But it is *māyā* in the form of mind, in the form of form. *Māyā*, or form, or mind, is created for a purpose, to help man evolve, not to bind him in illusion. The Hindu understands this. We want to help humanity, and simultaneously we know that we may well return in another physical body. So we are working not only for ourselves, but for our loved ones, not only now, but in the future as well. We are improving the world for future generations in which we will play a part. ¶Through our knowledge of reincarnation, we have a great love and understanding for every human being, for they have been our mothers, our fathers, our sons and daughters, our grandparents and companions in many past lives, or perhaps will be in a future incarnation. This expanded knowledge of the interrelatedness of humanity brings with it a deepened appreciation, helping us to understand why it is that some people seem so close to us though we hardly know them and others are strangers or even enemies after years of close association. To the Hindu, everyone younger is his brother or sister. Everyone older is his mother or father, and he maintains a deep respect for others. We have this knowledge by having lived through many hundreds of lives on this planet and having been associated with many thousands of people. We know that in our current pattern in this life we often attract those to us whom we have been with in past lives. So we have a great joy and happiness in meeting them again and a deep knowledge of our relationships, our psychic relationships, with them in past lives. ¶The Hindu believes in the law of *karma,* the ability to earn one's rewards as well as punishments. All this we can do ourselves with the help of our Gods and our personal relationship with our Ishṭa Devatā, the individual God that we have chosen, or rather that God who has chosen to love, guide and protect us through an incarnation. ¶In Hinduism there is no priest standing between the devotee and God. The priest is a servant of the God, just as is every other devotee. Even the *satguru,* the spiritual teacher, does not stand between the disciple and God, but seeks instead to strengthen the devotee's direct experiential relationship with the Divine. The Hindu thus finds a great joy in his relationship with God and the Gods. It is his relationship, and he alone is able to perpetuate it. No one can do this work for him or on his behalf. There is a great happiness there between the devotee and the God resident in the Hindu temple, which is the communication point with the God, as is the sacred home shrine.

Thursday
LESSON 249
The Joy of Pilgrimage

In our religious life, one of the most fulfilling aspects is pilgrimage. We have a joy in looking forward to a spiritual journey, and we experience a contentment while on our pilgrimage and later bask in the glowing aftermath of the *pūjās.* It is like going to see a great friend, a devotee's most loved friend—the Ishṭa Devatā. We travel to the far-off temple where this great friend is eminently present. At that particular temple, this personal God performs a certain function, offers a specific type of blessing to pilgrims who make the pilgrimage to that home. In this way, different temples become famous for answering certain types of prayers, such as requests for financial help, or prayers for the right mate in marriage, prayers to be entrusted with the raising of high-souled children, or help in matters of *yoga,* or help in inspiring *bhakti* and love. ¶The Hindu does not have the feeling of having to take a vacation to "get away from it all." We don't lead a life of mental confusions, religious contradictions and the frustrations that result from modern hurried living. We lead a moderate life, a religious life. In living a moderate life, we then look at our pilgrimage as a special moment, a cherished time of setting ordinary concerns aside and giving full stage to our religious longings. It is a time to take problems and prayers to our personal God. ¶Unlike the proud "free thinkers" who deem themselves emancipated, above the religious life, we Hindus feel that receiving the *darśana* from the Gods and the help that comes therein invigorates our being and inspires us to be even more diligent in our spiritual life. Unlike the rationalists who feel confident that within themselves lie all the resources to meet all needs, and that praying to Gods for help is a pathetic exercise in futility, the Hindu wisely submits to the Divine and thus avoids the abyss of disbelief. ¶All in life that one would want to "get away from" the Hindu takes with him on a pilgrimage to the temple, to the feet of his personal God, to the inner-plane being or Mahādeva, who needs no physical body with which to communicate with people—to the God who has a nerve system so sensitive and well developed that as it hovers over the stone image, which looks similar to how the Deity would look on the inner planes, this being of light can communicate with the pilgrims who visit the temple. This being of light, this Mahādeva, can and does absorb all of the dross the devotees have to offer, and gives back blessings which bring happiness and release to them. Thus, the pilgrimage is not travel in the ordinary sense of travel, but rather going to see a personal friend, one who is nearest and dearest, but does not live in a physical body. ¶The Hindu has another great joy—the certainty of liberation. Even in difficult times, we are solaced in the knowledge of our religion which tells us that no soul that ever existed or ever will exist in future extrapolations of time and space will ever fail to attain liberation. The Hindu knows that all souls will one day merge into God; and he knows that God, who created all souls, slowly guides our maturing into His likeness, brings us back to Himself, which is not separate from ourselves. The Hindu, through striving and personal development in this life on this planet, knows that liberation into God is the final goal. This knowing and this belief release us from any ego, from any superiority by which one person considers himself or herself as especially meriting God's grace while others are lost. For the Hindu, there is an assurance that all souls will eventually enjoy liberation, and that includes ourselves and all of our friends and family. We need never fear otherwise.

Friday
LESSON 250
The Joy of Mysticism

Then there is the joy of the mysticism of Hinduism. It is the world's most magical religion, offering worlds within worlds of esoteric discovery and perception. The inner worlds are what Hindu mystics tell of in the greatest richness and freedom of expression that exists on the planet. Mysticism in Hinduism is more out-front than in all the other religions of the world. As a result, it is enjoyed by more of the people in our religion. Mysticism is discussed more broadly and not limited to a few great souls or a handful of *pandits.* The mysticism of Hinduism is for all the people; yet, too, in its esoteric aspect it is protected at its core and kept sacred by being kept secret. How grand is the Hindu mystical tradition, with its *sādhanas* and *yogas,* with its wealth of understanding of the etheric bodies, of the *nāḍīs* and the *chakras,* of the aura and the *prāṇas,* of the various states of consciousness and levels of existence, and so much more. No other religion on the Earth can ever begin to equal Hinduism's mystical teachings; all that wealth is the rightful inheritance of each Hindu. ¶The Hindu enjoys all the facets of life as transmuted into a religious expression in art. The Hindu's art is a religious art—drawing, painting and sculpture of the Gods, the *devas,* and the saints of our religion. The music is devotional and depicts the tones of the higher *chakras,* echoes the voices of the Gods; and the dance emulates the movements of the Gods. We are never far away from sights, sounds and symbols of our religion. A mountaintop represents Lord Śiva; a hill represents Lord Murugan, Kārttikeya; and sugar cane fields represent Lord Gaṇeśa. Everything that one sees on the planet represents something religious. Art is not merely for egotistical and existential self-expression, but for spiritual expression, done consciously in service to the Divine. That is why one seldom sees or even knows the name of the artist of the great Hindu artistic creations. The artist is not creating in order to become famous or rich. He is surrendering his talents, serving his Gods and his religion through his art, and his art takes on a certain sacredness. ¶One great joy that the Hindu has is the appreciation for all other religions. Hinduism is theocentric, that means God-centric, whereas most other religions are prophet-centric, revolving around the personality of some living person or some person who once lived in history and interpreted religion to his culture in his time. Hinduism has no founder. It was never founded. It has neither a beginning nor an end. It is coexistent with man himself. That is why it is called the Sanātana Dharma, the Eternal Path. It is not one man's teaching or interpretation. It is not limited to a single facet of religion, but consists of the entire spectrum, seen in its various components as if through a prism. It does not say that this religion is wrong and this one right. It sees God everywhere, manifesting all the great religions. The Hindu can appreciate Buddha without becoming a Buddhist. He can understand Jesus without becoming a Christian. Therefore, the joys of all the religions of the world become the joys of the Hindu. ¶But as Hindus, we must first think of the joys and happiness within our own religion. Consider our blessings. Come closer to the Gods of our religion. The many Gods are in the Western world now and have circumferenced the planet with their *śakti* of radiant rays that penetrate with spiritual power, bringing harmony and culture, balancing out the *dharma* of the planet. ¶Hinduism is such a great religion. All practicing Hindus are very proud of their religion. Unfortunately, these days too many born into the religion are not all that proud to be Hindus, but this is slowly changing. Hindus are now welcoming into their religion others who are, of their own volition, adopting or converting into the Sanātana Dharma. They are proud enough of their faith to want others to share its wisdom, its mysticism, its scriptures, its broadmindedness, its magnificent temples and its final conclusions for all mankind. To all Hindus, who today are found in every country on the Earth, I say: Courage! Courage! Courage! Have the courage to know beyond a doubt that Hinduism is the greatest religion in the world. We must be proud of this.

Saturday
LESSON 251
Hinduism Can't Be Destroyed

It is false to think that one has to be born a Hindu in order to be a Hindu. That is a concept postulated by certain caste-based Hindu lineages and reinforced by the Christians in their effort to hinder the growth of our religion, to deprive it of new life, to hold it down while they in turn try to convert Hindus en masse to their religion. Swami Vivekananda (1863–1902), a Hindu monk and missionary who wrote extensively on the Hindu Dharma, when confronted by this same issue in the West would explain how Hindus who have been converted by force should not be denied an opportunity of returning to their ancestral religion. As for the case of those not born into Hinduism who might be interested to join it, he simply said, "Why, born aliens have been converted in the past by crowds, and the process is still going on." Dr. S. Radhakrishnan (1888–1975), the distinguished Hindu philosopher who became the second president of India, confirms this view in writing, "In a sense, Hinduism may be regarded as the first example in the world of a missionary religion. Only its missionary spirit is different from that associated with the proselytizing creeds. It did not regard as its mission to convert humanity to one opinion. For what counts is conduct and not belief. The ancient practice of *vrātyastoma,* described fully in the *Taṇḍya Brāhmaṇa,* shows that not only individuals but whole tribes were absorbed into Hinduism." ¶During the era of India's domination by alien religions, when Hinduism was scheduled to be destroyed, the attack was to be carried out in three ways. The first strategy was to convince the women to abandon their age-old *strī dharma*—of maintaining the home, its purity and ways of worship—thus drawing them away from the household in order to receive a so-called "higher education" or to teach in alien religious schools, thus denying future generations the mother's religious counsel and grounding in the *dharma.* The second strategy was to overtly break down the various castes of temple priests by enticing them to accept other, often higher-paying, occupations, thus leaving the temples unattended. ¶The third strategy was to convince Hindus that they had inherited a crude and outdated religion. This last attack was accomplished mainly through ridicule, by ridiculing every aspect of the religion that could possibly be ridiculed. For example, those who slandered Hinduism claimed it has no sacraments. Why, Hinduism has more sacraments, more sacred rites and ceremonies for its members, than perhaps any other religion in the world. These sacraments include the *nāmakaraṇa saṁskāra,* name-giving sacrament; *annaprāśana,* first feeding; *karṇavedha,* ear-piercing; *vidyārambha,* commencement of learning; *vivāha,* marriage; and many others. ¶Though India was politically dominated for generations by adherents of alien faiths, and though every attempt was made to discourage, weaken and crush the native religion, the carefully calculated, systematic assault failed to destroy Hinduism. Hinduism cannot be destroyed. It is the venerable eternal religion, the Sanātana Dharma. But it was an effective campaign that has left in its wake deep *saṁskāric* patterns, deep subconscious impressions, which still persist in the minds of the Indian people. It is going to be difficult to completely eradicate these impressions, but with the help of all the millions of Hindus throughout the world, in adhering to and extolling the benefits and joys of Hinduism and the gifts which it holds for mankind, this is possible and feasible, within the range of accomplishment, perhaps within this very generation.

Sunday
LESSON 252
Bringing In Ardent Seekers

Hindus should freely welcome sincere devotees into their religion, not those who already have a firm religion and are content, but those who are seeking, who believe, as millions in the West already believe, in the laws of *karma* and reincarnation and the existence of the ever-present God that permeates this planet and the universe. Hindus should freely embrace those who believe in the Gods and all we have been speaking about earlier, for whom other religious avenues have proved empty and fruitless. There are certain matured souls for whom the Sanātana Dharma can be the only true religion, who have no other religion and who will seek and seek until they come upon its profound truths, perhaps in an old scripture, or in a temple sanctum during *pūjā* or in the eyes of an awakened *siddha yogī*. These souls we must help. We must teach them of our religion and allow them to fully accept or reject it, to accept it because they know it, or to reject it because they know it and are not ready to meet Mahā Gaṇapati and humbly sit at the feet of this most profound Lord. ¶There are many lost souls on the planet today who die in the physical world—lose their physical body—wander on the astral plane a short time and are caught up immediately in another womb. They have no knowledge of other states of existence or of the workings of reincarnation. They have no time for the bliss of these in-between, astral states. They have no time for assessing their last life and preparing for the next, which they could then enter with new knowledge, no time for inner attunement with the Gods in the inner worlds between death and birth. Instead, they are caught in a constant cycle of flesh, making flesh and living in flesh, with the soul being immersed in ignorance and the darkness of the consciousness of flesh. Hinduism eradicates this cycle by offering knowledge of the states between life and death and then life again. It creates deep impressions within the mind of these individuals, which then bring them out of this syndrome so that they can enjoy months, years, in fact, of education and knowledge in the inner planes of consciousness between births, so that they can come back into a physical body a more awakened soul than when they left their last physical sheath at death. ¶We must not be reluctant to welcome these sincere Hindu souls and to assist them in finding the answers they seek and do not find elsewhere. It is our *dharma* to help them. Hinduism has always welcomed adoptives and converts. Bring in new people to the religion. Teach them. Help them. Counsel them. Proceed with confidence. Have courage, courage, courage.

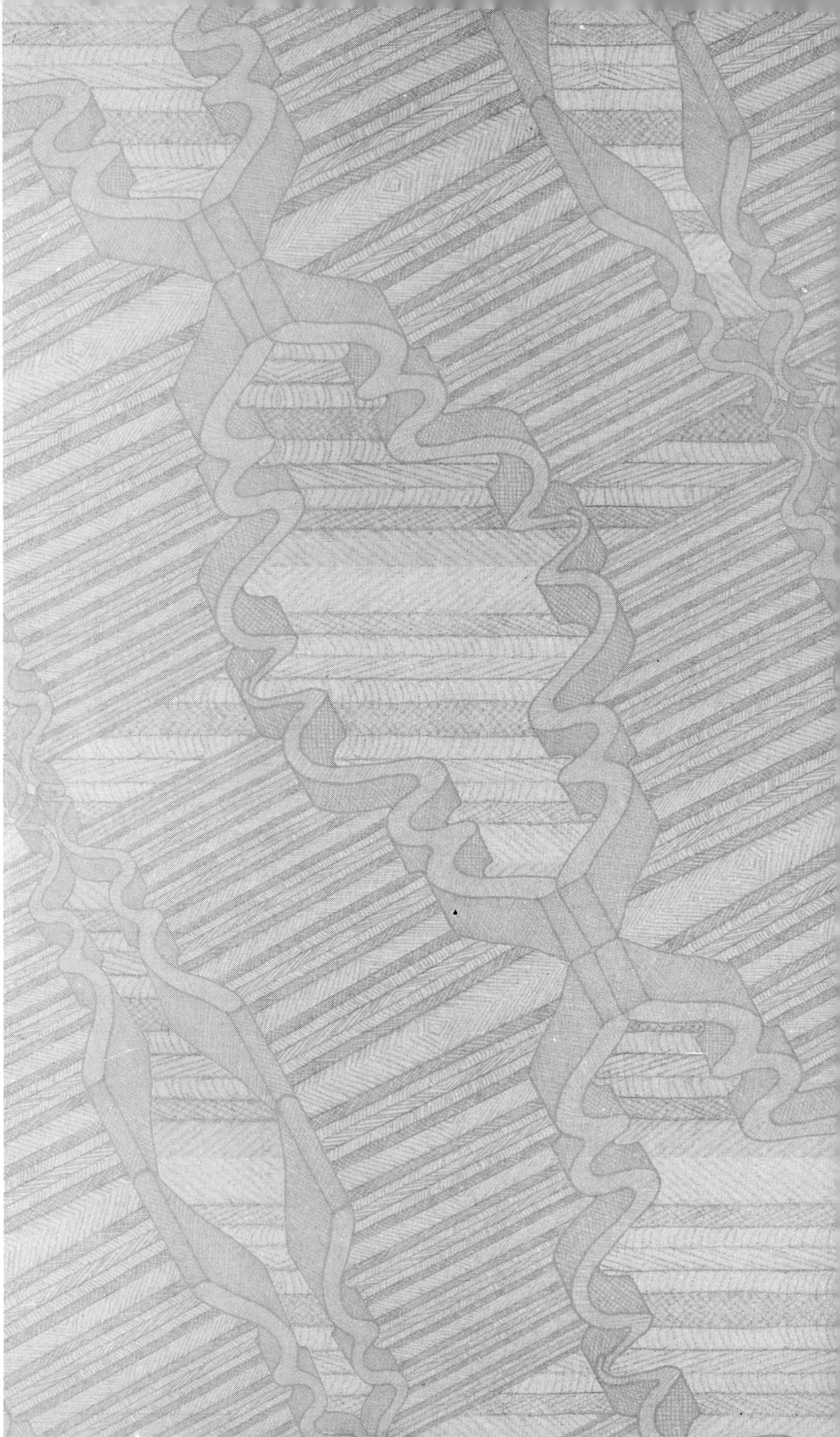

Dharma Niyatiśacha

धर्म नियतिश्च

Duty and Destiny

Let there be no neglect of Truth. Let there be no neglect of *dharma*. Let there be no neglect of welfare. Let there be no neglect of prosperity. Let there be no neglect of study and teaching. Let there be no neglect of the duties to the Gods and the ancestors.

Kṛishṇa Yajur Veda, Taittirīya Upanishad, 1.11.1. BO UPR, P. 537

Monday
LESSON 253
What Is Dharma?

One of the great joys of Hinduism is *dharma.* What is *dharma? Dharma* is to the individual what its normal development is to a seed—the orderly fulfillment of an inherent nature and destiny. *Dharma* means merit, morality, good conduct, religious duty and the way of life of the wise person. When people fulfill their *dharma,* they fulfill the very purpose of their life; and when they act against their *dharma,* they create new *karmas.* Just as we are born in a physical body with a certain outward appearance, our *dharma* is a certain accumulated pattern. We are expected to live through this *dharma* during a lifetime, understanding that all persons can be in their rightful place, doing their rightful *dharma* at the right time. The Hindu has this understanding. It's inbred. It offers a certain contentment in knowing that there is a rightful place for each soul in this vast universe. ¶*Dharma* is determined by the accumulated patterns of *karma,* the *saṁskāric* reactions to the experiences of *karma* throughout all the past lives, the sum of impressions that make up the seeds yet to be sprouted, which must be worked out through prayer, meditation, *sādhana* or *tapas* if they are not beneficial, but allowed to sprout if they are beneficial. These seeds, all collected together, make up the *dharma* of each individual. There are some who do not yet have a precise *dharma.* They have not collected up into themselves enough merit or demerit. Their options are great. They are still making—through their actions—impressions within their own minds in order to gather them together, to firm up their own mind to form a *dharma,* to fall into a certain kind of pattern. ¶*Dharma* is the heritage of all Hindus. It is working for the divine beings in the Second World and the Gods within the Third World. Hindu Dharma is working for the Gods, as opposed to working and living for our own personal wants and needs. Performing one's *dharma* properly is working in harmony with the divine plan of the universe, as laid out by the Gods. ¶Working for the Gods, being their employee, their servant or their slave, and not working for one's personal self, must be the prime occupation in life, whether the Hindu is a farmer, merchant, soldier or a king, a peasant, a *sādhu* or a *ṛishi.* All work done in the right consciousness, performing the right *dharma,* is in service of the Gods and is work of the Gods by the servants of the Gods. Working for one's religion, for

---

A man rakes banyan leaves on the temple steps in Nepal, a humble task which brings him deep fulfillment. In Hinduism a part of everyone's duty is seva, *selfless service, which includes helping with festival and temple duties, or volunteer work in an* āśrama *or other holy institution.*

the Deities and the *devas,* should be our occupation twenty-four hours a day, every day, during our waking hours on the physical plane and on the inner astral plane and higher mental planes at night. We should continue this work with an unbroken continuity. ¶To better understand the vast concept of *dharma,* look upon it as the natural process by which the inherent perfection of the soul is unfolded and realized. An acorn's natural pattern is to grow into a mighty oak, but the pattern for a rose is different. An acorn will never try to become a rose bush. Our good friend, Sita Ram Goel, once said, "Now I was made to see *dharma* as a multidimensional movement of man's inner law of being, his psychic evolution, his spiritual growth and his spontaneous building of an outer life for himself and the community in which he lives." In contrast, by performing an incorrect or *adharmic* pattern in life, the soul0 reaps more *karma* and is retarded for perhaps an entire lifetime. We call it righteousness and goodness and virtue when the *dharma* of a particular lifetime is performed correctly.

Tuesday
LESSON 254
Unfolding a Clear Pattern

The *dharma* of a person's life is set prior to birth according to the accumulated impressions of all previous lives. It is set as the most perfect path toward spiritual perfection in this life. A life spent in creating a new *karma* through not fulfilling the ordained pattern of *dharma* temporarily retards the soul's evolution. This retardation may not appear until future births, seemingly bypassed but not actually bypassed. ¶To avoid the potential catastrophes of *karma,* each Hindu must perform his *dharma,* live according to the natural Godward path. By following this important pattern of spiritual unfoldment, the devotee benefits and, in turn, benefits all others and, most importantly, serves the Gods and earns good merit, earns their grace and then deserves their boons. When spiritually awakened, the Hindu offers his every thought, word and deed in a consciousness of the Divine. All work is done for that high purpose. ¶To know one's *dharma* is a clear path. To be uncertain is a path of confusion. There is one God who knows the patterns of all humankind, whose superconscious mind is so intricate, encompassing and spanning the *yugas* of time, that each path for each individual is known, memorized and recorded indelibly in the inner ether of the *ākāśic* matter of His mind. Through the worship of this God, Lord Gaṇeśa, the venerable pope of the Hindu religion, the individual's *dharmic* pattern in this life is unfolded from within. It becomes clear. It becomes known. It is difficult for the modern, twenty-first-century Hindu to consciously know the correct *dharma*, but this can be made known to him through the worship of Lord Gaṇeśa. ¶If someone is not fortunate enough to have been born into a family that perpetuates the Sanātana Dharma, then he must perform *sādhana* and offer repeated prayers to this first God, Lord Gaṇeśa, whom all Hindus invoke before the other Gods and before any task is undertaken, this God whose knowledge remains supreme, penetrating most deeply through every avenue of the devotee's mind. Once the *dharma* is clear, is known, it must be faithfully performed throughout the life most willingly, thus destroying the seeds of *karma* through living out the pattern without creating a new *karma*, through performing good service, accruing good merit in fulfillment of the totalities of all of our multiple life patterns. This then makes the next life and the one after that joyous, brings good births well earned and well lived, through the graces of Mahā Gaṇapati, Lord Gaṇeśa, who sits upon the four-petaled lotus *mūlādhāra chakra* within the spine of every person. ¶As the divine being rises within and consciousness expands, a *kuṇḍalinī* coil is released and a certain power awakens from deep within. At the same time, conscience awakens, and the mind emerges into the *mūlādhāra chakra*, there to meet Mahā Gaṇapati, Lord Gaṇeśa, through whose eyes and mind the devotee enters into the joys and happinesses within the Hindu religion, the birthright of all humans. This is how the Sanātana Dharma perpetuates itself and progresses from generation to generation, from age to age. Of course, once well settled into *dharma*, through Lord Gaṇeśa, we will meet the other Gods. They will help maintain and fulfill our life in all avenues of culture and appreciation of that culture. It is only when each individual finds his own particular pattern in life, and clings to this pattern, that good future births are assured.

Wednesday
LESSON 255
Help From The Gods

What is a bad birth, one might wonder. It is being born into an area of the mind below the *mūlādhāra chakra* where the instinctive nature reigns supreme, where the intellectual nature runs amuck by pursuing dead-end sequences of thought and desire. This is considered a bad birth. It is where no consciousness of God or of the Gods exists, where there is no known pattern for life, no *dharma*, and where little or no knowledge of the laws of *karma* and reincarnation survive. This is a bad birth when within the *chakras* of our being, the centers of nerve force, thought and emotion, values of external existence remain supreme, and the many, many pitfalls of suffering, anguish, confusion, tears and sorṛow all exist. These areas of consciousness in the lower *chakras* below the *mūlādhāra* can reap birth after birth and are considered by the Hindu as births to be avoided. They are avoided through finding and then following unrelentingly one's *dharma* life after life. ¶The Hindu *dharma* is the clear pattern within the mind, earning the right to see the cumulative patterns of the *karmas* and the impressions of all past existences molded into a one pattern to be lived out in this life to the benefit of all patterns. Such a life is the fulfillment of all previous efforts and thus erases the uncomplimentary deeds and adds beneficial ones, so a next birth can be most rewardingly great and useful to the whole of mankind. This is the evolution of the soul, and the duty of the great God Gaṇeśa and of the Mahādevas who protect the soul, of the *devas* who guard and guide the soul and of the *ṛishis* and seers, saints and *satgurus* who are the guardians of mankind in this First World existence. ¶They assure that, little by little, this pattern unfolds through the performance of good *dharma*, through earning good *karma*. It does not take a deep understanding or a tremendous intellect to find one's perfect pattern among the many patterns of life. For Hindu souls, it does require being born into or gaining formal entrance into the Hindu religion, being properly introduced to the Gods and bearing the name of one of the Gods as one's own legal name. Then authority is given to make clear the pattern for this life, to receive the blessings and the protection of the benevolent God Gaṇeśa, protector of human evolution. This is one of the most basic benefits for all Hindus, for then we can serve the Gods well and work through our *karma* toward a greater *dharma* through working for the Gods. ¶We have one duty to perform, which is to pass our religion on to the next generation, the next and the next. And how do we do this? How is this done? It is done by causing the children to memorize the precepts of our scriptures. Our Śaivite scriptures are the heritage of the children. They own those scriptures. It is our duty to give them the scriptures. Among others, we now have the *Tirukural* in the English language, entitled *Weaver's Wisdom*. It must be memorized by them, by each and every one of them, along with the hundreds of Vedic verses in *Hinduism's Contemporary Catechism, Dancing with Śiva*. The teachings of our other scriptures should be familiar as well. That establishes them in their *dharma*. The sooner we get our scriptures into the minds of the children, the better we build the children into fine citizens. Crime is very expensive for any nation. Crime is very expensive for any family, for they suffer and the individual suffers. Nothing is gained by crime. Good citizenship comes from a good religious education. A good religious education starts with memory, and it is fulfilled in the realms of reason when the child is older and able to discuss his religion with his elders. We must educate the youth. We must educate them well in the Śaivite Hindu religion. Start with the *Tirukural*. Lord Murugan will help you. God Gaṇeśa will open doors and give you wisdom of how to proceed. Lord Murugan will give you the willpower—He is the God of Will—to perform this one supreme duty, and duty is also *dharma*, to pass our Śaivite religion on to the next generation, the next and the next.

Thursday
LESSON 256
Forces of Adharma

We all have our *dharma* to perform, each and every one of us. The child has his *dharma* to perform as a child. Unless the child has early training in his religious life, his religious patterns are not set firmly. It has to be taught to respect the *dharmic* mother and father as the first *gurus*. Parents teach mainly by example, and sadly some only teach what not to do rather than being religious models for their young. They don't understand that example is the most powerful and lasting lesson a parent can give to a child. Later the schoolteacher is the *guru*, and still later the *satguru* is the *guru* in the strict sense. The *satguru* more than often has to undo the erroneous, often angry and violent, examples given by parents and schoolteachers to the young ones, who thus learn of hurtfulness and anti-religiousness and immoral practices. It is up to the *satguru* to help heal the minds of the young of the fear and suppressed anger they naturally hold against parents who have inflicted emotional and bodily injury on them until they were physically big enough to resist. ¶There are a lot of influences in the world which deny *dharma*, which deny the Gods and which ignore the temples. You must never allow these worldly forces to affect you or your family, now or in the future. Don't let anyone take your religion away from you. We have to keep developing religion in our mind. We have to keep learning the language of our soul, which is one definition of religion. When religion leaves our mind, something comes in to replace it. What comes into our mind to replace the vacuum when religion goes? Greed, jealousy, hatred, anger, past regrets, despair, self-condemnation. We cease to feel good about ourselves. We are always discontented and restless, and we are always unhappy, jealous, angry and fretful. These are some of the lower emotions that replace religion when we allow religion to leave our mind. ¶There are many people in the world today intent on taking your religion away from you. Śaivites have the greatest and philosophically most comprehensive and deeply experiential religion in the world. Śaivites have moved their religion forward for five to ten thousand years. At no time in history has the Śaivite religion not been on this planet. The Tamil people especially have moved the Śaivite religion forward, year after year after year, through *bhakti.* And it is your religion. It is in your DNA, and no one can take that religion away from you. But you must steel your mind, make your mind strong through knowledge, through religious education.

Friday
LESSON 257
Charting A Course

When we set our *dharma* through the personal course of selecting a profession, we have to be very sure what we want to do through life; and it has to be in accordance with either *strī dharma* or *purusha dharma* to the best of our knowledge, and all of our family and relatives have to agree. For when we follow *dharma,* we are content; everyone in the community is happy. ¶Now, in this technological era, we have many choices of *dharma.* What would be some of them? To become a doctor would be a *dharma,* which is helping people, healing people mentally, emotionally and physically. To perform the *dharma* of a doctor, not just eight hours a day, but twenty-four hours a day, we have to be healing. Then the great healing forces from the great Gods of our religion come pouring through us, whether we are a medical doctor, an *āyurveda* healer, a nutritionist, a surgeon, a psychiatrist, a neurologist, or whatever we choose in that field as our *dharma.* This becomes our total pattern to be lived out in this birth. ¶What upsets *dharma* and makes *karma*? When we make *karma,* we either make negative burdens for ourselves, or we make helpful and useful *karmas* that bring us merit. For a youth to choose to be a doctor and then, in the middle of his career, decide he doesn't want to do that anymore, and make another choice in the middle of his life that he is going to now be a businessman and run a drugstore because it is more profitable to go into business—that would be abandoning *dharma* and making *karma, karma* which would have to be lived through, perhaps in another life. When that doctor made his decision to become a storekeeper, he started a new *dharma,* or a new *karma,* for which he was not trained from youth. He is, therefore, vulnerable to making many mistakes, because he has wandered off the pathway of *dharma.* ¶Why is the world in such a mess? Because people are not following *dharma.* They are *adharmic.* They are not following the path of *dharma.* They are following the path of *karma,* both bad *karma* and good *karma.* So, in our religion, the

Śaivite Hindu religion, we are bound to follow the path of *dharma* the best that we can understand it. We know it is unwise to do otherwise. And who teaches the wisdom of following the path of *dharma?* The grandfather, the grandmother, the father, the great uncle, the elders of the community, the family *guru,* the temple priest—they know how the *dharma* should be followed for a healthy, thriving society. When we make our choices in life, those choices should have the support of the family and the community. Then we are in the path of proper *dharma,* and it is easier for us to become successful in it since everyone is behind it. It is a difficult world in which we live, but we can go through it without being harmed by it by following the path of *svadharma,* the perfect personal pattern of an individual's life. ¶*Dharma* is something that only the Hindu religion, the Buddhist religion, the Jain religion, the Sikh religion and other Eastern religions know about. They know about the path of *dharma.* The other religions don't know too much about that path. But we know about the path of *dharma*—our duty to be fulfilled in this life, for family, friends, relatives, deceased relatives, community, *guru* and temple. We have, each and every one of us, a duty to this temple we are sitting in this morning, to see that it is cared for, supported and kept clean. That is one of the duties of our *dharma.* We have a duty to the community. We have a duty to our mother, duty to our father, duty to our *guru,* a duty to the world also. And good, religious people make good citizens of the world. ¶We hear a lot about human rights these days. It was in Sri Lanka in 1949 that I encountered the Eastern vision of human rights, learned that duty is greater than privilege, service is superior to security. Hindu Dharma is religion, duty and justice woven together, I discovered. I sometimes explain it as a simple box of controls which holds the actions of this life and those that preceded it and their corresponding reactions. Just what is the Hindu view on human rights? It is the right of all humans to be free enough to experience their experiences and learn from their ability to overcome, without holding resentments or indulging in anger, giving out harsh words, their misdeeds, sins and other wrongdoings and reactions to their former actions. From a mystical point of view, what happens to us is important, but not as important as how we react and respond to things, good or otherwise, that happen to us. The human rights of Gandhi, Sri Aurobindo, Martin Luther King and Nelson Mandela were terribly abused, yet they were not destroyed. Let us work for the most humane of human rights, but also teach that their absence in life need not destroy us. Greatness is in accepting whatever comes with open arms. All this abuse—which does exist despite the wishes of so many that it did not—can be a blessing when embraced by a pure soul. And we each have within us the power to accept, a power no one can deprive us of under any conditions.

Saturday
LESSON 258
The Caste System

I am often asked about *varṇa dharma*—the social structure of four classes and hundreds of subgroups—commonly known as the caste system, established in India in ancient times. Is the caste system still valid today? Caste—or at least discrimination on the basis of caste—has been thrown out of the culture of India, but people still hang on to it as an ego structure. The high caste people love to hurt the low caste people, so to speak, by ignoring them, treating them roughly. That's not the way it should be. In many areas of the world the caste system is distorted, and also very strong. If you find the high caste people in your society ignoring and not wanting to speak with and associate with the lower castes, those are nasty people, and those are people you should avoid. Spiritual people, even ordinary kindly people, would never think of behaving that way. ¶The original caste system was based on behavior, as it is now in countries where there is no overt caste system in effect. Those who beat their children, those who become angry and jealous, those who live in fear and those who feign humility are all of the lowest caste. Those who value memory and reason and use their willpower to benefit others—who control themselves and run an orderly home, support the temples and are respected by the lowest castes—are of the business caste. Those who protect the *dharma* and preserve the scriptures—who protect the temples and all the people, those who are respected by the other castes—are of the princely caste. Those who commune with the Gods and are priests in the temples—who are the disseminators of the highest knowledge and respected by all the other castes—are the priestly caste. These four groups make up a complete society anywhere in the world and at anytime in history. ¶The original caste system had these four divisions. The divisions were all based on the ability of the individual to manage his body, his mind and his emotions properly. If he stopped fulfilling the *dharma* of his caste, society would recognize that he had moved from one caste and was now in another. The original caste system was based on self-discipline through education and through personal *sādhana*. The original caste system was based on the unfoldment of the consciousness within each individual through the fourteen *chakras.* ¶People everywhere naturally divide themselves up into castes. We have the workers. You go to work, you work under somebody else—that happens all over the world—that's the *śudra* caste. We have the merchants, who are self-motivated. That's the *vaiśya* caste. We have the politicians and the lawmakers and the law-enforcement people. That's the *kshatriya* caste. And then you have the priests, the ministers, the missionaries. That's the *brahmin* caste. Every society has these four castes working within it in one way or another. In today's world, if one is not fulfilling the *dharma* of his born caste, then he changes castes. For instance, if a *brahmin* husband and wife are working eight to fifteen hours a day in a hospital under others, they are no longer of the *brahmin* caste, because they are not performing the duties of the *dharma* of that caste. They are workers, in the *śudra* caste. ¶We can see around us the deterioration of the system which has been abused beyond the point of recognition. Members of the *brahmin* caste are now beating their children, abusing their wives. Members of the *kshatriya* caste disrespect the laws of the land. Members of the business caste are deceptive and dishonest. All are confused, living in anger and in jealousy. No wonder their families break apart and their businesses fail. In the eyes of the Gods, most of those who adhere to the caste system that exists today are low caste. This is because they live in lower consciousness. They look at the world through the windows of the *chakras* below the *mūlādhāra.* These undeveloped humans are struggling through the lower *chakras,* trying to get out of the dark worlds of the mind. Let us not be deluded about what the *sapta ṛishis* had in mind when they casted humans according to the soul's unfoldment in one or more of the fourteen *chakras.* We should totally ignore the Hindu caste system as lived in India today and, through example, show a better and more wholesome path for modern society.

Sunday
LESSON 259
Dharma's Rewards

What happens if we follow *dharma?* The Gods, like our Supreme God Śiva, Lord Murugan, Lord Gaṇeśa and all the great Gods, reward us by giving us a good birth in the next life. A good birth is to be born into a family that follows *dharma,* that is loving and secure. We are also rewarded by being able to stay in the blissful Devaloka for a long time between births. We remain in that heaven world, in our etheric body, to enjoy, learn and gain knowledge and gain advancement for our soul as we prepare for the next birth on Earth. ¶So, there are great rewards for following the path of *dharma,* and there is equally great suffering for us if we follow the *adharmic* path, the path of *adharma* which creates *kukarma.* When we abandon *dharma,* we open ourselves to confusion, to self-condemnation. We are open to low-minded feelings, to jealousies and antagonisms and uncontrollable emotions. *Dharma* helps us to control our emotions, and our mind also. Do you want to live in these lower emotions, out of insecurity, to arouse hatred, jealousy, greed and all the negative states of mind? Of course not. By following the ancient path of *dharma,* we avoid all this suffering and mental pain and bring ourselves into positive, creative and productive states of consciousness, bringing us ever closer and closer to the holy feet of God Śiva. ¶We are in a technological age now. This technological age is fast moving. There are many temptations. There is television. There is the Internet, and soon things beyond Internet. There are things to see that children should not perhaps see at a young age. We must get hold of their minds early, at five years old, at six years old, at seven years old and cause them to memorize, even if they do not understand, the couplets of the *Tirukural* and the *ślokas* and Vedic verses of *Dancing with Śiva.* Later on, they will be grateful to you as parents and as elders. Still later on, these children will bless you, and the blessings of the children will be very comforting in your old age. ¶We must teach our children that the soul is immortal, created by Lord Śiva and destined to merge into Him in its absolute fulfillment. We must teach them about this world we live in and how to make their religion strong and vibrant in a technological age every day and tomorrow in their life. This is especially important for those Śaivite families who live beyond the borders of India and Sri Lanka. Those of you assembled here this morning are heirs to a rich and stable religious culture. If you stay with your religion, the future of your children is less uncertain. They will go to universities in other parts of the world. They will be exposed to the influence of other religions. They must be so sure of their religion, so knowledgeable in its tenets, that they can explain it intelligently to anyone and allow them to accept or reject the tenets of the Śaivite Hindu religion. Send them as missionaries out into the world, fully informed about Śaivism, our great God Śiva, Lord Murugan and Lord Gaṇeśa, and you will be doing a great benefit for the entire world. ¶All Śaivites throughout the world, the united Śaivites of the world, are linked together in a bond of love—Śiva-sambandham. God Śiva is immanent love and transcendent reality. Our religion tells us that the mature soul must lift up and take care of the young soul. Our religion tells us that we must go through the natural

Monday
LESSON 260
We Mold Our Own Future

Every action that we perform in life, every thought that we think, has its reaction. We may or may not be conscious of the reactions that will result from what we are doing or thinking. Many people spend a great deal of time acting only with the purpose of covering up the reactions to prior unsatisfactory actions of their own making. Hurt or puzzled, they often ask, "Why is this happening to me? What did I do to attract that? What did I do to cause that? Do I really deserve this? It doesn't seem fair!" ¶Were they to become enlightened and find the ability to live in their own intuitive, superconscious mind, they would see in that expanded state of consciousness all of the ingredients that came together out of the forgotten past to create the conditions through which they are passing in the now. They would observe that every action is like planting a seed. The fruit of that seed, harvested perhaps years later, is reaction. Like the seed, actions remain vibrating in the mind until fulfilled. It is not possible to trace past causes to current effects through analyzing or through the ordinary processes of reason, which result in uncertain conjecture. Only superconscious insight can accurately portray the chain of cause-and-effect relationships as a picture of what is. ¶Thus the wheel of *karma* continues, on and on and on, creating and recreating. The wheel of *karma* is simply the mechanism of the mind's action—your mind, everyone's mind. Through the study of the wheel of *karma*, which is a meditative study, you realize that you have created everything that is happening or has already happened to you. Everything that is coming your way in the future you will have created. Everything you will acquire your own wants will have brought into being. You are right now a sum total of millions of thoughts, feelings, desires and actions—all of them yours. Circumstance is not responsible for your condition, for you have made your circumstances consciously and unconsciously. There are no outside forces imposing themselves upon you. Whatever you attract to yourself of the world, though it seems to be external, is but a manifestation of your own inner nature. You are the author of all of your creations; and yet in the inner recesses of your being you are already the finished product at the same time. To understand this fully, you need *yoga*. ¶The study of *yoga* is reserved for the few who have the courage to seek the

---

After an accident in which she has broken her leg, a woman does not blame God. Though injured and confined to a wheelchair, she knows that this is her self-created karma *and trusts that Lord Śiva will guide her through the experience toward greater maturity and understanding.*

depths of their being, for the few who can overcome their experiences and their desires in deep meditation. Now, you may meet in your own subconscious, as soon as you sit down to practice meditation, all of the worldly desires latent within you, including several of which you perhaps have no conscious idea. If your meditation is successful, you will be able to throw out the unnecessary experiences or desires that are consuming your mind. When you do this and you travel past the world of desire, you will begin to break free of the wheel of *karma* which binds you to the specific reaction which must follow every action. To break free of this wheel of *karma,* you must have a strong, one-pointed mind. Your only key to help you attain this one-pointedness, this steadfastness, is your devotion to God, your devotion to the realization of the Truth. Few people remain steadfast enough under all circumstances and tests that life offers to realize the many causes and effects that are linked together in their lives. It is easy to study the law of *karma* and to appreciate it philosophically, but to realize it, to apply it to everything that happens to you, to understand the workings of it as the day goes by, requires an ability to which you must awaken. ¶Attachment, desire, craving, fear of loss—these are the self-created ropes that hold man in bondage to his lower states of mind. It is because man chooses to live in the ignorance of unfulfilled craving and unsatisfied desire that he suffers. How many of you have suffered over something that was anticipated and may never have taken place? You will remember then waking up out of the dream of your suffering and finding that things were all right after all, and that through your experience something within you remained the same.

Tuesday
LESSON 261
The Cause of Joy and Sorrow

Somewhere the idea was born that man should live in states of happiness and joy all of the time. But, in the first place, happiness and joy depend upon unhappiness and sorrow, even to be recognized or appreciated. If man would only know that whatever emotion transpires within him foreshadows its opposite. Secondly, suffering is a greater intensity, a higher vibration, than happiness. You do not learn much from your happinesses; you learn from the states of suffering, which awaken the higher consciousness of your soul. But suffering has no value for its own sake. When the mind recognizes it is suffering over something or other, it is time to practice meditation, to see into the causes, to expand your consciousness a little bit more so that you will grasp the workings of life and its *karmic* laws. Then you will attain to a greater intensity than either joy or suffering has to offer. You will view the wheel of life, of cause and effect, objectively. And you will not so quickly identify yourself with the lower emotions or the objects of your own mind's creation. ¶Then there are the people who, like a fish caught by a fisherman, grasp onto the hook, who step on the spiritual path, but spend their time flip-flopping in the water, tugging at the line, swimming first one way then the other, never really approaching the surface. Why? They live in their ego, that's all. Their consciousness is limited. The ego is just a trifle dumb. Have you observed an egotistical person? He is just a little dumb, isn't he—not aware of the layers and layers of wisdom within him. ¶It is the wise man who recognizes the importance of controlling the forces of his mind. His life is a struggle to make his philosophy real, to gain control of the cycles of experience which have tied him to the wheel of *karma*. You don't escape the chain of cause and effect by just sitting with your eyes closed, trying to keep awake, trying to meditate. The genuine practice of *yoga* involves meeting new challenges each day, having new realizations each day, becoming the boss of your mind, not allowing it to flop around at the end of the line. This type of diligent concentration will definitely change you from the inside out. You will begin to realize, more and more, that you are the creator of your life and every aspect of it. ¶But your incarnation on this planet is not complete until you have exhausted the wheel of *karma*, and it will not exhaust itself unless you gain control of it. The wheel of *karma*, of cause and effect, the world of form, is apparent only when you look at it. You only attain the natural state of your radiant inner being when you step off the wheel of *karma*. It is not natural for man to live bound to the lower states of mind, ignorant of the fact that God dwells within. But the hearing and understanding of this truth is only the first glimmer of the dawn, a preliminary awakening. The rest, the final realization, is up to you. It is up to you and you alone to penetrate the veil of illusion and realize the Self, the Absolute, beyond desire, beyond the experiences of the mind. It is up to you to realize God.

Wednesday
LESSON 262
How to Face Your Karma

If difficult things are happening to you and your mind is disturbed because of them and you have mental arguments within you because you can't accept your own *karma*, go to the feet of Lord Śiva in your mind, go to the feet of Lord Śiva in the temple with your physical body, and beg for the intelligence to place yourself firmly on the path of Sanātana Dharma. ¶Though it is true that we must work through all aspects and phases of past actions, there are ways of becoming excused from the punishments that drastic actions of the past impose upon the future. These ways are grace, *sādhana*, *tapas* and atonement through penance and the performance of good deeds, thus acquiring merit which registers as a new and positive *karma*, alleviating the heaviness of some of our past *karma*. Through seeking grace and through receiving it by performing *sādhana* and *tapas* and the doing of penance, the *karmas* are in themselves speeded up. The going through and meeting and reaping of rewards as well as displeasures embodied in past *karma* in the present is accelerated through these self-imposed actions. Therefore, the sages say, "Bear your *karma* cheerfully." And as the seeking of Self commences, the *karma* unfolds in all of its hideousness and glory, to be seen before the single eye and not reacted to by even a tremor within this physical and astral nerve system. The *yoga* must be that strong. Each time you blame another person for what has happened to you, or cast blame in any way, tell yourself, "This is my *karma* which I was born to face. I did not come into a physical body just to blame others for what happens to me. I was not born to live in a state of ignorance created by an inability to face my *karma*. I came here to spiritually unfold, to accept the *karmas* of this and all my past lives and to deal with them and handle them in a proper and a wonderful way." ¶Humility is intelligence; arrogance is ignorance. To accept one's *karma* and the responsibility for one's actions is strength. To blame another is weakness and foolishness. Let's begin by not advertising our ignorance. If you must blame what happens to you on your friend, your neighbor, your country, your community or the world, don't advertise it by speaking about it. Keep that ignorance to yourself. Limit it to the realm of thought. Harness your speech and at the same time work to remold your thinking and retrain your subconscious to actually accept this basic premise of Śaiva Siddhānta.

Thursday
LESSON 263
Take Full Responsibility

If you take responsibility for all that happens to you, then you will have the power to deal with your *karma* through the grace of Lord Śiva. He will give you the intelligence to deal with it as you worship Him in the Śiva temple, contact Him within as the Life of your life and find Him in meditation. Let's take an example. Say I am holding a plate of rice and curry and I pass it to you. All of a sudden the plate drops on the floor between us. I blame you, and you blame me. I don't want to be responsible for dropping the rice and curry, and you don't want to be responsible either. So, we blame each other. The rice and curry is scattered there on the floor. No one is going to clean it up until one of us takes responsibility and says, "I'm sorry I dropped the plate of rice and curry," and gets down on hands and knees and cleans it up. In the same way, only by taking responsibility, by recognizing what we have done as our own doing, can we begin cleaning up the results of our actions. Those who do take responsibility for their own *karma* have all the help in the world. ¶Pride, arrogance and an ungiving nature are characteristics of those who don't believe in the law of *karma.* These are qualities of those who do not take responsibility for their actions. They blame everything on someone or something other than themselves. This includes their mistakes and every unpleasant thing that has ever happened to them, is happening to them or may happen to them in the future. They live in the fears and the resentments born of their own ignorance. ¶Only through being born in a physical body can you experience certain kinds of *karmas* which cannot be fulfilled or experienced in your etheric/astral body. Therefore, between births those physical-body *karmas* live in seed form. Only in a physical body do you have all of the *chakras* functioning that will allow those *karmas* to manifest and be dealt with. Each birth is thus a precious window of opportunity. For heaven's sake don't blame your *karma* on somebody else and seek to escape from what you were born to deal with. That is the height of foolishness. Stop blaming and criticizing others, and take a good look at yourself. Stop excusing yourself and trying to make yourself look good in the eyes of others. Then a sense of strength will come up within you, a sense of independence and peace. Mental arguments will stop. Arrogance will vanish. Pride won't be there anymore. You will be a full person. All of your *chakras* will function properly. Your nerve system will quiet down, and intuitively you will be able to bear up under your *karmas* and deal with them positively. If it is your *karma* to be poor in this life, you will be rich by living within the income that you have. You will be content by having desires that you can afford. We make ourselves discontented, we make ourselves unhappy, we make ourselves useless creatures on this planet by allowing ourselves to live in an ignorant state.

Friday
LESSON 264
Good and Bad; Like Attracts Like

What do we mean when we say there is no good and no bad, only experience? We mean that in the highest sense, there is no good and bad *karma;* there is self-created experience that presents opportunities for spiritual advancement. If we can't draw lessons from the *karma,* then we resist or resent it, lashing out with mental, emotional or physical force. The original substance of that *karma* is spent and no longer exists, but our current reaction creates a new condition of harsh *karma* to face in the future. As long as we react to *karma*, we must repeat it. That is the law.¶Good or bad is just a door, going one way or the other. So I say, "There is no good, there is no bad; there is just a swinging door." Good deeds siphon the collective good deeds of other good deeds. When the door swings the other way, mistakes siphon the results of past mistakes. Hatreds, the accumulated results of hating, are pulled up from way down there. Thus, one of the major keys to understanding the importance of good conduct relates to the release of seed *karmas*. Performing *dharma*—acting with correct thought, word and deed—siphons the results of previous patterns of behavior from the past and causes those seeds to sprout in this life. Like attracts like. These patterns then aid the individual by bestowing clarity of mind and a life in which *yoga* can be performed and truth sought. In the practice of *yoga*, the negative seed *karmas* can actually be burned up without ever having to be lived through. ¶Conversely, *adharma*—wrong thought, word and deed—siphons the results of past misdeeds, like attracting like. These seed *karmas* begin to bear bitter fruit, resulting in a miserable life and state of mind. The individual is immersed in confusion, wrong patterns of thought and is, of course, in no position to practice *yoga*, follow *dharma* or realize truth. He is simply immersed in *saṁsāra*. ¶In His own way, Śiva is bringing you into realization, into knowledge of yourself and of Him. He has given you the world of experience. Study your experience. Learn from your experience. If it is painful, that is also good. In the fires of experience, which are both pain and pleasure, you are being purified. It is Śiva's duty to bring you forward into the fullness of yourself. In doing so, you must go through much pain, through much joy. Both register on the scale as the same intensity of emotion. It is what caused it that makes one more pleasurable than another. Don't be afraid of experience, and don't be afraid to go through your *karma*. Go through it with courage. ¶Of course, you can minimize reactions to unhappy experiences by performing selfless service, which will create good *karma*. This is what you have to do to progress your spiritual life. *Moksha*—enlightenment and liberation from rebirth—is the ultimate goal of all souls. The exit is through the crown *chakra*. Go forward without fear.

Saturday
LESSON 265
Three Kinds Of Karma

Karma is threefold: *sañchita, prārabdha* and *kriyamāna. Sañchita karma* means "accumulated actions." It is the sum of all *karmas* of this life and our past lives. *Prārabdha karma* means "actions begun; set in motion." It is that portion of *sañchita karma* that is bearing fruit and shaping the events and conditions of the current life, including the nature of our bodies, personal tendencies and associations. *Kriyamāna karma* means "actions being made." It is the *karma* we create and add to *sañchita* in this life by our thoughts, words and actions, or in the inner worlds between lives. While some *kriyamāna karmas* bear fruit in the current life, others are stored for future births. Each of these three types can be divided into two categories: *ārabdha* ("begun, undertaken;" *karma* that is "sprouting"), and *anārabdha* ("not commenced; dormant"), or "seed *karma.*" ¶In a famed analogy, *karma* is compared to rice in its various stages. *Sañchita karma,* the residue of one's total accumulated actions, is likened to rice that has been harvested and stored in a granary. From the stored rice, a small portion has been removed, husked and readied for cooking and eating. This is *prārabdha karma,* past actions that are shaping the events of the present. Meanwhile, new rice, mainly from the most recent harvest of *prārabdha karma,* is being planted that will yield a future crop and be added to the store of rice. This is *kriyamāna karma,* the consequences of current actions. ¶*Prārabdha karma* determines the time of birth, which dictates one's astrology, which in turn delineates the individual life pattern by influencing the release of these *karmas.* Three factors are fundamental: the nature of one's birth, the length of life and the nature of experiential patterns. Dormant *sañchita karma,* while not directly being acted upon, is a weighty and compelling force of potential energy, be it benign or gross, good or bad, slothful or inspirational. It is this dormant *karma* that explains why two people born at the same moment, and who thus have the same astrology, differ in their talents and tendencies. It is this held-back force of *sañchita karma* that the *yogī* seeks to burn out with his *kuṇḍalinī* flame, to disempower it within the *karmic* reservoir of *ānandamaya kośa,* the soul body. ¶Astrologers who understand *karma* well emphasize that one can influence his or her dormant *sañchita karma.* Further, one does have power over *karmas* being made, *kriyamāna.* But *karmas* set in motion, *prārabdha,* are binding. They form the gridwork of life and must be lived through. Facing them positively is the key to their resolution. Fighting them through resentment and the release of other negative emotions only creates more unseemly *sañchita karma* for the future. The law is: we must accept and bear our *karma* cheerfully.

Sunday
LESSON 266
Intricacies Of the Law

On resolving *karma,* our friend Tiru M. Arunachalam wrote, "Nonattachment to the fruits of action stops *kriyamāna* from accumulating. *Prārabdha* is experienced and ceases with this birth; and *sañchita* is burnt away by the *dīkshā* of the *guru.*" It is the *satguru* who holds the power to mitigate and redirect a person's *karma.* The *guru* always sees the good in a person and encourages that goodness. With his authority, this automatically mitigates the detrimental areas the person could fall into because of his past actions. ¶Naturally, *karma* also determines the circumstance of one's life in the Antarloka after death. The infallible law of *karma* continues for disembodied souls between births, though many *karmas* can only be fulfilled in physical incarnation. Thus, Earth is called Karma-kshetra, "arena of *karma.*" *Karma* is also binding, to varying degrees, for those who have attained *moksha* and are living in the Antarloka and for those who have attained residency in the Śivaloka until *viśvagrāsa,* ultimate merger in the Primal Soul, Parameśvara. ¶*Prārabdha karmas* fructify in a given lifetime, fortified by the ripe *karmas* that are experienced in the in-between. Some of what is learned in the Antarloka is used in the next birth, to know how to best face the *prārabdha karmas* as they manifest. Some of what is learned will only be used in future births. *Karma* made in the Antarloka, positive or negative, is added into the big *sañchita* basket; and, of course, some of it also bears fruit. ¶All *karmas* are either ripe or unripe, ready or unready. Of the *prārabdha karmas* that one is born with, some are immediately released, and others will be ready only in later years of life. This is why if a person commits suicide, the repercussions are drastic, because he has blocked and interrupted the fulfillment of the *prārabdha karmas* that he had set about to consume in this birth. Then it is like a string hopper in the inner worlds that must be unraveled when he arrives there unexpectedly. ¶The *prārabdha karmas,* as they ripen, open up as you go on through life. Similarly, of the *kriyamāna karmas* created, some are ripe and some are not ripe. Some immediately bear fruit and are consumed in this life. Others go to seed and enter the big *sañchita karma* bank to be experienced in future births as *prārabdha karma.* Whatever is not experienced and resolved in the current life is taken by you to the inner world as a basket of seeds. A mystical person who knows he is going to incarnate again can work on these seeds consciously.

Hiṁsā na Kartavyā

हिंस न कर्तव्या

To Do No Harm

Peace be to earth and to airy spaces! Peace be to heaven, peace to the waters, peace to the plants and peace to the trees! May all the Gods grant to me peace! By this invocation of peace may peace be diffused! By this invocation of peace may peace bring peace! With this peace the dreadful I now appease, with this peace the cruel I now appease. With this peace all evil I now appease, so that peace may prevail, happiness prevail! May everything for us be peaceful!

Atharva Veda 19.9.14. VE, P. 306

Monday
LESSON 267
The Hindu Way: To Do No Harm

Hindu wisdom, which inspires humans to live the ideals of compassion and nonviolence, is captured in one word, *ahiṁsā.* In Sanskrit *hiṁsā* is doing harm or causing injury. The "a" placed before the word negates it. Very simply, *ahiṁsā* is abstaining from causing harm or injury. It is gentleness and noninjury, whether physical, mental or emotional. It is good to know that nonviolence speaks only to the most extreme forms of forceful wrongdoing, while *ahiṁsā* goes much deeper to prohibit even the subtle abuse and the simple hurt. ¶In his commentary on the *Yoga Sūtras,* Sage Vyasa defines *ahiṁsā* as "the absence of injuriousness *(anabhidroha)* toward all living beings *(sarvabhuta)* in all respects *(sarvatha)* and for all times *(sarvada).*" He noted that a person who draws near one engaged in the true practice of *ahiṁsā* would be freed from all enmity. Similarly, Patanjali (*ca* 200 BCE) regards *ahiṁsā* as the *yogī's mahāvrata,* the great vow and foremost spiritual discipline, which those seeking Truth must follow strictly and without fail. This was not meant merely to condemn killing, but extended to harm caused by one's thoughts, words and deeds of all kinds—including injury to the natural environment. Even the intent to injure, even violence committed in a dream, is a violation of the principle of *ahiṁsā.* ¶Every belief creates certain attitudes. Those attitudes govern all of our actions. Man's actions can thus be traced to his inmost beliefs about himself and about the world around him. If those beliefs are erroneous, his actions will not be in tune with the universal *dharma.* For instance, the belief in the existence of an all-pervasive Divinity throughout the universe creates an attitude of reverence, benevolence and compassion for all animate and inanimate beings. The natural consequence of this belief is *ahiṁsā,* nonhurtfulness. The belief in the duality of heaven and hell, the light forces and the dark forces, creates the attitude that we must be on our guard, and that we are justified in inflicting injury, physically and emotionally, on others whom we judge to be bad, pagan or unworthy for other reasons. Such thinking leads to rationalizing so-called righteous wars and conflicts. We can sum this up from the Hindu, Buddhist and Jain traditions: *ahiṁsā* is higher consciousness, and *hiṁsā,* hurtfulness, is lower consciousness. ¶Devout Hindus oppose killing for several reasons. Belief in *karma* and reincar-

---

A hunter has stalked a few wild deer in the forest and is preparing to kill them for sport. His friend grabs the rifle, urging him to honor the life in these beautiful animals and to desist from the hunt, letting the deer live in peace.

nation are strong forces at work in the Hindu mind. They full well know that any thought, feeling or action sent out from themself to another will return to them through yet another in equal or amplified intensity. What we have done to others will be done to us, if not in this life then in another. The Hindu is thoroughly convinced that violence which he commits will return to him by a cosmic process that is unerring. Two thousand years ago South India's weaver saint Tiruvalluvar said it so simply, "All suffering recoils on the wrongdoer himself. Thus, those desiring not to suffer refrain from causing others pain" (*Tirukural* 320). A similar view can be found in the Jain *Acharāṅga Sūtra*: "To do harm to others is to do harm to oneself. You are he whom you intend to kill. You are he whom you intend to dominate. We corrupt ourselves as soon as we intend to corrupt others. We kill ourselves as soon as we intend to kill others."

Tuesday
LESSON 268
From Violence To Nonviolence

So many today are wondering how we might move from violence to nonviolence, how mankind might transform itself from approval of killing to opposition to it. There are millions of Hindus who are born into the Hindu religion because their parents and forefathers profess that faith, but who are not educated in the beliefs that will produce proper attitudes. Because they are Hindus, their desire to pursue the depth of their religion wells up often in later life. Through soul-searching, self-examination and psychological overhaul—not without a lot of mental pain attached—the old beliefs are replaced with new ones. A conversion has taken place within the subconscious mind. The computer program within the *mūlādhāra chakra*, which contains the memories of the deepest past, has been updated. Through this process, the meat-eater becomes a vegetarian, a hurtful person becomes kindly, *hiṁsā* becomes *ahiṁsā*. ¶The Hindu knows that at this time on this planet those of the lower nature, unevolved people, are society's antagonists. Being unevolved, they are of the lower nature, instinctive, self-assertive, confused, possessive and protective of their immediate environment. Others are their enemies. They are jealous, angry, fearful. Many take sport in killing for the sake of killing, thieving for the sake of theft, even if they do not need or use the spoils. This is the lower nature, and it is equally distributed among the peoples of the world, in every nation, society and neighborhood. Those of the higher nature—ten, fifteen or twenty percent of the population—live in protective environments. Their occupation is research, memory, education, which is reason; moving the world's goods here and there, which is will. Those of yet an even higher nature delve into the mysteries of the universe, and others work for universal peace and love on Earth, as groups and individuals. The Hindu knows that those of the lower nature will slowly, eventually, over an experiential period of time, come into the higher nature, and that those of the higher nature, who have worked so hard to get there, will avoid the lower nature and not allow themselves to be caught up in it again. Hindus believe in the progress of humanity, from an old age into a new age, from darkness into a consciousness of divine light. ¶Humans are essentially instinctive, intellectual and superconscious, or soul, persons. The instinctive nature is based on good and bad, mine and yours, up and down, pairs of opposites. The soul nature is based on oneness, humility, peace, compassion, love, helpfulness. The intellectual nature is based on trying to figure out both of these two. It juggles knowledge from the lower nature to the higher nature and from the higher nature to the lower nature. It works out formulas, finds solutions and processes knowledge. The key is *yoga*, yoking the energies of the soul with the energies of the physical body (the instinctive nature) and yoking the energies of the soul with the energies of the mind (the intellectual nature). Then, simply, one becomes consciously conscious in the soul. This is an experience to be experienced, and for the Hindu it is personal experience of God, which is essential for liberation. The Hindu strives to be consciously conscious of his soul. When those soulful qualities are unfolded, he is filled with a divine love and would not hurt a flea if he could help it. The *Yajur Veda* exclaims, "May all beings regard me with friendly eyes! May I look upon all creatures with friendly eyes! With a friend's eye may we regard each other!" (36.18. VE, P. 342)

Wednesday
LESSON 269
Peace Begins In the Home

What's the best way to teach peace to the world? The best way is to first teach families to be peaceful within their own home, to settle all arguments and contention before they sleep at night, even if they stay up for three days, so the children can see that peace can be attained and then maintained through the use of intelligence. Humans do not have horns or claws; nor do they have sharp teeth. Their weapon is their intelligence. Children must be taught through the example of parents and by learning the undeniable facts of life, the basic tenets—that an all-pervasive force holds this universe together, that we create with this force every minute, every hour, every day, and because time is a cycle, what we create comes back to us. Therefore, because we create in a physical universe while in a physical body, we must return to a physical body, in a new life after death, to face up to our creations, good, bad or mixed. Once they learn this, they are winners. It is up to the parents to create the peacemakers of the future. It is always up to the parents. And remember, we teach children in only one way—by our own example. ¶Parents must teach children to appreciate those who are different, those who believe differently; teach them the openness that they need to live in a pluralistic world where others have their unique ways, their life and culture; teach them the value of human diversity and the narrow-mindedness of a provincial outlook; give them the tools to live in a world of differences without feeling threatened, without forcing their ways or their will on others; teach them that it never helps to hurt another of our brothers or sisters. The *Atharva Veda* intones: "Peace be to the Earth and to airy spaces! Peace be to heaven, peace to the waters, peace to the plants and peace to the trees! May all Gods grant to me peace! By this invocation of peace may peace be diffused" (19.9.14. VE, P. 306). ¶When the injustice of killing happens no more, then and only then will the next *yuga* or human epoch commence in its fullness. The far-seeing *ṛishis* of our religion have predicted what we see today, so today is no worry to us. But the Hindu is bound by his intelligence to pass along to the next generation methods of improvement, pointing out the errors made in the past and outlining better directions for the future. A Hindu's method of saving the world is lifting up each individual within it and putting an end to the war in the home between parent and parent on the one hand, and parents and their offspring on the other. Ending the war in the home is the solution to ending the conflict in surrounding communities and, finally, wars between nations. A home where *ahiṁsā* abides is truly a home.

Thursday
LESSON 270
Finding Personal Peace

An individual can find total peace within himself, not through meditation alone—though peaceful actions must follow introspection—not through drugs, not through psychology or psychiatry, but through control. Peace is the natural state of the mind. It is there, inside, to be discovered in meditation and then radiated out to others. How do we bring individuals to this point? Let them go for one year without experiencing confusion in their thinking, covetousness of another's goods, even the urge to be hurtful to solve a problem, and not experiencing fear, anger or jealousy. After that year, they will be very peaceful persons. This is because of the soul knowledge they will have gained in overcoming these base instinctive forces, which will release their consciousness to the natural peace of the higher mind. ¶If the educational system promotes it in every community, the greatest potential for peace will be achieved. The educational system is controlled by the adults, so they have to come to terms with the fact that they must not be hurtful, physically, mentally or emotionally, and they must accept the basic principles of the Sanātana Dharma: all-pervasive energy, cause and effect, and coming back in a physical birth until all scores are settled. Once the adults accomplish this, these basic principles of life will naturally be passed on to the next generation. ¶But the fact is that even though mature souls may have achieved peace, others are coming up through the instinctive nature. In a complete humanity, there are always those of higher consciousness and those of lower consciousness. At this time on the planet it is the intrinsic duty of higher-consciousness people to be more self-assertive, let their voices be heard and take up the banner in a heroic way, join committees, enter government, while at the same time maintaining the peace within their own home and holding a benign reverence for all living beings. As the vibration of planet Earth changes, the mood of the people will change. ¶*Ahiṁsā* begins in the home, in the bedroom, in the kitchen, in the garden, in the living room. When *hiṁsā,* harmfulness, arises in the home, it must be settled before sleep, or else those *vṛittis,* those waves of the mind, which were disturbed by the creation of the situation will go to seed, to erupt at a later time in life. We cannot expect the children to control themselves if the parents do not control themselves. Those who attain a personal peace by controlling their instinctive nature become the spiritual leaders of human society. People who do become these leaders retroactively control the masses because of their spirit, their soul force—not because of their mind force, their cleverness, their deceptions, their political power, their money or contacts. They are the people in the higher consciousness who control lower consciousness by lifting up the masses, as parents are supposed to uplift their children. ¶Achieving a nonviolent world would simply mean that all individuals have to somehow or other reconcile their differences enough that the stress those differences produce can no longer take over their mind, body and emotions, causing them to perform injurious acts. Again, this would begin in the home. Peaceful homes breed gentle people. Gentle people follow *ahiṁsā.* Furthermore, the belief structure of each individual must allow for the acceptance of the eternal truths—returning to flesh to reabsorb back the *karmic* energies released in a previous life, and of course, the belief in the existence of an all-pervading power. As long as our beliefs are dualistic, we will continue to generate antagonism, and that will erupt here and there in violence. ¶At an international and national level, we must become more tolerant. Religious leaders and their congregations need to learn and teach tolerance for everyone and everything, and for other faiths. First this must be taught to the religious leaders themselves, the ministers, rabbis, imams, *ṛishis, swāmīs, āchāryas, bhikkus, sants* and priests. Tolerance and intolerance are basic attitudes found in our belief systems. These are things that one can learn. In our various nations, in the United Nations and other world organizations we can promote laws which recognize and take action against crimes of violence. The world must as a body come to the conclusion that such crimes are totally unacceptable. To abhor violence is a state of higher consciousness.

Saturday
LESSON 272
The Evolution Of Humanness

What is it that causes someone who was previously violent to become nonviolent? It is a matter of realizing what life is really all about and how harming others violates our own inner being. When an injurious act is committed, it makes a mark deep within the mind of the violator. Those individuals who become penitent bring higher energies into themselves, and these energies slowly heal this mark. But there is more to it than this. Certain kinds of spiritual therapy must go along with the penitent mood for a total healing to occur, which would be absolution. This therapy is finding a way to pay back society for the harm caused in that act of violence. It may be working as a nurse's aid or as a volunteer to help in the healing of people who have been victimized by the violent acts of others. The modern laws of community service are good, but for a total healing and change of heart, the service to the community should be directly related to the actual crime the person committed. Finally, over a long period of time, if the matter is totally resolved in the mind of the person and those who know him, then he would be as much a nonviolent person as he was previously a violent person. ¶Personal revelations or realizations can also bring about a transformation. One example that people are familiar with is the experience of astronauts who have orbited Earth. From their cosmic perspective they saw no borders, no divisions, only a one small planet, and this has tended to make them peacemakers. Their journey in space has been called "the overview effect" and would indeed be a revelation of higher consciousness. In deep states of consciousness such visions also happen and do change peoples' lives. But contemplative experiences come, for the most part, to contemplative people. And if we are referring to meditation and *yogic* practices here, they should not be performed by angry people, jealous people, confused people, lest the uplifted energies plummet and intensify the anger and other aspects of the lower nature. The better way would be for the angry, violent person to become religious and consistently do small religious acts, for these despicables will get their solace through remorse, repentance, reconciliation and finally absolution. Even the Gods will not, unless invoked, interfere and penetrate the sunken depths in which they live, in the *chakras* below the *mūlādhāra*, in the lower part of the body, down to the feet, *chakras* which spin counterclockwise. ¶Many people do have life-transforming mystical experiences, such as a soldier on a battlefield or someone who nearly dies. These experiences can also change our view of the universe. But transforming experiences generally come to really nice people, people endowed with love and trust. Maybe they are not too intelligent and get drawn into situations where they are overtaken by a fit of temper. But their remorse is immediate. A contrite or penitent reaction to hurting others is the sign of a higher-consciousness person. Maybe the *karma* the person caused is heavy, but his soul goes to work on the situation, and the healing process starts within his mind. Possibly the intensity of the violent mishap, which we might say is an uncontrolled mishap, itself creates a deep remorse which catalyzes the big awakening into higher consciousness. ¶We Hindus would look at that as a grace from the *guru* or a boon from the Gods, coming unbidden in the form of an inner revelation, bringing with it more permanent contact with inner-plane beings. This inner contact with greater beings, and the revelation they bestow, shortens the time sequence of the act and the absolution, which in some cases might take years, if someone was penitent, seeking atonement and absolution.

Saturday
LESSON 272
The Evolution Of Humanness

Ahiṁsā, nonhurtfulness, is the essence of *dharma,* and the *mūlādhāra chakra* sets the pattern of *dharma.* The *mūlādhāra chakra* is a very interesting *chakra,* because it is the base center of energy and consciousness, and consciousness is energy, ever creating, preserving and absorbing. *Karma* is the self-perpetuating principle of cause and effect, shaping our experiences as a result of how we use our energies, mentally, verbally or physically. So, once we narrow down the individual awareness from freedom without responsibility, which is the lower nature, into the consciousness of freedom with responsibility, which is the higher nature, the individual awareness, or consciousness, must pass through the portals of the *mūlādhāra chakra* and rest comfortably within the energies of its four petals. Four petals, of course, form a square. Three dimensionally, two squares put together with a space between can well be defined as a box. This box is defined as *dharma.* ¶Briefly, at this point on the path to enlightenment we put our cumulative *karmas* into a box called *dharma.* Once encased within *dharma,* the various *karmas* may fight each other. As the individual progresses on the path, the box lightens and rises. The box of *dharma* is the base from which the aspirant must live at this point. Strictly contained, he may rise through the hole in the top of the box in consciousness, or open a hole in the bottom of the box and seek freedom without responsibility in the world of darkness. To seek freedom in the *chakras* above is the San Mārga. To seal off the hole at the bottom of the box is his *sādhana,* penitent *tapas, japa, bhakti* and Sivathondu, all of which is eloquently explained in *Merging with Śiva.* ¶Who holds the lid on the box? Community, community pressures, both religious and secular. There are certain things you can do and certain things you can't do. The stronger *ahiṁsā* becomes at the family level, the more subtle it gets, and the violence gets more subtle, too. A careless word can cut the heart of someone you love, but someone not loved may not be wounded by anything less sharp than a knife. ¶Someone asks, "I am trying to seal off the *chakras* below the *mūlādhāra,* but whenever a trying situation comes up, the feelings of resentment and retaliation are paramount. What can I do?" When the feelings that come up amplify resentment, squelch reason and paralyze memory, we must assume that the box of *dharma* is empty and does not contain the cumulative *sukarmas* and *kukarmas* of this and past lives (the *kriyamāna and prārabdha karmas),* and that he is not bound by *dharma* at all, or that it has no influence in guiding his future *karmas.* There are no excuses on this path. This means that the person has really not yet come to Lord Gaṇeśa's feet. Therefore, *vrata*—he must take a vow and live up to it. ¶*Ahiṁsā* is a *vrata.* Rishi Patanjali called it the *mahāvrata,* or great oath. When it is not lived up to, there are consequences. Remorse must be felt, apologies made, penance endured and reconciliation accomplished. The ego experiences embarrassment. All this and more occurs, depending on the individual's sincerity, steadfastness and resolve never to reenter the lower nature of *hiṁsā,* hurtfulness, again.

Yuddhaḥ Śāntiścha
युद्धः शान्तिश्च

War and Peace

Let us have concord with our own people, and concord with people who are strangers to us; Aśvins, create between us and the strangers a unity of hearts. May we unite in our midst, unite in our purposes, and not fight against the divine spirit within us. Let not the battle-cry rise amidst many slain, nor the arrows of the War God fall with the break of day.

Atharva Veda 7.52.1-2. HV, P. 205

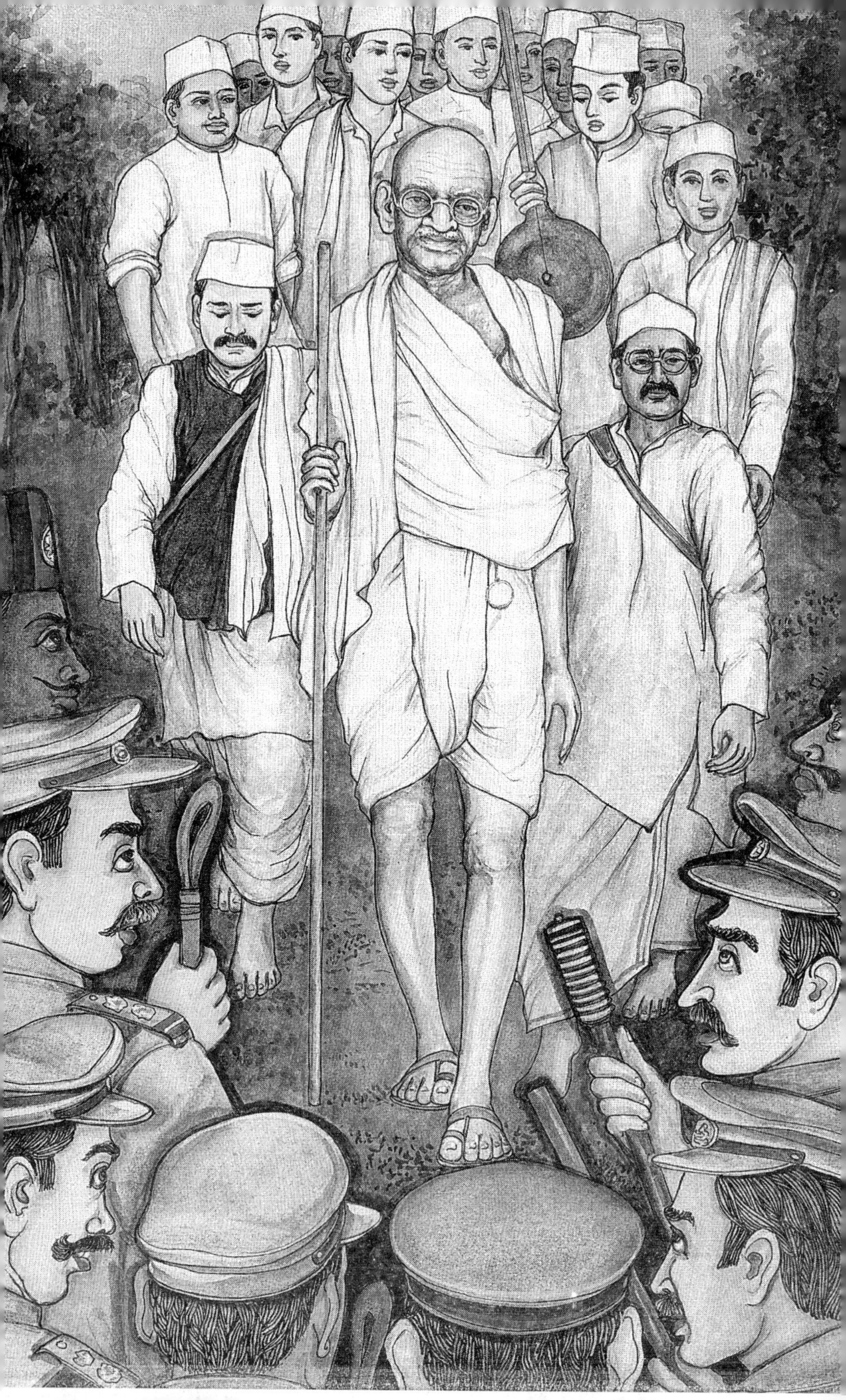

Monday
LESSON 274
Teaching of Life's Sanctity

Nonviolence has long been central to the religious traditions of India—especially Hinduism, Buddhism and Jainism. Religion in India has consistently upheld the sanctity of life, whether human, animal or, in the case of the Jains, elemental. There developed early in India an unparalleled concern for harmony among different life forms, and this led to a common ethos based on noninjuriousness and a minimal consumption of natural resources, in other words to compassion and simplicity. If *Homo sapiens* is to survive his present predicament, he will have to rediscover these two primary ethical virtues. ¶In order to understand the pervasive practice of nonviolence in Hinduism, one must investigate the meaning of life. Why is life sacred? For India's ancient thinkers, life is seen as the very stuff of the Divine, an emanation of the Source and part of a cosmic continuum. The nature of this continuum varies in Hindu thought. Some hold that the individual evolves up through life forms, taking more and more advanced incarnations which culminate in human life. Others believe that according to one's *karma* and *saṁskāras*, the process can even be reversed, that is, one can achieve a "lower" birth. Even those Indians who do not believe in reincarnation of an individual still hold that all that exists abides in the Divine. They further hold that each life form—even water and trees—possesses consciousness and energy. Whether the belief is that the life force of animals can evolve into human status, or that the opposite can also take place, or simply that all things enjoy their own consciousness, the result is the same—a reverence for life. ¶The human mind is exactly like a computer. Programs that go in are the beliefs. Their performance is the attitude, and the knowledge or the impetus that passes through both determines the output or the action. Children will learn the basic attitudes from their mothers and fathers by absorbing the beliefs that their mothers and fathers have placed into their subconscious mind, even prenatally. This is the first stage of writing the code, as a programmer would do in creating a new application. Later the child learns through observation, through seeing what the parents do and how they solve their problems, either reverently in the shrine room or hurtfully through arguments, contention, back-biting and getting one's way through emotional blackmail. By the age of six, the program is fin-

Mahatma Gandhi is shown on his famed Salt March, walking with supporters to a distant beach where he plans to collect sea salt in defiance of British tax laws. He is blocked by the British controlled Indian army, which intends to arrest and imprison him and the marchers.

ished, application complete, and beta testing begins. Children today face the world at this early age. Need we say more? Look at your own families. ¶Talk about peaceful means of dealing with problems, not allowing even your words to promote injury and harm. Let your words bring peace into others' lives and hearts. Work on your own consciousness. Purify yourself so that you are free from anger, free from hatred, free from wanting anyone to suffer, either at your own hand or in any other manner. Don't buy endangered plants, animals or products from exploited species, such as furs, ivory, reptile skin and tortoise shell. Volunteer your time to help groups who are sincerely working for a peaceful world. Learn more about other cultures and philosophies so your appreciation of them is genuine and deep. Work to strengthen your community and the people near you. Reduce stress in your life. Be joyful. Do all this and you will do much to bring peace and tranquility to your part of the world. This is what Mahatma Gandhi did, and look what a difference he made. ¶One person who lives *ahiṁsā* truly can be an instrument of peace for many. And you can make a difference, too, by affirming within yourself the vow not to injure others either physically, mentally or emotionally. Remember this one thing: peace and the choice to live the ideal of noninjury are in your own hands. ¶There is no longer a rural community or a national community. It is an international community. That change was well rooted in the planet a decade ago. When the Vietnam War stopped—the last big war of the twentieth century—that marked the beginning of the new era. People started using their minds to solve problems, and using their weaponry only for defensive measures.

Tuesday
LESSON 275
Peace and Righteous War

In Gandhian philosophy *ahiṁsā* means nonviolent action which leads to passive resistance in order to put a point across. Basically, he taught, don't hit your opponent over the head. If he tells you to do something, stall and don't obey and don't do it and frustrate him into submission. And yet, on the other hand, when a gang of tribals came in and raped the women in a village, Gandhi said there should not have been a man left alive in the village. They should have stood up for the village and protected it with their lives. ¶So, to me, that means if an intruder breaks into your house to rape the women or steal things, you have the right, even the duty, to defend your own, but you don't have the right to torture him. *Ahiṁsā* needs to be properly understood, in moderation. *Ahiṁsā* in the Jain religion has been taken to extremes. To explain nonviolence, you have to explain what violence is, as opposed to protecting yourself. Is it violent to own a dog who would put his teeth to the throat of a vicious intruder? I don't think it is. If nonviolence is to be something that the world is going to respect, we have to define it clearly and make it meaningful. ¶Not all of Earth's one billion Hindus are living in a perfect state of *ahiṁsā* all of the time. Sometimes conditions at hand may force a situation, a regrettable exception, where violence or killing seems to be necessary. Hindus, like other human beings, unfortunately do kill people. In self-defense or in order to protect his family or his village, the Hindu may have to hurt an intruder. Even then he would harbor no hatred in his heart. Hindus should never instigate an intrusion or instigate a death; nor seek revenge, nor plot retaliation for injuries received. They have their courts of justice, punishment for crimes and agencies for defending against the aggressor or the intruder. Before any personal use of force, so to speak, all other avenues of persuasion and intelligence would be looked into, as Hindus believe that intelligence is their best weapon. In following *dharma*, the only rigid rule is wisdom. My *satguru*, Siva Yogaswami, said, "It is a sin to kill the tiger in the jungle. But if he comes into the village, it may become your duty." A devout Hindu would give warnings to scare the tiger or would try to capture the tiger without injury. Probably it would be the most unreligious person in the village who would come forward to kill the tiger. ¶Many groups on the planet today advocate killing and violence and war for a righteous cause. They would not agree with the idea that violence, *hiṁsā*, is necessarily of the lower nature. But a righteous cause is only a matter of opinion, and going to war affects the lives of a great many innocent people. It's a big *karmic* responsibility. Combat through war, righteous or not, is lower consciousness. Religious values are left aside, to be picked up and continued when the war is over, or in the next life or the one after that. It is said that in ancient India meat would be fed to the soldiers during military campaigns, especially before combat, to bring them into lower consciousness so that they would forget their religious values. Most higher consciousness people will not fight even if their lives depend on it. They are conscientious objectors, and there have been many in every country who have been imprisoned or killed because they would not take up arms against their brother and sister humans. This is the strictest expression of Hinduism's law of *ahiṁsā*.

Wednesday
LESSON 276
Justification For Conflict

One of the most famous of Hindu writings, the *Bhagavad Gītā*, is often taken as Divine sanction for violence. It basically says that for the *kshatriya*, or soldier, war is *dharma*. Lord Kṛishṇa orders Arjuna to fight and do his *kshatriya dharma* in spite of his doubts and fears that what he is about to do is wrong, despite his dread of killing his own kinsmen. Arjuna says, "If they whose minds are depraved by the lust of power see no sin in the extirpation of their race, no crime in the murder of their friends, is that a reason why we should not resolve to turn away from such a crime—we who abhor the sin of extirpating our own kindred? On the destruction of a tribe the ancient virtue of the tribe and family is lost; with the loss of virtue, vice and impiety overwhelm the whole of a race. ...Woe is me! What a great crime are we prepared to commit! Alas that from the desire for sovereignty and pleasure we stand here ready to slay our own kin! I would rather patiently suffer that the sons of Dhritarashṭra, with their weapons in their hands, should come upon me and, unopposed, kill me unresisting in the field." ¶Kṛishṇa gradually convinces Arjuna to fight, beginning with the following argument. "Death is certain to all things which are born, and rebirth to all mortals; wherefore it doth not behoove thee to grieve about the inevitable. ...This spirit can never be destroyed in the mortal frame which it inhabiteth, hence it is unworthy for thee to be troubled for all these mortals. ...Thine enemies will speak of thee in words which are unworthy to be spoken, deprecating thy courage and abilities; what can be more dreadful than this! If thou art slain, thou shalt attain heaven; if victorious, the world shall be thy reward; wherefore, son of Kunti, arise with determination fixed for the battle. Make pleasure and pain, gain and loss, victory and defeat, the same to thee, and then prepare for battle, for thus and thus alone shalt thou in action still be free from sin" (from Chapter 1, Recension by W. Q. Judge, Theosophical University Press). ¶Hindus for a long time have taken this text as justification for war and conflicts of all kinds, including street riots and anarchy. It is indeed unfortunate that this particular composition has been championed to represent Hinduism rather than the four *Vedas*. At the turn of the twentieth century, the *Bhagavad Gītā* was not yet a popular book in America and Europe, but the *Upanishads* and *Vedas* were. When I was growing up in Hinduism, at about fifteen years of age, the *Gītā* was being slowly introduced in America and became an embarrassment in metaphysical circles throughout the country, as something to explain away.

"How could a religion based on *ahiṁsā* and such high ideals promote as a major scripture a story based on ruthless internecine war and violence?" Arjuna could be considered history's first conscientious objector. ¶Mystical seers, both Hindus and Western teachers, at that time, in an attempt to justify the *Gītā* as scripture, explained that Kṛishṇa represented Arjuna's higher self, and Arjuna himself was his lower self, or the external ego. Kṛishṇa encouraged Arjuna to kill out attachments to family, friends and foes, to become a *yogī* and realize Parabrahman. Teachers attempted to satisfy the minds of their followers that, in fact, the *Bhagavad Gītā* was an allegory of man's struggle within himself toward the highest realizations. Unconvincingly, contemporary *swāmīs* and astute commentators tried to justify God Kṛishṇa's urging his devotee to kill his friends, his relatives and his *guru*, that all would be well in the end because the soul never dies. I was never satisfied with this and found no alternative but to reject the book altogether, despite its many lofty chapters. I agree fully with those awakened Indian *swāmīs* who have called it *kolai nul*, the "book of carnage," a book that gives divine sanction to violence. ¶The *Bhagavad Gītā* was also known at that time as a historical poem, not a divinely revealed scripture at all. It is *smṛiti*, specifically Itihāsa, meaning a man-made history, a poem excerpted from the *Mahābhārata* epic. But all that aside, no matter how it is interpreted, whether it is revered by millions of Hindus or not, let us not be mistaken that the *Bhagavad Gītā* gives permission for violence. The *Mahābhārata* itself says, "*Ahiṁsā* is the highest *dharma.* It is the highest purification. It is also the highest truth from which all *dharma* proceeds" (18.1125.25). An eye for an eye and a tooth for a tooth is definitely not a part of true Hindu doctrine.

Thursday
LESSON 277
No Sanction For Terrorism

In every country there is the army, the navy, air force, police, the protectors of the country, the collective force of citizens that keep a country a country. This is *dharma.* In protection of family and nation, in armies and police forces which give security, it is indeed *dharmic* for *kshatriyas* to do their lawful duty, to use necessary force, even lethal force. But for this collective force of protectors, of peacemakers, of peacekeepers—which includes the law courts and the central administrative authorities who oversee the courts, the armies, the navies, the air force—would the priests be able to function? Would the businessmen be able to acquire and sell their goods? Would the farmers be able to plant their crops and harvest them? Could the children play fearlessly in the streets and countryside? No. The answer is obvious. ¶Those who take law into their own hands in the name of *dharma*, citing their case upon the *Mahābhārata*, are none but the lawbreakers, anarchists, the arsonists, the terrorists. The *Mahābhārata* gives no permission for anarchy. The *Mahābhārata* gives no permission for terrorism. The *Mahābhārata* gives no permission for looting and diluting the morals of society through prostitution, running drugs and the selling and buying of illegal arms. The Pāṇḍavas, the heroes of this ancient epic, were not rabble rousers. They were not inciting riots. Nor were they participating in extortion to run their war. Nor were they participating in the sale of drugs to finance their war. Nor were they participating in prostitution to win their war. Nor were they participating in enlisting women to help them fight their war. Nor were they having children learn to snare their victims. ¶Yes, *dharma* does extend to protecting one's country. But does it extend to taking a country from another, or to stealing lands? Were the Pāṇḍavas trying to do this? No, of course not. They were only protecting the status quo to remain sovereign over their kingdom. Let us not presume to take the *Mahābhārata* and *Rāmāyaṇa* as permission to do whatever one wants to do, for any cause whatsoever. Simply because it is said in certain Hindu texts that Kṛishṇa lied, stole some butter and dallied with the maidens does not give permission to the ordinary person to lie anytime he wants to, steal anytime he wants to or be promiscuous anytime he wants to and perhaps make all this a way of life. This definitely is not *dharma*. It is lawlessness, blatant lawlessness. In the modern age, to create a nation or even a business enterprise upon the death of another, upon lands confiscated, stolen, illegally acquired, usurped from another's realm, is definitely not Hindu *dharma*, and this is not *Mahābhārata*.

Friday
LESSON 278
Two Kinds Of People

I have often been asked how it is that some people work for peace and others seem always to work for contention. There are two kinds of children or souls that are born on this planet and are spoken of in our *Vedas* and other scriptures. Some come to Earth from up down and others from down up. This means that the children who come to Earth from up down come from a place in the inner world of higher consciousness, and the children who come to Earth from down up come to Earth from a place in the inner world of lower consciousness. We call the place of higher consciousness the Devaloka and the place of lower consciousness the Narakaloka. The Devaloka is a heaven world and the Narakaloka is not. ¶The Narakaloka exists wherever violence and hurtfulness take place, whether in the inner or outer world. We see such things in action on television. On the astral plane the terrible deeds perpetrated by Narakaloka people are much worse than in the physical world. Children who are born into Earth consciousness from the Narakaloka will not respond to meditation, *yoga* or any kind of quieting controls. They are strangers to self-discipline and enemies to their own parents. The parents of these offspring do have a challenge, to be sure, and are bound by the *karmic* implication of neglect to face up to it and make every effort to reform, lift up and thus enhance the learning of the young souls whose forces of deception, anger and resentment are stronger than their responsibilities to parents and society. Many such parents wisely direct their difficult offspring into agriculture, farming and nurturing nature, thus allowing them to blend with the forces of nature and rise into higher consciousness as they learn from the slow processes of nature. Some well-meaning but mistaken families demand of them a high education and suffer the results of their upbringing for a lifetime. ¶In contrast, children who are born into Earth consciousness from the Devaloka do respond to meditation, yoga and all kinds of methods of self-control. These are the gentle people. Self-control and personal advancement are the reasons they have taken a birth. There are ways to tell the difference between these two types of people. The mere fact that someone becomes penitent would show us that he is really a Devaloka person. This is because Narakaloka people don't become penitent. There is another way to tell the difference, and that is by looking into the eyes of the person. Narakaloka people generally have dull or sullen eyes, whereas Devaloka people have bright, clear, wide-open eyes. The former come from the world of darkness, the latter from the world of light. It is difficult to tell the difference at times, because the Narakaloka people are very cunning, and they will try to appear in the way they feel they should to measure up to your standards. They must be tested. ¶Peace will only come when the Narakaloka people are lifted up and made to obey the new standards in the world, standards which must be set by the Devaloka people. It is when the Devaloka people are in charge that peace will truly come; it can come in no other way. So, if the Devaloka people really desire to have peace on Earth, they should not be shy but take charge.

Saturday
LESSON 279
Curbing the Lower Natured

The problems of conflict reside within this low-minded group of people who only know retaliation as a way of life. To antagonize others is their sport. They must be curtained off and seen for what they are. Improvement has to come through their own self-effort. But they are always overly stimulated by doing so many mischievous acts and misdeeds that self-effort toward any kind of improvement is never even thought of. Yet, they must learn from their soul's evolution, and their own mistakes will be the teacher, for they are in the period of their evolution where they only learn from their own mistakes. ¶People of the lower nature cannot be made peaceful. They are not open to persuasion. They are sovereign in their own domain. There are many doors into lower consciousness, and if the Devaloka people get too involved with people of a lower nature, they may have violence awakened within them. Lower-consciousness people are always looking for recruits to bring into their world. This sounds like a sad story, but it is true nonetheless. You see it happening around you every day. ¶It would, of course, be wonderful to think that all people in this world are on the same level—and certainly they are in the deepest sense. But our sages and *ṛishis,* and wisdom itself, tell us that we cannot expect the same of everyone in this birth. By recognizing the differences in each soul's maturity, we also recognize the process of reincarnation, which gives us young souls and old souls. ¶People ask me from time to time, from the Hindu point of view, how to curtain off the lower-nature people. My answer is that people are curtained off from each other through their beliefs and the attitudes that they hold. Believing beyond a shadow of a doubt that a person is of the lower nature and is incorrigible in this life would create the attitude of avoiding his company, not antagonizing him, and this is the best protection. Societies all over the world are trying to control these people who have come to Earth from the world of darkness. This is one of the great concerns of all governments. ¶However, the problem is not only with people of the lower nature, it is also with people of the higher nature. They tend to be lazy. The more conscious a person is, the more responsible he or she should be. Therefore, the people of the higher nature should carry most of society's responsibility and not leave it to others. If the high-minded people really want peace, they have to all get to know each other and then join hands in love and trust and work together. In every religious organization on the Earth an emphasis to help people is put forward as a duty and a fulfillment. Many of the groups reach out for membership and bring people from the Narakaloka into their midst. It is not long before the lower-natured people turn their once-sincere and happy religious community into a devil's playground. They always begin by pitting people within the group against each other. If that is successful, then they pit their religious organization against another one. So, you can see that the Devaloka people have to join together, break down the barriers between themselves, work together, love and trust one another and protect their groups from this kind of intrusion. This is the first big doing. Once this is done, the rest will take care of itself quite naturally. ¶National and international peace movements are beneficial in that they keep the decision-making governments of the world aware of what the people want. They help the higher-consciousness people to become acquainted and to forge new principles for a global *dharma.*

Sunday
LESSON 280
Ahiṁsā in Business

I was once asked for my insights on applying *ahiṁsā* in the business world. *Ahiṁsā* in business is taught in a reverse way on American television: Titans, The West Wing, Dynasty, Falcon Crest, Dallas, LA Law—popular shows of our time. Their scriptwriters promoted *hiṁsā,* injuriousness, in business—"Save the Falcon Crest farm at any cost, save South Fork, save the corporation." Now the national news media reports attempts to save Microsoft, save the tobacco industry, save the hand gun manufacturers. The fight is on, and real-life court battles have taken the place of TV sitcoms which have long since been off the air. In both the TV and the real-life conflicts, whatever you do to your competitor is OK because it's only business. The plots weave in and out, with one scene of mental and emotional cruelty after another. ¶The Hindu business ethic is very clear. As the weaver Tiruvalluvar said, "Those businessmen will prosper whose business protects as their own the interests of others" (*Tirukural* 120). We should compete by having a better product and better methodologies of promoting and selling it, not by destroying our competitor's product and reputation. Character assassination is not part of *ahiṁsā*. It reaps bad benefits to the accusers. That is practiced by many today, even by Hindus who are off track in their perceptions of *ahiṁsā.* Hindus worldwide must know that American television is not the way business should be practiced. As some people teach you what you should do and other people teach you what you should not do, the popular television programs mentioned above clearly teach us what we should not do. The principles of *ahiṁsā* and other ethical teachings of Hinduism show us a better way. ¶Many corporations today are large, in fact larger than many small countries. Their management is like the deceptive, deceitful, arrogant, domineering king, or like the benevolent religious monarch, depending on whether there are people of lower consciousness or higher consciousness in charge. Cities, districts, provinces, counties, states and central governments all have many laws for ethical business practices, and none of those laws permit unfair trade, product assassination or inter-business competitive fights to the death. Each business is *dharmically* bound to serve the community, not take from the community like a vulture. When the stewardships of large corporations follow the law of the land and the principles of *ahiṁsā,* they put their energies into developing better products and better community service. When the leadership has a mind for corporate espionage, its energies are diverted, the products suffer and so does customer relations. The immediate profits in the short term might be gratifying, but in the long run, profits gained from wrong-doings are generally spent on wrong-doings. ¶*Ahiṁsā* always has the same consequences. And we know these benefits well. *Hiṁsā* always has the same consequences, too. It develops enemies, creates unseemly *karmas* which will surely return and affect the destiny of the future of the business enterprise. The perfect timing needed for success is defeated by inner reactions to the wrong-doings. A business enterprise which bases its strategies on hurtfulness cannot in good judgment hire employees who are in higher consciousness, lest they object to these tactics. Therefore, they attract employees who are of the same caliber as themselves, and they all practice *hiṁsā* among one another. Trickery, deceitfulness and deception are of the lower nature, products of the methodology of performing *hiṁsā*, hurtfulness, mentally and emotionally. The profits derived from *hiṁsā* policies are short-term and ill-spent. The profits derived from *ahiṁsā* policies are long-term and well spent.

Kshānti Śakti

क्षान्तिशक्ति

The Power Called Forgiveness

If we have injured space, the earth, or heaven, or if we have offended mother or father, from that may Agni, fire of the house, forgive us and guide us safely to the world of goodness.

Atharva Veda 6.120. VE, P. 636

Monday
LESSON 281
The Art of Forgiveness

The *Vedas* are full of verses which speak of the Divine within man, and therefore Hindu Dharma today implores us to let go of grudges, resentment and especially self-contempt. Most people today are working harder to correct the faults of others than they are their own. It is a thankless job. It truly is. Most are trying to recreate the relatively real world into being absolutely real. Another thankless job. The wise implore us to accept things as they are, to be happy and content at every point in time. They tell us: do not be discouraged in seeing the failings of others. Rather, let it help awaken your understanding of them as to where they are in consciousness and the suffering they must be going through. If others harm you in thought, word or deed, do not resent it. Rather, let it awaken compassion, kindness and forgiveness. Use it as a mirror to view your own frailties; then work diligently to bring your own thoughts, words and deeds into line with Hindu Dharma. ¶The secret is that we have to correct all matters within ourselves. We have to bear our *karmas*—the reactions to our actions—cheerfully. And what are the apparent injustices of life but the self-created reactions of our own past actions in this or a former life? The person of perfect understanding accepts all happenings in life as purposeful and good. We must be grateful to others for playing back to us our previous actions so that we can see our mistakes and experience the same feelings we must have caused in others. It is in this way that we are purified and trained not to commit the same *adharmic* acts again. ¶All the great ones have preached the art of forgiveness. First we must learn to forgive ourselves, to accept ourselves as we are and proceed with confidence. Many people live their whole lives immersed in guilt. It's a way of life passed on from generation to generation. It's like a passive fear, different from a threatening fear. Certain religions push people into fear and guilt. Therefore, if they don't feel guilty, they don't feel that they are being religious. Mary Baker Eddy once said God is love and was viciously attacked for it by the Christian community of her day, who believed with a vengeance that God is wrathful, fear invoking. Families who live in guilt pass it on to their children. People who live in a state of guilt don't give a lot, they don't produce a lot, and they don't move forward spiritually very far. ¶New energy is released for

---

In a modern hospital a surgeon attends a patient under operating room lights. Losing his composure, he harshly and unfairly scolds his nurse. Without reacting, she seeks a forgiving attitude, knowing this is today's* karma *and that the doctor is stressed by long hours and difficult cases.

a healthy future when we forgive ourselves. Yes, forgiveness is a powerful force. We must start with ourselves, for as long as we hold self-contempt, we are unable to forgive others, because everyone else is a reflection of ourself. We react to what we see in them that we are not ready to face up to in ourselves. ¶It is a great power to be able to look beyond ourselves and see others as they really are, how they really think and how they really feel. When we are wrapped up in our own individual ego, this is hard to do. We surmise that those we know are exactly like us, and we find fault with them when they are not. But eventually we break the shell of the ego—an act symbolized by smashing the rough, dark brown coconut in the temple, revealing the beauty of the pure, white fruit inside which represents our pristine spiritual nature. It takes a hard blow to subdue our ego, and this is never without pain. But we can remove the ego's hard shell painlessly through absolute surrender to Hindu Dharma, absolute surrender to our own soul, to God within us. External worship and internal worship, external surrender and internal surrender, bring about the softening of the ego and the unveiling of spirit.

Tuesday
LESSON 282
Congested Energies

What is resentment? Resentment is *prāṇic* force, subtle energy, that is congested. What is love? Love is *prāṇic* force that is flowing and uncongested. When someone performs an injustice toward us, he is giving us a conglomerate of congested *prāṇa*. If we were able to look at it in the astral world, we would see it as a confused mass of disharmonious colors and shapes. If we are unable to remain detached, we become upset and resentful. Instinctively this *prāṇa* is held by us and only released when we find it in our heart to forgive the person. At the moment of true forgiveness, the congested *prāṇa* is transferred back to the person who harmed or insulted us. ¶Now we can see that when we resent or hold something against someone, we are actually astrally connected to him and, in fact, holding back the *karma* that will automatically come to him as a result of his harmful act. If we forgive the offender, we release the congested energy. Then the unfailing *karmic* law begins to work. In other words, his actions will cause a reaction back on him, and we won't be involved in the process at all. That is why the *Tirukural*, a wonderful book written 2,200 years ago, tells us, "Though unjustly aggrieved, it is best to suffer the suffering and refrain from unrighteous retaliation. Let a man conquer by forbearance those who in their arrogance have wronged him" (157-8). ¶However, it would not be wise to accept the transgressor back in your life until true remorse is shown and resentment on his part is dissolved through apology and reconciliation. Otherwise, wisdom indicates he might just commit the same hurtful acts again. I was asked recently what we mean in *sūtra* 270 which says monastics forgive hurts quickly and inwardly, but not outwardly until the offender reconciles. The devotee who asked the question said he has taken a lot of physical and emotional abuse, as well as verbal abuse, from his family. He had forgiven them inwardly but wanted to know what their relationship should be, now that he had reached middle age. We forgive inwardly because we know the experience is the result of our *karma* that we have put into motion in the past. But we hold a friendly, firm wall between ourselves and the offenders, which means a friendly distance, because we know that it is their *kukarma,* too, which must be reconciled with apologies and with the assurance that the offense won't happen again. ¶To be affectionately detached—that is a power. That is a wisdom. But detachment does not mean running away from life or being insensitive or passively accepting harm to yourself or loved ones. When we have the ability to let go, through forgiveness, we are warmer, more friendly, more wholesome, more human and closer to our family and friends. ¶Just the opposite happens if we remain attached by resenting what happened in the past. Take the example of a teenager who sees a promising future ahead of him, then experiences begin to happen in his life, some of which are unpleasant. If these are not resolved, negative *prāṇa* begins piling up within his subconscious mind, *vāsanās* are made, and the future begins to diminish from view. Year after year, as he grows older, the past gets bigger and bigger and bigger, and the future gets smaller and smaller and smaller. Finally, there is so much resentment that the once joyful adolescent grows into a depressed and bitter adult. Eventually he develops cancer and dies lonely and miserable. ¶To have a happy future with your family and friends, don't ignore difficulties that come up between you. Sit down with them and talk things over. Stand on your own two feet, head up and spine straight and bring it all out in the open. Let them know how you feel about what they said or what they did. Especially in Asia, so many things are swept under the carpet, not talked about and left to smolder and mold there. But now, in today's world, we must clean up the mess in order to go along into a happy future. The basic foundation of Sanātana Dharma is *ahiṁsā,* nonhurtfulness, physically, mentally and emotionally. We must always remember this.

Wednesday
LESSON 283
Forgiving Is Health Giving

We recently learned that the oldest person in the world is a 118-year-old lady in Canada, who happens to be vegetarian. She is quite up in the news and in the *Guinness Book of Records.* In a study of her life and that of several others over age 110 it was asked, "How have they lived so long? Why are they still living? What is their secret?" The answer is that these elderly folk are optimistic. They see a future, and that keeps them living. They are easy-going, good-humored, contented and have a philosophy of forgiveness toward what anybody has done to them along the way. They are successful at flowing with the events of life and do not hold on to a lot of resentment or congested *prāṇas.* It is when hate and resentment become a way of life that we begin to worry and wonder what life is all about. Forgiving others is good for your health. ¶The wise have given a remedy, an effective penance, *prāyaśchitta,* that can be performed to get rid of the bundle of past resentment and experience forgiveness and the abundance of divine energy that comes as an aftermath. Write down in detail all the resentments, misunderstandings, conflicts and confusions that you are still holding onto. As you complete each page, crumple it up and burn it in a garbage can or fireplace. When the mind sees the fire consuming the paper, it intuits that the burden is gone. It is the emotion connected to the embedded experience that actually goes away. ¶Resentment is a terrible thing. It affects the astral body and then the physical. When there is a health problem, there may well be a forgiveness problem. Resentment is crippling to the astral body and the emotions, because when we resent others, we can't get them out of our mind—we are definitely attached to them. Resentment is equally distributed worldwide. Workers resent their bosses. Bosses resent the owners. Owners of companies resent the government. This is modern society today. This is all-pervasive ignorance, and ignorance added to ignorance makes ignorance stronger. One resentment adds to another in the subconscious mind. ¶We must begin the healing by first forgiving ourselves, by claiming our spiritual heritage, gaining a new image of ourselves as a beautiful, shining soul of radiant light. Then we can look at the world through the eyes of Hindu Dharma. The *Yajur Veda* expounds, "He who dwells in the light, yet is other than the light, whom the light does not know, whose body is the light, who controls the light from within—He is the soul within you" (*Bṛihadāraṇyaka Upanishad* 3.7.14, VE 708). ¶When this *vāsanā daha tantra,* subconscious purification by fire, is complete, you will never feel the same again. After this spiritual experience, religion, Hindu Dharma, will be foremost in your life. All other activities—business, social and family life—will circle around your newly found ideals. Many of the wealthiest people on our planet have kept their religion first, their family and business second and other activities third. Their timing was always right. They were magnetic and happy. Others were happy to be near them.

Thursday
LESSON 284
Well-Directed Willpower

Everyone has willpower. It is inherent to the makeup of the physical-astral-mental-emotional body. The center of willpower is the *maṇipūra chakra,* located at the solar plexus. Unlike other energies, the more willpower we use, the more willpower we have to use. Actually, by exerting our willpower, we store up new energy within the *maṇipūra chakra.* This happens when we work a little harder than we think we can, do a little more than we think we can do. By putting forth that extra effort, we build up a great willpower that we will always have with us, even in our next life, the next and the next. Willpower is free for the using, actually. ¶When we relate willpower to actions and compare actions to *dharma* or *adharma,* we find that *adharmic,* or unrighteous, actions bring uncomfortable results, and *dharmic* actions bring comfortable results. If we act wrongly toward others, people will act wrongly toward us. Then, if we are of a lower nature, we resent it and retaliate. This is a quality of the instinctive mind: "You strike me once, I'll strike you back twice. You make a remark to me that I don't like, and I will put you down behind your back. I will make up stories about you to get even and turn other people's minds against you." This is retaliation—a terrible negative force. When we use our willpower to retaliate against others, we do build up a bank account of willpower, to be sure, because we do have to put out extra effort. But we also build up a bank account of negative *karma* that will come back on us full force when we least expect it. When it does, if we remain locked in ignorance, we will resent that and retaliate against the person who plays our *karma* back to us, and the cycle will repeat itself again and again and again. ¶Those living in the higher nature know better. Belief in *karma* and reincarnation are strong forces in a Hindu. South India's Saint Tiruvalluvar said it so simply, "Worthless are those who injure others vengefully, while those who stoically endure are like stored gold. Just as the Earth bears those who dig into her, it is best to bear with those who despise us" (*Tirukural* 155-151). ¶Nevertheless, we see society tearing itself apart through retaliation. Respectable organizations retaliate against their leader, against each other. Countries divide and retaliate. Political parties retaliate. Vindictive law cases are professionally handled retaliation. To retaliate means to pay back injury with injury, to return like for like, evil for evil, an eye for an eye, a tooth for a tooth. It seems to be a part of humankind, though it is a negative part of humankind. It does not have to prevail. It is not spiritual. We would say it is demonic. We would say it is *asuric*. We would say it is unnecessary behavior, unacceptable behavior, a wrong use of willpower. People who have a lot of will can, if they wish, retaliate very, very well. They can ruin another person. But remember, the force will come back on them three times stronger than they gave it out, because their strong willpower will bring it back with vigor. This is the law.

Friday
LESSON 285
Deciding on A Better Way

The wise person chooses his actions according to *dharma*, which is quite specific as to how we must behave. Those who connive to retaliate after a misunderstanding comes up should know they are carving a destiny of unhappiness for themselves by digging a pit of remorse, self-condemnation and depression. They will fall into it in the far-off future. ¶Some might ask, "Does nonretaliation mean that one should not protect himself, his family, his community?" We are talking about revenge, not self-defense. To oppose the actions of an intruder to one's home or community at the time of the intrusion is very different from tracking him down later and vandalizing his home in retaliation. We cannot hurt another without getting hurt back in the future through some other way, generally through other people not even associated with the person we hurt. Those who offend us or commit crimes against us, we can be sure, will receive justice in an unerring manner through the law of *karma*. If the matter is a serious one, we can seek reconciliation through the laws of the land. In criminal cases, justice can be sought through the courts. It is not wise to take matters into our own hands and be the instrument of punishment, for by doing so we reap the same negative *karma* as the offender. Retaliation on a wide scale can be seen in cases of mob violence, terrorism and guerrilla warfare. ¶Therefore, it is wise to cultivate the powerful force of compassion, of righteous response, forgiveness, of admitting our own mistakes, of not lying our way out of a situation just to make ourself look good or putting others down so we can stand taller, so that we can save face. That is a face you would not want to save. It is a face not worth saving. ¶Those who accept the truth that retaliation is not the proper way to live, but are unable to stop trying to get even, are on the road to correcting themselves, especially if they feel remorseful about their impulses and actions. Through divine sight the soul perceives unwise actions, performed when in the lower nature, as a hindrance to spiritual progress. Penance received from a *guru* or *swāmī* and well performed by the devotee propels the soul into its natural state of bliss. All help is given by the divine *devas* to those seen performing a sincere penance. *Gurus* of every lineage receive the verbal confession of devotees and give out the appropriate penance, *prāyaśchitta.* They recognize divine absolution, knowing the penance has been fulfilled, when the inner aura is as bright as a new-born child's, the face happy and the testimony about the results of the penance discloses true atonement.

Saturday
LESSON 286
The Dalai Lama's Example

Speaking of nonretaliation, the peace-loving Dalai Lama, exiled leader of Tibetan Buddhism, is setting an extraordinary example of not striking back at antagonists. He has campaigned relentlessly for political assistance for his people's cause since 1959, when at age fifteen he fled across the Himalayas and into India for help. Even today he approaches the Chinese with care and respect, though he never forgets China's armed takeover of his nation in 1957 and the extermination of 1.2 million Tibetans by 1972. This humble being has never failed to exemplify the *dharma* of compassion, advocating "the kind of love you can have even for those who have done you harm." He once wrote: "My enemy is my best friend and my best teacher, because he gives me the opportunity to learn from adversity." ¶If there were anyone who could justifiably lash out in a vindictive way, it would be the Dalai Lama; but he has chosen a higher path. We listened to him appeal for Tibetan autonomy over the years at international conferences in Oxford, Moscow, Rio de Janeiro and Chicago, where he never deviated from his posture of love, trust and compassion, with full confidence that the divine law will finally manifest a righteous outcome, an agreeable solution. He also acknowledged that this persecution is a *karma* that his own people set in motion in the past. He is setting a noble pattern in the international arena, where spiritual people can forge, and are forging, new principles for a global *dharma.* ¶On an individual level, all can strive to give up the urge to "get even," heeding the Vedic admonition, "Here they say that a person consists of desires. And as is his desire, so is his will. And as is his will, so is his deed; and whatever deed he does, that he will reap" *(Śukla Yajur Veda, Bṛihadāraṇyaka Upani-*

shad 4.4.5. UPR, P. 272). Every belief creates certain attitudes. Our attitudes govern all of our actions. Belief in *karma;* reincarnation and the existence of an all-pervasive Divinity throughout the universe creates an attitude of reverence, benevolence and compassion for all beings. The Hindu or Buddhist who is consciously aware within his soul knows that he is the time traveller and may incarnate, take a body of flesh, in the society he most opposed in order to equalize his hates and fears into a greater understanding which would result in the release of ignorance. The knowledgeable Hindu is well aware of all these possibilities. The mystery is no mystery to the mystic. ¶*Ahiṁsā,* which the Dalai Lama exemplifies so courageously, is certainly not cowardice; it is wisdom. And wisdom is the cumulative knowledge of the existing divine laws of reincarnation, *karma, dharma* and the all-pervasiveness and sacredness of things, blended together within the psyche, the very soul, of the Hindu.

Sunday
LESSON 287
Realize That God Is Love

Śiva is Love and Love is Śiva. People often ask, "How can I worship God if I can't see God?" There was a young man who had formed an intense dislike for his father because his father disciplined him strongly when he was growing up. Every time the young man thought of his father, it was through feelings of resentment and confusion. Whenever his father was around, the son avoided him, and sharp words were often exchanged. However, his father put him through college, paying all the expenses. When the young man broke his leg playing football, the father visited him in the hospital every few days and paid the medical bills. But still the young man resented his father for what had happened years ago. He could not see that his father really loved him. His inner sight, feeling and emotion were blinded by his bitterness about the past. This story illustrates how mental barriers disable us from seeing people as they really are. And if we cannot correctly see the people around us, how can we expect to see God? We are often blinded by our "ignore-ance"—our great ability to ignore. ¶People who question the existence of God because they cannot see God must take the word of those who do see God. When they cannot do even this, they are obviously lost in their own delusions and confusions, unable to even see the love or accept the love of those who are closest to them. They most likely misjudge everything through their limited vision, clouded by resentments built up over the years. ¶We all see people with our two eyes, and we see into people with our hearts. When our heart is pure, holding no resentment, we can then see with our third eye. Someone having problems in seeing God should begin by worshiping his mother and father as divine. He can see them with his eyes and within his mind. This *sādhana* will clean up the person's heart and bring his thoughts, speech and actions into line with *dharma*. Then one day he will see that God Śiva truly is the Life within the life of everyone—of the whole universe, in fact. ¶The word *love* describes the free-flowing interchange of spiritual energy between people, between people and their things, between people and God and the Gods. Our scriptures clearly tell us that "Śiva is love, and love is Śiva." Therefore, our free-flowing love, or *bhakti*, is our own Śivaness in manifestation. Expressing this love is a profoundly auspicious and beginning form of living with Śiva that is complete, in and of itself.

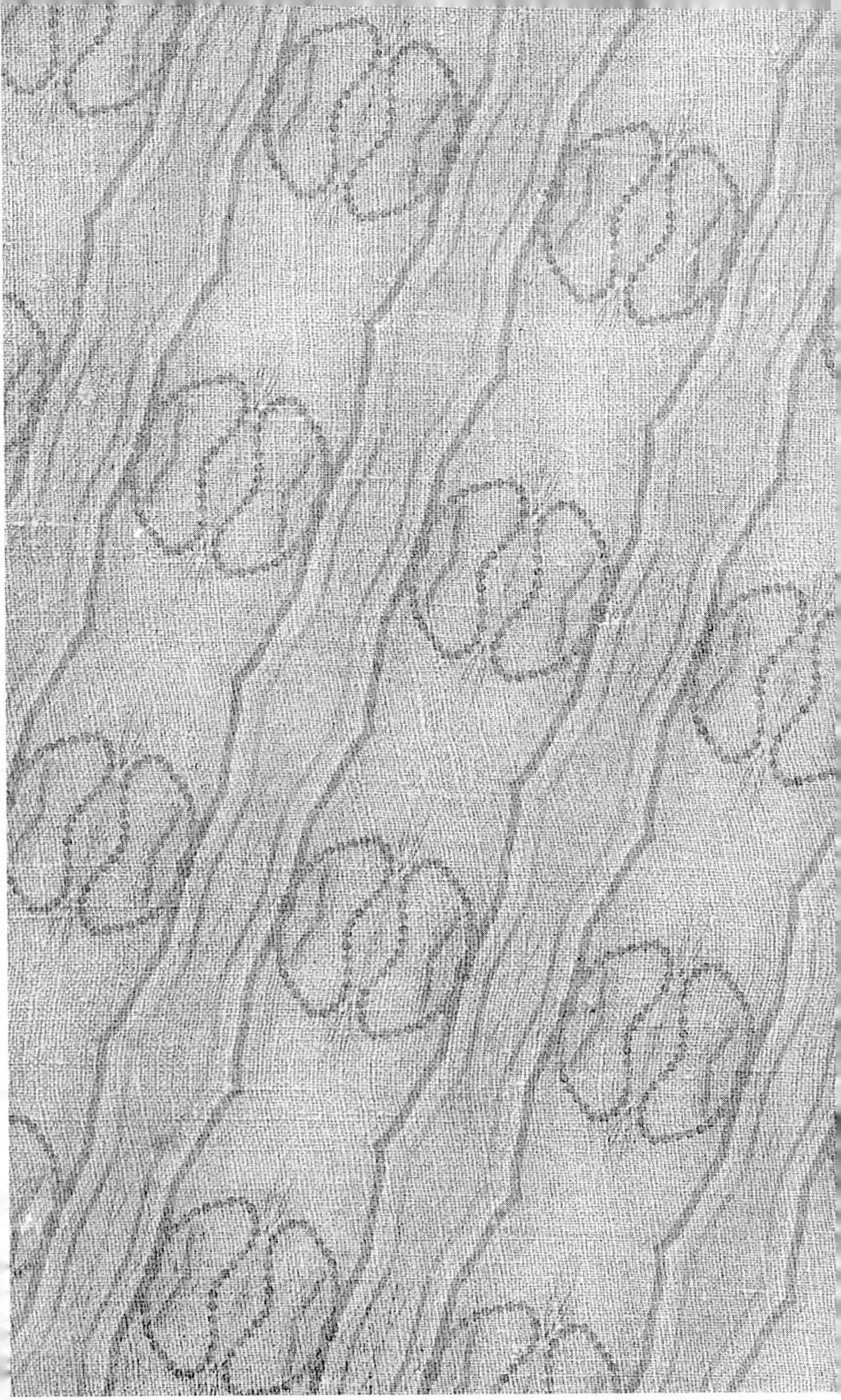

Kṛitajñatāṁ Pālaya; Samabhāvo Bhava

कृतज्ञतां पालय समभावो भव

Nurture Gratitude, Be Considerate

As from a tree covered with blossoms, the fragrance wafts far off, so also in the same way, the fragrance of a good deed blows its fragrance far off. Just as a juggler, when he steps upon an edge of a sword laid over a pit, speaks: "Softly! Softly! Or I shall come to harm and fall in the pit," so also one should keep himself away from an untruth!

Kṛishṇa Yajur Veda, Mahāṇārāyaṇa Upanishad. UPB, P. 253

Monday
LESSON 288
Half Full or Half Empty?

Much of life today is based on depreciation and denigration of public leaders, groups, governments, religions, corporations and even family members. This is negative living, always pointing out faults in no uncertain terms and ignoring the virtues. A Hawaiian civic leader lamented to us recently that people are cruel in their complaints. "It's OK to criticize," she said, "but they should be kindly when doing so!" ¶A story I was told decades ago relates. A *guru* was sitting with two disciples under a sprawling banyan tree in India. The older student inquired, "Gurujī, how long must I wait until I realize God?" The teacher responded, "Enlightenment is not something that can be predicted, but since you have asked," he leaned over and spoke in the right ear, "It will be twenty more lives." "Oh, no!" the youth cried in dismay, "I don't know if I can wait that long!" The other follower, naturally curious, asked of his own future. The *guru* whispered, "Liberation will come after you live as many lives as this banyan has leaves!" Hearing this, the seeker jumped to his feet and began to dance. Why? He was suddenly overcome by the assurance that he would ultimately be liberated. Ecstatic with appreciation, he transcended the mind and attained his liberation that very moment. ¶The first student was on the path of depreciation. For him the pot was half empty. The second followed the path of appreciation and was immersed in thankfulness. For him the pot was half full. "Some people complain because God put thorns on roses. Others praise Him for putting roses among the thorns." ¶Appreciation is a beautiful, soulful quality available to everyone in every circumstance—being thankful for life's little treasures, grateful for the opportunity to begin the day where you are, appreciating the perfect place your *karma* and God's grace have brought you to. Appreciation is life-giving. Depreciation without appreciation is heartlessly destructive. Yet, it is the all-too-common way of our times. When something is done that is good, helpful or loving, it is often overlooked, treated as something expected. No acknowledgement is shown, no gratitude expressed. But if a shortcoming is seen, everyone is swift to point it out! ¶The *Vedas,* the *Tirukural* and our many other holy texts indicate a better way. The wise ones knew that all people possess freedom of choice and the willpower to use it. Today that freedom is usually used, unwisely, to downgrade others,

---

Being grateful for God's gifts is a sign of spirituality. A sage tells two seekers they will live as many lives as there are leaves on the banyan tree. One rushes away in dismay, while the other dances, knowing that liberation is assured, and at that moment experiences freedom from saṁsāra.

as well as oneself. Ignorance seems to be almost as all-pervasive as God. We find it everywhere and within every situation. It does not have to be this way. ¶Gratitude is a quality of the soul. It does not depend on how much we possess. Its opposite, ingratitude, is a quality of the external ego. When we abide in soul consciousness, we give thanks for whatever we have, no matter how little or how much. When in ego consciousness, we are never grateful or satisfied, no matter how much we have.

Tuesday
LESSON 289
The Power Of Appreciation

I have faith in human integrity, in that unfailing "still small voice of the soul" which each who listens for can hear. We are essentially pure souls temporarily living in a physical body. We can and should use our God-given gift of free will encased in love to make a difference in the world today, even if it is in a small way. All of us making the same difference together do so in a big way. *Śishyas* should be grateful to their *gurus,* husbands to their wives, wives to their husbands, parents to their children, children to their parents, students to their teachers and teachers to their students. It's far more effective to praise others and appreciate what we have than to find fault and complain about what we don't have! ¶*Gratitude* and *appreciation* are the key virtues for a better life. They are the spell that is cast to dissolve hatred, hurt and sadness, the medicine which heals subjective states of mind, restoring self-respect, confidence and security. Shall we review them one at a time and consider a practice, a *sādhana,* for each? ¶First, gratitude. It is a feeling within the heart that we cannot suppress for long when overcome with abundant memories of all the good that has come into our lives. Most often, people remember the bad happenings, perhaps because they make the deepest impressions in the subconscious and are not expected. Good happenings are expected and therefore tend to be overlooked. ¶The *sādhana* here is to take out paper and pen and list all the good that has come into your life during the past five years. The list will grow as memory is stimulated. Should it not be possible to think of even one good thing, then write the affirmation several times, "I am a spiritual being of light maturing in the ocean of experience." Soon a good memory will come up, followed by more. Feelings of loving appreciation will begin to flow toward those who participated in the good times. Forgiveness then wells up for the bad times. Amazingly, on the day I was writing down these thoughts about gratitude, a Kauai islander handed me a paper on which was written the following wisdom from the Catholic mystic, Meister Eckhart: "If the only prayer you ever say in your entire life is thank you, it will be enough." ¶Now let's look at appreciation, turning our thanks toward the people in our lives. The *sādhana* of appreciation is to approach those you are grateful to and tell them, to their face, while looking deep into their eyes, how much you esteem and value them. Be specific. Find details to share so they know this is not a shallow compliment. Explain what each one has done to inspire this loving confrontation and convince each in turn that you are sincere. The look of a full smiling face, eyes shining and heart full of love, perhaps followed by a big hug, is convincing enough in itself. Words of appreciation are words people do not often hear. These loving confrontations do not happen nearly often enough among friends and relatives in today's world. ¶Loving appreciation is a life-changing force just waiting to be used. Express appreciation to community leaders, business associates, spiritual mentors, family members and friends as often as you can. Loving appreciation is a magic formula that works both ways. When we commend another, we are automatically uplifted.

Wednesday
LESSON 290
You Can Make A Difference

Here's a true story to show how effective a timely expression of appreciation may be. A young man tried the above practice on his rather gruff employer, whose heart melted when he heard the words, "One of the things that I appreciate most about you, sir, is your brilliance as an inventor. You have so much to teach me." After saying that and more, the youth urged the astonished elder to pass on the voicing of appreciation to another person. The man sat with his only son that same evening and awkwardly told him how much he appreciated his many fine qualities. "I never take time to say such sentimental things," he said, "but rather tend to keep to myself and be demanding and harsh because of the pressures of work. But please know that I do love you." The youth began sobbing and confessed, "Father, thank you so much. You can't imagine how glad and relieved I am to hear that. I was planning to commit suicide tomorrow because I thought you didn't care about me any more, or even like me. Now I won't." You never know how much difference your appreciation will make. ¶To prepare yourself for this *sādhana,* stand before a mirror and look at your face, right into your eyes, and say aloud, as if talking to another person: "I am grateful to you and appreciate your being in my life." Then describe to yourself in many sentences all the good you have done during the past five years. You can jog your memory by reading from your list of goodness that you made earlier. You will soon see the reflection in the mirror soften and begin to smile as it absorbs the happy feeling of your appreciation. Once this art is perfected between you and you, you can begin to appreciate others in the same way. Don't be shy. No one is shy when angry. Why be shy when we are happy and lovingly grateful? ¶There is a brave new world on the horizon for followers of *dharma,* one in which we are kindly to each other, trusting and aware of one another's feelings, a world in which we acknowledge our debt to others and express our thanksgiving, first in our silent heart and then outwardly. Gratitude is one of life's richest resources, containing the power to change people's lives. Its opposite is a disease that erodes all contentment and fills our life with emptiness and despair. Take heart. These *sādhanas* on gratitude and appreciation have worked wonders for many. Yes, each one of us can make a difference. The world is changing, and we can make it change for the better, or we can leave it in the hands of those who make changes for the "badder." It's our choice. ¶I appreciate you, our reader of *Living with Śiva,* you and other men and women, boys and girls who are strengthening Hinduism in hundreds of remote communities, upholding the Sanātana Dharma, being a beacon light to others on the path. It is you who are inspiring us to produce this series of books on contemporary Hinduism, giving us so many ideas and cheering us on. You are making a great difference by simply living the *dharma,* aspiring for self-transformation and speaking on these high principles that are so important to us all and to the future of humanity. ¶Just a little bit of kindness is so easy to express. Just a little bit of kindness heals the mind. And in this day and age, when so many are frustrated, troubled and need a little bit of help, appreciation and encouragement, your kindness can help. Your criticism, your gossip about them, hurts them and also hurts yourself. But the kindness that you express in what you do is healing unto you, too. So, see yourself as a being that always expresses kindness. What you think about, you become.

Thursday
LESSON 291
How to Be Happy

Look in the mirror. You have created your face through your many thoughts that have accumulated through this lifetime. Ask yourself, "Am I happy, or am I looking for others to make me happy?" Allow yourself to be kind; allow yourself to express the qualities, the beautiful qualities, of your soul. Your happiness then will come from within yourself, along with a deep contentment and inner peace and joy. Only a moment of thinking kindly about someone, and making a plan that will enable you to help your fellow man, even just a little bit, will awaken from your soul that deep, inner satisfaction, that depth of security you are really seeking. On the other hand, if you allow your mind to dwell in the realm of critical thinking, in the realm of gossiping, without the thought of helping others, you will feel insecure, unhappy. Nothing that could happen will bring you an inner satisfaction. You will be constantly desirous of acquiring, and that which you do acquire will not be satisfying to you. Why? Because there will be no love in your heart. If you find yourself in that state of mind, turn the energies around and find the quietness within you through being kind, being generous, being helpful. The doing brings its own reward. Only in the accomplishment of being big enough to understand the experiences of life that others go through, being tall enough to overlook the many, many things that you could take issue with and perhaps retaliate for, only in acquiring that depth which comes from your soul, can you truly find inner happiness and peace. ¶Go out into the world this week and let your light shine through your kind thoughts, but let each thought manifest itself in a physical deed of doing something for someone else. Lift their burdens just a little bit and, unknowingly perhaps, you may lift something that is burdening your mind. You erase and wipe clean the mirror of your own mind through helping another. We call this *karma yoga,* the deep practice of unwinding, through service, the selfish, self-centered, egotistical *vāsanās* of the lower nature that have been generated for many, many lives and which bind the soul in darkness. Through service and kindness, you can unwind the subconscious mind and gain a clear understanding of all laws of life. Your soul will shine forth. You will be that peace. You will radiate that inner happiness and be truly secure, simply by practicing being kind in thought, word and deed. ¶A sure indication of the manifestation of the soul nature on the physical plane is consideration for other people's feelings, consideration for other people's state of mind, which means appreciating their good qualities and overlooking their qualities that need improvement. Someone who is considerate is understanding. Those who are not considerate don't understand and don't understand that they don't understand. They don't understand, and they are not considerate and not appreciative, because they are wrapped up in their individual ego. Yet they expect everyone to be considerate of them.

Friday
LESSON 292
Consideration For Others

Consideration deals with the knowing principle. The opposite of consideration deals with the thinking principle. "I know what he means, and I know it is the best thing for me, but I don't think that it is right for me to do right now." That is how the thinking principle conflicts with the knowing principle within us. What does that create? It creates the individual, egotistical personality. ¶Consideration is a great principle to understand, and even a greater principle to unfold within yourself. If you can't be considerate of someone else's feelings, your soul is as if locked up in a little cage; and it can't get out, although it may be crying to express itself and hitting against that wall of the thinking mind which knows nothing at all about the qualities of the soul. ¶Knowing is the manifestation of your spiritual will. Consideration is also a manifestation of your spiritual will. When your spiritual will is awake, you have consideration for other people's feelings. When your spiritual will is awake, you give in on little things, and you have the power to hold firm on big issues, like keeping the twenty restraints and observances of the ancient Sanātana Dharma. You have an inner culture awakened within you. ¶Have you ever asked somebody to do some little thing, and he says "no"? He refuses to do it because he didn't think of it first, because he considers within himself that if he did do it, he would be falling under your domination? Why does he feel that way? It is because he has very little control over himself and is caught up in the thinking mind. But if you ask another type of individual to do something, it is done almost the minute you ask, he is so in tune with you. He has consideration for your feelings. He has consideration to the point where he doesn't want to upset the vibration around himself or around you by creating a situation. ¶By using the power of the thinking principle alone, we create situations for ourselves to face at another time, because each situation is of the subconscious mind and will manifest itself in life at a later date. Consideration is born of knowing, and knowing is a manifestation of your spiritual will, and your will shines forth when your soul begins to unfold itself. So, in order to be considerate, you have to exercise this knowing principle until it becomes manifest in your life every minute of every day. This is how to cultivate consideration. ¶How do we exercise our power to know? We have to look at people and ask ourself, "What do I know about my friends? What do I know about the depth of them? How deep are they?" We ponder, "What do I know about what I am reading—not just what I think about what I read? What do I really know about anything that I pick up and hold in my hand?" The knowing principle is very, very great. We study our mind: "If my intuition is working, do I know it is my intuition? If my subconscious mind is influencing my actions, do I know that I am attached to that state of mind?" What do you know? What do you not know? That is very important to know. ¶Going against what we know is a great pitfall. It is born from lack of consideration, lack of the ability to live in harmony with others, to fit into situations. Lacking consideration, we fail to fulfill the basic law of spiritual unfoldment: "Never miss an opportunity to serve." When we deliberately go against what we know, we create a burden that we don't want in our life, and we suffer under it. Then we ask, "Why do I feel so uninspired? I was doing so fine. I was so spiritual. I was feeling just wonderful. I felt all the life forces flowing through me, and all of a sudden it all stopped. Why did this have to happen to me? I thought I was doing fine. I was feeling so good." That's what I call a negative slump.

Saturday
LESSON 293
Emotional Slumps

Everybody falls into negative slumps at one time or another when they deny the God principle within themselves, when they deny their knowing power, absolutely, deliberately deny it, by allowing their thinking principle—what they themselves think as a little ego—to take hold and cancel off, just like an eraser on the blackboard of life, the soul's attempts to express itself. ¶For example, you are going along fine, just wonderful, you are feeling great, and a little opportunity to serve comes up and you miss it. You know you should, but you don't *think* it is quite the time, when it would be just as easy to fulfill whatever you know you should fulfill. But you think, "Well, this isn't exactly the best time for me." You have very good reasons to say no, excellent reasons, because the thinking mind is always filled with excellent reasons. They are wonderful for the time, but they wear out. That is why we don't exercise our memory and remember all the reasons we had for our actions. ¶If I asked why did you do this and that and those unseemly actions, you might say, "Yes, I know what you're thinking. I had a very good reason at the time, but I can't recall it just now." You don't want to remember the reason, because you know it was only an excuse sufficient for a time. Yet the action remains, along with the reason, which was a weak one, vibrating in the subconscious mind. If you accumulate two or three such incidents, pretty soon you fall into a negative slump, where you don't feel like doing anything and nothing seems to make sense to you in the spiritual world or any other world. You just drag along and say, "Oh my, the burdens of life are getting pretty heavy." Eventually that condition wears out, too, and you swing back and get a little light in you. That is why people turn to stimulants, excesses of chocolate, sugary yum-yums (the junk food business makes millions on the negative slumpers) and various innervating beverages, such as coffee and soft drinks, to pep up the physical body. But the body can take only so much of these negative slumps before it reacts and, in its reaction, becomes unhealthy. Finally it succumbs to disease; it is not at ease within itself because the subconscious mind is not at ease. ¶When you refrain from denying that soul source within you and fulfill what you know you should do, then you are filled and thrilled with life force. Your soul is shining out in the material plane. You don't go into negative slumps. You become like the people who don't just get up to do things, they jump up and are happy to do anything they have an opportunity to do. But deny your knowing principle, and it becomes an effort to do anything—even an effort to remember how you should respond and what you should do. ¶Many people know they should do certain things to help out, to help their families, their relatives and friends. But as the weeks go by, what they know they forget, because they really didn't want to do it in the first place. They didn't *think* they had time; they didn't *think* they could help; they didn't *think* they could afford it. They have so many limitations. They put their poor old soul into a cage. Excuse me, I am going to rephrase that. They put their poor *young* soul into a cage, because old souls manifest consideration. Young souls are just learning how. And this poor young soul climbs right into this little cage and sits, like a newborn baby, waiting for the subconscious mind—which has been filled with negative activity, negative thoughts and a negative approach to life—to unwind itself. But the soul within has to first watch itself wind up—and it winds up through the many lives, with all its negative creations, all of its thinking versus knowing, and thinking winning out every time. Then it has to unwind, and when it does unwind, pretty soon knowing gets stronger than thinking. Then we notice a spiritual unfoldment. Then we know that observation is taking hold. ¶Do you know how I can tell when someone is spiritually unfolding? When I suggest something, and he takes me up on the suggestion and observes and thinks of the next step before I think of it, I know that he is spiritually unfolding, because through his observation he is producing knowing, and through his knowing he is being considerate of his fellow man, just as he expects everyone to be considerate of him.

Sunday
LESSON 294
Getting Hold Of Your Mind

Those who are not considerate get very hurt when someone does not consider their feelings. Why? Because their feelings, their personality, are sticking out like antennas all over them, ready to be kinked up and twisted up when somebody is not considerate or loving toward them. Yet they don't show others the same consideration which they expect for themselves. ¶That is what creates the negative dream—everyone expecting everyone else to be very considerate of their feelings. And that is why we have etiquette books, to teach people to be considerate of other people's feelings—to teach those who really don't want to be considerate, but have to learn to be because they are out to build careers and make money, and they know they won't do so well unless they learn to be considerate, so they have to intellectually know how. But it is all surface. The word *insincere* describes the person who doesn't fulfill what he knows he should fulfill, but pretends that he does. We call him insincere. ¶That insincerity doesn't hurt anybody but himself, because you can't send out anything out into the world but that it comes back. When does it come back? It comes back later in life. He may get along fine when his body is young and healthy. He can be just as insincere as he wants to be, but later on in life he won't get along so fine, because the *karmic* rebounds start coming back, the reactions start coming back. They start coming back from other people, who become insincere with him. They also start coming back from deep within himself, from his conscience, when he learns that the way he had been was not right. Someday, unless he is fortunate enough to study *yoga* and clear it all up—perhaps through burning up the emotional memory patterns using the *vāsanā daha tantra*—he will suffer over it. And he will suffer over it a great deal. ¶The art of consideration is a real art, because it is a constant study. It really is a constant study. And it is a creative study. It is the art of learning how not to just get by; it is the art of learning how to fulfill your destiny through following the knowing principle inside you. ¶When you are in for the realization of the Self, you have to stop the cycles of hurt feelings and regrets. Just stop! You have to learn by exercising your knowing power and realize, "If I do this, it is going to have that kind of result. If I do that, which opposes my knowing of what I should do, I also have to know what kind of result that is going to create." Everything we do does have its consequences. It is up to you to sit down and meditate on such matters. That is what meditation is for. Meditation in the beginning stages is for getting a grip on your lower states of mind, so that the lower states of mind come under your control, so you learn to use your brain and don't loan it or rent it out. ¶When somebody causes you to do something that you don't feel that you want to do, or that you know is not the right way for you to behave, you are loaning out your brain to him. If somebody can make you feel antagonistic all day long because he didn't treat you right in the morning, he is using your brain, because he put that feeling into motion. He started something in you that you cannot conquer. But if, at the time of the incident, you straighten out the vibration with the person who made you feel antagonistic, by being considerate of his feelings, then you would be using your brain, and that is what you have to do. Maybe he is a young soul who will not learn to be considerate for a long, long time, and we couldn't expect that of him. That is why you have to meditate; that is why you have to get these things figured out—who's who on the scale of evolution. ¶Remember these three principles: 1) Your thinking is going to fight what you know. It is going to fight it all the time. You know you should do certain things, but you may not do them, because you have other reasons, and your other reasons will be good reasons, which you quickly forget because they are only good for the moment; 2) If you allow your knowing to dominate, you will be exercising your spiritual will. You will be alive. You will be dynamic. Spiritual forces will flow through you; 3) If you exercise your spiritual will, you will have a great power of observation and a great power over your own mind. No one will do your thinking for you. ¶After you have awakened your power of observation, your soul shines forth, and after meditation you will go into contemplation. You may think you are attaining high states of spiritual consciousness, but for real progress, your soul will have to manifest itself in what you do on the Earth all the time. So, these are your steps. Don't allow the thinking to fight the knowing. Don't allow the thinking to rule your willpower. Then you will be spiritual.

Vaishamyaṁ Prati Asahishṇutvam
वैषम्यं प्रति असहिष्णुत्वम्

Zero Tolerance for Disharmony

United your resolve, united your hearts, may your spirits be at one, that you may long together dwell in unity and concord!

Ṛig Veda 10.191.4. VB, P. 863

Monday
LESSON 295
Philosophers' Magic Barge

We are told that hundreds of years ago in the city of Madurai, known as the Athens of India for its cultural pre-eminence, there was constructed at the Meenakshi Somasundareśvara Śivan Koyil, within the vast temple tank, a magic boat called the Philosophers' Barge. *Ṛishis* came from the Himalayas, *pandits* from all corners of India and humble *bhakta siddhas* from the South to sit together and discuss life, illumination and release from mortality. This boat's singular magic was its extraordinary ability to expand to accommodate any number of people who conversed with an attitude of respect and harmony. But, miraculously, it grew smaller when discussion turned rancorous, and those who brought about the contention suddenly found themselves in the water, swimming to shore in embarrassment. In Śiva's temple, it seems, only nonargumentative discussion was allowed. ¶We have no magic boats today, …or perhaps we do. During a recent pilgrimage to India, I spoke to several large groups of devotees, including hundreds of *sādhus* of the Swaminarayan Fellowship, about zero tolerance for inharmonious conditions. Everyone found the message pertinent, yet difficult to practice, for there is no group of people on Earth for whom living in harmony is not a challenge at one time or another. But it is true that among my monastics we have zero tolerance for disharmonious conditions of any kind. ¶Harmony is the first and foremost rule of living in all spheres, but particularly in spiritual work, where it is an absolute must. Striving for harmony begins within the home and radiates out into all dimensions of life, enhancing and making joyous and sublime each relationship for every devotee. Thus, each strives to be considerate and kindly in thought, word and deed, to unfold the beautiful, giving qualities of the soul, to utter only that which is true, kind, helpful and necessary. The great Tamil saint, Tiruvalluvar, offers the following sage advice in *Tirukural* verse 100: "To utter harsh words when sweet ones would serve is like eating unripe fruit when ripe ones are at hand." Yes, this is the ideal. I was asked by the *swāmīs* in Gujarat, time after time, "But what if conflict and contention do arise?" My answer was that in our fellowship all work stops and the problem is attended to at once. It is each one's responsibility to follow this wisdom. Nothing could be more counterproductive and foolish

---

A spiritual family has zero tolerance for disharmonious conditions. A Hindu couple argue, with the towers of Meenakshi Temple behind, but later settle their differences before sleep. Their regained harmony is shown by their clasped hands.

than to continue work, especially religious work, while conflict prevails, for demonic forces have been unleashed that must be dispelled for any effort to be fruitful and long lasting. Any breach in the angelic force field of the home, monastery or workplace must be sealed off quickly. ¶Our approach is simple. We are all committed to the shared *sādhana* that all difficult feelings must be resolved before sleep, lest they give rise to mental argument, go to seed and germinate as unwanted, troublesome *vāsanās*, subconscious impressions, that cannot be totally erased but only softened and neutralized through the mystic processes of atonement. Disharmony is disruption of the harmonious *prāṇic* flow: anger, argument, back-biting, walking out of meetings, painful words and hurt feelings. The *Vedas* pray, "May our minds move in accord. May our thinking be in harmony—common the purpose and common the desire. May our prayers and worship be alike, and may our devotional offerings be one and the same" (*Ṛig Veda* 10.191.3. VE, P. 854). One of the principles of harmony is that the commitment to harmony has to be greater than any commitment to any particular issue or problem. Problems change, but the strength of harmony has to be the ultimate priority. This is a conceptual tool to use whenever differences arise.

Tuesday
LESSON 296
The Sādhana Of Resolution

If a disruption is not resolved before sleep, then a *kukarmaphala*, fruit of wrongdoing, will be created. The hurt feelings and mental arguments continue to fester until the matter is brought up and openly faced to be resolved. If not resolved within 72 hours, the problem germinates, and elders must take action under spiritual guidance to rectify the matter. The fact that all have chosen to avoid facing the difficulty shows that more serious remedies are required. ¶Resolution in all cases is accomplished through the *hṛī prāyaśchitta:* apology, the showing of remorse, talking together in small groups and giving gifts as tokens of reconciliation. Humility is the keynote. Sincere apology is offered for participating in argument or confusion, even if one was not necessarily to blame; the *karma* was there that attracted the situation. Harmony is reinstated by honestly accepting apologies, by forgiving and forgetting with the firm resolve to never bring up the matter again. Zero tolerance is based on the shared understanding that by working together on the firm foundation of love and trust all will progress in religious service and worship. Through these efforts, a *sukarmaphala*, fruit of right doing, is deliberately created. When two *śishyas* sit to settle a disharmony, it is sometimes helpful for an uninvolved third party to be present, even silently, to balance the energies. ¶*Sādhana*—personal transformation through self-effort—is the magic balm that soothes the nerve system, giving strength for each *śishya* to have forbearance with people and patience with circumstances. When *sādhana* is neglected, problems close in. Families find it difficult to see eye to eye. Hard feelings arise in even the simplest and well-intended encounters when the individuals have become too externalized. ¶There is a natural harmony within our monasteries, which families seek to emulate. Rarely is much discussion required when daily activities are being carried out, for the lines of authority based on seniority are always clear. This is the first boon for maintaining harmony among a group. Ours is a traditional hierarchical system of governance, upheld within our family and monastic communities, established when the *Vedas* were created. It is a system whereby the elders, in a loving manner, guide those younger than they. So, there is always an atmosphere of respect, loving harmony and meeting of minds. Never is scolding heard or feelings hurt or arguments provoked or sincere questions left unanswered. Here "love is the sum of the law," and the heartfelt feelings going out from the elders protect and support those who will one day themselves be elders. We create a secure and loving society in which intelligence overrides controversy and the only rigid rule is wisdom. Thus the *prāṇic* magnetism of the family or monastery is maintained and kept ever building for sustainable success and spirituality. ¶Yes, I can tell you from experience that zero tolerance for inharmonious conditions is a workable law and *sādhana* that can and should be adopted by all spiritual groups and individuals. My *satguru,* Siva Yogaswami, used to say, "It takes a lot of courage to be happy all the time." Most people, it seems, would rather be miserable. Think about it. They go through life getting their feelings hurt, resenting this or that and hurting the feelings of others in an endless cycle of unresolved emotion, asking a torrent of unanswerable rhetorical questions. Take today's average family: it's a composite of troubled individuals.

Wednesday
LESSON 297
Maintaining Magnetism

Today, more than ever, parents everywhere are concerned about keeping the family together. I have found that the key is to keep the *prāṇas* flowing harmoniously. A true family is a clan of individuals who love each other, which means they are bound together by positive *prāṇic* magnetism. When sons-in-law and daughters-in-law join the family, their *prāṇic* magnetism intermingles, and the family extends itself harmoniously, especially if the *jyotisha* compatibilities are good between the bride and her husband and the bride and her mother-in-law. This magnetism is maintained through the principle of zero tolerance for disharmonious conditions, to keep the *prāṇas* flowing within their homes in a positive, loving way. This means that if there is a disruption of the *prāṇas,* caused by interpersonal conflict—argument, angry words or worse—the matter must be settled among those involved before they retire to sleep, even if it means staying up all night. ¶What is *prāṇa? Prāṇa* is vital energy. There are three phases of the mind: instinctive, intellectual and superconscious. They comprise three different kinds of *prāṇa* in every human being: instinctive *prāṇa,* intellectual *prāṇa* and refined, superconscious *prāṇa,* also known as actinic energy. Instinctive *prāṇas* digest our food and maintain the functions of the physical body. They also give rise to the emotions of fear, anger, jealousy and other base instincts. The instinctive energies affect the mind, emotions and behavior. Without well-developed intellectual *prāṇas,* the mind is ruled by the lower nature and is easily influenced by others, often in a negative way. This is why children must be closely watched and guided during their formative years until their intellectual *prāṇas* develop in the form of good memory, discernment and willpower. The superconscious *prāṇas* bring through creativity, inspiration and intuition. These are the energies to be sought after and nurtured through various kinds of religious devotion and *sādhana.* ¶In nearly every home, all three kinds of *prāṇa* are at work. Little children are functioning mainly in the instinctive *prāṇas.* Students are in the intellectual *prāṇas.* Parents, hopefully, are functioning in the spiritual *prāṇas,* at least part of the time, drawing into the home the cosmic, actinic rays of the soul, while balancing all three forms of *prāṇa* within themselves. ¶It is the duty of the head of the house and his wife to take charge of all the three *prāṇas* within the home and keep them flowing harmoniously day after day after day after day. How do they do that? By prayer and regular, early-morning daily *sādhana,* bringing wisdom and other refined, actinic *prāṇas* through from the superconscious mind. When everyone is bound together with love, everything goes along fairly smoothly.

Thursday
LESSON 298
Keeping Peace With Yourself

The older children and young adults in the family must be taught that it is their responsibility, too, to see that the *prāṇas* are all flowing nicely in the home, so the little children and babies are protected. Young adults, having just come out of the instinctive mind themselves, are breaking the barriers into the intellect, experiencing these new *prāṇas* and beginning to think for themselves. This is the time when elders can guide them into the zero-tolerance-for-disharmonious-conditions philosophical outlook. Youths who have accepted the concept are most respectful of loving relationships. They tried it out and found for themselves that "Yes, we do have control over the instinctive mind" and "No, we won't allow it to run wild within our home, among our friends or in our associations with the community." They will be the ones to keep the flow of *prāṇas* harmonious. ¶Then the next step unfolds from within most naturally: zero tolerance for disharmonious conditions within our own self. This brings us back to my *guru's* wisdom: claim the strength to stop being miserable, to stop tolerating turmoil inside yourself. How is this accomplished? We have to boldly affirm, "I will not allow the instinctive mind that I experienced as a child to control me in any way. I will not allow anger to come up. I will not allow jealousy to dominate my thinking and make me feel inferior or superior to someone else. I will not allow fear to permeate my aura." ¶Then, each day before bedtime, settle any unresolved matters within yourself by performing the *vāsanā daha tantra*, "subconscious purification by fire." *Vāsanās* are sub-subconscious traits, complexes or subliminal tendencies which, as driving forces, color and motivate one's attitudes and actions. *Vāsanās* are conglomerates of subconscious impressions, *saṁskāras*, created through repeated or powerful experience. *Daha* means to burn, consume by fire, and a *tantra* is a method or technique, and the method here is to write out clearly all problems as well as emotional happenings, unhappy or happy, that are vibrating in the subconscious, instinctive-intellectual mind. When the eyes, through the intellectual mind or conscious mind, see the problem written down, the emotion attached to the memory begins to diminish. Then crumple up the paper and burn it in an ordinary fire, such as in a fireplace, urn or garbage can, to totally release some of life's burdens from the subconscious and dispel the suppressed emotions as the fire consumes the paper. ¶This simple *tantra* removes the *vāsanās* from the memory and emotional recesses along with the emotion, resentments, hurt feelings and misunderstandings. Soon the superconscious *prāṇas* will begin to flow, and our natural, peaceful self emerges, and we may be left wondering, "Why was I ever bothered about that trivial incident?" ¶What happens if we don't resolve inharmonious or congested matters within ourself before sleep? The condition will go to seed, and those *vṛittis,* waves of the mind, which were disturbed by the experiential creation of the situation, will form a *vāsanā* to germinate at a later time in life, perhaps many years in the future, or even in another lifetime. This daily mental maintenance, of course, requires discipline. It may be easier to simply drop off to sleep feeling angry, jealous, guilty, dejected or sorry for oneself. ¶Yes, zero tolerance for disharmonious conditions can be applied within oneself as well as among a family or any group of people. This practice can be established in one of two ways. Start with yourself and then carry it out to others. Or start with your relationships with others, smoothing out the *prāṇas* when they go a little crazy, and then finally apply it to yourself when you are convinced that this is the way life should be lived. Zero tolerance for disharmonious conditions is clearly the only way once one fully accepts the basic principles of the Sanātana Dharma: all-pervasive energy, cause and effect, and coming back in a physical birth until all scores are settled. ¶Remember the inspiring words of the *Atharva Veda,* "Let us have concord with our own people and concord with people who are strangers to us. Aśvins, create between us and the strangers a unity of hearts. May we unite in our midst, unite in our purposes and not fight against the divine spirit within us" (7.52.1-2. HV, P 205).

Friday
LESSON 299
Heal All Hurts Before Sleep

When an inharmonious condition arises in a seeker's life, it forms a deep, dark veil within his mind, inhibiting the progressive process of seeking inwardly. Shall he store it away and forget it, put it behind him and get on with life? That is a temporary relief, to be sure, only temporary insofar as retaliatory *karma* will come back in full force at another time as an even deeper, darker veil that will effectually stop the seeking. Only at this second round will the seeker, now knowing the effect of past causes, begin to perform *japa,* do *prāṇāyāma* and strenuous religious practices, such as penance and *kavadi,* beseeching Lord Śiva to lift the veiling doom. ¶The wise seeker obviously will endeavor to lift the dark veils once he realizes they never go away but always persist when he stores problems away. At the same time, he realizes that certain obstacles in his progressive life pattern are beginning to show. Thus, the super-wise seeker will not store a problem away when it arises, but handle it adroitly and magically heal all wounds before they fester. To be super wise on the path to enlightenment, one must have the *siddhi* of humility. ¶When an argument flares up in the home between mother and father, it affects all of the children. They feed on the *iḍā* and *piṅgalā prāṇas* of the mother and father. Super-wise parents heal their differences before they sleep at night, even if they have to stay up all night to do it. Failure to heal differences before sleep means that a first separation has occurred. ¶Domestic abuse is a difficult issue, but one we must confront openly. I urge you all to stand up and say it is no longer acceptable for a man to abuse his wife or for either the husband or the wife to abuse their children. This must stop. In order to heal the differences that arise within a marriage from time to time, both partners have to give in. The best place to do this is at the feet of their Gods in the temple or shrine room. There is no other solution. This is the only way. The method of giving in, yes, is to talk it over. A major emphasis is to see the other's point of view, finding points in the disturbance both can agree with. *Agreement* is the key word. The relationship between the husband and wife, who are also a mother and father or potential mother and father, has more lasting influence than their opposing opinions. Some relationships are easy and some are difficult. But resolving disagreements before nightfall is the aim. Some couples need to work harder at it than others. ¶Habits are formed through the repetition of the same events over and over again. No matter what you have seen or heard from parents, relatives, neighbors, friends or society itself, heal your differences before sleep, even if it takes all night. By doing this repeatedly, a new habit will be created. Don't go to sleep in anguish, holding on to anger, fear, confusion or ill feelings. The inconvenience of this wise remedy will cause each one to be careful of his or her words, thoughts and actions.

Saturday
LESSON 300
The Many Levels of Love

Those wondering how they could ever live with zero tolerance for all discord and disharmony need only realize that people are naturally tolerant with those they love. The good mother tolerates all the little problems her beloved infant brings into each day. The loving wife tolerates the faults and actions of her husband. A true friend tolerates another friend's foibles and even rough words. If we learn to love, we automatically learn to have perfect tolerance for those we love. The ancient *Tirukural* reminds us, "When friends do things that hurt you, attribute it to unawareness or to the privileges of friendship" (805). ¶Love comes in many forms. There is physical love, magnetic attraction. This is dualistic love, because if the other person responds, you feel very good, and if he does not respond, you don't like him. That is not the kind of love that is all encompassing. It is a very narrow form of love. It broadens a little bit with emotional love, which is the second kind of love. You love someone because he makes you happy, or you express love to make other people happy. But if someone doesn't make you happy or you are trying to make someone else happy and he just won't be happy, then you don't like him anymore. That is also a dualistic form of love. It is not all encompassing. Physical love and emotional love are companions. ¶Then there is intellectual love, which comes in and breaks it all up. In the intellect, if you love somebody and he doesn't agree with you, then you don't like him. That interrupts the physical love and the emotional love. Arguments start, sarcasm begins to well up. These are all forms of partial love. People experience this every day. ¶Spiritual love is the fourth kind. Somewhat hard to come by, it is the love from the soul body. Spiritual love transcends physical love, emotional love and mental love. It transcends all kinds of feelings. It has a feeling of its own, which is called bliss—the ever-flowing energy from Śiva out through your body, the ever-flowing energy from Śiva out through your mind, the ever-flowing energy of Śiva out through your emotions. Caught up in that ever-flowing energy, you can truly say to everyone, "I love you." And what does *you* mean? *You* means Śiva, because you are seeing Śiva in each one. What are you looking at when you say that? You are not looking at the body. You are not appreciating or depreciating the intellect. You are not even bothered about the emotions, whether you are liked or not liked, because you are seeing Śiva emanating out through the eyes, emanating out through the aura, emanating out through the skin. Śiva is there, and you are living with Śiva. ¶This great, Supreme God of all the Gods is limited in one respect: He cannot take Himself out of you or anyone else. So mentally say, "I love you," then ask yourself the question, "What does *you* mean?" Does *you* mean you like the body of the person? No. Does *you* mean you like the emotions of the person? No. Does *you* mean you like the intellect of the person? No. Does *you* mean you like somebody as long as they are always pleasing to you, always agreeing with you, never upsetting you, never pulling away from you? No. It means that you love their soul. It means that you love Śiva inside of them. The light within their eyes is Śiva's light. The light that lights up their thoughts is Śiva's light, and that is what you love. That love is all encompassing. That love is not partial love, half love or just a little bit of love given when it pleases you. It's not magnetic love; it's not intellectual love. You are not putting any demands on the other person at all. You are not expecting anything back. It is love for the sake of love. ¶There should be a unique English word for spiritual love, but there is not.

In Sanskrit we do have a word for divine love: *prema.* Therefore, we have to adjust our thinking when we say, "I love you," to this all-encompassing, beautiful love that radiates throughout the universe—the perfect universe where everything is in harmony and order. And even if it is seemingly out of harmony, you know it actually is in harmony because you are in the state of consciousness where harmony is, where peace is, where bliss is. Therefore, your Śaiva Siddhānta religion can work in your daily life.

Sunday
LESSON 301
The Hope of the World Is Love

Your Śaiva Siddhānta religion can be lived every minute of the day and all through the night. All you have to do is decide whether you are going to expect anything back from anyone. All you have to decide is what part of the person you love. If you love the soul, you love the whole person, no matter who the person is, no matter what he does, what he says, whether you know him or whether you don't know him, because he is the light of Śiva, the energy of Śiva, the love of Śiva walking around in human form. This is the kind of love that keeps you in harmony with everyone. ¶Love is expressed in so many different ways. It is a force, a vibration that you have to work at to keep it flowing. Everyone has human emotions, instinctive emotions. Love controls those emotions. Love is appreciation, which can be expressed through gratitude, kind words, and especially through kind thoughts, because unkind thoughts create unkind words which create unkind actions, and everything begins with a thought. Love is an inner happiness which you want to cultivate in someone else, and if you begin to work at cultivating an inner happiness in someone else, you will have it yourself. If you work to cultivate an inner happiness in yourself, it doesn't work so well. That's a selfish approach, and you are likely to bring up instinctive emotions and memories of the past, especially of the bad things that happened in the past. In expressing love, one has to be very careful to know that it is a building situation, and be very careful not to indulge in unkind words, unkind thoughts and sarcasm. Sarcasm is the first breakdown in relationships. Trying to change another person's character is also disastrous to a relationship. You have to accept everybody as they are. People change by the example of other people. Children learn first by the example people set for them. They follow that example—they don't learn by mere words in the beginning—and that carries out all through life. Everyone admires a hero; everyone needs a role model. So if you want to change someone else, be a role model for him. Then he will become like you eventually, but it takes time. Be forgiving, because love is also forgiving. And be compassionate, for love is also compassionate, along with showing gratitude and expressing appreciation. ¶Love says, "I'm sorry." Love says, "Thank you." Love is also generosity, because whomever you love you are generous toward. You have generosity; you give and you give and you give and you give. And according to the great law of *karma,* you can't give anything away but that it will come back to you. If you give love, it comes back to you double, and then you don't know what to do with that, so you give that away, and that comes back double, and again you don't know what to do with that, so you give that and it comes back double, and your whole family begins to flourish. The community begins to flourish. ¶Out of all the philosophies, out of all the psychological maneuverings and the psychiatric analyses, the hope of the world is love. It will be a wonderful day when all of us see that the hope of the world is love. You will discover ways yourself to express love. Love is decorating the home, bringing flowers into the home, arranging flowers in the home. It is cooking a wonderful meal and serving it properly. Love is cleaning and tidying up the home, bringing fresh air into the home so that those who come into the home are uplifted simply by being in the home. Love is taking care of the shrine room, bringing fresh water, fresh flowers and lighting incense, polishing the Deities, keeping them bright and shiny and dressing them in new clothing so that those who see and receive the *darśana* are uplifted. There are many physical ways we can express love. Love is bringing the whole family to the temple at auspicious times. Love is meeting with the family daily, solving all the little problems, sharing and talking and understanding each other's minds and where they are in their consciousness. Love is being patient with people who have problems until the problems go away by talking them through. Love is respecting the elders. Love is also respecting yourself, because unless you have self-respect, unless you respect yourself, which means having a good self image, you will find it difficult to respect others. And unless you love and respect others, you will definitely have a hard time living in harmony with the world around you.

Saddharmāvaśyakatā

सद्धर्मावश्यकता

Why We Need Religion

By means of the hymns one attains this world, by the sacrificial formulas the space in-between, by holy chant the world revealed by the sages. With the syllable Aum as his sole support, the wise man attains that which is peaceful, unageing, deathless, fearless—the Supreme.

Atharva Veda, Praśna Upanishad, 5.7. VE, P. 775

PEACE

Monday
LESSON 302
Vedānta, the Mountain Peak

As we progress on the spiritual path, we must have a clear intellectual understanding of the map leading to the eventual destination, as well as what is required to prepare ourselves and to take with us to complete the journey. To begin, we shall discuss Vedānta and Siddhānta, monism-pluralism, *advaita-dvaita* and the traditional part that *yoga* plays within the midst of Hindu Dharma. ¶Vedānta is a philosophy and an ideal. It sets its sights on the mountain peaks and declares emphatically these heights as man's true abode. Life as we normally live it, says Vedānta, is based on ignorance of our true nature. We are like pedigreed animals wallowing in the mud, believing we are swine, divine beings thinking ourselves to be mere humans. But once we recognize our true nature, we will rise up from the mud and leave behind, forever, our previous ignorant ways. Vedānta does not budge from its vision. It sees no excuse for the nonattainment of its ideals. No human weaknesses are recognized as reasons for falling short of the goal. They are but challenges. ¶Vedānta sees all men as equal. It makes the same declaration of truth to all men, regardless of their varying capabilities. Vedānta tells the instinctive man, the intellectual, the spiritual man, the man at the gallows and the man speaking from the pulpit each the same message—that he himself is the Truth that all men seek, that this world of experience and the role he is playing in it are based on ignorance of his true nature, that he is himself God, the Absolute. ¶Vedānta is the word of sages who have spoken out their realized truths, not based on needs of individual disciples or attached to a practical means of reaching followers. Vedānta is simply the goal, the final truths that man can attain to. The lofty Himalayan peak rises far above the surrounding country, breaking through the clouds, standing alone in silent declaration of its majesty. We may see this peak from a distant valley. We may know and learn much about it. Perhaps we even desire to reach this peak ourselves. Yet it remains so distant, giving us no clue of the path which could lead us to it. This is Advaita Vedānta in its purity—a mountain peak truly majestic, but so far aloft that for most it can only serve to inspire awe and deference toward heights that are out of our reach. ¶Vedānta, as an ideal and philosophy, can and perhaps should leave us just where it does, with a vision, a grand

---

A sister and brother are growing up in Germany, with the Berlin skyline behind them. While nonreligious youth run wild and vandalize property, they are grateful for their Hindu upbringing, which provides values and moral direction, teaching them the merits of a peaceful life.

vision, a grand vision of our potential, but a vision without a practical means of reaching it. The practical means, the carefully thought out and guided approach, belongs to another field of experience. And this we would call religion. It is the duty and purpose of religion to recognize the lofty goal, recognize the realistic capabilities, potential and present state of those seeking the goal, and provide a sensible and safe path toward that goal—a path that can take the strong to the final heights and yet not leave the weak on treacherous precipices along the way. Religion is the path, the only true path.

Tuesday
LESSON 303
There Are No Shortcuts

The idea of a shortcut that transcends religion and brings one quickly to the peak is a fallacy. We hear and read many stories of sages who have seemingly leapt from the valley to the peak on the power of tremendous austerities or rigorous mental control. Some of us may have heard of Ramana Maharshi or Rama Tirtha, great sages of India's recent past. We may recall that both of them climbed to the heights of Vedāntic truths while young, apparently unencumbered by traditional religious performance. Or at least this is the way we hear of them. True, they were both young when they reached great spiritual illumination. But their relationship with traditional religion needs clarification. In fact, each of these sages passed through religion, not around it. ¶For the would-be Vedāntin to shirk his religion, thinking he is following Ramana Maharshi or Rama Tirtha, is like the college dropout thinking that he is following the example of a graduate. The dropout and the graduate are similar in that they both have left college. But whereas the dropout was unable to absorb and fulfill the teachings of a college, and is unfit for anything that requires more than a high school diploma, the graduate has not only mastered the teachings but is the living fulfillment of the teachings. We could say that both Ramana Maharshi and Rama Tirtha were "A" students of the Hindu religion. How many people, as a fifteen-year-old child, like Ramana Maharshi, would walk each day to their village temple and prostrate before the image of God, weeping for the Lord's grace that he be able to live a pure and spiritual life as exemplified by his religion? How many of us could, as Rama Tirtha did from his earliest years, daily attend temple services, chant incessantly the holy words of his religion, read fervently his scriptures, become so enraptured with love of God that his pillow each morning would be soaking wet from tears of devotion inspired by his silent prayers? These are men of religion who dove so deeply into their religion that they became the very fulfillment, the very proof, of the power of religion. ¶And so it is with all the world's religions and the saints they have produced. There is no true path that leads away from religion. Hard work, diligence and perseverance in religious practices will be found as the spiritual foundation in the lives of all the world's great saints. In Hinduism, the word we use to denote religion, its theology and practices, is *Siddhānta*. Siddhānta is the path that one follows which leads to the mystic vision of Vedānta. When we read of the *yogas* of *bhakti*, *karma* and *rāja*, discipleship to a *guru*, the fulfillment of spiritual *dharma* and temple worship, these are all part of the path, part of Siddhānta.

Wednesday
LESSON 304
Vedānta and Religious Unity

In the West, we first received from India the philosophical teachings of Vedānta as if they exist separate from religion. There were, of course, some religious practices of Hinduism spoken of as methods to reach the Vedānta realizations. But it was all very low key, presented in a way that would not seem challenging or offensive to Western religions. This was fine and as it should be. But it also created misconceptions in the minds of those who earnestly did want to reach toward the Vedāntic truths. The West was given the impression that Vedānta was a mystic path which was independent of religion. *Yoga* was the word used to describe this "trans-religious" spiritual path to God. And this *yoga* could be adopted by anyone regardless of former or current religious involvement. The problem lies in the fact that many were left with the misconception that religion was unnecessary and perhaps unenlightened; whereas, in truth, *yoga* is an integral part of our ancient religious tradition. It is not now, nor was it ever, separate from the religious tradition that gave birth to it. *Yoga* is an advanced part of the Hindu religion, a religion which sees realization of the Vedāntic truths as the goal of man. ¶There is an important reason why many in the West were attracted to *yoga* and Vedānta philosophy. The idea of a spiritual path separate from religion comes very close to an ideal that many were, and still are today, seeking. This ideal is unity of world religions. This ideal is promoted by many *swāmīs* who declare that there is much in common between all religions, that there is, in fact, a meeting ground where all agree on certain basic spiritual truths. So, it would seem that the less important areas of difference could be overlooked and the commonly accepted truths proclaimed in unison. *Yoga* and Vedānta are said to be the answer, the meeting ground. ¶But in the final analysis, a spiritual path separate from religion neither fulfills the ideal of religious unity, nor is it really a spiritual path. It remains only a philosophy, a mental concept. Why? Because, for one, each religion knows all too well the true importance of the many seemingly less significant practices and rituals of their religion. They know that for most people the dutiful performance of these practices helps stabilize them in their spiritual lives. For some, any type of theology or philosophy, let alone mysticism, is beyond their realm of thinking. But what they can do, and need to do, are simple religious performances, the fruits of which will, later in life or in future lives, uplift them into deeper stages of spiritual life. To set aside this aspect of religion would be to destroy the religious life of millions. ¶Secondly, even those who are seemingly beyond the need for external religious practice, who would be inclined to accept a nonreligious spiritual path as their way, will eventually find themselves on unstable ground, and for many reasons. Each religion has a hierarchy of saints, angels and archangels which assist all of its followers from the inner planes, helping them through their difficult times, answering their prayers and supplications. When we leave the fold of religion, we remove ourselves from the benign influence of these great beings and actually open ourselves to much lesser, base influences which can disrupt our lives. Spiritual life, especially as one progresses into stages of mystical experience, is a very delicate process. Powerful forces are awakened in us that we may or may not always be able to perfectly control.

Thursday
LESSON 305
Unity at the Mountaintop

If we return to our analogy of the mountain peak, the path to it, religion, would be likened to a well-trodden trail. There are many people all along the way to assist in times of need. There are also those few in each religion who have walked the entire path, reached the summit and can lead others along the way. Those pursuing *yoga*, philosophy or mysticism separate from the foundation of day-to-day religion are like lone climbers treading through unknown territory, up unknown slopes. Theoretically they too can reach the summit. But realistically they do not. Mountain storms, unforeseen precipices, dead ends and untold other dangers and detours eventually claim such would-be seekers. Many fall into the crevice of intellectual rigidity and arrogant argumentativeness. ¶The path of *dharma,* which is India's word for religion, is the sure and proven path. They call it the eternal path, Sanātana Dharma. True religion does not discount mystic experience. Every true religion has produced its mystics. And it is here where religious unity is realized. The Zen master,

Christian mystic, master of Kabala, Sufi mystic, Shinto shaman, Hindu sage and Taoist recluse can all speak of unity. They can all look into each others' eyes and see no differences, but only oneness of spirit. For there is but one mountain peak that rises above the clouds. And all true seekers, regardless of their religion, must find their way to this one summit within themselves, sometimes transcending the religion of their birth. In mystic experience lies the unity of all religions. ¶Vedānta is an attempt to describe the experiences of the mystic. But how many actually attain to these final heights of realization? Many speak of them, but in the final analysis, too few ever reach them, for very few are willing to go through the rigorous efforts of purification. Few are willing to face each fault and weakness in their nature. Few are willing to take their scriptures, their spiritual leader's words and their own intuitive knowing to heart and apply and practice their religion every day, every hour, every minute. But this is what it takes. It takes this kind of dedication, this kind of unrelenting effort. ¶The mystic whom we see poised on the peak of God Realization is the man who once faced each experience that you now do. He didn't skip them or go around them. He had to deal with the same doubts, the same fears and the same confusions. He had those same experiences where all seems against you, and you seem so alone and ask, "Why am I the one who has these unsolvable problems, these totally confusing situations?" He didn't give in to that abyss of doubt. He threw himself at the feet of God when all seemed beyond hope. And hope appeared. He persevered, tried his best, made the decisions that made the most sense in spite of unclarity—and all the while continued his *sādhana,* continued his spiritual practices, until one by one the veils of confusion faded and clarity became constant. He is the man who strived so hard on the little things in life, as well as on the great challenges. He simply *did*—not spoke of, but *did*—what you know you should *do.* We are the carvers of our own future. God's grace, His love, is always blessing us in our efforts.

Friday
LESSON 306
Monistic Theism

In India's spiritual traditions there have been for ten thousand years or more two major streams of thought, one called *advaita* in Sanskrit, or monism in English, and the other called *dvaita* or theism. Our own tradition, known by many names—monistic theism, Advaita Siddhānta, monistic Śaiva Siddhānta or Advaita Īśvaravāda—embraces them both fully. I discovered that the path of monism and theism is the whole of life. As my *satguru* explained, it is the entire path. He compared it to an orchestra and an audience. Playing in an orchestra and being in the audience are two different experiences. The audience without the orchestra is not complete. They would be just sitting hearing nothing. The orchestra without the audience is not complete. They would be entertaining no one. So it is in the plane of duality. We have to practice duality in an intelligent way. Satguru Yogaswami had the full *advaitic* realization of the Self, Paraśiva, but at the same time he had the fullness of *dvaitic* devotion toward God, the Gods and his *guru.* ¶There was a Vedāntin in Jaffna, Sri Lanka, who was very pompous and looked down his nose at duality and temple worship. He did not have a great relationship with Śiva Yogaswami, who was always having fun with him in one way or another. One day Yogaswami saw the Vedāntin in the marketplace and, coming up from behind, tapped him on the shoulder. The man spun around and asked, "Who's there?" Yogaswami exclaimed, "What do you mean, 'Who's there?' Didn't you say there was only one!" Yogaswami had shown the Vedāntin that he could not keep the top of the mountain—the highest realizations of truth—separated from the bottom of it, the day-to-day world. He was making the point that the man had reached the summit only intellectually, through reasoning out the Vedic truths. Therefore, according to the same reasoning process, he had to reject the bottom of the mountain to maintain his arguments. This is the simplistic Vedānta philosophy, sometimes called the path of words, the *vāk mārga,* expounded by people who can eloquently explain Vedānta but have had no personal spiritual experience. They have attained the power to live a completely ordinary life as philosophically perfect *āṇava mārga* adepts. ¶By the example of his own life, Satguru Yogaswami showed that, having reached the top through realization, the seer cannot reject any part of the mountain, because he remembers his experiences at the bottom, his experiences in the middle and his experiences at the top. Yogaswami taught that we cannot reject direct experience. No one can take that away from us. It is recorded in the *ākāśa* forever. Therefore, *realization* is not synonymous with the word *understanding.* ¶When a musician is playing an instrument in an orchestra, he is having the experience of moving his fingers, arms and hands. The musician is hearing what he is playing and what everyone else is playing as well. Each player is realizing the unity of the entire orchestra. This is the experience of monism—that wonderful oneness. A member of the audience listening to the orchestra is not hearing just one instrument, but all playing together in unison. But he is only experiencing through his ears. That is the experience of theism—that wonderful twoness. ¶The orchestra can exist without the audience, but the audience cannot exist without the orchestra. That is why the monist can go on with his practices even if there is no temple close by to worship in. He can go on with his practices even without an image of God. The theist cannot do this. Without the image of God or a temple to worship within, he is lost. ¶Monistic theists are practical philosophers. They put the orchestra and the audience together. They have the grand experience of the fullness of life. They enjoy the top of the mountain and its bottom. They put monism into theism and bring theism into monism. They are the full persons on this planet. All the great *yogīs* and sages wandered from temple to temple worshiping externally, and in their internal worship realized God and the Gods within themselves.

Saturday
LESSON 307
Monism Without Theism?

Every monist, in deep or superficial conversation, will occasionally admit that the Gaṅgā is a sacred river and Mount Kailāsa is a sacred mountain. In admitting that, he is also somewhat of a theist at the time. Hindus believe that the Gaṅgā and Kailāsa are the ultimate temples. Most monists want to have their ashes put in the Gaṅgā when they die. Every Āgamic priest will tell us that Mount Kailāsa is at the top of the head and at the top of the world. He will explain this is where God is, in and above the *sahasrāra chakra.* This knowledge is right within the *pūjā* liturgy he chants. Therefore, when we find a monist who hides the fact that he is somewhat of a theist, we must question if his monistic outlook is sustained only by his intellectual abilities, clichés and cogent arguments. ¶Yes, following monism without theism makes it rather difficult to reconcile all life's experiences. But there are very few true monists. Many monists will not pass by a temple without a silent pause, even though they will argue that no one is home there. For the rare, nonreligious monist who goes deeply into monism and truly experiences it, theism comes up from within as a reward. This happened to Swami Vivekananda, who denied the reality of the Gods and Goddesses all his life, then changed his belief when he had a vision of the Goddess, Śakti, in the last days of his life. ¶To truly understand theism and monism, each should be taught separately, by the same teacher. The student is never given permission to make a choice between them. When each has been understood and there are no more questions, the teacher will blend them together in the mind of the devotee by requiring the practice of external and internalized worship. The theistic discipline is the external worship, and the monistic is the internal worship. ¶We are on the safe path of *yoga* when we are able to internalize the external worship. Otherwise, without this ability, devotees often just perform intellectual, mental gymnastics which result in no attainment whatsoever. Their nature begins to harden rather than soften. Their philosophical discussions become more rigid and unyielding. By blending monism into theism and theism into monism, the nature of devotees becomes soft and loving, as the spiritual unfoldment begins. They become wise and helpful to others as the maturing of their spirit progresses. Such persons have compassion for another's point of view, and all of the fine qualities of the soul come forward to be enjoyed and seen by others. ¶Monistic theism is a very detailed map of consciousness which has broadness and philosophically accepts all states of consciousness. The monistic theist does not turn away from the external world. He knows that Śiva's perfection lies everywhere within it. He attempts to expand his consciousness into the perfection within all three worlds. He attempts to experience the harmony of all of nature. He attempts to be one with Śiva's perfect universe, to live with Śiva. The monistic theist is the perfect Hindu in all respects. ¶Most Vedāntins are able to totally describe the country, or area of consciousness, in which they are residing. But because they do not practice much *yoga*, they are not all-pervasive enough in consciousness to understand the other countries on the planet, or other areas of the mind. For this reason their maps of the mind are relatively incomplete. Some draw lines into squares and shut out what they don't understand. Monistic theists draw lines into circles and take in the entire universe, including everything within everything.

Sunday
LESSON 308
Freedom and Responsibility

A human being has a dual and nondual component. He has belief. He has faith. He has love. But all of these fine qualities can be taken away through discouragement. His faith is faith in the unseen. His belief is belief in things that are not always intellectually rational. His love is love of all that is tender and beautiful. All of these fine qualities and many more work together in lifting up consciousness toward the ultimate reality of timelessness, causelessness and spacelessness. There is not one human being on the planet who will not eventually understand the monistic theist approach. This is because it is an intrinsic part of the human psyche. Everyone is a monistic theist in one way or another. ¶Historically, there have always been monists on one side and theists on the other. The one path that is made up of these two camps is monistic theism. It encompasses both. And, yes, it is the solution to many of the problems people face today. Śaiva Siddhānta is the final conclusion of the adepts, and it includes the true precepts of Vedānta. There can only be one final conclusion, and that is monistic theism. ¶The problem is that Vedānta as taught today gives privilege without the disciplines, creating *jñānīs* of intellect rather than realization. This privilege is taken as a boon by those of little spiritual attainment. Freedom without responsibility is another privilege given. This is also taken advantage of by the undisciplined; whereas discipline and responsibility should be taught and mastered before higher philosophy is delved into and practiced with any seriousness. The beginner should not be taught to rationalize on the nature of man and the universe from what he has memorized. He should be brought into the culture and community of Hinduism and establish a religious, fully committed, disciplined life before proceeding onward. We must become aware that the neo-Indian approach to Vedānta is very new, indeed. The true Vedāntists—those who have reached the ultimate realizations—have reached them by following the path of monistic theism. Modern Vedānta gives privilege without discipline, and the modern New Age movement gives freedom without responsibility. Is there a difference? ¶Monistic theism does not give privilege. It preaches a more pragmatic approach to life. Śaiva Siddhānta builds character within the individual—spiritually, socially, culturally, economically, karmically and dharmically. Aspirants have to meet a series of daily, monthly, yearly fulfillments. Truly, monistic theism is the path to *mukti* and merger. ¶The monistic Śaiva Siddhānta *bhaktar* can understand and appreciate the point of view of anyone, because his love of Śivaness in all extends his communication faculties. He is able to talk with each philosopher on his own level. When this happens, the feeling of sharing and giving exists. The *bhaktar* is wise enough to know that the other person may not understand his point of view. This ability is a great barometer for judging the attainment of any *bhaktar*, whether he can or cannot actually be one with—in empathy with, in heart and mind, in love and trust—rich man, poor man, beggar man, thief, doctor, lawyer, temple priest and in his heart make no differences. This is the true Śiva *bhaktar;* this is the true monistic theist; this is the true Śaiva Siddhāntin; this is the true Advaita Īśvaravāda adept, who lives the statement, "Lord Śiva is the Life within the life of everyone," as a fact, not a metaphor.

Devālayāḥ

देवालयाः

Palaces of the Gods

The rites of oblation, O lovers of truth, which the sages divined from the sacred verses, were variously expounded in the threefold Veda. Perform them with constant care. This is your path to the world of holy action.

Atharva Veda, Muṇḍaka Upanishad, 1.2.1. VE, P. 414

Monday
LESSON 309
Angelic Helpers

Good evening! It is wonderful to be in Mauritius and see how strong Śaivism is here. You have the advantage, not enjoyed in countries like Sri Lanka and Malaysia, that Hindus form the majority of the population of this beautiful island nation. This makes it possible for you to set a fine example to all the world, to courageously and dynamically teach and preach the Śaiva faith through your temple society and other fine institutions. I hope you will do this, and by doing so bring Śaivism positively into the technological age. ¶Tonight I want so speak about the great Gods of our ancient religion and the holy temples where we commune and communicate with these spiritual beings. A Hindu temple such as this one is filled with millions of *devas*. When someone is born into the Hindu religion, or formally accepted into the religion later in life, guardian *devas* in the unseen worlds are assigned to automatically protect and guide him through his Earthly life. These guardian *devas* in the heaven world cannot be seen by you with your physical eyes, but they can be seen and are seen by those who know how to use the psychic vision of their third eye. Nevertheless, you can feel their presence in your home. They surround you, they help you and they communicate with the great Gods of our religion to guide you through life. ¶There are three worlds of existence. The Third World is where the highest beings, such as Lord Gaṇeśa, Lord Murugan and our Great God Śiva, exist in shining bodies of golden light. This Third World is called the Śivaloka. The Second World of existence, or astral plane, is called the Devaloka. The great Gods have millions of helpers in the Devaloka who help each and every one of us. One or more of them is assigned to personally help you in this First World, which is the world of material or physical existence, called the Bhūloka. When we leave our physical body at night, we go into the Devaloka, the Second World, and commune with the *devas* there and with the Gods of our religion in the Śivaloka, the Third World. ¶Śaivism's most sacred substance, the holy ash, is the symbol of our religion, and we wear it across our forehead as a symbol of purity. But even more so, the *devas* in the Devaloka, in the Second World, can actually see this sacred substance on our forehead. They can actually hear the chanting of your sacred devotional hymns, your *Devarams*. They can actually see the flame

Hindu temples are homes of the Gods and the source of culture. This one lies in the Himalayan hill forest and houses a Śivaliṅga in the main sanctum and in nearby forest sanctuaries. Below are enshrined Naṭarāja, Gaṇeśa, Kālī, Vishṇu and Brahmā.

that is passed before the image that represents the Deity. This is why we wear this pure white ash, to alert the *devas* that we are members of this religion. This *vibhūti* is a sign, a way of saying, "We seek your help, and we seek your blessings." And by seeing the ash, they can distinguish your face. When they look into this world, it is like looking through a veil. They cannot see us too clearly. So we have signs and symbols to attract their attention, to earn their grace and their blessings. This is why it is important, especially when you come to the temple, to wear the sacred ash, so that you can be seen by the great beings in the inner worlds and attract their attention. They will respond. They will heal the aching mind.

Tuesday
LESSON 310
The Hindu Forehead Dot

Why do we wear the *pottu*, the red dot between our eyes? The dot worn on the forehead is a sign that one is a Hindu. It is called *bindi* in the Hindi language, *bindu* in Sanskrit and *pottu* in Tamil. In olden days, all Hindu men and women wore these marks, and they both also wore earrings. Today it is the women who are most faithful in wearing the *bindi*. The dot has a mystical meaning. It represents the third eye of spiritual sight, which sees things the physical eyes cannot see. Hindus seek to awaken their inner sight through *yoga*. The forehead dot is a reminder to use this spiritual vision to perceive and better understand life's inner workings—to see things not just physically, but with the "mind's eye" as well. With our third eye, we can see into the future. With our third eye, we can see into the next world, the Devaloka. With the third eye, we can see into the Third World, the Śivaloka. With our third eye, we can see into the past. It is an eye that we were born with and which is eternally awake, but we are usually unaware of its many functions. In most people it is clouded over with intellectual ignorance and disuse. When we are in a state of meditation and our entire mind is concentrated in the area of the third eye between our eyebrows, we see a red light begin to form. When we put a red dot between our eyebrows, the *pottu*, or *bindu*, as we are taught to do in the temple and at home, this enhances the use of the third eye, just as eyeglasses enhance the use of our two eyes. ¶There are many types of forehead marks, or *tilaka*, in addition to the simple dot. Each mark represents a particular sect or denomination of our vast religion. We have four major sects: Śaivism, Vaishṇavism, Śāktism and Smārtism. Vaishṇava Hindus, for example, wear a V-shaped *tilaka* made of clay. Elaborate *tilakas* are worn by Hindus mainly at religious events, though many wear the simple *bindi*, indicating they are Hindu, even in the general public. By these marks we know what a person believes, and therefore how to begin and conduct our conversations. ¶For Hindu women, the forehead dot is also a beauty mark, not unlike the black beauty mark European and American women once wore on the cheek. The red *bindi* is generally a sign of marriage. A black *bindi* is often worn before marriage to ward off the evil eye. The *bindi* is sometimes used as an exotic fashion statement, its color carefully chosen to complement the color of a lady's *sārī*. Ornate *bindis* are sometimes worn by actresses in popular American TV shows. ¶It is common in many religions to identify one's beliefs by wearing distinctive religious symbols. Often these are blessed in their temples, churches or synagogues. Jewish men wear the round skull cap, *yarmulka*. Christians wear a cross or medal on a necklace or coat lapel. In some countries, Muslim women still cover their face with a veil. ¶So, do not hesitate to wear the *bindi* on your forehead in the United States, Canada, Europe or any country of the world. It will distinguish you from all other people as a very special person, a Hindu, a knower of eternal truths. You will never be mistaken as belonging to another religion or to no religion at all. For boys and girls, men and women, the dot can be small or large depending on the circumstance. Recently a Canadian TV documentary distinguished the *bindi* by calling it a "cool dot." Times are changing, and to proudly wear the symbols that distinguish and define us is totally cool!

Wednesday
LESSON 311
The Nature Of God Śiva

The most important teaching of God Śiva is that He has three perfections. He is not only timeless, formless and spaceless. That Absolute Reality, Paraśiva, is but one of God Śiva's perfections. He also has an all-pervasive form which flows through all things—Satchidānanda. He pervades all form. There is no place that Śiva is not. And He has yet another perfection, which is a golden body of light in the Third World, a perfect body in which He is our Lord and Creator, the most wonderful and loving and perfect Being we can imagine. In the temple, when we invoke God Śiva, He comes in this golden body of light and blesses the people. He can see you. He can hear your prayers. He has created all the souls on this planet and all other planets in our universe, our holy scriptures tell us. ¶God Śiva is in all things and everywhere simultaneously, at every point in time. And yet, Śiva as Maheśvara, the Divine Dancer, Naṭarāja, has a body not unlike yours or mine, a body in which He can talk, a body in which He can think, a body in which He can see you and you can see Him, a body with legs, a body with arms. In this body He dances the eternal dance. I had a vision, once, of Śiva Naṭarāja dancing. I could hear the bells on His ankles. I could see His feet and legs. He is a beautiful dancer, and He dances in the Third World. ¶God Śiva is so close to us. He is closer than our breathing, nearer to us than our hands or feet. Yes, He is the very essence of our soul, and yet He has a body just like ours that lives in the Third World. In this body of light He can come into the inner sanctum of the temple, and He can look at us, and we can feel His *śakti*, His power and presence. He is our great God, the ruler of this universe. ¶Sometimes we hear the misconception that if you worship God Śiva He will take everything away from you. That is not true. That is anti-Śaivite propaganda. It is not true at all. God Śiva gives you everything, because He is the universal God described in the *Vedas* as the Life of your life. This unfavorable propaganda, which exists primarily in the north of India, but elsewhere, too, postulates that Śiva is only Rudra, the Destroyer. It makes people afraid of Śiva. There is never a reason to fear Śiva. He is a God of love, of compassion for all He has created. ¶Nothing has ever been destroyed by God Śiva but that He creates, constantly changes the form of and absorbs back to Himself His creations. For is not the ultimate absorption, after eons of time, the ultimate destruction of what was once created? This is the goal, is it not, for all to merge in oneness with our God Śiva? We are not destroyed by doing this. We are fulfilled! He does not take anything away from us, but that which would harm us. God Śiva takes from us greed and gives abundance. God Śiva takes from us lust and gives contentment. God Śiva takes from us anger and gives love. God Śiva takes from us jealousy and gives self-confidence and security. God Śiva is an ever-fulfilling God.

Thursday
LESSON 312
Temple Metaphysics

Our Supreme God Śiva has created the Mahādevas, the Gods, to help us, to protect us, to inspire us—such as Lord Murugan, Lord Gaṇeśa and many others. Gaṇeśa, above all others, is the God, the great Mahādeva, to be invoked before every act and especially worshiped and prayed to when changes occur in our lives as we move from the old established patterns into new ones. Lord Gaṇeśa is always there to steady our minds and open the proper doors as we evolve and progress. He never, ever fails. He is always there for us when we need Him. Lord Murugan was created by God Śiva's *śakti* and given a *vel* of spiritual discernment, a lance of divine intelligence. Pray to Lord Murugan to unravel the great mysteries of the universe. Pray to Lord Murugan to make you a spiritual person.

Pray to Lord Murugan to release you into the arms of Lord Śiva by teaching you more about your Śaivite religion. ¶The understanding of the reality of God and the Gods may help you to appreciate the importance of prayer and worship. Take, for instance, our hymns and chants—our *Devarams* and *bhajanas*, our *japa* and the many other ways we express the praises and love of God Śiva that we feel in our hearts. These hymns are actually heard by the subtle beings. *Devas* in the Second World come, hover around and near us and rejoice in our singing. If we are deeply devoted and inspired, then even the Mahādevas of the Third World will hover above the *devas* in their magnificent bodies of light, showering blessings to those who are singing or chanting prayerfully. ¶You may not be able to see these subtle beings, but you can feel their presence, feel a holy atmosphere around you. I'm sure that many of you here have felt this, perhaps while chanting Aum Namaḥ Śivāya. As long as somebody is saying "Aum Namaḥ Śivāya," the Śaivite religion exists on the planet in full force. Wake up in the morning saying "Aum Namaḥ Śivāya, Aum Namaḥ Śivāya." Go to sleep at night saying "Aum Namaḥ Śivāya, Aum Namaḥ Śivāya," and through the night you will leave your physical body and travel in the celestial spheres, where we are all together, learning, meditating and advancing ourselves spiritually. ¶On this Earth plane the Gods have a special home, and that is the holy temple. It is in the sanctified temple, where regular and proper *pūjā* is being performed in a pure way, that the Gods most easily manifest. You can go to a Hindu temple with your mind filled up with worries, you can be in a state of jealousy and anger, and leave the temple wondering what you were disturbed about, completely free from the mental burdens and feeling secure. So great are the divine psychiatrists, the Gods of our religion, who live in the Third World, who come from the Third World to this world where our priests perform the *pūjās* and invoke their presence over the stone image. ¶Hindus do not worship stone images. Don't let anyone ever convince you of that. It is absolutely false. Those who say such things simply do not understand the mystical workings of the temple, or they seek to ridicule our religion because they feel insecure about their own. Hindu priests invoke the Gods to come and manifest for a few minutes within the sanctum of the temple. The Deities do come in their subtle bodies of light. They hover in and above the stone image and bless the people. If you are psychic and your third eye is open, you can see the God there and have His personal *darśana*. Many of our ancient Śaivite saints, as well as contemporary devotees, have seen such visions of the Gods. They know from personal experience that God and the Gods do exist. ¶When we go to the temple, we leave with our mind filled with the *śakti* of the Deity. We are filled and thrilled with the *śakti* of the temple in every nerve current of our body. When we return to our home, we light an oil lamp, and that brings the power of the temple into the home. This simple act brings the *devas* in the Second World right into your home, where they can bless the rest of the family who perhaps did not go to the temple. With a little bit of study of the mysticism of Śaivism, we can easily understand how the unseen worlds operate in and through us.

Friday
LESSON 313
Talking to God During Pūjā

Many have wondered what the priest is saying when he is chanting in the Sanskrit language, which is the language of the *devas*, the celestial beings. When he is in the shrine chanting and performing *pūjā* with water, flowers and other offerings, you may wonder about the meaning of those very complex rituals. The priest's craft is very important to the proper working of the temple in our lives. He must be pure and follow strict disciplines so that the Gods will be drawn to the sanctum. Through his chanting, he is speaking to God and the Gods, saying, "O God, I am going to perform this *pūjā* at such-and-such a temple located in such-and-such a place in your universe of forms, and this *pūjā* will be for the purpose of such-and-such. I hope that you will consider this worship auspicious and grace it, and that you will grant our needs and our wishes and bring good things into the lives of everyone in this community. I pray that we will please you with our worship, making no errors and forgetting nothing that should be done. But if we do, Lord, please forgive us and make the blessings of this *pūjā* just as powerful as if we had done it perfectly, without error. We beseech you to come to this temple and hover over the stone image with your body of light and bless the people. Thus, I am offering you rice. I am offering you fruits and flowers. I am offering you all the fine things that we have, so that you will come and stay for awhile." ¶The priest's initial chants are basically letting God know the place and purpose of this day's worship. He intones, "We hope we are pure enough in our performance of the *pūjā* that we sanctify the atmosphere here, so that you will come and be our honored guest in this temple." Then he bathes the Deity image, dresses the Deity in fine clothes, and worships the Deity so that the God from the Third World will come into this finite body in the First World, this body made of stone. Our bodies are made with bones, but we are not our bones. The God's body in the temple is made of stone, but He is not that stone body. His Third-World form is a body of light. He is a great soul, just as we are also souls. ¶During the height of *pūjā,* the God comes with all of His *devas,* His celestial helpers. They take the problems or concerns out of your mind, harmonize the currents of your body and dissolve all the problems for you. When that happens, you walk out of the temple feeling you have been blessed, having forgotten the concerns that you went in with. ¶If you arrange for an *archana*—an optional personal *pūjā* generally held in-between the main *pūjās* of the day—the priest pronounces your name. He intones the name of your birth star, or *nakshātra,* and presents you to the God in a proper way. He says, "O Lord, this devotee humbly requests blessings for a particular problem or a special event. Please hear his prayers as he places them at your holy feet in the knowing that you will assist with the best possible outcome." "Would this work just as well if the priest chanted in English?" you might wonder. Yes, it would! In your mind you can talk to the God in English or in any other language, and He will understand. But the Sanskrit language has its own power, a spiritual vibration. It is a most ancient language, and far more subtle in its ability to communicate spiritual ideas and meanings. That is why it gives a good feeling to hear the ancient *mantras,* even if we don't understand them.

Saturday
LESSON 314
Approaching The Temple

Devotees ask, "Why do we circumambulate the temple?" When we come to the temple out of the world, off the street, we are often shrouded by negative vibrations, which can actually be seen in our aura. Our nerve system may be upset, especially now, in the technological age, when we often suffer from stress and strain, the insecurity of so many changes and the rapid pace of life. In order to prepare ourselves to enter the sanctum sanctorum of the temple, the great *maṇḍapa* inside, we walk clockwise around the temple very slowly. In this way we prepare our mind. We consciously drop off worldliness, letting the sufferings go, letting all disturbances leave our mind the best we can, and trying to reach deep inside of ourselves where peace exists eternally. We become as celestial as we can during the time we are walking around the temple, so that we can communicate with the celestial beings within the temple. ¶A Śiva temple marks an agreement between God Śiva and the people on the Earth as a meeting place where the three worlds can consciously commune. It is the home of Lord Śiva and many of the other Gods. Specifically sanctified, it possesses a ray of spiritual energy connecting the First World with the Śivaloka. My *satguru,* Siva Yogaswami of Sri Lanka, proclaimed, "O Lord, O Primal One who gives blessings to devotees, who has become the embodiment of Love, O Supreme Lord, Transcendent One who dwells in the temple, make me to live here like a God. In this world we may acquire a multitude of *siddhis,* but never stray from *bhakti's* path, nor disobey the words of *bhaktars.*" A holy Śiva temple must be approached with great reverence and humility, as God lives in the temple. Go into the temple as you would approach a great king, a governor, a president of a great realm, anticipating, with a little trepidation, your audience with Him. ¶The worship in the temple creates the culture in the land. The worship in the temple creates the wealth of the land. The worship in the temple creates the obedience to the divine law of God Śiva, the Śaiva Dharma. The ancient *Tirumantiram* conversely warns, "When in Śiva's temple worship ceases, harm befalls the ruler, scanty are the rains, theft and robbery abound in the land" (518). The greatest temples in the world are the homes of God Śiva, and within them there are private rooms and sanctums for Lord Gaṇeśa, Lord Murugan and others of the 330 million Gods of our Śaivite Hindu religion. Pray to God Śiva. Flock to the Śiva temples, and God Śiva will reward you, each and everyone of you, abundantly, as you perform His worship. ¶We just visited the great temple of Chidambaram, where God Śiva dances. The priests at the temple had their inner sanctum, the *garbhagṛiha,* scientifically tested. Scientists from the West came, made certain measurements and found that the inner sanctum was not only radioactive, but it also had the highest level of gravity on the planet. Yes, things are very heavy in the inner sanctum, much heavier than any other place in the temple or the surrounding area. And it was radioactive. This great power has been built up by thousands of years of worship there. ¶Why are Americans converting to the Śaivite religion? Because they have actually seen these mystical things happen, even in the new temples that are being constructed in the West or in their own meditations. They have actually seen the God come and hover over His First-World image. They have actually felt the rays of *śakti* coming out of the sanctum, cutting through their body, cutting through their aura, and their mind being cleansed and their whole life, even the atoms of their body, being inwardly changed. Therefore, the Americans, who want everything, also want the greatest of all things—the blessings of God Śiva.

Sunday
LESSON 315
Emissaries Of Lord Śiva

Worship God Śiva and you will be filled with love. Become a member of the united Śaivites of the world, who love one another, who take care of each other in England, in South Africa, in Nepal, in North America, in South America, in Mauritius, in Malaysia, in Java, in Fiji, in Trinidad and Tobago, in Guyana, in Suriname, in Sri Lanka and in India. It is this Śivasambhandam, this inner association of Śaivites the world over, that is the strength for Śaivites wherever they find themselves. In this technological age this must become an outer association as well. ¶I urge all Śaivites, devotees of God Śiva, to worship Him as the God of Love and, in doing so, to become beings of love. The great saints of our religion were Śiva *bhaktas.* They changed the world through their love of God. They did not need vast institutions to spread their message. They did not need riches or carts filled with books to spread their message. They did not need radio, television or the Internet. Their message spread because their minds were filled with direct knowledge, direct experience of God Śiva. Their message spread far and wide, though they perhaps never left their native village. They just evolved within it. You, too, are emissaries of Lord Śiva, and your love for Him is your greatest message. Simply love God Śiva and let that love radiate out into the world. ¶We cannot forget that Lord Śiva is the uncreated God. He is the closest to you. He is nearer than your breathing. He is nearer than your heartbeat. He is the very Self of you, each and every one of you. Śaivites love Śiva in that very way, as the Self of themselves. Being in all things simultaneously, at every point in time, God Śiva is in your fingers, He is in your eyes, He is in your heart, He is in your mind. As our great *satguru,* Śiva Yogaswami, said, "There is one thing that Lord Śiva cannot do. He can do everything, but there is one thing He cannot do. He cannot separate Himself from me." That is the only thing that God Śiva cannot do. He cannot take Himself out of you. ¶There are three things we must do: perform or attend *pūjā* every day in the home, attend a temple once a week and make a pilgrimage once a year. These three are the foundation of our Śaiva Siddhānta. Plus, for those who are able, meditation and certain *sādhanas* are part of this worship. External worship builds a vibration within us, and that vibration is taken within, into deep meditation—internalizing the worship in worshiping God and the Gods within you and contacting them within the higher *chakras* until you realize that you also have always been the all-pervasive energy that pervades the universe.

Daiva Prārthanā Preshaṇam
दैवप्रार्थनाप्रेषणम्

Sending Prayers To the Gods

All set for the kindling of the sacred fire, we hymn you, O Lord, with our verses, invoking your powerful grace. In your praise, O Lord, who reach highest heaven, we compose our song, eager to obtain your treasure divine!

Ṛig Veda 5.13.1-2. VE, P. 853

Monday
LESSON 316
The Boon of Prayer Writing

Shortly after the Kadavul Naṭarāja Deity arrived from India at Kauai Aadheenam, our monastery-temple complex on the Garden Island of Kauai, we received the wonderful boon of communicating with the inner worlds through written prayers. With this six-foot-tall bronze image of the Lord of Dance came tens of thousands of *devas.* It was revealed to us that these devonic helpers, though unseen to the physical eyes, are skilled in the art of fulfilling prayers. We were delighted to know that written prayers could be offered into their hands through the sacred fire that burns perpetually at Lord Naṭarāja's holy feet. In those early days of the beginning of the first Śiva temple in the United States, we felt blessed that this magical boon had come to us. Written prayers were offered up through the sacred temple fire and soon answered. The faith began to build among the devotees. The temple *yantra* was now fully activated. ¶But there was a problem. Sometimes, in devotees' emotional fervor, prayers were hastily scribbled out and could not be easily read. Seekers assumed that their requests and pleas for help or solace would be known by the Gods and *devas* who know them personally, and therefore they were not careful enough in composing their prayers, some even forgetting to sign their name or note the date. We soon learned that if prayers were not answered, it might be simply due to incompleteness or illegibility. We also became aware that sufficient explanation must be given for the inner-plane helpers to provide adequate assistance. ¶Here is why absolute clarity is necessary in each written prayer. The astral image of each prayer that arrives in the Second World, or astral plane, is an exact duplicate of its physical-plane counterpart, but not quite as clear—more like a carbon copy. So if the physical-plane original is not clear, its astral counterpart will be even less clear. It will be blurred, like trying to read a letter without one's eyeglasses. Even the astral counterparts of typewritten documents prepared in small type are difficult to read in the inner worlds, we were told. ¶To solve the problem of illegibility, the *devas* themselves gave a new script, which came through from the inner sky in Paris in the early '70s. The *devas* called this script Tyēīf. It is designed to look like bamboo leaves, arranged in an intricate pattern to form 135 characters or "images," the first twenty-six of which correspond to the English

Our loving Gaṇeśa, the rotund Deity honored by all Hindus, is approached with prayers and supplications by four traditionally dressed devotees, each from one of Sanātana Dharma's four primary denominations. Left to right, they are Śaivite, Vaishṇavite, Smārta and Śākta.

alphabet. Here is the word *Tyeīf* written in the *devas'* script:  ¶Writing and delivering prayers to the Devaloka through the sacred fire is an ancient Nātha Sampradāya practice. Today this method of communication is still employed in Shinto and Taoist temples in Japan, China, Singapore, Malaysia and other areas of Southeast Asia. The prayers are written down and placed in the temple fire. As the paper burns, the astral double of the prayer appears in the Devaloka. The prayer is then read by the *devas,* who proceed to carry out the devotee's requests. These temple *devas* are fully dedicated to assist all who come through the temple doors with their emotional, mental and physical problems. ¶It was made very clear to me, however, that prayers may only be sent to the Devaloka in a sanctified *havana kuṇḍa* where special arrangements have been made with the *devas.*

Tuesday
LESSON 317
Tantras of Communication

In our own Kailāsa Paramparā, there is a similar but uniquely different example of direct communion between the inner worlds and the outer. My *guru's guru's guru's guru,* known as the Rishi from the Himalayas, sat for meditation in a tea shop in Bangalore, South India, for seven years, never speaking a word or moving a muscle. Devotees flocked to this extraordinary sage, and with them came the normal quota of problems, questions, prayers and needs. Though they only spoke these needs in their own private thoughts, they were mystified by the way that answers came floating down on twisted-up slips of paper, from an unseen source above the *ṛishi's* head. Devotees would open up these messages to find the exact answers to their unspoken questions. Our prayers burned in the sacred fire are going in the opposite direction, and the answers are coming in more subtle, indirect ways that become obvious as satisfaction is experienced. ¶The knowledge of reincarnation, astral travel, channeling messages from the departed, auras and oh-so-many other psychic mysteries of the soul are an intrinsic part of the Western world in this age of communication, just as these phenomena have been an acknowledged part of life in the East since the dawn of mankind. Communicating with the Gods and their *devas,* invoking, courting and keeping happy angels and *devas* in home shrines has been at the core of nearly every religion in the world ever since religions have existed. ¶Methods of communication with one's guardian *devas,* their friends and associates and the Gods they so faithfully serve are many: the Ouija board, automatic writing, materialization seances, swinging pendulums, extracting knowledge from crystals, sending letters and gifts through sacred temple fires, clairvoyance, clairaudience, early-morning dreams, messages and predictions from entranced mediums, the readings of subtle signs, interpreting the sounds of lizards and crows, visiting psychic mentors, fortunetellers, palmists, astrologers, priests and shamans, exorcism, revelation of knowledge from deep meditation, and more. All of these are *tantras* of communication. A *tantra* is a method, preceded by learning, which often requires an initiation, but not always. ¶It is no accident that you and I are together and you are reading this book and have gotten this far. A great thought form and several *devas* accompany this book which you are now holding. They have guided you to it and are now with you, their inner mind and your inner mind communicating as you continue to read. This highly charged book is itself a doorway into the inner planes. Put it under your pillow when you sleep at night. Study it through the day and absorb the inner knowledge.

Wednesday
LESSON 318
How Prayers Are Answered

The Gods, their *devas* and your own guardian *devas* are ever ready to respond to requests for help and guidance. You may well ask, "How are prayers answered?" It is well known that religious people have guardian *devas*, or angels, helping them through their Earthly experience. Established families who have kept the continuity of togetherness generation after generation court the same *devonic* beings century after century in their home shrines. In our technological age it is difficult to maintain this kind of togetherness or to attend properly to the home shrine. Therefore, other means of communication with the *devonic* guardians must be used. ¶Those who worship in Śiva temples slowly gain acceptance into the *devonic* realms of the Gods, and one or two of the uncountable numbers of *devonic* intelligences often return with the devotee to his home. When this happens, the home immediately has within it the feeling of fullness. It is these guardian *devas* who are the first to receive the devotee's written prayers when they are transferred to the Devaloka through the sacred fire. They read each prayer carefully. If they cannot immediately respond, the prayer is given to a waiting dispatcher along with some personal advice about the individual or the family from their guardian *deva*. The dispatcher carries the prayer, along with the guardian *deva's* advice, to the group of *devonic* helpers who can best fulfill the request. ¶There are many groups of *devas* who sit in *saṅgam* circles, communicating with one another through thought transference. When they receive a prayer, read and understand it, through the power of consensus their group mind begins the process of fulfillment. After the prayer has been read and understood by each one present, it enters their inner minds. When this happens, the solution, *karmically* proper, is revealed to all. One or several of the *devas* is then seen to vanish from the group, on their way through inner space to execute the request. Because Earth time and astral time are different, the entire process takes about three Earth days from the time the prayer is offered until the time that it is fulfilled. ¶These *saṅgams* of *devas* configure themselves in circles of six, twelve, twenty-four and thirty-six. They dispatch many kinds of requests, some business, some health, some personal, some creative, some marital, some mental and others emotional. There is a *saṅgam* circle of *devas* for literally every department of life. These *saṅgams* service the needs of devotees in many temples and shrines in China, Japan, Southeast Asia, Hawaii, India, Africa, North America, Europe and other areas of our planet. ¶Before the Gods and *devas* can respond to your request, they must examine a time line extending ninety-nine years into the past and ninety-nine years into the future. Then they divide the possible decisions into nine groups to choose their course of helpfulness to your *karmic* pattern. Their duty is not to alter time or experience or to manipulate *karmas*, but to assist you in going through your natural *karmas* and to mitigate, nullify and soften the effects of *karmas* of the past that touch you in the present, whether they be good, mixed or bad. Therefore, it is important to delineate your state of mind as you write your prayer. ¶The *devas* surrounding all Nātha temples and shrines respond best to written requests. The Gods and *devas* do not normally read your thoughts—only the thoughts directed to them—and they never interfere in the natural *karmas* of individuals who come into these places of worship. Hindus often say, "God knows my need. He will fulfill it." This is generally true for those who have sufficient mental prowess and intensity of thought, the inner fire burning in the *maṇipūra chakra*, in the heart *chakra* and in the head. But in our day-to-day states of consciousness, it is most fruitful to clearly and precisely let our thoughts be known through the written word. This is the great boon the Nātha temples have to offer—the direct, intricately concise, two-way communication between this and the higher inner world.

Thursday
LESSON 319
Messages to Loved Ones

You may be wondering if you can send written prayers in Tyēīf to loved ones who have passed on to the inner world. The answer is, yes, you can. Your guardian *deva* will hand the prayer to the loved ones, relatives or close friends. They can be communicated with. Through such prayers, many devotees who are feeling badly about their behavioral patterns toward a departed member of their family apologize for misdemeanors performed during their relative's Earthly life. They make the apology by writing a letter in the magical Tyēīf script. It is received by a guardian *deva* and promptly delivered. Everything happens quite efficiently and rapidly in the inner world. In Japan and elsewhere in Asia not only are letters sent to the departed, but many gifts as well are placed in the sacred fire—gifts such as automobiles made of cardboard, money, food and more. The cardboard car and other items, when burned, will reappear in the astral world. ¶Those who have recently given up their physical bodies are easy to reach, because more often than not they are still close to Earth consciousness and enjoy receiving communication from loved ones in the form of written prayers. Souls who are well settled in the inner world but who are nearly ready to reincarnate are also easy to contact in this way. Souls who have attained *mukti,* freedom from rebirth, but who are not yet ready to enter into higher planes where they will no longer be involved with or communicate with those in Earth consciousness—because they have not yet finished helping their devotees to attain their highest potential in this lifetime—will also receive friendly messages from their loved ones on Earth. Many *chelas* communicate with their departed *gurus* in this way. ¶There is a vast inner network of devonic helpers, ever working, never sleeping. They are nourished on the *prāṇas* of the most refined morsels of Śiva consciousness. They never take time out even to eat a meal. There is a continuity of consciousness in the Devaloka that we do not experience in our earthly bodies. It is in the world of the Gods and their *devas* that the mass consciousness is guided through its evolution—the evolution of the *māyā* of the constant, interlaced action of creation, preservation and dissolution. This mighty group of soldiers of the within, preceptors of *dharma,* lords of *karma,* is ever active, available and ready to serve those who seek. ¶Sending prayers into the inner world through the sacred fire is simply a means of communicating with those powerful beings who do not possess a physical body. Using the Tyēīf script is as simple as writing then mailing a letter, sending an e-mail or a fax. Through this means, you can even communicate in Tyēīf with someone living in a physical body in a far-off place. They will receive your message from a dispatcher at night when they are out of the physical body during sleep and conscious on the astral plane. This is truly a magical way of reaching into the inner world and contacting friends and relatives asleep at night in a far-off place. ¶You are also an inner soul and can be seen by the *devas* in their world. They see you in your soul body. Psychic persons living in physical bodies can often see the *devas.*

Friday
LESSON 320
The Dharma Of Prayer

You may ask if the *devas* perform only good for us, and if they test us or punish us. All *devas* are under one of the Gods. When you write prayers to Lord Gaṇeśa, some of His *devas* go to work in finding a solution for you. It is the same for Lord Murugan. Lord Śiva is creator, preserver and destroyer of all that exists, but He also has tens of hundreds of thousands of *devas* who serve His devotees. All Śiva temples are *ahiṁsā,* benign. The temple *devas* who answer prayers are those who represent only two of Śiva's powers: that of creation and that of preservation. The innocent requests, void of malice toward others, are considered benign and acceptable. No request is fulfilled for a bad thing to happen—the death of an enemy, the failure of one person so that another can succeed, the displacement of a neighbor, the fall of business competitors, the injury of those who have injured us, the death of an infidel, equal retaliation for hurts received (the eye-for-an-eye, tooth-for-a-tooth philosophy). Any such retaliatory, hurtful, *hiṁsā* request is automatically placed into another sacred *homa* fire in the inner world by the first *deva* who reads it and sent back to the sender in tongues of fire to his heart to stimulate the fire of *tapas,* to soften his heart and to lift this young soul into higher consciousness, out from the *asuric* realms in which he lives. No, the Śiva temple's sacred fires can never be used for black magic, gray magic or the manipulation of other lives for the personal benefit of one's own. Hurtfulness, *hiṁsā,* is to be avoided, lest it stimulate the fires of *tapas* within the *hiṁsā* advocate and begin a process of purification that one might not be quite ready for. ¶There is no need to fear *tapas,* though it can be painful to see the malice wished on another come back to oneself. This is Śiva's mode of dissolution, a grace that burns away ill will and brings about a softening of the heart. It is one's own malice that must be faced and overcome and destroyed. When *tapas* begins, it will burn off the accumulated dross from the wrongdoings of many past lives and eventually lift the soul to higher consciousness. This is why we call higher consciousness "Śiva consciousness." But *tapas* is a painful process, one to be avoided by not wishing harm on another through the sacred fire. ¶You can gently purify yourself, while avoiding the burning fire of *tapas*, by following the disciplines of Śaivite religious life and *sādhana* such as the *yamas* and *niyamas*, the *pañcha nitya karmas*, scriptural study and other personal disciplines given by the Kailāsa Paramparā *satgurus*. These keep the fires of *tapas* only warm, not burning hot, and accomplish the same purpose over a prolonged period of time.

Saturday
LESSON 321
The Bamboo Tyēīf Font

Several years ago we created a Tyēīf font for the computer, to make it easy to write legible prayers in Tyēīf. On our website, at www.HimalayanAcademy.com/fonts/, you can download the font and also find out more about writing prayers. It is good for your powers of concentration to learn to read the Tyēīf script, but if you are using a computer, this is not really necessary, unless you want to write Tyēīf by hand, which many do. The easiest way to compose your prayer on a computer is to type in an English font, such as Geneva, and then select the text and change it to the Tyēīf font. Prayers written in Tyēīf have built-in confidentiality. You might leave a prayer to the *devas* on your desk. As few people read the Tyēīf script readily, confidentiality is ensured. ¶Should you be traveling and not have your computer with you, you can always write your prayers in Tyēīf the old-fashioned way, by hand. It is artistic to use a soft flow pen, and even more artistic to use a Japanese ink brush. If you want to be really modern, use a black, sharp-pointed pen. The Tyēīf script looks good coming from whatever plume you choose. Many devotees enjoy writing Tyēīf by hand in vertical columns from top to bottom. When writing by hand, this is quite acceptable. Always use black ink, never colors. Black translates to white or gray in the inner world, where the prayer appears reversed. The paper that is white becomes black, and the letters that are black become white. It is only by two or three *devas* holding it and putting their *prāṇas* into it that the prayer again becomes black on white as it appeared when it was sent. They do this only when they want to keep the document to study it. Many prayers are so simple that they can be easily memorized as they appear on the black background in white ink, and it is not worthwhile energizing them into a durable form. ¶If you use colored paper and colored ink in writing your prayers, your words could be unreadable, even using the Tyēīf script. Colored paper appears dark purplish-blue in the inner world, somewhat like the ashes of burned paper, still intact, but barely legible, ready to disintegrate at the first touch. Therefore, just sit down and write your prayer in Tyēīf with a black pen on white paper. ¶Typed documents—on one side of the page only—are acceptable and easily read in the inner world, as long as the size of the type is not too small. Typewritten prayers (again, on one side of the page) in English or any language are also acceptable to the *devas*, as are hand-printed prayers that are written with well-rounded, clearly formed letters. Be sure to sign the prayer and also include the date. ¶The writing of prayers can be done in several ways. Each devotee can write his or her own prayer about personal questions, needs or problems. One can pray for another person, for a group of people, or for a situation to clear up within a group or community, even for solutions to national or world problems. Every prayer received is answered in some way, however mysterious. Not one is neglected, ever. ¶The Gods and *devas* look very carefully into the *karma* of the devotee before taking any action. Because of this, it is always best to describe two or more alternatives that you would be satisfied with in each prayer, rather than insisting on only one solution. This is because your first preference may not be possible in your *karmic* pattern or, without your knowing, it may actually be the worst possible thing that could happen to you. In this case, your prayer would be answered with a non-answer. Therefore, it is wise to suggest two or more alternatives when making a request. For example, in seeking help in finding employment, you might suggest three places you would be content at, indicating first choice, second and third.

Sunday
LESSON 322
Guidelines For Prayers

We are reminded not to ask for services that the *devas* would normally provide, such as "Please help me," or "Please bless me, *devas*." These services are automatically performed by the guardian *devas* of each devout individual without asking. When not responding to requests, the devonic *saṅgams* send their *prāṇas*, with thoughts of help and healing, through the guardian *devas* of the devotee. They literally flood the guardian *devas* with *prāṇas* to be used by them to glorify the home and protect their wards in daily life in the physical world. This is a service given without asking. It refers to the flow of *prāṇic* energy to the devotee, as opposed to getting permission. To receive such blessings for yourself and to receive blessings to start a project are two different things. ¶Devonic helpers often do know what a devotee needs, but they are admonished by the *dharmic* law that requires that they must be asked before steps toward fulfillment can be taken. They are controlled by the worthy law of noninterference in the lives of those who do not pray. Prayer simply means politely asking. This ancient law is: "The devotee must first take one step toward the *guru.* Then the *guru* will take nine steps toward the devotee." Many guardian *devas* connected to the *saṅgam* groups of *devas* are inner-plane *gurus* of *karma,* and when asked they will fulfill their nine steps quite willingly and abundantly. ¶Clarity is essential for the *devas* to fulfill the petitions to the lasting satisfaction of each devotee. For complex issues, the explanations may need to be lengthy. Names and addresses of the various parties involved should be included. Along with your prayers, you can send typed documents, copies of contracts, etc., to clarify the subject. In this way you can make sure that the Gods and their *devas* are aware of the details of your prayer and understand your need fully. ¶Mail or fax your prayers to a temple that knows how to handle prayers through its sacred fire. At our temples we regularly receive and accept prayers for the sacred fire from members of the Hindu religion, for they have Hindu guardian *devas* who are prepared to help with their needs. Non-Hindus have guardian *devas* of other traditions and are not encouraged to write prayers to the Hindu *devas.* Prayers for the sacred fire can be sent to Saiva Siddhanta Church, Kadavul Hindu Temple, 107 Kaholalele Road, Kapaa, Hawaii, 96746-9304 USA. Write "prayer" on the outside of the envelope. All prayers are absolutely confidential, never read by the temple priests. It is traditional to give a gift of gratitude if a prayer is answered to your satisfaction, but not before. If you feel inclined to send a love offering with your prayers, for previous prayers answered, be sure to keep it outside the sealed envelope containing your prayers, as that will be placed into the sacred fire unopened. ¶One word of caution: it would be weakening to depend entirely on the inner-world *devas* to do everything for you. There are many, many things that you can do yourself to overcome difficulties and carve a positive future. They say, "When the will rises and commands, even the Gods are willing to obey." You have to use your willpower first, and try your very best to do the very best that you can. Then you get all the devonic help available. Don't just send in prayers and say, "Live my life for me, inner-world beings. I am not going to do anything. I will just sit back, put my feet up and let you do everything for me." It does not work that way.

Guru Śakti
गुरुशक्ति

The Spirit of the Guru

There is no one greater in the three worlds than the *guru*. It is he who grants divine knowledge and should be worshiped with supreme devotion.

Atharva Veda, Yoga-Śikha Upanishad, 5.53. YT, P. 26

Monday
LESSON 323
The Guru Tradition

In a traditional Śaivite family, the mother and the father are the first teachers, or *gurus,* of their children, teaching by example, explanation, giving advice and direction until their children are old enough to be sent to their next *guru,* in the arts, sciences, medicine and general education. Families that have a *satguru* will often choose the most promising religious young son to go to his *āśrama,* to study and learn the religion and become a *sannyāsin* or a family *pandit* in later years, depending on how his life works out. In this case, the mother and father, the first *gurus,* turn the entire direction of their son over to the *satguru,* the second *guru,* who then becomes mother and father in the eyes of the son, and in the eyes of his parents as well. ¶Hindu children are traditionally brought up respecting their parents. They follow certain in-house protocols of culture and conduct. Therefore, it is not difficult for an Asian man to live in an *āśrama* and follow the protocols of respect that monastic life demands. True *bhakti,* devotion, starts with your mother and father. You have to start there if you want a relationship with God and the Gods. Once the problems with mom and dad are resolved, then that love for the mother and father is transferred or extended to God, Gods and *guru.* It certainly doesn't mean that you no longer love your mother and father. It's just the opposite. You have more love, a deeper love, for everyone. Transferring the love of your family to your *guru* doesn't mean they no longer have your love, but that you've included your *guru* in the family. Love is inclusive, not exclusive, on the spiritual path. ¶To the traditional Śaivite, the *guru* is everything. As Satguru Siva Yogaswami sang, "Mother and father are Śiva. Sisters and brother are Śiva." Therefore, the *guru* is Śiva; and that is everything, because Śiva is everything. But the *satguru* is not your business partner, not your psychiatrist, not your psychologist, not your older brother, as Western persons may regard him. Western people who do not follow any protocol in their homes satisfactory for harmonious living should be careful not to transfer to the *guru* any disobedience and antagonism that they might have had for their parents. Many Western homes, in teaching by example, do so through reverse psychology, teaching what you shouldn't do rather than what you should do. Relating to a traditional *guru* is difficult for those brought up in this way. Respect for

---

A child's first gurus *are his parents, whose feet he touches in respect. Later he will find a* satguru, *a teacher of Sanātana Dharma, to guide him spiritually. Great* gurus *receive inspiration—shown by the ray of light—from Lord Śiva, seen as Dakshiṇamūrti beneath a Himalayan banyan.*

elders is not there. Neither is responsiveness. ¶From my monastic devotees especially I expect the razor's edge of attentiveness. I expect anticipated responses. This means that the *śishya* should read the mind of the *guru,* give the answer without forethought when a question is put. He must be sensitive and anticipate. It is not a schoolhouse relationship: five hours of study and then homework. It is a twenty-four-hour relationship. I expect to see the monastic in my dreams. The relationship with the *gṛihastha* devotees is different. My expectancy is that they will maintain the Śaiva Dharma as it is understood to be in the eyes of the community they are associating with. I also expect each of their male offspring to serve for at least six months, up to two years, at Kauai Aadheenam, in preparation for adult life. And I expect all members to perform four hours of *karma yoga* per week throughout life. ¶We are all involved in the *Nandinātha Sūtras,* which are the combined effort of all the *gurus* of our *paramparā,* with blessings from Maharishi Nandinatha himself. These aphorisms reflect the patterns of belief and behavior of every aspect of life for all those on the Kailāsa path. Nandinātha's great disciple, Rishi Tirumular, shows us in the *Tirumantiram* how well he was taught by his *guru* and how well he fulfilled his mission by going to South India to revive the monistic theism of Śaiva Siddhānta. The vast amount of knowledge in the *Tirumantiram,* which digests the *Āgamas* and *Vedas* and weaves them together in such an ingenious way, indicates a lot of deep meditation, training and *yoga* practice. It also indicates a great spirit, because he actually did what he was sent to do, so we actually have that great treatise today, over 2,200 years later. That shows us an unbroken continuity of what? Intellectual knowledge? No. Of spirit, the spirit of the *guru.*

Tuesday
LESSON 324
Continuity Of Spirit

Before books were invented, the traditional way of conveying information was through the spoken word. This is called *sampradāya. Sampradāya,* verbal teaching, was the method that all *satgurus* used. A *satguru* can only give his *śishya* as much as the *śishya* can hold in his mind at any one time. If the *śishya* comes with an empty cup, the cup is filled by the *guru.* But if the *śishya* comes with a cup that is already full, nothing more can be added by the *guru.* ¶Many *satgurus* work with their devotees in unseen ways. They have the ability to tune into the vibration of a devotee anywhere his physical body might be on the planet, feel how he is feeling and send blessings of protection and guidance. The *guru-śishya* system of training is personal and direct. Much is unspoken between them, so close is the mental attunement. The traditional observance of *brahmacharya* helps to stabilize this relationship. ¶An advanced *śishya* is one whose intuition is in absolute harmony with that of his *satguru.* This harmony does not occur in the beginning stages, however, when the devotee is probing the subject matter of the *guru's* teachings for answers. Only after he has conquered the fluctuating patterns of the thinking mind does an inner flow of harmony begin to become apparent to both *guru* and *śishya.* The *śishya* is expected to cultivate his inner life as well as his outer life. The more sincere and consistent he is with his inner work and his inner friends—God, Gods and *guru*—the more safe and secure and blessed he will be. Your relationship with your *guru* is growing stronger even now as you come to better know yourself and proceed in your study of these daily lessons. ¶Hindu temples sustain Hinduism around the world. Scriptures keep us always reminded of the path we are on and the path we are supposed to be on, but only from the *satguru* can you get the spirit, the *śakti,* the sustaining spirit, to make it all come to life in you, to make the temple meaningful and to complement the scriptures with your own sight, your own third-eye sight. Otherwise, it's just words. ¶Nāthas are not on the path of words. The Ṛishi wandered down from the Himalayas to Bangalore. What did he say? Nobody knows. Whom did he talk to? Nobody knows. Did he influence crowds of people? Perhaps, but he only had to influence one individual, Kadaitswami, to speak out to the world. Kadaitswami caught the spirit of the Rishi, who had caught the spirit of the previous *ṛishi,* the previous *ṛishi* and all the ones that preceded him. It is that spirit of *sampradāya* that makes the traditional teachings meaningful, that gives you the power to discriminate between what is real within those teachings and what is superfluous or just plain nonsense, that gives you the power to blend Siddhānta with Vedānta, *Vedas* with *Āgamas.* ¶The irreversible spirit of the *guru* carries through all of the *śishyas.* It is basically the only gift a *guru* can give—that sustaining spirit. He doesn't have to give knowledge, because that has already been written down. He doesn't have to build temples, because there are more than enough temples for everyone. The rare and precious gift that he can convey is the inner spirit of his religious heritage. That is his unique gift to the world. ¶Nāthas do not follow the way of words. Kadaitswami spoke to a lot of people. Who knows what he said? They didn't have tape recorders in those days, and doubtless he never wrote anything down, but the spirit carried through him to Chellappaguru, who didn't say an awful lot. He wasn't following the way of words either. He spoke only divine essences of the philosophy. He didn't write 3,000 verses like Rishi Tirumular did. Nor did he give lectures to crowds like Kadaitswami did. His spirit was passed on to Satguru Siva Yogaswami, who passed his spirit on to a lot of devotees. ¶We must remember that during the time of the British, all *gurus* had to keep a very low profile and that Yogaswami's great work started to flourish publicly only after the British left Sri Lanka. He passed his spirit on to lots of devotees, including me. If I had not journeyed to the northern part of Sri Lanka and gone to Śiva temples, worshiped there and received initiation from Yogaswami, would I have returned to America and built a Śiva temple or helped found over fifty other Hindu temples scattered around the world? No. Would we have a monastic community? No. Would we have an international Saiva Siddhanta Church? No. Would we have a Himalayan Academy? No. Would we have a Hindu Heritage Endowment? No. Would we have a HINDUISM TODAY magazine? No. Would we have family missions all over the world? No. Would we be sitting here right now? No. Only because of the existence of one *satguru* in this venerable line of *gurus,* I caught the spirit; and through this spirit the words manifest, the activities manifest, the devotees maintain that straight path, the disciplines bear fruit, the inner sight comes, and after it comes, it stays. Without *satgurus,* we would only have temples and scriptures. Without *satgurus,* we wouldn't have the spirit, and people would stop going to temples and stop reading the scriptures.

Wednesday
LESSON 325
Sustaining the Connection

A *satguru* doesn't need a lot of words to transmit the spirit to another person; but the *śishyas* have to be open and be kept open. The little bit of spirit extends like a slender fiber, a thin thread, from the *satguru* to the *śishya,* and it is easily broken. A little bit more of that association adds another strand, and we have two threads, then three, then four. They are gradually woven together through service, and a substantial string develops between the *guru* and the *śishya.* More strings are created, and they are finally woven together into a rope strong enough to pull a cart. You've seen in India the huge, thick ropes that pull a temple chariot. That is the ultimate goal of the *guru-śishya* relationship. ¶Upon the connection between *guru* and *śishya,* the spirit of the *paramparā* travels, the spirit of the *sampradāya* travels. It causes the words that are said to sink deep. They don't just bounce off the intellect; the message goes deep into the individual. Spiritual force doesn't just happen. It's a hand-me-down process, a process of transmission, just as the development of the human race didn't just happen. It was a hand-me-down from many, many fathers and mothers and many, many reincarnations that brought us all here. *Paramparā* is a spiritual force that moves from one person to another. I am not talking about the modern idea of bestowing *śakti* power, where somebody gets a little jolt and pays a little money and that's the end of the association with the teacher. *Paramparā* is like giving a devotee one end of a tiny silk thread. Now, if the devotee drops his end of the thread, the experiences are stopped and only words are left, just words, one word after another, another and another. The devotee then has to interpret the depth of the philosophy according to the depths of his inherent ignorance. What other measurement does he have? The relationship with the *guru* is a constant weaving in and out of one fiber of the thread added to another fiber, added to another fiber, added to another fiber, just like this *khadi kavi* robe we wear in our Order was woven. Each fiber is attached to another fiber, attached to another fiber, attached to another fiber, and finally we have a thread. Between the *guru* and *śishya* many threads are all woven together, and finally we have a firm rope that cannot be pulled apart or destroyed even by two people pulling against one another. That is *sampradāya.* That is *paramparā.* That is the magical power of the Nāthas. ¶As we look at this great line of *satgurus*—coming from Lord Śiva Himself through Nandinātha and countless ones before Nandinatha, to Rishi Tirumular and countless *ṛishis* after him to the Rishi of Bangalore, to Kadaitswami, Chellappaguru and Yogaswami—we see the same spiritual force flowing. We see an undaunted, rare succession of individuals who considered adversity as a boon from the Gods, wherein all the accumulated *karmas* to be wiped away come together in one place to be taken care of all at once. Nāthas don't run from adversity; nor do they resent it. They take it within themselves in meditation and deal with it, dissolve it in the clear white light within themselves, every tiny little bit of it. They consider it a boon from the Gods that it all came at one time rather than strung out over a period of many years. The mysterious Nāthas have their own way of handling almost everything, and much of that is revealed in the *Nandinātha Sūtras.* These *sūtras* have within them, summarized in short stanzas, all the knowledge that's within our catechism and creed, all the knowledge that's in our monastic *Holy Orders,* all the knowledge embodied in our Śaiva culture, in our *brahmacharya* course, and all the other books and lessons we have published and distributed throughout the years. They give codes of behavior, conduct, ways of living, ways of moving, ways of thinking, as well as the basic core of the monistic Śaiva Siddhānta taught by our Kailāsa Paramparā for eons and eons of time.

Thursday
LESSON 326
Why a Guru Is Necessary

Many of you have been studying with me for ten, twenty or thirty years. I want you to think and think through the rest of the day about the spirit of the *satguru.* Suppose you didn't have a *satguru.* You would be guided by the spirit of your intellect, or the spirit of your instinct, or the energies of confusion. The *satguru* only has one job, to keep his devotees on the right track. We do not follow the way of words, which is repeating from memory verses and stanzas of scripture with meager mental interpretations of their meaning. We follow the way of transformational spiritual unfoldment. We follow the *mārga* of *sādhana* and *tapas. Śishyas* move from one stage to another in spiritual unfoldment as they progress through the different petals of the higher *chakras* and come into one or more inner awakenings, one after another. They are not to settle down in any one or several of the *chakras* and consider, "This is a nice life. I like this part of my unfoldment, so I won't strive further." They can't do that, because the spirit of the *guru* drives them onward. He is constantly thinking and saying, "This is not good enough; you can do better." ¶Did Chellappaguru ever say to Yogaswami, "OK, now we've done enough. Let's just be ordinary"? No, he kept walking him around and feeding him, walking him around and feeding him, walking him around and feeding him, walking him around and feeding him, until finally Satguru Yogaswami was walking around and feeding everybody, walking around and feeding everybody, and eventually everybody was doing the same thing. Passing on that spiritual quality, we don't have any problems. We don't have to solve problems with words. Problems are tackled with words when you are following the path of words. This can be a long, long, tedious process. But when spiritual awakenings are there, problems are solved by lifting consciousness. The problem goes away, just automatically goes away. It is a do-it-yourself process, a mystical *tantra* not to be ignored. ¶Every Hindu needs a *satguru,* a preceptor. The *satguru* is as much a part of Hinduism as are the temples, as are the *Vedas* and our other great scriptures, because not everyone can see for themselves. They need someone to see ahead a little bit for them and to keep them on the right track and in the right mood. Because people are tribal, they need a guide. I've heard prominent *swāmīs* all through the years remark, "You all need a spiritual guide. If you don't want me, find somebody else, but you need someone to guide you through life." It could be a grandmother, it could be a grandfather, it could be your astrologer, a temple priest, a visiting *yogī* or a resident *swāmī* in your community, a *sādhu*, a *pandit* or a rare *satguru*—somebody that you will listen to and follow. The choice must be made after much consideration, after talking with parents, consulting elders and searching the heart. Once the choice is made, don't change your mind. Be loyal and give him or her all the love and devotion you have to give and more. Take advice and admonition as golden offerings and proceed in confidence. Many benefits will come from their guidance on the path of *dharma* for a fruitful and fulfilling life. ¶A heavy burden falls upon the preceptor, too. He or she must produce results and continue to do so. Preceptors are not entertainers, content to be lauded or bowed down to in adulation. Rather, they must benefit their followers' lives, lessen their *karmic* burdens and strengthen the family, hold marriages together, as well as seek out potential religious leaders and train them well. They must follow the *karmas* of each individual and each family year after year, and they must be there for devotees when needed most. They must demonstrate their *śānti* and bask in the bliss of attainment. They must be spirit, for spirit lives on.

Friday
LESSON 327
Guidance And Growth

When people do not have a guide, they wander around bumping into each other. They can't see the consequences of their actions. They perform good, bad and mixed actions and don't keep on the right track and therefore end up wandering around in circles. They don't listen to their mothers. They don't listen to their fathers. They don't listen to their spiritual guides. They don't listen to their local religious mentors. But they do listen to the hottest rock star, to their drug dealer and their gang leader. They do listen to the Miranda reading from the police officer before they have to listen to the local judge and later to their parole officer. Some have to listen to their AIDS or cancer counselor and make plans for an early departure. So, they *can* listen. Yes, listening is still functional. Am I communicating? Are we communicating? ¶Unfortunately, many children are raised by their parents these days to not listen to anyone. "Don't ask me. Make up your own mind," they are told, "I just want you to be happy." Children are raised to be confused. They are raised to be loners in a complicated world. They are raised to be lower-consciousness people. And in many schools they are raised to become educated criminals. Let's get back to the basics of raising children properly, giving them proper guidance. It is the *dharma* of the parents to raise their children properly, as it is the duty of the *satguru* to see that they do it. ¶It is the duty of the *śishya* to be responsive to the *satguru* and not resistive. I was impressed at an *āśrama* in India we visited recently with how responsive everybody was to their *guru.* The *guru* there merely looks, and devotees ask, "What can I do to serve?" The *guru* speaks, and everyone immediately responds. No resisting: "I have something else to do. You already gave me ten things to do. How can you possibly want me to stop now and do something else? Isn't there somebody else around here who can do it?" I saw none of that there. Maybe everybody was just on their good behavior because we were there, but it certainly took a lot of practice. They must have been practicing to be on their good behavior for about five years before we arrived. Wonderful responsiveness. Because of such responsiveness, the connection between the *śishya* and the *guru* maintains a systematic growth, and the spiritual life comes up within the individual which breaks all routine and yet works within routine, is beyond all intellectual and reasoning abilities yet works within the intellect and through reason, is unpredictable yet predictable in that it is consistently unpredictable. ¶However, we must remember that blind obedience is never the spiritual way. It is intelligent cooperation that is the binding force in a well-run *āśrama.* Intelligent cooperation means obtaining an extremely clear understanding of what is requested to be done before proceeding. Often this requires asking questions, discussing the direction or project, as one would do in a modern corporation, then, once all is understood, making the leader's direction your own direction. This is intelligent cooperation, not blind obedience. Those are the spiritual qualities that I see in all of you here at Kauai Aadheenam and which are manifesting in my *śishyas* all over the world.

Saturday
LESSON 328
The Mission Of the Nāthas

Responsiveness is the spiritual quality I look for in my devotees. Without that quality in life, nothing really works right. People settle down to an ordinary, routine job, and begin the process of hate, jealousy and revenge, hate, jealousy and revenge, hate, jealousy and revenge with their employer and with employees who work close to them. Nowadays even with their mothers and fathers and brothers and sisters this kind of competition goes on. Such negatively competitive people never make it to the top in any modern corporation or make much out of their lives. ¶In the *Nandinātha Sūtras* I make it very clear that competition—competitive games, competitive sports, competitive activities of all kinds—should not be stimulated within young people, or old people, because the winner-loser consciousness keeps the lower qualities active. I tell my devotees, be helpful to everyone; don't compete with anyone. Do the very best you can and appreciate others' doing the best that they can. You all have a lot to think about when you read the *Nandinātha Sūtras* and consider that the foundation of wisdom within them originated from deep within, 2,200 years ago, when Maharishi Nandinatha sat with his *śishya,* Tirumular, and said, "Go down to South India and teach about the glories of Lord Śiva. Teach that He is within you and you are within Him, that He is the Life of your life, and your soul was emanated from Him. Keep our monistic philosophy moving along down there. I can see that they have gotten a little bit confused." He didn't go to the airport and buy a ticket on a jet plane to South India. He had a long and arduous journey, probably on foot for the most part, and by bullock cart. Many, many things could have happened to him on the way. He could have faced many temptations. He could have been tempted by pretty girls bathing at the rivers. He could have been robbed. He could have been assaulted. He could have been killed, but because of his *tapas* and the good *karma* he had accumulated by being carefully obedient to his *guru,* the connection with his *guru,* the spiritual force, carried him like a magical carpet to where Chidambaram is today. He started his mission and he fulfilled his mission, and his mission is being fulfilled to this very day, right here in this room, and will continue to be fulfilled 2,200 years from now. ¶Nothing can stop the spiritual force. Death cannot stop it. The intellect cannot stop it. Once it begins, it continues. The instinct cannot stop it. Adversity cannot stop it. In the future, we envision pictures of our Nandinātha line of *satgurus* all the way around this room, then around, and then around, and then around. We can see ahead another 2,200 years. It's the same spiritual force, *śakti* of Śiva, flowing through the Nāthas. There are many Nāthas being born again as Nāthas to move things along, to improve conditions; and when things aren't going very well, more Nāthas will come to put a spiritual force into the world through such media as HINDUISM TODAY. This public service of our Nātha order has united the Hindus of the world, educated the Hindus of the world, so they can talk to one another in one voice, in one common forum, and look in the same way at *karma, dharma,* reincarnation, the *Vedas* and *Āgamas* and all these wonderful things that we are writing about in our international magazine. Hindus can now freely and knowledgeably speak about their religion and the four major denominations within it, understand one another in Asia, England, throughout the continents of Europe and Africa, North America, South America, and have better appreciation for their very great religion, which is put forth in HINDUISM TODAY in a simple, pragmatic way. This is all the work of the mysterious Nandinātha lineage.

Sunday
LESSON 329
Inner Bands Of Steel

If you ever become discouraged and wonder about the path, remember that there are three pillars of Hinduism that will keep you on the path: the *satguru*, the temple and the scriptures. Go to the temple, strengthen your relationship with your *guru* and begin studying the scriptures. Discouragement will go away and courage will come. Dark hours will go and bright hours will come. Problems will bend down as the intelligence from the spiritual force begins to come up. This is the way of the mysterious Nāthas, who don't follow the way of words. ¶Nāthas don't have any hype. We are not beating a drum or selling a *mantra* or selling a seminar or selling a promise. We just are who we are, doing what we are doing, and if anyone comes along to help, that is our *karma* at that point in time. We do the very best that we can with the facilities that we have. We don't sell healing. We make no promises. Nāthas do their job on a very broad scale and pay attention to every small detail at the same time. That's the working of the spiritual force that has come from Sage Yogaswami, Chellappaguru, Kadaitswami, the mysterious Ṛishi and those that preceded him, back to Tirumular and Maharishi Nandinatha and those that preceded them and those that preceded them and those that preceded them, for as long as people have walked on this planet. ¶Yes, there are three pillars of our great religion: *satgurus*, temples—Śiva temples, Murugan temples, Gaṇeśa temples—and the oldest scriptures in the world. But it's the spiritual force of the *satguru* that makes the religion come to life in the individual. Would we all be sitting here today if when I went to the Jaffna Peninsula to find my *guru* he wasn't there, and I just worshiped in a few temples for awhile and came back to the United States? No. We would not all be sitting here today. The temples don't give you that kind of spiritual force. The scriptures don't give you that kind of spiritual force. It is only the *satguru* that gives you the sustaining, spiritual force that makes life on this planet worthwhile and gives you the ability to prevail over all challenges and make a lasting difference, not only in yourself but in the lives of others. ¶Now we are all working together to bring Hinduism, especially Śaivism, into the twenty-first century. It is going to take all of our energies collectively to make that next big step, because there will be many changes. It is our job to bring the best of tradition into the twenty-first century, with clarity of thought and, most importantly, with the spirit and mysticism that go along with it. ¶Spirit expressed in a simple example would be, "I want to do my *haṭha yoga!* I want to get up in the morning and meditate!" Lack of spirit is, "I have to do my *haṭha yoga.* Oh, do I really have to? Maybe just today I won't get up and meditate." That's the instinctive mind talking. That's not the superconscious mind talking. "I want to"—that's the spiritual force. "Do I have to?" or "I should"—that's the instinctive-intellectual force. ¶Sitting here today thinking about our wonderful lineage of *gurus*, about what they said and what they didn't say, you will find that we don't know what some of them said and what they didn't say. But what they did, that's the important thing. And how did they do it? Through continuity of the spiritual force—one thread and then another thread, one fiber and then another fiber and another fiber, until a rope was built up that was stronger than any humans could pull apart. Bands of steel, generation after generation, that's the Nandinātha way, unbreakable bands of spiritual force. ¶It is important that newcomers to the Hindu faith, the young people especially, realize that in ancient times as well as today the family unit is complete only when it includes an ordained spiritual mentor, a *guru* or *pandit.* It is to him or her that the family turns in times of joy and celebration. It is to him or her that the family goes when *karmas* are heavy, when difficulties and confusions are encountered on the path and the proper course is unclear. This mentor's firmness and clarity are a stabilizing influence in the family's year-to-year life. For most, but not all Hindus, a family temple is also a necessity, as is a collection of sacred writings or scripture, often the teachings of contemporary masters. ¶We encourage all to receive, with enthusiasm, as one would a God, all Hindu religious leaders, when they come to your community. Show the proper protocol, rush forward, garland them with flowers, lay gifts at their feet in humble obeisance. They are the mainstay and powerhouse and source of all expressions of our beloved Sanātana Dharma and its followers.

Śaiva Maṭhavāsī

शैव मठवासी

Śiva's Monastics

Having transcended the desire for sons, the desire for wealth, the desire for worlds, they go about as mendicants. For the desire for sons is the desire for wealth, and the desire for wealth is the desire for worlds. All these are nothing but desires. He, the *ātman*, is not this, not this.

Śukla Yajur Veda, Bṛihadāraṇyaka Upanishad, 4.4.22. VE, P. 717

Monday
LESSON 330
Monastic Communities

Monks of every Hindu order are guided and guarded by unseen beings who look after their lives as if they were their own. Families are blessed who share in and support the renunciation of their sons born through them to perform a greater *dharma* than the *gṛihastha* life could ever offer. It is the monastic communities worldwide, of all religions, that sustain sanity on this planet. It is the monks living up to their vows who sustain the vibration of law and order in the communities and nations of the world. This is how the *devonic* world sees each monastic community worldwide. This is how it is and should always be. This is how humanity balances out its experiential *karmas* and avoids destroying itself as it passes through the darkness of the Kali Yuga. The monastic communities that surround the planet, fulfilling their *dharma*, compensate for the *adharma* that is so prevalent, thus ensuring that humanity does not self-destruct in these trying times. We must, for the sake of clarity, state here that monastic communities are either strictly male or strictly female. Coed mixed-group *āśramas* are not monastic communities, but classed traditionally as communes. ¶Our *Holy Orders of Sannyāsa* introduce monastic life in the following passages: "The two fundamental objectives of *sannyāsa*, renunciation, are to promote the spiritual progress of the individual, bringing him into God Realization, and to protect and perpetuate the religion. Renunciation and asceticism have been an integral component of Hindu culture from the earliest days, the most highly esteemed path of the Sanātana Dharma. *Sannyāsa* life has both an individual and a universal objective. At the individual level, it is a life of selflessness in which the *sannyāsin* has made the supreme sacrifice of renouncing all personal ambition, all involvement in worldly matters, that he might direct his consciousness and energies fully toward God Śiva. Guided by the *satguru* along the *sādhana mārga*, he unfolds through the years into deeper and deeper realizations. Ultimately, if he persists, he comes into direct knowing of Paraśiva, transcendent Reality. At the universal level, the *sannyāsins* foster the entire religion by preserving the truths of the Sanātana Dharma. Competent *swāmīs* are the teachers, the theologians, the exemplars of their faith, the torchbearers lighting the way for all. Paramaguru Sage Yogaswami sang: 'Hail, O *sannyāsin*, thou

Five vignettes capture the life of Śiva's maṭhavāsis *at Kauai Aadheenam in Hawaii. Their life of meditation and worship, shown by the* homa *ceremony conducted by Gurudeva, is balanced by computerized art and web work, philosophical seminars, publishing and gardening.*

who know'st no guile! Establish in thy heart and worship there the Taintless One—*Pañchākshara's* inmost core. Thou that regard'st all others as thyself—who in this world can be compared with thee?' "

Tuesday
LESSON 331
The Mission Of the Mission

A legacy of *devas* from the entire *paramparā* accompanies our monastic order, providing silent, unseen inner guidance and protection for old and young alike. As long as at least one person within the entire group of *maṭhavāsis* is going into and coming out of Paraśiva once a day, the doorway to the Third World remains open to the hereditary entourage of *devonic* forces that has been building up for over two thousand years. This is because the *brahmarandhra,* the door of Brahm at the top of the head, remains open when Paraśiva is daily experienced within a *maṭhavāsi* community. It could be within the oldest monk or within the youngest. This great realization occurring time and time again within someone day after day keeps the door of Brahm open for the entire *prāṇa chakravāla* of monastics, keeping vibrantly strong the inner, actinic connection with all *gurus* of our *paramparā,* as well as with other *sādhus, ṛishis* and saints who have reached these same attainments, and with the *sapta ṛishis* themselves who guide our order from deep within the inner *lokas.* ¶My Śaiva *swāmīs,* or Nātha *swāmīs,* are distinguished by their orange robes, gold Nātha earrings and three strands of *rudrāksha* beads. They are the Saiva Siddhanta Yoga Order, known as the Saiva Swami Sangam when they gather in ecclesiastical conclave. The *saṅgam* does not follow the protocol of unanimous decision. Rather, it works in intuitive one-mindedness to carry out instructions from the Kailāsa Pīṭham, our spiritual seat of authority, to better the Śaivite mission and the individuals dedicated to its success. ¶These *sannyāsins* are not looked upon as individuals so much as an integrated council, assembled and working in unison to perform a holy work as Sivanadiyars, servants of God Śiva. Guided by the *satguru,* the Saiva Swami Sangam forms the ecclesiastical body of our Hindu Church which works in a humble way to protect the purity of the faith among all Hindu sects, through inspiring publications and other means of encouragement. Specifically, our order's mission is to protect, preserve and promote the Śaivite Hindu religion as embodied in the Tamil culture, traditions and scriptures of South India and Sri Lanka. ¶Our monastic order follows the cenobitic pattern in which monastics live in community and work together toward common objectives. *Sannyāsins* of this order are not wandering *sādhus* or silent contemplatives, known as anchorites, rather they are members of a brotherhood working closely and industriously with their *satguru* and with their brother monastics. At the time of *sannyāsa dīkshā,* each has accepted the mission of the Kailāsa Paramparā as his own: to protect and perpetuate Śaivism; to serve Hindus the world over; to provide, teach and disseminate scripture, religious literature and practical instruction; to promote temple construction and to exemplify the dignity and enlightenment of our Nandinātha Sampradāya. Living under lifetime vows of renunciation, humility, purity, confidence and obedience, these *sannyāsins* are bound to fulfill their unique role in the Śaiva culture of religious exemplars and staunch defenders of the faith. Their ideal is to balance outward service (Sivathondu) and inward contemplation-realization (Śivajñāna) for a rich, fulfilling and useful life. ¶There are two other groups of monks within our monasteries: the yellow-robed *yogī tapasvins* and the white-robed *sādhakas,* living under renewable two-year vows of humility, purity, confidence and obedience.

Wednesday
LESSON 332
An Order of Renunciates

Sannyāsa is the life, way and traditions of those who have irrevocably renounced duties and obligations of the householder path, including personal property, wealth, ambitions, social position and family ties, in favor of the full-time monastic quest for divine awakening, Self Realization and spiritual upliftment of humanity. Traditionally, and in our order, this *dharma* is available to men under age twenty-five who meet certain strict qualifications. Some orders are more lenient and accept men into *sannyāsa* after age twenty-five. The rules pertaining to homeless anchorites are, for obvious reasons, more lenient. Other orders will accept widowers, and a few initiate women, though Hindu custom prefers that women who wish to follow the monastic path take simple vows of *brahmacharya* and not take *sannyāsa.* ¶Women in today's liberal Hindu orders who do take *sannyāsa* should wear white. Women donning orange robes is a new, very new, fashion. My perception over the past decades is that this generally does not work out well in the long run. Those women of history who have been recognized and honored as celibate seekers, as great souls, even as *gurus,* have worn the color white. This was then and is still the order of the day and will be far into the future for many very good esoteric reasons. ¶The householder naturally comes into the *sannyāsa āśrama,* stage of withdrawal, at age seventy-two, having lived through life's three prior stages: student (*brahmacharya*), householder (*gṛihastha*) and elder advisor (*vāṇaprastha*). This fourth stage is a time of turning inward, devoting oneself more fully to worship, introspection, scriptural study and meditation. This step for householder men and women may be ritually acknowledged in a home blessing but is not in any way construed as *sannyāsa dīkshā,* which is a monastic initiation. While traditions vary, after commencing the fourth stage of life, the elder husband and wife, now as brother and sister, turn more fully to religious pursuits while continuing their associations with the family, though they may seek accommodations that offer more privacy for their meditations and worship. ¶An elder man whose wife has passed on and whose children are grown may upon reaching age seventy-two take up the mendicant life fully and then diligently pursue his spiritual *sādhana* in a state of genuine renunciation and not in the midst of his relatives. This is expressed in *sūtra* 210: "Śiva's unmarried men and widowers may renounce the world after age seventy-two, severing all ties with their community and living as unordained, self-declared *sannyāsins* among the holy monks of India." *Sannyāsins* who were formerly married are not generally afforded the same respect as *sannyāsins* who never entered the family *dharma.* ¶Though it is sometimes done, it must be noted that it is against *dharma* for a householder to abandon his wife and children on the pretext of renouncing the world. Becoming a self-declared *sannyāsin* after age seventy-two is also not traditional, for one who has been divorced and whose former spouse is still living. Marriage is a lifetime commitment, and once taken cannot be rescinded.

Thursday
LESSON 333
Disciplined Leadership

Monastics are the religious leaders of Hinduism. Continuing this noble renunciate monastic tradition is essential for the perpetuation of the faith. Therefore, when a young boy expresses the desire to become a monk, parents should never discourage that inclination, but strongly encourage it in all ways. It is a great blessing for the family to have a son become a *sannyāsin.* Each father should guide his sons who express an inclination toward monastic life into learning more of *sannyāsa* by teaching them of the lives of great *yogīs* and *swāmīs,* encouraging them in the arts of meditation, *haṭha yoga* and personal purity, having them read and study the *Vedas,* and bringing them to receive the *darśana* and advice of the *satguru* and *swāmīs* whenever possible. They regard any son destined for the monastery not as their own child, but as the *satguru's* spiritual progeny in their trusted care. They work closely with the *satguru* in guiding his training so as to cultivate skills and character traits that will enhance his future as a monastic. Many devout families seek to birth a son for the monastery. Prior to conception, they mix with the *swāmīs* and pray to the Gods to bring through a soul destined to perpetuate the holy lineage. ¶Once a *brahmachārī* has entered the monastery under vows, he is a very special person living a very special life. He should be treated by everyone, including his own family, as a holy person. He now stands apart from family and former friends. Parents when visiting respect his chosen path and keep family problems from his knowledge. They exclude him from news of marriages, divorces, illness, deaths and other householder events. They should show great interest in what he is learning and speak of high philosophical matters. ¶A life of discipline is not an easy life, but it is a joyous one, with many soul-satisfying rewards. Monastics follow their rigorous twenty-four-hour protocol even in their dreams. Those who are born to perform this service are to be respected and not distracted by family pulls or the desires of former friends. They should be tested, yes, in their beginning years, to be assured that their commitment is firm, their energies secure and their loyalties well understood. Traditionally, at this time family and friends play an important role by bringing temptations to them and valid reasons why they should renounce renunciation. But when their robes turn to yellow or when in white the *rudrāksha* beads are worn, their path is clear and a new protocol on both sides must be firmly kept. All relationships have now changed. ¶The power of *brahmacharya* makes the monks very magnetic, and the temples they serve in powerful. Monastics are therefore careful to keep their distance and not become involved with devotees who attend the temples. In turn, the cultured devotees keep a respectful distance from the monks—physically, emotionally and psychically, not even thinking of them, let alone psychically pulling on them, even in their dreams. Nothing should happen to distract a monk from his chosen path. This code of nonintervention is even more strict for the monk's parents, who share in his renunciation of worldly life for the life of selfless service to the Sanātana Dharma.

Friday
LESSON 334
The Ideals Of Sannyāsa

The Śaiva *sannyāsin* states at the time of his initiation, "All that I have and all that I am I now give unto my God, my Gods and my *guru.* I have no family except the Divine Father Śiva and Mother Śakti who dwell in Kailāsa, and on Earth the *saṅgam* of Śaivite devotees." This is the ideal of not only the *swāmī,* but of all monastics. Therefore, a state of aloofness from blood ties must be maintained on the part of each monastic. This is reflected in the protocol of the monk's not referring to relatives as "my father," "my brother," "my mother," but by formal, impersonal names and common courtesy titles, such as Mr. Sivanesan, etc. This is an affectionate detachment, a lovingly detached attitude, from the *gṛihastha* community. It is a detachment from joint or extended family, which includes former friends, seeing *guru* as mother and father, and fellow monastics as family, *aadheenam devas* as dear relatives, and Gods as close, not far away. Each family learns to respect this renunciate attitude. This is the fabric of monastic life, both for *sannyāsins* and postulants, for in our community, all monastics are on the path of renunciation. Some have received *sannyāsa dīkshā* and others are preparing for it by fully living the life of the one who has renounced the world in one-pointed quest for service and God Realization. Because training must be given when the nature is still young and pliable, I do not accept candidates for monastic life who are over the age of twenty-five. ¶All must always remember that it is a family's greatest blessing for a son to become a *sannyāsin.* But a word of caution must follow. Though a young man may be raised and trained to one day become a monastic, it is he himself who must have the burning desire for ultimate, transcendent realization of Paraśiva. It is he who must have a heart full of selfless service and *vairāgya,* the spirit of renunciation. It is he who must have the *prārabdha karmas* that would allow him to be the ideal *sannyāsin* his parents would hope for. Becoming a monk is not simply a matter of moving from his family home into a monastery. Various tests must be met and passed. The entire monastic community has to be convinced of the young man's sincerity and strengthened by his presence. Such potential *sannyāsins* are watched closely and expected to dissociate themselves from *gṛihastha* impulses such as claiming "my things, my space, my career, my advancement and my exclusive duties." They are examined for the qualities of true *sannyāsa,* tested often as to their flexibility, their ability to instantly renounce attachment to position and job security without residual resentments, the fluidness to release awareness and move transparently from one area to the next as needs arise. ¶How does a monastic serve his *guru* in daily life? He must take every opportunity to be open. At the first level, that of a young aspirant, the mom and dad give him over and say, "The *guru* is now your mother and father. Go and be with him." Then it is up to the young man to think of his *guru* as mother and father and not think of them as his parents anymore. That is what they expect. They are thrilled that they could produce a son who could be a spiritual man, thrilled that their son might be accepted. The next step is on the part of the son himself. In living in the *āśrama* the son only sees the *guru* in his mind. He doesn't see anybody else. When he starts seeing others, finding fault and liking some more than others, that's when the trouble begins. Rather, he serves the *guru's* mission exclusively, in his whole mind, even while he is working with others. He treats everyone equally, with kindly, affectionate detachment. He fulfills each duty wholeheartedly and harbors no preferences for one type of service over another. He doesn't use the facility as a trade school to improve his skills, just in case monastic life doesn't work out. Finally he attracts the *guru's* attention, and the third stage begins. He is given special small tasks to accomplish by the *satguru,* and when successful given larger and more difficult tasks, as the *guru* guides him in strengthening his willpower. From that point on, his life unfolds from stage to stage as he purifies himself and brings forth his Divinity in his service and striving.

Saturday
LESSON 335
The Way of Old Souls

Wouldn't we have a wonderful world of living with Śiva if two thirds of the people on this planet were spiritual lights and had nothing on their mind but to spread the *dharma* of right thought, right speech and right action? It truly would be a global village, a haven, a wonderland. But during this *yuga,* it may not be possible, because younger souls inhabit the planet in abundance, and their only method of discipline among themselves is with the fist, the hatchet, the whip and harsh, insulting words. In this way they accrue much *karma* to be worked out in another birth. This makes a lot of sense, for if they did not make new *karma* they would not reincarnate and never become older souls. It is the tragedies, the hurts, the fears, the arguments that remain unresolved that goad the young souls onward. They learn by their own mistakes, but very slowly, taking the lessons out of their experiences and always blaming on others what has happened to them. This and most of the above is how we come to distinguish an old soul from one in the intermediate grade and those who are unverified. ¶The intermediate souls struggle with their emotions; they hurt themselves more than others. Misunderstanding is not their enemy. It is their teacher of new discoverings. Theirs is the never-ending search. Theirs is the never-ending, not-being-able-to-reach-the-end search. Unlike the young souls, their desires are well-defined. Unlike the young souls, their intellection has some development, maybe not keen but usable. For them, religion is an acceptable solution. They are not superstitious, meaning believing in what they do not understand, as are the young souls. They must be satisfied with adequate reasons of why, how and what the future holds. The intermediate souls all have to learn not to drag the past through life with them in the form of resentment, unforgivingness through unforgettability. This one lesson and this alone distinguishes them from their older examples. But they do look to the older souls for help and for solace, seeking to hold their hand, lean on their shoulder and share with them some of their experiential burdens. ¶Taking up *sannyāsa* as a young man and fulfilling the goals and disciplines of monastic life is for the older souls. These forgiving, intelligent beings rely on their memories of their past when they were young souls. They rely on their memories of the past when they were intermediate souls. They rely on their superconscious abilities to look through and see into every situation, every happening, of past, present and future. Their test, their supreme test, is to balance their inner and their outer life. So, they renounce the world, and in their renouncing, the world they renounced renounces them. Their humanness is still there, their striving is still there, and their seeking for elucidation is still there. But what is not there is the sense of their small self. The sense of the little I'go. The sense of "me and mine" is replaced by "us" and "ours." ¶Not all old souls are ready for holy orders of *sannyāsa,* but some of them are, and these rare few have special qualities. Loyalty to their lineage is one of the most important, and another is love in their will. This means that they do make happenings happen in the external world. They do effect change, but they do not claim reward or recognition. They do not sulk if appreciation is not forthcoming. They move on, ever impelled by their spirituality, that ever-moving force of inspiration that does good rather than harm, that ever-moving spiritual force that quells the external ego and gives credit to others. That rewarding ability to see into the future, prepare for it and to guide others into it is theirs to develop. ¶Young souls merge with each other. Intermediate souls merge with projects and learning new things, merging with the mind and the intellect. Older souls, seeking the Self beyond the mind, merge with the Spirit and with things spiritual. For them, a pure and nearly perfect life calls. They intuitively know that the profound merger of *jīva* in Śiva is no easy task, to be accomplished in a weekend seminar or *yoga* class. So they go farther, they renounce, they take up the ideals of the four *Vedas*—not to parrot them, but to live them, just as did the *ṛishis* of yore. That leads to the path of the renouncer, to the *sannyāsin* in the Indian tradition.

¶Though it may not be your *dharma* to formally renounce the world, you can benefit your search immensely by knowing how the great ones seek to live and respond to life. You can find ways in the midst of your life to follow their example. ¶Realize that the *sannyāsins*, the *sādhus* and the host of nameless mendicants from the traditional orders of Hinduism do have built within them the spiritual, social, cultural structure that has survived siege and pestilence within the countries they serve. But most importantly, these three million soldiers of the within have survived the siege of their lower self, the pestilence of their own mind, and risen above to the heights. This book, *Living with Śiva*, contains within it the wisdom which, once read and understood, becomes knowledge to make the conquest of all conquests, the victory over the instinctive-intellectual mind and all that it contains. All this and more is summed up so eloquently in the "Song of the *Sannyāsin*," in Sunday's lesson, a stirring poem by Srila Sri Swami Vivekananda Maharaj (1863-1902), composed in July, 1885, at Thousand Island Park, New York. I advise my monastic followers to live it, just live it, and try to fulfill in your life these high ideals. To all readers of this book, I say, proceed with confidence along the path of *sādhana*, through which dancing with Śiva, living with Śiva and merging with Śiva is assured and certain. That's the way it is, and that is the way it is.

Sunday

LESSON 336

Song of the Sannyāsin

Wake up the note! the song that had its birth
Far off, where worldly taint could never reach,
In mountain caves and glades of forest deep,
Whose calm no sigh for lust or wealth or fame
Could ever dare to break; where rolled the stream
Of knowledge, truth and bliss that follows both.
Sing high that note, *sannyāsin* bold! Say
"Om Tat Sat, Om!"

Strike off thy fetters! bonds that bind thee down,
Of shining gold, or darker, baser ore—
Love, hate; good, bad; and all the dual throng.
Know slave is slave, caressed or whipped, not free;
For fetters, though of gold, are not less strong to bind.
Then off with them, *sannyāsin* bold! Say
"Om Tat Sat, Om!"

Let darkness go; the will-o'-the-wisp that leads

With blinking light to pile more gloom on gloom.
This thirst for life forever quench; it drags
From birth to death, and death to birth, the soul.
He conquers all who conquers self.
Know this and never yield, *sannyāsin* bold! Say
"Om Tat Sat, Om!"

"Who sows must reap," they say, "and cause must bring
The sure effect: good, good; bad, bad; and none
Escapes the law. But whoso wears a form
Must wear the chain." Too true; but far beyond
Both name and form is *ātman*, ever free.
Know thou art That, *sannyāsin* bold! Say
"Om Tat Sat, Om!"

They know not truth who dream such vacant dreams
As father, mother, children, wife and friend.
The sexless Self—whose father He? whose child?
Whose friend, whose foe, is He who is but One?
The Self is all in all—none else exists;
And thou art That, *sannyāsin* bold! Say
"Om Tat Sat, Om!"

There is but One: the Free, the Knower, Self,
Without a name, without a form or stain.
In Him is *māyā*, dreaming all this dream.
The Witness, He appears as nature, soul.
Know thou art That, *sannyāsin* bold! Say
"Om Tat Sat, Om!"

Where seekest thou? That freedom, friend, this world
Nor that can give. In books and temples, vain
Thy search. Thine only is the hand that holds
The rope that drags thee on. Then cease lament.
Let go thy hold, *sannyāsin* bold! Say
"Om Tat Sat, Om!"

Say, "Peace to all. From me no danger be
To aught that lives. In those that dwell on high,
In those that lowly creep—I am the Self in all!
All life, both here and there, do I renounce,
All heavens and earths and hells, all hopes and fears."
Thus cut thy bonds, *sannyāsin* bold! Say
"Om Tat Sat, Om!"

Heed then no more how body lives or goes.
Its task is done: let *karma* float it down.

Let one put garlands on, another kick
This frame: say naught. No praise or blame can be
Where praiser, praised, and blamer, blamed, are one.
Thus be thou calm, *sannyāsin* bold! Say
"Om Tat Sat, Om!"

Truth never comes where lust and fame and greed
Of gain reside. No man who thinks of woman
As his wife can ever perfect be;
Nor he who owns the least of things, nor he
Whom anger Chains, can ever pass through *māyā's* gates.
So, give these up, *sannyāsin* bold! Say
"Om Tat Sat, Om!"

Have thou no home. What home can hold thee, friend?
The sky thy roof, the grass thy bed, and food
What chance may bring—well cooked or ill, judge not.
No food or drink can taint that noble Self
Which knows Itself. Like rolling river free
Thou ever be, *sannyāsin* bold! Say
"Om Tat Sat, Om!"

Few only know the truth. The rest will hate
And laugh at thee, great one; but pay no heed.
Go thou, the free, from place to place, and help
Them out of darkness, *māyā's* veil. Without
The fear of pain or search for pleasure, go
Beyond them both, *sannyāsin* bold! Say
"Om Tat Sat, Om!"

Thus day by day, till *karma's* power's spent,
Release the soul forever. No more is birth,
Nor I, nor thou, nor God, nor man. The "I"
Has All become, the All is "I" and Bliss.
Know thou art That, *sannyāsin* bold! Say
"Om Tat Sat, Om!"

"Song of the *Sannyāsin*" by Swami Vivekananda is quoted, with written permission, from ***Inspired Talks, My Master and Other Writings;*** copyright 1958 by Swami Nikhilananda, trustee of the estate of Swami Vivekananda; published by the Ramakrishna-Vivekananda Center of New York.

Śaiva Saṁpradāya Śikshaṇam
शैव संप्रदाय शिक्षणम्

Passing On Our Heritage

I know not how to stretch the threads or weave or discern the pattern of those who weave in the contest. Whose son will be the one to speak so well as to surpass, advancing from below, his father?

Ṛig Veda 6.9.2. VE, P. 331-332

YAMAS
NIYAMAS
1. Remorse
2. Contentment
3. Giving
4. Faith
5. Worship
6. Scriptural Listening
7. Cognition
8. Sacred Vows
9. Recitation
10. Austerity
Sri Ganesha

Monday
LESSON 337
Tools for Education

Education is a major issue in religious communities around the world today, including our own Hindu communities. Those who value their traditions everywhere are worried. They see all too clearly that children are learning another culture, or a nonculture, instead of absorbing the precious things in the various heritages. Elders, mothers and fathers, teachers and spiritual leaders are all wondering the same thing about traditional values: "How are we going to pass them along, assure that they will survive?" ¶The Swaminarayan Fellowship has one good answer: involvement of youth at all levels. They know the importance of inculturalization. Individual families have another answer: keep kids out of public schools, use home-schooling systems, of which there are many these days. India is seeking answers, too, and is striving for a balance that incorporates Western knowledge and Eastern wisdom—not an easy goal to accomplish, and as yet unaccomplished for India's 250 million school children. It's even hard to offer them wholesome Hindu literature, since so many books for children and other educational tools are heavily slanted toward violence. Many will excuse it when a God slays a demon or when an indignant sage destroys some evil person, but to my thinking that is also violence, making such stories unacceptable for the minds of our young ones. Presenting violence as a good thing, even a somehow holy thing, definitely causes problems in today's society, where hurtfulness is seen as a simple and legitimate solution to many problems. Many parents are at a loss as to how to solve the problems that surround the education of their youth. One solution they turn to is sending them off to boarding school. This is not a great answer. This is not even a good answer. ¶Śaivites of the world are now uniting in one common cause: to pass on the knowledge of Śaivism to the next generation. They are protecting the minds of their children, saturating the minds of their children, educating the minds of their children, penetrating the minds of their children with the knowledge of our great God Śiva, with the knowledge of Lord Gaṇeśa, Lord Murugan, the *devonic* worlds, the powerful temples of our religion in which God Śiva in His etheric body comes personally and blesses the devotees. ¶Where is religion preserved? It is preserved in the minds of children, recorded in the brain cells of our youth, stored

Each of us has a duty to pass our heritage on to the next generation. Here a teacher is sharing the ancient philosophy with a young class. On the blackboard she has outlined the ancient Hindu ethical principles we must follow to be good human beings and high-minded Hindus.

there for the future. We must teach the Śaiva Dharma to our children. For this we need more Śaivite courses, more Śaivite schools and more Śaivite parents willing to teach the young ones. We owe it to the next generation, the next, the next and the next. Share your knowledge with them. Have them memorize a consistent and logical approach to Śaivite Hinduism. Then their life experiences are imprinted intelligently as they draw upon those memories to control their *karma* and *dharma.* ¶In the ancient days, the Śaivite kings, the *mahārājas,* were responsible for the religion. They saw to it that the priests performed their duties, that the *pandits* added to the store of knowledge, that the temples were built and maintained and that religion flourished throughout the land and remained alive in the minds and hearts of the people. This was the *dharma* of the *kshatriya* caste, headed by the kings, their ministers and heads of state. When the Śaivite kings fell from power, the entire caste system was, for all practical purposes, left there on the battlefields. Decades have passed, and now we are in a technological age where computers and machinery replace more burdensome work, where caste is a matter of choice, not birth, where the common man and woman have replaced the royal powers as the protectors of Śaivism.

Tuesday
LESSON 338
The First 24 Years

There are no more *mahārājas* to defend the Śaiva Dharma for the people, and therefore the people themselves have taken up the scepter. Together they have to work to preserve and publish scriptures. Together they have to found Śaivite schools and universities in which the knowledge of their forefathers will be safeguarded and disseminated. It is not enough to be born into a Śaivite home. Education and training are now more essential than ever before if Śaiva souls being born today are to grow up into the fullness of the Śaiva Samayam. ¶In our efforts to preserve Śaivism, we have but one paramount duty to perform, and that is to pass Śaivism on to the next generation. How do we do this? By capturing and holding the minds of our youth for their first twenty-four years, holding them close, as was done in the traditional *gurukula,* exposing them to a broad yet specific knowledge and immersing them in the most wonderful impressions of our great religion. Children during the *brahmacharya āśrama,* we could say, are on the *kuṭumba mārga,* the stage of being trained by their parents, of being educated, of developing into useful members of society. After age twenty-four, they can be freely released with the confidence that they will contend well in a demanding world, that they will always have their faith to guide and strengthen them when *karmas* become intense or alien influences encroach. ¶We of the older generation are already set in our ways. Our patterns were established years ago when early impressions impregnated and influenced our minds. We can still learn, we can study, but our formative years are largely past. It is now the children who must be thought of, for they will be here when we pass away. We can devise ways to let them benefit from our experience, good and bad. To do this, we must hold them firmly for twenty-four years as they go through two natural twelve-year cycles of life, impressing on them the intricacies of the Śaiva Samayam before they are exposed to any alien faith or belief. Having done that, our duty is complete, and we can rest assured that Śaivism will be perpetuated by our children, by our children's children and on into the future of the world, on into the new age of space. ¶However, it must be said, and said boldly, that not all Śaivites are performing this important duty. Rather than becoming the first *gurus*, as mother and father, as is traditional, they send the youth off to school, away from home, without chaperoning, and make the world his *guru*. From there he falls naturally into *āṇava mārga*, the path of being his own person, looking out for "number one." ¶If we fail and let a single generation slip by, the entire religion will be threatened. It only takes one generation to let our religion begin a fall into disuse. I gave this message on Śaivite education to over 300,000 devotees during a 1981 tour of Sri Lanka and India. It was an important message at the time, well received, and today is no less relevant. I pointed out in no uncertain terms that for many decades Hindus have been sending their children to Catholic schools. They do this because the Catholics run very fine educational institutions and programs throughout India and Sri Lanka and elsewhere, and each family naturally wants its children to have the best education. The children do get a good discipline and education, but it is a Catholic education, an education ultimately designed to bring young boys and girls into the Catholic religion, designed to persuade them of the Christian view of life, of the Christian view of God and salvation, and of all the Christian beliefs. ¶Hindu parents should not send their children to Christian missionary schools, nor to schools founded in the name of any other religion who seek to influence them, even in subtle ways, such as through symbols and peer missionaries who chide and taunt Hindu children about their culture, their beliefs, their dress or their symbols. These schools have a detrimental effect on the subconscious minds of the children, steadily turning them away from Hindu beliefs. When they slowly absorb the attitudes of another faith, slowly their belief structure is altered, and gradually their actions at home reflect this change.

Wednesday
LESSON 339
Contradictory Teachings

We know from modern psychology how important early impressions are. The first impressions that go into the minds of young people mold and influence their entire life. While a child is learning history in a Catholic school, learning geometry, learning mathematics, he is also being taught the teachings of the Catholic Church. The teachings of the Catholic Church are not the Śaiva Dharma. They are drastically different, in some ways even opposite, from the Śaiva Dharma..What has happened? In order to gain an education for their children so they can grow up and earn money, so they can compete with their peers in the West, the parents have sacrificed the soul of the child and prepared him for a poor birth in his next life. ¶It happens in this way. The child goes to school each day and listens to the teachings of the Catholics about God and Jesus and Mary. He learns from the *Catholic Catechism* that the soul goes to heaven or to hell after one birth on this Earth, that those who do not accept Jesus as their savior suffer eternally in hell, where the physical body burns forever without being consumed, that one must not worship idols, that other religions are not God's true path. ¶Then the child returns home, and his parents try to undo these impressions by telling him that there is no eternal hell and no original sin, that non-Christians do not suffer in hell, that Śiva is a God of love, that *karma* does exist and souls do incarnate many, many times upon the Earth. This young mind, not having matured into reason as yet, simply becomes confused. At school he hears that his parents just don't understand, and he should therefore not listen to them about religious matters. At home his parents tell him that in certain matters he should not listen to the nuns, should not believe the good fathers, that Śaivism is his religion, and is a wonderful religion, that it is all right to wear holy ash. Imagine a child who goes to school and is taught all day, six or eight hours a day, that he should believe the Catholic beliefs. He is taught that there is no reincarnation, that there is no *karma*, that Hinduism is a pagan religion, that the Catholic religion is the only true religion in the world, that his parents are wrong, that his forefathers were wrong, that the *ṛishis* and *satgurus* are also wrong. And then, for an hour or so at night, if he is lucky, the parents teach that the Catholic Church is wrong, that he should go there only for the secular education, that he should disregard all the other instruction, not listen to the holy fathers and nuns but ignore them when they talk about their religion. ¶A true story was related to me by Pundit K.N. Navaratnam, Jyotisha Shastri, a close devotee of my *satguru.* "As a young boy growing up in Jaffna, I received my primary school education in a Christian school. The teacher impressed upon me in religious classes that the Hindu Gods were all evil devils. We were told when passing the Hindu temples to spit and swear at these evil images. Many times I followed my teacher's instructions and indeed did these inappropriate deeds—until one day I spat at an image of Lord Gaṇeśa and immediately fell to the ground and suffered a serious head wound. My cousin was studying in a Catholic convent with many other students who were born as Hindus. Every morning they were taken to the church for prayers. On the way the students passed a Hindu temple where they were told to spit and swear in the direction of the temple. This was a cruel and dishonest attempt at conversion to a different faith."

Thursday
LESSON 340
Neglecting The First Duty

What happens to a child who receives such contradictory training? He doesn't know whom or what to believe. He pulls away from the Christian religion he learned at school. He pulls away from the Śaivite religion he learned at home. He grows up without a religion. He does not have the good Catholic fathers to turn to; nor can he turn to his parents' religion when in need of spiritual advice, for Śaivism has been discredited in his mind. He is thus denied a religion in this life. As one Catholic Father confided, "The Hindu children in our school may never become Catholics, but they also will never be good Hindus." The child who once attended home *pūjā* with joy and respected the visiting *swāmī* no longer shows him *praṇāmas*, resists *pūjā* time, challenges parental decisions and slowly takes over the home, relegating the parents to second-class citizenship within it. All in the home are consigned to dance around the contrary feelings of such children in order to avoid their threats of unchaperoned dating, leaving home, even suicide. As a result, these spiritual orphans are growing up without a religion and turning to drugs, turning to crime, turning to existentialism and Western rationalism, even terrorism, for some semblance of security, turning to divorce and even suicide in increasing numbers when life becomes difficult to face. Their lack of religious life is creating a very serious *karma*, taking them into the consciousness of the seven lower worlds. This *karma* is the responsibility of our Śaivite community, of each and every one of us. We will all reap the bad *karma* generated by our neglect. ¶Those who have been educated in Christian schools have little respect for the *swāmīs, pandits* and *gurus* of Śaivism. They don't respect the sanctity of our temples. They may go into a temple to fulfill the social customs, but in their hearts they don't believe that the Gods live in the temple, because they have been told in school that the stone Deities are just stones, that *pūjās* are just primitive rituals. You love your children and you should not sacrifice their minds for an education, for a little money. That money will be ill-gotten, for you played the Christians for fools in order to get it. Do the Christians believe our beliefs? No. Do the Jews? No. Do the Muslims? No. They do not believe a single one of our central beliefs, which are *karma,* reincarnation, the existence of God everywhere, the absence of an eternal hell and the assurance that every soul, without exception, will attain liberation. ¶All religions are not the same. They are not equal. They have different spiritual goals and, therefore, different attainments reached by their followers. We must not forget this, especially these days when it is fashionable to ignore the differences and to claim that all religions are one. We must not be taken in by those who make such claims. The religions of the world are all great, but they are not all the same. Their beliefs are different, and since beliefs create attitudes, they hold different attitudes toward life and death, and toward the soul and God, too. Our collective beliefs create our collective attitudes and thus perpetuate the culture. ¶Yes, we have but one duty to perform: to pass our religion on to the next generation, the next, the next and the next. How is this done? Through Śaivite education, building more schools. We must educate our youth well. The alternative is to allow Śaivism to be conquered by atheism, to be conquered by Christianity, to be conquered by Islam, to be conquered by existentialism and Western rationalism, materialism and secular humanism, and to be conquered by the liberal neo-Indian postulations which seek to cut the roots of tradition. Our only hope lies in educating the children, the young minds which are open and eager to learn, but which are being enticed away from their heritage. Hold them close, protect them, love them dearly and give them the treasures of Śaivism. That is the greatest gift you can offer them. Everything else will perish. Everything else will decay. ¶You can remember this next time a Christian missionary comes to your door. Welcome him with "Namaste." Tell him or her, "We are Hindus. We have a catechism of our own. We have a creed and an affirmation of faith in our religion, too. We have our scriptures, our *Holy Bible of the Śaivite Hindu*

Religion. We have religious leaders and institutions, and a tradition that is vastly more ancient than any other. We have our holy temples and our great Gods. We are proud to be Śaivites. We are proud to worship God Śiva and the Gods. We have all this and more. Thank you very much." And then close the door!

Friday
LESSON 341
What to Teach The Youth

Behind many past wars and before us today we find unconscionable conversion efforts that infringe on the rights of not only the individual, but of groups and nations. When religions set out with a consciousness of conquest and make inroads on each other, this naturally becomes a major concern to families, communities and nations. Is it not the right of each of the world religions to declare dedication to their incontestable lawbooks of shoulds and should nots, holy texts telling us how to pray, meditate and behave? Freedom to choose one's religion as well as freedom to leave it if one wishes is a fundamental human right, and it is a human wrong to deny or even limit it. This may seem obvious, but it is not a freedom many people of the world fully enjoy. ¶Because they love their children, devout Śaivites do not put them into Christian schools but provide Śaivite schooling which fills young minds with Śaivite lore, Śaivite history, Śaivite art, knowledge of the *Vedas* and the *Śaiva Āgamas.* Such children, nurtured from birth in their religion and taught the sacred scriptures and songs from an early age, grow into the great ambassadors of Śaivite Hinduism and joyfully carry it out into the rest of the world. This is the plan and the thrust of the devotees of God Śiva in 1981, 1982, 1990 and on beyond the year 2000. They know that there is no place where we can go but that God Śiva is there ahead of us—there already. They know that nothing has existence except that God Śiva created it. These Sivathondars are vowed to protect, preserve and promote the Śaiva Dharma on this planet. ¶In *Dancing with Śiva, Hinduism's Contemporary Catechism* all of this that I have been speaking about is neatly explained through short questions and answers which are easy to understand, to commit to memory and to teach to children and adults alike so that they can talk intelligently in foreign countries about their religion and benefit themselves as well as others. ¶A child's mind is like a computer disc or a recording cassette. It is a blank tape, capable of recording confusing sounds or beautiful melodies. It is up to us to make those first and lasting impressions. That tape is very difficult to edit later. What should we teach to our young boys and girls? What do we record in their mental computer? *Dancing with Śiva*—beautifully illustrated because children also learn through their eyes—contains a foundation of religious study to be memorized by boys and girls from six to sixteen years of age, to be discussed by the family, to be expounded upon by the father and explained by the mother. ¶This book answers the question, "What should I teach my children about Śaivism?" We must teach the children about our purpose on this Earth, our relationship with God, our ultimate destiny—all according to the *Tirumantiram, Tirukural,* the *Vedic* and *Āgamic* scriptures of monistic Śaiva Siddhānta. We must teach our children, as did *mahāsiddha* Tirumular 2,200 years ago, that the soul is immortal, created by God Śiva and destined to merge back in Him. We must teach our children about this world we live in and about the other belief structures they will encounter throughout life. We must teach our children how to make their religion strong and vibrant in a technological age. These instructions are important for all Śaivite families. ¶Those of you here in Asia have a rich and stable religious culture. Therefore the future of your children is less uncertain. In other parts of the world, Śaivite children are not benefiting from a temple in the village, from a grandmother who can explain things or a grandfather to expound. Yet, though children here have all these advantages, still the temptations are there to adopt wayward Western ways and Christian attitudes. We must work to overcome such magnetic forces by educating our children, both those who are living here in Sri Lanka and India and those who are citizens of other nations in the world. They will then grow up to teach their children and thus perpetuate the Śaivite Hindu religion into the next generation, the next and the next. ¶Yes, united Śaivites of the world, we need to pass on to the next generation the importance of *dharma* and of good conduct, especially *ahiṁsā,* fundamental principles of the Hindu faith. *Ahiṁsā* means noninjury physically, mentally and emotionally. We need to explain to them the secret of the mysteries of the holy Śiva temple. We need to take them often to the *kovils, mandirs,* shrines, *āśramas, aadheenams, maṭhas,* sacred places and rivers so they become well grounded in their devotion. We need to carefully explain to them the purpose of, and the results that can be obtained through, home *pūjā,* having *archanas, abhishekas* and *homas* performed in their behalf in Śiva temples. We need to teach them how to pray to God and the Gods. We need to foster in them a deep reverence for our scriptures and our saints and sages.

Saturday
LESSON 342
Preparation For Adult Life

Very importantly, we must inculcate in youth a respect for family life, for marriage as a sacred union undertaken for the mutual spiritual advancement of husband and wife. They have to be counseled and counseled well in how married life is to be faced, what attitudes they should hold toward sex, how to keep a marriage strong and joyful, how to combat the pressures they will face in this modern world, especially if they come to live beyond the borders of our holy land. We must also inculcate in them a knowledge of monastic life, so they may understand and revere the *satgurus* and *swāmīs* of Śaivism. Śaivite monasticism was a powerful spiritual force in the world when the *mahārājās* supported the monastics, and it will continue to be so through the support of the families, their children and their children's children. All this is accomplished through religious education. We call upon the youth of India, the youth of Sri Lanka, the youth of Malaysia and all other countries where Śaivites are living to consider the two paths. We call upon those rare few to accept the *dharma* of the Śaivite monastic and serve their God and religion through a selfless life, preaching and teaching throughout the world. There is a great need here. Too many Asian families relinquish their children to become Catholic priests and Protestant ministers and not enough encourage them to become Hindu *sādhakas*, *yogīs* and *swāmīs*. ¶The youth must be taught that Śaivism is not only the oldest religion in the world, but a vibrant and dynamic religion in this technological age. They must come to know its wisdom is for the farmer as well as for the computer programmer, for our ancestors and for our descendants. Śaivism is the Eternal Path, the Sanātana Dharma. The youth working in science, working in space exploration, working in electronics, working in business, working closely with members of different religions, will encounter many challenges. They must be carefully taught how to remain within the bounds of their religion and their beliefs without being dissuaded, without accepting ridicule from those who have yet to comprehend Śaivism. We must teach the Śaivite youth who are now growing up around the world about the Hindu festivals and holy days, making these auspicious days vibrant and alive in their memories. We must explain to them the meanings behind every observance so they are not just following blindly. ¶Symbols are an important part of bringing Śaivism into the hearts of the youth. Symbols carry great significance, and young people love and understand symbols. We should have Śaivite symbols abundantly around us, in the shrine room and throughout the home. The Prāṇava Aum, *swastika, Śivaliṅga, tripuṇḍra* and *pottu, aṅkuśa, tiruvadi, nāga, vel, kalaśa, vaṭa, rudrāksha, seval, triśūla, kamaṇḍalu, trikoṇa, bilva, shaṭkoṇa, konrai, homa, kuttuvilaku* and *mankolam.* ¶We should have a *kuttuvilaku,* or oil lamp, in our shrine room. We should have pictures of the Deities and their *vahanas,* Nandi, peacock and mouse, in our home, sacred flowers and trees in our garden. We should, of course, wear the holy ash and *pottu,* our sacred jewelry and prayer beads, and see that our young people do also. All Śaivites should become initiated into the Pañchākshara Mantra and chant it daily upon a *mālā* of *rudrāksha* beads. Sights, scents, sounds, tastes and religious symbols—it is through these ways our religion is understood by the next generation.

Sunday
LESSON 343
Affirming Basic Human Values

I spoke on global education in January of 1990 at the Global Forum for Human Survival, Development and Environment in Moscow. My message to the 700 religious and political leaders there was that we need, in the century ahead, to teach all children tolerance, openness to different ways of life, different beliefs, different customs of dress and language. We need to stop teaching them to fear those who are different from themselves, stop teaching them hatred for peoples of other colors and other religions, stop teaching them to see the world as a field of conflict and instead instill in them an informed appreciation and a joyous reverence for the grand diversity we find around us. Modern education can do that, provided the approach is changed. ¶Basic human Vedic values should be taught to every child and every student. These eternal values have nothing to do with race, creed, caste, politics or ethnic culture. Learning how to read and write is not the ultimate goal. The ultimate goal of education is also knowing what to read and what to write, as well as how to live in tune with nature, in harmony with the universe and at peace with oneself and one's fellow man. A great Hindu saint once wrote, "Those who cannot live in harmony with the world, though they have learned many things, are still ignorant" (*Tirukural* 140). ¶The big question today that spiritual and political leaders are facing is how the peoples of the world are to live on this planet in harmony, and how to correct the errors of the past and the resentments that still linger, to ensure survival of humankind in the future. Education, they know, will play a key role, but only if educators focus first on human values which make us all better people, and secondly on technical know-how. ¶The human values we are speaking of here are known by all the tribal peoples, as they are inwardly a part of the knowledge within each of us. These principles must be cultivated, however, to manifest in any society, community, village or family. Global education must reach all the peoples, including the tribals, in our worldwide global village. It cannot be one-sided on the part of those who have the resources teaching others what they think they need to know. Rather, all voices must be heard, of the tribal and the industrialist. But will they be heard? Perhaps yes! The intelligentsia of industrialized societies are realizing that they don't really have all the answers and that traditional tribal communities have something to teach after all. We have simple problems on this planet—food for survival, water, air, shelter and health care. The tribals are well aware of each of these and had them under control before they were conquered. In the same spirit that the modern pharmacologist journeys into the Amazon forests to discover medicines used for centuries that he can apply to world health care, so we in our various spheres of knowledge need to more and more rediscover the old ways and bring them forward. ¶In Russia, some bright young students asked me, "What can Hinduism offer in contributing to world peace and global education?" I explained that Hinduism offers a unified vision of man and nature in which there is reverence, not dominion or carelessness. Mother Earth, sustainer of life, is a key Vedic idea. Respect for Earth, for life in its many forms, is found in the American Indian nations, in the Hawaiian religion, the African tribes and the many other indigenous peoples. It was lost by many in recent centuries, but now its depth is being discovered again. ¶While the family is suffering a lot in many parts of the world, I explained, it is still very strong in Hindu society. We have to keep it that way, and teach the world by our example that it is the family that nurtures the individual and stabilizes the religion and hence the nation. Only by keeping a strong sense of family can humankind hope for a secure future.

Śaiva Saṁskṛiti
शैव संस्कृति

Śaivite Culture

May the Goddess of culture, associated with the models of other cultures, may the Goddess of wisdom in company with men, ordinary and intellectual, may the fire divine, and may the Goddess of divine speech with masters of language come to bless us and enshrine our hearts.

Ṛig Veda 7.2.8. RVP, P. 2,355

Monday
LESSON 344
Śaivism Has Everything

Good evening, everyone! Vanakkam. Anbe Sivamayam Satyame Parasivam. God Śiva is Immanent Love and Transcendent Reality. The American devotees of our great God Śiva are very happy to be here today at this beautiful temple in Sri Lanka. It is so inspiring to see this temple being well maintained, improved, managed in a responsible way and filled with Śaivite souls. Your open and lovely faces remind me of beings in the Devaloka. We feel blessed here. ¶Śaivism is the greatest religion in the world, and we are all very fortunate and proud to be Śaivites. Why is it great among all the world's great religions? It has the most ancient culture on the planet. It has scriptures that are utterly profound. It has sacred hymns that stir the soul. It has unparalleled disciplines of *yoga* and meditation. It has magnificent temples that are truly holy. It has devoted sages and holy men and women to guide our life and lead us to Lord Gaṇeśa, who leads us to Lord Murugan and finally to the Supreme God, Śiva. Śaivism has God and the Gods. It has *charyā, kriyā, yoga* and *jñāna.* It has so many enlightened beliefs, including *karma* and reincarnation. That is why I call our religion the greatest in all the world. ¶I believe that this oldest religion of the farthest past is also the religion of the future, the religion best suited to the technological age. I think we should present Hinduism as it is today, as a vibrant religion of the present. Then it will survive into glorious futures. We need inspired people to serve Śaivism with a strong will and a positive mind. In this effort, all differences must be set aside so we can work together on powerful programs that will bring progress; and that progress will inspire others, make them enthusiastic, show them that Śaivism can be brought into the technological age for the good of the next generation, the next and the next. ¶What happens when a religion is lost in yesterday and not brought forward to guide its followers today and on into the future? All kinds of problems arise. The youth begin to think religion is obsolete, abandon it and become immersed in worldliness, often in activities that are *adharmic.* They leave the Śaivite path, the Śaiva Neri. Families break up, friends argue, and people fight within themselves and with one another. Poor citizens are raised in the absence of ethics. Unrest and discontentment reign, and the entire nation suffers. So many problems arise when reli-

Here a vīṇā *player is seated in the granite-pillared outer chambers of a local temple, playing for her God. Her music is a spiritual art which draws her close to Lord Śiva, whose Holy Foot in the subtle world blesses her with His divine touch.*

gion is lost, when people don't know the right things to do. They become unhappy, restless, unstable. They have nothing to lean on, no place to turn in difficult times. This leads to abuse, to divorce, to suicide, to disease, to murder and dozens of sad experiences and hellish states of mind. ¶People who do have a religion live a very different life. Recently a large sum of money was spent to conduct a vast survey on the effects of religion in people's lives in America. Thousands of people from every walk of life were interviewed throughout the United States as to their religion, their jobs and their family life. It was found that those with a religion and who really followed that religion were happier, wealthier and healthier than those who had no spiritual life. The researchers concluded that nonreligious people were less happy in their home life, less successful in their businesses and personal relationships, and more prone to anxiety, stresses and strains. We have to take that information seriously and determine to live our spiritual life fully, in all its dimensions. We have to realize that there are serious problems awaiting us if we are half-hearted and live a double standard. Therefore, it is important, both for the individual and the country, that we preserve the Śaiva Dharma and bring it forward into the technological age.

Tuesday
LESSON 345
A Religion Of the Future

Many years ago I was given a beautiful description of Śaivism. I was told that Śaivism is like *ghee.* The cow eats grass all day and from it produces gallons of white milk. The dairyman separates out the rich cream. The cream is then churned into sweet butter. Finally, the butter is boiled to produce a tiny amount of *ghee,* the essence of milk. Like *ghee,* Śaivism is the essence of religion. ¶In the past decades I have found that instead of preserving and enjoying this *ghee,* people are pouring it into a brass pot and diluting it with Western rationalism, diluting it with liberal Hinduism, diluting it with unorthodox practices and beliefs of all kinds. That precious *ghee* has been turned into a greasy water which is not fit for anything except to be thrown out. Therefore, I call upon the united Śaivites of the world to protect, preserve and promote the Śaiva Samayam by bringing a stop to this dilution of our religion. This dilution is caused by Western influences, by the efforts of alien religions to convert our members, by liberal-Hindu thinking which seeks to destroy the traditions of temple worship and sectarian customs and, most importantly, by our own neglect. ¶Only the united Śaivites of the world can solve these problems. It is not enough to understand these problems or to complain about them. Objecting is not enough. We have to have a plan, a purpose, persistence and push. We have to put that plan forward with a positive mind, a practical approach and a dynamic will in order to make Śaivism the religion of the future, bringing it out of the agricultural era and into the technological age. ¶Here in Sri Lanka there is a misconception that in order to progress, in order to move into the age of technology, we have to abandon our religion, give up our culture. That is a false concept. Religion does not conflict with technology, but enhances it, gives it balance and purpose. As soon as a young man or woman gets a Western education, he or she assumes that the old traditions don't apply anymore and becomes ashamed to worship God and the Gods. Where are the spiritual leaders who can explain that this need not be so? It is too bad that our religious leaders aren't teaching the fact that Śaivism is the one religion on the planet best suited to this great age, which agrees most closely with the most advanced postulations of modern science, yet it is itself even more advanced. ¶In Bali, the technological age did not conquer religion. Rather, Śaivite religious leaders harnessed technology to serve their distinct way of life. There the Śaivite traditions have been valued and protected. On American national television a few months ago, a beautiful program on Bali's Śiva festival, Ekadaśa Rudra, was shown—a massive celebration held for ten days only once every hundred years. A Balinese high priest was interviewed. He was proud to be a Śaivite and told the reporter, "We use technology here in Bali. We are not overcome by technology." I am afraid to say that technology is overcoming many of us here in Sri Lanka. It is a dangerous trend. Unless we reverse it through education, it will gather momentum, and changes will come more and more quickly, not positive changes, but negative ones that destroy the religious character of people and nations.

Wednesday
LESSON 346
Double Standards

Devout Hindus have a hard time dividing life into the sacred and the profane. It is life, and it is all divine expression. Thus, Hindu art is sacred art, Hindu music is devotional music. Even business, for the devout Hindu, is not just livelihood but a way of serving God, the community and helping mankind. ¶But we must admit that not all Hindus live the life as fully as they might. There has evolved a double standard in the modern world. There are those who are consistent as Hindus in the temple as well as at home, whose home life is consistent with their behavior in the temple, whether they live in Europe or in an Indian village.

There are also those who are Hindus when it is convenient and something else when it is not. A good, hard look at oneself once in a while is beneficial, especially at the time of year when many Hindus send Christmas cards. Do they send greetings to acknowledge the holy days of Islam or Judaism? No. But, having been educated in Christian schools, they feel it's all right to send Christmas cards. Christian on the inside and Hindu on the outside—it's a double standard. Rice and curry at the temple, a Big Mac beef burger on the way home. Of course, we would always encourage friendly gestures of goodwill and polite exchanges of good wishes with school mates, neighbors, colleagues, business and professional associates or customers who are members of another community, but that can be done without compromising our Hindu identity. There are perfectly neutral and secularized season's greetings cards, devoid of religious expression. ¶Fortunately, the duplicity is changing. Hindus are getting more confident about living their culture, even in the West. A recent speaking tour in Canada and California brought to my attention an awakening in the older generation (for the sake of their children, they explained), and that is to be one hundred percent Hindu all the time, living the culture at home, in the workplace, the temple and even in dreams. One temple I visited in Toronto had set up a dress code for the devotees: elegant Hindu attire for ladies—no shorts, slacks, skirts, etc., and only traditional attire for men. Those who don't comply are not admitted. Yes, there was at first some reaction, management told me. Even now, there are some who just won't come to the temple if they can't worship the Lord in T-shirts and tight jeans. But so many others who don't appreciate the double standard and previously would stay away—because worshipers were dressing so immodestly—have since replaced the dropouts. The strictness has brought other boons along with it, such as a one-hour, absolutely silent meditation by two or three hundred people prior to the evening *pūjā*. The management prides itself on cleanliness, decorum and discipline. My group arrived there shortly after a feeding of several thousand. The kitchen was immaculate. So was the dining room. Similar efforts to bring forward the whole of our tradition are underway in other communities as well. ¶There is an old saying, "Clothes make the man." And it must be equally true that clothes make the woman. Dress codes are a growing issue in many temples throughout the world, and in *āśramas* and *maṭhas*, too. This is being discussed not only in Hinduism but in other religions as well. ¶In international airports all over the world we see so many kinds of clothing. Airports are beginning to look like backstage at the opera—a flamboyant array—not of actors pretending to be who they are not, but an array of people whose clothing declares who they are. A materialist wears his shirt and tie. The Muslims are elegantly dressed. The colorful African tribals, stately Japanese Shintoists and modest Buddhists are in their traditional garb. Catholics dress demurely; Protestants informally. You can spot an existentialist just like that. And of course, you can never miss the punk rockers or the hippies. A *kurta* shirt, shawl and loosely fitted pants are definitely Hindu, and go well with the wife's wearing a *sārī* or *puñjābi.*

Thursday
LESSON 347
Upholding Your Faith

The clothing we wear shapes our attitudes, cultural behavior and the friendships we hold. Clothes do affect our moods and emotions and make a declaration of who we are. My recommendation is to be who you are and let the world know it, even in the workplace, unless a dress code does not permit this, of course. This includes wearing the sacred forehead marks and Hindu jewelry, wedding pendant, toe rings, earrings and beads. The message is: don't be afraid to be a Hindu, which includes dressing like a Hindu. ¶Boldly proclaim your faith to the world. Others proclaim theirs. I will never forget seeing the many spiritual and parliamentary leaders in Moscow at the Global Forum on Human Survival in January of 1991. Many were dressed in Western suits and ties, and it was hard to tell who among them were from the West, or from Africa or India, and harder still to tell who was a religious person and who a politician. But at the Millennium Peace Summit of Religious Leaders at the United Nations General Assembly Hall in New York in 2000, there were so many, perhaps most, who wore their native dress. I knew instantly who they were, where they were from and what they represented. They carried the stronger message and showed by their clothes that they were proud of their tradition, and that they intended to preserve it. That kind of strength is good to see in a world that has mistaken drab uniformity for security. ¶This is what temple societies and elders and *swāmīs* and *gurus* are all thinking deeply about—"Should my *aśrama* look like a hippie commune, or a serious place of *yoga?* Should our temples look like advertisements for Levi-Strauss acid-washed jeans?" Many say, "Well, God in the temple doesn't care how I'm dressed. It's how I am on the inside that counts." This is a weak excuse. We cannot be one way on the inside and another on the outside. It's all us, inside and out. Even in elegant restaurants, a coat and tie is required. They will lend these to you at the door. Just as is done today at temples in Bali, we loan wrap-arounds and shawls to those who walk into our temples wearing T-shirts and shorts. Perhaps the way things are heading, one day the Gods in the temples will have the dress of the day: a baseball cap turned backwards, a T-shirt, baggy pants. Perhaps that would satisfy the issue and end the controversy. What do you think? ¶Women say that they think and act and move differently when they are dressed in a *sārī* than in Western casual clothing. Another point—men look nicer in the traditional Indian outfit than they do in Western coats, shirts and trousers. But many are shy to wear Hindu clothing, especially the men. They need not be. Last summer a girl we know was scared to death to go to college in her *puñjābis*. But she tried it. Within four days some of the American coeds came up and asked, "What do you call that outfit? We want one like it, too. It's so beautiful." So much for our fears! ¶Swami Vivekananda noted, "The *sārī* of our women and the *choga* and turban of our men defy comparison as regards beauty in dress. The tight dresses cannot approach in loveliness the loose ones that fall in natural folds." Hindus dressed like Hindus behave like Hindus. Don't underestimate the power of our dress, how it influences our attitudes, feelings and even the company we keep. This is food for thought, isn't it? Think about it.

Friday
LESSON 348
Beware of Detractors

Every nation, village, organization, society and even small group has certain goals to accomplish, ideals to live by and a mission it seeks to fulfill. But every organization and group, large or small, has something else as well: detractors. They are usually friendly, kindly, sociable and fun to be with. They're often intellectually bright and more sophisticated than most. They can be the life of the party, the ones who get things going, serve the *prasāda* and talk a mile a minute. They are often popular, welcomed onto every committee and board of trustees, because people feel their energy and inspiration will implement the objectives of the organization, be they building a temple, promoting a publication, saving the rain forests or reorganizing Hindu society into traditional ways of life, culture and arts. ¶Their special social skills promote them quickly through the ranks. Once in an influential position, they speak wisely on subjects irrelevant to the central purpose of the organization. Given the chance, they can turn a not-so-wealthy *āśrama* into an up-and-coming business, thus diluting the original holy impulse of selfless, humble service. Of course, they do perform worship, but in most cases it is not genuine, and just enough to keep them in with a religious group. Given a project, they may balk or procrastinate—delaying a mailing to the point that when it arrives it is useless, or refraining from doing it at all. They are never without a good reason for their actions, having been educated in the venerable "Book of Excuses." At meetings they are quite competent to tell in compelling terms why a project that all wish to manifest is not possible. They are equally capable of making everyone question the mission of the organization and their part in it. They politic to redefine the group's chartered purpose, to make it fit into their own ideas. These *rājas* of reason have many ruses to discourage others from fitting in, and will go to great efforts to bring up irrelevant alternatives and possibilities which cloud the group's thinking and undermine its commitments. All this may seem overstated, perhaps over-generalized, but from my experience I assure you that it is not. ¶These, my friends, are detractors. Though they may appear to be allies, they are not. The worst of them, I would say, are guided by asuric forces which seek to undermine, erode and create confusion. Detractors also endeavor to control and then stifle the religious leaders—the *swāmīs*, *pandits*, priests and the *guru*—by setting schedules as to whom they should or should not meet, what they should and should not say. If they can, they will cleverly edit a religious institution's written works into oblivion and relegate the founder to being a feeble figurehead, a mere picture hanging on the wall. ¶Detractors are something to be deeply concerned about. Don't hope that they will one day turn around and be defenders of faith. They won't. By divine, *dharmic* law, devotees who are dedicated to the goals of their group are wrong to associate with detractors, who often seek to replace the religious agenda with a social one. Rather, they must be dissociated from and seen as foes to the forces of *dharma*, antagonists who do not allow others to preserve the thrust of the founder's goals. Every group should rigorously test each one within it to determine who is vowed to fulfill the goals of the organization and who will hamper them every step of the way, resist and refuse to fit in fully, and politic to cause others to do the same. Their favorite mode of operation is the erosion method, continually taking up time, even if it's only five minutes today and eight minutes tomorrow. Their presence is always a burden, as they deter, delay and inhibit the mission by their remarkable irrelevancies and intolerable subtle obstinacy. *Asuric* invasion comes through such detractors, who rely on anger, pouting, gossip, backbiting and emotional upheavals to get their way. Once having been admitted into the central fold, they employ these means of motivation even more openly than before, to the utter distress of devotees who are humbly striving to follow *dharma* and to fulfill the stated mission of the organization. Now, I am not saying these are all necessarily bad people, though some are definitely there to intentionally infiltrate, dilute and destroy. Others may have, in their own minds, perfectly good intentions and may be entirely unaware of their negative effect on the group. But that does not excuse them. It is important to stress that for religious service to be effective, there must be absolute group harmony. For words to go deep and lives to be changed for the better, everyone's *prāṇas* must be flowing together on an equal wavelength. All must be kindred in their vows and unified in their determination to fulfill the goals of the *āśrama*, society, temple or mission. ¶The big question remains: how to get rid of detractors once they are discovered. Quite probably they have made many friends, are tied into key projects, have contributed a great deal of money and gained a position of control. If detractors are discovered, don't confront them. Don't accuse them. Don't try to persuade or convince them to be different. Don't expect them to change. Be persistent in maintaining the original goals of the institution. Uphold the *dharma* and be unified with those who are loyal. Quietly let the detractors go their way, or into another group that is more suited to them. Without them, the mission will soar. Religious organizations must not tolerate domination by wealthy or influential patrons or members who do not support the shared goals. An indigent widow's single rupee in the *huṇḍi* and a billionaire's one million should have equal weight in the minds of the trustees.

Saturday
LESSON 349
Respecting Temple Priests

In the past months, we have talked to many groups about the abuse of women and children, of animals and our environment. And there is yet another kind of abuse whose victims have silently suffered without our concern, without our intervention, and mostly without our even knowing about it. I'm speaking of our temple priests, who are being mistreated and abused all over the world. This is a distressing problem that I hear about nearly every week and am working steadily to solve. ¶It is time that we talked about this atrocity. Hindu priests, known as *pujārīs*, are being mistreated, humiliated and bashed—emotionally, mentally and even physically—by temple managers, trustees and sometimes even devotees. We all know that this is not right. Still, with few exceptions, no one is objecting, except of course the priests themselves. Their objections and efforts to provide for their own security go largely unheard, as they are looked down upon by management as uneducated, simple people who merely perform rote rituals. In truth, they are a noble army of soldiers of the within, who are the heart of Hinduism's spiritual leadership. ¶Priest bashing is a popular sport outside of India. Back in India, priests have their *saṅga* and elders to stand up for them. Outside India, when a priest falls into disfavor, the slightest infractions are used against him, and serious accusations are quickly levelled to blacken his name, hurt him and force him out. Accusation of wrongdoing in handling money is a favorite ploy and usually the first to be used. The list goes on, giving management the license to yell at him, push him, ignore his needs, embarrass him in front of his peers and humiliate him in public. In Australia, a priest spent two weeks in the hospital following an incident of severe and traumatic public humiliation. There have been too many cases for us to take lightly the *hiṁsā* hurts inflicted upon priests serving in foreign lands. With a sympathetic attorney's help, one priests' group in California formed their own organization for protection, but this is still the exception. ¶It is bad enough inside India, but even worse outside. At least in India the priest is on home ground, knows the rules of the region and has moral, emotional and even legal support available. And, of course, he has his extended family to turn to. Outside of India, many priests have none of these support systems. Many priests are isolated and vulnerable in so many ways—often living alone, with only a temporary visa. Many don't know the laws and customs of the country they serve in, and may not know the language too well, so they are often at the mercy of the temple managers for everything. They are disadvantaged in another way, too: if a priest has to return to his village, he will face a second humiliation as elders and peers make him answer up to the gossip, insinuations and accusations that have accumulated against him. ¶Yes, bashing Hindu temple priests is a worldwide tragedy, and those who perpetrate these acts are also bashing the Sanātana Dharma. But abusing priests is not to be taken lightly. Those who can invoke blessings from the Gods can also invoke curses from asuric forces of this planet for their own protection when angered, embarrassed and deeply hurt. Hindu temple priests deserve respect for the richness of their holy profession, the dignity of their office and the importance of their function. They should not be mistreated or interfered with. They have earned the same respect that any professional in "the real world" enjoys.

When *swāmī* bashing was in vogue years ago, *swāmīs* took it seriously. They got to know each other better, stood up for each other and put a stop to the nonsense. ¶Women today are taking such a stand against their own husbands who take sadistic joy in battering them repeatedly. When these transgressions are brought before the public, changes are often set in motion. Attitudes change. Soon the media changes its ways of reporting on abuse. Laws eventually change. We have seen this happen with child abuse, with racial abuse, with sexual abuse. The time has now come for us all to change our attitudes about abusing temple priests. This will require temple managers to adjust their thinking. It will also require the international priesthood of Sanātana Dharma to take a firm stand against their molesters and refuse to meekly submit, day in and day out, to harassment or to being relegated to janitorial work and the handling of shoes. Some priests work fourteen hours a day and more. They are treated like servants of the manager rather than servants of the temple Gods. Let's put an end to this shameful mistreatment and the bad *karma* that it creates. Let's honor, love and respect our priests. Let's make our priests happy. Happy priest, happy temple, happy Gods, happy devotees. That's the way it works.

Sunday
LESSON 350
The Path of Commitment

Commitment is a big word and a very scary word to many people nowadays. The word *commitment* means responsibility. The word *commitment* brings up our willpower. Many people think the word *commitment* is too limiting. We can sum up commitment in one word, *dharma*. The path of *dharma* is the path of one commitment after another commitment. In between the commitments is fulfillment of the commitment, which is another word for duty. We are here to realize God Śiva within ourself. We are here to resolve all the *karmas* we put in motion in past lives. We are here to manage our affairs so properly that eventually we do not have to come back into a physical body anymore. This takes tremendous commitment, and our great Hindu religion gives us the knowledge of how to be committed. ¶If your religion is not manifesting daily in your life, then basically you don't have a religion. You just have some sort of Indian culture which will eventually go away and be replaced with another kind of a culture, because it doesn't really matter to you. Someone asked me recently, "How do I know what to be committed to?" The answer: "What do you believe in?" Belief is a magical thing. It's like a vitamin; it permeates your whole system. A belief can be taken away and another belief can replace it, or the belief can be strengthened through commitment. Be committed to your beliefs, or find beliefs that you can be committed to, then build on them. Then you will leave your footprints on the San Mārga of time. Otherwise, you are just sitting in one place, making no progress. Nothing is happening in your life. The *karmas* aren't working right, and you are not able to face life. ¶If you feel, day after day, that you are in the right place at the right time, doing the right thing, then I would say you are a being who is fully committed to the spiritual path. If, day after day, you feel you don't know whether you are in the right place or not, and things are always "happening to you," that you are like a little boat on the great ocean of life being tossed around, here and there, then you should look within yourself and find out where you stand on the scale of life itself. What are your basic beliefs? What are your basic commitments? Ask yourself. ¶There are many things to be committed to. Youths should be committed to an education that prepares them for what they plan to do in the future. Mothers should be committed to raising their children, making them good citizens, though some mothers don't care whether their children are good citizens or not. They just don't care. They are not even committed to raising their own children. They give them over to somebody else to raise: "Here, you do it." Day-care centers are opening up all across the nation, though statistics show that children educated in day-care centers are terrible students when they get into school—discouraged, undisciplined, unruly students. Husbands should be committed to raising up their family, taking care of their wife and children. That is a commitment that they have to fulfill. If they don't fulfill it, they are making an unworthy *karma*. But many husbands are not even committed to that. ¶Commitment and *dharma* are just about the same. *Dharma* brings law and order into life, gives us rules to follow and guides us along. Where does commitment come from? Commitment comes from the soul. The intellectual mind is going this way and that way all the time, controlled or antagonized by other people's opinions most of the time and by how society is thinking. Commitment comes from the soul. It is a quality of the soul which you can teach to the next generation. Another quality of the soul is observation. Still another intuitive quality of the soul is creativity, which should be encouraged in every child. Through commitment, the soul dominates the intellect and the intellect dominates the instinctive mind. This is religion in action. This is living with Śiva.

Hindu Ekatā

हिन्दु एकता

Hindu Solidarity

Gather together, converse together! Your minds be of one accord, just as in harmony the Gods of old took their ritual shares of oblation! United be your counsel, united your assembly, united your spirit and thoughts! A single plan do I lay before you; a single oblation do I offer!

Ṛig Veda 10.191.2-3. VE, P. 854

Monday
LESSON 351
Hinduism In America

Namaste to each and every one here at this Cultural Center tonight in California. We invoke Lord Gaṇeśa's blessings to guide us through our evening together. We are glad to see you all sitting on the floor on these beautiful carpets in the traditional way. You are obviously taking pride in bringing more and more of the great heritage of India to America. ¶Tonight we are going to discuss an issue that is essential to the future of Hinduism in America, I would even say in the world. It is a complex matter, but in brief it may be defined as the relationship of Hindus to Hindus, of Vaishṇavites to Śaivites, of northern traditions to southern. I call it Hindu solidarity, and I can assure you that there is no single more challenging or significant lesson that we as members of the world's oldest religion have to learn. If we can achieve this, and we can, many of our problems will be solved, and Hinduism will take a new place of pride in North America. ¶Hindu solidarity is not a new idea. Mahatma Gandhi literally gave his life to religious unity. Of course, his greatest efforts were focused on the more serious conflicts between Hindus and Muslims, but he was a man for whom unity—but not uniformity—among Hindus was the rock upon which harmony between members of all religions must be based. To him this goal was considered a prerequisite for freedom and for prosperity. Gandhi took religious harmony so seriously that it became for him the fulfillment, the "ultimate triumph of Truth." Of course, from the 1982 film shown in major cities around the world, you know that Gandhi faced many disappointments, many setbacks. Yet he never despaired. Though we, too, encounter obstacles in this effort, we must not lose heart, but carry on with courage and determination. ¶Gandhi did not force his will on others, but used humility, penance, prayer and purity to convey his ideals to others, to awaken in them the same love, the same tolerance, the same dependence on God. Gandhi followed Swami Vivekananda in impressing America with principles of tolerance, understanding, forbearance and nonviolence—all Hindu ideals. While Swami Vivekananda became known to relatively few here in the West, Gandhi captured the imagination and hearts of all Americans, if not the whole world. He is really a hero in this country, and our own freedom fighters, Martin Luther King and others, took their guidance from him. When he failed,

Hindu solidarity is shown by the respect for forms of worship of the Divine. Devotees of one lineage, whether followers of Śiva, Vishṇu or Durgā, honor the followers of other other denominations. Below a devotee of Lord Śiva is tying a flower garland around a stone Śivaliṅga.

Gandhi would say, "Let us ask for help from God, the All-Powerful, and tell Him that we, His tiny creatures, have failed to do what we ought to do. We hate one another. We distrust one another. We fly at one another's throat, and we even become assassins. Let us ask Him to purge our hearts of all hatred in us. Let us ask God in all humility to give us sense, to give us wisdom." ¶The people of America sincerely want the Hindu religion here. And all the Asian Hindus who have come to America, now numbering in the millions, also want the Hindu religion here. They are not all in agreement as to what it is; nor do they even understand the deeper tenets of Hinduism. But the general feeling among them is, "We want Hinduism here in America." In a recent publication, I believe it was *U.S. News and World Report*, statistics were given showing that in American today one person in twenty-five is associated with Hinduism, *yoga* or meditation. Of course, we have millions of other Americans who are atheists, born without any religion at all. There are tens of millions who are Jews, Muslims and Buddhists. Buddhism is very popular in the United States, and Islam is the fastest growing religion. You can see that we are not really a Christian country. We are a mosaic of all races, all religions. The Founding Fathers of America arrived seeking a new world, a new hope, freedom from unenlightened European monarchies. They consciously did not create a Christian nation. Their freedom of religion policy was for all the religions of the world. Much of their symbolism and thinking was derived from the Masonic Lodge and the Deist movement of the times. ¶Thomas Jefferson himself said that the freedoms were to extend to the Hindus, the Muslims and others. He wrote in his autobiography, "[When] the [Virginia] bill for establishing religious freedom... was finally passed, a singular proposition proved that its protection of opinion was meant to be universal. Where the preamble declares that coercion is a departure from the plan of the holy author of our religion, an amendment was proposed, by inserting the words *Jesus Christ,* so that it should read 'a departure from the plan of Jesus Christ, the holy author of our religion.' The insertion was rejected by a great majority, in proof that they meant to comprehend within the mantle of its protection the Jew and the Gentile, the Christian and Mahometan, the Hindoo and infidel of every denomination."

Tuesday
LESSON 352
Sectarianism Is Healthy

Those who followed in the decades after the US Constitution was ratified were divided one from another because of language, religion and culture. They spoke different languages, followed many different customs and promoted many different religious beliefs. In spite of all this, they worked with and solved the problems. They set their differences aside through the separation of church and state and created friendships by not entering into discussions of church and state, business and politics. They solved the problems and decided not to talk much about religion and decided to work together for a new world, a new nation, a new democracy that the entire world is now beginning to emulate. This is because they came to the conclusion that they must be united to exist, and that working together was imperative for survival in the new world. And this is how the American people work together today. They don't speak about religion or politics in corporations or businesses. ¶There are good lessons for Hindus in these historical happenings, for the founding fathers of this nation did not destroy their heritage. The Lutherans coming over here from Germany and Denmark did not forsake the traditions of the Lutheran religion; rather, they strengthened them. The Baptists strengthened their religion. The Methodists became strong. The Catholics from Ireland and Italy became very strong here. That's what they did. What they did not do is just as important. They did not create a liberal Christianity in which everyone was expected to blend with other creeds for the sake of unity. They did not dismantle or dilute their religion. They did not compromise all their culture so they could "fit in." Nor did the Buddhists, the Taoists, the Shintoists or the Confucianists seek to combine all the sects of their faiths into one. They did not do this. They did not take an axe to that tree. They did not chop away at its roots. They didn't do that. They knew that individual ways of worship are important, that individual customs are important, important enough to preserve. ¶Many Hindus wrongly believe there is just one Christianity which all Christians support. This is simply not true. There are 33,500 sects within Christianity in this country alone, as published by the highly regarded Dr. David Bartlett. Imagine that! More than 33,500, each having its own separate identity, its own individual beliefs, creeds, doctrines and ways of worship. This is very important to remember. Of course, they are in the ninth and tenth generation now, and everyone speaks English. ¶Recently, while dedicating Flint's Paśchimā Kāśī Śrī Viśvanātha Temple, Congressman Riley of the state of Michigan and I were on the same platform and he told the gathered crowd, "America is often called a melting pot. But that's not exactly true. It is more of a mosaic, where everyone fits together and nurtures their own individuality." Here we have the great cultures of many countries, and we appreciate all the cultures of every country and want the best of each culture from each country. ¶Now we come to Hindu solidarity. I call it "solidarity in diversity." Solidarity in diversity is really a better term than unity in diversity, just like the mosaic is more accurate than the melting pot. In America we have Śaivite Hindus, Vaishṇava Hindus, Śākta Hindus, Smārta Hindus, liberal Hindus, agnostic Hindus and anti-Hindu Hindus, all working together for Hindu solidarity, a grand Hindu front competent to master and reform Hinduism today. ¶There are different theologies, different philosophies and different scriptures for each of the various Hindu sects. We do not have 33,500 divisions to deal with like the Christians, but we do have a few major ones. Some liberal Hindus would like to get rid of these, but there is no reason why in America and the other countries of the world the major Hindu sects cannot live in harmony. Many *swāmīs* join with me in this thinking, as do other Hindu leaders. They know that unity does not mean sameness. Sameness in religion is not healthy, not natural. Sameness is a most common, dull, uninspired and unenlightened solution, for it reduces that which is vital with differences, rich in philosophical interpretation and background, to a common denominator. Such a solution would be very harmful to Hinduism in the world, and many of us are firmly against that idea. Hinduism has always taken pride in its broadness. All of history proclaims this to be true. In this most advanced age of civilization shall we abandon that lofty view? Shall we take a sumptuous feast with its rich variety of curries and chutneys and dals and stir it all together into an unappealing stew? Certainly not. I certainly hope not.

Wednesday
LESSON 353
Solidarity, Not Sameness

Hindu solidarity is not an original idea. It has become very popular in India itself. Whatever our background, we can and we must maintain our sectarian roots and heritage, cultivate our differences and become strong within them, as the Christians did. There exists a common bond between all Hindus. What is that bond? Number one, it is the belief in *karma* and *dharma*. The Śaivites and the Vaishṇavites, the Śāktas and the Smārtas all believe in *karma* and *dharma*. Number two is reincarnation. Number three is the all-pervasiveness of God and the sanctity of the *Vedas.* If we accept these three basic beliefs—along with tolerance for all the religions of the world coupled with the belief that all people, whatever their spiritual path, will one day attain to knowledge of God—then we can say, "Yes, we are Hindus." ¶Though the branches of Hinduism are many and different, the roots are common to us all. We share so much, and we can never forget this. Sharing a common heritage, we can then, with confidence, follow our own path. If that path is liberal Hindu, fine. If that path is Śaivite Hindu, Vaishṇava Hindu or Śākta Hindu, fine. Let each follow his own path. Let each perfect himself and purify himself within the context of his individual way. We must know and get the strength from the heritage of our roots. That is a real strength; that is a genuine Hindu solidarity. It is not strength for us all to call out for others to be exactly as we are. A tree has one trunk, one root system, but for survival its branches must reach in many directions. The different directions are not a weakness in the tree. In fact, its very life depends on this diversity. The very life of Hinduism has always depended on a similar diversity. That is why I say it is not uniformity or sameness that we seek together. It is solidarity, the strength which comes from appreciating and cultivating our differences, not denying them or trying to restrain or even destroy them altogether. ¶It is a strange fact that there are temples today that enshrine three Supreme Gods within them—Śiva, Vishṇu and Śakti. This never used to happen, because people were secure and firm in their beliefs. Imagine, three Supreme Gods in one temple. Who can understand such a thing? This is a new phenomenon. It is not *Āgamic.* It is not traditional. It is like having three prima donnas on one stage, and the only result will be confusion, strife and unhappiness. What are the children going to think about this? As they are growing up, they will say, "When you make up your mind, Mom and Dad, who is Supreme God, let us know. In the meantime, we are going to live, have fun and be Americans. Hey, when you decide, let us know." ¶First we need to know, deep inside ourselves, who is the Supreme God. Is He Śiva? Is He Vishṇu, Kṛishṇa, or is She Durgā? Having made that determination, we can gather like-minded people together to design and build a temple to our Supreme God. There is no power in a temple to more than one Supreme God, no power at all. Better not to build such a place, which will just be a social hall. That is not religion. That is opportunistic compromise. That is politics trying to run religion. Rather, build a temple to Śiva and worship there with your whole heart. Build a temple to Vishṇu and worship there with your whole heart. Build a temple to Śakti and worship there with your whole heart. But don't compromise, don't confuse yourselves and your children by trying to please everyone in every temple. Let there be good, strong temples to Śiva and good strong temples to Kṛishṇa and to Vishṇu and to Śakti. Each devotee can then worship God or Goddess properly, with full commitment and devotion.

Thursday
LESSON 354
The Demise Of Pagan Faiths

There have been civilizations that have become ashamed of and then abandoned their religion and their temples because of Christian and Communist propaganda. Where is the Greek religion today? Their temples are mere monuments. Where is the Native American religion today, with all of its mysticism? And where is the religion of the Native Hawaiian people today? They practiced a profound religion that was in many respects very similar to Hinduism. They worshiped Lord Gaṇeśa, and called Him God Lono. They worshiped Lord Subramaṇya and they called Him God Ku, who is our Kumāra. Their Goddess Pele was Pārvatī, whom they feared. Their Supreme God, our Lord Śiva, was called God Kane, represented by a single upright sacred stone, much like our *liṅga.* ¶Then, about a hundred and fifty years ago, Christians came in force to Hawaii. They set about to convert all of the "pagan" Hawaiians. They set up printing presses and schools. They convinced the queens and kings to close the temple doors, which they did. What followed is a sad history of decline and fall. The 1,500-year-old Polynesian culture dwindled and died. Intermarriage began. Today, 200 years later, the language, the culture, the religion, the worship and the race are nearly gone. Of the 500,000 Hawaiians that Captain Cook encountered in 1772, only about 500 are left today. There are virtually no pure Hawaiians anymore, all because the temple doors were closed. Such is the vulturism that the Christians, in their commercial, colonial, imperial expansion, perpetuated on the Hawaiian people. We live in Hawaii. We know all of this. ¶We do not want Hinduism in mainland America to suffer that fate, and so we urge all of you to protect yourselves from the forces that may try to demean and destroy our Hindu temples. By protecting the temples, we protect the religion. Proceed with confidence. With a united will, a solidarity, a Hindu front, we are a loving fortress unto ourselves. ¶You are all to be commended for your efforts to open the temple doors in this community. I ask each and every one of you to bring your heritage, the best you understand it, all of it, here to the United States of America. Don't try to create a new religion here, a Neo-

Indian religion. The one you have is perfectly fine, the best in the world. Those of you who have been educated in Christian schools, your minds have been turned against Hinduism at a young age by the clever teachers in the school, and thoughts have gone into the subconscious mind that are there militating against your bringing up temples and bringing the culture here, thinking it may be not quite right to do. Release those thoughts from the subconscious mind and realize that we are all in a country that grants us religious freedom through its constitution. It is our privilege and duty to claim that religious freedom, to enforce that religious freedom, to implement it and not be shy about our faith. This is not a shy country. ¶I visited the Hindu temple in Flint, Michigan, a few days ago. Someone had written in the sand in front of the temple, "Jesus Saves." I inquired, "How long has that been there?" They said a few days. I asked, "Why didn't you take your foot and rub that out? No one has the right to come on this property and write such things in front of a Hindu temple." Everyone was too shy. We need strength, not shyness when these kinds of things happen. We rubbed it out. ¶How do we show that strength? We have to go to the Christian ministers in that community and tell them politely but firmly that their children are desecrating our temple and demand that this stop. We have to ask them to talk to their congregations, to explain Hinduism to their congregations and tell them that we are not putting up with this sort of nonsense and harassment. If one of the children of the Hindu community went to the Baptist church and wrote "Hare Kṛishṇa" or "Śiva Śiva" on the sand in front of the church, you would hear about it from the Baptists. They would come right over here saying, "I would like to talk to the spiritual leader of this organization about a very important subject." Then you would have to tell your children not to antagonize the Christians or desecrate their property. ¶We also have to question our children as to any and all badgering by Christians in their school. This taunting in public schools violates the First Amendment of our Constitution, which guarantees the right to religious freedom. Such abuse should not be allowed in the schoolyard, in the halls, before or after class, in the cafeteria or in the bathrooms. When a child threatens another child, saying his soul will perish or burn forever in Hell, is that not a serious crime? After all, the soul is more important than the body, and if it's a crime to threaten to harm someone's body, should it also not be considered a crime to threaten harm to another's soul, a crime which starts with the priest or minister's speaking out hatred and bigotry from behind his pulpit? ¶These are called hate crimes, and more laws are being passed to prevent them. But until the laws are clear, parents should know that complaint is a great power. Hindus, Jews, Muslims, Jains and Buddhists are rising up in one voice and speaking with parents, parish priests, ministers, school teachers, principals and boards of education to give children release from the religious taunting and badgering which they have to put up with day in and day out. How is it possible to study and receive a good education under such unhealthy, antagonistic conditions? We cannot let fear paralyze us. Go to the Christians and state your case. Proceed with confidence. You will prevail.

Friday
LESSON 355
Strength of Commitment

What is our strength? One Supreme God and many Gods. First we have to decide who is the Supreme God. Are you a member of the Śaivite Hindu religion? The Vaishṇavite Hindu religion? The Śākta Hindu religion? The Smārta Hindu religion? Having made that decision, you will have hope and peace of mind. You will have solace when you need it, and something to pass on to your children. Knowledge is strength. Commitment is strength. Knowing where you stand and what you are, that is strength. Worshiping many Gods is our way, but they are not all the Supreme God. They are His helpers, His creations. There is only one Supreme God, though we call Him by various names. The many Gods, the Mahādevas, will help us. They are specialists created by God. ¶Hinduism today is a religion of today and tomorrow. It is not just a religion of history books and yesterday. Our religion gives us strength today. It is a religion which worships one Supreme God, with vast scriptures that prescribe the worship and illumine our minds with knowledge about the one Supreme God. Never forget this. Never forsake your Vedic Hindu Dharma, but fulfill it, and you will be rewarded, generation after generation after generation. ¶There is a movement from within Hinduism itself which poses yet another threat to our religion, a threat to all the sects. I call it "liberal Hinduism." Liberal Hinduism is a "Chellappa stew," a confused mixture of many things thrown into a one bowl. This movement was started by your forefathers, and it has to be corrected by us through being good Śaivites in this life. ¶What does liberal Hinduism teach? It teaches that it is not necessary to go to the temple, that *yoga* is not necessary, that all religions are one, that we need not listen to the *swāmīs,* and that sectarianism is wrong. What the followers of liberal Hinduism don't seem to realize is that if they destroy the temples, the sects and the *swāmīs,* they will be destroying Hinduism itself. ¶Liberal Hindus hold an idea that all religions are one. They must not have studied the various religions, or they would have to conclude, as we did in America after years of comparative research, that all religions are not one, not at all alike. I was told that all religions are fundamentally one when I was young, and I believed it until I found out years later that it is a lie. All religions are good insofar as they teach devotion and good conduct, but they are not one. The Christians know that their religion is totally different from Hinduism. They live under no illusions, because they know that the very foundations of Śaivism—namely, *karma,* reincarnation, *yoga,* God's existence in all things and the soul's ultimate merger in God—these beliefs are not their beliefs. Did you know that for a Christian to believe in any of these things is heresy? Absolute heresy. There is very little beyond a belief in a Supreme God and some good moral laws that is common to nearly all religions, but there are many, many differences. ¶As Śaivites, we love everyone. We appreciate and encourage all religious paths. That is our way. But that does not mean that we should abandon our beliefs and practices to embrace Islam or Buddhism. That does not mean that we should put Jesus on the altar in our shrine room, which is exactly what the liberal Hindus do. I was at a Śaivite institution the other day and was shocked to find that Jesus, Kṛishṇa and Buddha were there together on the altar in the prayer room. There was no image of Gaṇeśa or Murugan or Śiva, yet they called themselves Śaivites. I asked what it meant. They explained, "We believe in all religions, Swāmī." They were worshiping every God except their own! That complacent syncretism is the result of faulty, liberal Hindu thinking. ¶The Christians don't have Lord Gaṇeśa presiding over Sunday services. Of course not. It would be unthinkable. For Śaivites to put Jesus or Mary on the altar is an invitation to every Christian missionary to enter your home, to enter the minds of your children. It is the first sign of the breaking of your faith. That is certainly how the Christians take it. They will see you as a prime target, and they will say among themselves, "It won't be long now."

Saturday
LESSON 356
Liberal Hinduism

Liberal Hindus preach against sectarianism—against Śaivism, Vaishṇavism, Śāktism and orthodox Smārtism. They teach that sectarianism is some kind of antiquated evil, an unenlightened view of life, a thing of the past. They are absolutely wrong. Sectarianism is the strength of religion. If you ask a liberal Hindu what he is, he will tell you, "I am everything. I am a Christian. I am a Jew. I am a Buddhist." Of course, the Christians know full well that he is not a Christian. The Jews are certain that he is not Jewish, and the Buddhists will tell you that he does not follow the Buddha's path. In the West they think he sounds stupid. ¶The liberal Hindus are out to destroy sectarianism, to break down Śaivism, Vaishṇavism and Śāktism—all in the name of modernization or to unite the people for some political reason. The same thing is happening in America, where liberal Hindus are trying to coax everyone away from their sect into a one group so they can have more political power in their lobbying in Washington. It is a sad thing that people go right along with this line of thinking, giving up thousands of years of beautiful tradition for no reason at all. It is totally insidious. So, here we have the Christian forces working against Hinduism, the Muslim forces working against Hinduism, the atheistic forces working against Hinduism and now, worst of all, the liberal Hindu forces working against Hinduism, which is worse because they are working from within the religion itself. ¶What is the solution? We have to define the boundaries of each sect in order to protect and preserve this most ancient of all the world's religions. We have to realize that the liberal Hindus are just creating another sect, and we must refuse to join their modern sect. We want nothing to do with those who call for the end of sectarianism. Those who abandon Śaivism to embrace this liberal Hindu path will later take the next natural step and give up Hinduism altogether, calling themselves nothing, or calling themselves everything, which amounts to the same thing. ¶To understand how liberal Hinduism fits in, it is helpful to use the Western terms *orthodox, reform* and *liberal,* because this is a problem that all of the great religions have had to face. Śaivism is the orthodox and original form of the Sanātana Dharma, the eternal path. Vaishṇavism and Śāktism are the reform sects which developed later but retained most of the ancient patterns of practice and belief. Liberal Hinduism is the liberal branch which postulates a form of the religion which is entirely unorthodox and diverges from the path set down by our Gods, by our scriptures, by our *ṛishis* and other holy men. ¶The Tamil people should take a lesson from the fate of the Jewish religion. The liberal Jewish movement is bringing about the end of the race, which means the end of the religion. It is doing this through its modernistic concepts, through its sweeping compromise of the duties and disciplines set down for Jews to follow, through its disregard for Jewish ethics, values and practices. We have to take heed. It is happening in India and in Sri Lanka, too. ¶What is not well understood here is that in America traditional, sectarian religious people and groups are respected, provided they are firm in their convictions and are really leading a religious life and not harming others. It is human to respect strength and conviction. Śaivites who are firm and proud of their religion will be respected wherever they go throughout the world. But people do not respect those who don't know what they believe or those who will say they believe one thing in order to get something, in order to fit in, or for whatever reason, while in their heart they believe something entirely different. Liberal groups do not receive the same respect. They are not looked up to but are ignored and then absorbed back into society. ¶The American Śaivites want the true Śaiva Samayam, not a watered-down, intellectual concoction created by a few discontented Hindus in order to get along with Western scholars. People are becoming more educated, more enlightened, and they realize that the orthodox Śaiva Dharma is far more profound and rewarding to their soul. They love and want to worship Lord Śiva. They love Lord Gaṇeśa and go to Lord Murugan for help. What is the solution? We have to preserve scripture and temple worship.

Sunday
LESSON 357
Realities Of Worship

We approach the temple in a much different way, a humble way. We believe that the Deity lives in the temple, that He comes from the inner worlds, hovers over the stone image in His golden body of light and, as the priest invokes Him, blesses those present. Everyone is elated. Everyone feels His holy presence, and an advanced soul may even see Him there. So, we approach the Deity with a pure mind. We approach Him in trepidation. We want to look our best, for when He takes over the stone image in the sanctum and sends forth His rays of blessing, we don't want to look disrespectful in His eyes. We therefore prepare the body and the mind before going to the temple. We get our aura looking just right. The aura is the sum of vibrations that emanate out around the body. The colors of the aura are dark or light depending on the nature of our thoughts and emotions. We prepare our aura by chanting *mantras,* hymns and prayers. We prepare our body by bathing and dressing simply and properly, not in the sexy way that young girls are dressing nowadays. Then we go to the temple, and the Deity actually comes on the inner planes and blesses us, listens to our prayers, clears our minds and calms our emotions. ¶We take that holy vibration home, back into the community, where we respect our elders and they guide us wisely. Then culture flourishes, because culture has its source right there in the temple. When culture is flooding out of the temple, our actions are productive and our minds are creative, our speech is pure, our hearts rejoice and we become good citizens. Religion makes us good citizens, because we are peaceful inside and want peace in our land. Peace comes first from the individual. It is unrealistic to expect peace from our neighbors unless we are peaceful first, unless we make ourselves peaceful through right living, right worship and right religious culture in the home. ¶How can we destroy all of this? It's simple. Stop going to the temple. Culture will begin to go. Refinement and love will begin to go. Arguments will be heard in the homes. Divorces will fill the courts. Stress and mental illness will become the common experience—all because we stopped that one, great, mystical practice—temple worship. ¶The temple is the great psychiatrist of the Hindu religion. When we forget that, we suffer the consequences of our neglect, personally and as a nation. The temple has mystical powers that surpass the greatest psychiatrists on the planet. Our priesthoods have the tools to invoke and perpetuate this power. The temple can not only analyze your problem, it can give absolution. You can leave the temple wondering what it was that was bothering you on the way to seek the help of the Deity—so complete is the power of the temple. ¶We are proud to say that we worship God and the Gods. We object to the liberal Hindu propaganda which denies the existence of our Gods and installs its limited knowledge in their place. We object to the notion that all religions are one, and we believe that for us Śaivism is the greatest religion on the Earth and has no equal. I think that Śaivite leaders should rise up against liberal Hinduism and remove it from the minds of the children and the general population. It is a cancer for which there is no miraculous cure, so it has to be surgically removed to preserve Śaivism. That is the only solution available. ¶Well, you can see that our religion is faced with a lot of serious problems. Yet, there are good, sensible solutions if we, the united Śaivites of the world, all pitch in and work together and have a little selfless sacrifice to offer. I feel the spirit coming up among Lord Śiva's devotees. But it is not enough. More has to be done. We need religious leaders to come forward from among the *gṛihastha* community, tens of thousands of men and women who have something to offer, who can serve and teach the Śaiva Dharma. We need Śaivite schools of a fine caliber to be built and managed by devout Śaivites. We need all of you to spread the religion to the next generation, many of whom are not receiving proper religious training. We need field workers and teachers and missionaries to serve Lord Śiva in His work. This is necessary in the technological age, necessary in order that Śaivism will be the religion of the future, not of the past.

Hindu Dharmārtham Śakto Bhava

हिन्दुधर्मार्थं शक्तो भव

Stand Strong For Hinduism

May the mid-region free us from all fear, and both Heaven and Earth make us secure. Let there be for us no fear from behind, no fear from in front, no fear from the north or the south. Let there be no fear from friend, no fear from foe, no fear from the known, no fear from what lies before us unknown, let there be no fear for us from night, no fear from day. Let all the quarters be my friends.

Atharva Veda 19.15.5–6. HV, P. 105

Monday
LESSON 358
Are You A Hindu?

This afternoon we had a nice visit with a fine young man here at my *āśrama* in Sri Lanka. During the conversation, I encouraged him to stand strong for Hinduism. "When you stand strong for your religion, you are strong," he was told. Today there are many Hindus from India and Sri Lanka in the United States and Europe who when asked, "Are you a Hindu?" reply, "No, I'm not really a Hindu. I'm nonsectarian, universal, a follower of all religions. I'm a little bit of everything, and a little bit of everybody. Please don't classify me in any particular way." Are these the words of a strong person? No. Too much of this kind of thinking makes the individual weak-minded. Religion, above all else, should bring personal strength and commitment to the individual. When a Hindu is totally noncommittal, releasing his loyalties as he goes along through life, disclaiming his religion for the sake of so-called unity with other people or for business or social reasons, he can easily be taken in, converted to other people's beliefs. Even when it is just a way to get along with others, by seeming uncertain of his path, he opens himself to alien influences of all kinds. ¶In America the beautiful, the land of the money, anything is possible. It is possible to get money. But to get it at the expense of disclaiming one's religion to the public is a very great expense. Young adults hear their parents disclaiming their religion by saying, "Oh, I am a Christian. I am a Muslim. I am a Buddhist. I am a follower of all religions. All religions are one." All religions are not one. They are very, very different. They all worship and talk about God, yes, but they do not all lead their followers to the same spiritual goal. The Christians are not seeking God within themselves. They do not see God as all-pervasive. Nor do they see God in all things. Their religion does not value the methods of *yoga* which bring Hindus into God Realization. Their religion does not have the mysticism of worshiping God and the Gods in the temple. Jews, Christians and Muslims do not believe that there is more than one life or that there is such a thing as *karma*. They simply do not accept these beliefs. They are heresy to them. These are a few of the basic and foremost beliefs that make our religion and theirs very, very, different indeed. ¶Many Asian Hindus traveling to America, Europe or Africa for business reasons think that in order to fit in, to be accepted, they must deny their

---

A traditional temple vocalist, oduvar, *sings a* Devaram *hymn by Saint Sambandar. Holding wooden cymbals, he stands before the Kumbhalavalai Gaṇeśa Temple in Alaveddy, Sri Lanka, near Gurudeva's Sri Subramuniya Ashram. Gaṇeśa blesses his song with a shower of flowers.*

religion. The Jews, Christians and Muslims did not deny their faith when they found themselves in alien countries, yet their businesses flourish. But too many Hindus say, "I am a Muslim. I am a Jew. I am a Christian. I am a Hindu. I am a universalist." These are very naive statements. The Muslims do not think these Hindus are Muslim. The Jews do not think that they are Jewish. The Christians know they are not Christians. And the Hindus know they were born Hindu and will die as Hindus, and that they are disclaiming their own sacred heritage for the sake of money and social or intellectual acceptance. How deceptive! How shallow! The message should go out loud and strong: Stand strong for Hinduism, and when you do you will be strong yourself. Yes! Stand strong for Hinduism. Stand strong for Hinduism. Religion is within your heart and mind. ¶If there were no humans with thinking minds on the planet, there would be no religion at all. Religion does not exist outside of a person's mind and spirit. Religion lies within the human mind. If we want to preserve the world's oldest religion, the Sanātana Dharma, which goes back in time as far as man himself, then we must preserve it within our minds, protect it in our hearts and then slowly, steadily spread its great wisdom out into the minds of others. The dignity of the Hindu people must be preserved, not surrendered on the altar of material gain.

Tuesday
LESSON 359
One Duty To Perform

Every Hindu has but one great obligation, and that is to pass his religion on to the next generation of Hindus. That's all he has to do, pass his religion on to the next generation. Then that generation passes it on to their next generation. If we lose a single generation inbetween, the whole religion is lost in an area of the world. How many religions have existed on this planet? Thousands of them. What happened to the Zoroastrian religion? It barely exists now. What happened to the religion of the ancient Greeks? They must have missed several generations. The ancient Mayan, Hawaiian, Druid and Egyptian religions are all virtually forgotten but for the history books. ¶The great men and women in our history have withstood the most severe challenges to our religion and sacrificed their energies, even their lives, that it would not be lost to invaders who sought to destroy it. It is easy to be courageous when an enemy is on the attack, because the threat is so obvious. Today the threat is more subtle, but no less terrible. In fact, it is really a greater threat than Hinduism has ever had to face before, because an enemy is not destroying the religion. It is being surrendered by the Hindus themselves through neglect, through fear, through desire for land and gold, but mostly through ignorance of the religion itself. If Hindus really understood how deep into their soul their religion penetrates, if they knew how superior it is to any other spiritual path on the Earth today, they would not abandon it so easily but cherish and foster it into its great potential. They would not remain silent when asked about their religion, but speak out boldly its great truths. They would not hesitate to stand strong for Hinduism. ¶How can Hindus in the modern, mechanized world pass their religion to the next generation when they are not proud enough of it to announce it openly to business associates and all who ask? When the Muslim seeks employment, he is proud to say, "I worship Allah." The Christian is proud to say, "I worship Jesus Christ." But too often the Hindu is not proud to say, "I worship Lord Gaṇeśa." In our great religion there is one Supreme God and many Gods. The average Hindu today is not proud of this. He feels others will reject him, will not employ him, will not like him. Of course, this might be true. It might be very true. Then he should seek out people who do respect Hinduism. These are the people to associate with.

Wednesday
LESSON 360
Vedānta and Christianity

Tens of thousands of America's and Europe's younger generation have come to believe in the basic tenets of Hinduism. There are hundreds of thousands of the older generation who believe in reincarnation and the laws of *karma.* These two beliefs have pulled them away from the Abrahamic religions. But unless the Hindu organizations in every country who teach reincarnation and *karma* take these fine, dedicated half-Hindu people one step further and convert them fully into the Hindu religion, a disservice through neglect has been committed. ¶Yes, native-born Americans want to know more about *karma* and reincarnation and God's all-pervasiveness. They have not been satisfied with the postulations taught by the Abrahamic faiths. They do not believe in a wrathful God who punishes souls in Hell for eternity. They do not believe that non-Christians will suffer forever for their "wrongful beliefs." Many Americans are adopting the Hindu view of life. Even scientists are looking to Hinduism for deeper understanding as to the nature of the universe. Ironically, born Hindus are trying to be like Western people just when Westerners are appreciating the beauties of Hinduism. Yes, hundreds of thousands of sincere seekers in the United States, Europe, Canada, Australia and elsewhere are turning toward Hinduism, pulling away from their former religions and finding themselves in an in-between state, an abyss which offers them no further guidance from Indian *swāmīs* or community acceptance by Hindu groups. ¶It is postulated by some that Vedānta makes a Christian a better Christian. Because of that postulation Vedānta has been widely accepted throughout the world. "Study Vedānta," seekers are told, "and it will make you a more enlightened Christian." This is simply not true. When you study Vedānta, you learn about *karma* and reincarnation, you begin to understand that God is within you and within all things, and that the immortal soul of man is one with the Absolute God. These are not Christian beliefs. These beliefs are a strong threat to Catholic and Protestant Christian doctrine, so strong, in fact, that in 1870 the First Vatican Council condemned five beliefs as the single most sensitive area threatening the Catholic faith of the day, and even in recent times the Vatican has described their encroachment as a grave crisis. Among those condemned beliefs is the belief that God exists in the world, in all things. To believe that God is everywhere and that all things are His Sacred Being makes an individual an apostate to his religion, according to the mandates of the Catholics and most Christian churches. ¶Isn't that interesting? Certainly the Catholics do not agree that studying Vedānta makes one a better Catholic. Certainly the Methodists, Baptists, Lutherans and evangelicals do not hold that the study of Vedānta makes one a better Christian. Quite the opposite, the study of Vedānta will make a Christian a heretic to his own religion. So successful were the Vedānta *swāmīs* in promulgating the notion that Vedānta can be studied by people of all religions, that they have become a threat to the existence of the Catholic and Protestant churches. That is how different Christianity is from traditional Hinduism. ¶Hinduism has come a long way in North America and Europe through the tireless efforts of the Vedānta *swāmīs*, the Sivananda *swāmīs* and others. They are to be commended for their efforts and insight, and for succeeding in putting the precepts of Hinduism on the map of the world's consciousness. However, one step further must be taken.

Thursday
LESSON 361
Welcoming Newcomers

Only if we bring seekers into Hinduism properly through the *nāmakaraṇa saṁskāra*, our name-giving sacrament, will they truly become a part of this time-honored tradition and be able to raise their children as Hindus. If we do not, they will have nothing to offer their children but an empty, negative abyss to slowly fall into when they grow up. We owe it to the next generation, the next, the next and the next to take these sincere Hindu souls in Western bodies fully into our religion, train them and help them to become established in one sect or another. It should be insisted upon that their children do not grow up without a religion, for that would prove harmful both to the individual and to Hindu society as a whole. ¶Societies which do not foster religion foster crime by default. Crime is very expensive for an individual, for a community and for a nation. When we neglect religious training, we allow crime to gain a foothold on the youth, and we pay for that neglect dearly. Therefore, I say that this next step must be taken, and taken fully, by all the *swāmīs* throughout the United States, Canada, Europe and around the world. ¶We beseech all Hindu organizations worldwide to open their hearts and doors to these fine souls. This is a very serious situation. There are hundreds of thousands of people who have been dislodged from their parents' religion through their belief in reincarnation, *karma* and the knowledge of God's all pervasiveness, and yet they have not been fully taken into the Hindu religion or its community of devotees. Why? Because of color? Yes, that is partly true. Many Indian people say, "You have to be born a Hindu to be a Hindu. You cannot adopt the Hindu religion. You have to be born a Hindu to be a Hindu." This, of course, is not true. Other Indian Hindus say, "You have to be born in India and in a caste to be a Hindu." This also is not true. What about all of you who were born and live here in Sri Lanka? What about the Hindus in Bali, those in Malaysia or the Hindus born in Trinidad, Nepal, Europe, Guyana, Suriname and elsewhere? Are they not Hindus? ¶We did some research on this erroneous statement: "You cannot convert to Hinduism." We studied dozens of books and noted down all of the quotes that we could find that said, "You have to be born a Hindu to be a Hindu" or "You have to be born in India to be a Hindu." We found that these two quotes were only in the books authored by Christians. These statements, we concluded, were nothing more than Christian propaganda against the Hindu religion. Presumably, the Christians knew that if they could stop or at least slow down the growth of Hinduism through conversion, they would make more progress in their own conversions and in a few generations perhaps destroy Hinduism. We did not find these statements in a single book written by a Hindu author. ¶In fact, eminent Hindu authors have said that you can convert to Hinduism. Swami Vivekananda proclaimed, "Born aliens have been converted in the past by crowds, and the process is still going on." Even if you only adopt Hindu practices, believe in reincarnation and *karma* and do a *pūjā* once a day, you are a Hindu and will be accepted by Hindu society. Unfortunately, a minority of Hindus of Indian origin, educated in Christian schools, and even a few Western-influenced *swāmīs* and *pandits* and one or two Śaṅkarāchāryas, echo this misinformation with conviction. We can now see how the Christian propaganda has negatively influenced the growth of Hinduism worldwide. Their propaganda has infiltrated, diluted and destroyed the Hindu's faith in his own religion.

Friday
LESSON 362
A Crisis Of Identity

This confusion about Hinduism, what it is and is not and who is a Hindu and who is not, occurs in San Francisco, New York, Chennai, Mumbai, New Delhi and in London. It is mainly in the larger cities in India, the United States and Europe that people are not upholding the Sanātana Dharma anymore and are surrendering it, the most precious thing in their life, to adopt an ecumenical philosophy. The sad thing is that no one is objecting. Yes, no one is objecting. It doesn't seem to bother anybody at all. No one bothers when a Hindu denies his religious heritage in order to be accepted into a place of employment, or while working with fellow employees. No one bothers when that same Hindu returns home and performs *pūjā* in the closet shrine among the shoes. The shrine is in the closet so the door can be quickly closed in case non-Hindu visitors arrive. Isn't this terrible? ¶But these same Hindus expect their sons and daughters to believe in the religion that they are publicly denouncing. They expect their sons and daughters to worship in the closet shrine they hide at home. The children today just will not accept this deception. Modern education teaches people to think for themselves. They will soon reject Hinduism and maybe their parents, too. Yes, youth do reject it, and they are rejecting it more and more each year that this deceptive attitude continues on the part of the elders. Having rejected their Hinduism, the young people are not adopting another religion. What then are they doing? They are living as nonreligious people. ¶When the pressures of mechanized industrial society get too difficult for them, when they need God and need the strength of their childhood faith, they will have no place to turn—not even to their parents. They may even seek escape in committing suicide, by hanging themselves, poisoning themselves. It's happening now, happening more and more as the years go by. And now divorce is widespread among Hindus. The elders sit in judgment and proclaim, "Divorce is wrong. Therefore, you shouldn't get a divorce. You are breaking the rules by getting a divorce." Too many elders have already broken the rules by not standing strong for their religion, and they are not listened to. Our fellow Hindus should not be harshly judged and cast out when things go wrong in their life. The elders should offer gentle advice and help in as many ways as possible to make up for any wrong that has been done. When the younger generation fails, the elders must share their strength with them to make them succeed, drawing on the wisdom of Sanātana Dharma. ¶But it is never too late to stand strong for Hinduism. Hindu societies have to provide marriage counselors, people who go to the homes and counsel the couples before the relationship comes to the point of planning for divorce. Yes, we must provide professionally trained men and women to help a troubled couple before they go to the attorney, and others who can counsel our troubled youth, our elderly and our poor. Every Hindu who needs help must be able to find it somewhere within his own religion. Who can provide that help? The elders can and must.

Saturday
LESSON 363
Ministers Are Needed

There are many professions that emerged in India during the Rāj: the profession of the attorney, the profession of the engineer, the profession of the modern businessman, the scientist and more. However, the most respected profession, that of religious minister, was not allowed to develop. Under the British rule the profession of the religious ministers was not made popular. Why? We can assume it would have made Hinduism strong and its people self-sufficient. It would have increased its self-respect. Slowly the Anglican Christian government drew devotees away from the temple and philosopher, and teachers away from the religion into the secular world. Slowly they drew the women out of the homes into jobs, and the priests out of the temples into better-paying professions. ¶A law student has no authority in the courts. He cannot approach the judge. He can sit in the courtroom and listen. But as soon as he passes his bar examination, he gains authority. He can then wield his authority in the courts. There is a parallel to this in religion. The average follower does not have religious authority, but the appointed or ordained minister has been given authority by all the members and other ministers. The Muslims have ministers with authority, the Buddhists have priests with great authority, and so do the Christians. They all have their churches, temples and houses of worship where the ministers and priests do their work. The modern church system is a social, economical, cultural and religious structure. A minister of a church or of a Muslim mosque, Buddhist temple or Jewish synagogue has a certain well-defined authority and can effectively help the members of his congregation, much more so than can the ordinary person. ¶The modern church system gives authority to well-educated people, to the most devout and committed people, to perform their ministry. Once Hindu men or women have this kind of authority, it is possible to approach the president of a country, the Pope in Rome or any other important person in government as representatives of the religion. They can freely communicate with other religious leaders: a Muslim imam, a Christian minister, a Buddhist priest on an equal basis. They can lecture around the world and do much more than they could before being ordained. This is because they have been given the authority by their congregation and other clergy persons. Hindus of all sects need their religious leaders in every country to serve the community, to teach and represent the religion at local and international venues, to stand strong for Hinduism on equal footing with all major religions of the world. Hindus need their religious leaders to perform the rites of passage, to manage the temples, to counsel and console, to uphold family values, to stop the suicides, to stop the divorces, to stop the murders, to stop the wife and child abuse, so that the community is strong and stable.

Sunday
LESSON 364
Sannyāsins Are Needed

There are hundreds of thousands of *sannyāsins,* Hindu monks, throughout North India. But where are the *sannyāsins* that have been produced by the Hindu community of northern Sri Lanka? Where are they? The community produces attorneys. The community produces businessmen. The community produces freedom fighters. Why not produce a *swāmī* also? Is that too much to ask? It's not too much to ask. It is part of Hindu culture to dedicate a son to religious orders. This same community, however, has given many, many of their young men to the Catholic Church to become its priests. This is difficult to understand. It really is. ¶A young man before the age of twenty-five should be allowed to make a personal decision whether he wants to follow the path of the *sannyāsin* or the path of the householder. He should never be forced into employment to earn a big dowry in order to marry off his sisters. It is a sin if he is forced to work in the world if his calling is to find God and serve his people through Hinduism. It is a sin, when the calling of his soul is to realize God, to force him into a marriage. The best thing for the family, for the community and for all of humanity would be to let those rare souls seek out God, take their holy vows of *sannyāsa* and bring light and love back into a hurting world through their awakened being. ¶The Hindu community in Sri Lanka should produce spiritual leaders from among its young men. It has quite enough of all the other kinds of professions. It should again produce great *swāmīs,* as well as many *gṛihastha* missionaries and ministers. We asked this young man sitting here before me an hour ago, "How many people of your age go to the religious meetings and events?" He said, "Very few of us do." The parents should bring their young men with them by the hundreds to listen to visiting *swāmīs* and participate in other functions. Hindus around the world have to stand up for Hinduism, support it by their efforts, their interest, their resources of time and money and talent. ¶Last week while in Chennai, Swami Chinmayananda, a friend of mine for over twenty years, and I were talking together. A young man came in during our conversation and told Swami that he was preparing to go to school and then asked Swami for his blessings. Swami inquired of him what he would do after finishing with schooling. He said, "Then I will be married." Swami inquired, "Then what?" "Then I'll raise the children." Swami asked again, "Then what?" "I will go on with my profession." Swami persisted, "Then what?" He went on like that until finally the young man said, "Well, then I will die." Swami then said to him. "You should do some useful service and help me in my mission before you marry. There are enough children being born in India today—that can wait a little. Come to me after your schooling and we will do some useful work for God and our people together." ¶The point is that all things in life must be centered around religion. Only the spiritual matters of life live on. Everything else in life is destined to perish. This body will perish. This personality will perish. But our religion will live on and grow inside of us as we evolve from life to life. It is the duty of each Hindu, young or old, to help the religion progress from generation to generation. We help Hinduism live on by serving and guiding others. For true and lasting happiness, religion must be the basis of everything in life, around which all other interests and desires revolve. So many people are against religion these days. It is up to religious people to make it popular again. ¶India and Sri Lanka are in between being agricultural countries and technological countries. We have to bring Hinduism into the technological age. It has to be reiterated, reedited and reexplained. We must teach how the worship of Lord Gaṇeśa can help people run their computer better, help them become a better typist, help them handle the stress and strain that come from dealing with traffic and coping with people of all kinds. Hinduism has to be retranslated, updated into this industrial and technological era. Who can do that? Only the intelligent older people like yourselves. Intelligent older people can take this on and help me in this reformation, and then we will together pass it to the next generation. Soon the Hindus of all sects will become strong and proud of their religion. ¶Let us now affirm: "Lord Śiva loves and cares for all of His devotees. He always has and He always will." "Lord Śiva loves and care for all of His devotees. He always has and He always will." Let's work together, and let's begin now.

Monday
LESSON 365
You Can Make A Difference

It is important that all of you here with me tonight band together and do what you can to make a difference. It is important that you immediately refrain from following the patterns taught to you or your parents by the British Christians. One such pattern is that if one person in the community comes up, cut him down, malign him, criticize him until all heads are leveled. In the modern, industrial society everyone tries to lift everyone else up. People are proud of an individual in the community who comes up, and they help the next one behind him to succeed as well. They are proud of their religious leaders, too. Not so here, because if anyone does want to help out spiritually they have to be quiet and conceal themselves, lest they be maligned. Nobody is standing up to defend the religion; nobody is allowing anybody else to stand up, either. This has to change, and change fast it will. ¶Yes, the tide has to change. It has to change, no matter how painful it might be to praise people rather than criticize them, and to support and to protect them. The tide has to change. It has to change no matter how painful it might be to admit that we worship many Gods as well as one supreme God. The time has come for Hindus to be openly proud of their religion—the oldest religion on the planet. The time has come for Hindus to proclaim their beliefs and to defend their beliefs. The time has come for Hindus to stand up for Hinduism, no matter what the cost. The results will be a younger generation which respects the older generation again. The results will be a younger generation proud to be called Hindu. The results will be a younger generation eager to pass the tenets of Hinduism on to the next generation in a proud and a dynamic and a wonderful way. The time is now—begin! ¶Western nations are becoming truly pluralistic. These are days of truth. They are days of correction of wrongdoing, days of Self Realization, which cannot be hidden under a cloak of deception. Believe me, no Christian or Muslim looks at the Vedic-Āgamic goal of *ātmajñāna,* Self Realization, in the same way Hindus do. The days are gone when it is necessary to observe Christmas in the *āśrama* and sing non-Hindu hymns at *satsaṅga.* There was a time to hide the Vedic Truth beneath a basket and behind a cross, but now is a time to shout Self Realization from the rooftops. Self Realization is, in fact, what all people on the planet have come here to experience. ¶The Self within all is the sustainer of all, yet it acts not in that sustaining and is itself unsustained. It sustains our thoughts, our emotions, our physical universe, yet it lies mysteriously beyond them all, perfectly obvious to the knower, perfectly invisible to most. It is and yet it is not. Hindus need nothing else to hide behind than this Paramātman. Certainly we no longer need to define ourselves in a Christian or a Muslim way, or any other way but our own. So, no need to send out Christmas cards this year or have a tree in the *āśrama,* right? ¶In looking back on all the wonderful aspects of Hinduism that have been spoken of tonight on the beautiful island of Sri Lanka, it is clear that Hinduism is the answer for the future generations on this planet. It is the answer for the New Age, for the dawning Sat Yuga. The gracious Sanātana Dharma, our great religion, has all the answers. It has always had all of the answers in every age, for there was never an age when it did not exist. The time has now passed for many and is quickly passing for everyone when they can deny their Hindu heritage, when they can be afraid to admit their belief in Hinduism or even the simple fact that they are a Hindu. The time has come for Hindus of all races, all nations, of all cultures, of all sects to stand up and let the peoples of the world know of the great religion of which they are one of the staunch adherents. Take courage, courage, courage into your own hands and proceed with confidence. Stand strong for Hinduism.

The soul is born and unfolds in a body, with dreams and desires and the food of life. And then it is reborn in new bodies, in accordance with its former works. The quality of the soul determines its future body; earthy or airy, heavy or light.

Kṛishṇa Yajur Veda, Śvetāśvatara Upanishad, 5.11-12. UPM, P. 94

There is nothing higher than *dharma.* Verily, that which is *dharma* is truth.

Śukla Yajur Veda, Bṛihadāraṇyaka Upanishad 1.4.14. BO UPH, P. 84

Whatever world the man of purified mind desires, whatever desires he wishes to fulfill, all these he attains. Therefore, let whoever is desirous of prosperity worship the man of Self Realization.

Atharva Veda, Muṇḍaka Upanishad 3.1.10. EH P. 178

Now, there are, of a truth, three worlds: the world of men, the world of the fathers, and the world of the Gods. The world of the Gods is verily the best of worlds. *Śukla Yajur Veda, Bṛihadāraṇyaka Upanishad* 1.5.16. UPH, P. 89

Many are the lovely flowers of worship offered to the *guru,* but none lovelier than nonkilling. Respect for life is the highest worship, the bright lamp, the sweet garland and unwavering devotion.

Tirumantiram V. 197. TM

May noble wisdom come to us from all sides, undeceived, unhindered, overflowing, so that the *devas* may always help us onward, unceasing in their care, our Guardians day by day. Ours be the blissful love of *devas* who desire straight life; about us may the grace of *devas* lie. We have approached the *devas* for friendship; may they prolong our life to the full, so that we may live. *Ṛig Veda* 1.89.1-2. HV, P. 109

Having realized with mind and heart, having become wise, you will no longer move on the path of death. Therefore, they call renunciation the ardor surpassing all others.

Kṛishṇa Yajur Veda, Mahāṇārāyaṇa Upanishad 537–8. VE, P. 439

Of lords the Lord Supreme, of kings the King, of Gods the God, Him let us worship—transcendent, Lord of all worlds and wholly worthy of worship. *Kṛishṇa Yajur Veda, Śvetāsvatara Upanishad* 6.7. VE P. 156

Those who in penance and faith dwell in the forest, peaceful and wise, living a mendicant's life, free from passion depart through the door of the sun to the place of the immortal Person, the imperishable Self.
Atharva Veda, Muṇḍaka Upanishad 1.2.11. VE P. 415

Mind is indeed the source of bondage and also the source of liberation. To be bound to things of this world—this is bondage. To be free from them—this is liberation. *Kṛishṇa Yajur Veda, Maitrī Upanishad* 6.34. UPM, P. 104

If you have doubt concerning conduct, follow the example of high souls who are competent to judge, devout, not led by others, not harsh, but lovers of virtue. *Kṛishṇa Yajur Veda, Taittirīya Upanishad* 1.11.4. BO UPR, P. 539

The rites of oblation, O lovers of truth, which the sages divined from the sacred verses, were variously expounded in the threefold *Veda*. Perform them with constant care. This is your path to the world of holy action. *Atharva Veda, Muṇḍaka Upanishad.* 1.2.1. VE, P. 414

Let him approach with humility a *guru* who is learned in the scriptures and established in Brahman. To such a seeker, whose mind is tranquil and senses controlled, and who has approached him in the proper manner, let the learned *guru* impart the science of Brahman, through which the true, Imperishable Being is realized.
Atharva Veda, Muṇḍaka Upanishad 1.2.12–13. EH, P. 157

Yes, may the man who within his home pleases you all his days with songs and with offerings receive a rich reward, be loaded with your gifts! To him be happiness! This is our prayer. *Ṛig Veda* 4.4.7. VE 845

Like the cry of watchful birds swimming in water, like the loud claps of thundering rain clouds, like the joyful streams gushing from the mountain, so have our hymns sounded forth to the Lord.
Ṛig Veda 10.68.1. VE, P. 812

Without regard for themselves, without urges and efforts, absorbed in contemplation and established in the higher Self, they endeavor to remove evil deeds and surrender their bodies by renunciation.
Śukla Yajur Veda, Jābāla Upanishad, 6. VE, P. 441

Nandinātha Sūtrāṇi

नन्दिनाथसूत्राणि

PART FOUR

Hinduism's Nandinātha Sūtras

SUCCINCTLY, BOLDLY, THESE NANDINĀTHA SŪTRAS DESCRIBE HOW PEOPLE LIVED AND INTERRELATED WITH ONE ANOTHER WHEN LIFE WAS SIMPLER, WHEN FAMILIES AND VILLAGES WERE CLOSE-KNIT, AND LOVE AND PEACE, RESPECT AND WISDOM PREvailed. There is no new knowledge contained herein. Each *sūtra* proclaims an ancient wisdom and protocol which, when followed, brings that same simplicity, community support, peace, harmony and refinement of enduring relationships into daily life. Each of these *sūtras*, one to be read each day of the year, is a thread of purity, many from the historic past into the present, some from contemporary times. Even today, in the fifty-second Hindu century, these precepts define the daily life of hundreds of millions of well-bred and well-raised Asian people. These 365 *sūtras* are a distilled summation of *The Master Course*, a profound 3,000 page trilogy of *Dancing with Śiva, Living with Śiva* and *Merging with Śiva*, which contain the traditional Śaiva philosophy, culture and ways of meditation. They are the venerable *ghee* of our lineage.

While they are law, these *sūtras* are not commandments. They simply describe what devout Hindus do. Naturally, my expectations are that my close followers will heed and earnestly try to put into practice all 365 *sūtras*. However, eighteen of the aphorisms speak against practices that are, in wisdom, always avoided. In fact, I have used the word *forbidden* in each of these character-building, character-maintaining precepts to distinguish them from the rest. Fulfilling them, we have found, allows for inner freedom that is unsurpassed. Stress, often a by-product of guilt, has no home in individuals who never allow themselves to participate in any of these unwholesome areas. "It is wise to fear that which is to be feared."

Many who read these *sūtras* will wonder to themselves or even among friends, "Why do we need to follow such strict traditions and disciplines? Aren't they a bit old-fashioned?" My answer is: before the two world wars, many traditions similar to these were followed even in the United States, regarding raising of children, man-and-wife relationships, women rarely working outside the home, and thus not neglecting their children, etc. It was during World War II, when women began working in the world, that the breakdown of traditional culture occurred, setting a trend that is now being followed in almost every nation. The nonculture, or the destruction of culture which *is* nonculture, has become the "culture" which everyone follows. Hence the avalanche of promiscuity, divorce, suicide, various excesses and abuses—murder, theft, wife-beating, drug abuse, unstable, ever-shifting cohabitation as a substitute for marriage and the shameful neglect of children. Everyone's security is threatened.

When my *satguru,* Sage Yogaswami, was asked half a century ago why we should follow the old ways, he answered simply, "The railway engine pulls many coaches. Can it do so if it runs off the track? No. Great people have shown the path. We must follow it." Though perhaps challenging, the disciplines and guidelines described here create happy individuals, harmonious families and secure nations. Sage Yogaswami, the venerable *satguru* of the Tamil people of the island nation of Sri Lanka, made still another observation that points to the first reason for these *sūtras:* "Because of worldliness, the light in the faces of the young has become less bright these days. The way is very long, and you must go forward slowly, keeping to the path, not walking on the thorns by its sides." These *sūtras* define the path and the thorns that lie on either side of it. There is a second reason for these *sūtras.* When you take them as a total whole, you will glimpse the ideal community. Such a community is able to work together, love together, trust together, create together, serve Śiva together, worship together, live together in a productive harmony and ongoing creativity, as they each experience birth, life, death and birth again.

Thirdly, Hindus have spread throughout the world, relocating themselves because of employment opportunities, ethnic disputes, violence and economic deprivation within their homelands. Because of this diaspora, it has become necessary to restate the law of the culture, the protocol and modes of behavior that their forefathers knew and lived so well. At this trying time in history, these *Nandinātha Sūtras* came forth as a boon from the Gods to followers who, in their time of need, in the seriousness of their search, were asking for advice and guidance as to how they should behave with one another, how they should relate and interrelate with their husbands and wives, children, with fellow devotees, widows, widowers, divorcées and divorcés, and with *satguru, āchāryas, swāmīs, yogīs* and *sādhakas, brahmachārīs* and *brahmachāriṇīs.*

In reading the *sūtras,* you will notice that the vast majority are addressed to "All Śiva's followers," "Devotees of Śiva," etc. These are universally applicable to all Śaivites. A smaller number of *sūtras,* addressed to "My followers," are specific disciplines for those who look to me as their *guru.* A few *sūtras,* even more specific, are addressed to members of my Saiva Siddhanta Church or to my initiates. You will also notice that about one-seventh of the *sūtras* are addressed to monastics, and may wonder why they are included here. The answer is that it is important that families understand my expectations for the monastics, and the other way around—and that all be continually reminded of the lofty monastic *dharma.* It is the balance between the monastic community and the family community that stabilizes spiritual life in the physical world, in matters of marriage, business, politics, money and health.

I have articulated these *sūtrās* in clear, simple English so that they can easily be translated and unambiguously understood. However, obscurities do arise with the interpretation and application of even basic, straightforward precepts, and this will also happen with these *sūtrās.* They shall be upheld, enforced and simply explained by my order of *āchāryas* and *swāmīs,* by senior *sādhakas* and by elders. But all final interpretations and deductions, clarifications of apparent contradictions, settling of disputes and unraveling of subtle questions shall be made only by myself and my *ādi āchāryas* of our Śaiva Siddhānta Yoga Order. These four *ādi āchāryas* are duly ordained and authorized to give interpretations of these *sūtras.* While I live, my word shall be absolutely final. Future *satgurus* of our *paramparā,* lineage, will progress the understanding of these precepts from century to century.

And now I shall address ardent seekers who have become acquainted with me through dreams, visions, publications, lectures, the Internet, personal encounters or hearing of me from others. I challenge you to boldly go forth in your spiritual quest with firm determination. These 365 *sūtras* give the protocol and practices, as well as the attainments—the end in view. Live up to each one of them. Within these *sūtras* are restraints, encouragement, admonitions, enlightened coaching, even reprimands. There is much nourishment here for the intelligent soul who is pushing forward into peace and tranquility, having conquered the trials and tribulations of the yesterdays, and is now willing to bear his or her *karma* cheerfully and push onward. Study these *sūtras* that I have unfolded and adjust your life accordingly. Be unwavering in your commitment. You know the rightness of these guidelines for good conduct in your heart of hearts, soul of soul. Your inner ear hears and your inner eye sees the truth of each one. To adjust your life to their wisdom is the discipline toward being able to come close to and then truly dance, live and merge with Śiva. In applying these principles to your life, remember, above all, the only rigid rule is wisdom, for wisdom is the timely application of knowledge.

Dhārmika Jīvanam

धार्मिक जीवनम्

Section One

Right Living

Saṁsāra, the transmigration of life, takes place in one's own mind. Let one therefore keep the mind pure, for what a man thinks, that he becomes: this is a mystery of Eternity.

Maitrī Upanishad 6.34. UPM, P.103

Spiritual evolution is achieved by yoga *and striving. Devotees perform* tapas, *holding pots of fire, meditating for long hours, rolling around the temple in hot sand and carrying* kavadi. Devas *bless their efforts from the inner planes, while the baser worlds remain below and apart.*

The Purpose of Life

SŪTRA 1: LIFE'S HIGHEST PURPOSE

Śiva's followers strive for God Realization as the first and foremost goal of life. They learn to dance with Śiva, live with Śiva, merge with Śiva. Deep within, they discover their eternal, immortal oneness with God. Aum.

SŪTRA 2: FOUR NOBLE GOALS

Śiva's followers are ever mindful that life's purpose is to wholeheartedly serve God, Gods and *guru* and fulfill the four traditional Hindu goals: duty *(dharma)*, wealth *(artha)*, love *(kāma)* and liberation *(moksha)*. Aum.

SŪTRA 3: SEEING ŚIVA'S ENERGY IN ALL

Śiva's devotees bask contentedly in Śiva consciousness, seeing the pure life energy in every person, animal, bird, reptile, fish, insect, plant, tree and even microscopic intelligence as Supreme God Śiva Himself. Aum.

SŪTRA 4: ONENESS WITH THE SATGURU

Śiva's devotees strive to be inwardly one with their *satguru,* acknowledging the paramount need for a spiritual preceptor to guide them on the upward climb, the straight path that leads to Lord Śiva's holy feet. Aum.

SŪTRA 5: SEEKING WHILE STRONG

Śiva's devotees heed the ancient wisdom: "The physical body does not last forever. Age prowls like a leopard. Before the limbs lose their vitality, one should take to the auspicious path to the Self." Aum Namaḥ Śivāya.

Facing Life's Challenges

SŪTRA 6: LIVING CONTEMPLATIVELY

Śiva's devotees cultivate a contemplative nature by meditating daily, seeking the light, drawing the lesson from each experience and identifying with infinite intelligence, not with body, emotion or intellect. Aum.

SŪTRA 7: ACCEPTING OUR KARMA

Śiva's devotees accept all experiences, however difficult, as their self-created *karma*, without cringing or complaining. Theirs is the power of surrender, accepting what is as it is and dealing with it courageously. Aum.

SŪTRA 8: FLOWING WITH THE RIVER OF LIFE

Śiva's devotees live vibrantly in the eternity of the moment and flow with the river of life by giving up negative attachments, releasing the pains, injustices, fears and regrets that bind consciousness in the past. Aum.

SŪTRA 9: PURPOSE, PLAN, PERSISTENCE AND PUSH

Śiva's devotees approach each enterprise with deliberate thoughtfulness, and act only after careful consideration. They succeed in every undertaking by having a clear purpose, a wise plan, persistence and push. Aum.

SŪTRA 10: MOVING THE FORCES OF THE WORLD

Śiva's devotees, by remaining steadfast on the path, upholding the *yamas* and *niyamas* and relying on their indomitable will, move the forces of the world, and are not moved or affected by them. Aum Namaḥ Śivāya.

Yoga in Action

SŪTRA 11: THE LION-HEARTED ONES

Those who live with Śiva fulfill life's purposes by placing heavy demands on themselves from within themselves, never shirking their duty to religion, family, community or planet. *Jai,* they are the lion-hearted. Aum.

SŪTRA 12: EXCELLENCE AND NONCOMPETITIVENESS

Those who live with Śiva endeavor to be their best in whatever they do, to excel and make a difference. Even so, they remain apart from the demeaning and contentious "winners and losers" spirit of competition. Aum.

SŪTRA 13: TEACHING THE FIVE PRECEPTS AND PRACTICES

Those who live with Śiva teach children the five precepts: God as All in all, temples, *karma,* reincarnation/liberation, scripture/preceptor; and five practices: virtue, worship, holy days, sacraments and pilgrimage. Aum.

SŪTRA 14: GUIDING AND NURTURING CHILDREN

Those who live with Śiva personally guide their children's spiritual and secular education. They teach and model respect, share what happens each day, have fun together and shower love and hugs upon them. Aum.

SŪTRA 15: ZERO TOLERANCE FOR DISCORD

Those who live with Śiva have zero tolerance for disharmonious conditions. In the home and beyond, they settle differences when others can only disagree. *Jai,* they are all instruments of peace. Aum Namaḥ Śivāya.

The True Values of Life

SŪTRA 16: GIVING AND GRATITUDE

Those who live with Śiva render to those in need help that is loving, selfless and free from all expectation of repayment. They are constantly grateful for all they have, never complaining about what they don't possess. Aum.

SŪTRA 17: BEINGS OF JOY AND COMPASSION

Those who live with Śiva are honorable, cheerful, modest and full of courtesy. Having removed the darkness of anger, fear, jealousy and contempt for others, their faces radiate the kindly compassion of their soul. Aum.

SŪTRA 18: SEEKING INNER LIGHT AND STILLNESS

Those who live with Śiva attend close to His mystery. While others seek "name and fame, sex and money," they seek the clear white light within, find refuge in the stillness and hold Truth in the palm of their hand. Aum.

SŪTRA 19: GUARDING AGAINST INSTINCTS AND INTELLECT

Those who live with Śiva keep the mountaintop perspective that life on Earth is an opportunity for spiritual progress. They never lose sight of this truth by becoming infatuated with instinctive-intellectual pursuits. Aum.

SŪTRA 20: DIRECTING THE POWER OF DESIRE

Those who live with Śiva know the great power of desire and thought, and choose theirs wisely. They also know the infinitely greater power of those who conquer desire by desiring only to know God. Aum Namaḥ Śivāya.

Spiritual Disciplines

SŪTRA 21: HOLDING A DAILY VIGIL

Worshipers of Śiva perform a one-hour daily vigil, ideally before sunrise, in a clean, quiet place, after bathing and donning fresh clothing and holy ash. This vigil is optional on weekends and when traveling or ill. Aum.

SŪTRA 22: MORNING SĀDHANAS

Worshipers of Śiva, during their daily *sādhana* vigil, conduct or attend *pūjā*, chant the Guru Mantra and 108 repetitions of their *mantra,* study scripture and perform *haṭha yoga,* concentration and meditation. Aum.

SŪTRA 23: YOGA AS A LIFELONG EFFORT

Worshipers of Śiva practice basic *yogas (bhakti, karma, haṭha* and *japa)* as their *guru* instructs, throughout life and more as life goes on. They know self-mastery yokes the fire within with That which quells the fire. Aum.

SŪTRA 24: CAUTION WITH ADVANCED YOGAS

Worshipers of Śiva who qualify may perform advanced *yogas (kriyā, rāja* and *kuṇḍalinī),* but only with their *guru's* guidance, for unless harnessed, *kuṇḍalinī* can manifest base desires, disease, egotism and joylessness. Aum.

SŪTRA 25: WARNINGS AGAINST ANGER

Worshipers of Śiva who are victim to anger or hatred refrain from meditation, *japa* and *kuṇḍalinī yoga.* They confess sins, do penance and engage in *bhakti* and *karma* yoga to raise consciousness. Aum Namaḥ Śivāya.

Personal Disciplines

SŪTRA 26: SHARING RICE WITH OTHERS

Lovers of Śiva, before preparing any meal, place in a vessel one handful of uncooked rice. This modest sharing is offered at their *satguru's tiruvadi* each full-moon day to be shared by him with the less fortunate. Aum.

SŪTRA 27: DAILY OFFERINGS FOR THE TEMPLE

Lovers of Śiva keep a box in their shrine into which they place a few coins each day for their favorite temple. They bring or send this love offering to their Śaiva temple each year during its Mahāśivarātri festival. Aum.

SŪTRA 28: KAVADI AND OTHER PENANCE

Lovers of Śiva so inclined may perform *kavadi* during Murugan festivals where custom allows. They may also lie on beds of nails, walk on fire and undertake other penances to build character and atone for sins. Aum.

SŪTRA 29: KEEPING CLEAN SURROUNDINGS

Lovers of Śiva keep their home and work environment clean and uncluttered to maintain a spiritual vibration and not attract negative forces. They seek fresh air and sunshine and surround themselves with beauty. Aum.

SŪTRA 30: INSTRUCTIONS FOR SLEEP

Lovers of Śiva sleep with the head placed south or east after chanting and meditating to prepare for a great journey to the inner worlds. If awakened, they sit up and meditate before returning to sleep. Aum Namaḥ Śivāya.

The Nature of God

SŪTRA 31: A PHILOSOPHY WORTHY OF PRIDE

Śiva's followers take pride in the fact that the philosophical basis of their peerless lineage lies in the unity of Siddhānta and Vedānta. This mysterious dance of dualism and nondualism is called monistic theism. Aum.

SŪTRA 32: LIVING AND PREACHING ŚIVA'S PATH

Śiva's followers of my lineage study, live and preach to the world our peerless theological doctrine, called by various names: monistic theism, Advaita Īśvaravāda, Advaita Siddhānta and Śuddha Śaiva Siddhānta. Aum.

SŪTRA 33: GOD'S UNMANIFEST REALITY

Śiva's followers all believe that Lord Śiva is God, whose Absolute Being, Paraśiva, transcends time, form and space. The *yogī* silently exclaims, "It is not this. It is not that." Yea, such an inscrutable God is God Śiva. Aum.

SŪTRA 34: GOD'S MANIFEST NATURE OF LOVE

Śiva's followers all believe that Lord Śiva is God, whose immanent nature of love, Parāśakti, is the substratum, primal substance or pure consciousness flowing through all form as energy, existence, knowledge and bliss. Aum.

SŪTRA 35: GOD'S IMMANENT NATURE AS PERSONAL LORD

Śiva's followers all believe that Lord Śiva is God, whose immanent nature is the Primal Soul, Supreme Mahādeva, Parameśvara, author of *Vedas* and *Āgamas,* creator, preserver and destroyer of all that exists. Aum Namaḥ Śivāya.

The Nature of Souls and World

SŪTRA 36: GAṆAPATI, FIRST AMONG THE GODS

Śiva's followers all believe in the Mahādeva Lord Gaṇeśa, son of Śiva-Śakti, to whom they must first supplicate before beginning any worship or task. His rule is compassionate. His law is just. Justice is His mind. Aum.

SŪTRA 37: MURUGAN, LORD OF YOGA AND HARMONY

Śiva's followers all believe in the Mahādeva Kārttikeya, Son of Śiva-Śakti, whose *vel* of grace dissolves the bondages of ignorance. The *yogī,* locked in lotus, venerates Murugan. Thus restrained, his mind becomes calm. Aum.

SŪTRA 38: GOD CREATES SOULS WHO ARE ONE WITH HIM

Śiva's followers all believe that each soul is created by Lord Śiva and is identical to Him, and that this identity will be fully realized by all souls when the bondage of *āṇava, karma* and *māyā* is removed by His grace. Aum.

SŪTRA 39: THE GROSS, SUBTLE AND CAUSAL PLANES

Śiva's followers all believe in three worlds: the gross plane, where souls take on physical bodies; the subtle plane, where souls take on astral bodies; and the causal plane, where souls exist in their self-effulgent form. Aum.

SŪTRA 40: KARMA, REINCARNATION AND LIBERATION

Śiva's followers all believe in the law of *karma*—that one must reap the effects of all actions he has caused—and that each soul reincarnates until all *karmas* are resolved and *moksha,* liberation, is attained. Aum Namaḥ Śivāya.

Evil and Expressions of Faith

SŪTRA 41: THE FOUR PROGRESSIVE STAGES OF THE PATH

Śiva's followers all believe that the performance of *charyā*, virtuous living; *kriyā*, temple worship; and *yoga*, leading to Paraśiva through the grace of the living *satguru*, is absolutely necessary to bring forth *jñāna*, wisdom. Aum.

SŪTRA 42: THE ILLUSION OF EVIL

Śiva's followers all believe there is no intrinsic evil. Evil has no source, unless the source of evil's seeming be ignorance itself. They are truly compassionate, knowing that ultimately there is no good or bad. All is Śiva's will. Aum.

SŪTRA 43: TEMPLE WORSHIP CONNECTS THREE WORLDS

Śiva's followers all believe that religion is the harmonious working together of the three worlds and that this harmony can be created through temple worship, wherein the beings of all three worlds can communicate. Aum.

SŪTRA 44: ŚAIVISM'S MOST POWERFUL VEDIC MANTRA

Śiva's followers all believe in the Pañchākshara Mantra, the five sacred syllables Namaḥ Śivāya, as Śaivism's foremost and essential *mantra*. The secret of Namaḥ Śivāya is to hear it from the right lips at the right time. Aum.

SŪTRA 45: ŚIVA IS IN ALL AND BEYOND ALL

Śiva's followers hold as their affirmation of faith *Anbe Sivamayam Satyame Parasivam*, "God Śiva is immanent love and transcendent reality," a perfect summary of Śaiva Siddhānta's exquisite truth. Aum Namaḥ Śivāya.

Nītividyā

नीतिविद्या

Section Two

Ethics

Only by a tranquil mind does one destroy all action, good or bad. Once the self is pacified, one abides in the Self and attains everlasting bliss. If the mind becomes as firmly established in Brahman as it is usually attached to the sense objects, who, then, will not be released from bondage?

Kṛishṇa Yajur Veda, Maitrī Upanishad 6.34. VE, P. 422

The ethical path defined by the yamas *and* niyamas *takes this seeker step by step toward his goal. At first he is agitated and distracted, then learns of discipline, advancing into his internal* yogas *and worship of the Gods. All the while, he inwardly stands apart as a witness to his own life.*

Yamas: Ten Classical Restraints

SŪTRA 46: NONINJURY AND TRUTHFULNESS

All devotees of Śiva practice *ahiṁsā,* not harming others by thought, word or deed, even in their dreams. Adhering to *satya,* truthfulness, they do not lie, deceive, betray promises or keep secrets from loved ones. Aum.

SŪTRA 47: NONSTEALING AND SEXUAL PURITY

All devotees of Śiva uphold *asteya,* never stealing, coveting, cheating or entering into debt. They practice sexual purity, *brahmacharya,* controlling lust by remaining celibate when single and faithful in marriage. Aum.

SŪTRA 48: PATIENCE AND STEADFASTNESS

All devotees of Śiva exercise *kshamā,* restraining intolerance with people and impatience with circumstances. They foster *dhṛiti,* steadfastness, overcoming nonperseverance, fear, indecision and changeableness. Aum.

SŪTRA 49: COMPASSION AND STRAIGHTFORWARDNESS

All devotees of Śiva practice *dayā,* compassion, conquering callous, cruel, insensitive feelings toward all beings. Maintaining *ārjava,* they are straightforward and honest, renouncing deception and wrongdoing. Aum.

SŪTRA 50: MODERATE APPETITE AND PURITY

All devotees of Śiva observe *mitahāra,* moderation in appetite, not eating too much or consuming meat, fish, shellfish, fowl or eggs. They uphold *śaucha,* avoiding impurity in body, mind and speech. Aum Namaḥ Śivāya.

Niyamas: Ten Classical Observances

SŪTRA 51: REMORSE AND CONTENTMENT

All Śiva's devotees, upholding the expression of *hrī,* remorse, are modest and show shame for misdeeds. They nurture *santosha,* seeking joy and serenity in life. Thus, theirs is a happy, sweet-tempered, fulfilling path. Aum.

SŪTRA 52: CHARITY AND FAITH

All Śiva's devotees practice *dāna,* tithing and giving generously, creatively, without thought of reward. They sustain an unshakable faith, *āstikya,* believing in God, Gods, *guru* and the Vedic path to enlightenment. Aum.

SŪTRA 53: WORSHIP AND SCRIPTURAL STUDY

All Śiva's devotees cultivate *bhakti* and family harmony in daily ritual and reflection, Iśvarapūjana. Upholding *siddhānta śravaṇa,* they hear the scriptures, study the teachings and listen to the wise of their lineage. Aum.

SŪTRA 54: COGNITION AND VOWS

All Śiva's devotees acquire *mati,* divine cognition and an indomitable will and intellect, under their *satguru's* guidance. They observe *vratas,* religious vows, rules and observances, and never waver in fulfilling them. Aum.

SŪTRA 55: INCANTATION AND SACRIFICE

All Śiva's devotees do *japa* daily, counting recitations on *rudrāksha* beads. Embracing *tapas* through simple austerities, they sacrifice often, carry out penances as needed and perform *sādhana* regularly. Aum Namaḥ Śivāya.

Ahiṁsā, the Foremost Discipline

SŪTRA 56: NONINJURY

Śiva's devotees do not intentionally kill or harm any person or creature. Nonviolence, physically, mentally and emotionally, is their highest code. Full of compassion, they are never a source of fear or hurtfulness. Aum.

SŪTRA 57: SUICIDE

Śiva's devotees are forbidden to escape life's experience through suicide. However, in cases of terminal illness, under strict community regulation, tradition does allow fasting as a means of *mors voluntaria religiosa.* Aum.

SŪTRA 58: ABORTION

Devout Hindus all know abortion is, by Vedic edict, a sin against *dharma* fraught with *karmic* repercussions. Scripture allows it only to prevent the mother's death, for it is a greater sin for a child to kill the mother. Aum.

SŪTRA 59: PORNOGRAPHY

Śiva's devotees are forbidden to speak of, listen to or look at exhibitions of pornography. This *adharma* is addictive, erodes self-esteem and teaches that degrading women, men and children is acceptable behavior. Aum.

SŪTRA 60: PURITY OF SPEECH

Śiva's devotees speak only what is true, kind, helpful and necessary. They never use profane language, bear false witness, engage in slander, gossip or backbiting, or even listen to such debasing talk. Aum Namaḥ Śivāya.

Regrettable Exceptions to Ahiṁsā

SŪTRA 61: EXCEPTIONS TO AHIṀSĀ

Śiva's devotees, when unable to observe *ahiṁsā* perfectly, may claim three exceptions to preserve one life over another. But these must be used sparingly, reluctantly, after the noninjurious options have been tried. Aum.

SŪTRA 62: SELF-DEFENSE AND LAW ENFORCEMENT

Śiva's devotees faced with imminent danger may elect to injure or kill to protect their life or that of another, or to defend the community as a soldier or a law officer in the line of duty. This is *ahiṁsā's* first exception. Aum.

SŪTRA 63: PRESERVING LIFE AND HEALTH

Śiva's devotees may elect to preserve the life and health of a person or animal under their care by forfeiting the life of organisms, such as worms or microbes, that pose a threat. This is the second exception to *ahiṁsā*. Aum.

SŪTRA 64: PREDATORS AND PESTS

Śiva's devotees may elect to protect the home, the village and the nation by eradicating predators, pests, bacteria and disease-carrying creatures that threaten health or safety. This is *ahiṁsā's* third and last exception. Aum.

SŪTRA 65: NONINJURIOUS SOLUTIONS

Śiva's devotees uphold the principle not to kill even household pests, but to stop their entry, not to kill garden insects or predators, but keep them away by natural means. This is the highest ideal. Aum Namaḥ Śivāya.

Reverence for the Environment

SŪTRA 66: PROTECTING CREATURES, DEFENDING RIGHTS

All Śiva's devotees are stewards of trees and plants, fish and birds, bees and reptiles, animals and creatures of every shape and kind. They respect and defend the rights of humans of every caste, creed, color and sex. Aum.

SŪTRA 67: HONORING THE VALUES OF OTHERS

All Śiva's devotees think globally and act locally as interracial, international citizens of the Earth. They honor and value all human cultures, faiths, languages and peoples, never offending one to promote another. Aum.

SŪTRA 68: PRESERVING THIS DIVINE ABODE

All Śiva's devotees honor and revere the world around them as God's creation and work for the protection of the Earth's diversity and resources to achieve the goal of a secure, sustainable and lasting environment. Aum.

SŪTRA 69: RESPECTING EARTH'S PLANTS AND ANIMALS

All Śiva's devotees refuse to acquire or condone the use of endangered plants, animals or products from exploited species, such as furs, ivory, reptile skin, tortoise shell, or items produced using cruel animal testing. Aum.

SŪTRA 70: CONSERVING THE GIFTS OF NATURE

All Śiva's devotees are frugal and resourceful, avoiding waste and conserving nature's precious resources. They wisely store a three-to-twelve-month supply of food according to the family's means. Aum Namaḥ Śivāya.

Self-Control

SŪTRA 71: SEXUAL FAITHFULNESS

Devout Hindus observe the eightfold celibacy toward everyone but their spouse, renouncing sexual fantasy, glorification, flirtation, lustful glances, secret love talk, amorous longing, rendezvous and intercourse. Aum.

SŪTRA 72: ACCEPTING PRAISE AND BLAME

It is well known that all Śiva's devotees can absorb any amount of praise. But those who can withstand mental, emotional persecution, even physical torment, with the same infinite capacity are Śiva's truest devotees. Aum.

SŪTRA 73: LIVING IN TRADITIONAL SURROUNDINGS

Śiva's devotees, in their homes, endeavor to surround themselves with Śaiva images, music and song. In the world they may enjoy the arts of other cultures but strictly avoid lower-world artistic expressions. Aum.

SŪTRA 74: WISE USE OF TELEVISION

Śiva's devotees may watch television and other media for recreation and to keep informed about the world, limiting viewing to about two hours a day. They avoid nudity, foul language, crudeness and excessive violence. Aum.

SŪTRA 75: COMPUTERS

Śiva's devotees know computers and the Internet are boons from the Gods and approach them as tools, not toys. They moderate leisure use, minimize Web browsing and never play violent games. Aum Namaḥ Śivāya.

Worldly Activities

SŪTRA 76: GAMBLING IS FORBIDDEN

Śiva's devotees are forbidden to indulge in gambling or games of chance with payment or risk, even through others or for employment. Gambling erodes society, assuring the loss of many for the gain of a few. Aum.

SŪTRA 77: THE CURSE OF BAD MONEY

Śiva's devotees, knowing that bad money is cursed and can never do good deeds, refuse funds gained by fraud, bribery, theft, dealing arms or drugs, profiting from abortion or divorce, and all dark, devious means. Aum.

SŪTRA 78: BRIBERY IS FORBIDDEN

Śiva's devotees are forbidden to accept bribes; nor do they offer bribes to others, no matter how seemingly necessary, expedient or culturally accepted this practice may be. *Jai,* they fight for the mercy of honesty! Aum.

SŪTRA 79: GUARDING AGAINST PRIDE

Śiva's devotees treasure humility. They never boast, point with their index finger or assume prideful postures, such as with arms folded and chin held high, or with one foot resting on the knee when sitting. Aum.

SŪTRA 80: AVOIDING LOW-MINDED COMPANY

Śiva's devotees avoid thieves and addicts, those who are promiscuous, who feign devotion, who are ungrateful, against religion, selfish, abusive, ill-tempered, vicious or who possess many impurities. Aum Namaḥ Śivāya.

Gṛihastha Dharmaḥ

गृहस्थधर्मः

Section Three
The Family Path

Earth, ether, sky! May we be proud possessors of fine children, proud possessors of fine heroes, and be well nourished by fine food.

Yajur Veda, 8.53. HV, P. 91

A husband and wife are seen through the wooden doorway of their home, which they have decorated traditionally with auspicious symbols: tripuṇḍra, kolams *and fresh mango leaves on a string. Their infant plays near the family's shrine where Lord Gaṇeśa rules and resides.*

Instructions for Men

SŪTRA 81: MODESTY WITH WOMEN

Devout Hindu men speak to and associate mostly with men. Conversation with women, especially the wives of other men, is not prolonged. To avoid intimacy, one's gaze is directed at the hairline, not into the eyes. Aum.

SŪTRA 82: RESPECT FOR WOMEN

All Śiva's men devotees go out of their way to express respect, bordering on reverence, for women. They never demean them in speech, watch vulgar or erotic shows, or associate with lustful or promiscuous women. Aum.

SŪTRA 83: KINDLINESS TOWARD WOMEN

Śiva's men devotees never argue with women, antagonize, disrespect, tease or abuse them in any way. They are always kindly, protective, helpful and understanding, honoring the mother spirit within women. Aum.

SŪTRA 84: WEARING TRADITIONAL CLOTHING

Śiva's men devotees dress, whenever appropriate, in impeccable traditional Hindu attire, always at home, in the temple and at religious/cultural events. Their outer elegance is equaled only by their inner dignity. Aum.

SŪTRA 85: THE HOME AS REFUGE

Śiva's men devotees, on arriving home from work, immediately bathe and enter their shrine for the blessings of Gods and *guru* to dispel worldly forces and regain the state of Śiva consciousness. Aum Namaḥ Śivāya.

Instructions for Husbands

SŪTRA 86: CARING FOR ONE'S WIFE

Each of Śiva's married men devotees loves and cares for his wife, despite any shortcomings. He is forbidden to strike or speak harshly to her or ignore her needs. If he does, he must seek family and professional help. Aum.

SŪTRA 87: RESTRAINT WITH OTHER WOMEN

Śiva's married men, in the workplace and in the world, hold a courteous aloofness toward all women, whether young, older, single, married, divorced or widowed. They reserve their affections for wife and family. Aum.

SŪTRA 88: COMMUNICATING DAILY

When away from home, each of Śiva's married men devotees contacts his wife every day to express his love and inquire about her day. He avoids rowdy company and never visits another woman's home alone. Aum.

SŪTRA 89: FULFILLING ALL HER NEEDS AND WANTS

Śiva's devotees who are husbands practice the mystical law of caring for and giving the wife all she needs and all she wants, thus releasing her *śakti* energy from within, making him contented, successful and magnetic. Aum.

SŪTRA 90: FAMILY TOGETHERNESS

Each of Śiva's devotees who is a husband spends time with his wife and children daily. Monday is a family evening at home. One night monthly is devoted to the wife alone in an activity of her choice. Aum Namaḥ Śivāya.

Instructions for Women

SŪTRA 91: WOMEN'S ATTIRE

Śiva's women devotees wear, whenever appropriate, traditional Hindu attire, always at home and in the temple, adding rich jewelry for cultural events. Ever modest and elegant, they never expose breasts or thighs. Aum.

SŪTRA 92: MODESTY WITH MEN

Devout Hindu women associate mostly with women. Conversation with males, especially married men, is by custom limited. Intimate exchange of energies is avoided by looking at the hairline, not into the eyes. Aum.

SŪTRA 93: HER MONTHLY RETREAT

Śiva's women devotees, by custom, rest and regenerate physical forces during menses, refraining from heavy or demanding work. On these days they do not enter temples or home shrines, or approach holy men. Aum.

SŪTRA 94: UPHOLDING FEMININE DHARMA

Devout Hindu women are fulfilled in living and passing on the *dharma* to the youth as their special duty, unlike those who, swayed by feminist thinking, feel unfulfilled and criticize Hinduism as being male dominated. Aum.

SŪTRA 95: NOT CONTROLLING MEN EMOTIONALLY

Śiva's women devotees never become angry with a man, maliciously belittle or verbally abuse him, or use other emotional controls, such as disdain, accusation, crying, or prolonged pouting or silence. Aum Namaḥ Śivāya.

Instructions for Wives

SŪTRA 96: SHE WORSHIPS HER WEDDING PENDANT

Each of Śiva's married women devotees each morning worships her wedding pendant, for it betokens her dear husband, whom she reveres as Śiva Himself, and the spiritual bond and goals she shares with him. Aum.

SŪTRA 97: BEING MODEST WITH OTHER MEN

Śiva's married women maintain a kindly and modest reserve toward all men, be they young, older, single, married, divorced or widowed. They shower all their love and attention on their husband and family. Aum.

SŪTRA 98: FULFILLING MORNING DUTIES

Each of Śiva's married women devotees observes the custom of arising before her husband, to bathe, ready the shrine and prepare his morning beverage. First up and last to retire, she is in charge of her home. Aum.

SŪTRA 99: MEALTIME CUSTOMS

Each of Śiva's married women devotees joyously observes at mealtimes the ancient custom of serving her husband and family first. When they are satisfied, she is fulfilled and only then sits down for her own meal. Aum.

SŪTRA 100: TAKING ACTION IF ABUSED

Each of Śiva's married women loves and serves her husband, despite any shortcomings. But if he ever strikes her or the children, she is duty-bound to seek help from family, friends and community. Aum Namaḥ Śivāya.

Instructions for the Widowed

SŪTRA 101: REMARRYING AFTER WIDOWHOOD

Śiva's widowed followers may remarry, provided it is a spiritual union, astrologically compatible, blessed by their preceptor and their religious community. If they remarry, they are no longer considered widowed. Aum.

SŪTRA 102: PURSUING THE PATH OF SĀDHANA

Śiva's widowed devotees who choose not to remarry practice strict continence. They dedicate their lives to God and transmute sexual forces into the higher *chakras* through *sādhana,* worship and *brahmacharya.* Aum.

SŪTRA 103: WIDOWS' SIMPLE DRESS

Śiva's widowed devotees choosing not to remarry traditionally wear unprovocative white clothing, not yellow or orange. They wear no cosmetics, marriage pendant or elaborate jewelry. Their deportment is demure. Aum.

SŪTRA 104: WIDOWHOOD'S INNER OPPORTUNITY

Śiva's devotees who are widows or widowers happily throw themselves into *yoga* practices. Though their loss is great, so too is their opportunity for religious service and the attainment of the highest spiritual goals. Aum.

SŪTRA 105: SIGNS OF THE WIDOWED'S INTENT

Śiva's widowed devotees not intending to remarry wear holy ash and the forehead mark of sandalpaste, but not red powder. Those wishing to remarry may wear jewelry, cosmetics and colorful clothing. Aum Namaḥ Śivāya.

Instructions for the Unmarried

SŪTRA 106: CHASTITY AND MARRIAGE TO A ŚAIVITE

Śiva's young devotees take the celibacy vow and remain virgin until marriage. For lasting happiness and mutual spiritual purpose, they seek to marry a Śaivite wisely chosen by their parents, *satguru* and themselves. Aum.

SŪTRA 107: LIVING VIRTUOUSLY WHEN SINGLE

Śiva's unmarried adolescent and adult devotees are all considered *brahmachārīs* or *brahmachāriṇīs,* bound to the wise restraints of chastity that tradition prescribes, whether they have taken a celibacy vow or not. Aum.

SŪTRA 108: THE BRAHMACHĀRIṆĪ PATH

Śiva's women devotees electing not to marry may live the *brahmachāriṇī's* celibate life, keeping simple vows and always wearing white. By this the world knows they are unavailable, having chosen the path of devotion. Aum.

SŪTRA 109: THE BRAHMACHĀRĪ PATH

Śiva's men devotees choosing not to marry may take up celibate life, keeping simple vows and wearing white. To be a *swāmī* candidate, they must begin an 8-to-12-year period of monastic training before the age of 25. Aum.

SŪTRA 110: THE FIRST STEP OF RENUNCIATION

Śiva's young men devotees inclined to throw down the world and enter the monastery should read and accept the *Holy Orders of Sannyāsa* and adjust themselves to its ideals before requesting training. Aum Namaḥ Śivāya.

Arranging Marriages

SŪTRA 111: CONSIDERATIONS FOR MATCHMAKING

Śiva's followers arrange the marriages of their children, seeking sameness of lineage, astrological compatibility, harmony of the two families, total consent of both boy and girl and, foremost, their *satguru's* blessings. Aum.

SŪTRA 112: FORCED MARRIAGE IS PROHIBITED

Śiva's followers are forbidden to force any marriage arrangement that overrides astrological incompatibility, the couple's feelings or the *guru's* advice. To do so would bind them to a life of unsolvable problems. Aum.

SŪTRA 113: KEEPING WEDDING COSTS REASONABLE

Weddings are spiritual events among Śiva's followers. Ceremonies must never burden the families financially and, while the bride may bring wealth to the marriage, families are forbidden to demand or pay dowries. Aum.

SŪTRA 114: THE WRITTEN MARRIAGE COVENANT

Śiva's followers compose a written promise to one another before marriage, defining the duties, responsibilities and expectations of their life together. At key junctures in life, they rewrite this vital agreement. Aum.

SŪTRA 115: THE ALL-IMPORTANT SUPPORT GROUP

Each marriage within a Śaivite community enjoys support, strength and encouragement from the *satguru* and all of Śiva's followers, and counsel from elders when needed, especially in times of trial. Aum Namaḥ Śivāya.

Sustaining Marriages

SŪTRA 116: THE PURPOSE OF MARRIAGE

Śiva's followers look upon their marriage as a spiritual partnership for the purpose of uplifting each other and bringing through higher souls. It is a union not only of a man and woman, but of two entire families. Aum.

SŪTRA 117: SUPPORTING RELIGIOUS OBSERVANCES

Śiva's married followers all encourage their spouses to ardently fulfill *sādhana,* religious service, meditation, *yoga,* ritual worship, festivals and pilgrimage. They never discourage such noble expressions of *dharma.* Aum.

SŪTRA 118: TRADITIONS OF CONJUGAL LIFE

Śiva's followers who are married regulate their sex life according to traditionally accepted standards. They confine their affectionate looks to one another and do not hold hands, embrace, caress or kiss in public. Aum.

SŪTRA 119: ADULTERY AND FIDELITY

Śiva's followers are forbidden by Sanātana Dharma to commit adultery or even steal the affections of another's spouse. They treasure fidelity and know that transgressions are rewarded with pain, guilt and remorse. Aum.

SŪTRA 120: CELIBACY IN MARRIED LIFE

Śiva's followers who have raised their family may, by mutual consent and with *satguru's* blessings, choose to live in celibacy, as brother and sister, and thus transmute their vital energies into the Divine. Aum Namaḥ Śivāya.

About Divorce

SŪTRA 121: VALID CAUSES FOR SEPARATION

In marriages of Śiva's followers, adultery, severe neglect, verbal abuse and abandonment may be valid causes for separation but not divorce. Spiritual law recognizes no divorce, and separation is hoped to be temporary. Aum.

SŪTRA 122: THE ONLY REASON TO DIVORCE

In marriages of Śiva's followers, divorce by man's law may be resorted to in cases of persistent physical abuse to protect the abused spouse. This is the singular regrettable exception to the permanence of marriage. Aum.

SŪTRA 123: REMARRIAGE IS DISCOURAGED

Any of Śiva's followers who is divorced is by tradition encouraged to not remarry but rather adopt the path of celibacy. They know that marriage is a Godly covenant ideally made with only one spouse in a lifetime. Aum.

SŪTRA 124: NOT ATTENDING RITES OF PASSAGE

Śiva's traditional priests require that divorced and widowed followers protect auspiciousness by not attending rites of passage, except funerals. However, they may help with preparations and participate in receptions. Aum.

SŪTRA 125: DIVORCE AND ŚAIVA CHURCH MEMBERSHIP

In divorce cases in my Church, except when caused by chronic abuse, the spouse initiating the divorce process is no longer a member. He or she is kept apart and urged to seek out a more lenient lineage. Aum Namaḥ Śivāya.

Hospitality

SŪTRA 126: THE GUEST IS GOD IN ŚAIVA HOMES

Hospitality flows from Śiva's followers like sweet music from a *vīṇā*. Guests are treated as Gods. Friends, relatives, acquaintances, even strangers, are humbled by the overwhelming, ever-willing attention received. Aum.

SŪTRA 127: SERVING THE HOLY ONES

Śiva's followers serve holy men and women of all lineages, providing food, money and clothes according to their means. They lovingly care for these living archives of Sanātana Dharma and treat them amicably. Aum.

SŪTRA 128: CLOSENESS WITH OTHER FAMILIES

Śiva's followers who are householders joyously visit one another's homes and grow together in Godliness. Some religious ceremony or *karma yoga* is a part of their every gathering. They live as one spiritual family. Aum.

SŪTRA 129: RESPECTING ELDERS, NURTURING THE YOUNG

Śiva's followers honor elders for their wisdom, guidance and compassion. Those who are younger, whatever their age, never disrespect those older than they. Those older nurture and encourage all who are younger. Aum.

SŪTRA 130: HELPING ONE ANOTHER

Śiva's followers see that the spirit of helping and taking care of one another prevails between family and family, monastery and family. The group helps the individual, and the individual helps the group. Aum Namaḥ Śivāya.

Household Ethics

SŪTRA 131: THE HUSBAND'S DHARMA

Each of Śiva's married men followers strives to fulfill male *dharma,* safeguarding the integrity of society and the family through protecting and providing abundantly for his beloved wife, children and parents. Aum.

SŪTRA 132: THE WIFE'S DHARMA

Each of Śiva's married women followers strives to fulfill female *dharma,* perpetuating the race, family and the faith through remaining in the home to nurture, guide and strengthen her dear husband and children. Aum.

SŪTRA 133: THE STRENGTH OF THE EXTENDED FAMILY

Śiva's followers know the most stable societies are based on the extended family. They often merge individuals with families and families with families in one home or complex, for economy, sharing and religiousness. Aum.

SŪTRA 134: CARING FOR ELDERS

Śiva's followers who are householders care for their parents and close relatives all through life. The elderly especially must be comforted, honored at auspicious times and never left alone for extended periods. Aum.

SŪTRA 135: LIMITING THE STAY OF GUESTS

Śiva's householder followers, to protect family sanctity and avoid magnetic entanglements, do not allow adult guests in their home for more than three nights who are not part of their extended family. Aum Namaḥ Śivāya.

Raising Worthy Children

SŪTRA 136: NURTURING CHILDREN, MEETING DAILY

Śiva's followers use astrology, tradition and wise counsel to cultivate each child's inherent talents and higher nature. They hold family meetings daily to share, plan, express love and discuss issues with mutual respect. Aum.

SŪTRA 137: TAKING TIME TO TRAIN THE YOUTH

Śiva's followers who are parents take time to train boys in technical skills, girls in homemaking, and both in music, health, cooking and home management. They celebrate improvements instead of focusing on mistakes. Aum.

SŪTRA 138: NOT GOVERNING THROUGH FEAR

Śiva's followers never govern youth through fear. They are forbidden to spank or hit them, use harsh or angry words, neglect or abuse them. They know you can't make children do better by making them feel worse. Aum.

SŪTRA 139: TEACHING AND MODELING GOOD CONDUCT

Śiva's followers love their children, govern them in a kind but firm way and model the five family practices: proper conduct, home worship, religious discussion, continuous self-study and following a preceptor. Aum.

SŪTRA 140: TIMELY OBSERVANCE OF SACRAMENTS

Śiva's followers provide their children the essential sacraments at the proper times, especially name-giving, first feeding, head-shaving, ear-piercing, first learning, rites of puberty and marriage. Aum Namaḥ Śivāya.

Preserving Family Unity

SŪTRA 141: LOGICAL, POSITIVE DISCIPLINE

Śiva's followers direct children through affirmations, meaningful chores and rules that are clear and understood, teaching that mistakes are opportunities to learn, and focusing on solutions instead of punishment. Aum.

SŪTRA 142: INSPIRING BELONGING AND DIGNITY

Śiva's followers encourage and inspire children so they always feel they belong and are significant. If upsets occur, parents use loving, positive strategies such as time-out, logical consequences and denial of privileges. Aum.

SŪTRA 143: TRAINING YOUTH IN MONEY MANAGEMENT

Śiva's followers who are parents preserve family unity and teach responsibility by not granting youth financial independence. Money is given only for approved expenses, and change is returned with accounting. Aum.

SŪTRA 144: POOLING INCOMES FOR FAMILY UNITY

Śiva's followers require unmarried progeny living with them who have finished school and are employed to submit, after tithing, all earnings to the family fund. Once betrothed, they manage their own earnings. Aum.

SŪTRA 145: DISCIPLINING WITH LOVE

Śiva's followers, knowing that misbehaving children are discouraged, take time for play and encouragement, and ensure that discipline is respectful, reasonable and not based on blame, shame or pain. Aum Namaḥ Śivāya.

Preparing Youth for Adult Life

SŪTRA 146: GROWING UP IN THE FAMILY OCCUPATION

Śiva's followers abide by the tradition of bringing sons and daughters into the family skills, profession or business by involving them from a young age. This is family *dharma*, family bonding, family perpetuation. Aum.

SŪTRA 147: PROVIDING EARLY SEX EDUCATION

Śiva's followers teach their sons and daughters, between ages four and ten, about the cycles of life and the principles of virtue, and when puberty arrives, require them to take the sacred vow of celibacy until marriage. Aum.

SŪTRA 148: CHERISHING CHASTITY

Śiva's young followers are taught to protect their chastity as a treasure and to save sexual intimacy for their future spouse. If a premarital affair does occur, a marriage of the young couple is seriously considered. Aum.

SŪTRA 149: RESPONSIBLE CHAPERONING

Śiva's followers accept the serious responsibility of guiding the private and social life of their children. They chaperone and monitor friendships to help ensure that young ones grow up safe and celibate. Aum.

SŪTRA 150: YOUTH ENTERING MY ŚAIVA CHURCH

My devotees require children to decide before age twenty whether to enter Saiva Siddhanta Church of their own volition or to choose another path. If they go away, they are always welcome back. Aum Namaḥ Śivāya.

Duties of Young Adults

SŪTRA 151: BRINGING OTHERS TO THE ŚAIVA PATH

Śiva's followers who are adolescents use their youthful aggressiveness to teach the Śaiva Dharma, inspire and uplift others, bring seekers into their lineage and welcome strayed members back into the Hindu fold. Aum.

SŪTRA 152: BRINGING JOY TO THEIR PARENTS

Śiva's young adult followers realize they have a debt to their parents for their birth, early raising and education, which they repay with obedience and affection, giving joy, practical assistance and satisfaction. Aum.

SŪTRA 153: THE IDEAL YOUTH-PARENT RELATIONSHIP

Śiva's young adult followers esteem their mother and father. In respecting their parents, they respect themselves and keep the doors open to parental aid and advice on the churning sea of adolescent experience. Aum.

SŪTRA 154: NEVER BENDING TO PEER PRESSURE

Śiva's adolescent followers hold their own among their peers and are leaders. To bend to peer pressure and offend the *dharma* shows weakness of character and parental neglect. Nothing but shame can follow. Aum.

SŪTRA 155: PATH CHOOSING FOR YOUNG MEN

Śiva's young men followers are free to pursue their born destiny of either renunciation or family life. This choice of two traditional paths is their birthright. Following either, they follow *dharma*. Aum Namaḥ Śivāya.

About Wealth

SŪTRA 156: TRUE WEALTH

Devout Hindus remain dignified in deprivation and humble in prosperity. Knowing that one can be spiritually rich in poverty and spiritually impoverished in affluence, they live bountifully in either world. Aum.

SŪTRA 157: BUILDING ECONOMIC SECURITY

Śiva's householder devotees strive to own their home and save for retirement. They live within their means in dwellings suitable to their wealth and are regular and completely honest in paying their tithe and taxes. Aum.

SŪTRA 158: RESPONSIBLE MONEY MANAGEMENT

Śiva's devotees keep a monthly budget and regulate expenses according to their revenues. They never abuse credit or indulge in extravagant buying, for they know that spending in excess of income invites misery. Aum.

SŪTRA 159: HANDLING MONEY WISELY

Śiva's devotees keep a regular monthly and yearly accounting of income and expenses, and accurate records of all transactions. In every business deal, they make sure that all parties are benefited and are content. Aum.

SŪTRA 160: ENDOWMENTS AND WILLS

Śiva's devotees dutifully save for their future through Hindu Heritage Endowment and prepare a formal, final will and testament, even when young, that provides funds for their family and temple. Aum Namaḥ Śivāya.

God's Money

SŪTRA 161: ONE-TENTH BELONGS TO ŚIVA

Śiva's close devotees take a vow and joyously tithe ten percent of their gross income to their lineage monthly. This is God's money. Using it otherwise is forbidden—a *karma* reaping loss exceeding all anticipated gain. Aum.

SŪTRA 162: TITHING IS THE FIRST OBLIGATION

My close devotees consider tithing their first expense. They provide a written reconciliation each April, including with it all unremitted tithing. Those behind in tithing are counseled to help them fulfill the vow. Aum.

SŪTRA 163: TITHING'S MANY BLESSINGS

Śiva's close devotees delight in the unfailing law that by tithing freely and wholeheartedly, with a consciousness of plenty, they become receptive to God's blessings and draw to them abundance and happy experiences. Aum.

SŪTRA 164: DHARMIC USES OF MONEY

Śiva's close devotees of means utilize their wealth to strengthen their community and their lineage, to support temples, publish books, establish endowments and scholarships, and to sponsor elaborate rituals. Aum.

SŪTRA 165: ANNUAL MONETARY GIFT TO THE SATGURU

Śiva's close devotees observe the tradition of expressing appreciation to their *satguru* by giving an annual love offering at Guru Pūrṇimā in July-August, thus enabling him to help others on the path. Aum Namaḥ Śivāya.

Guidelines for Business

SŪTRA 166: BUSINESS AMONG MEMBERS

My Church members may employ other members, provided payment is made promptly each Friday. They may receive blessings to go into business with one another if their relationships are harmonious and spiritual. Aum.

SŪTRA 167: CONTRACTS AND ARBITRATION

My worldly-wise devotees never enter into business transactions without a written contract. In cases of dispute, they avoid courts of law and seek judgment from an arbitration board within their community. Aum.

SŪTRA 168: NOT BORROWING OR GIVING CREDIT

My devotees, to safeguard harmony, never borrow or lend money among themselves or give credit to one another, even for interest. They may do business together, but only through immediate cash transactions. Aum.

SŪTRA 169: TREATMENT OF EMPLOYEES AND SERVANTS

My devotees treat servants and employees honorably, as they would members of their own family, never neglecting or taking advantage of them. They provide conditions that are safe, healthful and uplifting. Aum.

SŪTRA 170: BORROWING FROM OTHERS

My wise devotees never borrow from a monastery or temple. They may borrow belongings from other devotees, provided objects are returned within twenty-four hours after the purpose is fulfilled. Aum Namaḥ Śivāya.

Politics and Vocation

SŪTRA 171: SERVING COMMUNITY AND COUNTRY

Śiva's devotees are patriotic to their nation and concerned about ecology. They strive to give to, advance, support and defend their community and country, never living as outsiders or as predators upon them. Aum.

SŪTRA 172: ENTERING POLITICS

Śiva's devotees who qualify may, with vigor and indomitable will, enter into politics, overcome opposition and rise to the top to shower good fortune, peace, justice, interracial harmony and care on all people. Aum.

SŪTRA 173: RULES FOR POLITICAL ACTIVISM

Śiva's devotees freely pursue the politics of their choice, but never subscribe to doctrines that advocate violent revolution or deny religion. My followers do not organize among themselves for political purposes. Aum.

SŪTRA 174: PURSUING BENEVOLENT VOCATIONS

Śiva's devotees conscientiously choose professions that are helpful and beneficial to all, never destructive, divisive or exploitive. Yea, they are ministers of the Divine, missionaries of a future tranquility yet to be seen. Aum.

SŪTRA 175: MIGRATING FOR SPIRITUAL SECURITY

In the event of famine, invasion, tyranny or extreme conditions threatening wealth or life, my devotees may migrate to a place free of harassment where their spiritual life can continue unhindered. Aum Namaḥ Śivāya.

Edicts for Parliamentarians

SŪTRA 176: MAINTAINING FAIRNESS AND INTEGRITY

Śiva's devotees who are parliamentarians live in full conformity with the sacred scriptures, extend protection to all the people as they would to their own children and never bend to bribery, graft or corruption. Aum.

SŪTRA 177: PROMOTING SPIRITUAL VALUES

Śiva's devotees who are parliamentarians take pains to spread lofty religious tenets and tolerant human values among their constituents. They commission competent people who will enhance all the great world faiths. Aum.

SŪTRA 178: JUSTICE AND IMPARTIALITY

Śiva's devotees who are parliamentarians have as their platform justice for all and enmity toward none. They know that to show favoritism for one group over another is to sow the seeds of their own downfall. Aum.

SŪTRA 179: POLITICAL PERSEVERANCE

Śiva's devotees who are parliamentarians face and work through each challenge that comes and are never forced to abdicate. They maintain their office for as long as possible, then seek for the highest next position. Aum.

SŪTRA 180: NURTURING ALL FAITHS EQUALLY

Śiva's devotees who are parliamentarians grant equal boons to each spiritual sect under their aegis as if it were their own. They know a society is only as free as the freedom enjoyed by its minorities. Aum Namaḥ Śivāya.

Edicts for Scientists

SŪTRA 181: KEEPING SCIENCE ETHICAL

Śiva's devotees who are scientists are protectors of humanity and stewards of the Earth. They must never compromise their ethics for financial rewards or release inventions before proven safe and beneficial. Aum.

SŪTRA 182: HARNESSING SCIENCE WITH RELIGION

Śiva's devotees who are scientifically and alchemistically inclined naturally approach each investigation in awe, consider themselves servants of the Divine and subjugate themselves to the guidance of their preceptor. Aum.

SŪTRA 183: NONINJURIOUS SCIENCE

Śiva's devotees who are scientists or medical researchers refuse to participate in product testing that is harmful to the subject. They are forbidden to take part in any enterprise that promotes death or destruction. Aum.

SŪTRA 184: GUARDIANS OF EARTH AND HER PEOPLE

Śiva's devotees who are scientists concentrate their energies on bettering the world, conserving its resources and enabling humans to live in harmony with nature and one another. They are noble examples to mankind. Aum.

SŪTRA 185: PROTECTING SCIENTIFIC DISCOVERIES

Śiva's devotees who are scientists must resist the urge to share everything they discover. Certain knowledge has proven dangerous and hurtful to mankind, especially in the hands of the unscrupulous. Aum Namaḥ Śivāya.

Vyakti Jīvanam

व्यक्तिजीवनम्

Section Four

Personal Life

What is needful? Righteousness and sacred learning and teaching; truth and sacred learning and teaching; meditation and sacred learning and teaching; self-control and sacred learning and teaching; peace and sacred learning and teaching; ritual and sacred learning and teaching; humanity and sacred learning and teaching.

Kṛishṇa Yajur Veda, Taittarīya Upanishad 1.9. UPM, P. 109

n aspirant reads from the ancient scriptures of his lineage and chants on his holy rudrāksha *eads as part of a daily* sādhana. *Lord Gaṇeśa hovers nearby, holding His noose in one hand nd blessing the seeker's inner efforts with His other hand, held in the "fear not"* abhaya mudrā.

Diet and Food

SŪTRA 186: THE ĀYURVEDIC VEGETARIAN DIET

Śiva's devotees cook and eat in the balanced, varied, vegetarian, Indian *āyurvedic* manner, enjoying healthy, unprocessed, freshly cooked foods. Occasionally, they may partake of cuisine from other world cultures. Aum.

SŪTRA 187: MEALTIME TRADITIONS

Śiva's devotees eat with their fingers to energize food. They chew well and include the six tastes daily (sweet, salty, sour, pungent, bitter and astringent) and a balance of protein and carbohydrates at all meals. Aum.

SŪTRA 188: GOOD EATING HABITS

Śiva's devotees adhere to the *āyurvedic* principles of eating at regular times, only when hungry, always seated, at a moderate pace; never between meals, in a disturbed atmosphere or when angry or emotionally upset. Aum.

SŪTRA 189: UNFANATICAL VEGETARIANISM

Śiva's devotees are forbidden to eat meat, fish, shellfish, fowl or eggs, but they may regard as regrettable exceptions unseen traces of nonfleshy ingredients, such as eggs and gelatin, in packaged or restaurant foods. Aum.

SŪTRA 190: GOOD FOOD FOR GOOD HEALTH

Śiva's devotees know that a good diet is the best medicine. They drink two liters of water daily, minimize fried foods and avoid junk foods, white rice, white flour, processed sugar and degraded oils. Aum Namaḥ Śivāya.

Health and Exercise

SŪTRA 191: NOT EATING TOO MUCH

Śiva's devotees eat in moderation. Meals seldom exceed what two hands cupped together can hold. If hunger persists, another handful may be taken. Eating right extends life and maintains higher consciousness. Aum.

SŪTRA 192: FASTING FOR HEALTH AND PENANCE

Śiva's devotees may fast for twenty-four hours on water, herb teas or fruit juices each Friday or twice a month on *pradosha.* Longer fasting, such as a festival penance, is done only with the *guru's* or a doctor's sanction. Aum.

SŪTRA 193: CHOOSING APPROPRIATE HEALING ARTS

Śiva's devotees know wellness is balance. If the imbalance called illness occurs, they apply self-healing, then resort as needed to such arts as *āyurveda,* acupuncture, chiropractic, allopathy, *prāṇic* healing or massage. Aum.

SŪTRA 194: WEARING THE BODY LIKE A SANDAL

Śiva's devotees do not indulge in inordinate concerns about food, undue physical worries or extensive personal health studies other than *āyurveda.* They avoid extreme diets, except under medical supervision. Aum.

SŪTRA 195: EXERCISING DAILY

Śiva's devotees keep strong and healthy by exercising at least one half hour each day through such activities as brisk walking, swimming, dancing, salutations to the sun, *haṭha yoga* and vigorous work. Aum Namaḥ Śivāya.

Tobacco and Drugs

SŪTRA 196: FORBIDDING TOBACCO

Śiva's devotees are forbidden to smoke, chew tobacco or inhale snuff. They know nicotine's deadly, addictive power and value health and longevity as primary to fulfilling good *karmas* and serving the community. Aum.

SŪTRA 197: NOT USING DANGEROUS DRUGS

Śiva's devotees are forbidden to use drugs of abuse, such as cocaine, heroin, amphetamines, barbiturates, psychedelics and marijuana, unless prescribed by a licensed physician. They know their devastating effects. Aum.

SŪTRA 198: CHILDREN SAY NO TO DRUGS

Śiva's devotees educate their children to say no to any and all known or unknown illicit drugs offered to them, whether by friends or strangers. Pure and well informed by caring parents, children avoid these dangers. Aum.

SŪTRA 199: CHEMICAL CHAOS

Śiva's devotees know that drugs may awaken simultaneously the *chakra* of divine love and those of fear, confusion and malice, producing vast mood swings and a stunted intellect. They dread this chemical chaos. Aum.

SŪTRA 200: THE DEMONIC DRUG CULTURE

Śiva's devotees stand against drugs and never mix with those who use them or listen to talk extolling them. The drug culture and its demonic music erode the very fabric of human character and culture. Aum Namaḥ Śivāya.

Alcohol

SŪTRA 201: MODERATION WITH ALCOHOL

All strong and intoxicating distilled alcohols are forbidden to Śiva's devotees. They may moderately partake of the family of wines and beers, including honey mead, for these are wholesome when properly enjoyed. Aum.

SŪTRA 202: NOT DRINKING ALONE OR WHEN UPSET

Even in moderation, Śiva's devotees do not drink alcohol in solitude, when depressed, angry or under extreme stress. When one is emotionally unstable, alcohol inhibits the ability to confront and solve problems. Aum.

SŪTRA 203: MONITORING DRINKING AMONG PEERS

Śiva's devotees gently enforce temperance among peers whenever necessary. They know that those unable to observe moderation may have to abstain entirely and restrict themselves to nonalcoholic beverages. Aum.

SŪTRA 204: WOMEN DO NOT DRINK IN PUBLIC

All Hindu women, respecting customs of decorum and demureness, refrain from drinking alcohol in public. During pregnancy, they abstain completely to protect the health and well-being of their unborn child. Aum.

SŪTRA 205: TOTAL ABSTINENCE FOR SOME

Śiva's devotees know that if, despite the help of peers or elders, alcohol becomes a spiritual obstacle or a burden to family or community, the preceptor is duty-bound to deny the privilege altogether. Aum Namaḥ Śivāya.

The Four Stages of Life

SŪTRA 206: LIFE'S FOUR SEASONS

Śiva's ardent souls honor and conscientiously fulfill the duties of each of life's four progressive stages of *dharma:* student (age 12–24), householder (24–48), respected elder (48–72) and religious solitaire after age 72. Aum.

SŪTRA 207: TWO PSYCHOLOGICAL JUNCTURES

Śiva's ardent souls recognize that the natural human life span is 120 years. They confidently plan ahead at each 40-year juncture. Elders counsel, as needed, persons in life transitions, around 40 and 80 years of age. Aum.

SŪTRA 208: AGING WITH DIGNITY

Śiva's ardent souls grow old gracefully, without fear, knowing that the soul is immortal and the mental body does not age, but becomes stronger and more mature, as do the emotions, if regulated stage by stage. Aum.

SŪTRA 209: SELFLESS DUTIES AFTER RETIREMENT

Śiva's ardent souls intensify religious disciplines after retirement, give guidance to younger generations, teach, encourage, uplift, serve the community in various ways and support endowments to educate the young. Aum.

SŪTRA 210: RENUNCIATION AFTER AGE 72

Śiva's unmarried men and widowers may renounce the world after age 72, severing all ties with their community and living as unordained, self-declared *sannyāsins* among the holy monks of India. Aum Namaḥ Śivāya.

Approaching Death

SŪTRA 211: FACING THE PAST TO PREPARE FOR DEATH

Śiva's devotees give spiritual counseling to the terminally ill who are blessed with the knowledge of death's approach, showing ways to resolve the past so that Śiva consciousness is their bridge during transition. Aum.

SŪTRA 212: FORGIVING AND SEEKING FORGIVENESS

Śiva's devotees facing death perform *vāsanā daha tantra,* reconcile with and seek forgiveness from anyone they have offended, lest they leave unresolved *kukarmas* to go to seed and bear bitter fruit in future births. Aum.

SŪTRA 213: DRAWING WITHIN, RELEASING THE WORLD

Śiva's devotees who are dying concentrate on their *mantra* and find solace in the holy Vedic teachings on the soul's immortality, ever seeking the highest realizations as they consciously, joyously release the world. Aum.

SŪTRA 214: SEEKING A NATURAL DEATH AT HOME

Śiva's devotees welcome life-saving medical interventions, but in their last days avoid heroic, artificial perpetuation of life and prefer not to die in a hospital but at home with loved ones, who keep prayerful vigil. Aum.

SŪTRA 215: THE MOMENT OF GRAND DEPARTURE

Śiva's devotees strive at the moment of death to depart the body through the crown *chakra* and consciously enter the clear white light and beyond. A perfect transition culminates in God realization. Aum Namaḥ Śivāya.

Death's Aftermath

SŪTRA 216: CREMATION AND DISPERSAL OF ASHES

Devout Hindus always cremate their dead. Burial is forbidden by tradition. Embalming is never permitted, and no autopsy is performed unless required by law. Ashes are ceremoniously committed to a river or ocean. Aum.

SŪTRA 217: THE MYSTICAL BENEFIT OF CREMATION

Śiva's devotees arrange swift cremation, ideally within 24 hours. The fire and accompanying rites sever ties to earthly life and give momentum to the soul, granting at least momentary access to superconscious realms. Aum.

SŪTRA 218: FUNERAL RITES AND REMEMBRANCES

At the death of a Śiva devotee, family and friends gather for funeral rites in the home. They prepare the body and arrange for cremation. On the seventh day, the deceased's picture is honored, and food is offered. Aum.

SŪTRA 219: MEMORIAL RITES FOR THE DEPARTED

Family and friends of a deceased Śiva devotee hold amemorial on the thirty-first day after the transition and again one year later, cleaning the home and making food offerings to ancestors and to the departed. Aum.

SŪTRA 220: JOYFULLY RELEASING THE DEPARTED

Knowing that the soul is deathless, Śiva's devotees never suffer undue or prolonged sorrow for the departed, lest they bind these souls to Earth. They rejoice in the continuing journey of loved ones. Aum Namaḥ Śivāya.

Ādhyātmika Pārasparyam
आध्यात्मिक पारस्पर्यम्

Section Five

Spiritual Interaction

Śiva is knowledge, and knowledge is the *satguru.* Thus the same result is obtained by worshiping Śiva, knowledge and the *guru.* The *guru* is the abode of all divine beings and all *mantras.* Hence man should bow down and obey the instructions of the *guru* with all humility.

Chandrajñāna Āgama, Kriyāpāda, 2.9. BO CJ, P. 12

Seven śishyas *gather in the forest at their* satguru's *feet. The great radiance of his illumination shines out in a glowing nimbus, or auric halo. The* swāmī's *words are empowered by a psychic inner ray which touches the core of each seeker, awakening in them the same light and love.*

Respect for Saints and Dignitaries

SŪTRA 221: GREETING THE GURU AND HIS MONASTICS

All Śiva's devotees prostrate before their *satguru,* reverently touch the feet of his *āchāryas* and *swāmīs,* and greet *yogīs* and *sādhakas* with their palms pressed together and head slightly bowed. This is tradition. Aum.

SŪTRA 222: HOSTING A VISITING SWĀMĪ

Hearing of a venerated *swāmī's* arrival, Śiva's devotees joyously rush to the outskirts of town to welcome him. On his departure, they accompany him there and, with gifts, money and good wishes, bid him farewell. Aum.

SŪTRA 223: VENERATING WORTHY LEADERS

Devout Hindus honor a *satguru,* a head of state, a respected elder, a learned scholar, a renunciate or ascetic of any lineage. Upon his entrance, they stand, rush forward, bow appropriately and offer kind words. Aum.

SŪTRA 224: ŚIVA IS MOST EASILY SEEN IN THE SATGURU

Śiva's devotees know that God exists equally in all souls but is most apparent in the enlightened master. Thus, they revere their own *satguru* as Śiva Himself, but do not worship anyone as an incarnation of Śiva. Aum.

SŪTRA 225: TOUCHING THE FEET OF HOLY ONES

Sincere Śiva devotees never fail to bow down or gently touch the feet of a *satguru* or holy person of any order dressed in monastic robes. They prostrate only to their own *satguru.* This is the tradition. Aum Namaḥ Śivāya.

Social Injunctions

SŪTRA 226: RESTRAINING GESTURES OF AFFECTION

All Śiva's adult devotees refrain from touching adolescents or adults of the opposite sex, other than near relatives or older persons. They do not embrace or shake hands except when required by social etiquette. Aum.

SŪTRA 227: MODESTY BETWEEN GENDERS

All Śiva's devotees who are no longer children remain apart from the opposite sex when attending temples and public gatherings. Upon entering, women always sit on the left side, and men occupy the right side. Aum.

SŪTRA 228: GUIDELINES FOR GARLANDING OTHERS

Devotees of Śiva do not garland members of the opposite sex, other than their spouse or blood relatives. Women never garland a *swāmī, yogī* or *sādhaka,* but may freely and lovingly garland their own *satguru.* Aum.

SŪTRA 229: FAMILY RETREAT AFTER A BIRTH OR DEATH

Śiva's devotees observe a thirty-one-day retreat after the birth or death of a family member, not entering temples or home shrines, not attending *pūjā* or religious events, but continuing their *japa,* study and meditations. Aum.

SŪTRA 230: CASTING ASIDE THE CASTE SYSTEM

Śiva's devotees are forbidden to perpetuate the restrictions and abuses of the Indian caste system. Instead, they base respect and status on attainment, knowledge, behavior and spiritual maturity. Aum Namaḥ Śivāya.

Interfaith Harmony

SŪTRA 231: INTERACTING WITH OTHER FAITHS

Śiva's devotees properly respect and address virtuous persons of all religious traditions. They may support and participate in interfaith gatherings from time to time with leaders and members of all religions. Aum.

SŪTRA 232: NOT DEMEANING OTHER SECTS OR RELIGIONS

Śiva's devotees do not speak disrespectfully about other Hindu lineages, their beliefs, Gods, sacred sites, scriptures, or holy men and women. Nor do they disparage other religions. They refuse to listen to such talk. Aum.

SŪTRA 233: RESTRAINING INVOLVEMENT WITH OTHER FAITHS

Śiva's devotees avoid the enchantment of other ways, be they ancient or modern. They remain friendly toward but apart from other religions, except when their members sincerely approach Hinduism for its wisdom. Aum.

SŪTRA 234: MAINTAINING A HINDU SOLIDARITY

Śiva's devotees know that for eons our religion has come forward to recreate a Hindu unity. Therefore, they are dedicated to building whenever necessary, and keeping strong always, an invincible Hindu solidarity. Aum.

SŪTRA 235: HARMONY BETWEEN DENOMINATIONS

Śiva's devotees, with hearts as big as the sky, love and accept Smārta, Śākta and Vaishṇava Hindus as brothers and sisters, even if not accepted by them, and keep harmony by not discussing differences. Aum Namaḥ Śivāya.

Avoiding Alien Influences

SŪTRA 236: SAFEGUARDING ONE'S BELIEFS

Śiva's devotees, one-pointed in striving on their chosen path, do not join or study with any esoteric, religious, secular humanist, atheist, existentialist or self-improvement group that might undermine their beliefs. Aum.

SŪTRA 237: DEALING WITH DETRACTORS

Śiva's devotees never listen to talk intended to deter them from their commitment, devotion or duty unless willing and able to turn the detractor's mind around by debating the truths of the Śaivite Hindu religion. Aum.

SŪTRA 238: NOT SENDING YOUTH TO OTHER FAITHS' SCHOOLS

Śiva's devotees never educate their children in institutions that would instill or force on them the teachings of alien religions. They know that the early impressions of youth go deep and can never be totally erased. Aum.

SŪTRA 239: KEEPING GOOD, RELIGIOUS COMPANY

Śiva's devotees do not mix with dogmatic or militant Hindus, or with anyone who would infiltrate, dilute and destroy their faith. They associate closely with devout people whose beliefs are similar to their own. Aum.

SŪTRA 240: TRUTH IN THE PALM OF THEIR HAND

My devotees know that everything they need to fulfill their quest for liberation is found in our consummate Nandinātha Sampradāya. With the final conclusions in their grasp, they look no further. Aum Namaḥ Śivāya.

Devotion to the Satguru

SŪTRA 241: PROTOCOLS FOR HONORING THE SATGURU

Śiva's devotees daily offer fruit or flowers in love and prostrate before their *satguru,* or to his sandals or the direction in which he abides. They chant the Guru Mantra when approaching any *satguru* for *darśana.* Aum.

SŪTRA 242: THE SATGURU AND ŚIVA ARE ONE

Śiva's devotees look upon their *satguru* as the embodiment of Śiva, offering service and reverence equally to both, making no distinction between the two. So live His truest devotees. This is pure Śaiva tradition. Aum.

SŪTRA 243: SEEKING INNER UNITY WITH THE SATGURU

Śiva's devotees meditate each morning upon their *satguru's* inner form, striving earnestly to know his temperament, the contents of his heart and his essential nature, which is eternal, peaceful and unattached. Aum.

SŪTRA 244: BLESSINGS FROM AND SERVICE TO THE SATGURU

Śiva's devotees hasten to receive their *satguru's* food leavings and the sanctified waters from his holy feet or sandals. They know that in serving the enlightened master, the whole world is served and *dharma* is fulfilled. Aum.

SŪTRA 245: SEEKING SATGURU DARŚANA AND INITIATION

Śiva's devotees emulate the awakened qualities they see in their *satguru,* seek initiation and daily strive to fathom his realization of Paraśiva, which is his priceless gift, attainable by no other means. Aum Namaḥ Śivāya.

Working with the Satguru

SŪTRA 246: NURTURING THE GURU-ŚISHYA RELATIONSHIP

Śiva's devotees seek their *satguru's* blessings, act in harmony with his will, trust in his supreme wisdom, seek refuge in his grace and rush forward to rededicate themselves each year during the month of the *guru*. Aum.

SŪTRA 247: OBEY YOUR GURU, OBEY YOUR GURU...

Śiva's devotees obey their *satguru*, carrying out his directions, expressed or implied, with intelligent cooperation, without delay. They keep no secrets from him, nor advise others how to manipulate his decisions. Aum.

SŪTRA 248: ...OBEY YOUR GURU

Śiva's devotees trustingly heed their *satguru's* counsel without even subtly attempting to change his mind. If he declines to give blessings for an endeavor, they accept that as his blessing and proceed no further. Aum.

SŪTRA 249: SEEKING SANCTION FOR SEVERE AUSTERITIES

Śiva's devotees regularly perform spiritual practices on their own, but undertake serious penance and rigorous austerities only with their *satguru's* express permission, guidance, empowerment and spiritual protection. Aum.

SŪTRA 250: CUSTOMS FOR RECEIVING THE SATGURU

Śiva's devotees, upon the *satguru's* entrance or arrival, cease worldly activity and conversation. They rise, rush forward to greet him, offer him a seat of honor and expectantly await his instructions. Aum Namaḥ Śivāya.

In the Satguru's Presence

SŪTRA 251: NEVER CRITICIZING OR CONTENDING

Śiva's devotees are forbidden by tradition to criticize their *satguru,* even behind his back, or to argue with him, contradict or correct him. They may, however, request clarification and offer additional information. Aum.

SŪTRA 252: SHOWING RESPECT TO THE PRECEPTOR

Śiva's devotees never stand or sit above their *satguru,* walk or drive ahead of him, take a place of authority or instruct others in his presence unless invited. All Hindus are sensitive in a *guru's* lofty company. Aum.

SŪTRA 253: UNSEEMLY BEHAVIORS TO AVOID

Śiva's devotees never utter words of falsehood or contempt before their *satguru.* Nor do they deceive him, address him as an equal, imitate his dress or deportment or speak excessively or pridefully in his presence. Aum.

SŪTRA 254: HONORING THE SATGURU'S PRESENCE

When with the *satguru,* devotees do not initiate conversation or ask questions unless he gives permission. If he prefers silence, silence is the message, the pure nectar from the deep well of his ineffable attainment. Aum.

SŪTRA 255: NO TOLERANCE FOR SLANDER

Śiva's devotees never listen to criticism of their *satguru.* If slander is heard, they extol the *guru* and warn the trespasser of his encroachment. If he persists in ignorance, they leave in eloquent silence. Aum Namaḥ Śivāya.

Dhārmika Saṁskṛiti

धार्मिक संस्कृति

Section Six

Religious Culture

May Earth on which men offer to the Gods the sacrifice and decorous oblations, where dwells the human race on nourishment proper to the requirements of its nature—may this great Earth assure us life and breath, permitting us to come to ripe old age.

Atharva Veda 12.1.22. VE

A contemporary priest, complete with t-shirt, performs āratī *to our global and cosmic God, indicated by Earth and stars. Lord Gaṇeśa's reality is shown by the* mūrti's *transformation from inanimate bronze at the bottom to living flesh at the top.*

Temples and Priesthood

SŪTRA 256: OUR HOLY GATHERING PLACES

My devotees revere Kauai Aadheenam's San Marga Iraivan Temple as their center of the universe, our Śaiva *dharmaśālas* as sites of learning and service, and mission houses as places of study, worship and assembly. Aum.

SŪTRA 257: FOUR VEHICLES OF SERVICE

My devotees give full energy and dedication to Saiva Siddhanta Church, Himalayan Academy, HINDUISM TODAY and Hindu Heritage Endowment. These four form a mighty, unified force for Sanātana Dharma. Aum.

SŪTRA 258: OUR SACRED PRIESTS

My Church honors our *maṭhavāsis* as its official priesthood. For *samskāras* and special festivals we may engage closely devoted Tamil priests, as well as hereditary Śivāchāryas, who preside at all temple consecrations. Aum.

SŪTRA 259: THE VEDIC SCIENCE OF TEMPLE BUILDING

My devotees perpetuate in our temples the architecture set forth in the *Śaiva Āgamas* and *Vāstu Śāstras*, and exemplified in the sanctuaries of South India, to create holy places where even the stones have sanctity. Aum.

SŪTRA 260: APPROPRIATE PLACES OF WORSHIP

My devotees worship at their home shrines, *dharmaśālas*, Kauai Aadheenam and all Śaivite temples. They do not attend temples of other denominations except on pilgrimage or as required socially. Aum Namaḥ Śivāya.

Weekly Gatherings

SŪTRA 261: THE IMPORTANCE OF FAMILY MISSIONS

My congregation is organized into local missions to nurture religious life through shared worship, extended family gatherings, sacraments and community service, in accordance with the *Śaiva Dharma Śāstras.* Aum.

SŪTRA 262: CONNECTING WITH THE INNER WORLDS

My devotees rush to family gatherings for *bhajana, havana satsaṅga* and fellowship, to worship devoutly and sing loudly in praise of God, Gods and *guru.* They attend Śaivite temples weekly and during festivals. Aum.

SŪTRA 263: EXPRESSING DEVOTION WITH SONG

At gatherings among themselves, my devotees sing from our Śaiva Church hymnal, primarily Sage Yogaswami's *Natchintanai.* When with devotees of other sects, they enthusiastically join in their devotional songs. Aum.

SŪTRA 264: DECISION-MAKING BY CONSENSUS

My devotees abide by "consensualocracy." All involved in a decision must unanimously agree and obtain the *guru's* blessings before proceeding. No votes are taken based on the majority superceding the minority. Aum.

SŪTRA 265: EDICTS FROM THE SEAT OF AUTHORITY

My devotees never apply the principle of unanimous agreement to sovereign edicts issued from Kauai Aadheenam's seat of power. Such proclamations are the uncontestable law of the *satguru.* Aum Namaḥ Śivāya.

New Members

SŪTRA 266: SHARING THE TEACHINGS WITH OTHERS

All my devotees reach out for new members by enthusiastically printing and distributing Hindu literature and putting sacred texts of our lineage into libraries, bookstores and educational institutions worldwide. Aum.

SŪTRA 267: AN ELITE AND STEADFAST ASSOCIATION

All within my Saiva Siddhanta Church are stalwart and dedicated. Not one is half-hearted or equivocal. Each is a jewel, important to me and to each other. Thus, strictness is necessary when accepting new members. Aum.

SŪTRA 268: EMBRACING NEWCOMERS

All within my Saiva Siddhanta Church accept newcomers as part of their own family. They care for, teach, gently guide and prepare these souls for their first initiation. Yea, they too were once new members. Aum.

SŪTRA 269: THE PROBATIONARY FIRST YEAR

All within my Śaiva Church who sponsor new members are responsible for their strengths and failures during the probationary year, their study for initiation and their merger with others as milk poured into milk. Aum.

SŪTRA 270: THE QUEST FOR MONASTIC CANDIDATES

All my devotees search for souls ripe to enter the monastery, realizing that the core of my Śaiva Church is its Śaiva Siddhānta Yoga Order, and many old souls are being born to perpetuate our lineage. Aum Namaḥ Śivāya.

Coming Home to Śaivism

SŪTRA 271: REACHING OUT TO ŚAIVITE SOULS

My ardent devotees relentlessly search for Śaivite souls, finding them, drawing them to Śiva and their *satguru* and, when necessary, helping them convert to Śaivism from the faiths or philosophies they have rejected. Aum.

SŪTRA 272: SPECIAL ATTENTION TO ARDHA-HINDUS

My ardent devotees reach out to seekers who, half-converted, bear a Hindu first name. Gently they assist them through a full and ethical conversion from any and all former faiths, then accept them wholeheartedly. Aum.

SŪTRA 273: SEVERING FORMER RELIGIOUS TIES

My ardent devotees of other religions or lineages who seek to enter my Śaiva Church must, with authorized guidance, formally sever all loyalties by talking with former preceptors and gaining a written release. Aum.

SŪTRA 274: CONVERSION FROM OTHER HINDU SECTS

My ardent devotees affirm that even seekers from within the Hindu fold must convert to enter our strict Śaiva Church. All former commitments and memberships must be dissolved before new ones can be made. Aum.

SŪTRA 275: THE TRANSFORMATION CALLED CONVERSION

My ardent devotees well know that *conversion* means a change of one belief structure into another and is never without some degree of fire and pain. Counseling is necessary in this soul-searching time. Aum Namaḥ Śivāya.

Detractors and Adversaries

SŪTRA 276: SHUNNING ENEMIES

My devotees abide by the custom of shunning those who oppose, criticize or attack their lineage. By not interacting with detractors, they forestall conflict and thus protect their lineage as well as themselves. Aum.

SŪTRA 277: THE MEANING OF SHUNNING

My devotees realize that shunning means tactful avoidance, exclusion, ignoring and ostracizing. Thus a firm, protective wall of silence is built between our lineage and its detractors, whether individuals or groups. Aum.

SŪTRA 278: WHEN TO STOP SHUNNING

My devotees who refuse to shun those who should be shunned should themselves be shunned. But none shall shun those who have reconciled with the preceptor and been publicly welcomed back into association. Aum.

SŪTRA 279: WELCOMING BACK THOSE WHO RECONCILE

My devotees extend every effort to welcome and bring back into the lineage those seeking to reenter its fold, having formerly left, provided they show grief, remorse and repentance, and reconcile with the *satguru*. Aum.

SŪTRA 280: WITHDRAWING FROM ERRANT MONASTICS

My devotees know that any monastic who abandons his sacred vows and leaves the monastery or is dismissed should be shunned and treated as an outsider until he rights himself with his preceptor. Aum Namaḥ Śivāya.

Raising Sons for the Monastery

SŪTRA 281: CONCEIVING SONS FOR THE MONASTERY

Each Saiva Siddhanta Church family prays to birth a son for the monastery. Prior to conception, parents mix with the *swāmīs* and beseech the Gods to bring through a divine soul destined to perpetuate our lineage. Aum.

SŪTRA 282: NURTURING MONASTIC INCLINATIONS

My devotees with sons inclined toward monastic life wholeheartedly encourage these noble aspirations. Fathers and young sons live as monastery guests periodically to nurture monastic patterns and tendencies. Aum.

SŪTRA 283: SATGURU GUIDES THE LIFE OF DEDICATED SONS

My devotees regard any son destined for the monastery not as their own child, but as the *satguru's* progeny in their trusted care. All details of his upbringing, training and education are to be guided by the preceptor. Aum.

SŪTRA 284: PARENTS OF MONASTICS EXPECT NO PRIVILEGES

My devotees with a monastic son never claim special access or privileges based on blood ties. They dissociate from him and do not involve themselves in his life or seek to influence our Śaiva Church through him. Aum.

SŪTRA 285: SERVING TWO YEARS IN THE MONASTERY

My family devotees raise their sons to be worthy of entering my monastery for two years to serve, study and grow in character as they live the monk's selfless life. This is the ideal for all young men. Aum Namaḥ Śivāya.

Sacred Scriptures

SŪTRA 286: OUR SCRIPTURAL BEDROCK, VEDAS AND ĀGAMAS

All my devotees recognize that the primary scriptural authority of our Nandinātha lineage derives from the *Śaiva Āgamas* and the four noble *Vedas,* which include the *Upanishads.* Ours is a Vedic-Āgamic tradition. Aum.

SŪTRA 287: OUR ŚAIVITE HINDU BIBLE

All my devotees revere as scripture *The Holy Bible of the Śaivite Hindu Religion*—which includes excerpts from the *Vedas,* the *Āgamas, Tirumantiram, Tirumurai* and *Tirukural*—and guide their lives by its wisdom. Aum.

SŪTRA 288: THE TEACHINGS OF PRISTINE TAMIL SAINTS

My Hindu Church decrees as true Tamil Śaiva saints the great ones who upheld *dharma, ahiṁsā* and monistic Śaiva Siddhānta through the ages. We revere their words as scripture and bestow our heartfelt *praṇāmas.* Aum.

SŪTRA 289: SAGE YOGASWAMI'S PROFOUND HYMNS

All my devotees revere as sacred scripture the songs and sayings of Satguru Siva Yogaswami, called *Natchintanai,* which embody the teachings of our lineage, commanding one and all to "Know thy Self by thy self." Aum.

SŪTRA 290: MY TRILOGY AND OTHER LEGACY WORKS

All my devotees revere as sacred scripture *Dancing with Śiva, Living with Śiva, Merging with Śiva, Lemurian Scrolls* and my other authorized texts and discourses, including *Śaiva Dharma Śāstras.* Aum Namaḥ Śivāya.

Temple Worship

SŪTRA 291: THE DEDICATED HOME SHRINE ROOM

All my devotees must have an absolutely breathtaking home shrine, used solely for meditation and worship of Śivaliṅga, Naṭarāja, Murugan, Gaṇeśa and the *satguru's tiruvadi.* This is the home's most beautiful room. Aum.

SŪTRA 292: AUTHORIZATION TO PERFORM WORSHIP RITES

My initiated devotees perform the Śaiva *ātmārtha pūjā,* but only in home shrines, not in temples. Unless formally, traditionally authorized, they are prohibited to learn, teach or perform the *parārtha* temple *pūjā.* Aum.

SŪTRA 293: LIVING NEAR ŚAIVA TEMPLES

My devotees wisely settle in areas where Gaṇeśa, Murugan or Śiva temples exist for their frequent pilgrimage, worship and spiritual security. None should live farther than a day's journey from such sacred sanctuaries. Aum.

SŪTRA 294: PILGRIMAGE TO ŚIVA'S SPECIAL ABODES

My devotees hold as most sacred and pilgrimage to each at least once: Śiva's San Mārga Iraivan Temple on Kauai, His Himālayan and Gangetic abodes, His five elemental temples and the Madurai Meenakshi citadel. Aum.

SŪTRA 295: VISITING SHRINES TO GODS AND GURUS

My devotees all revere and pilgrimage to Nallur and Murugan's six South Indian temples, Gaṇeśa's many temples and shrines, especially Kumbhalavalai, and the *samādhi* shrines of our lineage. Aum Namaḥ Śivāya.

Symbols, Mantras and Names

SŪTRA 296: WEARING THE EMBLEMS OF ŚAIVISM

All Śiva's devotees, men and women, boys and girls, wear holy ash and the proper forehead mark for religious events and in public when appropriate. They wear a single *rudrāksha* bead on the neck at all times. Aum.

SŪTRA 297: BENEDICTIONS FOR GREETING AND PARTING

All my devotees greet others by saying *Aum Namaḥ Śivāya, Aum Śivāya* or the more general benedictions *vanakkam, namaste* or *namaskāra.* These, or the sweet expression *Aum, Aum,* also serve when parting. Aum.

SŪTRA 298: ŚAIVISM'S AFFIRMATION OF FAITH

Just before sleep, all my devotees utter: "Anbe Sivamayam Satyame Parasivam," while pondering the great depths of this affirmation. Upon awakening, their first words are "Anbe Sivamayam Satyame Parasivam." Aum.

SŪTRA 299: SACRED MANTRAS FOR MEALS AND GATHERINGS

All my devotees chant the Bhojana Mantra before each meal, offering thankful praise to God, Gods and *guru.* They chant the Vedic Śānti Mantra to begin and end all meetings, invoking peace and one-mindedness. Aum.

SŪTRA 300: PROUDLY USING ONE'S ŚAIVITE NAME

All my devotees bear and legally register their Śaivite Hindu name, first and last, and use it proudly each day in all circumstances, never concealing or altering it to adjust to non-Hindu cultures. Aum Namaḥ Śivāya.

Cultural Accomplishments

SŪTRA 301: DEVELOPING A USEFUL CRAFT

All my devotees are encouraged to learn a skill requiring the use of their hands, such as pottery, sewing, weaving, painting, gardening, baking or the building arts, to manifest creative benefits for family and community. Aum.

SŪTRA 302: MUSIC, ART, DRAMA AND THE DANCE

All my devotees are encouraged to perfect a cultural accomplishment, be it a form of art, singing, drama, dance or a musical instrument of Śiva's ensemble—*vīṇā, mṛidaṅgam, tambūra*, cymbals and bamboo flute. Aum.

SŪTRA 303: USING OUR MYSTICAL LANGUAGES

All my devotees are encouraged to embrace Sanskrit as their language of ritual worship, Shūm Tyēīf as their language of meditation and the Tyēīf script for offering prayers to the *devas* through the sacred *homa* fire. Aum.

SŪTRA 304: HINDUISM'S SACRED CALENDAR

All my devotees are encouraged to use the South Indian lunar calendar as a daily guide to auspicious planning for travel, business, innovation, ceremony and major life events. Our year begins with the month of Aries. Aum.

SŪTRA 305: LIVING THE SUBLIME TAMIL ŚAIVA CULTURE

All my devotees are encouraged to adopt the gestures, attitudes, customs, ways of worship, dress and refinements of Tamil Śaiva protocol. They learn by living and studying with traditional Śaivites. Aum Namaḥ Śivāya.

Spiritual Study

SŪTRA 306: THE MASTER COURSE AS DAILY GUIDE

My devotees avidly study *The Master Course* as their lifetime *sādhana,* allowing its mystical and practical teachings to light their inner path. In these profound lessons they discover the meaning of life's many lessons. Aum.

SŪTRA 307: SELF-MASTERY THROUGH INTROSPECTION

My devotees study the five states of mind: conscious, subconscious, sub-subconscious, subsuperconscious and superconscious. They let go of negative attachments and become master of mind, body and emotions. Aum.

SŪTRA 308: REMOLDING THE SUBCONSCIOUS

My devotees succeed by remolding subconscious magnetic forces. They purge the dross through *vāsanā daha tantra*—writing and burning past transgressions and current problems—then use positive affirmations. Aum.

SŪTRA 309: RĀJA YOGA, THE ROYAL PATH TO REALIZATION

My devotees learn and perfect the five steps to enlightenment: attention, concentration, meditation, contemplation and finally *samādhi,* wherein they realize the unspeakable Truth known only by the knower. Aum.

SŪTRA 310: FATHOMING OUR SUBTLE NATURE

My devotees study these three to discover the mysteries of being: the subtle bodies of man, the aura, which is a rainbow of thought and feeling, and the twenty-one *chakras,* or centers of consciousness. Aum Namaḥ Śivāya.

Occultism

SŪTRA 311: AVOIDING THE ADVICE OF PSYCHICS

My devotees do not counsel with trance mediums, clairvoyants, past- and future-life readers or psychic mentors. Nor do they consult astrologers or palmists other than those approved by their preceptor. Aum.

SŪTRA 312: CAUTION AGAINST DABBLING IN THE OCCULT

My devotees may spontaneously experience but do not practice clairvoyance, clairaudience, astral projection, lucid dreaming, trance mediumship, mind-reading, fortunetelling, magic or other distracting occult arts. Aum.

SŪTRA 313: SHIELDING FROM ASTRAL FORCES

My devotees are under the *satguru's* psychic protection and remain untouched by negative occult forces. Those who are as yet susceptible to such afflictions should seek relief through *pūjā*, prayer and penance. Aum.

SŪTRA 314: DREAMS ARE TO BE FORGOTTEN

My devotees do not indulge in remembrance or interpretation of dreams, unless as a special discipline from their *guru*. They intentionally forget their dreams and positively concern themselves with waking life. Aum.

SŪTRA 315: SENDING PRAYERS TO THE INNER WORLDS

My devotees practice the ancient rite of sending prayers to the *devas* and Gods through the sacred fire, but only during auspicious times at Church missions and temples designated by the preceptor. Aum Namaḥ Śivāya.

Sannyāsa Dharma

संन्यासधर्म

Section Seven

The Monastic Path

The ascetic who wears discolored robes, whose head is shaved, who does not possess anything, who is pure and free from hatred, who lives on alms, he becomes absorbed in Brahman.

Śukla Yajur Veda, Jābāla Upanishad 5. VE

A sannyāsin *is a Hindu monk, one who has thrown down worldliness, renounced name and fame, possessions, family and desires of all kinds, to find the Self within. The* swāmī *is walking pensively along the trails of the high Himalayas. Two* mālās *of ruddy* rudrāksha *beads adorn his neck.*

Monastic Holy Orders

SŪTRA 316: MONASTIC LIFE'S FOURFOLD PURPOSE

Śiva's monastics lead a joyous, contented, steadfast, humble life. Their purpose is contemplation upon and love of Śiva, to maintain Śiva consciousness, realize the Self and uplift others while serving their *satguru.* Aum.

SŪTRA 317: VOWS FOR CONTEMPLATIVE LIVING

Śiva's monastics who are *sādhakas* and *yogīs* uphold, and renew every two years, the four vows of humility, purity, confidence and obedience. *Swāmīs* uphold for life these four and a fifth vow of renunciation. Aum.

SŪTRA 318: HOLDING FAST TO THE TRUEST TREASURES

Śiva's monastics never fail to take refuge in their God, their *guru* and their Great Oath. This is the highest path they have chosen, the culmination of numberless lives, perhaps the last in the cycle of reincarnation. Aum.

SŪTRA 319: THEIR PAST IS SMALL, THEIR FUTURE IS LARGE

Śiva's monastics walk bravely into the future, letting go of the past and letting what is be. Through *yoga* their *kuṇḍalinī* rises, expanding consciousness, changing values and creating magical happenings around them. Aum.

SŪTRA 320: LIVING IN THE SPIRIT OF TOGETHERNESS

My Śaiva monastics embrace a selfless life in which all work their minds together to keep the monastery strong. They never follow an individual path, remaining remote or aloof from brother *maṭhavāsis.* Aum Namaḥ Śivāya.

Monastic Mission

SŪTRA 321: PRESERVING THE THREE PILLARS OF ŚAIVISM

Śiva's monastics valiantly bring Śaivism into the future of futures. The fullness of their mission lies in our faith's three pillars—temples, scriptures and *satgurus*—which they are vowed to protect, preserve and promote. Aum.

SŪTRA 322: REMAINING ABOVE CORRUPTION AND CONTROL

Śiva's monastics never compromise their ideals or rules for material or political gain, nor come under the control of the rich or influential. Vows prohibit them from being told what to think, say or do except by their order. Aum.

SŪTRA 323: FEARLESS DEFENDERS OF HINDUISM

Śiva's monastics are unfettered and fearless, wholeheartedly and boldly supporting the ancient Sanātana Dharma against all who would infiltrate, dilute and destroy it. Yea, they are defenders of all Hindu sects. Aum.

SŪTRA 324: SELFLESS SERVICE LEADS TO SELF-MASTERY

Śiva's monastic disciples regard themselves as the full-time slaves of Śiva, servants of the servants of the Lord. They are masters of mind, body and emotion, divine rulers of their instinctive and intellectual forces. Aum.

SŪTRA 325: PURE VESSELS FOR THE DIVINE

My monastics strive to keep Lord Śiva foremost in their mind and heart, seeking pure emptiness, *kāīf.* Having mastered the Shūm-Tyēīf language of meditation, they are vessels for God's gracious will. Aum Namaḥ Śivāya.

Monastic Spirit

SŪTRA 326: RĀJA YOGA IN ACTION

Śiva's monastics—*āchāryas, swāmīs, yogīs* and *sādhakas*—are precise, concentrated, serenely centered, eager to serve and tireless in every task, held back to rest only by others. *Jai,* they carry their *yoga* into action. Aum.

SŪTRA 327: SERVING DYNAMICALLY SINCE TIME BEGAN

Śiva's monastics are strong-willed, gentle in intellect, rushing forward in youthful, happy ways. Every desire they have is for the welfare of others. Yea, this group is the religion's core and has been for eons of time. Aum.

SŪTRA 328: THE WHOLE WORLD IS THEIR FAMILY

Śiva's monastics who have separated themselves from family to pursue a divine life do so in a spirit of love. They look upon this not as losing their dear family of a few but as gaining all of humanity as their kin. Aum.

SŪTRA 329: FIRST THINGS FIRST

Śiva's monastics tread the path of experiential *yoga.* They never allow intellectual studies or interests to overshadow their inner life. They are men of God and the Gods first, teachers, scholars or artisans second. Aum.

SŪTRA 330: FACING KARMA IN WISDOM

Śiva's monastics, knowing the law of *karma,* accept as their own *karma* all that comes. They forgive others of all offenses inwardly at once, but outwardly only after transgressors sincerely reconcile. Aum Namaḥ Śivāya.

Monastic Attitudes

SŪTRA 331: ENCOURAGING OTHER QUALIFIED MONASTICS

Śiva's monastics support *sādhus, yogīs, swāmīs* and *gurus* of other orders, male or female, even if their beliefs differ, as long as they promote the *Vedas,* the Hindu religion and the renunciate ideals of monasticism. Aum.

SŪTRA 332: REMAINING APART FROM THE UNQUALIFIED

Śiva's monastics restrain their support for *sannyāsins* in saffron robes who are married, who have personal income, live with birth family, deny or dilute Hinduism, have left their *guru* or are known philanderers. Aum.

SŪTRA 333: SUPPORTING HINDU PRIESTS AND PANDITS

Śiva's monastics honor and support the good causes of Hindu lay ministers, priests and *pandits* of all lineages to create a dynamic solidarity in diversity to carry Sanātana Dharma to each succeeding generation. Aum.

SŪTRA 334: HUMILITY IS THEIR HALLMARK

Śiva's monastics never boast of their accomplishments, knowledge, position, equipment, money they handle, places they have been or people they know. Self-effacement—yea, self-erasement—is their hallmark. Aum.

SŪTRA 335: OVERCOMING THE FOUR OBSTACLES

Śiva's monastics regard sex, money, food and clothes as the prime challenge to their spiritual quest, harboring the potential to reinvolve them in the world. Thus, they restrain themselves accordingly. Aum Namaḥ Śivāya.

Monastic Restrictions

SŪTRA 336: NEVER INDULGING IN SEXUAL FANTASY

All Śiva's monastics strictly avoid sexual fantasy, knowing that it opens the door to the progressive stages of glorifying sex, flirting, desirous glances, love talk, pining, deciding to have sex and finally intercourse. Aum.

SŪTRA 337: RESERVE TOWARD WOMEN

All Śiva's monastics honor all older women as their mother and younger women as their sisters. Intensely renounced, modest and reserved, they avoid extended conversation and exchange of subtle energies. Aum.

SŪTRA 338: THEIR LIKES ARE THEIR DISLIKES

All Śiva's monastics firmly uphold the spirit of nonownership, never adopting the householder attitudes of claiming their own space, timing, tools, friends, ambitions, likes and dislikes. Yea, they are unattached. Aum.

SŪTRA 339: THE PROBLEMS OF TODAY END TODAY

All Śiva's monastics treasure harmony as their way of life. They stop work, attend to and resolve before sleep any inharmonious conditions that may arise, knowing that creativity lies dormant while conflict prevails. Aum.

SŪTRA 340: QUALIFICATION TO PERFORM TEMPLE PŪJĀ

All my Śaiva monastics who qualify may perform the *parārtha pūjā* in their temples. Should they not renew their vows or be dismissed, they are prohibited to perform or teach this *pūjā* thenceforth. Aum Namaḥ Śivāya.

Monastic Personal Care

SŪTRA 341: SIMPLE CLOTHING FOR SIMPLE MAṬHAVĀSIS

Śiva's monastics wear robes of cotton or wool—hand-spun, hand-woven and unsewn. Other clothing should be made of simple, unadorned cotton, wool or synthetics, in traditional North or South Indian style. Aum.

SŪTRA 342: LUNAR RETREATS FROM GUESTS AND THE PUBLIC

Śiva's monastics observe the full, new and half moons and the day after each as retreats for *sādhana*, study, rest, personal care and *āśrama* upkeep, plus a fortnight's retreat at the end of each of the year's three seasons. Aum.

SŪTRA 343: DISCIPLINES FOR SLEEP

My monastics sleep six to eight hours a day for rejuvenation and astral duties. They refuse a soft bed and sleep on a firm floor mattress, ideally on a *neem* plank. This custom may be relaxed when ill or traveling. Aum.

SŪTRA 344: KEEPING LITTLE, OWNING NOTHING

Śiva's monastics have no more personal belongings than they can easily carry in two bags, one in each hand. By tradition, they have little, and even these few things they do not own. Yea, they are true mendicants. Aum.

SŪTRA 345: NURTURING NEW MONASTICS

Śiva's monastics look upon newcomers to the monasteries as their potential spiritual heirs, to care for, tenderly nurture and train. They know it is their duty to pass on the wisdom of their years. Aum Namaḥ Śivāya.

Monastic Travel and Retreat

SŪTRA 346: RECEIVING NO PERSONAL GIFTS

My Śaiva monastics do not accept personal gifts of any kind, but they may receive offerings on behalf of the monastery and support during pilgrimage, including fruit, flowers, food, lodging and travel expenses. Aum.

SŪTRA 347: OVERNIGHT STAYS WHEN TRAVELING

My Śaiva monastics while traveling may reside and take meals in *āśramas,* temples, hotels or homes of worthy initiated families of our Saiva Siddhanta Church. Their sojourn in homes must never exceed three nights. Aum.

SŪTRA 348: MALES SERVE MY MAṬHAVĀSIS

My Śaiva monastics are all males, our ancient tradition ordains. When they visit homes, temples or *āśramas,* all service to them, such as meals, travel assistance, laundry and visitor hosting, shall be carried out by males. Aum.

SŪTRA 349: FOOD GUIDELINES FOR TRAVELING MONASTICS

My Śaiva monastics when traveling may partake of food prepared at home by devout families and delivered to them. They may also cook for themselves, or enjoy meals in restaurants, whether served by men or women. Aum.

SŪTRA 350: THE TRADITION OF MOVING IN PAIRS

My Śaiva monastics, whether in or outside the monastery, perform ministry only in pairs. They never travel alone. Exceptions are made in dire emergencies and for those on the *nirvāṇa sādhaka* path. Aum Namaḥ Śivāya.

Monastics and the World

SŪTRA 351: REMAINING ALOOF FROM INTRIGUE

My Śaiva monastics stand apart from intrigue, corruption and cunning. They never act as go-betweens, spies, agents or bearers of false witness and cannot be bought, influenced, or obligated by the rich or powerful. Aum.

SŪTRA 352: STAYING OUT OF SOCIAL SERVICE AND POLITICS

My Śaiva monastics are assigned to religious work alone and, except to bless, advise and counsel, do not involve themselves with secular events or social service. Nor do they vote in elections or seek to influence politics. Aum.

SŪTRA 353: CIRCUMSTANCES REQUIRING A SECOND MONK

My Śaiva monastics follow the tradition of not holding serious or lengthy private conversations in person or by telephone without another monk present. Gracious, impersonal small talk in public is, of course, allowed. Aum.

SŪTRA 354: THE TRADITION OF NOT TOUCHING

My Śaiva monastics maintain a strict nontouching policy. They do not shake hands or embrace. However, if someone unaware of their protocol initiates such contact, they do not recoil, but respond appropriately. Aum.

SŪTRA 355: DEMURENESS IN CONVERSATIONS

My Śaiva monastics, in respect, stand no closer than an arm's length during conversations. When speaking to men and women together, they direct their attention mostly to the men, as is traditional. Aum Namaḥ Śivāya.

Instructions for Swāmīs

SŪTRA 356: UPHOLDING YOGASWAMI'S AND MY TEACHINGS

My *swāmīs* know there is strength and guidance in orthodoxy and avoid adopting the new for its own sake or because the old seems an arduous path. They uphold traditions that have survived the trials of time. Aum.

SŪTRA 357: PRESERVING THE AUTONOMY OF OUR LINEAGE

My *swāmīs* rigidly maintain the Nandinātha Sampradāya as independent and absolutely separate from the Smārta *daśanāmī* orders and all other lineages. Yea, this autonomy shall endure until the end of time. Aum.

SŪTRA 358: MY SWĀMĪS DO NOT SPEAK OF THEIR PAST

My *swāmīs* never speak of their past or the personal self they have renounced. Those who know tradition do not ask, for one never looks for the source of a *ṛishi* or a river. These always remain shrouded in mystery. Aum.

SŪTRA 359: REMAINING APART FROM FAMILY MATTERS

My *swāmīs* do not participate in births, weddings or other intimate householder events, always remaining aloof from such activities. Nor do they attend funeral rites, except those of brother monks and *satgurus*. Aum.

SŪTRA 360: THE BROTHERHOOD OF RENUNCIATES

All those in saffron robes who have braved death to the world are the brethren of my *swāmīs*, who appropriately honor authentic male *swāmīs* older than themselves and touch their feet in homage. Aum Namaḥ Śivāya.

Instructions for Āchāryas

SŪTRA 361: THE SACRED DUTY OF MY ĀCHĀRYAS

My *sannyāsins* who are *āchāryas* are the supreme architects of our *sampradāya's* future and the fulfillers of these *Nandinātha Sūtras.* They carry this responsibility on top of their head. Yea, they are chosen ones. Aum.

SŪTRA 362: TAKING RESPONSIBILITY FOR CHURCH KARMAS

My *sannyāsins* who are *āchāryas* realize that they are not beyond the laws of the land, but must work within them, even to the point of apologizing should misconduct occur on the part of Saiva Siddhanta Church. Aum.

SŪTRA 363: NEVER DEMEANING OTHERS

My *sannyāsins* who are *āchāryas* nurture each devotee equally. They never make others their servants, order them about, shout at them, snap their fingers, clap their hands, nor strike or demean them at any time. Aum.

SŪTRA 364: MY ĀCHĀRYAS SPREAD LOVE AND LIGHT

My *sannyāsins* who are *āchāryas,* filled with love and helpfulness, promote joy and harmony among the congregation. They never anger, incite fear or take advantage of a person's health, wealth or well-being. Aum.

SŪTRA 365: THE END IS ONLY THE BEGINNING

Numberless successors of the Nandinātha lineage have gone before me. Numberless shall follow. I have woven these 365 threads of wisdom, but there is infinitely more to know of the mysterious Nāthas. Aum Namaḥ Śivāya.

Ādhāra Granthāḥ

आधार ग्रन्थाः

Resources

Haṭha Yoga

हठयोग

RESOURCE ONE

Haṭha Yoga

Iḍā is the Gaṅga of the lower world, *piṅgalā* the river Yamunā, and between iḍā and *piṅgalā* is *sushumṇā*, the subtle river Sarasvatī. It is said that to bathe in the confluence of the three rivers leads to the Great Result.

Śukla Yajur Veda, Trishikhi Brāhmaṇa Upanishad, 316-317

HAṬHA YOGA IS A SYSTEM OF BODILY POSTURES, OR *ĀSANAS,* CREATED AS A METHOD FOR THE *YOGĪ* PRACTICING *YOGA* FOR LONG HOURS EACH DAY, PERFORMING *JAPA* AND MEDITATION, TO EXERCISE AND KEEP THE PHYSICAL BODY HEALTHY SO THAT his meditations could continue uninhibited by disease or weakness. That is how it was explained to me long ago. The great, fully illumined *ṛishis* of old, in order to serve mankind, completely inwardly motivated the external world for good upon good upon good, as do the great *ṛishis* of India today as well. They sat in their caves, in forests or on river banks to think upon the *karma* of the masses and take it into their minds by understanding mankind's predicaments. The impact of the cause-and-effect actions would affect their physical body. Outside of meditation, they would perform their routine of *āsanas* to untie the knots of these *karmas* they had taken onto themselves, and the villages and the countries and the individuals within them would improve. These great *yogīs* were, indeed, not unlike the Gods. The purpose of *haṭha yoga* today again is the same—to keep the physical body, emotional body, astral body and mental body harmonious, healthy and happy so that awareness can soar within to the heights of divine realization.

Haṭha yoga has come along with advaita yoga from the Sanskrit *ṛishis,* and has been on Earth thousands of years. Each teacher of *haṭha yoga* teaches from the perspective of where he is in consciousness. For example, the *advaitist,* or pure monist, uses techniques of *haṭha yoga* to nurture the *advaita* philosophy within his students. The *dvaitist,* or *dualist,* uses the techniques of *haṭha yoga* to make somebody healthy, to heal kidney problems and for general limbering up of the individual.

In 1969 we performed *haṭha yoga* in the Himalayas above Darjeeling, at 13,000 feet, on India's Tibet/Nepal border. It was there that I was blessed with a very great unfoldment of blending all the major *haṭha yoga* techniques and practices into a concise system captured in Shūm, our language of meditation. This took place in the presence of over seventy-five devotees who had gathered from several countries, the largest such group to ever pilgrimage to India, we were told at the time.

Haṭha yoga as it is generally being taught now in the Americas and

---

On the edge of a rock cliff, a limber yogī *performs* haṭha yoga *alone in the stillness of morning. Behind him, near the border between Canada and the United States, the famed Niagara Falls cascades over the rocks, dwarfing the tourist boat below which keeps a respectful distance.*

in Europe is quite different than it originally was. The presentation of *haṭha yoga* in Shūm molds it into its original simplicity. The Shūm language perspective of *haṭha yoga* is of the Nandinātha Sampradāya. It is a more mystical perspective than ordinarily seen today. In our *haṭha yoga* we work with color, we work with sound and with the subtle emotions and feelings of the body when going from one *āsana* to another. That is the difference. Each *āsana* carefully executed, with regulated breathing, the visualization of color and the hearing of the inner sound, slowly unties the knotted *vāsanās* within the subconscious mind and releases awareness from there to mountaintop consciousness. *Haṭha yoga* opens up the consciousness, because when the height of the energy, the zenith, is reached in each posture and we change to the next posture, a small or large adjustment occurs within the physical and astral nerve system.

True, there are those who regard it as a means of health, longevity, fitness, stamina or disease abatement. *Haṭha yoga*, or *banasana* as we call it in Shūm, is a harmless way of exercising the body, and it does produce all of these results. The results come more readily to those who have a subconscious foundation of Vedānta and a background of Siddhānta, temple worship. By this I mean the born Hindu who was raised in a religious home, worshiping in the home shrine, going to the temple with his parents, which is Siddhānta, and if fortunate, learning Vedānta. *Haṭha yoga* blends Vedānta and Siddhānta in the psyche of the devotee, as does *japa*, laying the foundation for deep meditation on Siddhānta and Vedānta. European and American devotees, even without having had these privileges, when practicing *haṭha yoga* become healthy and experience a certain mental peace. These are my observations over the past fifty years. *Haṭha yoga* and the basic techniques of *prāṇāyāma* should not be overdone. They are totally safe in moderation. And *japa* with the universal *mantra Aum* is beneficial to those of all religions and faiths and beliefs and nonreligions and all ism's.

Traditionally, *haṭha yoga*, or *āsana*, is the third step in the eightfold *yoga* system outlined by Ṛishi Patanjali in his *Yoga Sūtras*. It is preceded by *yama* and *niyama*, the moral restraints and spiritual observances. Many people practice it today without having been established in the *yamas* and *niyamas*. Yet, the results, obtained slowly, bring them into the *yamas* and *niyamas*, which are the foundation of *yoga* in Hinduism.

The great *gurus*, *ṛishis* and *swāmīs* who came from India and taught *haṭha yoga* at the turn of the twentieth century, guided the inquiring souls in a traditional way. At the turn of the '60s those who came from India teaching *mantras* and high-powered *prāṇāyāma* techniques led them astray. The *yamas and niyamas,* as well as *haṭha yoga,* should precede *mantra yoga.* You need the *ha-ṭha,* meaning "sun-moon," before *mantra japa* should be done. And you need the *yamas* and *niyamas* before *japa* should be done. Once the *yamas* and the *niyamas* and the *ha* and the *ṭha* are all functioning properly, then we can begin performing *japa.*

Twenty-four *āsanas* are taught in our Himalayan Academy. Though there are many more in complex *haṭha yoga* systems, I chose these as an adequate number to be gone through in succession to transfer awareness from the external areas of the nerve system to the inner areas of the nerve system and give a general exercise to the physical body through the performance of them each day. Each position holds awareness in one area of the mind or another. The names given to these positions in the Shūm language name not only the physical position, but also the area of the mind in which awareness is held.

There are two phases in performing *haṭha yoga.* The first is physical, learning to loosen up the body and to properly attain the posture. Once the body can assume the various postures, the second phase can be mastered, moving rhythmically from one *āsana* to another when the energy flow within the *āsana* itself is at its high point. Thus the building of the energy within the body feeds the astral body and brings mental, emotional and physical health. It takes about a half an hour a day to perform the series of twenty-four *āsanas* well, or just ten minutes as a minimum. Group *haṭha yoga* is also good.

The *kriyās,* such as the cleansing of the mucous membranes of the sinuses and of the digestive tract, are an integral part of *haṭha yoga* for many people. This is beneficial for the health, preservation and longevity of the physical body, as is *āyurveda,* which is actually a part of this form of *yoga.* From the Nāthas came *haṭha yoga.* And from it came these various disciplines, which enable you to go into the *prāṇāyāmas,* then into concentration and meditation. But you should prove to your *guru* that you are disciplined first. Truly, *haṭha yoga* is the beginning of all *yogas.* It is the ideal exercise for human beings.

Haṭha yoga is an excellent preparation for meditation. Though meditation can be performed without doing *haṭha yoga āsanas,* it is an aid, a great helping hand, especially for the beginning student. One of the greatest benefits is that it makes the devotee aware of his nerve system—first that he has one, second that it has three or four sections, and third that the nerve feelings within his feet are different from those of his hands and again different from those in his head, and so on. Through this study, he learns that the nerve system and awareness and energy are all synonymous. He becomes aware that he is aware, that he can move awareness from one area to another. Therefore, in daily life he begins to do just that—move awareness out of unhappy conditions of the mind into happy ones, deliberately and at will, for when man equates awareness with the nerve system and with energy, he has, therefore, willpower and can become aware of what he wants to be aware of at will.

Singling Out Seeds of Desire

There is a classic question, "What way is there to control our desires and thus stay balanced?" Years ago, in 1950, I answered this concisely in an aphorism of *Cognizantability,* which you can read in *Merging with Śiva.* Here is that aphorism: "The seed of desire is a false concept in relation to corresponding objects. The conscious mind throws into its subconscious a series of erroneous thoughts based upon a false concept. This creates a deep-rooted desire or complex. Single out the seed of desire by disregarding all other corresponding erroneous thoughts. Then destroy that seed through understanding its relation in itself, and to all other corresponding thoughts. The deep-rooted desire or complex will then vanish."

Our deep-rooted desires or complexes—which are the battle within everyone during certain periods of life—must be defused first. But in order to defuse them, we have to find them. In other words, we have to bring our mind to a point where we can concentrate without any effort, where our mind is so calm and so quiet that we have effortless concentration. In other words, we have to bring our mind to a point where the subconscious mind itself is concentrated, giving birth to an inner peace which surpasses all understanding. In order to do this, the system of *haṭha yoga* was unfolded to very great teachers many thousands of years ago and handed down from teacher to teacher; and one of my teachers handed it down to me.

Haṭha yoga is a system of handling the physical body so that you quiet it through the subconscious mind. *Haṭha yoga* is founded on the principle of holding the body in a traditional posture until the nerve currents figuratively speaking, get tuned up to a perfect pitch. It is like tuning the strings on a *vīṇā.* If you tune the *vīṇā* just right, each string will be in harmony with the others. In *haṭha yoga* we remain in each posture, each *āsana,* until the whole nature is tuned up to that posture. Change into another position and the whole nature will get tuned up to that position, therefore bringing calmness by tuning up the body.

For instance, I extend my right arm out to the side and hold it there. For the first thirty seconds the arm may feel very comfortable , and I will feel all the nerve currents adjusting themselves to that position. After thirty or forty seconds, the arm will begin to feel heavy, and the part of the subconscious mind that controls the body will say, "All the nerve currents have been tuned up to this position. It is time to move to another position." At this point, I move into another position, while visualizing the corresponding color. I again feel the nerve currents readjusting and tuning up to that position. Then the corresponding part of the subconscious mind will again inform me that the arm has been there long enough, and I should move into another position. After going through three positions, this arm feels entirely different from the other arm. It feels alive and vibrant, like a well-tuned *vīṇā,* while the other arm feels ordinary, like any old *vīṇā* that has been lying around.

This is how *haṭha yoga* works: no stretching, no straining, no pulling, no stressing, as the whole body is tuned up to a perfect pitch. You will find that if you practice this series of *āsanas* regularly over a period of time, you will be able to concentrate without any effort whatsoever. In other words, you will be in an automatic state of concentration. You will be alive consciously and much more alive subconsciously than you have ever experienced if you practice this form of *haṭha yoga* consistently and live a balanced, *dharmic* life in keeping with the *yamas* and *niyamas.*

When the body is tuned up through the correct practice of *haṭha yoga,* systematically over a long period of time, the mind becomes so acute that the student is able to single out the seed of desire by disregarding all other corresponding erroneous thoughts. In other words, in the practice of this alone, he is beginning to burn out the seeds of desire from within. When a student practices *haṭha yoga* past the elementary stages, he is watched by his teacher, who observes the progress by evaluating his vibrations, the effect on the skin, etc. Ideally, the student is becoming more spiritual by perfecting the physical body. Through this practice, the physical body will become supple, healthy and good looking. If a person is too heavy, the metabolism will adjust itself. If a person is too light, it will adjust accordingly. Through this practice, the body is becoming a perfect vehicle for the soul to live in. The tensions that have been built up through the years become fleeting, the mind becomes alive and he is able to single out the seed of desire and, in the light of understanding, destroy it. What does that do? That gives birth to a great wisdom through the subconscious mind. In other words, you don't have to think to know. You know, and thinking is a result. Then you are able to become affectionately detached in all of your relations and find a greater love through understanding.

Health and Longevity

Haṭha yoga, coupled with *āyurveda,* regulates the heat of the body, and it is the heat of the body that prevents and wards off disease and all health problems. Therefore, *Haṭha yoga* and *āyurveda,* which balance the energies of the entire body, should be practiced throughout one's lifetime for health and well-being. Satguru Siva Yogaswami, knowing all this, often said a fever is a blessing. From the *haṭha yoga* perspective, it is the heat that destroys, or fries, the germs. It also relaxes the muscle tissue and harmonizes the central and sympathetic nervous system, not unlike taking a very hot bath.

Haṭha yoga and *āyurveda* also produce heat in the body. They work together. There is a formula for increasing the heat of the body in winter and reducing it in summer. When people are discouraged or depressed, the heat of the body goes down. When they are angry and excited, the heat of the body goes up. This is an unregulated heat, guided by emotion. When we eat certain foods, the heat of the body goes up. Other foods make the heat of the body go down. This fluctuation has its corresponding effects on the moods and emotions. It is the regulation and balance of this heat that *haṭha yoga* and *āyurveda* seek for a healthy and productive life. *Haṭha yoga* can cure diseases that can be cured through the balancing of the *iḍā* and the *piṅgalā,* which often brings a diet change, eating good foods according to the guidelines of *āyurveda.*

Acupuncture and massage are also a part of *haṭha yoga,* a part of the same science of *ha* and *ṭha.* Acupuncture, which also works directly on the nervous system, is a refinement of it, as is moving the *praṇas* of the body through *tai chi chuan. Haṭha yoga* does not end with the *haṭha yoga āsanas.* All the rest are part of it, as are hot and cold baths, mineral baths, hot sand and proper foods. *Haṭha yoga* takes in *āyurveda* and *āyurveda* takes in *haṭha yoga.* They are all of a one interrelated system, just like dance. Dance is not only the movement of the body; it is exercise, rhythm, drama, the knowledge of music, knowledge of timing and more. It's an all-inclusive art. Similarly, *āyurveda* does not stand alone. It's a part of *haṭha yoga.* It is the science of life. I would recommend chiropractic to also be a part of the practice of *haṭha yoga.* The tendons are the inhibiting factor. There is no greater healing to be released into the body than through *haṭha yoga, āyurveda,* acupuncture and chiropractic.

When *iḍā* and *piṅgalā* are balanced, the *sushumṇā* is activated. *Haṭha yoga* balances the *iḍā* and the *piṅgalā* because it balances the entire body in which the *iḍā* and *piṅgalā* run. When the *iḍā* and the *piṅgalā* are balanced, the devotee is very present. He is very present. He is not conscious of the past, not conscious of the future. Many take the activation of the *sushumṇā* as the cultivation of *kuṇḍalinī. Sushumṇā* is the spiritual force. It is also the healing force, the primal energy, not only within the physical body, but the astral and mental bodies as well. All self-healings are done through the *sushumṇā* current. It is neither hot nor cold. It is of itself, unto itself, ever present. It gives the all-pervading feeling of the now consciousness. It is *rāja yoga* practice that awakens the *kuṇḍalinī* and guides its journey through the *chakras.* The *kuṇḍalinī* permanently alters consciousness by slowly expanding it into superconscious realms. It is the hot fire that burns cold, that cuts through the force centers which the *sushumṇā* holds together and energizes.

It is the fire which burns hot, through the *iḍā* and *piṅgalā,* if it has been forced into action through premature *rāja yoga* practices. But it burns as a cool fire through the *sushumṇā,* altering consciousness all the way, if the devotee has been properly prepared for many years. This preparation is done by performing *charyā,* which is *karma yoga; kriyā,* which is *bhakti yoga,* unqualified surrender; and *japa yoga,* unceasing repetition of *mantras;* with a firm Śaivite Hindu religious-cultural background firmly implanted in the subconscious mind and followed as a way of life. That is why *haṭha* is the basis of *yoga* which all the *swāmīs* teach. Then from that you go to *karma* yoga, to *bhakti yoga, japa yoga, rāja yoga* and finally to *jñāna.*

When the *iḍā* and *piṅgalā* —the *ha* and the *ṭha*—are balanced, the spiritual force is there, the pure life energy, *sushumṇā,* and it actually seems to rise up the spine, because the *iḍā* and *piṅgalā* balance from the base of the spine up to the nape of the neck. A great peace pervades the seeker, a feeling of nowness, happiness, contentment—but there is no altering of consciousness.

Through the *sushumṇā* current, the energy continually flows down through the top of the head to the base of the spine. It carries with it the *karma* of this life, determining the character of the person, the form and shape of the body. It is the life force that is in tune with the entire universe, feeding through not only the *iḍā* and *piṅgalā* but all the organs of the astral body and mental body. It is this current that one goes into in deep sleep and wakes up energized.

Now, this has nothing to do with the *kuṇḍalinī* force. The *sushumṇā* is not an altering-of-consciousness force. It is a sustaining-of-consciousness force. It is the force of sanity. Therefore, performing *haṭha yoga,* especially in the modern age, when we can become so externalized through emotional upheavals and overt mental activity, brings one back to oneself. We could say the *sushumṇā* is the *purusha* force, the soul force. It is where the *jīva* lives in the physical body.

Untying Karmic Knots

God Śiva created the soul perfect, but the mischievous actions of the *jīvas,* embodied souls, manifest various entanglements, *karmas,* actions and reactions. Fresh *karmas* are embedded in the sympathetic nerve system, and if serious, in the central nerve system. *Haṭha yoga* is the healer, the first-aid kit, for the results of mischievous actions of Śiva's *jīvas.*

Iḍā and *piṅgalā* are the tools of the *jīva* to express its creativity and work through its various *karmas* of each birth. The nervous system is the vehicle for the soul's experience of *karma,* the back-and-forth battle within the physical, sensual universe. Therefore it needs to be strong. *Haṭha yoga* is exercise for the nervous system, the only science for this purpose, reaping a strong network in which the soul can go through these experiences. *Haṭha yoga* balance brings the *sushumṇā* into prominence, keeps the system healthy by being balanced and being fed by the *sushumṇā.* It is the *kuṇḍalinī* force rising through the nervous system that builds a new nerve system.

Haṭha yoga can also be of psychological, mental benefit. It is a do-it-yourself psychological tool, a harmless antidote to physical, mental and emotional diseases. It is a harmless remedy for uneasiness. *Haṭha yoga* exercises the physical body and the emotional body, which is the astral body, in a controlled and a systematic way. A byproduct of this is a certain amount of benefit to the mental body. Its conscious and subconscious states of mind become quiescent. Superconsciousness temporarily prevails. That makes it the first of the *yogas* and the last of the *yogas.* The *jñāni* will practice *haṭha yoga,* the *rāja yogī* would, so would the *bhakti yogī,* so would the *karma yogī,* as would all who own a physical body. It is all-inclusive and will amplify the results of all the other *yogas* that are going on. It would lead one to the Hindu temple, to the Gods. They are the great psychologists and psychiatrists for the Hindu. Because *haṭha yoga* really does stimulate the *kuṇḍalinī śakti,* Lord Ganeśa is stimulated within the *mūlādhāra chakra,* and one is drawn to Lord Gaṇeśa in a temple, or to a picture of Him.

If we are flowing through an area of the mind where we are aware of the emotional area of the nerve system, if we are having mental arguments with ourselves and we sit down and begin to practice the *haṭha yoga āsanas,* we become aware of energy in its natural state. We cease being aware of energy in its mirage of vibrations of the external nerve system. We have, in effect, shifted gears from the external to the internal after doing a few *āsanas.* This does not mean that after we finish our *haṭha yoga* session that we cannot get up and go into another room and continue the argument with ourself, or go back into the confused area of the mind of fears, worries or doubts.

If you have a negative experience with someone, *haṭha yoga* can help you regain a balance. If someone antagonizes you, you feel it in your solar plexus and nervous system. You can either swim ten laps, run a mile or perform *haṭha yoga* to regain your inner balance. It harmonizes the forces of the physical and emotional bodies. It does not erase the incident from the mind. Nor does it resolve the matter. That requires other practical steps, such as sitting down and talking it over with the person or performing *vāsanā daha tantra.* You still remember the situation, and if you start recollecting it, you stir up the memory in the solar plexus. You can swim ten laps, run a mile or perform *haṭha yoga* to again regain your poise. So, we can clearly see that *haṭha yoga* is a yoking of the physical, emotional and mental bodies. As its name indicates, the *yoga* of *ha* and *ṭha,* sun and moon, *piṅgalā* and *iḍā,* creates a unified body.

Karmas manifest in the nervous system, be they good, bad or mixed. This is all most desirable for the individual, in that it compels him to use his self-propelling force. All small and large tensions in the body are the result of mixed *karmas* and bad *karmas* that have not been resolved. Positive *karmas* create no tensions within the body. They dispel disease, harmonize the nerve system and keep the muscles relaxed. *Karmas* are forces leading to fulfillment, set in motion by the individual himself somewhere in his past. The performance of *haṭha yoga*, balancing of the *ha* and the *ṭha*, untangles the nerve system and regulates the timing of these *karmas*, so that they do not, in their fulfillment, reentangle the nerve system.

Congested, unresolved, seeking-to-be-dissolved *karma* manifests as knots in the nerve system which can be seen as darkness or redness in the aura. You can carefully work with them through *haṭha yoga*, *āyurveda*, massage, chiropractic and acupuncture. With this union of approaches, results will be obtained that will be very satisfactory. Resolution can be stimulated through loosening the *karmas* through *haṭha yoga*. Then, when they come up in the mind or in interpersonal relationships, the use of spiritual journaling, *vāsanā daha tantra;* the use of *bhakti yoga* techniques, putting the problems at the feet of the Deities and sending prayers to the *devas;* the practice of *karma yoga*, selfless service; and of *japa yoga* will eventually resolve these *karmas* by dissolving the emotion connected to the memory patterns.

Young people, before the age of twenty-five, in the *brahmacharya āśrama*, are generally more consistent with their *haṭha yoga* practices than older people. This is not just because they are young, but because few of their *prārabdha karmas* have manifested. From twenty-five to fifty, the *prārabdha karmas* of this life manifest in their fullness. This is the time when *haṭha yoga* is most beneficial. Some of the *karmas* created in past lives manifest first in the astral body, then in the physical body. Through *haṭha yoga* and simple *prāṇāyāma*, they can be conquered in the astral body itself. However, if they are persistent *karmas*, manifesting in the physical body as tensions, *haṭha yoga* becomes a total life- and environment-changing process.

Often people give up *haṭha yoga* to stop the process of change. Others persist and finally dissolve the *karmas* systematically, one after the other. We often see people begin on the spiritual path and then abruptly leave it, burying themselves in their moods and emotions. The regular practice of *haṭha yoga* is self-discipline, which is a basic aid in character building. A good character and strong willpower are essential to advance oneself spiritually. *Haṭha yoga* may be done all through life. If a person gives it up, he suffers the consequences. It is the most perfect form of exercise. But it is certainly not the *yoga* of all *yogas*. It is a physical, mental, emotional, intellectual harmonization. When you have taken unto yourself many responsibilities and divided your awareness, *haṭha yoga* often becomes one of your last priorities and you may neglect it and, in a sense, sacrifice your body for your duties. But that does not mean that you are going to be rewarded with a lot of health or longevity. You will have to compensate by doing a lot of walking. I think that *haṭha yoga* is the overlord of all exercises. Each posture affects a certain organ and a state of mind connected to that organ.

Karma can be experienced externally, or internally in a softened way, through *haṭha yoga.* It is according to the nature of the *karma* that the devotee experiences one kind of release or another. Small *karmas* can be totally dissolved within oneself. Large, negative and mixed *karmas* would return, and if there is a lesson to be learned will be experienced in the outside world but mitigated or softened through *haṭha yoga* and the *vāsanā daha tantra,* which if practiced regularly do bring flashes of superconsciousness into the person's understanding mechanism.

There is still another kind of *karma* that people carry, and that is the *karma* of other people. Certain people are parasitic and want someone else to live their life for them. These kinds of *karmas* can be very heavy on the nerve system. But they can be resolved and thrown off immediately through *haṭha yoga.* We cannot help but help our loved ones with their *karmic* experiences. Therefore, the *haṭha yoga* and basic *prāṇāyāma* techniques and all that we have explained so far keep the motherly and fatherly people of this world helpful but unburdened.

Western Seekers

The millions of people who practice *haṭha yoga* just to stay limber and beautiful are also on the path of mitigating mixed and negative *karmas.* Even the time that they use performing *haṭha yoga* keeps them out of mischief. Anyone who is practicing *haṭha yoga,* no matter what his basic belief system is, is exposed to basic tenets of Hinduism. He becomes attracted to books on *haṭha yoga,* written in India, which are full of Hinduism. *Haṭha yoga* has come to be a basic household *yoga* in the modern world. This is a break-away from tradition, but it has worked out well.

Many seekers delve into elaborate, high-powered *prāṇāyāmas,* breathing practices. But you don't need elaborate or high-powered *prāṇāyāmas* for effective *haṭha yoga.* The simplest are the best. There are two ways to practice *prāṇāyāma.* One is to control and regulate the breath, which in turn regulates the *prāṇas.* The other is to use the breath and the *prāṇas* to awaken the *kuṇḍalinī* fire. This is *rāja yoga*, not *haṭha yoga*. *Haṭha yoga* is balancing the heat and cold that already exist within the body. *Rāja yoga* is awakening the fire to deliberately burn out *karmas* that have not yet manifested in this life—good, bad and mixed—or which may not manifest until another life. There is a great difference here. Many other *yogas* have to be gone through and perfected before *rāja yoga* should be practiced. A university medical school does not put a scalpel in the hand of a novice. In *rāja yoga*, the patient is himself. He must be well prepared.

What is the phenomenon of spontaneous, uncontrollable movements and shaking of the body that seekers sometimes display? These "*kriyās*" are similar to other emotional releases, like laughing and crying, depression and demobilization of physical functions through the loss of the will. They come spontaneously, often unbidden, and are more often experienced by those who do not have a firm philosophical Sanātana Dharma foundation within their subconscious mind. These actions are wrongly thought to be desirable signs of spiritual progress, but in reality they are unnecessary shaking and jerking of the body. In Śaiva Siddhānta, this is not a part of spiritual practice, but is considered a fairly primitive release, as is speaking in tongues, the primal scream and incomprehensible trances which, as described by the *ṛishis*, one goes into as a fool and comes out of as a fool. None of these are transforming to consciousness; they are emotional releases.

A regular regime of *haṭha yoga* can help harmonize and stabilize those kinds of outbursts. It harmonizes the heat and cold, which harmonizes the ups and downs of emotion. The full intent of a developing society is to foster controls. *Haṭha yoga* is a control. So are the basic *prāṇāyāmas*. They add to a flourishing society. We are not in favor of going back to primitive, uncontrolled outbursts and fostering departures from society by individuals with no structure whatsoever to sustain themselves. This is the cultish nuisance which society deplores today.

The Nerve System

In *haṭha yoga* we are moving our awareness from an external part of the nerve system to an internal part of the nerve system. In doing so, the physical cells adjust. It takes time for the physical body to change. Therefore, *haṭha yoga* and *āyurvedic* nutrition for meditation should be worked on consistently over a period of time for positive results to manifest—at least one year or a year and a half.

As we move awareness into the internal nerve system, the physical body begins to respond. It begins to become lighter. The muscles begin to relax. There have been people who have experienced states of superconsciousness which enabled them to immediately to sit in lotus position, *padmāsana;* whereas previously they couldn't sit in that position at all. The superconscious system completely dominated the external nerve system with a rush of bouncing energy, and that internal nerve system took over the physical body temporarily.

This is what we want to accomplish. We want to be living in the inner nerve system and have it motivate the forces of the physical body, rather than living in the external nerve system, which should basically take care of the functions of elimination, keeping the blood circulating and the other instinctive functions of the body. Because we become conscious of the nerve system as being the physical body, we relinquish our consciousness of skin and bones as being the physical body. That's also what we do when we learn to dance. It is the nerve system that dances. The physical body's movement is only a reaction. Therefore, one could dance sitting still, not moving at all.

From a mystical perspective, the nerve system is the area of the mind within man's body through which energy bounces. It is through the nerve system that we become aware of three worlds: the external world, objects, things, people; the world of thought, concepts, precepts, light; and the world of rarefied space, of inner space in the internal areas of the mind. Energy bounding through the nerve system is encased in an energy sheath which disseminates highly charged actinic energy into another type of energy called actinodic force, and then into odic force.

The subtle nerve system is unseen by any type of physical mechanism, in the same way electricity is unseen. This is called the psychic nerve system. The physical nerve system can be seen, as this energy becomes translated into odic force. These nerve systems in depth in the external working together cause man to be what he is as man.

A good way to portray the inner nerve currents would be with the example of an onion. You have one skin on top of another skin on top of another skin on top of another skin—or like a gem stone, for instance a diamond. You have one layer on top of another layer on top of another layer on top of another layer. Esoterically, nerve currents are not like a bunch of little wires. That is only seeming. That is the way it looks when you look from the external world in, but when you look from the inner world out, you see them in sheaths or layers, completely covering the entire being of man, one vibratory rate to another that awareness is moving through. It's not flowing out one little channel and another, so to speak. Nerve currents are like great rooms of a house rather than the hallways. Try to experience for yourself this new way of looking at nerve currents. Visualize yourself as an onion.

The practice of *haṭha yoga āsanas* makes us aware of the totality of the nerve system, both the inner realms of the nerve system and the external. Man in everyday life is only aware of his external nerve system. He is not aware of the internal, and he is not aware that he is unaware of the internal areas of the nerve system. He is only aware of the external, of what he sees and what is in the immediate range of his feeling mechanism, his emotional mechanism and intellectual mechanism, and he generally is programmed to feel and see more or less the same things all the time. That's why he wishes to go on a vacation, so he can see and feel different, or exercise other areas of the nerve system. The practice of *haṭha yoga* brings awareness of the other areas of the nerve system which are active all the time, and thus brings a certain improvement in physical health and emotional relaxation, simply because awareness is transferred from one area of the nerve system into another, and mental peace is felt because he is aware of the area of the nerve system which is peaceful.

Haṭha yoga āsanas loosen the muscles around the bones and increase the circulation of the blood, causing man to be aware of the nerve system as it flows through the physical body only. Man in everyday life is aware of the nerve system as it flows through the emotions or through the intellect. A new, challenging idea comes to him, and he begins to go into the thinking area of the mind. If he becomes confused in that area, it reacts back emotionally on him. Many, many hours of the day, he is not aware of the physical body or the energies flowing through it. *Haṭha yoga* brings awareness right to the physical body, right into the spine, where energy begins flowing through the physical body, the emotions and the mind. He studies these energies and becomes what is called perceptive, or he becomes aware in the area of the mind that is refined.

Threefold Purpose

In summary, the purpose of *haṭha yoga* as taught in the Himalayan Academy is threefold. 1) First is self-discipline. To regulate the study into a daily practice, the seeker has to actually perform this discipline with his physical body each day. This regulates his time and builds a good habit pattern for his approach to meditation. 2) Second is control of awareness. Immediately the seeker gains the ability to detach awareness from that which it is aware of and fulfill the first step of the basic philosophy. 3) Third is mastery of the nerve system and preparation for meditation. *Haṭha yoga* makes the seeker aware of the inner nerve system as opposed to the outer nerve system. Thus it sets the stage for him to begin his meditations in the correct area of the nerve system. In one area of the nerve system we approach daily life. In another area of the nerve system we approach meditation. Awareness travels between the two. The mature, unfolded mystic is fully conscious of both areas of the nerve system and therefore is within himself while doing his daily duties.

Twenty-Four Haṭha Yoga Āsanas

A System of Body Tuning and Preparation for Meditation

PRESENTED HERE ARE EIGHT SETS OF THREE POSTURES TO BE PERFORMED IN SERIES. THESE RELATIVELY EASY *ĀSANAS* CONSTITUTE A BALANCED SYSTEM FOR DAILY USE. EACH POSE IS TO BE HELD IN RELAXED STILLNESS FOR 30 TO 120 SECONDS, WITHout straining. As maximum stretch and flexibility are achieved, subtle stimulation of the physical and psychic nerve system occurs.

Perform the postures daily in the privacy of your own room, without drawing attention to yourself. Naturally, they should not be performed after meals. Don't worry if you can't perform the poses perfectly, or if some are difficult for you. Do the best you can. Progress at your own pace. With practice, you will find the body becoming more supple, reflecting the mind's flexibility, alertness and freedom from subconscious repressions. By controlling breath we control thought and life energy, or *prāṇa. Yogīs* call this *prāṇāyāma*. The *prāṇāyāma* for these *āsanas* is simple: breathe in for nine equal counts (ideally counting with the heartbeat), then hold one count, breathe out nine counts, hold one, and so on.

Each set includes a color visualization to quiet the mind and intensify healing. The color described at the top of each page is the color to visualize while in the poses on that page. Mentally fill your body with that color, from your head to your toes; or imagine yourself suspended in space, surrounded on all sides by the color. If you discover tensions in the body or mind, visualize them flowing away as you exhale. At the end of your *yoga* session, sit quietly and plunge into meditation. Tradition sets the best times for *haṭha yoga* at dawn, noon and twilight. Minimally, only twelve minutes of time is needed.

Cautions: Anyone with neck or back problems should abstain from poses that place strain on the spine, such as the headstand and the shoulder stand. For best results, *haṭha yoga* should be taught by a qualified teacher. The instructions given here are a rudimentary aid.

At dawn a devotee practices an advanced haṭha yoga āsana *as part of a series that will prepare him for meditation. Each day in his shrine room, where Lord Gaṇeśa has been installed in a stone wall, he follows a one-hour spiritual routine of* yoga, *worship and meditation.*

Set One

Visualize deep, ruby red for physical vitality.

1. Bend the right leg back around the thigh and tuck the right foot along the contour of the buttocks. Bring the left leg in front of the torso, tucking it close to the groin. Hands are on the knees, in the *ākāśa mudra,* palms up, thumb and index fingers touching. Keep the spine, the powerhouse of the body, straight and the head erect and balanced at the top of the spine.

2. Assume the same posture as in *āsana* one, but with the leg positions reversed. Remember to keep the spine erect and the head balanced atop the spine. Become aware of the breath, equalized as nine counts in, holding one count, and nine counts out. Flood your mind and body with ruby red throughout this set. Do not strain; try to relax into the pose, letting go of all anxieties.

3. Tuck the right leg into the groin area, then place the left leg in front of it. This is a variation of the accomplished pose, *siddhāsana,* सिद्धासन. If possible, keep both legs resting fully on the floor. Try to sense the energy of the inner and outer nerve system building up to a high point as you sustain each pose. When this peak is felt, gracefully shift during the out-breath to the next *āsana.*

Set Two

Visualize marigold orange for pure, selfless service.

4. From the last pose of set one straighten the left leg, lean forward and grasp the left foot with the thumb and index fingers of both hands. This is the *jānu śīrshāsana*, जानुशीर्षासन, head-to-knee pose. Relax into the position, letting the head drop lower and lower. In full flexibility the head rests on the knee, elbows lower to the floor, and the torso rests on the leg.

5. Perform the same pose on the right side. Do not strain; rather relax into the pose, letting all anxieties depart. Remain conscious of your breath and mentally surround yourself with the color orange. Be perfectly at ease, one with Śiva's perfect universe.

6. Extend both legs into the forward bend, *paśchimottānāsana*, पश्चिमोत्तानासन. Grasp the toes with the thumb and index fingers and let the head gently lower to the knees. In the ideal pose, the legs are straight and elbows will lower to the floor.

Set Three

Visualize sun-glow yellow for purified intellect.

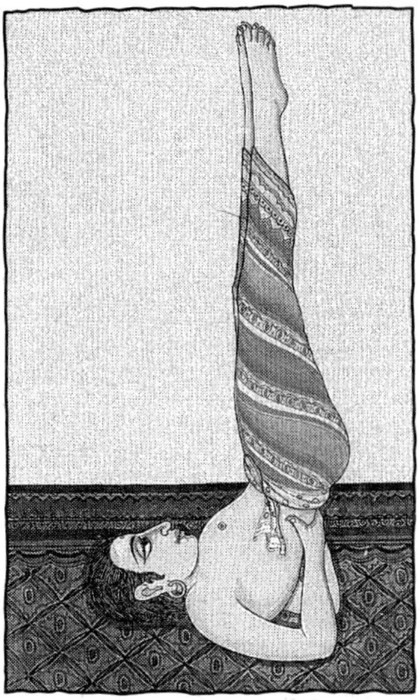

7. Lying face-up on the floor, raise the legs and—with the hands in the mid-back region to support the body—raise the torso until the entire body is vertical over the shoulders. This is the shoulder stand, *sarvāṅgāsana,* सर्वाङ्गासन. Keep the spine straight, feet together, torso perpendicular to the floor. Visualize yellow. ¶As you perform the *haṭha yoga āsanas,* put out of your mind all thoughts relating to your work, family, friends, associates, problems and challenges that normally concern you. Relax. Relax. Relax. Be completely at peace with yourself and fully enjoy this contemplative art.

8. Lower the legs slowly over the head until the toes touch the floor. Then lower the arms, palms down. This is the plough pose, *halāsana,* हलासन.

9. End the set with the corpse pose, *śarvāsana,* शर्वासन, by lowering the legs to the floor in front of you. Let the hands rest loosely by the sides, palms down. Every muscle is relaxed. Imagine you are floating in the ocean, without a worry in the world.

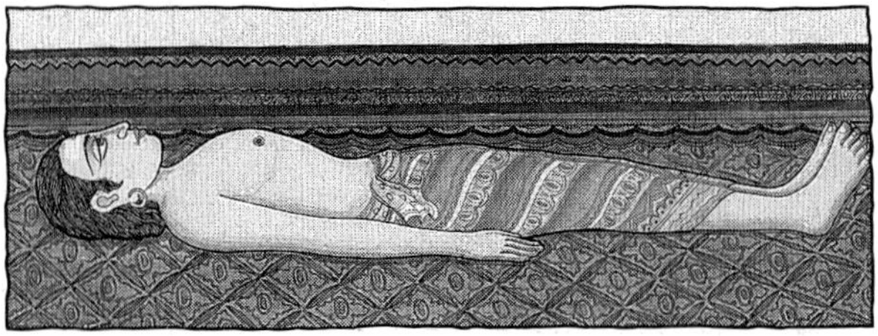

Set Four *Visualize emerald green for physical/emotional health.*

10. Kneel and spread the feet apart, and sit between the ankles, hands on the knees, palms down. This is the heroic pose, *vīrāsana,* वीरासन. Visualize emerald green. In all poses, breathe deeply, fully and diaphragmatically. Let go of tensions in the solar plexus until you are breathing as a baby breathes—not by moving the chest, but by allowing the diaphragm to lower and expand naturally. Think of the action of a bellows which, when expanded, creates a vacuum and allows air to enter. Do not force the breath; relax the body and quiet the mind.

11. Still kneeling, arch back as far as possible until the head touches the floor behind you. This is the couch pose, *paryaṅkāsana,* पर्यङ्कासन. Hold the palms together over the chest in *namaskāra.*

12. When you reach the height of energy, bring the torso up (ideally without aid from the arms) and bend forward until the forehead touches the floor, palms down near the head, buttocks on the floor between the ankles.

Set Five

Visualize bright royal blue for peace of mind.

13. Move the upper body forward, inhale, arch the back slowly and extend the arms until straight, in the cobra pose, *bhujaṅg-āsana,* भुजङ्गासन. Hold the pose for two or three breaths, then lower the torso gracefully, one vertebrae at a time starting at the base of the spine.

14. Bring the legs up, reach back and clasp the ankles. Inhale as you pull the legs up and raise the head and upper body into the bow pose, *dhanurāsana,* धनुरासन. Look up and back. Hold for two or three rounds of breathing. Visualize royal blue. Exhale as you release the legs and lower to the full prone position.

15. Rise into a kneeling position, buttocks on the ankles, and lower the upper body to the floor, in the *pañchāṅga praṇāmāsana,* पञ्चाङ्गप्रणामासन, "five-limb prostration," forehead touching the floor, arms forward, palms down.

Set Six *Visualize purple for the outpouring of spiritual knowledge.*

16. From the last *āsana,* move the body forward and form a triangle of fore-arms and head, hands clasped behind the head, fingers interwoven. The hair-line touches the floor. Raise the body slowly, keeping the knees bent. Pause, then extend the legs vertically into the headstand, *sālamba śīrshāsana,* सालम्ब शीर्षासन. Keep most of the body weight on the arms, not the head.

17. When ready to come down, bend and tuck in the knees and carefully lower into the curled pelvic pose. Remain for at least eight cycles of breath to allow the blood to equalize. Fill your mind with purple.

18. Slowly rise into the upright pelvic pose, hands on knees, palms down. Keep the head down momentarily against the chest in a *bandha,* or lock, and then straighten the neck.

Set Seven *Visualize lavender to purify* karma *through divine sight.*

19. Sit on the left hip and place the right foot over the left knee. Insert the left arm under the bent right knee. Extend the right arm behind the back and clasp the left hand with the right, or, as an easier alternative, grasp the right knee with the left arm. Keep the spine as straight as possible. This is the spinal twist, *matsyendrāsana,* मत्स्येन्द्रासन. Turn the head slowly to the left each time you inhale, and back to the right as you exhale.

20. Repeat the spinal twist pose on the opposite side, visualizing lavender. In each *āsana,* be totally at ease. Harnessing the breath's three phases (inhalation, retention and exhalation) directs the flow of calming and relaxing body and mind.

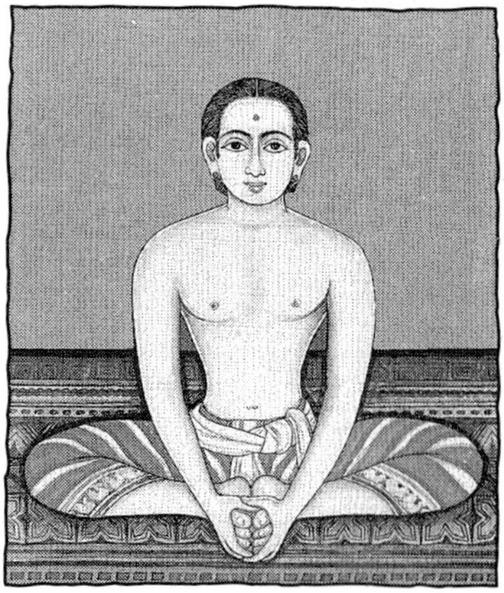

21. Coming out of the twist, bring the soles together and hold the feet with both hands in the bound-eagle pose, *baddha koṇāsana,* बद्धकोणासन. Let the knees lower to the floor. Free the mind of thoughts and tensions, and you will be more aware, more alive, more serene.

Set Eight *Visualize white for purity in thought, word and deed.*

22. Extend the right leg and place the left ankle high on the right thigh. Stretch forward and clasp the right foot with the thumb and index finger. Visualize white. This is a variation of the head-to-knee pose, *janu śīr-shāsana,* जानुशीर्षासन.

23. Repeat this same procedure on the left side, with the right foot on the left thigh. *Āsanas* elongate, tone and strengthen muscle tissue, massage the organs, stimulate the nerves and balance the *piṅgalā* and *iḍā nāḍīs.*

24. Finally, assume the lotus posture, *padmāsana,* पद्मासन. The right foot is already on the left thigh. To complete the lotus, carefully place the left foot on the right thigh. Spine straight with the hands resting in the lap, palms open, right hand on top, with the thumbs gently touching in *dhyāna mudra.* When physical tensions are released through *haṭha yoga,* mental-emotional tensions are automatically dissolved. This is a great secret and a wonderful tool that you can use every day of your life.

Daśamāṁśa

दशमांश

RESOURCE TWO

Religion's Dues

When a man is born, whoever he may be, there is born simultaneously a debt to the Gods, to the sages, to the ancestors and to men.

Śukla Yajur Veda, Śatapatha Brāhmaṇa, 1.7.2.1 VE, 393

NOW WE SHALL EXPLAIN HOW THE SPIRITUAL PRACTICE OF TITHING, PAYING MONTHLY RELIGIOUS DUES OF TEN PERCENT, CREATES WEALTH OVER TIME FOR INDIVIDUALS AND FAMILIES ALIKE—A WEALTH THAT IS BLESSED TO NEVER GAIN LOSSES, but to perpetuate itself generation after generation. Read on and learn! Tithing is giving ten percent, not a dollar more, not a dollar less; not a rupee more, not a rupee less; not a pound more, not a pound less; not a lira more, not a lira less.

God's Money

Everything—from a lump of carbon to a dazzling diamond, a molecule of oxygen to the galactic explosion of a star gone supernova—is of the Being of God. We place lesser and greater value upon things usually dependent upon our interests. Ultimately, we would have to say that everything is God's, including what we manufacture from native elements. Indeed, if all the trillions of dollars, rupees, yen, pounds, rubles, Deutschmarks and francs, and all the precious metals and gems were gathered and compressed together into one giant cube, any Hindu would readily have to admit that man's money and the planet's minerals are really God's.

So, in the first sense, God's money is the sum of all monetary values. Connecting this idealistic perspective to a practical one, where we as individuals are engaged in the *dharmic* pursuit of wealth, God's money is what we dedicate to God, as our religious dues, to perpetuate His greater spiritual design for our planet. This is also true for our personal use of time. God's time is what we dedicate, as roughly ten percent of our time, toward service that furthers our religion. This is outside of the time spent in our personal spiritual practices: home *pūjā*, scripture reading, *japa*, *sādhana* and meditation.

This resource is about joyously returning each month ten percent of our earnings and gifts to God for our own spiritual upliftment and economic welfare, and for the support and perpetuation of our Hindu religion, the Sanātana Dharma, the "Eternal Path." This is the spiritual practice, the unfolding process, of *daśamāṁśa*. In the West it is known as tithe, which means "a tenth." Among the world's religions and faiths, it is

Knowing that all of life's bounty and abundance comes from God, Hindus take joy in giving back a generous portion. Here men, women and children bring baskets of fruit, cloth, jewelry, foods and money to lay at Lord Śiva's Holy Feet for Śaivism to flourish on the Earth.

an ancient common denominator. In the earliest known historical civilizations, Egypt, Sumeria (Mesopotamia) and the Indus Valley, all of which were theocracies, or "God-governed," the totality of the annual produce of the land was, in principle, pledged to the Gods in their temples, then redistributed to the populace.

Imagine the phenomenal results if the ancient practice of *daśamāṁśa* were fully revitalized today. There are over a billion Hindus worldwide. Some 940 million live in India. A large percentage of those, say 600 million, are financially poor—the per capita annual income in India is around US$444. Yet, even if each offered one dollar (which is only a little more than two thousanth's of one percent) as God's money every year, that would total $600 million annually for Hindu institutions from the poor sector alone. If a full ten percent were paid, the amount would be $26.64 billion each year. The remaining 330 million Hindus in India, being mostly in the newly formed middle class (paying, say, an average of $400 tithe per year), would provide an additional annual fund pool of $132 billion. This does not take into account over sixty million Hindus living outside India, some of whom, especially in Western countries, make very high salaries, many as doctors or engineers, and even dot com founders making hundreds of millions. This ancient spiritual levying of *daśamāṁśa*, religion's dues, would give Hinduism some $150 billion dollars each year. Since *daśamāṁśa* is paid by each individual to the institution of his choice, the distribution of the money would be fairly evenly widespread.

Hinduism, having fully entered the 21st century, urgently needs this monetary strength. Hinduism is incalculably rich in religious knowledge, mystic ceremony and spiritual experience. This inner treasure house of Hinduism will never diminish. But the great periphery that touches every Hindu's life does need constant sustenance. Our temples should look like exquisitely wrought jewelry, worthy earthly abodes for God and the Gods, spiritually uplifting for devotees. Our monasteries and lecture halls, schools and cultural centers should glow with inviting beauty and radiate the best the Hindu mind can offer to the world. All Hindus should be well educated in their faith and have every facility available for advancing spiritually, socially, economically and culturally. In the past, the present and into the future, the practice of *daśamāṁśa* has no equal in instilling closeness to God through our *dharma* of gaining wealth, and in a steady provisioning of our religion. It is a proven system needed now.

In this brief presentation, we also outline the benefits an individual or an organizational body will gain from giving God's money. Saiva Siddhanta Church has been managed for almost fifty years on a tithing basis. It achieves results of people's lives unfolding into a greater spirituality, financial security and religious fellowship. These are day-by-day rewards, not easily summed up in a few sentences. But they distill down to the fact that members, largely because they practice *daśamāṁśa*, are happy, healthy, at peace within themselves and among themselves and energetically enthusiastic about advancing their religion. They have cultivated a deep sense of selflessness that recognizes God in all dimensions of their lives. The practice of giving God's money, religion's dues, has become a doorway into tangible inner experience.

Hinduism has always celebrated the merits of giving, both of wealth and knowledge. The householder gives to the children, the poor and the *sādhus*, the children give to the parents in old age, the elderly give to the community, the student and *sādhus* give to the *guru*, and the *guru* gives to all. It is so much a part of our soul nature to give. Every time we give, more of our soul nature is expressed. Yet, when it comes to our hard-earned money, which in Hinduism we call *artha*, "wealth," it is sometimes difficult to give, especially on a regular basis and to a society or institution we may not have a voice in governing. Nevertheless, it is our *dharma* to give of our *artha*. Only by our generous contributions, individually and as a group, will Hinduism flourish and grow from strength to strength. On that the scriptures are unequivocal.

> The powerful man should give to one in straits;
> let him consider the road that lies ahead!
> Riches revolve like a chariot's wheels,
> coming to one man now, then to another.
>
> *Ṛig Veda*, 10.117.5. VE, P. 850-851

To not give generously and regularly is to be unduly self-interested, a condition that will cloud our divine nature and make us feel guilty and stressful. The practice of tithing will do just the opposite: create positive *karma* of abundance and financial opportunity, cultivate family and community bonding and enhance healthy states of mind. And a group that is jointly paying religious dues will enjoy a fulfillment, accomplishment and spiritual joy that is collective.

Examples

An excellent example of the practice of tithing is a group of devotees of Lord Murugan who, to support His temple, generously gave an even larger portion of their income than ten percent. They are the Chettiar salt merchants of Tamil Nadu, South India, who 400 years ago began dedicating one-eighth or 15 percent of their earnings to Lord Palani of the Palani Hills Temple. Recorded testimony of the merchants states that, because of the payment of religious dues, their businesses prospered to the extent that even the *mahārāja* took favorable notice. In the Hindu traditions of South India, donating to charity a fixed percentage of one's income is called *makimai* in the Tamil language.

A contemporary example of tithing is the Swaminarayan Fellowship, whose leader, Sri Sri Sri Pramukh Swami Maharaj, was accorded the Renaissance Award by HINDUISM TODAY and named 1995 Hindu of the Year. His congregation of hundreds of thousands all pay their religious dues through *daśamāṁśa*. With so many dedicated Fellowship devotees paying their tithe to their *guru*, and on top of that giving gold each year in measure equal to his weight, plus selflessly contributing vast quantities of their time and encouraging their children to do the same, that all adds up to a truly powerful force in the world. On the strength of a tithing membership, they built a $4 million temple in the middle of London, inaugurated in August of 1995. They support a strict monastic order of over 650 *sādhus*, run numerous social services and are single-handedly educating millions of people all over the world in the cultural sophistication of India's wonderful Hindu traditions. If more Hindus were to follow their tithing example, Hinduism would be even stronger than it is today. We look forward to an abundant future in the decades to come.

Hindu Children

Here is a story that demonstrates the spirit of *daśamāṁśa*. A businessman in Texas had made several large gifts to the temple and to local charities. Few calls to him for contributions ever failed to receive a willing response. His generosity to community causes was well known to many people who were identified with the organizations he supported. One evening he was introduced as the key speaker at a banquet. The chairman told of a number of instances when the man's generosity had helped to make financial campaigns successful. When the Texas businessman arose to begin his address, he was evidently embarrassed. "I want to make it clear that I do

not deserve credit for what I give to my temple or to any cause in our community," he said. "The way I look at it is that I have contributed none of my own money. The money all belongs to God; for, you see, I am a tither, having in early childhood taken my tithing vow, my *daśama bhāga vrata.*" Most long-time tithers are humble about their regular habit of setting aside a tenth of their income, especially if they started the habit at an early age. For they truly have come to feel that they are but the stewards of God's money and pay their religion's dues with a heart full of gratitude for their abundance, whether large or small.

A California financier related the story of how he began the habit of tithing. He was one of four boys, all about twelve years of age, who were received into membership of a Hindu society. At the conclusion of the *pūjā*, an observer remarked to a respected temple elder, "That was certainly a very auspicious event, wasn't it, Sir?" "To what do you refer?" the trustee inquired. "Why, those four boys coming forward into membership and surrendering themselves to our Gods," the man replied. "Yes, it was," the trustee commented, "but they did not bring fruit and flowers as an offering, nor did they give anything to the *huṇḍi.*"

One of the boys (the financier) overheard the conversation. Later he approached the elder and asked what he would traditionally be expected to give when coming to *pūjās* and for the support of the temple. The elder explained that every Hindu should bring fruit and flowers when coming to a *pūjā* and that it is a spiritual privilege to pay one-tenth of one's income to God in appreciation for His blessings. The elder asked how much the boy was earning. He replied that his part-time wages were only $35.00 each week. The elder suggested that the lad think of $3.50 a week as his contribution for the support of the temple and that he should take the *daśama bhāga vrata* before he begins to set aside his *daśamāṁśa.* In Sanskrit, *vrata* means vow or pledge, *daśama* means tenth, and *bhāga* means part or share, the elder told the boy. *Daśamāṁśa* means tithe, and *tithe* means a tenth. Immediately setting aside the tithe as soon as money is received sanctifies the remaining balance. Once the money has thus been blessed, it would be difficult to use it for a profligate, *adharmic* purpose.

The elder explained to the boy that this is a custom as old as our Hindu religion and that many other religions practice it as well. Thus, the taking of the *daśama bhāga vrata* and then beginning to pay *daśamāṁśa,* religion's dues, can be a very important part of every modern Hindu's life. The lad was pleased to hear that *daśamāṁśa* was an ancient religious practice of giving one-tenth of one's income back to God and the Gods to perpetuate their work on Earth. At the next auspicious occasion in the temple, the boy prostrated before God, Gods and a picture of his *guru* and took his *vrata* without hesitation. A few elders witnessed the event, smiled and signed his certificate. All were pleased to see the brightness on his face as he put the envelope with the $3.50 into the *huṇḍi* before he left the temple. He was now truly one of the congregation in his heart and in the hearts of all.

Now the pattern was set and the boy began the life-long habit of setting aside one-tenth of his income for God's work. Years later, as a seasoned businessman, he declared that he had never ceased to tithe. He felt that he was helped personally more by tithing than by any other habit he had observed throughout his life. It is important to note that the financier began tithing as a boy. Many of the men and women who tithe in this generation say that they also began the practice in their early youth.

Tithing ought to begin in childhood. If boys and girls have the example of their parents to encourage them, the decision to tithe will not be a difficult one to make. Devout children who have been raised in a kindly manner readily respond to the suggestion that God has given us so much that it is only right that we should set aside a portion of all we receive and bring it as an offering to the temple for its support. This is one way of thanking God and the Gods for their goodness. And this is the only way that we truly bless the remaining nine-tenths. Yes, the pattern of a lifetime can best be set by carefully teaching a young person to begin tithing with the first money he or she is given or earns.

Paying Religion's Dues Monthly

Many Hindus have never learned to give systematically. They follow no plan in facing their responsibility to the temple they worship in, the society they belong to or the community they live in. Tithing provides a spiritual plan for meeting these responsibilities. The key is to regularly, on a monthly schedule, set aside in a special saving account or envelope one-tenth of one's income as soon as it is received; then, again on a monthly schedule, to give that sum to a religious organization of one's own choosing.

Most Hindus give if they are specifically asked for a contribution and their name is published. Others give generously if they hear the temple needs an extra amount to pay a deficit. Many such persons feel virtuous if they are enabled to pull the temple out of what they think is a "financial hole." They fail to consider that the deficit would never have occurred if they, and others, had voluntarily and regularly contributed their share during the first week of each month. Some Hindus give only if they like the priest, others if they are supporting some phase or all of a special festival. Still others only give out of a sense of appreciation for prayers being answered.

We were acquainted with a negligent Hindu in London who never failed to boast about how he had helped to erect a temple, even though he had not attended a *pūjā* for many years. Yet, he often bragged that he had helped build the temple. We came to believe he had given a very substantial sum for the building. He had left such an impression with so many people. But one day someone took it upon himself to look into the past financial records of the temple and discovered that the man had contributed the "magnanimous" total of $101! All this time he had avoided his responsibilities to the Gods and to their temple by giving the false impression that he had given so much that he should not be expected to contribute any more.

The Rediscovery of Tithing

Our young generation of modern Hindus are awakening to an awareness of the need for a fuller and more dedicated life in God consciousness. The trends in current civilization in this technological age indicate that we must go deeper into our faith and into ourselves if we are to spiritually unfold and experience the bliss that is ours to enjoy. Thoughtful contemporary Hindus are made aware every day of the conflicting forces which war in the world during this time in the *Kali Yuga.* They know that it is a time which cries out for a more complete surrender of money, time and talents to the will of God and our Gods. They are also well aware that it is the religious institutions that keep the knowledge of Hinduism alive in the world and that the temples provide open doors for devotees. Many Hindus conclude that they must teach their children the spiritual merits of tithing from their gifts and later from their earnings.

Money has assumed a place of increasing importance in the life of everyone this century. With each passing year fewer people live the kind of existence in which they themselves produce the basic necessities of life. Money has become the buying power to satisfy almost every physical demand. Even the farmer has come to rely upon money. Only a few decades ago the tiller of the soil raised the food which met the needs of his family. The power to work his fields came from animals which themselves had their subsistence in the land. But now he needs money to operate a farm. He buys rather than raises much of his food. Money pays for the electric power to operate his machinery and for the fuel to run his tractor. His clothing is bought at a store, and his recreation is purchased by the investment he makes in a radio or television.

What has happened in recent years to the farmer has long been the experience of millions of workers who earn their livelihood in the factory or the office. For many people the possession of money has become an end in itself in life. The growing importance of money has turned the focus of attention from the true source of the world's goods. The man who worked the fields to produce the necessities for sustenance was in a position to observe the creating and sustaining power of God and the Gods in his life. When he was dependent upon the rainfall, the sun and the fertile earth for his well-being, it was natural to recognize loving Gods. But such recognition becomes more difficult when money is the source of one's physical and psychological satisfaction. It is harder to see God and the Gods at work in the product of a machine or a factory. Then man is tempted to give his worshipful devotion to a pay envelope or a checkbook. That means money to him. It is the source of his personal comforts and pleasures.

A New Standard Is Needed

In this technological age people are tempted to believe that their skills and ingenuity which produce material commodities come from themselves alone. They either assume the absence of God's power in the world, or God and the Gods are pushed back so far in their mind that no vital contact is felt with these great beings or even their own Divinity. A new standard is needed to put God consciousness first.

When Hindu children recognize God's creative gifts by setting aside a tithe from their gift or income immediately upon receiving it, before any money is spent for themselves or others, they express their conviction that God is the giver of all that they have. Each young person inwardly admits that the product of the mine or the fertile field can only be explained by the long creative process which is the direct result of the existence of God and the Gods that Hindus gratefully acknowledge. The money that the computer engineer, the baker or the manufacturer earns has its ultimate source in those elements which man did not and could not create. Each occupation or profession engaging the efforts of mankind deals with factors beyond the range of man's ability to make.

Children who pay their tithe learn that God continues to be the owner of the material possessions entrusted to them. They know that the final title to property or money does not rest with the individual, but with God. They learn that people may be stewards of worldly possessions for many years; yet, inevitably they must surrender that stewardship at the end of their earthly life. The trust is then transferred to some other person. They slowly come to realize through experience that people do not own the material world; they are merely its stewards.

Honoring God by Sharing

American-born entrepreneur William Colgate was a tither throughout his long and successful business career. He gave not merely one-tenth of the earnings of Colgate's Soap Products; he gave two-tenths, then three-tenths and finally five-tenths of all his income to the work of God in the world. During the latter days of his life, he revealed the origin of his devotion to the principle of tithing. When he was sixteen years old, he left home to find employment in New York City. He had previously worked in a soap manufacturing shop. When he told the captain of the canal boat he was traveling on that he planned to make soap in New York, the man gave him this advice: "Someone will soon be the leading soap maker in New York. You can be that person. But you must never lose sight of the fact that the soap you make has been given to you by God. Honor Him by sharing what you earn. Begin by tithing on all you receive." William Colgate felt the urge to tithe because he recognized that God was the giver of all that he possessed, not only of opportunity, but even of the elements used in the manufacture of his products.

QUESTIONS AND ANSWERS ON RELIGION'S DUES

How can tithing help eliminate debt? My finances are a mess. Tithing helps to establish order in mind and affairs; and when order exists, debt is vanquished. All conditions that are not in order are eliminated. New avenues of supply open up. Intuition is strengthened. Giving opens the door for receiving.

Shall I tithe before my debts are paid? Yes, tithing is the best-known and most practical method of consecrating all your finances to God. You can tithe your way out of debt if you do it through prayer and in the spirit of love and understanding. Practiced properly, tithing will help solve the conditions that create debt. This has been accomplished by thousands of others; it can be done by you. The tithes that you lay at God's lotus feet in loving consecration may be likened to drops of water that, drawn up by the sun, form rain clouds and descend again to Earth in refreshing showers.

Should I tithe on the money I borrow to consolidate debt? No. Nor should you use borrowed money for any purpose other than that for which it was secured.

If I am tithing and my debt becomes heavy, should I stop? A few do tithe for years and, when their expenses become heavy, stop in order to meet their bills. In stopping tithing their desires increase and debts are piled so high that there seems to be no way out. This also leads to a worldliness that causes a distance between themselves and their religious institutions.

Would it be wiser for me to wait before deciding to tithe? If you feel an inner urge to tithe, now is the time to make a start. Those who wait until they feel they have abundance to spare usually never begin.

Won't tithing change my accustomed standard of living? In Hinduism, one's standard of living is measured by the four aims: *dharma* (virtuous conduct), *artha* (wealth), *kāma* (enjoyment) and *moksha* (liberation). *Dharma* governs *artha* and *kāma* so that they are not overly self-centered. Tithing is a *dharmic* act. Your standard of living will be spiritually higher, and in many cases the tither's standards are raised culturally and financially as well.

Will my income improve if I depend totally on God to help? As you tithe faithfully and your affairs become established in divine order, your visible supply will increase. You will be able to avoid debt and to learn to live as befits a child of God. The tithe always returns to you, the tither, as further prosperity and abundance for you and for your loved ones. You can't give anything away but that it eventually comes back to you, even God's money.

Then tithing is an act of faith. Is this correct? Yes, tithing is an act of faith. When you give love with your religious dues, you become receptive to God's blessing of love. Tithing is a positive use of the law of *karma*. When you give freely and joyously with the consciousness of plenty, you draw back to yourself abundance and many happy experiences. This spirit of giving magnetizes the unseen *devas* of the inner worlds who then can give to you by opening opportunities for you.

Will I be convinced once I experience the positive effects of* karma *in my life as a result of tithing? People are most aware of the negative *karmic* effects in their life. But when they become free in their giving, they experience more in return. In conforming to the divine law of *karma*, wonderful things occur in their lives. *Karmic* effects (being either positive, negative or mixed) are created unknowingly by most Hindus and knowingly by some. To use this law to your best advantage, ask for divine guidance and wisdom in spending your money. You will be delighted to see how much more you can do with it and all the benefits that will return to you.

Tithing for the Self-Employed

Is there one key to successful tithing for the self-employed? Yes. It is to separate one's business finances from one's family finances. This is done by maintaining two checking accounts, one for the business and one for the family.

How do the self-employed calculate their tithe? An owner or partner tithes on the income he receives from the business. Firstly, he tithes on his monthly draw from the business. Secondly, he tithes on his share of any net profits earned for the year which exceed his monthly draw.

Please give an example to illustrate this concept for someone who owns his own business. Firstly, a theoretical owner of a sole proprietorship draws $2,500 a month from the business by writing a check on his business account, depositing it in his personal account, then he writes a tithing check for $250. Secondly, in January the year-end financial statements for the business are completed and show a net profit after taxes of $45,000. Since he has already drawn $30,000 during the year, the net profit exceeds his monthly draw by $15,000. Therefore, he needs to tithe $1,500 on this amount. To do this he draws an extra $1,500 from the business, deposits it in his personal account and writes a tithing check for the full $1,500.

If my business is not earning a profit, should I still tithe? It is even more important to be tithing on one's family income if one's business is not doing well.

I know this is rather technical, but how do I adjust my tithe if the amount I have drawn from the business during the year exceeds my share of the business's net profit? This is carried forward and adjusted from one year to the next. For example, say in 1995 your year's draw exceeds your share of the net profit by $10,000. In 1996 your profit share exceeds your draw by $8,000, and in 1997 your profit share exceeds your draw by $15,000. The extra tithe at the end of 1995 is zero, 1996 is zero and 1997 is 10 percent of the $13,000, or $1,300.

Tithing and the Hindu Institution

I have not even given a dollar or a rupee to the temple for a long time. Now I am being encouraged to tithe? When you ceased to give, did you not feel as though you had closed an inner door? Many devotees give a little something as a means of opening the way into a larger measure of loving, living and giving, even if they do not tithe.

How do I decide where to pay my religious dues? The most obvious choice is the Hindu leader or institution that is most relevant to your spiritual life and represents the tradition you find solace in. This benefactor could be in your community, or 10,000 miles away. Or there may be a temple in your community that you and your family worship that would be strengthened and encouraged by your support. If you are not blessed with such an association and do not know exactly where your religious dues would best be used to promote Sanātana Dharma, you can begin by giving to one or more Hindu Heritage Endowment funds of your choice, or create a new fund to benefit one or more institutions of your choice. HHE is a very special foundation designed to support India's diverse spiritual paths and traditions. Begin right away paying ten percent of your income to HHE. Then in the months ahead find the exact institution or project that you feel most inclined to strengthen by your strength.

With this in mind, should I look carefully into each institution? Yes! Tithing should be approached much like investing in the stock market for a secure return. Religious leaders have a duty to perform in spending the money wisely, as do corporate presidents. Choose an institution that will grow and bring spiritual dividends.

Is there a responsibility on receiver as well as the giver? Yes! Both are stewards of God's money. Wisely choose a worthy temple, Hindu church or institution that you feel good about paying your tithe to.

Ways and Means of Giving

My tithe will not be much to begin with. Will the leaders judge me because of this? A religious leader does not or should not judge the offerings of devotees. Hindus give according to their means. If a devotee's circumstances dictate a small tithe, then that tithe is worth great value to God, for the wealthy can easily afford to tithe. Tithing is totally fair; for each one is paying his religious dues of ten percent of his income, small or large. Someone earning $300 a month or someone earning $300,000 dollars a month are giving the same proportionate amount.

Is tithing a gift? The religions of the world don't look at the tithe that they receive as a gift. They look at it as a payment. More than often, those who cannot pay their tithe also do not pay their creditors.

Is it appropriate to give more than ten percent? After the dues of tithing are paid, further religious giving can take place, such as sponsoring temple construction and supporting other religious endeavors. There is a big difference between *daśamāṁśa,* which is an obligation or payment, and religious giving from the remaining 90%. Many tithers give five to ten percent above and beyond their tithe for building funds and other inspiring projects. This is especially frequent in the case of single men and women.

Does tithing include produce grown on one's property for non-commercial purposes? Yes, give a tenth of any food you grow: one coconut for every ten, one banana for every ten. This is only proper, for the one coconut, one banana are not your own. They belong to God and the Gods.

What about tithing of one's time? Tithing can and should also be applied to time, skills and talents. For example, if a devotee is a carpenter or seamstress, those skills may help a local Hindu institution. Everyone, no matter what their skills, can and should give ten percent of their time each week in service to their religious institution. We calculate it as four hours a week, which is ten percent of a forty-hour work week, which amounts to 208 hours a year. It is also acceptable to tithe one's time in intense projects all at once, rather than each week. For example, many of the devotees who helped build the Swaminarayan temple in London took time off from their professions for a full month and labored twelve hours a day to build that magnificent edifice. It has been our experience that those who tithe openly, honestly, spontaneously also give 10 percent of their time in service. Those who live beyond their means, juggle their income and manipulate don't have time to give 10 percent of their time for religious service. That has been our experience.

Shall I tithe on my monthly social security check? Yes. As the amount of your social security check has no direct relationship to the amount of social security withholdings over the years from your paychecks, it is best to look at what was withheld as a tax that you paid to the government for the privilege of receiving social security in your retirement years. Your employers have also contributed to the social security program based on the wages they paid to you. It is even possible that the amount of your total social security withholdings is only a small fraction of what you receive back from social security in monthly checks.

What is the difference between gross and net income? Gross income is your salary or wages before any deductions are taken. Net income is the amount after deductions which, of course, is the amount of the paycheck. Deductions are withholdings for federal and state taxes, social security and other such items. The tithe is calculated as ten percent of the gross income.

The Proper Spirit of Tithing

What are some of the abuses of tithing? Many clever people who are in business create "tithing shelters." They only pay themselves a little bit out of their own business, and the rest of the profits go toward business expenses, like the rent, the food and everything. In other words, they establish a tithing shelter, so they won't have to give much tithe. Finally, their conscience will come up and hurt and they will straighten out their methodology. Others are happy to tithe because they save on taxes. They figure out right to the penny, right to the rupee, how much tax they save by how much they tithe. That is also not the spirit of tithing. There are those who have taken a pledge to tithe who, instead of tithing monthly, actually use God's money for two or three months to get interest or to pay debts, then finally regather the funds together and tithe with a great effort. Bargaining and manipulating in that way is not the spirit of *daśamaṁsa.*

Devotees of our organization tithe freely, wholeheartedly, without thought of such matters. The Singaporeans or the Malaysians get no tax benefits from tithing. They tithe because of their heart, and therefore, *puṇya,* good merit, comes back to them. So, we can see it as a spiritual practice, not an intellectual practice. Tithing is a very simple practice, giving the first payment first—giving one-tenth of God's money back to God. Someone gives you ten dollars; one dollar goes to God, and the rest is for you. If you get a paycheck for $1,000 before deductions and $700 after deductions, you don't say to yourself, "Well, I can't give $100 of the $1,000, because some was deducted for social security and other benefits." No, tithing is on gross income and the right way is to give the full $100.

What is the best attitude to keep in mind to avoid such abuse? Tithing, giving one-tenth of one's income, possessions or time, is a deeply religious commitment. It is not a business proposition. It is a religious commitment, based on the principle that 100 percent of one's energy comes from God, 100 percent of one's belonging comes from God, 100 percent of one's activity and creativity comes from God. God gives back 90 percent. And God and the Gods keep 10 percent for their work. What is their work? Uplifting humanity through religious organizations of all kinds.

There is a great *swāmī* in India who began his entire organization largely on income from coconuts. Of every thirty coconuts that religious growers take off their trees, they give him three. They don't give excuses and say, "Swāmī only needs two out of every thirty coconuts, because I am saving one coconut out of that batch for my social security." They don't look at all the coconuts and say, "I'll give Swāmī the smallest ones, the ones that I cannot sell." No. Because they are true devotees, they take three of the best coconuts and give them to the *swāmī*. The *swāmī* sells those coconuts to help support his religious institutions. And through this practice the entire community has come up.

There is another Guru Mahāsannidhānam in South India. His local devotees give 10 percent of the rice they harvest. They don't count each grain. They simply take a 10 percent portion and present it to the *swāmī*. We have been at his *āśrama* and seen rice piled twelve to fifteen feet high in the great hall.

Begin Tithing, Then Take Your Vow

If you, as an adult, have not already taken the tithing vow yourself, there is no better time than now. But first begin tithing for six months or more to set the pattern in your own mind that, "yes," you can in the long run actually fulfill this commitment. Once you have convinced yourself, then set an auspicious date to take the vrata.

Include your children. If they believe in the divine laws of *Sanātana Dharma* and have faith in the principle of *daśamāṁśa*, they may be ready to begin tithing. Once they also feel comfortable and fulfilled with this ancient religious practice and you feel they are ready, let them take their *daśama bhāga vrata*. Those taking the vow should repeat the following paragraph in the home shrine or temple before God and the Gods, family, *guru* or a respected elder. Repeat the *daśama bhāga vrata*, the vow to pay religion's dues, three times and create a covenant to tithe. We have enclosed here a *vrata* certificate to document the vow taking. It can be photocopied and enlarged, signed and then framed or kept safely with other valuable papers.

O Divine beings of all three worlds, let us bring our minds to rest in the darśana *of Him who has one tusk. Let us meditate on Him who has the form of an elephant with a curved trunk. May He guide us always along the right path. I, ________________ [name of devotee], believe in you, the one Supreme God, Lord Śiva, and the Gods of our Śaivite faith, and in the Śaiva Dharma. In love and trust I recognize your goodness in providing for my every material and spiritual need. I accept the principle of* daśamāṁśa *(giving one-tenth of my gross income) as the method by which I may acknowledge my gratitude to you, Lord Śiva, and share in helping you fulfill and perpetuate your work on Earth. As an act of dedication, I am resolved this day to begin (continue) the regular practice of tithing.*

Announce Your Intent to Tithe

After you have made your *vrata,* tell the trustees of your temple, Hindu church or society about the decision to pay your *daśamāṁśa,* your religious dues, to their organization during the first week of each month. They will be pleased that they have been chosen by you and be able to plan your contributions into their yearly budgets.

SOUND FINANCIAL PRACTICES

Once you have been inspired to tithe regularly, there are a few financial practices that will assist you. These have been developed over several decades of tithing experience.

1. Make Tithing Your First Budgetary Expense

Put tithing at the top of your household budget list. We suggest that you purchase a book on household budgeting from your local bookstore and, if you don't already have one, purchase a household budget program for your computer. Putting our *daśamāṁśa* first creates a fine feeling and presence of God in our home and lives. We know that our income, as it goes toward home, food, clothing, education, entertainment and culture, is sanctified because ten percent was dedicated to God. As we enjoy our home, its furnishings and the bounty of our life style, we can also feel content that God's work, the welfare of Hinduism and our local Hindu institution are well provided for.

Everybody dreads the time near the beginning of the month when they sit down to pay the bills. Try not to treat the setting aside of God's money as paying one of the bills. Why not create a separate time at the beginning of the month when God's money is calculated and the check is written or cash placed in an envelope? This will help create the proper spirit and attitude. While calculating your *daśamāṁśa,* think how it is helping your religion, your fellow Hindus, yourself and your family now and in the future. Try to sense how you are both a steward of God's money and a partner with God Śiva and the Gods in earning and providing for the family, the community, the nation and the religion.

2. Complete a Formal, Written Reconciliation Annually

For your and the institution's records, it is important to execute a "*daśamāṁśa* reconciliation" once a year. We have provided two sample forms for this procedure, one for individual use and one for self-employed businesses or partnerships (you may photocopy and enlarge these for actual use). These reconciliations give tithers a clear record of their tithing for the year and enable benefiting institutions to create realistic financial plans based on the tithing of its members.

Nandinātha Sūtras on God's Money

SŪTRA 161: ONE-TENTH BELONGS TO ŚIVA

Śiva's close devotees take a vow and joyously tithe ten percent of their gross income to their lineage monthly. This is God's money. Using it otherwise is forbidden—a *karma* reaping loss exceeding all anticipated gain. Aum.

SŪTRA 162: TITHING IS THE FIRST OBLIGATION

My close devotees consider tithing their first expense. They provide a written reconciliation each April, including with it all unremitted tithing. Those behind in tithing are counseled to help them fulfill the vow. Aum.

SŪTRA 163: TITHING'S MANY BLESSINGS

Śiva's close devotees delight in the unfailing law that by tithing freely and wholeheartedly, with a consciousness of plenty, they become receptive to God's blessings and draw to them abundance and happy experiences. Aum.

Tiruvalluvar's *Tirukuṛaḷ* on Earning and Utilizing Wealth

KURAL 81:

The whole purpose of earning wealth and maintaining
a home is to provide hospitality to guests.

KURAL 85:

If a man eats only after attending to guests' needs,
what further sowing will his fertile fields require?

KURAL 87:

Charity's merit cannot be measured by gifts given.
It is measured by measuring the receiver's merits.

Personal Tithing Reconciliation

JANUARY TO DECEMBER, YEAR: ________

Member completing this form:

Name: ____________________

Address: ____________________

____

Beneficiary organization:

Name: ____________________

Address: ____________________

____

1. **Regular Gross Income** — 1.________
   Your salary (before any taxes are deducted) plus interest and dividend income from bank accounts and investments
2. **Business Income**
   a. The amount of funds drawn out of the business during this period (line 2 of your Business Tithing Reconciliation) if applicable — 2a.________
   b. Cumulative net profit less drawings (line 4 of your Business Tithing Reconciliation) if applicable — 2b.________
3. **Special Income** — 3.________
   Such as inheritance or cash gifts at birthdays or other times
4. **Capital Gains** — 4.________
   Gains on investments, the sale of a house, car or other possessions (For example, on a house sale the tithe is 10% of the difference between your sales price and the original price—this is referred to as the "capital gain.")
5. **Total Income** — 5.________
   Add together lines 1, 2(a), 2(b), 3 and 4 and enter the total here.
6. **Tithe Due** — 6.________
   Divide the amount on line 5 by 10 and enter it here. This is the amount of tithe due on your income for this period.
7. **Previous Overpaid Tithing** — 7.________
   Enter the amount of any tithe overpaid from last year here.
8. **Tithe Paid** — 8.________
   List the tithe you actually paid on the current period's income here.
9. **Total Underpaid (or Overpaid)** — 9.________
   Subtract lines 7 and 8 from line 6 and enter the amount here. Place the number in parentheses if it is a negative number and you have overpaid.
   Check one box below.

- ❑ Line 9 is zero (0) and shows my tithe due and the tithe paid to the organization are equal.
- ❑ Line 9 shows my tithe paid exceeds the tithe due by the amount shown. Please carry this forward to the next reconciliation.
- ❑ Line 9 shows my tithe is underpaid. I am enclosing the underpaid tithing.

Signature: ____________________ **Date:** ________

I took my *daśama bhāga vrata* on (date): ____________________

Note: Please make one copy of your completed form for your records and send the original to the beneficiary organization.

Business Tithing Reconciliation

JANUARY TO DECEMBER, YEAR: ________

Member completing this form:

Name: ______________________________

Address: ______________________________

____

Beneficiary organization:

Name: ______________________________

Address: ______________________________

____

1. **Net Profit** 1.__________

   If a sole proprietorship, write the total amount of net profit earned by the business during the year. If a partnership, write the share of net profit earned by this partner.

2. **Funds Drawn** 2.__________

   Write the amount of funds drawn out of the business by this owner/partner for personal use during the year. (Enter this amount on line 2a of your Personal Tithing Reconciliation.)

3. **Drawings Exceeding Net Profits** 3.__________

   Subtract line 2 from line 1. If a negative number, your drawings exceeded your share of net profits for the year.

4. **Carry-over from Previous Year** 4.__________

   If at the end of the previous year your cumulative drawings exceeded your cumulative net profit share, enter the amount on this line. (This amount, if any, is found on line 5 of last year's Business Tithing Reconciliation and is to be entered only if it is a negative number.)

5. **Cumulative Balance** 5.__________

   Add together lines 3 and 4. This is the cumulative balance between your share of net profit and funds actually drawn at the end of this year. Check one box below.

   ❑ Line 5 is negative and shows I have a credit to forward to next year's Business Tithing Reconciliation. (Enter zero on line 2b of the Personal Tithing Reconciliation.)

   ❑ Line 5 is positive and shows I have undrawn income on which tithe is owed. (Enter this amount on line 2b of the Personal Tithing Reconciliation.)

Signature: ______________________________ **Date:** __________

I took my *daśama bhāga vrata* on (date): ______________________________

NOTES:

1. Individuals who are self-employed complete both this Business Tithing Reconciliation and the Personal Tithing Reconciliation and submit both together to the beneficiary organization.

3. Please make one copy of your completed form for your own records and send the original to the beneficiary organization.

Conclusion

Nirvahaṇam

निर्वहणम्

ALL THAT IS ELUCIDATED IN *LIVING WITH ŚIVA* IS THE TRADITIONAL PATH OF *DHARMA* FOLLOWED NOT ONLY BY HINDUS BUT, IN LARGE PART, BY ALL ASIAN PEOPLES. IT SHOWS THE WAY OF WISDOM, PAINTS A PICTURE OF AN IDEAL, CULTURED LIFE TO be lived when the spiritual nature illumines the intellect and dispels ignorance, when the mind holds the instincts in check and overcomes brutality, when striving for perfection brings the soul to realization of the Self within. Śaivite Hinduism is the greatest religion in the world. It has the *Vedas.* It has the *Āgamas.* It has the *Devarams.* It has the mystical knowledge of *yoga,* methods and techniques to help everyone find God within themselves. It has the wisdom of its *swāmīs, āchāryas* and *ṛishis* of yore, from the Himalayas to the South of India. It has Nirguṇa Brahman and Saguṇa Brahman, transcendent God and immanent, personal God. It has the world's oldest and largest active temples, the liturgy and science of invoking the Gods to enter the inner sanctum, and it has the great *aadheenam* tradition of venerable masters to sustain the temples, the pandits, the scriptures and populace. It has happy festivals and holy sacraments. It has *mantra* and *tantra* and *yantra.* It has *charyā, kriyā, yoga* and *jñāna,* in that order, the order of the progression of the soul. It has *karma* and reincarnation. It humbles itself by recognizing and honoring all other paths as part and parcel of the human experience toward God. All this and more make Śaivism exceedingly great. It makes us humble to be a small part of so great a spiritual tradition, to have the joy and privilege of living with Śiva. We end with the conclusive words of my *satguru,* Sage Yogaswami:

> *When your body and mind become attuned to the spiritual laws, your soul will be freed to contemplate on the blissful Self. Vedānta and Siddhānta are not separate paths, but are essential facets of the Luminous One.*

Glossary

Śabda Kośaḥ

शब्दकोशः

aadheenakarthar: **ஆதீனகர்த்தர்** The *aadheenam* head, or pontiff, also called the Guru Mahāsannidhānam. See: *aadheenam, monastery.*

aadheenam: **ஆதீனம்** "Ownership possession, dependence; endowment, foundation, institution," Śaiva monastery. A Śaivite Hindu monastery and temple complex in the South Indian Śaiva Siddhānta tradition. The *aadheenam* head, or pontiff, is called the *guru mahāsannidhānam* or *aadheenakarthar.* See: *monastery.*

abjure: To give up or renounce, often under oath; to abstain from.

abortion: Any deliberate procedure that removes or induces the expulsion of an embryo or fetus before it is viable. Not condoned in Hinduism except to save the mother's life.

Abrahamic religions: The religions descending from Abraham, a biblical patriarch regarded by Jews as the founder of the Hebrew people through his son Isaac and by Muslims as the founder of the Arab people through his son Ishmael; thus, Judaism, Christianity and Islam.

Absolute: Lower case (absolute): real, not dependent on anything else, not relative. Upper case (Absolute): Ultimate Reality, the unmanifest, unchanging and transcendent Paraśiva—utterly nonrelational to even the most subtle level of consciousness. It is the Self God, the essence of man's soul. See: *Paraśiva.*

absolution (to absolve): Forgiveness. A freeing from guilt so as to relieve someone from obligation or penalty. **—atone:** to compensate or make up for a wrongdoing. Atonement can only be done by the person himself, while absolution is granted by others, such as a family head, judge or jury. Exoneration, the taking away of all blame and all personal karmic burden, can only be given by God Śiva. Society would naturally acknowledge and accept this inner transformation by forgiving and forgetting. See: *penance, sin.*

abstinence: Voluntary restraint from something undesirable or harmful.

āchārya: आचार्य "Going toward;" "approaching." A highly respected teacher. The wise one who practices what he preaches. A title generally bestowed through *dīkshā* and ordination, such as in the Śivāchārya priest tradition. In the context of this book, a senior *swāmī* of the Saiva Siddhanta Yoga Order, founded by Satguru Sivaya Subramuniyaswami in 1949. Having completed at least 24 years of service under Gurudeva while observing *brahmacharya sādhana,* these specially ordained *swāmīs* are the acknowledged examples for younger monks. ***—ādi āchāryas:*** Four *āchāryas* of the Saiva Siddhanta Yoga Order ordained as an ongoing, self-perpetuating group chosen from among the *āchāryas* to determine the course of the future of the Order and lay membership of Saiva Siddhanta Church. Their major duty is to exemplify the Śaiva ideals and keep the teaching programs and publications purely in line with those of the *paramparā* and *sampradāya.*

actinic: Spiritual, creating light. Adjective derived from the Greek *aktis,* "ray." Of or pertaining to consciousness in its pure, unadulterated state. Actinic force is the superconscious mind and not a force which comes from the superconcious mind. Commonly known as life, spirit, it can be seen as the light in man's eyes; it is the force that leaves man when he leaves his odic physical body behind. It is not opposite to odic force, it is different than odic force as light is different than water but shines through it. Actinic force flows freely through odic force. See: *kośa, odic.*

acupuncture: An essential component of traditional Chinese medicine consisting of the practice of puncturing the body with very thin needles, or applying consistent massage pressure (called *acupressure)* at specific points along established pathways of subtle energy, called meridians, to cure disease, balance energies or relieve pain. *Āyurveda* has its own system of acupuncture. See: *meridian.*

adharma: अधर्म Negative, opposite of *dharma.* Deeds thoughts or words that transgress divine law. Unrighteousness, irreligiousness; demerit. See: *dharma, sin.*

adultery: Sexual intercourse between a married man or a woman who is not one's own wife or husband. Adultery is spoken of in Hindu *śāstras* as a serious breach of *dharma.* See: *sexuality.*

advaita: अद्वैत "Non dual; not twofold." Nonduality or monism. The philosophical doctrine that Ultimate Reality consists of a one principal substance, or God. Opposite of *dvaita,* dualism. See: *dvaita-advaita, Vedānta.*

Advaita Īśvaravāda: अद्वैत ईश्वरवाद "Nondual and Personal-God-as-Ruler doctrine." The Sanskrit equivalent of *monistic theism.* A general term that describes the philosophy of the *Vedas* and *Śaiva Āgamas,* which posits simultaneously the ultimate oneness of all things and the reality of the personal Deity. See: *Advaita, Advaita Siddhānta, monistic theism.*

Advaita Siddhānta: अद्वैत सिद्धान्त "Nondual ultimate

conclusions." Śaivite philosophy codified in the *Āgamas* which has at its core the nondual (*advaitic*) identity of God, soul and world. This monistic-theistic philosophy, unlike the Sankara, or Smārta view, holds that *māyā* (the principle of manifestation) is not an obstacle to God Realization, but God's own power and presence guiding the soul's evolution to perfection. While Advaita Vedānta stresses *Upanishadic* philosophy, Advaita Siddhānta adds to this a strong emphasis on internal and external worship, *yoga sādhanas* and *tapas*. *Advaita Siddhānta* is a term used in South India to distinguish Tirumular's school from the pluralistic Siddhānta of Meykandar and Aghoraśiva. This unified Vedic-Āgamic doctrine is also known as *Śuddha Śaiva Siddhānta*. It is the philosophy on which this text is based. See: *Advaita Īśvaravāda, dvaita-advaita, monistic theism, Śaiva Siddhānta.*

Advaita Vedānta: अद्वैत वेदान्त "Nondual end (or essence) of the *Vedas*." The nondual final conclusions of the *Vedas*. Commonly names the various Indian monistic schools, most prominently that of Sankara, that arose from the *Upanishads* and related texts. See: *Vedānta.*

affectionate detachment: The power and wisdom of love born of understanding. Not becoming engrossed in the problems or negative attachments of others. As opposed to "running away" from the world or being insensitively aloof, affectionate detachment allows for more genuine, wholesome relationships with people and things.

affirmation: *Dṛidhavāchana*. "Firm statement." A positive declaration or assertion. A statement repeated regularly while concentrating on the meaning and mental images invoked, often used to attain a desired result.

affirmation of faith: A brief statement of one's faith and essential beliefs. See: *Anbe Sivamayam Satyame Parasivam.*

Āgama: आगम The tradition that has "come down." An enormous collection of Sanskrit scriptures which, along with the *Vedas*, are revered as *śruti* (revealed scripture). Dating uncertain. The *Āgamas* are the primary source and authority for ritual, *yoga* and temple construction. See: *Śaiva Āgamas, śruti.*

agni: अग्नि "Fire." 1) One of the five elements, *pañchabhūta*. 2) God of the element fire, invoked through Vedic ritual known as *yajña, agnikāraka, homa* and *havana*. See: *havana, homa.*

ahiṁsā: अहिंसा "Noninjury," nonviolence or nonhurtfulness. Refraining from causing harm to others, physically, mentally or emotionally. *Ahiṁsā* is the first and most important of the *yamas* (restraints). It is the cardinal virtue upon which all others depend. See: *yama-niyama.*

ājñā chakra: आज्ञाचक्र "Command wheel." The third-eye center. See: *chakra.*

ākāśa: आकाश "Space." The sky. Free, open space. Ether, the fifth and most subtle of the five elements—earth, air, fire, water and ether. Empirically, the rarefied space or ethereal fluid plasma that pervades the universes, inner and outer. Esoterically, mind, the superconscious strata holding all that potentially or actually exists, wherein all transactions are recorded and can be read by clairvoyants. It is through psychic entry into this transcendental *ākāśa* that cosmic knowledge is gathered, and the entire circle of time—past, present and future—can be known.

all-pervasive: Diffused throughout or existing in every part of the universe. See: *Satchidānanda.*

amends: Recompensation, making up for injury or loss caused to another. This is done through sincere apology, expressing regrets, contrition, public penance, such as *kavadi*, and ample gifts. See: *penance.*

anabhidroha: अनभिद्रोह "Absence of injuriousness."

ānanda: आनन्द "Bliss." The pure joy—ecstasy or enstasy—of God-consciousness or spiritual experience. See: *God Realization, Satchidānanda.*

ānandamaya kośa: आनन्दमयकोश "Bliss body." The body of the soul, which ultimately merges with Śiva. See: *soul, kośa.*

Anandamayi Ma (Ānandamāyī Mā): आनन्दमायीमा Godly *yoginī* and mystic Bengali saint known for her purity and *sādhanas*, including not eating unless fed by her devotees (1896-1982).

āṇava: आणव "Fragment; atom; minuteness, individuality." God's veiling power that provides individualness, or individual ego, to each soul, making the soul seem apart and distinct from God and the universe. See: *āṇava mala, evolution of the soul, grace, mala, soul.*

āṇava mala: आणवमल "Impurity of smallness; finitizing principle." The fetter or individualizing veil of duality that enshrouds the soul. It is the source of finitude and ignorance, the most basic of the three bonds (*āṇava, karma, māyā*) which temporarily limit the soul. The presence of *āṇava mala* is what causes the misapprehension about the nature of God, soul and world, the notion of being separate and distinct from God and the universe. See: *āṇava, evolution of the soul, grace, mala, soul.*

āṇava mārga: आणवमार्ग "Path of ignorance." The path of egoity, separateness, self-indulgence, self-interest and selfishness. See: *āṇava mala.*

Anbe Sivamayam Satyame Parasivam: அன்பே சிவமயம் சத்தியமே பரசிவம் Tamil for "God Śiva is Immanent Love and Transcendent Reality." The affirmation of faith which capsulizes the entire creed of monistic Śaiva Siddhānta. In Sanskrit it is *Premaiva Śivamaya, Satyam eva Paraśivaḥ.*

anchorite: "Hermit." A monk or aspirant who lives alone and apart from society, as contrasted with *cenobite*, a member of a religious order living in a monastery or convent. See: *monk.*

animate-inanimate: From the Latin animatus, "to make alive, fill with breath." These terms indicate the two poles of manifest existence, that which has movement and life (most expressly animals and other "living" beings) and that which is devoid of movement (such as minerals and, to a lesser degree, plants). From a deeper view, however, all existence is alive with movement and possessed of the potent, divine energy of the cosmos.

aṅkuśa: अंकुश Goad, symbol of Lord Gaṇeśa's power to remove obstacles from the devotee's path, and to spur the dullards onward.

anna dāna: अन्नदान "Giving food." The Hindu tradition, also called *yajña*, of holding mass feedings for guest and for the poor. It is a source of great merit, especially if an exceptionally great soul happens to partake of the meal and his hunger is satisfied. See: *yama-niyama.*

annaprāśana: अन्नप्राशन "Feeding." The childhood sacrament of first solid food. See: *saṁskāras of childhood.*

Antarloka: अन्तर्लोक "Inner plane," or "in-between world." The astral plane, or Second World. See: *astral plane.*

Antoinette, Marie (1755-1793): Queen of France from 1774, wife of Louis XVI, and daughter of Maria Theresa and Francis I of Austria. During the French Revolution she and her husband were accused of treason. She was guillotined on October 16, 1793.

anugraha śakti: अनुग्रहशक्ति "Graceful or favoring power." Revealing grace. God Śiva's power of illumination, through which the soul is freed from the bonds of *āṇava, karma* and *māyā* and ultimately attains liberation, *moksha*. Specifically, *anugraha* descends on the soul as *śaktipāta*, the *dīkshā* (initiation) from a *satguru. Anugraha* is a key concept in Śaiva Siddhānta. It comes when *āṇava mala*, the shell of finitude which surrounds the soul, reaches a state of ripeness, *malaparipāka*. See: *āṇava, grace, Naṭarāja, śaktinipāta.*

aphorism: A terse and well-qualified, easy-to-remember statement of a truth placed in the subconscious mind.

āratī: आरती "Light." The circling or waving of a lamp—usually fed with *ghee*, camphor or oil—before a holy person or the temple Deity at the high point of *pūjā*. The flame is then presented to the devotees, each passing his or her hands through it and bringing them to the eyes three times, thereby receiving the blessings. *Āratī* can also be performed as the briefest form of *pūjā*. See: *archana, pūjā.*

arbitrate: To give a judgment or decision in a dispute; mediate.

archana: अर्चन A special, personal, abbreviated *pūjā* done by temple priests in which the name, birthstar and family lineage of a devotee are recited to invoke individual guidance and blessings. *Archana* also refers to chanting the names of the Deity, which is a central part of every pūjā. See: *pūjā.*

***ardha*-Hindu:** अर्धहिन्दु "Half-Hindu." A devotee who has adopted Hindu belief and culture to a great extent but has not formally entered the religion through ceremony and taking a Hindu first and last name. Also refers to Easterners born into the faith who adopt non-Hindu names.

ārjava: आर्जव "Honesty." See: *yama-niyama.*

Arjuna: अर्जुन A hero of the *Mahābhārata* and the central figure of the *Bhagavad Gītā*. See: *Bhagavad Gītā.*

artha: अर्थ "Goal" or "purpose;" wealth, substance, property, money. See: *four traditional goals.*

artificial perpetuation of life: See: *heroic measures.*

arul: அருள் "Grace." The third of the three stages of the *sakala avasthai* when the soul yearns for the grace of God, *śaktinipāta*. At this stage the soul seeks *pati-jñānam*, knowledge of God. See: *pati-jñānam, sakala avasthā, śaktinipāta.*

āsana: आसन "Seat; posture." In *haṭha yoga*, any of numerous poses prescribed to balance and tune up the subtle energies of mind and body for meditation and to promote health and longevity. See: *haṭha yoga, rāja yoga, yoga.*

ascetic: A person who leads a life of contemplation and rigorous self-denial, shunning comforts and pleasures for religious purposes. See: *monk.*

ashṭāṅga yoga: अष्टाङ्गयोग "Eight-limbed union." The classical *rāja yoga* system of eight progressive stages or steps as described in the *Yoga Sutras* of Sage Patanjali (often termed *rāja yoga)* and in numerous Hindu scriptures including various *Upanishads* and the *Tirumantiram* by Saint Tirumular. The eight limbs are: restraints (*yama*), observances (*niyama*), postures (*āsana*), breath control (*prāṇāyāma*), sense withdrawal (*pratyāhāra*), concentration (*dhāraṇā*), meditation (*dhyāna*) and contemplation (*samādhi/ Self Realization*). See: *rāja yoga, yoga, yama-niyama, āsana, prāṇāyāma, samādhi.*

aspirant: A person who strives for some high achievement.

aspiration: A desire for some high achievement.

āśrama: आश्रम "Place of striving." From *śram*, "to exert energy." Hermitage; order of the life. Holy sanctuary; the residence and teaching center of a *sādhu*, saint, *swāmī*, ascetic or *guru*; often includes lodging for students. Also names life's four stages. See: *āśrama dharma, sādhana.*

āśrama dharma: आश्रमधर्म "Laws of life development." Meritorious way of life appropriate to each of its four successive stages *(āśramas)*, observing which one lives in harmony with nature and life, allowing the body, emotions and mind to develop and undergo their natural cycles in a most positive way. The four stages are: —1) ***brahmacharya:*** Studentship, from age 12 to 24. —2) ***gṛihastha:*** Householder, from 24 to 48. —3) ***vānaprastha:*** Elder advisor, from 48 to 72. —4) ***sannyāsa:*** Religious solitary, from 72 onward. See: *dharma, gṛihastha dharma, sannyāsa dharma.*

asteya: अस्तेय "Nonstealing." See: *yama-niyama.*

āstikya: आस्तिक्य "Faith." See: *faith, śraddhā, yama-niyama.*

astral body: The subtle, nonphysical body *(sūkshma śarīra)* in which the soul functions in the astral plane, the inner world also called Antarloka. The astral body includes the *prāṇic* sheath *(prāṇamaya kośa)*, the instinctive-intellectual sheath *(manomaya kośa)* and the cognitive sheath *(vijñānamaya kośa)*—with the *prāṇic* sheath discarded at the death of the physical body.

astral entity: Any being in the astral plane. See: *astral* *plane.*

astral plane: From the word astral, meaning "of the stars." Belonging to the subtle, non-physical dimension also known as the Antarloka, or Second World. "Astral forces" exist in the Second World but can be felt psychically in the First. See also: *loka, three worlds.*

astral projection: The practice of consciously directing one's activities when out of the physical body and functioning in the astral body, including the ability to direct attention to and visit other people who are also in their astral body, or visit a remote location, experiencing the activities there and retaining knowledge of such experiences after returning to the state of wakeful, physical consciousness. See: *astral plane.*

astral shell: The odic astral form which a soul leaves behind in the astral plane when it enters into a new physical birth. The astral shell soon disintegrates as creative forces generate a new physical and astral body.

astrology: Science of celestial influences. See: *jyotisha.*

aśubha: अशुभ "Inauspicious," "gloomy." See: *śubha.*

asura: असुर "Evil spirit; demon." (Opposite of *sura:* "*deva*; God.") A being of the lower astral plane, Naraka. *Asuras* can and do interact with the physical plane, causing major and minor problems in people's lives. *Asuras* do evolve and do not remain permanently in this state. See: *Naraka.*

asuric: Of the nature of an *asura*, "not spiritual."

atala chakra: अतल चक्र "Bottomless region." The first *chakra* below the *mūlādhāra*, at the hip level. Region of fear and lust. See: *chakra, Naraka.*

atheism: The rejection of all religion or religious belief, or simply the belief that God or Gods do not exist. See: *materialism.*

ātman: आत्मन् "The soul; the breath; the principle of life and sensation." The soul in its entirety—as the soul body *(ānandamaya kośa)* and its essence (Parāśakti and Paraśiva). One of Hinduism's most fundamental tenets is that we are the *ātman*, not the physical body, emotions, external mind or personality. See: *Paramātman, kośa, soul.*

ātmārtha pūjā: आत्मार्थपूजा "Personal worship rite." Home *pūjā*—Sanskrit liturgy performed in the home shrine. See: *pūjā.*

ātura sannyāsa: आतुरसंन्यास "Renunciation while suffering." See: *sannyāsa.*

attachments: That which one holds onto or clings to with the energy of possessiveness, which is a natural function of the inner and outer ego of an individual. As one unfolds through the *chakras*, the force of attachment naturally diminishes through *sādhana, tapas* and the grace of the *guru.*

Aum: ॐ or ओम् Often spelled *Om.* The mystic syllable of Hinduism, placed at the beginning of most sacred writings. As a *mantra*, it is pronounced *aw* (as in *law*), *oo* (as in *zoo*), *mm.* Aum represents the Divine, and is associated with Lord Gaṇeśa, for its initial sound "aa," vibrates within the *mūlādhāra*, the *chakra* at the base of the spine upon which this God sits. The second sound of this *mantra*, "oo," vibrates within the throat and chest *chakras*, the realm of Lord Murugan, or Kumāra. The third sound, "mm," vibrates within the cranial *chakras*, *ājñā* and *sahasrāra*, where the Supreme God, Śiva, reigns.

aura: The luminous colorful field of subtle energy radiating within and around the human body, extending out from three to seven feet. The colors of the aura change constantly according to the ebb and flow of one's state of consciousness, thoughts, moods and emotions. Higher, benevolent feelings create bright pastels; base, negative feelings are darker in color. The aura consists of three aspects, the *prāṇa-aura*, the outer aura and the inner aura. The *prāṇa-aura* is the reflection of the physical body, the life force. The outer aura extends beyond the physical body and changes continuously, reflecting the individual's moment-to-moment panorama of thought and emotion.

Aurobindo Ghosh: A prolific Bengali writer and poet, pantheistic philosopher and *yoga* mystic, widely known as Sri Aurobindo (1872-1950). He perceived the modern global crisis as marking a period of transition from a dark age to a more enlightened one, when Hinduism will play a preponderant role. He founded the Auroville community in Pondichery, based on *purṇa* (integral) *yoga* and contributed much to this century's Hindu revival.

auspicious: *Maṅgala.* Favorable, of good omen, foreboding well. One of the central concepts in Hindu life. Astrology defines a method for determining times that are favorable for various human endeavors. See: *jyotisha.*

austerity: Self-denial and discipline, physical or mental, performed for various reasons, including acquiring powers *(siddhis)*, attaining grace, conquering the instinctive nature and burning the seeds of past *karmas.* Ranging from simple deprivations, such as foregoing a meal, to severe disciplines, called *tapas*, such as always standing, never sitting or lying down, even for sleep. See: *penance, tapas.*

Auvaiyar: ஔவையார் A woman saint of Tamil Nadu (ca 800 ce), a contemporary of Saint Sundarar, devotee of Lord Gaṇeśa and Kārttikeya, or Murugan, and one of the greatest literary figures in ancient India. (See Chapter 17.) Among the most famous are Atti Chudi, Konrai Ventan, Ulaka Niti, Muturai and Nalvali. Her Tamil primer is studied by children to this day. An earlier traditional date for Auvaiyar of 200 bce is from a story about her and Saint Tiruvalluvar.

avasthā: अवस्था (Tamil: *avasthai.*) "Condition or state" of consciousness or experience. 1) Any of three stages of the soul's evolution from the point of its creation to final merger in the Primal Soul. 2) The states of consciousness as discussed in the *Māṇḍūkya Upanishad: jāgrat* (or *vaiśvānara*), "wakefulness;" *svapna* (or *taijasa*), "dreaming;" *sushupti*, "deep sleep;" and *turīya*, "the fourth" state, of superconsciousness. A fifth state, "beyond *turīya*," is *turīyātīta.* See: *kevala avasthā, sakala avasthā, śuddha avasthā.*

avatāra: अवतार "Descent." A God born in a human (or animal) body. A central concept of Śāktism, Smārtism and Vaishṇavism. See: *incarnation, Ishṭa Devatā.*

awareness: *Sākshin,* or *chit.* Individual consciousness, perception, knowing; the witness of perception, the "inner eye of the soul." The soul's ability to sense, see or know and to be conscious of this knowing. When awareness is indrawn *(pratyak chetana),* various states of *samādhi* may occur. Awareness is known in the Āgamas as *chitśakti,* the "power of awareness," the inner self and eternal witness. See: *consciousness.*

ayanāṁśa: अयनांश "Portion" *(aṁśa)* of the solstice *(ayana),* meaning the deviation of the zodiac from the equinoctial position of zero degrees Aries—or the amount of the precession of the equinoxes since the zero degrees Aries vernal equinox, which defines the difference between the Vedic and Western (or tropical) zodiacs. The Western system marks zero degrees Aries at the vernal equinox. The Vedic system adjusts for the precession and marks the (current) vernal equinox at about 6 degrees of the sign of Pisces, or roughly 23 degrees. The exact *ayanāṁśa* is not known, so a number of *ayanāṁśas* are put forth by various astronomers and well known astrologers. Lahiri created the official *ayanāṁśa* approved by the government of India. It counts the beginning of the zodiac as exactly 180 degrees opposite the star Chitra (Alpha Virgo in the Western system, the star Spica). Most older *ayanāṁśas* are Revati-paksha, or relating to the star Revati.

āyurveda: आयुर्वेद "Science of life," "science of longevity." A holistic system of medicine and health native to ancient India. The aims of *āyurveda* are *āyus,* "long life," and *ārogya,* "diseaselessness," which facilitate progress toward ultimate spiritual goals. Health is achieved by balancing energies (especially the *doshas,* bodily humors) at all levels of being.

Being: Upper case: God's essential divine nature—Pure Consciousness, Absolute Reality and Primal Soul (God's nature as a divine Person). Lower case: the essential nature of a person, that within which never changes; existence. See: *Śiva.*

beta testing: The final testing of new computer software, performed by persons other than software developers, before it is released for sale.

Bhagavad Gītā: भगवद् गीता "The Lord's Song." One of the most popular of Hindu writings, a conversation between Lord Kṛishṇa and Arjuna on the brink of the great battle at Kurukshetra. In this central episode of the epic *Mahābhārata* (part of the Sixth Book), Kṛishṇa illumines the warrior-prince Arjuna on *yoga,* asceticism, *dharma* and the manifold spiritual path. See: *Mahābhārata.*

bhajana: भजन Spiritual song. Individual or group singing of devotional songs, hymns and chants.

bhakta: भक्त (Tamil: *Bhaktar.*) "Devotee." A worshiper. One who is surrendered to the Divine. See: *bhakti, bhakti yoga, devotee, guru bhakti.*

bhakti: भक्ति "Devotion." Surrender to God, Gods or *guru. Bhakti* extends from the simplest expression of devotion to the ego-decimating principle of *prapatti,* which is total surrender. *Bhakti* is the foundation of all sects of Hinduism, as well as *yoga* schools throughout the world. See: *bhakti yoga, darśana, prasāda.*

bhakti yoga: भक्तियोग "Union through devotion." *Bhakti yoga* is the practice of devotional disciplines, worship, prayer, chanting and singing with the aim of awakening love in the heart and opening oneself to God's grace. *Bhakti* may be directed toward God, Gods or *guru. Bhakti yoga* is embodied in Patanjali's *Yoga Darśana* in the second limb, *niyamas* (observances), as devotion (Īśvarapraṇidhāna).

bhikku: A Buddhist monk, or any of the first disciples of Buddha.

Bhojana Mantra: भोजन मन्त्र "Food-blessing chant." As each meal is served, reciting the food-blessing chant, silently or aloud as a group, is an expression of gratitude, an acknowledgement of food's ultimate source and an invocation of spiritual benefits. Its recitation prepares one for partaking of the Supreme Lord's abundance, which should occur in the right state of mind and emotion. Food, the magical source of *prāṇa,* is an umbilical connection to the cosmos, the lifeline of embodied souls, nature's means of nourishment. This chant is given in the spirit of a beggar humbly seeking alms. Water—a *prāṇic* bridge between the subtle and physical universes—is used in four ways in preparing to eat. First the mouth is rinsed. Then water is used to rinse the banana leaf or plate. Water from one's drinking cup is poured into the right hand to rinse it, as food is, whenever possible, taken with the hand, rather than with chopsticks or fork and spoon. Finally, water is sprinkled in a circle around the food with the right hand, creating a force field of purification and protection and invoking harmony of all five bodily *prāṇas.* In the South of India, a little bit from each food item is placed on the upper left corner of the plate as an offering to Gaṇeśa before taking one's first bite.

bilva: बिल्व Wood-apple (or bael) tree, Aegle marmelos, sacred to Lord Śiva. Its leaves, picked in threes, are offered in the worship of the Śivaliṅga. The delicious fruit when unripe is used medicinally.

bindu: बिन्दु "A drop, small particle, dot." Small dot worn on the forehead between the eyebrows, or in the middle of the forehead, made of red powder *(kuṅkuma),* sandalpaste, clay, cosmetics or other substance. The *bindu* is known as pottu in Tamil, and as *bindi* in Hindi. *Bindu* is also a term for semen. See: *tilaka.*

blackmail: Payment extorted to prevent disclosure of information that would bring disgrace or ruin if made public.

boon: *Varadāna.* A welcome blessing, a gracious benefit received. An unexpected gift or bonus. See: *grace.*

brahmachārī: ब्रह्मचारी An unmarried male spiritual

aspirant who practices continence, observes religious disciplines, including *sādhana*, devotion and service and who may be under simple vows. Names also a young man in the student stage, age 12-24, or until marriage. See: *āśrama dharma, monk.*

brahmacharya: **ब्रह्मचर्य** See: *yama-niyama.*

brahmacharya āśrama: **ब्रह्मचर्य आश्रम** See: *āśrama dharma.*

brahmacharya vrata: **ब्रह्मचर्य व्रत** "Celibacy vow." The verbal pledge given before members of one's religious community to remain chaste until marriage, for a specified period of time, or for life. It also includes restraining the base instincts of anger, jealousy, greed, selfishness, etc.

brahmachāriṇī: **ब्रह्मचारिणी** Feminine counterpart of *brahmachārī.*

Brahmadhvara: **ब्रह्मध्वर** The door to the seven *chakras* and the *Narakaloka* just below the *mūlādhāra*. In order for the higher *chakras* to come into power, this door must be shut, making it impossible for fears, hatreds, angers and jealousies to arise. *Sādhana* and right thought, word and deed are among the aids in this accomplishment. See: *Naraka.*

Brahman: **ब्रह्मन्** "Supreme Being; Expansive Spirit." From the root *bṛih*, "to grow, increase, expand." Name of God or Supreme Deity in the *Vedas*, where He is described as 1) the Transcendent Absolute, 2) the all-pervading energy and 3) the Supreme Lord or Primal Soul. These three correspond to Śiva in His three perfections. Thus, Śaivites know Brahman and Śiva to be one and the same God: ***—Nirguṇa Brahman,*** God "without qualities" (*guṇa*), i.e., formless, Absolute Reality, Parabrahman, or Paraśiva—totally transcending *guṇa* (quality), manifest existence and even Parāśakti, all of which exhibit perceivable qualities; ***—Saguṇa Brahman,*** God "with qualities;" Śiva in His perfections of Parāśakti and Parameśvara—God as superconscious, omnipresent, all-knowing, all-loving and all-powerful. The term Brahman is not to be confused with 1) *Brahmā*, the Creator God; 2) *Brāhmaṇa*, Vedic texts, nor with 3) *brāhmaṇa*, Hindu priest caste (English spelling: *brāhmin*). See: *Parāśakti, Paraśiva.*

Brahmarandhra: **ब्रह्मरन्ध्र** See: *door of Brahman.*

brāhmin (brāhmaṇa): **ब्राह्मण** "Mature or evolved soul." The class of pious souls of exceptional learning. From *Brāhman*, "growth, expansion, evolution, development, swelling of the spirit or soul." See: *caste.*

bhāshya: **भाष्य** "Speech, discussion." Commentary on a text. Hindu philosophies are largely founded upon the interpretations, or *bhāshyas*, of primary scripture. Other types of commentaries include: *vṛitti*, a brief commentary on aphorisms; *tippani*, like a *vṛitti* but less formal, explains difficult words or phrases; *vārttika*, a critical study and elaboration of a *bhāshya;* and *tika* or *vyakhyana*, an explanation of a *bhāshya* or *śāstra* in simpler language.

birthstar: See: *nakshatra.*

Bṛihadāraṇyaka Upanishad: **बृहदारण्यक उपनिषद्** One of the major *Upanishads*, part of the *Śatapatha Brāhmaṇa* of the *Yajur Veda*. Ascribed to Sage Yājñavalkya, it teaches modes of worship, meditation and the identity of the individual self with the Supreme Self. See: *Upanishad.*

Buddha: **बुद्ध** "The enlightened." Usually refers to Siddhartha Gautama (ca 624-544 bce), a prince born of the Śākya clan—a Śaivite Hindu tribe that lived in eastern India on the Nepalese border. He renounced the world and became a monk. After his enlightenment he preached the doctrines upon which followers later founded Buddhism. See: *Buddhism.*

Buddhism: The religion based on the teachings of Siddhārtha Gautama, known as the Buddha (ca 624–544 BCE). He refuted the idea of man's having an immortal soul and did not preach of any Supreme Deity. Instead he taught that man should seek to overcome greed, hatred and delusion and attain enlightenment through realizing the Four Noble Truths and following the Eightfold Path. See: *Buddha.*

caste: A hierarchical system, called *varṇa dharma* (or *jāti dharma*), established in India in ancient times, which determined the privileges, status, rights and duties of the many occupational groups, wherein status is determined by heredity. There are four main classes (*varṇas*)—*brāhmin, kshatriya, vaiśya* and *śūdra*—and innumerable castes, called *jāti*. The four *varṇas* are as follows. ***—brāhmin (brāhmaṇa):*** "Mature, evolved soul." Scholarly, pious souls of exceptional learning. Hindu scriptures traditionally invest the *brāhmin* class with the responsibility of religious leadership, including teaching and priestly duties. ***—kshatriya:*** "Governing; endowed with sovereignty." Lawmakers and law enforcers and military, also known as *rājanya*. ***—vaiśya:*** "Landowner, merchant." Businessmen, financiers, industrialists; employers. Those engaged in business, commerce and agriculture. ***—śūdra:*** "Worker, servant." Skilled artisans and laborers.

Catholicism: The doctrine, system and practice of the Catholic Church; a major Christian denomination.

celibacy: Complete sexual abstinence. Also the state of a person who has vowed to remain unmarried. Celibacy is abstinence from the eight degrees of sexual activity: fantasy *(smaraṇa)*, glorification *(kīrtana)*, flirtation *(keli)*, glances *(prekshaṇa)*, secret talk *(guhya bhāshana)*, longing *(kāma saṁkalpa)*, rendezvous *(adhyavāsāya)* and intercourse *(kriyā nivṛitti)*. See: *brahmachārī, ojas, tejas, transmutation, yama-niyama.*

cenobite: A member of a monastery community.

cenobitic: Belonging to a monastery community.

ceremony: From the Latin *caerimonia*, "awe; reverent rite." A formal rite established by custom or authority as proper to special occasions.

chakra: **चक्र** "Wheel." Any of the nerve plexes or centers of force and consciousness located within the inner bodies of man. In the physical body there are corresponding nerve plexuses, ganglia and glands. The seven principal *chakras* can be seen psychically as colorful, multi-petaled wheels or lotuses. They are situated along the spinal cord from the base to the cranial chamber. The seven principle chakras, from lowest to highest, are: 1) ***mūlādhāra*** (base of spine): memory, time and space; 2) ***svādhishṭhāna*** (below navel): reason; 3) ***maṇipūra*** (solar plexus): willpower; 4) ***anāhata*** (heart center): direct cognition; 5) ***viśuddha*** (throat): divine love; 6) ***ājñā*** (third eye): divine sight; 7) ***sahasrāra*** (crown of head): illumination, Godliness. ¶Additionally, seven *chakras*, barely visible, exist below the spine. They are seats of instinctive consciousness, the origin of jealousy, hatred, envy, guilt, sorrow, etc. They constitute the lower or hellish world, called *Naraka* or *pātāla*. From highest to lowest they are 1) ***atala*** (hips): fear and lust; 2) ***vitala*** (thighs): raging anger; 3) ***sutala*** (knees): retaliatory jealousy; 4) ***talātala*** (calves): prolonged mental confusion; 5) ***rasātala*** (ankles): selfishness; 6) ***mahātala*** (feet): absence of conscience; 7) ***pātāla*** (located in the soles of the feet): murder and malice. ¶Seven *chakras*, or conglomerates of *nāḍīs*, exist within and above the *sahasrāra*, as the seven levels of the rarified dimensions of *paranāda*, the first *tattva* and the highest stratum of sound. From lowest to highest they are: 1) ***vyāpinī:*** "all-pervasive;" 2) ***vyomāṅga:*** "space-bodied;" 3) ***anantā:*** "infinity;" 4) ***anāthā:*** having "no master;" 5) ***anāśritā:*** "independent;" 6) ***samanā:*** "uniform, synchronous;" 7) ***unmanā:*** "ecstatic, trans-mental." See: *Naraka* (also: *individual chakra entries).*

chakravāla: चक्रवाल "Circle," "an assembly." A circle or gathering of devotees, seated clockwise according to age or seniority in their fellowship. This clear acknowledgement of heirarchy by all parties helps keeps associations and interactions harmonious, as the lines of responsibility, respect or elders and nurturing of those young are clear. When such a group sit together, they send their *prāṇas*, positive energies, clockwise around the circle for the upliftment of all.

Çhāndogya Upanishad: छान्दोग्य उपनिषद् One of the major *Upanishads*, it consists of eight chapters of the *Çhāndogya Brāhmaṇa* of the *Sāma Veda*. It teaches the origin and significance of *Aum*, the importance of the *Sāma Veda*, the Self, meditation and life after death. See: *Upanishad.*

channeling: the practice of serving as a medium through which a spirit guide communicates with living persons.

charyā: चर्या "Conduct stage." Stage of service and character building. See: *pāda, Śaiva Siddhānta, Śaivism.*

chat room: A virtual place to participate in a real-time computer-to-computer teletype conversation over a network.

chelā: चेला "Disciple." (Hindi.) A disciple of a *guru;* synonym for Sanskrit *śishya*. The feminine equivalent is *chelinā* or *chelī*.

Chellappaswami: செல்லப்பாசுவாமி "Wealthy father." (Also known as Chellapaguru.) Reclusive *siddha* and 160th *satguru* (1840-1915) of the Nandinātha Sampradāya's Kailāsa Paramparā. Lived on Sri Lanka's Jaffna peninsula near Nallur Kandaswāmī Temple in a small hut where today there is a small *samādhi* shrine. Among his disciples was Sage Yogaswami, whom he trained intensely for five years and initiated as his successor. See: *Kailāsa Paramparā, Nātha Sampradāya.*

Chettiar: செட்டியார் The name of the merchant caste of South India and Sri Lanka.

Chidambaram: சிதம்பரம் "Hall of Consciousness." A very famous South Indian Śiva Naṭarāja temple. See: *Naṭarāja.*

chiropractic: A modern health system which holds that disease results from a lack of normal nerve function and which employs adjustment of body structures, such as the spinal column, as the means of restoration, thus relieving pain, discomfort and disease which result from improper skeletal alignment.

chlorofluorocarbons: A substance used in refrigeration and air conditioning appliances that is known to deplete Earth's stratospheric ozone layer and is, in some countries, now illegal and being phased out.

choga: (Bengali) A long loose men's shirt, similar to the kurta or kafni.

Christ: See: *Jesus Christ.*

Christian-Judaic: See: *Judaic-Christian.*

circadian rhythm: The natural cycle of biological activity or function over an approximate 24-hour period, as well as the movement of subtle energy throughout the body as it is influenced by the rising and setting of the sun. Traditional Chinese medicine establishes that *chi*, or vital energy, moves from one major meridian to another every two hours, repeating every 24 hours: 11PM-1AM: gall bladder; 1-3AM: liver (during the time of deepest sleep, the liver is most actively cleansing the blood); 3-5AM: lung (in traditional cultures, people wake up and take the first breath of the day during this period); 5-7AM: large intestine (depending upon the quantity of food taken during the day, the first bowel movement usually occurs during this period); 7-9AM: stomach (breakfast is usually taken during this period); 9-11AM: spleen; 11AM-1PM: heart; 1-3PM: small intestine (lunch is usually digested during this period); 3-5PM: bladder; 5-7PM: kidney; 7-9PM: pericardium; 9-11PM: *san jiao* ("triple warmer"). See: *acupuncture, meridian.*

clairaudience: "Clear-hearing." Psychic or divine hearing, *divyaśravana*. The ability to hear the inner currents of the nervous system, the *Aum* and other mystic tones. Hearing in one's mind the words of inner-plane beings or earthly beings not physically present. Also, hearing the *nādanāḍī śakti* through the day or while in meditation.

clairvoyance: "Clear-seeing." Psychic or divine sight, *divyadṛishṭi*. The ability to look into the inner worlds and see auras, *chakras, nāḍīs*, thought forms, nonphysical people and subtle forces. See: *ākāśa, clairaudience.*

clear white light: See: *light.*

clemency: A disposition to show mercy or leniency, especially towards an offender or enemy.

cloistered: Secluded, as in a monastery.

cognition: Knowing; perception. Knowledge reached through intuitive, superconscious faculties rather than through intellect alone.

cognizant: Informed or aware of something.

cognize: To take notice of something.

communism: The social and economic system which emerged around the turn of the 20th century in present-day Russia as "a hypothetical stage of socialism, as formulated by Marx, Engels, Lenin and others, to be characterized by a classless and stateless society and the equal distribution of economic goods and to be achieved by revolutionary and dictatorial, rather than gradualistic, means" *(Webster's Dictionary)*. Communism is proudly atheistic and seeks to liberate mankind from superstition and "spiritual bondage."

complacent: Self-satisfied and unconcerned.

conception: Power to imagine, conceive or create. Moment when a pregnancy is begun, a new earthly body generated.

confession: An admission, acknowledgement; as of guilt or wrongdoing.

Confucius: Chinese philosopher and teacher (552-479 BCE), founder of the Confucianist faith, whose *Analects* contain a collection of his sayings and dialogues. His teachings on social ethics are the basis of Chinese education, and religion.

conscience: The inner sense of right and wrong, sometimes called "the knowing voice of the soul." However, the conscience is affected by the individual's training and belief patterns, and is therefore not necessarily a perfect reflection of *dharma*. It is the subconscious of the person—the sum total of past impressions and training—that defines the credal structure and colors the conscience and either clearly reflects or distorts superconscious wisdom. See: *creed, dharma, mind (individual).*

conscious mind: The external, everyday state of consciousness. See: *mind.*

consciousness: *Chitta* or *chaitanya*. 1) A synonym for mind-stuff, *chitta;* or 2) the condition or power of perception, awareness, apprehension. There are myriad of gradations of consciousness, from the simple sentience of inanimate matter to the consciousness of basic life forms, to the higher consciousness of human embodiment, to omniscient states of superconsciousness, leading to immersion in the One universal consciousness, Parāśakti. See: *awareness, mind.*

consensualocracy: Government or management by intelligent cooperation, based on a shared vision and adherence to *dharma. Ahiṁsā*, nonhurtfulness—spiritually, physically, emotionally and mentally—is the keynote of this tribal/family system of rule.

consummate: Perfect; complete in every way.

contemplation: Religious or mystical absorption beyond meditation. See: *rāja yoga, samādhi.*

contention: Strife, dispute, quarrel.

contentious: Likely to cause or involving intense debate; quarrelsome.

Cook, Captain James: British navigator and explorer (1728-1779) who commanded major voyages exploring and claiming many islands of the Pacific Ocean for England in her Christian Colonialist campaign.

cosmic: Universal; vast. Of, or relating to, the cosmos or entire universe.

Cosmic Soul: Purusha or Parameśvara. Primal Soul. The Universal Being; Personal God. See: *Parameśvara, Primal Soul, purusha, Śiva.*

cosmos: The universe, or whole of creation, especially with reference to its order, harmony and completeness. See: loka, three worlds.

creation: The act of creating, especially bringing the world into ordered existence. Also, all of created existence, the cosmos. Creation, according to the monistic-theistic view, is an emanation or extension of God, the Creator. It is Himself in another form, and not inherently something other than Him. See: *damaru.*

Creator: He who brings about creation. Śiva as one of His five powers. See: *creation, Naṭarāja, Parameśvara.*

creed: *Śraddhādhāraṇā.* An authoritative formulation of the beliefs of a religion. See: *conscience.*

cremation: *Dahana.* Burning of the dead. Cremation is the traditional manner of disposing of bodily remains, having the positive effect of releasing the soul most quickly from any lingering attachment to the earth plane. Note that the remains of enlightened masters are sometimes buried or sealed in a special tomb called a *samādhi.* This is done in acknowledgement of the extraordinary attainment of such a soul, whose very body, having become holy, is revered as a sacred presence, *sānnidhya,* and which not infrequently becomes the spiritual seed of a temple or place of pilgrimage. See: *reincarnation.*

crown chakra: *Sahasrāra chakra.* The thousand-petaled cranial center of divine consciousness. See: *chakra, sahasrāra chakra.*

crux: The essential, deciding or difficult point. Latin "cross." Originally a mark indicating a difficult textual problem in books.

crystal: A mineral, especially a transparent form of quartz, having a crystalline structure.

crystal-gazing: An occult practice for divining the future by gazing into a crystal ball.

culminate: To bring to the highest point, to the greatest intensity, or to completion.

Curie, Madame (Marie Sklodowska Curie, 1867-1934): a Polish chemist and physicist, born in Warsaw. In France, she and her husband Pierre discovered polonium and radium, jointly earning the 1903 Nobel prize in Physics. In 1911 she received the Nobel Prize in Chemistry, becoming the first person to be awarded a second Nobel Prize.

cyberspace: the electronic medium of computer networks in which online communication takes place; the Internet or Web.

cynical: Scornful of others' motives or integrity.

dakshiṇā: **दक्षिणा** A fee or gift to a priest given at the completion of any rite; also given to *gurus* as a token of appreciation for their spiritual blessings.

Dakshiṇāmūrti: **दक्षिणामूर्ति** "South-facing form." Lord Śiva depicted sitting under a pīpala (bo) tree, silently teaching four *ṛishis* at His feet.

Dalai Lama:-The traditional high priest of Tibetan Buddhism, or Lamaism, a spiritual and political authority. The term is Mongolian: *dalai,* ocean + *blama,* chief, "preceptor with oceanic wisdom." An honorary title bestowed by the Mongolian prince Altan Khan on the third head of the Gelukpa school in 1578.

dāna: **दान** Generosity, giving. See: *yama-niyama.*

Dancing with Śiva: The first book in Gurudeva's *Master Course* trilogy. Subtitled *Hinduism's Contemporary Catechism, Dancing* is a remarkable sourcebook expounding the Śaivite Hindu outlook on life in the form of questions and answers. It covers every subject on Śaivism, especially the philosophical depths, answers seekers' questions on the nature of God and the Gods, the soul, *dharma,* life's ultimate goal, Hindu denominations, theology, the *satguru,* temple worship, *karma,* spiritual unfoldment, the inner worlds, good and evil, the duties of family life, monastic life and more. It is clearly written and lavishly illustrated, expertly woven with 600 verses from the *Vedas, Āgamas* and other holy texts, 165 South Indian paintings, 40 original graphics, a 40-page timeline of India's history and a 190-page lexicon of English, Sanskrit and Tamil. Released in 1997.

darśana: **दर्शन** "Vision, sight." Seeing the Divine. Beholding, with inner or outer vision, a temple image, Deity, holy person or place, with the desire to inwardly contact and receive the grace and blessings of the venerated being or beings. Even beholding a photograph in the proper spirit is a form of *darśana.* Not only does the devotee seek to see the Divine, but to be seen as well, to stand humbly in the awakened gaze of the holy one, even if for an instant, such as in a crowded temple when thousands of worshipers file quickly past the enshrined Lord. Gods and *gurus* are thus said to "give" *darśana,* and devotees "take" *darśana,* with the eyes being the mystic locus through which energy is exchanged. This direct and personal two-sided apprehension is a central and highly sought-after experience of Hindu faith. Also: "point of view," doctrine or philosophy.

daśama bhāga vrata: **दशमभागव्रत** "One-tenth-part vow." A promise that tithers make before God, Gods and their family or peers to tithe regularly each month, for a specified time, or for life. See also: *daśamāṁśa.*

daśamāṁśa: **दशमांश** "One-tenth sharing." The traditional Hindu practice of tithing, giving one-tenth of one's income to a religious institution. It was formerly widespread in India. In ancient times the term makimai was used in Tamil Nadu. See also: *daśama bhāga vrata.*

Daśanāmī: **दशनामी** "Ten names." Ten monastic orders organized by Adi Sankara (ca 800): Āraṇya, Vāna, Giri, Pārvata, Sāgara, Tīrtha, Āśrama, Bhārati, Pūrī and Sarasvatī. Also refers to *sannyāsins* of these orders, each of whom bears his order's name, with *ānanda* often attached to the religious name. For example, Rāmānanda Tīrtha. Traditionally, each order is associated with one of the main Śaṅkarāchārya *pīṭhas.* See: *Sankara, Smārtism.*

dayā: **दया** "Compassion." See: *yama-niyama.*

death: The soul's detaching itself from the physical body and continuing on in the subtle body *(sūkshma śarīra)* with the same desires, aspirations and activities as when it lived in a physical body. See: *reincarnation.*

decadence: Decay. A condition, process or period of declining morals.

deceit (deception): The act of representing as true what is known to be false. A dishonest action.

degraded oils: See: *oils, degraded.*

Deism: From the Latin, *Deus, "God."* A rationalist tradition dating back to English Lord Herbert of Cherbury (d. 1648), who defined the Five Articles of English Deists as: belief in a single supreme God; humanity's duty to revere God; linkage of worship with practical morality; that God will forgive us if we repent and abandon our sins; good works will be rewarded (and punishment for evil) both in life and after death. Deism rejects reliance on revealed religion, on religious authority and on the infalibility scriptures such as the Bible and the Koran. Deism has no special places of worship, no priesthood and no heirachy of authority. Deism was greatly influential among politicians, scientists and philosophers during the later 17th century and 18th century in England, France, Germany and the United States. Many of America's founding fathers were Deists, including John Quincy Adams, Benjamin Franklin, Thomas Jefferson, James Madison and George Washington. Deists were instrumental in creating the principle of separation of church and state, and the religious freedom clauses of the First Amendment. Source: www.religioustolerance.org/deism.

Deity: "God." The image or *mūrti* installed in a temple or the Mahādeva the *mūrti* represents. See: *pūjā.*

delinquent: Failing to do what law or duty requires.

demon: See: *asura.*

deterrent: Something that prevents or discourages action; frightens away.

detractor: One who takes away from the positive qualities of a group.

deva: **देव** "Shining one." An angelic being living in the higher astral plane, in a subtle, nonphysical body. *Deva* is also used in scripture to mean "God" or "Deity." See: *Mahādeva.*

Devaloka: **देवलोक** "Plane of radiant beings." A synonym of Maharloka, the higher astral plane, realm of *anāhata chakra.* See: *loka.*

Devaram: **தேவாரம்** The collected devotional hymns composed by Saints Tirujnana Sambandar (ca 600) Tirunavakarasu (Appar), a contemporary of Sambandar, and Sundaramurti (ca 800). These make up the first seven books of the *Tirumurai*. See: *Tirumurai*.

devonic: Angelic, heavenly, spiritual. Of the nature of the higher worlds, in tune with the refined energies of the higher *chakras* or centers of consciousness. Of or relating to the *devas*. Implies that something is divinely guided. See: *deva*.

devotee: A person strongly dedicated to something or someone, such as to a God or a *guru*. The term *disciple* implies an even deeper commitment. See: *bhakta, bhakti, guru bhakti*.

devout: Strongly attached to religion or religious obligations. See: *bhakti*.

dharma: धर्म "Righteousness." From *dhṛi*, "to sustain; carry, hold." Hence *dharma* is "that which contains or upholds the cosmos." *Dharma*, religion, is a complex and comprehensive term with many meanings, including divine law, law of being, way of righteousness, ethics, duty, responsibility, virtue, justice, goodness and truth. Essentially, *dharma* is the orderly fulfillment of an inherent nature or destiny. Relating to the soul, it is the mode of conduct most conducive to spiritual advancement, the right and righteous path. There are four principal kinds of dharma, known collectively as *chaturdharma:* "four religious laws:" 1) *ṛita:* "Universal law." The inherent order of the cosmos. 2) *varṇa dharma:* "Law of one's kind." Social duty. 3) *āśrama dharma:* "Duties of life's stages." Human or developmental *dharma*. The natural process of maturing from childhood to old age through fulfillment of the duties of each of the four stages of life—*brahmachārī* (student), *gṛihastha* (householder), *vānaprastha* (elder advisor) and *sannyāsa* (religious solitaire). 4) *svadharma:* "Personal path, pattern or obligation." One's perfect individual pattern through life, according to one's own particular physical, mental and emotional nature. See: *four traditional goals*.

dharmaśāla: धर्मशाला "Abode of righteousness." A monastery or *āśrama*, offering religious training for monks and in some cases lay persons on pilgrimage or religious retreat. In *Living with Śiva*, it specifically refers to branch monasteries of Kauai Aadheenam.

dhoti: धोती (Hindi) A long, unstitched cloth wound about the lower part of the body, and sometimes passed between the legs and tucked into the waist. A traditional Hindu apparel for men.

dhṛiti: धृति "Steadfastness." See: *yama-niyama*.

diaphragm: The muscular partition between the abdomen and chest cavity, instrumental in breathing.

diaphragmatic breathing: Deep regulated breathing from the diaphragm, at the solar plexus region, as opposed to the upper chest.

diaspora: From the Greek, "scattering." A dispersion of religious or ethnic group(s) to foreign countries, such as the scattering of Jews when driven out of the land of Israel, or Hindus driven from Sri Lanka, Pakistan and Bangladesh.

difi: (Shūm) The space aspect of the mind. The perspective of space travel, *devas* and Gods; inner communication. Pronounced *dee-fee*. See: *Shūm, Shūm perspectives*.

dīkshā: दीक्षा "Initiation." Solemn induction by which one is entered into a new realm of spiritual awareness and practice by a teacher or preceptor through the transmission of blessings. Denotes initial or deepened connection with the teacher and his lineage and is usually accompanied by ceremony. Initiation, revered as a moment of awakening, may be conferred by a touch, a word, a look or a thought. See: *grace, śaktinipāta*.

Dīpāvali: दीपावली "Row of Lights." A very popular home and community festival during which Hindus of all denominations light oil or electric lights and set off fireworks in a joyful celebration of the victory of good over evil, light over darkness. It is a Hindu solidarity day and is considered the greatest national festival of India. In several countries, including Nepal, Malaysia, Singapore, Sri Lanka and Trinidad and Tobago, it is an inter-religious event and a national holiday. It occurs in October-November.

disincarnate: Having no physical body; of the astral plane; astral beings. See: *astral body, astral plane*.

dissipate: Here, to let loose more than often the vital sexual energies, which must be transmuted in order to make progress in spiritual life. Dissipation occurs through excessive talk, and through loss of the vital fluids, such as through masturbation or excessive intercourse only for pleasure, with no intention of conceiving a child. See: *actinic, odic, transmutation*.

dissolution: Dissolving or breaking up into parts. An alternative term for destruction. See: *Naṭarāja*.

Divine: Godlike; supremely good or beautiful.

Divinity: A God, or Deity. Also the spiriuality or holiness that pervades the universe and is most easily felt in the presence of a holy man or in a temple.

dogma: An authoritative principle, belief, or statement of ideas or opinion, especially one considered to be absolutely true.

door of *Brahman:* *Brahmarandhra;* also called *nirvāna chakra*. A subtle or esoteric aperture in the crown of the head, the opening of *sushumṇā nāḍī* through which *kuṇḍalinī* enters in ultimate Self Realization, and the spirit escapes at death. Only the spirits of the truly pure leave the body in this way. *Saṁsārīs* take a downward course. See: *jñāna, kuṇḍalinī*.

dosai: தோசை An Indian crepe, a crisp, paper-thin pancake, generally made with soaked, slightly fermented ground rice and urad dal, water and spices.

dowry: Money or property brought by a bride to her husband at marriage. A tradition that exists in most cultures in some form, but which in India has been carried to abusive extremes, where the bride's family must pay exorbitant sums of money to the groom's family to buy a husband for their daughter. Dowry is outlawed now in India.

dross: Rubbish, waste matter; useless byproduct.

drudgery: Work that may be tedious, menial, hard or unpleasant.

Druid: An ancient Celtic priest, magician or soothsayer of Britain, Ireland and Gaul (ancient region corresponding roughly to modern-day France and Belgium).

dual: Having or composed of two parts or kinds.

dualism: See: *dvaita-advaita.*

duality: A state or condition of being dual.

dvaita-advaita: द्वैत अद्वैत "Dual-nondual; twoness-not twoness." Among the most important categories in the classification of Hindu philosophies. *Dvaita* and *advaita* define two ends of a vast spectrum. ***—dvaita:*** The doctrine of dualism, according to which reality is ultimately composed of two irreducible principles, entities, truths, etc. God and soul, for example, are seen as eternally separate. **—dualistic:** Of or relating to dualism, concepts, writings, theories which treat dualities (good-and-evil, high-and-low, them-and-us) as fixed, rather than transcendable. **—pluralism:** A form of nonmonism which emphasizes three or more eternally separate realities, e.g., God, soul and world. ***—advaita:*** The doctrine of nondualism or monism, that reality is ultimately composed of one whole principle, substance or God, with no independent parts. In essence, all is God. **—monistic theism:** A dipolar view which encompasses both monism and dualism. See: *monistic theism.*

dysfunctional: Abnormal, impaired, not functioning completely.

ego: The external personality or sense of "I" and "mine." Broadly, individual identity. In Śaiva Siddhānta and other schools, the ego is equated with the *tattva* of *ahaṁkāra,* "I-maker," which bestows the sense of I-ness, individuality and separateness from God. See: *āṇava mala.*

egocentric: Placing one's own ego in the center of all values and experiences.

egoism: The tendency to be self-centered; egotism, conceit.

egoity: Self-interest, selfishness See: *āṇava mala.*

egotist: One who is selfish, conceited or boastful.

Eckhart, Meister Johannes: German theologian (1260-1327) regarded as the founder of Catholic mysticism in Germany. His influential works concern the union of the individual soul with God.

elastic: Flexible, able to stretch and immediately return to an original length or shape.

elemental temples: Five temples in South India, each enshrining one of the Pañchatattva Liṅgas, five sacred emblems of Lord Śiva representing the five basic elements: earth *(pṛithivī),* water *(āpas),* fire *(tejas),* air *(vāyu)* and ether *(ākāśa).* 1) The Earth Liṅga is enshrined in the Ekambareśvara Temple at Kanchipuram. 2) The Water Liṅga is worshiped at Jambukeśvara Temple in Trichy. 3) The Fire Liṅga is venerated at the Arunchaleśvara Temple in Tiruvannamalai. 4) The Air Liṅga is venerated at the Śrī Kalahasti Temple, north of Tirupati. 5) The Ākāśa Liṅga is enshrined at the stunning Śrī Naṭarāja Temple of Chidambaram.

emanation: "Flowing out from." *Ābhāsa.* Shining forth from a source, emission or issuing from. A monistic doctrine of creation whereby God issues forth manifestation like rays from the sun or sparks from a fire.

embryo: The early development of a human/animal within the womb, up to the end of the second month. An undeveloped plant within a seed.

Emerson, Ralph Waldo: American poet, essayist and philosopher (1803-1882), a central figure of American transcendentalism. Enamored of Indian thought, he was instrumental in popularizing the *Bhagavad Gītā* and the *Upanishads* in the US.

eminent: High; above others in stature, rank or achievement. Renowned or distinguished; prominent, conspicuous. Not to be confused with: 1) *imminent,* about to happen; 2) *emanate,* to issue from; 3) *immanent,* inherent or indwelling.

emkaef: (Shūm) No awareness, state beyond that of singular awareness. Not a word for Self Realization, but the entry into that nonexperience. Pronounced *eem-kaw-eef.* See: *Shūm.*

emotional body: See: *kośa.*

enlightened: Having attained enlightenment, Self Realization. A *jñānī* or *jīvanmukta.* See: *jñāna, Self Realization.*

enlightenment: For Śaiva monists, Self Realization, *samādhi* without seed *(nirvikalpa samādhi);* the ultimate attainment, sometimes referred to as Paramātma *darśana,* or as *ātma darśana,* "Self vision" (a term which appears in Patanjali's *Yoga Sūtras).* Enlightenment is the experience-nonexperience resulting in the realization of one's transcendent Self, Paraśiva, which exists beyond time, form and space. Each tradition has its own understanding of enlightenment, often indicated by unique terms. See: *God Realization, kuṇḍalinī, Self Realization.*

enmity: Active or aggressive, deep-seated hatred or ill will, often mutual between two parties.

equivocal: Uncertain; undecided; doubtful.

esoteric: Hard to understand or secret. Teaching intended for a chosen few, as an inner group of initiates. Abtruse or private.

essence (essential): The most important, ultimate, real and unchanging nature of a thing or being. **—essence of the soul:** See: *ātman, soul.*

eternity: Time without beginning or end.

ether: *Ākāśa.* Space, the most subtle of the five elements. See: *ākāśa.*

ethereal: Highly refined, light, invisible.

etheric: Having to do with ether or space.

ethics: The code or system of morals of a nation, people, philosophy, religion, etc. See: *dharma, yama-niyama.*

ethnic: Pertaining to, or designating a large group or groups of people with the same culture, race, religion, or national heritage.

evil: That which is bad, morally wrong, causing harm, pain, misery. In Western religions, evil is often thought of as a moral antagonism to God. Hindus hold that evil, known in Sanskrit as *pāpa, pāpman* or *dushṭā,* is the result of unvirtuous acts *(pāpa* or *adharma)* caused by the instinctive-intellectual mind dominating and obscuring deeper, spiritual intelligence. The evil-doer is viewed as a young soul, ignorant of the value of right thought, speech and action, unable to live in the world without becoming entangled in *māyā*. —**intrinsic evil:** Inherent, inborn badness. Hinduism holds that there is no intrinsic evil, and the real nature of man is his divine, soul nature, which is goodness. See: *hell, karma, pāpa, sin.*

evolution of the soul: *Adhyātma prasāra.* In Śaiva Siddhānta, the soul's evolution is a progressive unfoldment, growth and maturing toward its inherent, divine destiny, which is complete merger with Śiva. The soul is not created at the moment of conception of a physical body. Rather, it is created in the Śivaloka. It evolves by taking on denser and denser sheaths—cognitive, instinctive-intellectual and *prāṇic*—until finally it takes birth in physical form in the Bhūloka. Then it experiences many lives, maturing through the reincarnation process. There are young souls just beginning to evolve, and old souls nearing the end of their earthly sojourn. See: *mala, moksha, reincarnation, saṁsāra, viśvagrāsa.*

excruciating: Intensely painful, agonizing.

existence: "Coming or standing forth." Being; reality; that which is.

existentialism: A philosophy that emphasizes the uniqueness and isolation of the individual experience in a hostile or indifferent universe, regards human existence as unexplainable, and stresses freedom of choice and responsibility for the consequences of one's acts.

existentialist: Pertaining to, or believing in, the philosophy of *existentialism.*

exuberant: Full of unrestrained enthusiasm or joy.

faith: Trust or belief. Conviction. From the Latin *fidere*, "to trust." *Faith* in its broadest sense means "religion, *dharma.*" More specifically, it is the essential element of religion—the belief in phenomena beyond the pale of the five senses, distinguishing it sharply from rationalism. Faith is established through intuitive or transcendent experience of an individual, study of scripture and hearing the testimony of the many wise *ṛishis* speaking out the same truths over thousands of years. This inner conviction is based in the divine sight of the third eye center, *ājñā chakra.* Rightly founded, faith transcends reason, but does not conflict with reason. Faith also means confidence, as in the testimony and reputation of other people. The Sanskrit equivalent is *śraddhā.* Synonyms include *āstikya, viśvāsa, dharma* and *mati.*

family life: See: *gṛihastha āśrama, extended family, joint family.*

family practices: See: *five family practices.*

fast: To abstain from all or certain foods, as in observance of a vow or holy day. Hindus fast in various ways. A simple fast may consist of merely avoiding certain foods for a day or more, such as when vegetarians avoid *tamasic* or *rajasic* foods or when nonvegetarians abstain from fish, fowl and meats. A moderate fast would involve avoiding heavier foods, or taking only juices, teas and other liquids. Such fasts are sometimes observed only during the day, and a normal meal is permitted after sunset. Serious fasting, which is done under supervision, involves taking only water for a number of days and requires a cessation of most external activities.

fetus: A human/animal embryo more than eight weeks after conception until birth.

First World: The physical universe, called Bhūloka, of gross or material substance in which phenomena are perceived by the five senses. See: *loka.*

five family practices: *Pañcha kuṭumba sādhana,* or five parenting guidelines. 1) **Good Conduct—Dharmachāra:** Loving fathers and mothers, knowing they are the greatest influence in a child's life, behave the way their dear children should when adults. They never anger or argue before young ones. Father in a *dhotī*, mother in a *sārī* at home, all sing to God, Gods and *guru.* 2) **Home Worship—Dharma Svagṛiha:** Loving fathers and mothers establish a separate shrine room in the home for God, Gods and guardian *devas* of the family. Ideally it should be large enough for all the dear children. It is a sacred place for scriptural study, a refuge from the karmic storms of life.3) **Talking About Religion—Dharma Sambhāshana:** Loving fathers and mothers speak Vedic precepts while driving, eating and playing. This helps dear children understand experiences in right perspective. Parents know many worldly voices are blaring, and their *dharmic* voice must be stronger. 4) **Continuing Self-Study—Dharma Svādhyāya:** Loving fathers and mothers keep informed by studying the *Vedas, Āgamas* and sacred literature, listening to *swāmīs* and *pandits.* Youth face a world they will one day own, thus parents prepare their dear children to guide their own future progeny. 5) **Following a Spiritual Preceptor—Dharma Saṅga:** Loving fathers and mothers choose a preceptor, a traditional satguru, and lineage to follow. They support their lineage with all their heart, energy and service. He in turn provides them clear guidance for a successful life, material and religious.

five states of mind: The conscious, subconscious, subsubconscious, subsuperconscious and superconscious mind. See: *mind (five states).*

forbearance: Self-control; responding with patience and compassion, especially under provocation. Endurance; tolerance. See: *yama-niyama.*

forehead marks: See: *tilaka.*

force field: A region of space through which a force, for example, an electric current, is operative. Here the term is used in reference to psychic energies, both positive and negative, that are generated by the emotions, the mind, the higher or lower *chakras* or emanate from the inner higher or lower worlds. Positive psychic force fields, such as those surrounding and protecting a temple, an *ashram* or harmonious home, are built up by worship, invoking of the Deities, *sādhana, tapas* and disciplined living, attracting divine spirits, or *devas.* Negative force fields, such as found in the worst areas of a city or within an inharmonious home, are built up by anger, violence, lust and outbursts of such lower emotions, attracting evil spirits, or *asuras.* See: *odic, actinic, prāṇa.*

formless: Philosophically, *atattva,* beyond the realm of form or substance. Used in attempting to describe the wondersome, indescribable Absolute, which is "timeless, formless and spaceless." God Śiva has form and is formless. He is the immanent Pure Consciousness or pure form. He is the Personal Lord manifesting as innumerable forms; and He is the impersonal, transcendent Absolute beyond all form. Thus we know Śiva in three perfections, two of form and one formless. See: *Paraśiva, Satchidānanda.*

four traditional goals: *Chaturvarga,* "four-fold good," or *purushārtha,* "human goals or purposes." The four pursuits in which humans may legitimately engage, a basic principle of Hindu ethics. 1) ***dharma*** **("Righteous living"):** The fulfillment of virtue, good works, duties and responsibilities, restraints and observances—performing one's part in the service and upliftment of society. This includes pursuit of truth under a guru of a particular *paramparā* and *sampradāya.* See: *dharma.* 2) ***artha*** **("Wealth"):** Material welfare and abundance, money, property, possessions. Artha is the pursuit of wealth, guided by dharma. It includes the basic needs—food, money, clothing and shelter—and extends to the wealth required to maintain a comfortable home, raise a family, fulfill a successful career and perform religious duties. See: *yajña.* 3) ***kāma*** **("Pleasure, love; enjoyment"):** Earthly love, aesthetic and cultural fulfillment, pleasures of the world (including sexual), the joys of family, intellectual satisfaction. Enjoyment of happiness, security, creativity, usefulness and inspiration. 4) ***moksha*** **("Liberation"):** Freedom from rebirth through the ultimate attainment, realization of the Self God, Paraśiva. The spiritual attainments and superconscious joys, attending renunciation and *yoga* leading to Self Realization. *Moksha* comes through the fulfillment of *dharma, artha* and *kāma* in the current or past lives, so that one is no longer attached to worldly joys or sorrows.

fundamentalism: Any religious creed or philosophical persuasion marked by extreme dogmatism and intolerance. There are fundamentalist denominations within many religions, believing in a literal interpretation of their scripture as the exclusive truth, the one and only way which all souls must follow to attain salvation. Historically, fundamentalism, especially when coupled with evangelical zeal, has led to aggression, even violence, against nonbelievers.

Gaṇapati: गणपति "Leader of the *gaṇas.*" A surname of *Gaṇeśa.*

Gandhi: गन्धी Mohandas Karamchand Gandhi (1869-1948), the Hindu nationalist leader whose strategy of nonviolent resistance won India's freedom from British colonial rule. Often honored as *Mahātma* ("great soul").

Gaṇeśa: गणेश "Lord of Categories." (From *gaṇ,* "to count or reckon," and *Īśa,* "lord.") Or: "Lord of attendants *(gaṇa),*" synonymous with *Gaṇapati.* Gaṇeśa is a Mahādeva, the beloved elephant-faced Deity honored by Hindus of every sect. He is the Lord of Obstacles (Vighneśvara), revered for His great wisdom and invoked first before any undertaking, for He knows all intricacies of each soul's *karma* and the perfect path of *dharma* that makes action successful. He sits on the *mūlādhāra chakra* and is easy of access. See: *gaṇa, Gaṇapati, Mahādeva.*

Gaṇeśa Chaturthī: गणेश चतुर्थी Birthday of Lord Gaṇeśa, a ten-day festival of August-September that culminates in a spectacular parade called Gaṇeśa Visarjana. It is a time of rejoicing, when all Hindus worship together.

Gaṅgā sādhana: गंगासाधन A practice for unburdening the mind, performed by releasing the energy of unwanted thoughts. An internal cleansing *sādhana* of sitting quietly by a river or stream and listening to the Aum sound as the water flows over the rocks. When a thought arises, it is mentally placed into a leaf held in the right hand, then gently tossed into the water. Then a flower is offered to thank the water for carrying away the thought. This is a subconscious cleansing process of letting go of hurts, anger, problems or whatever it is that rises in the mind to disturb the meditation.

Ganges *(Gaṅgā):* गंगा India's most sacred river, 1,557 miles long, arising in the Himalayas above Haridwar under the name Bhagīratha, and being named Gaṅgā after joining the Alakanada (where the Sarasvatī is said to join them underground). It flows southeast across the densely populated Gangetic plain, joining its sister Yamunā (or Jumnā) at Prayaga (Allahabad) and ending at the Bay of Bengal.

Gangetic: Near to or on the banks of the Ganges river in North India.

Gangetic abodes of Śiva: Ancient pilgrimage places that devotees strive to visit at least once in a lifetime, including the sacred Viśvanātha Temple of Varanasi (on the banks of the Gaṅgā between the Varaṇā and Asī Rivers); Gaṅgotri Temple at the source of the Gaṅga (near Kedarnath), and the sacred temples in the cities of Hardwar and Rishikesh.

garbhagṛiha: गर्भगृह The "innermost chamber," sanctum sanctorum, of a Hindu temple, where the primary *mūrti* is installed. It is a small, cave-like room, usually made of granite stone, to which only priests are permitted access. Esoterically it represents the cranial chamber. See: *temple.*

gauche: Someone lacking grace or social tack; awkward,

clumsy.

ghee: घी Hindi for clarified butter; *ghṛita* in Sanskrit. Butter that has been boiled and strained. An important sacred substance used in temple lamps and offered in fire ceremony, *yajña.* It is also used as a food with many *āyurvedic* virtues. See: *yajña.*

Gibran, Kahlil: Lebanese mystic, poet, dramatist and artist (1888-1931), best known for *The Prophet.*

Gītā: गीता "Song." Foreshortened title of *Bhagavad Gītā.* See: *Bhagavad Gītā.*

gluttony: Excessiveness in eating or drinking.

God Realization: Direct and personal experience of the Divine within oneself. It can refer to either 1) *savikalpa samādhi* ("enstasy with form") in its various levels, from the experience of inner light to the realization of Satchidānanda, the pure consciousness or primal substance flowing through all form, or 2) *nirvikalpa samādhi* ("enstasy without form"), union with the transcendent Absolute, Paraśiva, the Self God, beyond time, form and space. In *The Master Course* trilogy, the expression *God Realization* is used to name both of the above *samādhis,* whereas *Self Realization* refers only to *nirvikalpa samādhi.* See: *rāja yoga, samādhi, Self Realization.*

God: Supernal being. Either the Supreme God, Śiva, or one of the Mahādevas, great souls, who are among His creation. See: *Gods, Mahādeva, Śiva.*

Gods: Mahādevas, "great beings of light." The plural of *God* refers to extremely advanced beings existing in their self-effulgent soul bodies in the causal plane. The meaning of *Gods* is best seen in the phrase, "God and the Gods," referring to the Supreme God—Śiva—and the Mahādevas, who are His creation. See: *Mahādeva.*

grace: "Benevolence, love, giving," from the Latin *gratia,* "favor," "goodwill." God's power of revealment, *anugraha śakti* ("kindness, showing favor"), by which souls are awakened to their true, Divine nature. Grace in the unripe stages of the spiritual journey is experienced by the devotee as receiving gifts or boons, often unbidden, from God. The mature soul finds himself surrounded by grace. He sees all of God's actions as grace, whether they be seemingly pleasant and helpful or not. See: *śaktinipāta.*

gratification: Indulging in what is desired.

Great Oath: The Śaiva *sannyāsin's* vow of renunciation, the *mahāvrata* of the Śaivite pathfinders. It is the relinquishment of the world, desire and ego. It is detachment founded in knowledge of the magnetic nature of body, mind and emotion, a knowledge which inclines the soul toward noninvolvement with external forms and, in time, summons forth realization of Paraśiva, Absolute Reality. See: *sannyāsa.*

gṛihastha: गृहस्थ "Householder." Family man or woman. Family of a married couple and other relatives. Pertaining to family life. The purely masculine form of the word is *gṛihasthin,* and the feminine *gṛihasthī. Gṛihasthī* also names the home itself. See: *āśrama dharma.*

gṛihastha āśrama: गृहस्थ आश्रम "Householder stage." See: *āśrama dharma.*

gṛihastha dharma: गृहस्थधर्म "Householder law." The virtues and ideals of family life. See: *āśrama dharma.*

gross: Dense, coarse, unrefined, crude; carnal, sensual; lacking sensitivity.

guarantor: A person or corporation that makes or gives assurance or pledge.

guṇa: गुण "Strand; quality." The three constituent principles of prakṛiti, primal nature. The three *guṇas* are: —***sattva:*** "Purity," quiescent, rarified, translucent, pervasive, reflecting the light of Pure Consciousness. —***rajas:*** "Passion," inherent in energy, movement, action, emotion, life. —***tamas:*** "Darkness," inertia, density, the force of contraction, resistance and dissolution. The *guṇas* are integral to Hindu thought, as all things are composed of the combination of these qualities of nature, including *āyurveda,* arts, environments and personalities. See: *āyurveda.*

guru: गुरु "Weighty one," indicating an authority of great knowledge or skill. A title for a teacher or guide in any subject, such as music, dance, sculpture, but especially religion. According to the *Advayatāraka Upanishad* (14-18), *guru* means "dispeller *(gu)* of darkness *(ru).*" See: *guru-śishya system, satguru.*

guru bhakti: गुरुभक्ति Devotion to the teacher. The attitude of humility, love and ideation held by a student in any field of study. In the spiritual realm, the devotee strives to see the *guru* as his higher Self. By attuning himself to the *satguru's* inner nature and wisdom, the disciple slowly transforms his own nature to ultimately attain the same peace and enlightenment his *guru* has achieved. *Guru bhakti* is expressed through serving the *guru,* meditating on his form, working closely with his mind and obeying his instructions. See: *guru, satguru, guru-śishya system.*

Gurudeva: गुरुदेव "Divine" or "radiant preceptor." From *guru,* "teacher" and *deva,* "angel." An affectionate, respectful title for the *satguru.* See: *guru, satguru, deva.*

Guru Mahāsannidhānam: गुरु महासन्निधानम् Spiritual head of a traditional *aadheenam.* See: *aadheenakartar.*

guru paramparā: गुरुपरंपरा "Preceptorial succession" (literally, "from one teacher to another"). A line of spiritual *gurus* in authentic succession of initiation; the chain of mystical power and authorized continuity, passed from *guru* to *guru.* See: *sampradāya.*

Guru Pūrṇimā: गुरु पूर्णिमा Occurring on the full moon of July, a day of rededication to all that the *guru* represents. It is occasioned by *pādapūjā*—ritual worship of the *guru's* sandals, which represent his holy feet. See: *guru-śishya system.*

***guru-śishya* system:** गुरुशिष्य "Master-disciple" system. An important educational system of Hinduism whereby the teacher conveys his knowledge and tradition to a student. Such knowledge, whether it be Vedic-Āgamic art, architecture or spirituality, is imparted through the developing relationship between *guru* and disciple. See: *guru, guru bhakti, satguru.*

guruthondu: குருதொண்டு "Service to the *guru.*" In *Living with Śiva, guruthondu* refers to the period of service that all young men of Gurudeva's Śaiva Church are expected to fulfill in a monastery, at least six months and ideally two years, prior to marriage. It also refers to the three-hour period that monastics devote in specific projects, working under the *guru's* direction, performed as a personal vigil, preceded and ended with a ceremony in the temple.

harmonize: To bring about agreement or harmony.

haṭha yoga: **हठयोग** "Forceful yoga." *Haṭha yoga* is a system of physical and mental exercise developed in ancient times as a means of rejuvenation by *ṛishis* and *tapasvins* who meditated for long hours, and used today in preparing the body and mind for meditation. In the West, *haṭha yoga* has been superficially adopted as a health-promoting, limbering, stress-reducing form of exercise, often included in aerobic routines. Esoterically, *ha* and *ṭha,* respectively, indicate the microcosmic sun *(ha)* and moon *(ṭha),* which symbolize the masculine current, *piṅgalā nāḍī,* and feminine current, *iḍā nāḍī,* in the human body. See: *āsana, kuṇḍalinī, nāḍī, yoga, rāja yoga.*

Haṭha Yoga Pradīpikā: **हठयोगप्रदीपिका** "Light on *haṭha yoga.*" A 14th-century text of 389 verses by Svatmarama Yogin which describes the philosophy and practices of *haṭha yoga.* It is widely used in *yoga* schools today.

havana: **हवन** "Making oblations through fire." The Vedic fire ritual. Same as *homa.* Can also refer to the offering place, or *kuṇḍa. Havis* and *havya* name the offerings. See: *homa.*

havana kuṇḍa: **हवन कुण्ड** "Offering pit." The fire pit, usually lined with bricks, into which offerings are placed during *havana,* or *homa,* rites.

heart *chakra:* *Anāhata chakra.* Center of direct cognition. See: *chakra.*

heaven: The celestial spheres, including the causal plane and the higher realms of the subtle plane, where souls rest and learn between births, and mature souls continue to evolve after *moksha. Heaven* is often used by translators as an equivalent to the Sanskrit *Svarga.* See: *loka.*

hedonist: Dedicated to or obsessed with the pursuit of pleasure.

heinous: Grossly wicked or reprehensible; abominable.

hell: *Naraka.* An unhappy, mentally and emotionally congested, distressful area of consciousness. Hell is a state of mind that can be experienced on the physical plane or in the sub-astral plane (Naraka) after death of the physical body. It is accompanied by the tormented emotions of hatred, remorse, resentment, fear, jealousy and self-condemnation. However, in the Hindu view, the hellish experience is not permanent, but a temporary condition of one's own making. See: *asura, Naraka.*

heresy: An opinion or belief that is strongly at variance with beliefs, customs within an established religion.

heroic measures: Medical intervention that provides breathing or heart function for someone whose body cannot sustain these processes on its own. Such measures today include cardiopulmonary resuscitation (CPR) and artificial respiration by human or by machine. Heroic measures span the gamut from emergency intervention, such as in an auto accident or a near drowning, to applying mechanical devices to the body of an elderly person who has suffered organ failure who would expire without such intrusion. Such heroic measures are welcomed in the event of accident or disease as temporary measures when recovery is likely, but they are not advised as long-term life support with little or no hope of recovery, especially in advanced years when death is immanent. It is the latter artifical extension of life beyond the natural capacity of the body to sustain itself or recover from an injury that *Living with Śiva* advises against.

higher-nature, lower nature: Expressions indicating man's refined, soulful qualities on the one hand, and his base, instinctive qualities on the other. See: *kośa, mind (five states), soul.*

Himalayan abodes of Śiva: These renowned pilgrimage sites include Mount Kailāśa (in Tibet) and Lake Manasarovar at its base; Kedarnath (in Garhwal, Uttara Pradesh) and Amarnath, the ice Liṅga cave temple in Kashmir.

Himalayan Academy: An educational and publishing institution of Saiva Siddhanta Church founded by Sivaya Subramuniyaswami in 1957. The Academy's objective is to spread the teachings of Sanātana Ḍharma through the monthly magazine HINDUISM TODAY, Innersearch travel-study programs, *The Master Course* trilogy of *Dancing with Śiva, Living with Śīva and Merging with Śiva,* as well as other publications and web resources, all as a public service to Hindus worldwide. See: *Hinduism Today, Subramuniyaswami.*

Himālayas: **हिमालय** "Abode of snow." The mountain system extending along the India-Tibet border and through Pakistan, Nepal and Bhutan.

hiṁsā: **हिंसा** "Injury;" "harm;" "hurt." Injuriousness, hostility—mental, verbal or physical. See: *ahiṁsā.*

Hindu: **हिन्दु** A follower of, or relating to, Hinduism. Generally, one is understood to be a Hindu by being born into a Hindu family and practicing the faith, or by professing oneself a Hindu. Acceptance into the fold is recognized through the name-giving sacrament, a temple ceremony called *nāmakaraṇa saṁskāra,* given to born Hindus shortly after birth, and to Hindus by choice who have proven their sincerity and been accepted by a Hindu community. Full conversion is completed through disavowal of previous religious affiliations and legal change of name. While traditions vary greatly, all Hindus rely on the *Vedas* as scriptural authority and generally attest to the following nine principles: 1) There exists a one, all-pervasive Supreme Being who is both immanent and transcendent, both creator and unmanifest Reality. 2) The universe undergoes endless cycles of creation, preservation and dissolution. 3) All souls are evolving toward God and will ultimately find *moksha:* spiritual knowledge and liberation from the cycle of rebirth. Not a single soul will be eternally deprived of this destiny. 4) *Karma* is the law of cause and effect by which each individual creates his own destiny by his thoughts, words and deeds. 5) The soul reincarnates, evolving through many births until all *karmas* have been resolved. 6) Divine beings exist in unseen worlds, and temple worship, rituals, sacraments, as well as personal devotionals, create a communion with these *devas* and Gods. 7) A spiritually awakened master or *satguru* is essential to know the transcendent Absolute, as are personal discipline, good conduct, purification, self-inquiry and meditation. 8) All life is sacred, to be loved and revered, and therefore one should practice *ahiṁsā,* nonviolence. 9) No particular religion teaches the only and exclusive way to salvation above all others. Rather, all genuine religious paths are facets of God's pure love and light, deserving tolerance and understanding. See: *Hinduism.*

Hindu Heritage Endowment: A publicly supported charitable foundation established by Satguru Sivaya Subramuniyaswami in December, 1993, as a public service. Its philanthropic mission is to set up and maintain secure, professionally managed endowments to offer financial support for individuals, religious leaders and institutions of all lineages of Sanātana Dharma. www.HHEonline.org

Hindu solidarity: Hindu unity in diversity. A major contemporary theme according to which Hindu denominations are mutually supportive and work together in harmony, while taking care not to obscure or lessen their distinctions or unique virtues. The underlying belief is that Hinduism will be strong if each of its sects, and lineages is vibrant. See: *Hinduism.*

Hinduism (Hindu Dharma): हिन्दुधर्म India's indigenous religious and cultural system, followed today by nearly one billion adherents, mostly in India, but with large diaspora in many other countries. Also called Sanātana Dharma (Eternal religion) and Vaidika Dharma (Religion of the *Vedas.*) Hinduism is the world's most ancient religion and encompasses a broad spectrum of philosophies ranging from pluralistic theism to absolute monism. It is a family of myriad faiths with four primary denominations: Śaivism, Vaishṇavism, Śāktism and Smārtism. These four hold such divergent beliefs that each is a complete and independent religion. Yet, they share a vast heritage of culture and belief—*karma, dharma,* reincarnation, all-pervasive Divinity, temple worship, sacraments, manifold Deities, the *guru-śishya* tradition and a reliance on the *Vedas* as scriptural authority. From the rich soil of Hinduism have sprung other traditions, including Jainism, Buddhism and Sikhism, which rejected the *Vedas* and thus emerged as completely distinct religions, dissociated from Hinduism, while still sharing many philosophical insights and cultural values with their parent faith. See: *Hindu.*

Hinduism Today: The Hindu family magazine founded by Sivaya Subramuniyaswami in 1979, published bimonthly by Himalayan Academy to affirm Sanātana Dharma and record the modern history of a billion-strong global religion in renaissance, reaching 150,000 readers in over 100 countries. See: *Himalayan Academy.*

Hispanic: Latin American; relating to their culture.

holy ash: See: *vibhūti.*

holy feet: The feet of God, a God, *satguru* or any holy person, often represented by venerable sandals, called *śrī pādukā* in Sanskrit and *tiruvadi* in Tamil. The feet of a Divinity are considered especially precious as they represent the point of contact of the Divine and the physical, and are thus revered as the source of grace. The sandals or feet of the *guru* are the object of worship on his *jayantī* (birthday), on Guru Pūrṇimā and other special occasions. See: *satguru.*

Holy Kural: See: *Tirukural.*

holy orders: A divine ordination or covenant, conferring religious authority. Vows that members of a religious body make, especially a monastic body or order, such as the vows (holy orders of renunciation) made by a *sannyāsin* at the time of his initiation *(sannyāsa dīkshā),* which establish a covenant with the ancient holy order of *sannyāsa.* See: *sannyāsa dīkshā.*

homa: होम "Fire-offering." A sacred ceremony in which the Gods are offered oblations through the medium of fire in a sanctified fire pit, *homakuṇḍa,* usually made of earthen bricks. *Homa* rites are enjoined in the *Vedas, Āgamas* and *Dharma* and *Gṛihya Śāstras.* See: *agni.*

Homo sapiens: Human beings, man; the species including all existing races of mankind.

hosting guests: Hospitality toward special guests in Hindu homes is extraordinary. It follows the Vedic edict that the guest is God in one of many forms. Therefore, greetings and hospitality are offered as if to a God. ¶While each visitor, whether close or distant, is treated with love and generosity, a protocol is observed on special occasions for honored guests in the South Indian/Sri Lankan Hindu tradition. The house is decorated with *tombais* (ornaments made from palm leaves) and mango leaves above the front door. Outside the front door on the porch are set a *kuttuvilaku* (standing oil lamp) and *kumbha* (water pot with five mango leaves and a decorated coconut, representing Lord Gaṇeśa). *Kolams* (floor decorations made from colored rice flour) are drawn at the threshold or gate of the home. ¶Guests are greeted at the door with offerings of *vibhuti, kuṅkuma* and *chandana,* then sprinkled lightly with rose water and given a small candy. They then enter the home and are led into the shrine room where the elder man of the house performs *āratī* to Gaṇeśa, Murugan and Śiva. Following the *ārati,* everyone goes into the communal room of the house and arranges themselves in a *chakravāla,* or a circle according to age, first the men, then the ladies, each younger sitting to his or her elder's left. The most senior male leads everyone in a peaceful invocation, then *bhājanas* are led and sung by all. Other activities follow. ¶For meals, mats are laid on the floor in two lines, one side for men and another for ladies. Banana leaves are placed before each person, sometimes on top of plates. The lady of the house and the youngest women serve everyone. Salt is first placed at the top right corner of each leaf, followed by the curries and rice with *sambar.* Seconds are offered until everyone is satisfied. After the initial rice with *sambar,* rice is served with *rāsam* and then with curd, or yogurt, as well as more salt, if necessary, and pickles. Tumblers of water and *rāsam* are available for each guest (although usually water only is served nowadays). *Kesari, payasam* or other sweets and tea are served after the meal. When the meal is concluded, very special guests would be offered a bowl of water to wash their hands where they sit. Hands are never washed in the kitchen sink, but the bathroom is okay. In Asia a special sink is most often located in the room where meals are taken. The hostess, standing and facing East, gives each married lady *kuṅkuma* and all guests a gift upon their departure, often as simple as a few betel leaves or a candy. Friends, relatives and casual guests are treated according to a more informal protocol.

hrī: ह्री "Remorse; modesty." See: *yama-niyama.*

humility: Modesty in behavior, attitude, or spirit; not arrogant or prideful.

huṇḍi: हुण्डि "Offering box," from hun, "to sacrifice." A strong box inside Hindu temples into which devotees place their contributions.

hymns: Songs of praise to God, Gods or guru.

hypocrisy: Professing beliefs, feelings, or virtues that one does not hold or possess; false pretensions.

icçhā śakti: इच्छाशक्ति "Desire; will."

ice: See: *methamphetamine.*

iḍā nāḍī: इडानाडी "Soothing channel." The feminine psychic current flowing along the spine. See: *kuṇḍalinī, nāḍī, odic, piṅgalā.*

ideology: A set of doctrines or beliefs that form the basis of a system of thought, often used to mean narrow-minded or uncritical adherence to such a system.

immanent: Indwelling; inherent and operating within. Relating to God, the term *immanent* means present in all things and throughout the universe, not aloof or distant. Not to be confused with *imminent,* about to happen; *emanate,* to issue from; *eminent,* high in rank.

immemorial (from time immemorial): From a time so distant that it extends beyond history or human memory.

imminent: Threatening to happen without delay; impending.

impetus: A push that stimulates activity. Driving force; motive, incentive.

impulse: A sudden wish or urge that prompts an unplanned act or feeling.

impurity: A state of immorality, pollution or sin. Uncleanliness.

inanimate: See: *animate-inanimate.*

inauspicious: Not favorable. Not a good time to perform certain actions or undertake projects. Ill-omened.

incantation: *Japa* or *mantraprayoga.* The chanting of prayers, verses or formulas for magical or mystical purposes. Also such chants *(mantra).* See: *mantra.*

incarnation: From *incarnate,* "made flesh." The soul's taking on a human body. **—divine incarnation:** The concept of *avatāra.* The Supreme Being's (or other Mahādeva's) taking of human birth, generally to re-establish *dharma.* This doctrine is important to several Hindu sects, notably Vaishṇavism, but not held by most Śaivites. See: *avatāra, Vaishṇavism.*

indigent: Impoverished; poor; needy; destitute.

indomitable: Not easily discouraged, defeated or subdued. Unconquerable.

Indra: इन्द्र "Ruler." Vedic God of rain and thunder, warrior king of the devas. A great, inner-plane being who is invoked in hundreds of Vedic hymns.

I-ness: The conceiving of oneself as an "I," or ego, which Hinduism considers a state to be transcended. See: *āṇava mala, mind (individual).*

infidel: One who has no religious beliefs, or who rejects a particular religion.

infiltrate: To gradually penetrate so as to counteract or seize control from within.

infinitesimal: Infinitely small; too small to be measured.

inhibit: To hold back, restrain, prohibit or forbid. To suppress.

initiation (to initiate): Entering into; admission as a member. In Hinduism, initiation from a qualified preceptor is considered invaluable for spiritual progress. See: *dīkshā, śaktinpāta, sannyāsa dīkshā.*

innate: Naturally inborn; not acquired. That which belongs to the inherent nature or constitution of a being or thing.

inner light: A moonlight-like glow that can be seen inside the head or throughout the body when the *vṛittis,* mental fluctuations, have been sufficiently quieted. To be able to see and bask in the inner light is a milestone on the path. See: *vṛitti.*

inner planes: Inner worlds or regions of existence.

innerversity: Learning from within. A word coined by Sivaya Subramuniyaswami which indicates turning inward, through *yoga* concentration and meditation, to the vast superconscious state of mind; whence knowledge can be unfolded.

insignia: Plural of the Latin *insigne.* Signs or symbols of identity, rank or office, such as a badge, staff or emblem.

instinctive: "Natural" or "innate." From the Latin *instinctus,* participle of *instingere,* "impelling," pricking," "instigating." The drives and impulses that order the animal world and the physical and lower *astral* aspects of humans—for example, self-preservation, procreation, hunger and thirst, as well as the emotions of greed, hatred, anger, fear, lust and jealousy. See: *mind, yama-niyama.*

instinctive mind: *Manas chitta.* The lower mind, which controls the basic faculties of perception, movement, as well as ordinary thought and emotion. *Manas chitta* is of the *manomaya kośa.* See: *kośa, yama-niyama, mind.*

instinctive-intellectual mind: The mind in ordinary consciousness, when actions are based either upon instinctive emotional desires and fears or intellectual concepts and reason. See: *astral body, instinctive mind, kośa, odic force, soul, subtle body, vāsanā.*

intellect: The power to reason or understand; power of thought; mental acumen. See: *intellectual mind, mind.*

intellectual mind: *Buddhi chitta.* The faculty of reason and logical thinking. It is the source of discriminating thought, rather than the ordinary, impulsive thought processes of the lower or instinctive mind, called *manas chitta. Buddhi chitta* is of the *manomaya kośa.* See: *mind.*

internalize: To take something inside of oneself.

internalized worship: *Yoga.* Worship or contact with God and Gods via meditation and contemplation rather than through external ritual. This is the *yogī's* path, preceded by the *charyā* and *kriyā pādas.* See: *meditation, yoga.*

intimacy: Privacy; closeness marked by informality.

intone: To speak with a singing tone or with a particular intonation.

intrinsic: Inward; essential; inherent. Belonging to the real nature of a being or thing.

intuit: To know or sense without resorting to rational processes.

intuition (to intuit): Direct understanding or cognition, which bypasses the process of reason. Intuition is a far superior source of knowing than reason, but it does not contradict reason. See: *cognition, mind (five states).*

Iraivan: இறைவன் "Worshipful one; divine one." One of the most ancient Tamil epithets for God. See: *Iraivan Temple.*

Iraivan Temple: A chola-style white-granite Iraivan Temple, hand-carved in Bangalore, India, established on Hawaii's Garden Island of Kauai. In the sanctum sanctorum, the Supreme God, Śiva (Parameśvara-Parāśakti-Paraśiva), will be enshrined as a massive 700-pound, single-pointed earthkeeper quartz crystal. See: *San Mārga Sanctuary.*

irul: இருள் "Darkness." The first of three stages of the *sakala avasthai* where the soul's impetus is toward *pāśa-jñānam,* knowledge and experience of the world. See: *pāśa-jñānam, sakala avasthā.*

iruvinaioppu: இருவினையொப்பு "Balance." The balance which emerges in the life of a soul in the stage of *marul,* or *paśu-jñānam,* the second stage of the *sakala avasthai,* when the soul turns toward the good and holy, becomes centered within himself, unaffected by the ups and downs in life. See: *marul, paśu-jñānam, sakala avasthā.*

Ishṭa Devatā: इष्टदेवता "Cherished" or "chosen Deity." The Deity that is the object of one's special pious attention. *Ishṭa Devatā* is a concept common to all Hindu sects. See: *Śakti, Śiva.*

Islam: The religion founded by Prophet Muhammed in Arabia about 625 CE. Islam connotes submission to Allah, the name for God in this religion. Adherents, known as Muslims, follow the "Five Pillars" enjoined in their scripture, the *Koran:* faith in Allah, praying five times daily facing Mecca, giving of alms, fasting during the month of Ramadan, and pilgrimage. Islam has over one billion followers, mostly in the Middle East, Pakistan, Africa, Indonesia, China, Russia and neighboring countries.

island abode of Śiva: A renowned pilgrimage site that devotees strive to visit at least once in a lifetime. Iraivan Temple is situated on the banks of the historically famous Wailua River on the Garden Island of Kauai in the Hawaii island chain. See: *Iraivan Temple, San Mārga Sanctuary.*

Īśvara: ईश्वर "Highest Lord." Supreme or Personal God. See: *Parameśvara.*

Īśvarapūjana: ईश्वरपूजन "Worship." See: *yama-niyama.*

Itihāsa: इतिहास "So it was." Epic history, particularly the *Rāmāyaṇa* and *Mahābhārata* (of which the *Bhagavad Gītā* is a part). This term sometimes encompasses the *Purāṇas,* especially the *Skānda Purāṇa* and the *Bhāgavata Purāṇa* (or *Śrīmad Bhāgavatam).* See: *Mahābhārata, Rāmāyaṇa, Smṛiti.*

jagadāchārya: जगदाचार्य "World teacher."

jaggery: A dark, crude sugar made from the sap of certain species of palm.

Jainism: *(Jaina)* जैन An ancient non-Vedic religion of India made prominent by the teachings of Mahāvīra ("Great Hero"), ca 500 BCE. The Jain *Āgamas* teach reverence for all life, vegetarianism and strict renunciation for ascetics. Jains focus great emphasis on the fact that all souls may attain liberation, each by their own effort. Their great historic saints, called Tīrthaṅkaras ("Ford-Crossers"), are objects of worship, of whom Mahāvīra was the 24th and last. Jains number about six million today, living mostly in India.

japa: जप "Recitation" or "incantation." Practice of concentrated repetition of a *mantra,* often while counting the repetitions on a *mālā* or strand of beads. It may be done silently or aloud. Sometimes known as *mantra yoga.* A major *sādhana* in Hindu spiritual practice, from the simple utterance of a few names of God to extraordinary feats of repeating sacred syllables millions of times for years on end. See: *mantra, yama-niyama, yoga.*

Jesus Christ: A teacher and prophet in the first century of this era whose teachings are the basis of Christianity.

Jew: An adherent of Judaism, or descendant of such adherents. See: *Judaism.*

jīva: जीव "Living, existing." From *jīv,* "to live." The individual soul, *ātman,* bound by the three *malas (āṇava, karma* and *māyā).* The individuated self *(jīva-ātman)* as opposed to the transcendental Self *(parama ātman).* The *jīvanmukta* is one who is "liberated while living." See: *ātman, evolution of the soul, purusha, soul.*

jñāna: ज्ञान "Knowledge; wisdom." (Tamil: *jñānam)* The matured state of the soul. It is the wisdom that comes as an aftermath of the *kuṇḍalinī* breaking through the door of *Brahman* into the realization of Paraśiva, Absolute Reality. The repeated *samādhis* of Paraśiva ever deepen this flow of divine knowing which establishes the knower in an extraordinary point of reference, totally different from those who have not attained this enlightenment. *Jñāna* is sometimes misunderstood as book knowledge, as a maturity or awakening that comes from simply understanding a complex philosophical system or systems. Those who define *jñāna* in this way deny that the path is a progression of *charyā-kriyā-yoga-jñāna* or of *karma-bhakti-rāja-jñāna.* Rather, they say that one can choose one's own path, and that each leads to the ultimate goal. See: *God Realization, door of Brahman, Self Realization, samādhi.*

jñāna dāna: ज्ञानदान "Gifts of wisdom." The *karma yoga* of printing, sponsoring and distributing Hindu religious literature, pamphlets and books, free of charge as a way of helping others spiritually. See: *yama-niyama.*

jñāna mārga: ज्ञानमार्ग See: *jñāna pāda.*

jñāna pāda: ज्ञानपाद "Stage of wisdom." According to the Śaiva Siddhānta *ṛishis, jñāna* is the last of the four successive *pādas* (stages) of spiritual unfoldment. It is the culmination of the third stage, the *yoga pāda.* Also names the knowledge section of each *Āgama.* See: *jñāna, pāda.*

jñānī: ज्ञानी "Sage." One who possesses *jñāna.* See: *jñāna.*

Judaic-Christian: Concerned with two of the three religions descended from Abraham, Judaism and Christianty, especially in the sense of their shared beliefs.

Judaism: The religion of over 12 million adherents worldwide (over half in the United States), first of the Abrahamic faiths, founded about 3,700 years ago in Canaan (now Israel) by Abraham, who started the lineage, and in Egypt by Moses, who emancipated the enslaved Jewish tribes. Its major scripture is the *Torah.*

jyotisha: ज्योतिष From *jyoti,* "light." "The science of the lights (or stars)." Hindu astrology, the knowledge and practice of analyzing events and circumstances, delineating character and determining auspicious moments, according to the positions and movements of heavenly bodies. In calculating horoscopes, *jyotisha* uses the sidereal (fixed-star) system, whereas Western astrology uses the tropical (fixed-date) method.

Kabala: A body of mystical teachings of rabbinical origin, partially based on an esoteric interpretation of the Hebrew scriptures.

Kadaitswami: கடையிற்சுவாமி MarMarketplace *swāmī.*" A *satguru* of the Nandinātha Sampradāya's Kailāsa Paramparā. Born ca 1804; died 1891. Renouncing his career as a judge in Bangalore, South India, Kadaitswami became a *sannyāsin* and trained under the "Rishi from the Himālayas," who then sent him on mission to Sri Lanka. He performed severe *tapas* on an island off the coast of Jaffna, awakening many *siddhis.* For decades he spurred the Sri Lankan Śaivites to greater spirituality through his inspired talks and demonstration of *siddhis.* He initiated Chellappaswami as the next *satguru* in the *paramparā.* Kadaitswami's name given at his initiation was Muthyanandaswami. See: *Kailāsa Paramparā, Nātha Sampradāya.*

kadhi kavi: காதிகாவ "Hand made saffron color." Hand-spun, hand woven cloth, ocher in color, worn by Hindu renunciates. A Tamil term referring to the color taken on by robes of *sādhus* who sit, meditate or live on the banks of the Ganges. The Sanskrit equivalent is *kāshāya.*

kahuna: "Deep one." A priest in the Native Hawaiian religion: 1) *Kahuna pule* officiated in the temples *(heiau)* and performed rites for the inauguration of houses. 2) Healer *kahunas* were medicine men who, depending on their specialty, delivered babies, treated sick children, and plied the arts of magic, diagnosis with fingertips, psychic reading and contacting the spirits of illness. 3) *Kaula kahunas* were reclusive ascetic prophets who lived aloof from society. A rare few *kahuna* lineages are carried forth today.

kaif: (Shūm) The state of awareness being aware of itself. Pronounced *kaw-eef.* See: *Shūm.*

Kailas (Kailāsa): कैलास "Crystalline," or "abode of bliss." The four-faced Himālayan peak (22,028 feet) in Western Tibet; the earthly abode of Lord Śiva. Associated with Mount Meru, the legendary center of the universe, it is an important pilgrimage destination for all Hindus, as well as for Tibetan Buddhists. Kailāsa is represented in Śāktism by a certain three-dimensional form of the Śrī Chakra yantra (also called kailāsa chakra). See: *Śrī Chakra.*

Kailāsa Paramparā: कैलासपरंपरा A spiritual lineage of 162 *siddhas,* a major stream of the Nandinātha Sampradāya, proponents of the ancient philosophy of monistic Śaiva Siddhānta. The first of these masters that history recalls was Maharishi Nandinatha (or Nandikesvara) 2,250 years ago, *satguru* to the great Tirumular, ca 200 BCE, and seven other disciples (as stated in the *Tirumantiram).* The lineage continued down the centuries and is alive today—the first recent *siddha* is known as the Rishi from the Himalayas," so named because he descended from those holy mountains. In South India, he initiated Kadaitswami (ca 1804–1891), who in turn initiated Chellappaswami

(1840–1915). Chellappan passed the mantle of authority to sage Yogaswami (1872–1964), who in 1949 initiated the present *satguru*, Sivaya Subramuniyaswami. See: *Nātha Sampradāya, Patanjali, Tirumular, Yogaswami.*

kalaśa: कलश "Water pot; pitcher; jar." In temple rites, a pot of water, *kalaśa*, topped with mango leaves and a husked coconut represents the Deity during special *pūjās*. *Kalaśa* also names the pot-like spires that adorn temple roofs.

Kali Yuga: कलियुग "Dark Age." The Kali Yuga is the last age in the repetitive cycle of four phases of time our solar system passes through. It is comparable to the darkest part of the night, as the forces of ignorance are in full power and many subtle faculties of the soul are obscured. See: *mahāpralaya, yuga.*

kamaṇḍalu: कमण्डलु "Vessel, water jar." Traditionally earthen or wooden, carried by *sannyāsins*, it symbolizes the renunciate's simple, self-contained life. The tree from which *kamaṇḍalus* are traditionally made is the *kamaṇḍalutaru*. See: *sannyāsa dharma, sannyāsin.*

Kane: The central, primary God of the Hawaiians, Lord of procreation, associated with dawn, sun and sky, creator of the three worlds (upper heaven, lower heaven and earth) and the beings within them.

Kant, Immanuel: German philosopher (1724-1804) whose classic works include *Critique of Pure Reason* (1781) and *Critique of Practical Reason* (1788).

karma: कर्म "Action," "deed." One of the most important principles in Hindu thought, *karma* refers to 1) any act or deed; 2) the principle of cause and effect; 3) a consequence or "fruit of action" *(karmaphala)* or "after effect" *(uttaraphala)*, which sooner or later returns upon the doer. What we sow, we shall reap in this or future lives. Selfish, hateful acts *(pāpakarma* or *kukarma)* will bring suffering. Benevolent actions *(puṇyakarma* or *sukarma)* will bring loving reactions. *Karma* is threefold: *sañchita, prārabdha* and *kriyamāna*. ***—sañchita karma:*** "Accumulated actions." The sum of all *karmas* of this life and past lives. ***—prārabdha karma:*** "Actions begun; set in motion." That portion of *sañchita karma* that is bearing fruit and shaping the events and conditions of the current life, including the nature of one's bodies, personal tendencies and associations. ***—kriyamāna karma:*** "Being made." The *karma* being created and added to *sañchita* in this life by one's thoughts, words and actions, or in the inner worlds between lives. *Kriyamāna karma* is also called *āgāmi*, "coming, arriving," and *vartamāna*, "current, revolving, set in motion." While some *kriyamāna karmas* bear fruit in the current life, others are stored for future births. See: *āṇava, fate, mala, māyā, moksha, pāśa, sin, soul.*

karma yoga: कर्मयोग "Union through action." Selfless service. See: *yoga.*

karṇavedha: कर्णवेध "Ear-piercing." See: *saṁskāras of childhood.*

Kārttikeya: कार्त्तिकेय Child of the Pleiades, from *Kṛittikā*, "Pleiades." Second son of Śiva, brother of Gaṇeśa. A great Mahādeva worshiped in all parts of India and the world. Also known as Muruga, Kumāra, Skanda, Shaṇmukhanātha, Subramaṇya and more, He is the God who guides that part of evolution which is religion, the transformation of the instinctive into a divine wisdom through the practice of *yoga*. See: *Muruga, Pleiades, Veda.*

Kauai: Northernmost of the Hawaiian islands; 553 sq. mi., pop. 50,000.

Kauai Aadheenam: Monastery-temple complex founded by Sivaya Subramuniyaswami in 1970; international headquarters of Saiva Siddhanta Church.

kavadi: காவடி A penance offered to Lord Murugan-Kārttikeya, especially during Tai Pusam, consisting of carrying in procession a heavy, beautifully decorated, wooden object from which pots of milk hang which are to be used for His *abhisheka*. The participant's tongue and other parts of the body are often pierced with small silver spears or hooks. See: *penance.*

kevala avasthā: केवल अवस्था "Stage of oneness, aloneness." (Tamil: *avasthai.)* In Śaiva Siddhānta, the first of three stages of the soul's evolution, a state beginning with its emanation or spawning by Lord Śiva as an etheric form unaware of itself, a spark of the Divine shrouded in a cloud of darkness known as *āṇava*. Here the soul is likened to a seed hidden in the ground, yet to germinate and unfold its potential. See: *āṇava, avasthā, evolution of the soul, sakala avasthā, soul, śuddha avasthā.*

konrai: கொண்றை The Golden Shower tree, Cassia fistula; symbol of Śiva's cascading, abundant, golden grace.

kośa: कोश "Sheath; vessel, container; layer." Philosophically, five sheaths through which the soul functions simultaneously in the various planes or levels of existence. They are sometimes compared to the layers of an onion. The *kośas*, in order of increasing subtlety, are as follows. ***—annamaya kośa:*** "Sheath composed of food." The physical or odic body, coarsest of sheaths in comparison to the faculties of the soul, yet indispensable for evolution and Self Realization, because only within it can all fourteen *chakras* fully function. See: *chakra.* ***—prāṇamaya kośa:*** "Sheath composed of *prāṇa* (vital force)." Also known as the *prāṇic* or health body, or the etheric body or etheric double, it coexists within the physical body as its source of life, breath and vitality, and is its connection with the astral body. *Prāṇa* moves in the *prāṇamaya kośa* as five primary currents or *vayus*, "vital airs or winds." *Prāṇamaya kośa* disintegrates at death along with the physical body. See: *prāṇa.* ***—manomaya kośa:*** "Mind-formed sheath." The lower astral body, from *manas*, "thought, will, wish." The instinctive-intellectual sheath of ordinary thought, desire and emotion. It is the seat of the *indriyas*, sensory and motor organs, respectively called *jñānendriyas* and *karmendriyas*. The *manomaya kośa* takes form as the physical body develops and is discarded in the inner worlds before rebirth. It is understood in two layers: 1) the odic-causal sheath *(buddhi)* and 2) the odic-astral sheath *(manas).* See: *indriya, manas.* ***—vijñānamaya kośa:*** "Sheath of cognition." The mental or cognitive-intuitive sheath, also called the actinodic sheath. It is the vehicle of higher thought, *vijñāna*—understanding, knowing, direct cognition, wisdom, intuition and creativity. ***—ānandamaya kośa:*** "Body of bliss." The intuitive-superconscious sheath or actinic-causal body. This inmost soul form *(svarūpa)* is the ultimate foundation of all life, intelligence and higher faculties. Its essence is Parāśakti (Pure Consciousness) and Paraśiva (the Absolute). See: *actinic, actinodic, manomaya kośa, odic, soul, subtle body.*

Kṛishṇa: कृष्ण "Black." Also related to *kṛishṭiḥ,* "drawing, attracting." One of the most popular Gods of the Hindu pantheon. He is worshiped by Vaishṇavas as the eighth *avatāra* incarnation of Vishṇu. He is best known as the Supreme Personage celebrated in the *Mahābhārata,* and specifically in the *Bhagavad Gītā.* In Gauḍīya Vaishṇavism, Kṛishṇa is the Godhead.

kṛishṇadāna: कृष्णदान "Black gifts." Bad money, funds derived through *adharmic* activities, which should not be received as donations by institutions, temples or *āśramas.* Bad money can never do good. It has a curse upon it. See: *yama-niyama.*

kriyā: क्रिया "Action." 1) In a general sense, *kriyā* can refer to doing of any kind. Specifically, it names religious action, especially rites or ceremonies. 2) In *yoga* terminology, *kriyā* names involuntary physical movements occuring during meditation that are pretended or caused by lack of emotional self-control or by the premature or unharnessed arousal of the *kuṇḍalinī.* 3) Various traditional *haṭha yoga* techniques for cleansing the mucous membranes. 4) The second stage of the Śaiva path, religious action, or *kriyā pāda.* See: *kriyā pāda.*

kriyā mārga: क्रियामार्ग See *kriyā pāda.*

kriyā pāda: क्रियापाद् "Stage of religious action; worship." The stage of worship and devotion, second of four progressive stages of maturation on the Śaiva Siddhānta path of attainment. See: *pāda.*

kriyā yoga: क्रियायोग "Action union." A term for various schools of meditative *yoga* practice emphasizing *prāṇāyāma,* breathing techniques, to accelerate spiritual progress, aggressively breaking awareness free of day-to-day consciousness and arousing the *kuṇḍalinī* with the goal of expanded consciousness and self transformation. Paramahansa Yogananda (1893-1952), who taught *kriyā yoga,* called it the "airplane route" to God. The modern revival of this ancient meditation system is said to have begun with the deathless *avatāra* Babaji in 1861.

kriyamāna karma: क्रियमानकर्म "Actions being made." See: *karma.*

kshamā: क्षमा "Patience." See: *yama-niyama.*

kshatriya: क्षत्रिय "Governing; sovereign." See: *caste.*

Ku: The Hawaiian Deity worshiped for prosperity, good fishing, abundant crops, good will, noble offspring, righteous leaders and victory in battle. In the Hindu pantheon, Ku is known as Kumāra, Skanda or Kārttikeya .

kukarma: कुकर्म "Unwholesome acts," or the fruit therefrom. See: *karma.*

kulaguru: कुलगुरु "Family preceptor" or "teacher." The *kulaguru* guides the joint and extended family, particularly through the heads of families, and provides spiritual education. He may or may not be a *satguru.*

kumbhābhisheka: कुम्भाभिषेक "Water pot ablution." The formal consecration of a new temple and its periodic reconsecration, usually at twelve-year intervals, following renovation, extensive cleaning and renewal. The rites culminate with the priests' pouring sanctified water over the temple spires, which resemble an inverted pot, or *kumbha.* Leading up to the consecration, during the construction of a temple, the following rituals are performed by the *sthapati* (architect) assisted by the temple priest: 1) *pañcha silanyasa:* setting five stones in the foundation at the northeast corner of the main sanctum; 2) *prathama silanyasa:* laying of first stone on foundation bed; 3) *nilayasthapanam:* placement of the door frame; 4) *garbhanyasam:* encasement of a cubical silver or gold box of gems, silver, gold and herbs; 5) *sthupi sthapanam:* placement of the tower capstone; 6) *nethron meelanam:* awakening the Deity by completing the chiseling of the eyes with a gold chisel dipped in milk and honey; 7) *mulalinga sthapanam:* installing the Deity.

Kumbhalavalai: கும்பிழாவளை A large and popular temple to Lord Gaṇeśa located in Alaveddy, Northern Sri Lanka, near Gurudeva's Sri Subramuniya Ashram.

kuṇḍalinī: कुण्डलिनी "She who is coiled; serpent power." The primordial cosmic energy in every individual which, at first, lies coiled like a serpent at the base of the spine and eventually, through the practice of *yoga,* rises up the *sushumṇā nāḍī.* As it rises, the *kuṇḍalinī* awakens each successive *chakra. Nirvikalpa samādhi,* enlightenment, comes as it pierces through the door of Brahman at the core of the *sahasrāra* and enters it. *Kuṇḍalinī śakti* then returns to rest in any one of the seven *chakras.* Śivasāyujya, perpetual Śiva consciousness, is complete when the *kuṇḍalinī* arrives back in the *sahasrāra* and remains coiled in this crown *chakra.* See: *chakra, door of Brahman, samādhi, nāḍī, tantra.*

kuṇḍalinī śakti: कुण्डलिनीशक्ति The pure (neither masculine nor feminine) force that flows through the *sushumṇā nāḍī.* See: *kuṇḍalinī, sushumṇā nāḍī.*

kuṇḍalinī yoga: कुण्डलिनीयोग "Uniting the serpent power." Advanced meditative practices and *sādhana* techniques, a part of *rāja yoga,* performed to deliberately arouse the *kuṇḍalinī* power and guide it up the spine into the crown *chakra, sahasrāra.* In its highest form, this *yoga* is the natural result of *sādhanas* and *tapas* well performed, rather than a distinct system of striving and teaching in its own right.

Kural: குறள் See: *Tirukural.*

***kurta* shirt:** Traditional men's shirt of India, usually thigh length and collarless.

kuttuvilaku: குத்துவிளக்கு A standing lamp found in the temple, shrine room or home. It is made of metal, with several wicks fed by *ghee* or special oils. Used to light the home and used in *pūjā*. Part of temple and shrine altars, the standing lamp is sometimes worshiped as the divine light, Parāśakti or Parajyoti. Returning from the temple and lighting one's *kuttuvilaku* courts the accompanying *devas* to remain in the home and channels the vibration of the temple sanctum sanctorum into the home shrine. Called *dīpastambha* in Sanskrit.

Lahiri Ayanāṁśa: लहिरि अयनांश *See: ayanāṁśa.*

Lao Tzu: Chinese philosopher (6th century BCE), author of *Tao-te Ching,* traditionally regarded as the founder of Taoism. See: Taoism.

Lemurian Scrolls: A work like none other on the planet, *Lemurian Scrolls* came to Gurudeva in a series of clairvoyant revelations during 1973-1974 in answer to his need, inwardly expressed, for the ancient ideal pattern on which to begin molding his several Śaivite monasteries in the Western world. Thus, as a boon from the Gods, Gurudeva began developing the *siddhi,* or psychic ability, to perceive and read from a series of ancient manuscripts with his inner eye. These were presented to him by a librarian on the astral plane, and as Gurudeva read from them, he dictated them word by word to a scribe who recorded them on paper. The manuscripts, written some two million years ago, unfolded the nature of life in Śaivite monasteries in the Tretā and Dvāpara Yugas. This text, along with subsequent writings, gave Gurudeva the pattern of culture and administration that he sought for his own monasteries. In addition, they disclosed much new knowledge about how man came to this planet, journeying millions of years ago from the Pleiades and other planets to further the soul's unfoldment. *Lemurian Scrolls* was for 25 years entrusted only to the resident monastics of Gurudeva's monasteries, until 1998 when they were released to the world. These angelic prophecies, exquisitely illustrated, overwhelm the reader with a sense of his divine origin, purpose and destiny and have the power to motivate a profound rededication to anyone's spiritual quest.

liberal Hinduism: A synonym for Smārtism and the closely related neo-Indian religion. See: *neo-Indian religion, Smārtism.*

liberation: *Moksha,* release from the bonds of *pāśa,* after which the soul is liberated from *saṁsāra* (the round of births and deaths). In Śaiva Siddhānta, *pāśa* is the three-fold bondage of *āṇava, karma* and *māyā,* which limit and confine the soul to the reincarnational cycle so that it may evolve. *Moksha* is freedom from the fettering power of these bonds, which do not cease to exist, but no longer have the power to fetter or bind the soul. See: *mala, moksha, pāśa, reincarnation, Self Realization, soul.*

light: In an ordinary sense, a form of energy which makes physical objects visible to the eye. In a religious-mystical sense, light also illumines inner objects (i.e., mental images). —**inner light:** light perceived inside the head and body, of which there are varying intensities. When the *karmas* have been sufficiently quieted, the meditator can see and enjoy inner light independently of mental images.

linchpin: A central, key element; a locking pin inserted in a hole at the end of an axle or other shaft to prevent a wheel from slipping off.

lineage: A direct line of ancestors and descendants or predecessors and successors.

liturgy: The proper, prescribed forms of ritual.

loka: लोक "World, habitat, realm, or plane of existence." From *loc,* "to shine, be bright, visible." See: *three worlds.*

Lono: The Hawaiian God of weather, worshiped to bring the rains and dispense fertility. One of four primary Gods, along with Ku, Kane and Kanaloa. Lono, also the God of harvest, is known as Gaṇeśa in the Hindu tradition.

lotus flower: An aquatic plant *(Nelumbo nucifera)* native to southern Asia and Australia, with large leaves, fragrant, pinkish flowers, a broad, rounded, perforated seedpod, and fleshy rhizomes.

lotus pose: *Padmāsana.* The most famous of *haṭha yoga* poses and the optimum position for meditation. The legs are crossed, turning the soles of the feet up, which then resemble a lotus flower. See: *āsana, haṭha yoga, padmāsana.*

lucid dreaming: The practice of remaining conscious in the dream state and directing the course of one's dream.

lunar calendar: A calendar based primarily on the cycles of the moon rather than the sun. For example, a month is from one full moon to the next or from the new moon to the next new moon. There are both lunar and solar based calendars in India, though today the solar is becoming prevalent. See: *ayanāṁśa, pañchāṅga.*

macrocosm: "Great world" or "universe." See: *microcosm-macrocosm, three worlds.*

Madurai Meenakshi citadel: The labyrinthine Meenakshi-Sundareśvara temple, on the Vagai River in Madurai, the Athens of India. This edifice holds two temples, one to Śiva and one to Śakti. The tall *gopuras,* thousand-pillared hall, sacred tanks and shrines vibrate with thousands of years of worship at this seven-walled citadel.

magnetized: Having been made magnetic. As certain physical elements are magnetized with *actinodic* power within a shrine through the chanting of *mantras* and by various other means.

mahā: महा An adjective or prefix meaning "great."

Mahābhārata: महाभारत "Great Epic of India." The

world's longest epic poem. It revolves around the conflict between two royal families, the Pāṇḍavas and Kauravas, and their great battle of Kurukshetra near modern Delhi in approximately 1424 BCE. The *Mahābhārata* is revered as scripture by Vaishṇavites and Smārtas. See: *Bhagavad Gītā, Itihāsa.*

Mahādeva: महादेव "Great shining one;" "God." Referring either to God Śiva or any of the highly evolved beings who live in the Śivaloka in their natural, effulgent soul bodies. God Śiva in His perfection as Primal Soul is one of the Mahādevas, yet He is unique and incomparable in that He alone is uncreated, the Father-Mother and Destiny of all other Mahādevas. He is called Parameśvara, "Supreme God." He is the Primal Soul, whereas the other Gods are individual souls. It is said in scripture that there are 330 million Gods. See: *Gods, Parameśvara, Śiva, deva.*

mahāprasthāna: महाप्रस्थान "Great departure." Death. See: *transition.*

mahārāja: महाराज "Great king." Indian monarch. Title of respect for political or (in modern times) spiritual leaders.

Maharshi (or Maharishi): महर्षि "Great seer." Title for the greatest and most influential of *siddhas.*

mahāsamādhi: महासमाधि "Great enstasy." The death, or giving up of the physical body, of a great soul, an event occasioned by tremendous blessings. Also names the shrine in which the remains of a great soul are entombed. See: *cremation, death.*

Mahāśivarātri: महाशिवरात्रि "Śiva's great night." Śaivism's foremost festival, celebrated on the night before the new moon in February-March. Fasting and an all-night vigil are observed as well as other disciplines: chanting, praying, meditating and worshiping Śiva as the Source and Self of all that exists.

mahātala: महातल Sixth netherworld. Region of consciencelessness. See: *chakra.*

mahā vāsanā daha tantra: महावासनादहतन्त्र "Great purification by fire." See: *vāsanā daha tantra.*

Maheśvara: महेश्वर "Great Lord." In Śaiva Siddhānta, the name of Śiva's energy of veiling grace, one of five aspects of Parameśvara, the Primal Soul. *Maheśvara* is also a popular epithet for Lord Śiva as Primal Soul and personal Lord. See: *Naṭarāja, Parameśvara.*

makimai: மகிமை The Hindu tradition of regularly giving to a temple or *āśrama* a fixed percentage of one's income. Fifteen percent, approximately one sixth, was the *makimai* established in South India by the Chettiar community around Palani Temple and now practiced by the Malaka Chettiars of Malaysia. See: *tithe.*

mala: मल "Impurity." An important term in Śaivism referring to three bonds, called *pāśa—āṇava, karma,* and *māyā*—which limit the soul, preventing it from knowing its true, divine nature. See: *āṇava, karma, liberation, māyā, pāśa.*

mālā: माला "Garland." A strand of beads for holy recitation, *japa,* usually made of *rudrāksha, tulasī,* sandalwood or crystal. Also a flower garland.

malaparipakam: மலபரிபாகம் "Ripening of bonds." The state attained after the three *malas, āṇava, karma* and *māyā,* are brought under control during *marul,* the second stage of the *sakala avasthai.* At this time, the Lord's concealing grace, *tirodhāna śakti,* has accomplished its work, giving way to *anugraha,* His revealing grace, leading to the descent of grace, *śaktinipāta.* See: *āṇava, anugraha, karma, mala, marul, māyā, sakala avasthā, śaktinipāta, tirodhāna śakti.*

manifest: To show or reveal. Perceivable or knowable, therefore having form. The opposite of unmanifest or transcendent. See: *formless.*

maṇipūra chakra: मणिपूरचक्र "Wheel of the jewelled city." Solar-plexus center of willpower. See: *chakra.*

mankolam: மாங்கோலம் "Mango design." The paisley, a stylized image of the mango, symbol of auspiciousness, associated with Lord Gaṇeśa.

manomaya kośa: मनोमयकोश See: *kośa.*

maṇḍapa: मण्डप From *maṇḍ,* "to deck, adorn." Temple precinct; a temple compound, open hall or chamber. In entering a large temple, one passes through a series of *maṇḍapas,* each named according to its position, e.g., *mukhamaṇḍapa,* "facing chamber." In some temples, *maṇḍapas* are concentrically arranged.

mānsāhāra: मांसाहार "Meat-eating."

mānsāhārī: मांसाहारी "Meat-eater." One who follows a nonvegetarian diet. See: *vegetarian.*

mantra: मन्त्र "Mystic formula." A sound, syllable, word or phrase endowed with special power, usually drawn from scripture. *Mantras* are chanted loudly during *pūjā* to invoke the Gods and establish a force field. Certain *mantras* are repeated softly or mentally for *japa,* the subtle tones quieting the mind, harmonizing the inner bodies and stimulating latent spiritual qualities. Hinduism's universal *mantra* is Aum. To be truly efficacious, such *mantras* must be bestowed by the preceptor through initiation. See: *Aum, incantation, japa, pūjā.*

Manu Dharma Śāstra: मनुधर्मशास्त्र "Sage Manu's law book." An encyclopedic treatise of 2,685 verses on Hindu law assembled as early as 600 bce. Among its major features are the support of *varṇa dharma, āśrama dharma, strī dharma* and seeing the Self in all beings. Despite its caste-based restrictions, which determine one's life unrelentlingly from birth to death, it remains the source of much of modern Hindu culture and law. These "Laws of Manu" are the oldest and considered the most authoritative of the greater body of *Dharma Śāstras.* The text is widely available today in several languages. See: *caste, dharma.*

Manu Saṁhitā: मनु संहिता "Verses of Manu." Alternate term for *Manu Dharma Śāstras.*

mārga: मार्ग "Path; way." From *mārg,* "to seek." See: *pāda.*

marriage (or wedding) pendant: A gold ornament worn by the Hindu wife around the neck representing her vows of matrimony. Known as *maṅgala sūtra* in Sanskrit, and *tali* in Tamil. She reveres it as an image of her husband and ritually worships it during her morning devotions.

marul: மருள் "Confusion." The second of the three

stages of the *sakala avasthai* when the soul is "caught" between the world and God and begins to seek knowledge of its own true nature, *paśu-jñānam.* See: *paśu-jñānam, sakala avasthā.*

Masonic Lodge: A society or body of Freemasons. A fraternal, all-male order derived from the organized guilds of stoneworkers in the Middle Ages, who unlike other classes of people, were allowed to travel freely from country to country. In the 1700s, with the decline of stoneworking arts, fraternity lodges were opened to honorary Masons who were not stoneworkers. Freemasonry teaches moral philosophy and welcomes members of all faiths.

Master Course, The: A trilogy of three masterful volumes by Satguru Sivaya Subramuniyaswami—*Dancing with Śiva, Hinduism's Contemporary Catechism; Living with Śiva, Hinduism's Contemporary Culture;* and *Merging with Śiva, Hinduism's Contemporary Metaphysics*—constituting a daily study of 365 lessons, one for each day of the year, undertaken privately or as a correspondence study with Himalayan Academy. See: *Dancing with Śiva, Merging with Śiva.*

masturbation: Manipulating one's own genitals, or the genitals of another, for sexual gratification. See: *celibacy, dissipation, ojas, tejas, transmutation.*

materialism (materialistic): The doctrine that matter is the only reality, that all life, thought and feelings are but the effects of movements of matter, and that there exist no worlds but the physical. Materialists usually hold that there is no God—a cosmic, material, prime mover perhaps, but no personal God. An Indian school of thought which propounded this view were the Chārvākas. See: *atheism, worldly.*

maṭha: मठ "Monastery." See: *monastery.*

maṭhavāsi: मठवासि "Monastery dweller." A monastic. See: *monk.*

mati: मति "Cognition, understanding; conviction." See: *yama-niyama.*

maya: मय "Consisting of; made of," as in *manomaya,* "made of mind."

māyā: माया "Artfulness," "illusion," "phantom" or "mirific energy." The substance emanated from Śiva through which the world of form is manifested. Hence all creation is termed *māyā.* It is the cosmic creative force, the principle of manifestation, ever in the process of creation, preservation and dissolution. *Māyā* is a key concept in Hinduism, originally meaning "supernatural power; God's mirific energy." See: *mala, mind (universal).*

Mayan: An advanced civilization that thrived 3,000 years ago in southern Mexico, Guatemala and northern Brazil. The Mayans were adept in astrology, mathematics and agriculture. They built great cities and temples out of stone and believed in many nature Gods.

mayil: மயில் "Peacock." See: *mayūra.*

mayūra: मयूर "Peacock." (*Mayil* in Tamil.) The *vāhana,* or mount, of Lord Kārttikeya, symbolizing effulgent beauty and religion in full glory. The peacock is able to control powerful snakes, such as the cobra, symbolizing the soulful domination of the instinctive elements—or control of the *kuṇḍalinī,* which is *yoga.* See: *Kārttikeya.*

meditation: *Dhyāna.* Sustained concentration. Meditation describes a quiet, alert, powerfully concentrated state wherein new knowledge and insights are awakened from within as awareness focuses one-pointedly on an object or specific line of thought. See: *internalized worship, rāja yoga, Satchidānanda.*

mendicant: A beggar; a wandering monk, or *sādhu,* who lives on alms. See: *sādhu.*

medium: A person who communicates with the departed or with agents of another world or dimension. See: *mediumship.*

mediumship: The phenomenon in which a person goes into a trance and allows a disincarnate, astral being to enter or take control of his body, often to convey verbal messages to others in attendance, as in a seance.

menopause: The permanent cessation of menstruation, normally occurring between ages 40 and 55. The decline in ovarian hormones may result in unpleasant effects, such as hot flashes, and may be coupled with midlife emotional crises, leading to a variety of health problems.

menopause, male: The male equivalent of female menopause, the mid-life passage also termed virapause and andropause, physiological, chemical and hormonal, changes, particularly the decrease in the body's production of testosterone. Generally occurring in the late forties or early fifties, the timing is generally parallel, as for women, with the *vāṇaprastha āśrama,* the life stage of withdrawal into higher pursuits. Without proper psychological preparation, this can be a difficult passage, accompanied by mood swings, fatigue, depression, feelings of inadequacy and loss of purpose and direction in life. See: *menopause.*

mental body (sheath): The higher-mind layer of the subtle or astral body in which the soul functions in Maharloka of the Antarloka or subtle plane. In Sanskrit, the mental body is *vijñānamaya kośa,* "sheath of cognition." See: *kośa, subtle body.*

mental plane: The refined strata of the subtle world. Here the soul is shrouded in the mental or cognitive sheath, called *vijñānamaya kośa.*

Merging with Śiva: The third book in Gurudeva's *Master Course* trilogy, this tome is aptly subtitled *Hinduism's Contemporary Metaphysics.* It explores the metaphysics of the soul, written directly, intimately, to the seeker on the path of enlightenment. *Merging with Śiva* consists of 365 daily lessons comprising Gurudeva's inspired talks, dictations and writings on *yoga* and mysticism from 1950 to 2001. It's about God, about the mystical realm of the fourteen *chakras,* the *yogic* path, the human aura, *karma,* force fields, thought and the states of mind, the two paths, living a pure life, clearing the subconscious, meditation and Self Realization. Released in 1999, it is custom illustrated with 71 original South Indian paintings.

meridian: The passageways of vital energy, known as *chi* in Chinese and *prāṇa* in Sanskrit, as well as blood flow through the body. It is an important component of traditional Chinese medicine. Meridians act as the route for circulating *chi* and blood, connecting viscera with extremities and for communication between the upper/lower and interior/exterior parts of the body. Most of the major meridians are subtly governed by a physical organ. The major meridians of the human body are: governing vessel, large intestine, conception vessel, pericardium, heart, stomach, kidney, spleen, liver, lung, gall bladder, bladder, small intestine, and *san jiao* ("triple warmer"). See: *acupuncture, circadian rhythm.*

metaphysics: The philosophy that examines the nature of reality, especially those aspects of reality beyond the realm of physical perception, or impossible to investigate by intellectual scientific study.

methamphetamine: A highly toxic, synthetic chemical often used illicitly as a stimulant. Also called crystal meth, ice, methedrine and speed. This drug of abuse is one of the most addictive and popular on the streets today. An average dose causes a rush of energy and sense of euphoria that, unlike other drugs, can easily be hidden from observers. Consistent abuse of this drug is known to result in inability to hold a job, alienation of family and friends, violent crime, domestic abuse, stealing and other illegal acivities to support the habit, excessive persistent insomnia lasting from a couple of days to a week and causes permanent damage to the brain. Clandestine "meth" laboratories are exceedingly dangerous. Police officers and drug enforcement agents must exercise extreme caution when entering a suspected methamphetamine laboratory, often in a home, due to the volatile and lethal nature of the chemicals used in the drug's production. At such sites, chemicals are usually airborne in life-threatening quantities. They contaminate clothing, especially footwear, and often cause spontaneous explosions.

microcosm-macrocosm: "Little world" or "miniature universe" as compared with "great world." *Microcosm* refers to the internal source of something larger or more external (macrocosm). In Hindu cosmology, the outer world is a macrocosm of the inner world, which is its microcosm and is mystically larger and more complex than the physical universe and functions at a higher rate of vibration and even a different rate of time. The microcosm precedes the macrocosm. Thus, the guiding principle of the Bhūloka comes from the Antarloka and Śivaloka. Consciousness precedes physical form. In the *tantric* tradition, the body of man is viewed as a microcosm of the entire divine creation.

mind (five states): A view of the mind in five parts. **—conscious mind:** *Jāgrat chitta* ("wakeful consciousness"). The ordinary, waking, thinking state of mind in which the majority of people function most of the day. **—subconscious mind:** *Saṁskāra chitta* ("impression mind"). The part of mind "beneath" the conscious mind, the storehouse or recorder of all experience (whether remembered consciously or not)—the holder of past impressions, reactions and desires. Also, the seat of involuntary physiological processes. **—subsubconscious mind:** *Vāsanā chitta* ("mind of subliminal traits"). The area of the subconscious mind formed when two thoughts or experiences of the same rate of intensity are sent into the subconscious at different times and, intermingling, give rise to a new and totally different rate of vibration. This subconscious formation later causes the external mind to react to situations according to these accumulated vibrations, be they positive, negative or mixed. **—superconscious mind:** *Kāraṇa chitta.* The mind of light, the all-knowing intelligence of the soul. The Sanskrit term is *turīya,* "the fourth," meaning the condition beyond the states of wakefulness *(jāgrat),* "dream" *(svapna),* and "deep sleep" *(sushupti).* At its deepest level, the superconscious is Parāśakti, or Satchidānanda, the Divine Mind of God Śiva. In Sanskrit, there are numerous terms for the various levels and states of superconsciousness. Specific superconscious states such as: *viśvachaitanya* ("universal consciousness"), *advaita chaitanya* ("nondual consciousness"), *adhyātma chetanā* ("spiritual consciousness"). **—subsuperconscious mind:** *Anukāraṇa chitta.* The superconscious mind working through the conscious and subconscious states, which brings forth intuition, clarity and insight. See: *chitta, consciousness, saṁskāra, Satchidānanda, vāsanā.*

mind (three phases): A perspective of mind as instinctive, intellectual and superconscious. **—instinctive mind.** *Manas chitta,* the seat of desire and governor of sensory and motor organs. **—intellectual mind.** *Buddhi chitta,* the faculty of thought and intelligence. **—superconscious mind:** *Kāraṇa chitta,* the stratum of intuition, benevolence and spiritual sustenance. Its most refined essence is Parāsakti, or Satchidānanda, all-knowing, omnipresent consciousness, the One transcendental, self-luminous, divine mind common to all souls. See: *awareness, consciousness.*

mind (universal): In the most profound sense, mind is the sum of all things, all energies and manifestations, all forms, subtle and gross, sacred and mundane. It is the inner and outer cosmos. Mind is *māyā.* It is the material matrix. It is everything but That, the Self within, Paraśiva, which is timeless, formless, causeless, spaceless, known by the knower only after Self Realization. The Self is the indescribable, unnameable, Ultimate Reality. Mind in its subtlest form is undifferentiated Pure Consciousness, primal substance (called Parāśakti or Satchidānanda), out of which emerge the myriad forms of existence, both psychic and material. See: *chitta, consciousness, māyā.*

Mirabai (Mīrābāī): मीराबाई A Vaishṇava saint (ca 1420), poetess and mystic, said to be a Rājput princess who abandoned the world in surrender to Lord Kṛishṇa. Her life story and songs are popular today, especially in Gujarat.

Miranda reading: A mandatory, formal, legal, verbal

warning given by police in the US to a person who has been taken into custody advising of his right to remain silent and to have legal counsel.

mitāhāra: मिताहार "Measured eating; moderate appetite." A requisite to good health and an essential for success in *yoga.* The ideal portion per meal is described as no more than would fill the two hands held side by side and slightly cupped piled high, an amount called a *kuḍava.* All the six tastes should be within these foods (sweet, salty, sour, pungent, bitter and astringent), which should be vegetarian, well cooked and highly nutritious. See: *yama-niyama.*

moksha: मोक्ष "Liberation." Release from transmigration, *saṁsāra,* the round of births and deaths, which occurs after *karma* has been resolved and *nirvikalpa samādhi*—realization of the Self, Paraśiva—has been attained. Same as *mukti.* See: *four traditional goals, kuṇḍalinī, Paraśiva.*

monastery: "Place of solitariness." *Maṭha.* The age-old tradition, carried forward from Lemurian times into the Hindu culture of India, a sacred residence where those of the same gender live under strict vows and work out their birth *karmas* in community toward realization of the Self. In monasteries, dedicated to transmutation of the sexual energies, celibacy is strictly upheld and there is no fraternizing with the opposite sex. The purpose of the monastery is to create an environment in which the monastic can balance the male and female energies *(piṅgala* and *iḍā)* within himself so that he lives in the spiritual, or *sushumṇā,* energy, which cannot be maintained in close association with the opposite sex. The monastic, whether a monk or a nun, is in a sense neither male nor female, but a pure soul being. See: *āśrama, nāḍī.*

monastic: A monk or nun (based on the Greek *monos,* "alone"). A man or woman who has withdrawn from the world and lives an austere, religious life, either alone or with others in a monastery. (Not to be confused with *monistic,* having to do with the doctrine of monism.) A monastery-dweller is a *maṭhavāsi,* and *sādhu* is a rough equivalent for mendicant. See also: *monastery, monk, sannyāsin.*

monism: "Doctrine of oneness." 1) The philosophical view that there is only one ultimate substance or principle. 2) The view that reality is a unified whole without independent parts. See: *dvaita-advaita.*

monistic theism: Advaita Īśvaravāda. Monism is the doctrine that reality is a one whole or existence without independent parts. Theism is the belief that God exists as a real, conscious, personal Supreme Being. Monistic theism is the dipolar doctrine, also called panentheism, that embraces both monism and theism, two perspectives ordinarily considered contradictory or mutually exclusive, since theism implies dualism. Monistic theism simultaneously accepts that God has a personal form, that He creates, pervades and *is* all that exists—and that He ultimately transcends all existence and that the soul is, in essence, one with God. Advaita Siddhānta (monistic Śaiva Siddhānta, or Advaita Īśvaravāda Śaiva Siddhānta) is a specific form of monistic theism. See: *advaita, Advaita Īśvaravāda, Advaita Siddhānta, dvaita-advaita.*

monk: A celibate man wholly dedicated to religious life, either cenobitic (residing with others in a monastery) or anchoritic (living alone, as a hermit or mendicant). Literally, "one who lives alone" (from the Greek *monos,* "alone"). A synonym for *monastic.* Its feminine counterpart is *nun.* See: *monastic, sannyāsin.*

mors voluntaria religiosa: Latin for "religious self-willed death," a tradition in many religions which, with the sanction of community elders and religious leaders, offers the aged person who knows the end of physical life is near to voluntarily, peacefully and slowly end his life by fasting. Known in Hinduism as *prayopaveśa.*

mortal sin: In the Abrahamic religions, a transgression that, if unexpiated in this one and only life, deprives the soul from closeness to God for eternity. Most Christian denominations, as well as Islam and mid-line conservative Judaism, believe that mortal sin will always automatically and inexorably condemn the sinner to eternal punishment. See: *sin.*

Mount Kailas: One of the most famous peaks in the Himalayas. See: *Kailas.*

Mount Tamalpais: A magnificent mountain in Marin County near San Francisco, California. A place of special power, it provides excellent hiking along with some of the most outstanding lookout points in California.

mṛidaṅga: मृदङ्ग (Tamil: *mṛidaṅgam*) A South Indian concert drum, barrel-shaped and played on both ends.

mukti: मुक्ति "Release." A synonym for *moksha.* See: *moksha.*

mūlādhāra chakra: मूलाधारचक्र "Root-support wheel." The four-petaled psychic center at the base of the spine which governs memory. See: *chakra.*

mumia: The force of dissolution or withdrawal of life force from organic substances and living organisms. For example, as soon as vegetables are picked, the force of dissolution, *mumia,* sets in. Therefore, the food should be cooked and eaten as soon after picking as possible, before the *mumia* force gets strong. *Mumia,* as it causes the breakdown of the cells, is an impure force. When food that is breaking down is regularly eaten, the body and mind become sluggish.

Muṇḍaka Upanishad: मुण्डक उपनिषद् Belongs to the *Atharva Veda* and teaches the difference between the intellectual study of the *Vedas* and their supplementary texts and the intuitive knowledge by which God is known.

mundane: Worldly, especially as distinguished from heavenly or spiritual. Ordinary. From Latin *mundus* "world;" *mundanus* "worldly."

Murugan: முருகன் "Beautiful one," a favorite name of Kārttikeya among the Tamils of South India, Sri Lanka and elsewhere. See: *Kārttikeya.*

Murugan's South Indian abodes: A series of six temples

to be visited in specified order, a life-changing pilgrimage called Arupadai Veedu: Tirupparankundram, known as the mount of beauty; Tiruchendur, abode of fulfillment; Palani Hills, the mount of meditation; Swamimalai, the abode of Kumara Guru; Tiruttani, the sport on the hills; and Palamadirsolai, the fruit grove of grace.

mūshika: मूषिक From *mūsh*, "to steal." The mouse, Lord Gaṇeśa's mount, traditionally associated with abundance. Symbolically, the mouse carries Gaṇeśa's grace into every corner of the mind. See: *Gaṇeśa.*

mystic: One who understands religious mysteries or occult rites and practices. Inspiring a sense of mystery and wonder.

mysticism: Spirituality; the pursuit of direct spiritual or religious experience. Spiritual discipline aimed at union or communion with Ultimate Reality or God through deep meditation or trance-like contemplation. From the Greek *mystikos*, "of mysteries." Characterized by the belief that Truth transcends intellectual processes and must be attained through transcendent means. See: *clairaudience, clairvoyance, psychic, trance.*

nāḍī: नाडी "Conduit;" "river." A nerve fiber or energy channel of the subtle (inner) bodies of man. It is said there are 72,000. These interconnect the *chakras*. The three main *nāḍīs* are named *iḍā, piṅgalā* and *sushumṇā*. —***iḍā:*** Also known as *chandra* ("moon") *nāḍī*, it is pink in color and flows downward, ending on the left side of the body. This current is feminine in nature and is the channel of physical-emotional energy. —***piṅgaḷā:*** Also known as *sūrya* ("sun") *nāḍī*, it is blue in color and flows upward, ending on the right side of the body. This current is masculine in nature and is the channel of intellectual-mental energy. —***sushumṇā:*** The major nerve current which passes through the spinal column from the *mūlādhāra chakra* at the base to the *sahasrāra* at the crown of the head. It is the channel of *kuṇḍalinī*. Through *yoga*, the *kuṇḍalinī* energy lying dormant in the *mūlādhāra* is awakened and made to rise up this channel through each *chakra* to the *sahasrāra chakra*. See: *chakra, kuṇḍalinī, rāja yoga.*

nāga: नाग "Snake," often the cobra; symbol of the *kuṇḍalinī* coiled on the four petals of the *mūlādhāra chakra*. See: *kuṇḍalinī, mūlādhāra chakra.*

nakshatra: नक्षत्र "Star cluster." Central to astrological determinations, the *nakshatras* are 27 star-clusters, constellations arranged along the ecliptic, or path of the sun. An individual's *nakshatra*, or birth star, is the constellation the moon was aligned with at the time of birth. See: *jyotisha.*

Namaḥ Śivāya: नमः शिवाय "Adoration (homage) to Śiva." The supreme *mantra* of Śaivism, known as the *Pañchākshara*, or "five syllables." *Na* is the Lord's veiling grace; *Ma* is the world; *Śi* is Śiva; *Vā* is His revealing grace; *Ya* is the soul. The syllables also represent the physical body: *Na* the legs, *Ma* the stomach, *Śi* the shoulders, *Vā* the mouth and *Ya* the eyes. Embodying the essence of Śaiva Siddhānta, it is found in the center of the central *Veda* (the *Yajur*). ¶In a second rendering, Na-Ma Śi-Vā-Ya corresponds to *Śiva's* five actions, reflected in the symbolism of Lord Naṭarāja as follows. *Na* represents *saṁhāra*, destruction or dissolution, corresponding to the hand which which holds a blazing flame. *Ma* stands for His concealing grace, *tirodhāna śakti*, symbolized by Lord Naṭarāja's planted foot. *Vā* indicates revealing grace, *anugraha śakti*, by which souls return to Him, reflected in the left front hand in the elephant trunk pose, *gajahasta*, pointing to His left foot, source of revealing grace. *Śi* stands for *sṛishṭi*, creation, and Śiva's back right hand holding the drum. *Ya* stands for Śiva's power of *stithi*, preservation and protection, shown in His hand gesturing *abhaya*, "fear not." ¶Na-Ma Śi-Vā-Ya also stands for the five elements: *Na* as earth; *Ma*, water; *Śi*, fire; *Vā*, air; and *Ya*, *ākāśa*. See: *mantra, japa.*

nāmakaraṇa: नामकरण "Name giving." See: *saṁskāras of childhood.*

namaskāra: नमस्कार "Reverent salutations." Traditional Hindu verbal greeting and *mudrā* where the palms are joined together and held before the heart or raised to the level of the forehead. The *mudrā* is also called *añjali*. It is a devotional gesture made equally before a temple Deity, holy person, friend or even momentary acquaintance.

namaste: नमस्ते "Reverent salutations to you." A traditional verbal greeting. A form of *namas*, meaning "bowing, obeisance." See: *namaskāra.*

Nandi: नन्दि "The joyful." A white bull with a black tail, the *vāhana*, or mount, of Lord Śiva, symbol of the powerful instinctive force tamed by Him. Nandi is the perfect devotee, the soul of man, kneeling humbly before God Śiva, ever concentrated on Him. The ideal and goal of the Śiva *bhakta* is to behold Śiva in all.

Nandinatha, Maharishi: नन्दिनाथ महर्षि (ca 250 BCE) A synonym of *Nandikeśvara*. The first *siddha satguru* of the major stream of the Nandinātha Sampradāya, the *Kailāsa Paramparā*, recorded in Panini's book of grammar as the teacher of *ṛishis* Patanjali, Vyaghrapada and Vasishtha. Among its representatives today is Satguru Sivaya Subramuniyaswami. See: *Kailāsa Paramparā, Nātha Sampradāya.*

Nandinātha Sampradāya: नन्दिनाथसंप्रदाय See: *Nātha Sampradāya.*

Naraka: नरक Abode of darkness. Literally, "pertaining to man." The nether worlds. Equivalent to the Western term *hell*, a gross region of the Antarloka. Naraka is a congested, distressful area where demonic beings and young souls may sojourn until they resolve the darksome *karmas* they have created. Here beings suffer the consequences of their own misdeeds in previous lives. *Naraka* is understood as having seven regions, called *tala*, corresponding to the states of consciousness of the seven lower *chakras*. They are described as places of torment, pain, darkness, confusion and disease, but these are only temporary abodes for the evolving soul. Hinduism has no eternal hell. See: *asura, hell.*

Naṭarāja: नटराज "King of Dance," or "King of Dancers." God as the Cosmic Dancer. Perhaps Hinduism's richest and most eloquent symbol, Naṭarāja represents Śiva, the Primal Soul, Parameśvara, as the power, energy and life of all that exists. This is Śiva's intricate state of Being in Manifestation. The dance of Śiva as Naṭeśa, Lord of Dancers, is the rhythmic movement of the entire cosmos. All that is, whether sentient or insentient, pulsates in His body, and He within it. Both male and female elements are depicted in this icon—as also shown in Ardhanārīśvara, the "half-female God," symbol of the inseparable nature of Śiva-Śakti. See: *Namaḥ Śivāya, Parāśakti Parameśvara, Parāśakti, Paraśiva.*

Natchintanai: நற்சிந்தனை The collected songs of Sage Yogaswami (1872-1964) of Jaffna, Sri Lanka, extolling the power of the *satguru,* worship of Lord Śiva, adherance to the path of *dharma* and striving for the attainment of Self Realization. See: *Kailāsa Paramparā, Yogaswami.*

Nātha: नाथ "Master, lord; adept." An ancient Himalayan tradition of Śaiva-*yoga* mysticism, whose first historically known exponent was Nandikesvara (ca 250 BCE). *Nātha*—Self-Realized adept—designates the extraordinary ascetic masters (or devotees) of this school. Through their practice of *siddha yoga* they have attained tremendous powers, *siddhis,* and are sometimes called *siddha yogīs* (accomplished or fully enlightened ones). The words of such beings penetrate deeply into the psyche of their devotees, causing mystical awakenings. Like all *tantrics,* Nāthas have refused to recognize caste distinctions in spiritual pursuits. Their *satgurus* initiate from the lowest to the highest, according to spiritual worthiness. *Nātha* also designates any follower of the Nātha tradition. The *Nāthas* are considered the source of *haṭha* as well as *rāja yoga.* See: *Kailāsa Paramparā, Nātha Sampradāya.*

Nātha Sampradāya: नाथसंप्रदाय "Traditional doctrine of the masters." *Sampradāya* means a living stream of tradition or theology. Nātha Sampradāya is a philosophical and *yogic* tradition of Śaivism whose origins are unknown. This oldest of Śaivite *sampradāyas* existing today consists of two major streams: the Nandinātha and the Ādinātha. The Nandinātha Sampradāya has had as exponents Maharishi Nandinatha and his disciples: Patanjali (author of the *Yoga Sūtras)* and Tirumular (author of *Tirumantiram).* Among its representatives today are the successive *siddhars* of the Kailāsa Paramparā. The Ādinātha lineage's known exponents are Maharishi Adinatha, Matsyendranatha and Gorakshanatha, who founded a well-known order of *yogīs.* See: *Kailāsa Paramparā, Nātha, Śaivism, sampradāya.*

Nayanar: நாயனார் "One who shows the way." The 63 canonized Tamil saints of South India, as documented in the *Periyapurāṇam* by Sekkilar (ca 1140). All but a few were householders, honored as exemplars of radical devotion to Lord Śiva, though their biographies are perhaps historically inaccurate and the actions of some were violent, even heinous. Several contributed to the Śaiva Siddhānta scriptural compendium called *Tirumurai.*

negative attachment: A fear, worry or doubt about the future or a lingering regret about the past that keeps one from "flowing with the river of life," living fully in the moment as an independent, spiritual being, facing each experience in the light of understanding.

Nehru, Jawaharlal: A major political influence in India's movement for independence, Nehru (1889-1964) was born in Allahabad, educated at Harvard. With Mahatma Gandhi he helped negotiate India's freedom from Britain. After the formation of Pakistan in August, 1947, he became Prime Minister of India.

neo: A prefix meaning new and different; modified.

neo-Indian religion: *Navabhārata Dharma.* A modern form of liberal Hinduism that carries forward basic Hindu cultural values—such as dress, diet and the arts—while allowing religious values to subside. It emerged after the British Rāj, when India declared itself an independent, secular state. It was cultivated by the Macaulay education system, implanted in India by the British, which aggressively undermined Hindu thought and belief. Neo-Indian religion encourages Hindus to follow any combination of theological, scriptural, *sādhana* and worship patterns, regardless of sectarian or religious origin. Extending out of and beyond the Smārta system of worshiping the Gods of each major sect, it incorporates holy icons from all religions, including Jesus, Mother Mary and Buddha. Many *Navabhāratis* choose to not call themselves Hindus but to declare themselves members of all the world's religions. See: *Smārtism.*

nerves: Cordlike bundles of fibers made up of neurons through which impulses pass between the brain, central nervous system and other parts of the body. Here also names the fibrous network of inner bodies.

nervous system: The system of the brain, spinal cord, nerves, ganglia and parts of the receptor and effector organs that regulates the body's responses to internal and external stimuli.

New Age: According to *Webster's New World Dictionary:* "Of or pertaining to a cultural movement popular in the 1980s [and '90s] characterized by a concern with spiritual consciousness, and variously combining belief in reincarnation and astrology with such practices as meditation, vegetarianism and holistic medicine."

Nightingale, Florence: English hospital administrator (1820-1910) born in Florence, Italy, was influential in modernizing training for nursing. In 1854 during the Crimean War she organized a new type of hospital unit, introducing sanitary reforms, and securing necessary supplies. In 1907 she became the first woman to receive the British Order of Merit.

Nirguṇa Brahman: निर्गुणब्रह्मन् "God without qualities." See: *Brahman.*

nirvāṇa sādhaka: निर्वण साधक Title for a senior *sād-*

haka in Saiva Siddhanta Church who has followed the pattern of wearing white throughout monastic life and not entering the auxiliary training of the *natyam*. *Nirvāna sādhakas* may qualify for holy orders of *sannyāsa* after age 72.

***nirvāṇī* and *upadeśī*:** निर्वाणी उपदेशी *Nirvāṇī* means "extinguished one," and *upadeśī* means "teacher." In general, *nirvāṇi* refers to a liberated soul, or to a certain class of monk. *Upadeśī* refers to a teacher, generally a renunciate. In *The Master Course*, these two terms have special meaning, similar to the Buddhist *arhat* and *bodhisattva*, naming the two earthly modes of the realized, liberated soul. After full illumination, the *jīvanmukta* has the choice to return to the world to help others along the path. This is the way of the *upadeśī* (or *bodhisattva)*, exemplified by the benevolent *satguru* who leads seekers to the goal of God Realization. He may found and direct institutions and monastic lineages. The *nirvāṇī* (or *arhat)* abides at the pinnacle of consciousness, shunning all worldly involvement. He is typified by the silent ascetic, the reclusive sage. See: *satguru, viśvagrāsa.*

***nirvikalpa samādhi*:** निर्विकल्पसमाधि "Undifferentiated trance, enstasy *(samādhi)* without form or seed." The realization of the Self, Paraśiva, a state of oneness beyond all change or diversity; beyond time, form and space. The prefix *vi-* connotes "change, differentiation." *Kalpa* means "order, arrangement; a period of time." Thus *vikalpa* means "diversity, thought; difference of perception, distinction." *Nir* means "without." See: *rāja yoga, samādhi, Self Realization.*

***niyama*:** नियम "Restraint." See: *yama-niyama.*

nondualism: "Not two-ness." Monistic philosophy. See: *advaita, monism, monistic theism, Vedānta.*

nonsectarian: Not limited to or associated with a particular religious denomination.

observation: The act of being aware, recording or noting things.

occult: Hidden, or kept secret; revealed only after initiation. See: *mysticism.*

occultism: The study of, and attempted control over, the supernatural.

odic: Spiritually magnetic—of or pertaining to consciousness within *aśuddha māyā*, the realm of the physical and lower astral planes. Odic force in its rareified state is *prakṛiti*, the primary gross energy of nature, manifesting in the three *guṇas: sattva, rajas* and *tamas.* All matter, earth, air, fire and water, as well as thought, are odic force. It is the force of attraction and repulsion between people, people and their things, and manifests as masculine (aggressive) and feminine (passive), arising from the *piṅgalā* and *iḍā* currents. These two currents *(nāḍī)* are found within the spine of the subtle body. Odic force is a magnetic, sticky, binding substance that people seek to develop when they want to bind themselves together, such as in partnerships, marriage, *guru-śishya* relationships and friendships. It, of itself, is stagnant and unflowing. Odic energy is the combined emanation of the *prāṇamaya* and *annamaya kośas.* See: *actinic, kośa, subtle body.*

officiate: Performing duties and responsibilities of an officer or priest.

oils, degraded: Describes oils that have been overused or overheated in the cooking process to the point of toxicity, such as in deep-frying, or that are exceedingly high in saturated fat or cholesterol, or that have been found to be unhealthy to use in cooking. The unhealthiest oils include coconut oil, cottonseed oil, rapeseed (canola) oil, palm oil, corn oil, peanut oil and all hydrogenated oils, as well as others. The most healthy cooking oils are *ghee* (clarified butter), olive oil and sesame oil. Olive oil and sesame oil are also nutritious in salads and other raw dishes. Flaxseed oil also has many health advantages, but it should never be heated.

***ojas*:** ओजस् "Vigor, force, strength, vitality." In *āyurveda*, the underlying life-sap or fluid-essence of the *dhatus*, the seven tissue systems of the body—plasma, blood, muscle, fat, bone, nerves and reproductive tissue. *Ojas* pervades every part of the body and underlies all physical capacities. It is not a physical substance, but exists on a subtle level. *Ojas* is depleted by excessive sex, drugs, talking, loud music, emotional burnout and insufficient rest. Signs of diminished *ojas* are fear, worry, sensory organ pain, poor complexion, cheerlessness, harshness, emaciation, immune system disorders and easily contracting of diseases (all the symptoms of the modern disease AIDS). Conservation of the vital sexual fluids increases the store of *ojas*, strengthens the immune system and enhances health and the quality of one's consciousness. See: *āyurveda, tejas, transmutation.*

***olai*:** ஓலை "Leaf." An ancient form of Indian books used in India, made of strips of fronds from the palmyra *(triṇḍruma)* and talipot *(tālapatra,* "fan-leaf") palms. Prepared birch bark *(bhūrja pattra)* was the medium in the North. The pages were loosely tied, with cord passed between one or two holes and usually bound between wooden covers. Ink made from lampblack or charcoal was applied with a reed pen. Or, more commonly in the South, the letters were scribed with a stylus, then rubbed with powdered lampblack. These books average about 2 inches high and 8 inches wide and up to 11 or 12 inches thick, wound with string and generally protected in colored cloth.

old soul: One who has reincarnated many times, experienced much and is therefore further along the path. Old souls may be recognized by their qualities of compassion, self-effacement and wisdom. See: *evolution of the soul, soul.*

***Om*:** ओम् "Yes, verily." The most sacred *mantra* of Hinduism. An alternate transliteration of *Aum.* See: *Aum.*

omnipotent: All-powerful. Able to do anything.

omnipresent: Present everywhere and in all things.

omniscient: Possessing infinite knowledge, all-knowing.

oneness: Quality or state of being one. Unity, identity, especially in spite of appearances to the contrary—e.g., the oneness of soul and God. See: *monism.*

opinionated knowledge: A faculty of memory stored in the memory gridwork of the subconscious mind which provides a platform for the intellect, developing an ego. Knowledge gained through the study, hearing and quoting of opinions of others. Looking at the world through the eyes of others.

ordain (ordination): To confer the duties and responsibilities, authority and spiritual power of a religious office, such as priest, minister or *satguru,* through religious ceremony or mystical initiation. See: *dīkshā.*

orthodox: "Of right (correct) opinion." Conforming to established doctrines or beliefs. Opposite of *heterodox,* "different opinion."

P

pāda: पाद "The foot" (of men and animals); quarter-part, section; stage; path. Names the major sections of the Āgamic texts and the corresponding stages of practice and unfoldment on the path to *moksha,* liberation. According to Śaiva Siddhānta, there are four *pādas,* which are successive and cumulative; i.e. in accomplishing each one the soul prepares itself for the next. (In Tamil, Śaiva Siddhānta is also known as *Nalu-pāda,* "four-stage," *Śaivam*). ***—charyā pāda*** (or ***mārga):*** "Good conduct stage." The first stage where one learns to live righteously, serve selflessly, performing *karma yoga.* It is also known as *dāsa mārga,* "servitor's path," a time when the aspirant relates to God as a servant to a master. Traditional acts of *charyā* include cleaning the temple, lighting lamps and collecting flowers for worship. Worship at this stage is mostly external. ***—kriyā pāda*** (or ***mārga):*** "Religious action; worship stage." Stage of *bhakti yoga,* of cultivating devotion through performing *pūjā* and regular daily *sādhana.* It is also known as the *satputra mārga,* "true son's way," as the soul now relates to God as a son to his father. A central practice of the *kriyā pāda* is performing daily *pūjā.* ***—yoga pāda*** (or ***mārga):*** Having matured in the *charyā* and *kriyā pādas,* the soul now turns to internalized worship and *rāja yoga* under the guidance of a *satguru.* It is a time of *sādhana* and serious striving when realization of the Self is the goal. It is the *sakhā mārga,* "way of the friend," for now God is looked upon as an intimate friend. ***—jñāna pāda*** (or ***mārga):*** "Stage of wisdom." Once the soul has attained Realization, it is henceforth a wise one who lives out the life of the body, shedding blessings on mankind. This stage is also called the San Mārga, "true path," on which God is our dearest beloved. The *Tirumantiram* describes the fulfillment of each stage as follows. In *charyā,* the soul forges a kindred tie in "God's world" *(sālokya).* In *kriyā* it attains "nearness" *(sāmīpya)* to Him. In *yoga* it attains "likeness" *(sārūpya)* with Him. In *jñāna* the soul enjoys the ultimate bliss of identity *(sāyujya)* with Śiva.

padmāsana: पद्मासन "Lotus posture." The most famous *haṭha yoga āsana,* the optimum pose for sustained meditation. The legs are crossed, the soles of the feet upward, resembling a lotus flower. Sitting in this pose balances and quiets the intellectual-emotional energies. See: *lotus pose, rāja yoga, yoga.*

pagan: The pre-Christian religion of Europe, akin to shamanism and other of the world's indigenous faiths, which have survived to this day despite organized persecution. Pagans are gradually surfacing again, and have acknowledged a kinship with Hinduism. The term *pagan* is used negatively by Semitic faiths to indicate a follower of another religion, or of no religion. See: *mysticism, shamanism.*

pañcha nitya karma(s): पञ्चनित्यकर्म "Five constant duties." A traditional regimen of religious practice for Hindus: 1) *dharma* (virtuous living), 2) *upāsanā* (worship), 3) *utsava* (holy days), 4) *tīrthayātrā* (pilgrimage) and 5) *saṁskāras* (sacraments.) See: *dharma, pilgrimage, saṁskāra.*

Pañchākshara Mantra: पञ्चाक्षरमन्त्र "Five-lettered chant." Śaivism's most sacred *mantra.* See: *Namaḥ Śivāya.*

pañchāṅga: पञ्चांग "Five limbs, or parts." (Tamil: *pañchāṅgam*) The name of the traditional Hindu almanac, so named because of its five basic elements—*tithi, nakshatra, kāraṇa, yoga* and *vara* (or *vasara).* It provides information about unseen astrological factors, which influence the subtle environment. *Pañchāṅgams* are used to determine the optimum times for all activities. See: *jyotisha, lunar calendar.*

paṇḍara: पण्डर An informal order of independent priests, often self-taught and self-appointed, who emerge within a community to perform *pūjās* at a sacred tree, a simple shrine or a temple.

pandit (paṇḍita): पण्डित A Hindu religious scholar or theologian, a man well versed in philosophy, liturgy, religious law and sacred science.

pantheon: All the Gods of a religion together.

pāpa: पाप "Wickedness; sin, crime." 1) Bad or evil. 2) Wrongful action. 3) Demerit earned through wrongdoing. *Pāpa* includes all forms of wrongdoing, from the simplest infraction to the most heinous crime, such as premeditated murder. Each act of *pāpa* carries its *karmic* consequence, *karmaphala,* "fruit of action," for which scriptures delineate specific penance for expiation. *Pāpa* is the opposite of *puṇya* (merit, virtue). See: *evil, karma, penance, puṇya, sin.*

Parabrahman: परब्रह्मन् "Supreme (or transcendent) God." A synonym for Nirguṇa Brahman, Absolute Reality, beyond time, form and space. Same as Paraśiva. See: *Brahman, Paraśiva.*

paramaguru: परमगुरु "Grand preceptor." The *guru* of a disciple's *guru.*

Paramātman: परमात्मन् "Supreme Self," or "transcendent soul." Paraśiva, Absolute Reality, the one transcendent Self of every soul. Contrasted with *ātman,* which includes all three aspects of the soul: *Paraśiva, Parāśakti* and *ānandamaya kośa.* See: *ātman, kośa, soul.*

Parameśvara: परमेश्वर "Supreme Lord or Ruler." God

Śiva's third perfection, Supreme Mahādeva, Śiva-Śakti, mother of the universe. In this perfection as Personal, father-mother God, Śiva is a person—who has a body, with head, arms and legs, etc.—who acts, wills, blesses, gives *darśana*, guides, creates, preserves, reabsorbs, obscures and enlightens. In Truth, it is Śiva-Śakti who does all. The term *Primal Soul*, Paramapurusha, designates Parameśvara as the original, uncreated soul, the creator of all other souls. Parameśvara has many other names and epithets, including those denoting the five divine actions: Sadāśiva, the revealer; Maheśvara, the obscurer; Brahmā, the creator; Vishṇu the preserver; and Rudra the destroyer. See: *Naṭarāja*.

paramparā: परंपरा "Uninterrupted succession." A lineage. See: *guru paramparā*.

parārtha pūjā: परार्थपूजा "Public liturgy and worship." See: *pūjā*.

Parāśakti: पराशक्ति "Supreme power; primal energy." God Śiva's second perfection, which is impersonal, immanent, and with form—the all-pervasive Pure Consciousness and Primal Substance of all that exists. There are many other descriptive names for Parāśakti—Satchidānanda ("existence-consciousness-bliss"), light, silence, divine mind, superconsciousness and more. Parāśakti can be experienced by the diligent *yogī* or meditator as a merging in, or identification with, the underlying oneness flowing through all form. The experience is called *savikalpa samādhi*. See: *rāja yoga, Śakti, Satchidānanda*.

Paraśiva: परशिव "Transcendent Śiva." The Self God, Śiva's first perfection, Absolute Reality. God Śiva as *That* which is beyond the grasp of consciousness, transcends time, form and space and defies description. To merge with Him in mystic union is the goal of all incarnated souls, the reason for their living on this planet, and the deepest meaning of their experiences. Attainment of this is called Self Realization or *nirvikalpa samādhi*. See: *samādhi, Śiva*.

pāśa: पाश "Tether; noose." (Tamil: *pāśam*) The whole of existence, manifest and unmanifest. That which binds or limits the soul and keeps it (for a time) from manifesting its full potential. *Pāśa* consists of the soul's three-fold bondage of *āṇava, karma* and *māyā*. See: *liberation, mala, Pati-paśu-pāśa*.

pāśa-jñānam: பாசஞானம் "Knowledge of the world." That which is sought for by the soul in the first stage of the *sakala avasthai*, known as *irul*. See: *irul, sakala avasthā*.

paśu: पशु "Cow, cattle, kine; fettered individual." Refers to animals or beasts, including man. In philosophy, the soul. Śiva as Lord of Creatures is called Paśupati. See: *pāśa, Pati-paśu-pāśa*.

paśu-jñānam: பசுஞானம் "Soul-knowledge." The object of seeking in the second stage of the *sakala avasthai*, called *marul*. See: *marul, sakala avasthā*.

pātāla chakra: पाताल चक्र "Fallen" or "sinful region." The seventh *chakra* below the *mūlādhāra*, centered in the soles of the feet. Corresponds to the seventh and lowest astral netherworld beneath the earth's surface, called Kākola ("black poison") or Pātāla. This is the realm in which misguided souls indulge in destruction for the sake of destruction, of torture, and of murder for the sake of murder. *Pātāla* also names the netherworld in general, and is a synonym for *Naraka*. See: *chakra, loka, Naraka*.

Patanjali: पतञ्जलि A Śaivite Nātha *siddha* (ca 200 BCE) who codified the ancient *yoga* philosophy which outlines the path to enlightenment through purification, control and transcendence of the mind. One of the six classical philosophical systems *(darśanas)* of Hinduism, known as Yoga Darśana. His great work, the *Yoga Sūtras*, comprises some 200 aphorisms delineating *ashṭāṅga* (eight-limbed), *rāja* (kingly) or *siddha* (perfection) *yoga*. Still today it is the foremost text on meditative *yoga*. Different from the namesake grammarian. See: *rāja yoga, yoga*.

Pati: पति "Master; lord; owner." An appellation of God Śiva indicating His commanding relationship with souls as caring ruler and helpful guide. In Śaiva Siddhānta the title is part of the analogy of cowherd *(pati)*, cows *(paśu*, souls) and the tether *(pāśa—āṇava, karma* and *māyā)* by which cows are tied. See: *Pati-paśu-pāśa, Śiva*.

Pati-jñānam: பதிஞானம் "Knowledge of God," sought for by the soul in the third stage of the *sakala avasthai*, called *arul*. See: *arul, sakala avasthā, śaktinipāta*.

Pati-paśu-pāśa: पति पशु पाश Literally: "Master, cow and tether." These are the three primary elements *(padārtha*, or *tattvatrayī)* of Śaiva Siddhānta philosophy: God, soul and world—Divinity, man and cosmos—seen as a mystically and intricately interrelated unity. Pati is God, envisioned as a cowherd. *Paśu* is the soul, envisioned as a cow. *Pāśa* is the all-important force or fetter by which God brings souls along the path to Truth. The various schools of Hinduism define the rapport among the three in varying ways. For pluralistic Śaiva Siddhāntins they are three beginningless verities, self-existent, eternal entities. For monistic Śaiva Siddhāntins, *paśu* and *pāśa* are the emanational creation of Pati, Lord Śiva, and He alone is eternal reality. See: *pāśa, Śaiva Siddhānta, soul*.

payasam: பாயசம் A cooked, milk-based, pudding dessert often served at special festive occasions, generally made from tapioca or rice.

penance: *Prāyaśchitta*. Atonement, expiation. An act of devotion *(bhakti)*, austerity *(tapas)* or discipline *(sukṛitya)* undertaken to soften or nullify the anticipated reaction of a past action. Penance is uncomfortable *karma* inflicted upon oneself to mitigate one's *karmic* burden caused by wrongful actions *(kukarma)*. It includes such acts as prostrating 108 times, fasting, self-denial, or carrying *kavadi* (public penance), as well as more extreme austerities, or *tapas*. Penance is often suggested by spiritual leaders and elders. Penitence or repentance, suffering regret for misdeeds, is called *anutāpa*, meaning "to heat." —***bāla tāḍayati prāyaśchitta:*** "Child-beating penance," performed to mitigate the *pāpa*, sometimes called sin, accrued by having beaten a child. First, the adult counts the number of slaps or hits—with cane, stick, strap, hand, or fist—that he (or she) administered to children in the past. Then he meditates on the extent of harm he caused and in what ways. He lets the reality of this live with him for a week or two. (He may, at first, deny it, rationalize it, explain it away to himself, tell himself that there are a dozen reasons why striking a child was necessary, useful, customary and therefore acceptable. But all is Śiva, and no violence toward another human being, let alone our own flesh and blood, is acceptable.) Once acceptance is complete, while looking into a large mirror, he administers upon his own body five hits for each one he gave to a child, with hand, cane, belt, etc., in the exact area of the body where the hurt was felt by the child. This may take time, and it should be painful. Thus, looking in the mirror, he slaps himself five times for every slap he gave each child, pinches himself five times for every pinch given, etc. ¶After this phase of the *prāyaśchitta* has been completed and the abuser feels much relieved of the heavy *karmas*, the abuser must 1) apologize to all the children he has abused and assure them that he will no longer ever use corporal punishment, but instead use positive discipline. 2) Then he assures the children under his influence that he will protect them from such brutality at home and in school. 3) Next, he writes to his *satguru* or other mentor about his penance, indicating if the guilt has passed and inner peace has returned. He includes a handwritten pledge, *vrata*, stating: A) that he will never inflict such abuse ever again; and B) that he will notify the school that children must be treated with respect and kindness and receive no beating of any kind, and that any misbehavior by children under his care should be reported to him by teachers so that appropriate discipline can be administered at home. 4) Once the mentor responds, the penance is complete. ***—pushpa prāyaśchitta:*** "Flower penance." Those who have been physically abused are as much in need of penance to mitigate the experience as are those who abused them. Each person—child or adult—who has been beaten at any time, no matter how long ago, is enjoined to put up in the shrine room a picture of the person or persons by whom they were beaten, be it a father, mother or teacher. Then, every day for thirty-one days, he or she places a flower in front of each picture and, while doing so, sincerely forgiving the person in heart and mind. If no picture is available then some symbol or possession can be substituted, or even a paper with the name written on it. ***—krodha prāyaśchitta:*** "Anger penance." Anger arises from the second *chakra* below the *mūlādhāra*, the *vitala chakra*, and when that force center begins to vibrate, it vibrates in many different ways, spinning counterclockwise, causing disturbance to the natural *śānti* that otherwise prevails. Below are the some of the various faces of anger that the *vitala chakra* gives rise to. For each, a monetary sum is paid to compensate, as a form of penance, for allowing oneself to sink into this hurtful, unwholesome state of mind. Angry emotions that are suppressed: US$.10. Raising one's voice to emphasize a point: $.25. Pouting and turning the head away: $.50. Saying unkind things, unnecessary snide remarks: $.75. Sharp comments uttered in a raspy voice: $1.00. Long, brooding silences (an expression of anger that appears peaceful but is a way of cutting a person out of one's life): $2.00. (Mental arguments happen during those silences, deafening silences, loud deafening silences, during which thought swirls around how to retaliate or refute the other person's point.) A deeply cutting remark or hurtful insinuation or criticism of a personal nature: $2.50. A long, angry dissertation as to how others are totally wrong and how matters cannot continue in this way any longer: $4.00. An angry rage in which the aura turns black-red, or a jealous outburst in which one emphasizes, "I am in command. You are the serfs. You obey me, because you fear me." Or "You are wrong, and I don't like you. You did something terrible, unforgivable, stupid...(and such hateful things)" $5.00. For the wealthy, each of these amounts can be doubled; for the very wealthy, quadrupled. A jar labeled "Krodha Prāyaśchitta" is established in the shrine room to receive the payments. The sum collected is sent to a charity on the first Sunday of each month. See: *evil, kavadi, pāpa, prāyaśchitta, sin, tapas.*

perfections: Qualities, aspects, nature or dimensions that are perfect. God Śiva's three perfections are Paraśiva (Absolute Reality), Parāśakti (Pure Consciousness) and Parameśvara (Primal Soul). Though spoken of as three-fold for the sake of understanding, God Śiva ever remains a one transcendent-immanent Being. See: *Parameśvara, Parāśakti, Paraśiva, Śiva.*

perplexity: Puzzlement; the state of being confused, uncertain, befuddled.

pilgrimage: *Tīrthayātrā,* one of the five sacred duties *(pañcha nitya karmas)* of the Hindu, is to journey periodically to one of the innumerable holy spots in India or other countries. Preceded by fasting and continence, it is a time of austerity and purification, when all worldly concerns are set aside and God becomes one's singular focus. Streams of devout pilgrims are received daily at the many ancient holy sites *(tīrthas)* in India, and tens of thousands at festival times. See: *pañcha nitya karma.*

piṅgalā nāḍī: पिंगला नाडी "Tawny channel." The masculine psychic current flowing along the spine. See: *kuṇḍalinī, nāḍī, rāja yoga.*

plexus: A structure consisting of interwoven parts; a network. Especially of nerves, blood vessels, or lymphatic nodes.

Plotinus: (205-270CE) Egyptian-born Greek philosopher who founded Neo-Platonism, a revival of Platonism, in the Roman Empire. He taught *ahiṁsā,* vegetarianism, *karma,* reincarnation and belief in an immanent and transcendent Supreme Being.

pluralism (pluralistic): Any doctrine that holds existence to be composed of three or more distinct and irreducible components, such as God, souls and world. See: *dvaita-advaita.*

polarize: To turn, grow, think, feel in a certain way as a result of attraction or repulsion. In *The Master Course,* often to consciously align individual spiritual forces with the higher cosmic forces, also to attract and sustain the presence of divine beings.

Polynesian: Referring a group of islands in the Pacific, east of Australia and the Philippines, or to its peoples, languages or cultures.

pornography: Pictures, writings, movies or other media that present sexual matters in a manner intended to incite lust.

positive discipline: A system of raising children with love, respect and dignity, as a compassionate alternative to traditional punitive methods. Based on the books by author Jane Nelsen ED.D., it offers practical guidelines for parents and teachers to help children develop self-discipline, responsibility through firm but kindly guidance and mutual respect.

potluck: Whatever is available, with little or no choice.

pradosha: प्रदोष The auspicious 3-hour period, 1½ hours before and after sunset. *Pradosha* especially refers to this period on the 13th *(trayodaśī) tithi* of each fortnight, an optimum time of the month for meditation. Its observance, prepared for by fasting, is called *pradosha vrata.* See: *fast, tithi.*

prāṇa: प्राण Vital energy or life principle. Literally, "vital air," from the root *praṇ,* "to breathe." The interrelated odic and actinic forces. The sum total of all energy and forces. *Prāṇa* in the human body moves in the *prāṇamaya kośa* as five primary life currents known as *vāyus,* "vital airs or winds." These are *prāṇa* (outgoing breath), *apāna* (incoming breath), *vyāna* (retained breath), *udāna* (ascending breath) and *samāna* (equalizing breath). Each governs crucial bodily functions, and all bodily energies are modifications of these. Usually *prāṇa* refers to the life principle, but sometimes denotes energy, power or the animating force of the cosmos, the sum total of all energy and forces.

prāṇa chakravāla: प्राणचक्रवाल "Energized circle or assembly." See: *chakravāla.*

Praṇava: प्रणव "Humming." The *mantra Aum,* denoting God as the Primal Sound. It can be heard as the sound of one's own nerve system, like the sound of an electrical transformer or a swarm of bees. The meditator is taught to inwardly transform this sound into the inner light which lights the thoughts, and bask in this blissful consciousness. *Praṇava* is also known as the sound of the *nādanāḍī śakti.* See: *Aum.*

prāṇāyāma: प्राणायाम "Breath control." See: *rāja yoga.*

prāṇic body: The subtle, life-giving sheath called *prāṇamaya kośa.* See: *kośa.*

prārabdha karma: प्रारब्धकर्म "Action that has been unleashed or aroused." See: *karma.*

prasāda: प्रसाद "Clarity, brightness; grace." 1) The virtue of serenity and graciousness. 2) Food offered to the Deity or the *guru,* or the blessed remnants of such food. 3) Any propitiatory offering. See: *sacrament.*

prāyaśchitta: प्रायश्चित्त "Predominant thought or aim." Penance. Acts of atonement. See: *penance.*

prāyopaveśa: प्रायोपवेश "Resolving to die through fasting." Self-willed death by fasting. See: *suicide.*

precept: A commandment meant as a rule of action or conduct.

preceptor: Highly respected teacher and head of a spiritual order and clan; the equivalent of the word *satguru.*

Pretaloka: प्रेतलोक "World of the departed." The realm of the earth-bound souls. This lower region of Bhuvarloka is an astral duplicate of the physical world. See: *loka.*

Primal Soul: The uncreated, original, perfect soul—Śiva Parameśvara—who emanates from Himself the inner and outer universes and an infinite plurality of individual souls whose essence is identical with His essence. God in His personal aspect as Lord and Creator, depicted in many forms: Naṭarāja by Śaivites, Vishṇu by Vaishṇavites, Devī by Śāktas. See: *Naṭarāja, Parameśvara.*

Primal Substance: The fundamental energy and rarified form from which the manifest world in its infinite diversity is derived. See: *Parāśakti.*

processed sugar: See: *sugar, processed.*

procrastination: Postponing or needless delaying.

promiscuity: Engaging in sex indiscriminantly or with many partners. Not confining one's sexual relationship to one person.

prostitute: A person who solicits and accepts payment for sexual acts.

prostrate: Lying face down, as in submission or adoration. See: *prostration.*

prostration: *praṇāma:* प्रणाम "Obeisance; bowing down." Reverent salutation in which the head or body is bowed. ***—ashṭāṅga praṇāma:*** "Eight-limbed obeisance." The full body form for men, in which the hands, chest, forehead, knees and feet touch the ground. (Same as *śashṭāṅga praṇāma.*) ***—pañchāṅga praṇāma:*** "Five-limbed obeisance." The woman's form of prostration, in which the hands, head and legs touch the ground (with the ankles crossed, right over the left). A more exacting term for prostration is *praṇipāta,* "falling down in obeisance." See: *bhakti, namaskāra.*

protocol (cultural): A code of correct conduct for any procedure. A code of correct etiquette and cultured behavior among the members of a particular ethnic, religious or social group, often unwritten and passed on by example from generation to generation. For instance, there is a protocol for properly and humbly approaching a *guru, swāmī* or other holy person. Likewise, there is a protocol for respectfully receiving an important foreign diplomat.

pseudo: A prefix meaning false, sham, pretended.

psyche: The soul.

psychiatrist: A medical specialist who treats mental and emotional disorders.

psychic: "Of the psyche or soul." Sensitive to spiritual processes and energies. Inwardly or intuitively aware of nonphysical realities; able to use powers such as clairvoyance, clairaudience and precognition. Nonphysical, subtle; pertaining to the deeper aspects of man. See: *mysticism, odic.*

psychic entanglements: See: *psychic tubes.*

psychic tubes: Channels of astral matter which connect a man and woman who have had sexual intercourse. Such connections persist for a 12-year period, though they are greatly diminished after 6 years. Psychic tubes also persist between child and mother up until age 24. Through the process of *brahmacharya* all such connections are gradually dissolved and a new connection established with the *guru.* See: *brahmacharya.*

psychoanalyze: To interpret mental and emotional processes as results of unconscious impulses, repressed experiences and conflicts, etc.

psychologist: A person schooled in understanding of mental and emotional processes and behavior and treating disorders according to one or another of the various modern theories of human behavior.

psychology: The intellectual study of mental processes and behavior. The emotional and behavioral characteristics of an individual, or an activity.

psychometry: The ability of one's nervous system or psychic faculty to register and interpret vibrations from objects.

puberty: The stage of adolescence at which one becomes physiologically capable of sexual reproduction.

pūjā: पूजा "Worship, adoration." An Āgamic rite of worship performed in the home, temple or shrine, to the *mūrti, śrī pādukā,* or other consecrated object, or to a person, such as the *satguru.* Its inner purpose is to purify the atmosphere around the object worshiped, establish a connection with the inner worlds and invoke the presence of God, Gods or one's *guru.*

pujārī: पुजारी "Worshiper." A general term for Hindu temple priests, as well as anyone performing *pūjā. Pujārī* (sometimes *pūjārī)* is the Hindi form of the Sanskrit *pūjaka; pūsārī* in Tamil. *Archaka* is another term for the officiant priest used in the southern tradition. *Purohita* is a Smārta *brāhmin* priest who specializes in domestic rites. See: *pūjā.*

punarjanma: पुनर्जन्म "Reincarnation." From *punaḥ,* "again and again," and *janma,* "taking birth." See: *reincarnation.*

punjabi: A woman's outfit of India, a term derived from Punjab, a northern state in India. In current form it is a modest pant suit for women with a *kurta* upper garment with a widened bottom designed to sit on.

puṇya: पुण्य "Holy; virtuous; auspicious." 1) Good or righteous. 2) Meritorious action. 3) Merit earned through right thought, word and action. *Puṇya* includes all forms of doing good, from the simplest helpful deed to a lifetime of conscientious beneficence. Each act of *puṇya* carries its *karmic* consequence, *karmaphala,* "fruit of action"—the positive reward of actions, words and deeds that are in keeping with *dharma.* (Opposite of *pāpa.)* See: *karma, pāpa, penance.*

Pure Consciousness: See: mind (universal), *Parāśakti, Satchidānanda.*

purity-impurity: *Śaucha-aśaucha.* Purity and its opposite, pollution, are a fundamental part of Hindu culture. While they refer to physical cleanliness, their more important meanings extend to social, ceremonial, mental, emotional, psychic and spiritual contamination. Freedom from all forms of contamination is a key to Hindu spirituality, and is one of the *yamas.* Physical purity requires a clean and well-ordered environment, *yogic* purging of the internal organs and frequent cleansing with water. Mental purity derives from meditation, right living and right thinking. Emotional purity depends on control of the mind, clearing the subconscious and keeping good company. Spiritual purity is achieved through following the *yamas* and *niyamas,* study of the *Vedas* and other scriptures, pilgrimage, meditation, *jāpa, tapas* and *ahiṁsā.* See: *dharma, pāpa, penance, puṇya, yama-niyama.*

purusha: पुरुष "The spirit that dwells in the body/in the universe." Person; spirit; man. Metaphysically, the soul, neither male nor female. Also used in Yoga and Sāṅkhya for the transcendent Self. A synonym for *ātman. Purusha* can also refer to the Supreme Being or Soul, as it often does in the *Upanishads.*

purusha dharma: पुरुषधर्म "A man's code of duty and conduct." See: *dharma.*

Radhakrishnan, Dr. S. (Rādhākṛishṇan): राधाकृष्णन् (1888-1975) President of India from 1962 to 1967, a scholar, philosopher, prolific writer, compelling speaker and effective spokesman of Hinduism. Along with Vivekānanda, Tagore, Aurobindo and others, he helped stimulate the current Hindu revival by making Hinduism better known and appreciated at home and abroad, especially in the intellectual world. He was a foremost proponent of panentheism.

rāja yoga: राजयोग "King of *yogas.*" Also known as *ashṭāṅga yoga,* "eight-limbed *yoga.*" The classical *yoga* system of eight progressive stages to Illumination as described in various *yoga Upanishads,* the *Tirumantiram* and, most notably, in the *Yoga Sūtras* of Patañjali. The eight limbs are: 1) ***—yama:*** "Restraint." Virtuous and moral living, which brings purity of mind, freedom from anger, jealousy and subconscious confusion which would inhibit the process of meditation. 2) ***—niyama:*** "Observance." Religious practices which cultivate the qualities of the higher nature, such as devotion, cognition, humility and contentment—inducing the refinement of nature and control of mind needed to concentrate and ultimately plunge into *samādhi.* 3) ***—āsana:*** "Seat" or "posture." A sound body is needed for success in meditation. This is attained through *haṭha yoga,* the postures of which balance the energies of mind and body, promoting health and serenity, e.g., *padmāsana,* the "lotus pose," for meditation. 4) ***—prāṇāyāma:*** "Mastering life force." Breath control, which quiets the *chitta* and balances *iḍā* and *piṅgalā.*

Science of controlling *prāṇa* through breathing techniques in which the length of inhalation, retention and exhalation is modulated. *Prāṇāyāma* prepares the mind for deep meditation. 5) —***pratyāhāra:*** "Withdrawal." The practice of withdrawing consciousness from the physical senses first, such as not hearing noise while meditating, then progressively receding from emotions, intellect and eventually from individual consciousness itself in order to merge into the Universal. 6) —***dhāraṇā:*** "Concentration." Focusing the mind on a single object or line of thought, not allowing it to wander. The guiding of the flow of consciousness. When concentration is sustained long and deeply enough, meditation naturally follows. 7) —***dhyāna:*** "Meditation." A quiet, alert, powerfully concentrated state wherein new knowledge and insight pour into the field of consciousness. This state is possible once the subconscious mind has been cleared or quieted. 8) —***samādhi:*** (contemplation/God Realization) "Enstasy," which means "standing within one's self." "Sameness, contemplation." The state of true *yoga*, in which the meditator and the object of meditation are one. See: *āsana, enlightenment, enstasy, samādhi, yoga.*

rajas: रजस् "Passion; activity." See: *guṇa.*

Ramakrishna (Rāmakṛishṇa): रामकृष्ण (1836–1886) One of the great saints and mystics of modern Hinduism, and a proponent of monistic theism—fervent devotee of Mother Kālī and staunch monist who taught oneness and the pursuit of *nirvikalpa samādhi*, realization of the Absolute. He was *guru* to the great Swami Vivekananda (1863–1902), who internationalized Hindu thought and philosophy.

Ramana Maharshi: ரமண மகரிஷி (1879-1950) Hindu Advaita renunciate renaissance saint of Tiruvannamalai, South India.

Rama Tirtha (Rāma Tīrtha): रामतीर्थ One of the first Indian monks (1873-1906) to bring *yoga* and Vedānta to the West, he lectured throughout Japan and America, spreading "practical Vedānta."

Rāmāyaṇa: रामायण "Life of Rāma." One of India's two grand epics (Itihāsa) along with the *Mahābhārata*. It is Valmiki's tragic love story of Rāma and Sītā, whose exemplary lives have helped set high standards of dignity and nobility as an integral part of Hindu Dharma. Astronomical data in the story puts Rāma's reign at about 2015 bce.

rasātala chakra: रसातल चक्र "Subterranean region." The fifth *chakra* below the *mūlādhāra*, centered in the ankles. Corresponds to the fifth astral netherworld beneath the earth's surface, called Ṛijīsha ("expelled") or Rasātala. Region of selfishness, self-centeredness and possessiveness. *Rasā* means "earth, soil; moisture." See: *chakra, Naraka.*

realm: A kingdom, region, area or sphere. See: *loka.*

reconcile: To settle or resolve, as a dispute. To make consistent or compatible, e.g., two conflicting ideas.

reconciliation: Harmonization of quarrels or mending of differences.

reincarnate: To take birth in another body, having lived and died before.

reincarnation: "Re-entering the flesh." *Punarjanma;* metempsychosis. The process wherein souls take on a physical body through the birth process. The cycle of reincarnation ends when *karma* has been resolved and the Self God (Paraśiva) has been realized. This condition of release is called *moksha*. Then the soul continues to evolve and mature, but without the need to return to physical existence. See: *evolution of the soul, karma, moksha, saṁsāra, soul.*

relative: Quality or object which is meaningful only in relation to something else. Not absolute.

relative reality: *Māyā*. That which is ever changing and changeable. Describes the nature of manifest existence, indicating that it is not an illusion but is also not Absolute Reality, which is eternal and unchanging. See: *absolute, māyā.*

religion: From Latin *religare*, "to bind back." Any system of belief in and worship of suprahuman beings or powers and/or a Supreme Being or Power. Religion is a structured vehicle for soul advancement which often includes theology, scripture, spiritual and moral practices, priesthood and liturgy. See: *Hinduism.*

remorse: Deep, painful regret or guilt over a wrong one has done. Moral anguish. See: *penance.*

renunciation: See: *sannyāsa.*

repressions: Experiences, desires or inner conflicts residing in the subconscious mind and hidden from the conscious mind. Suppressed desires.

resent (resentment): A feeling of ill-will, indignation or hostility from a sense of having been wronged.

retaliate: To pay back an injury like for like, to get even.

righteous indignation: A standing up for *dharma*, a show of angry displeasure on personal moral or religious principles, accompanied in its lower forms by a vain sense of superiority.

ṛishi: ऋषि "Seer." A term for an enlightened being, emphasizing psychic perception and visionary wisdom. In the Vedic age, *ṛishis* lived in forest or mountain retreats, either alone or with disciples. These *ṛishis* were great souls who were the inspired conveyers of the *Vedas*. Seven outstanding *ṛishis* (the *sapta ṛishis*) mentioned in the *Ṛig Veda* are said to still guide mankind from the inner worlds.

Rishi from the Himalayas: The first known *satguru* of the Kailāsa Parampāra in recent history (ca 1770-1840) famous for having entered a teashop in a village near Bangalore where he sat down, entered into deep *samādhi* and did not move or speak for seven years. Streams of devotees came for his *darśana*. Their unspoken prayers and questions were mysteriously answered in dreams or in messages on paper that manifested in the air and floated down to the floor. One day he suddenly arose and left the village, later to pass his power to Siddhar Kadaitswami (1804-1891).

rite (or ritual): A religious ceremony. See: *sacrament, saṁskāra.*

rites of passage: Sacraments marking crucial stages of life. See: *saṁskāra.*

rites of passage, not attending: As the *Nandinātha Sūtras* indicate, rites of passage, sacraments or *saṁskāras* are special moments in life that are preciously guarded by all members of the community. Thus, tradition indicates certain restrictions as to who may attend, though those who do not attend may participate in preparations and receptions afterwards. Those who refrain from attending rites of passage include widows and widowers, *brahmachārīs* and *brahmachāriṇīs* and anyone who has been divorced. The reason is to protect the impressionable subconscious mind of those receiving the sacrament from the impressions of the possibilities of renunciation, widowhood and divorce. Funeral rites, however, are open to everyone, though a couple just married within the past year will stay away. Other important funeral customs are: 1) a son who would normally light the pyre for his parents will not if his wife is pregnant. Instead, a cousin or brother will take his place; 2) when a widow is at her husband's funeral rites, the other widows of the village gather around her, not the married couples. Note that if a widowed person remarries, he or she is no longer considered a widow or widower and may attend rites of passage with his or her new spouse. See: *saṁskāras.*

ritual: A religious ceremony conducted according to some prescribed order.

Rudra: रुद्र "Controller of terrific powers;" or "red, shining one." The name of Śiva as the God of dissolution, the universal force of reabsorption. *Rudra-Śiva* is revered both as the "terrifying one" and the "lord of tears," for He wields and controls the terrific powers which may cause lamentation among humans. See: *Naṭarāja, Śiva.*

śabda kośa: शब्दकोश "Sheath of sounds, or words." Vocabulary; a dictionary or glossary of terms.

sacrament: 1) Holy rite, especially one solemnized in a formal, consecrated manner which is a bonding between the recipient and God, Gods or *guru.* This includes rites of passage *(saṁskāra),* ceremonies sanctifying crucial events or stages of life. 2) *Prasāda.* Sacred substances, grace-filled gifts, blessed in sacred ceremony or by a holy person. See: *prasāda, saṁskāra.*

sacrifice: *Yajña.* 1) Making offerings to a Deity as an expression of homage and devotion. 2) Giving up something, often one's own possession, advantage or preference, to serve a higher purpose. The literal meaning of *sacrifice* is "to make sacred," implying an act of worship. It is the most common translation of the term *yajña,* from the verb *yuj,* "to worship." In Hinduism, all of life is a sacrifice—called *jīvayajña,* a giving of oneself—through which comes true spiritual fulfillment. *Tyāga,* the power of detachment, is an essential quality of true sacrifice.

sādhaka: साधक From *sadh,* "going straight to the goal." A spiritual aspirant; a devotee who performs *sādhana.* A serious seeker who has undertaken spiritual disciplines, is usually celibate and under the guidance of a *guru.* He wears white and may be under simple vows, but is not a *yogi* or *sannyāsin.* In Gurudeva's monastic communities, *sādhakas,* or postulants, abide by four vows—obedience, humility, purity and confidence, which they renew every two years. See: *sādhana.*

sādhana: साधन "Effective means of attainment." Self-effort, spiritual discipline; the way. Religious or spiritual disciplines, such as *pūjā, yoga,* meditation, *japa,* fasting and austerity. The effect of *sādhana* is the building of willpower, faith and confidence in oneself and in God, Gods and *guru. Sādhana* harnesses and transmutes the instinctive-intellectual nature, allowing progressive spiritual unfoldment into the superconscious realizations and innate abilities of the soul. See: *pāda, rāja yoga, sādhana mārga, spiritual unfoldment.*

sādhana mārga: साधनमार्ग "The way of *sādhana.*" A phrase used by Sage Yogaswami to name his prescription for seekers of Truth—a path of intense effort, spiritual discipline and consistent inner transformation, as opposed to theoretical and intellectual learning. See: *pāda, sādhana, spiritual unfoldment.*

sādhu: साधु "Virtuous one; straight, unerring." A holy man dedicated to the search for God. A *sādhu* may or may not be a *yogī* or a *sannyāsin,* or be connected in any way with a *guru* or legitimate lineage. *Sādhus* usually have no fixed abode and travel unattached from place to place, often living on alms. The feminine form is *sādhvī.*

saffron: An orange yellow, traditional color of the Hindu monk, said to originate from the mud of the Gaṅgā discoloring their white robes.

sage: A person respected for his spiritual wisdom and judgement.

Saguṇa Brahman: सगुणब्रह्मन् "God with qualities." The Personal Lord. See: *Brahman, Parameśvara.*

sahasradala padma: सहस्रदलपद्म "Thousand-petaled lotus." Another name for the *sahasrāra,* or crown, *chakra.* See: *sahasrāra chakra, chakra.*

sahasrāra chakra: सहस्रारचक्र "Thousand-spoked wheel." The cranial psychic force center. See: *chakra.*

saint: A holy person. See: *Nayanar.*

Śaiva: शैव Of or relating to Śaivism or its adherents, of whom there are about 400 million in the world today. Same as *Śaivite.* See: *Śaivism.*

Śaiva Āgamas: शैव आगम The sectarian revealed scriptures of the *Śaivas.* Strongly theistic, they identify Śiva as the Supreme Lord, immanent and transcendent. They fall in two main divisions: the 64 *Kashmīr Śaiva Āgamas* and the 28 *Śaiva Siddhānta Āgamas.* The latter group are the fundamental sectarian scriptures of Śaiva Siddhānta. The *Śaiva Āgama* scriptures, above all else, are the connecting strand through all the schools of Śaivism. The *Āgamas* themselves express that they are entirely consistent with the teachings of the *Veda,* that they contain the essence of the *Veda,* and must be studied with the same high degree of devotion. See: *Āgama, Vedas.*

Śaiva Dharma: शैव धर्म Another name for Śaivism. See:

Śaivism.

Śaiva Dharma Śāstras: शैव दर्म शास्त्र Saiva Siddhanta Church's *Book of Discipline*, detailing policies, membership rules and mission guidelines.

Śaiva Neri: சைவநெறி "Śaiva path." Tamil term for Śaivism. See: *Śaivism.*

Śaiva Samayam: சைவ சமயம் "Śaivite religion." See: *Saivism.*

Śaiva Siddhānta: शैवसिद्धान्त "Final conclusions of Śaivism." The most widespread and influential Śaivite school today, predominant especially among the Tamil people in Sri Lanka and South India. It is the formalized theology of the divine revelations contained in the twenty-eight *Śaiva Āgamas.* Other sacred scriptures include the *Tirumantiram* and the voluminous collection of devotional hymns, the *Tirumurai,* and the masterpiece on ethics and statecraft, the *Tirukural.* For Śaiva Siddhāntins, Śiva is the totality of all, understood in three perfections: Parameśvara (the Personal Creator Lord), Parāśakti (the substratum of form) and Paraśiva (Absolute Reality which transcends all). Souls and world are identical in essence with Śiva, yet also differ in that they are evolving. A pluralistic stream arose in the Middle Ages from the teachings of Aghoraśiva and Meykandar. For Aghoraśiva's school (ca 1150) Śiva is not the material cause of the universe, and the soul attains perfect "sameness" with Śiva upon liberation. Meykandar's (ca 1250) pluralistic school denies that souls ever attain perfect sameness or unity with Śiva. See: *Śaivism.*

Saiva Siddhanta Church: "Church of God Śiva's Revealed Truth," founded in 1949 by Satguru Sivaya Subramuniyaswami.

Saiva Siddhanta Yoga Order: Ecclesiastical body of lifetime renunciate swāmīs of Saiva Siddhanta Church. This *saṅgam* was founded by Satguru Sivaya Subramuniyaswami in 1949.

Śaivism *(Śaiva):* शैव The religion followed by those who worship Śiva as supreme God. Oldest of the four sects of Hinduism. The earliest historical evidence of Śaivism is from the 8,000-year-old Indus Valley civilization in the form of the famous seal of Śiva as Lord Paśupati, seated in a *yogic* pose. There are many schools of Śaivism, six of which are Śaiva Śiddhānta, Pāśupata Śaivism, Kashmīr Śaivism, Vīra Śaivism, Siddha Siddhānta and Śiva Advaita. They are based firmly on the *Vedas* and *Śaiva Āgamas,* and thus have much in common, including the following principal doctrines: 1) the five powers of Śiva—creation, preservation, destruction, revealing and concealing grace; 2) The three categories: Pati, *paśu* and *pāśa* ("God, souls and bonds"); 3) the three bonds: *āṇava, karma* and *māyā;* 4) the three-fold power of Śiva: *icçhā śakti, kriyā śakti* and *jñāna śakti;* 5) the thirty-six *tattvas,* or categories of existence; 6) the need for initiation from a *satguru;* 7) the power of *mantra;* 8) the four *pādas* (stages): *charyā* (selfless service), *kriyā* (devotion), *yoga* (meditation), and *jñāna* (illumination); 9) the belief in the Pañchākshara as the foremost *mantra,* and in *rudrāksha* and *vibhūti* as sacred aids to faith; 10) the beliefs in *satguru* (preceptor), Śivaliṅga (object of worship) and *saṅgama* (company of holy persons). See: *Śaivism.*

Śaivite (Śaiva): शैव Of or relating to Śaivism. See: *Śaivism.*

sakala avasthā: सकल अवस्था "Stage of embodied being." (Tamil: *avasthai.)* In Śaiva Siddhānta, the second of three stages of the soul's evolution, when it is engaged in the world through the senses as it first develops a mental, then emotional and astral body, and finally a physical body, entering the cycles of birth, death and rebirth under the veiling powers of *karma* and *māya.* Progress through *sakala avasthā* is measured in three stages: 1) *irul,* "darkness;" when the impetus is toward *pāśa,* knowledge and experience of the world *(pāśa-jñānam);* 2) *marul,* "confusion;" caught between the world and God, the soul begins to turn within for knowledge of its own nature *(paśu-jñānam);* and 3) *arul,* "grace," when the soul seeks to know God (Pati-*jñānam*); and receive His grace. See: *avasthā, evolution of the soul, kevala avasthā, śuddha avasthā.*

Śākta: शाक्त Of or relating to Śāktism. See: *Śāktism.*

Śakti: शक्ति "Power, energy." The active power or manifest energy of Śiva that pervades all of existence. Its most refined aspect is Parāśakti, or Satchidānanda, the pure consciousness and primal substratum of all form. In Śaiva Siddhānta, Śiva is All, and His divine energy, Śakti, is inseparable from Him. Śakti is most easily experienced by devotees as the sublime, bliss-inducing energy that emanates from a holy person or sanctified Hindu temple. See: *kuṇḍalinī, Parāśakti, Śāktism.*

śaktinipāta: शक्तिनिपात "Descent of grace," occuring during the advanced stage of the soul's evolution called *arul,* at the end of the *sakala avasthai. Śaktinipāta* is two-fold: the internal descent is recognized as a tremendous yearning for Śiva; the outer descent of grace is the appearance of a *satguru.* At this stage, the devotee increasingly wants to devote himself to all that is spiritual and holy. Same as *śaktipāta.* See: *arul, grace, sakala avasthā, śaktipāta.*

Śāktism (Śākta): शाक्त "Doctrine of power." The religion followed by those who worship the Supreme as the Divine Mother—Śakti or Devī—in Her many forms, both gentle and fierce. Śāktism is one of the four primary sects of Hinduism. Śāktism's first historical signs are thousands of female statuettes dated ca 5500 BCE recovered at the Mehrgarh village in India. In philosophy and practice, Śāktism greatly resembles Śaivism, both faiths promulgating, for example, the same ultimate goals of *advaitic* union with Śiva and *moksha.* But Śāktas worship Śakti as the Supreme Being exclusively, as the dynamic aspect of Divinity, while Śiva is considered solely transcendent and is not worshiped. There are many forms of Śāktism, with endless varieties of practices which seek to capture divine energy or power for spiritual transformation. See: *Śakti, tantric.*

salutations to the sun: *Sūrya namaskāra.* A group of eight or more *yoga āsanas,* postures, performed in methodic sequence in the morning while facing and saluting the sun. The sequence incorporates stretching and limbering exercises with controlled breathing and reverent concentration as a daily regimen for good health and as a preparation for meditation.

samādhi: समाधि From verb-root with prepositional prefixes samādhā "to hold together completely." "Enstasy," which means "standing within one's Self." "Sameness; contemplation; union, wholeness; completion, accomplishment." *Samādhi* is the state of true *yoga,* in which the meditator and the object of meditation are one. *Samādhi* is of two levels. The first is *savikalpa samādhi* ("enstasy with form" or "seed"), identification or oneness with the essence of an object. Its highest form is the realization of the primal substratum or pure consciousness, Satchidānanda. The second is *nirvikalpa samādhi* ("enstasy without form" or "seed"), identification with the Self, in which all modes of consciousness are transcended and Absolute Reality, Paraśiva, beyond time, form and space, is experienced. This brings in its aftermath a complete transformation of consciousness. Note that *samādhi* differs from *samyama.* See: *God Realization, kuṇḍalinī, Paraśiva, rāja yoga, samyama, Satchidānanda, Self Realization, trance.*

samayam: சமயம் "Religion."

sampradāya: संप्रदाय "Tradition," "transmission;" a philosophical or religious doctrine or lineage. A living stream of tradition or theology within Hinduism, passed on by oral training and initiation. The term derives from the verb *sampradā,* meaning "to give out," "render," grant, bestow or confer; to hand down by tradition; to bequeath.

saṁsāra: संसार "Flow." The phenomenal world. Transmigratory existence, fraught with impermanence and change. The cycle of birth, death and rebirth; the total pattern of successive earthly lives experienced by a soul. A term similar to *punarjanma* (reincarnation), but with broader connotations. See: *evolution of the soul, karma, reincarnation.*

saṁskāra: संस्कार "Impression, activator; sanctification, preparation." 1) The imprints left on the subconscious mind by experience (from this or previous lives), which then color all of life, one's nature, responses, states of mind, etc. 2) A sacrament or rite done to mark a significant transition of life, such as namegiving, first feeding, commencement of learning, coming of age and marriage. See: *mind (five states), sacrament.*

saṁskāras* of birth:** From the rite of conception to the blessings of the new-born child. ***—garbhādhāna: "Womb-placing." Rite of conception, where physical union is consecrated with the intent of bringing into physical birth an advanced soul. ***—punsavana:*** "Male rite; bringing forth a male." A rite performed during the third month of pregnancy consisting of prayers for a son and for the well-being of mother and child. A custom, found in all societies, based on the need for men to defend the country, run the family business and support the parents in old age. The need for male children in such societies is also based on the fact that women outlive men and leave the family to join their husband's family. ***—sīmantonnayana:*** "Hair-parting." A ceremony held between the fourth and seventh months in which the husband combs his wife's hair and expresses his love and support. ***—jātakarma:*** "Rite of birth." The father welcomes and blesses the new-born child and feeds it a taste of *ghee* and honey. See: *saṁskāra.*

saṁskāras* of childhood:** From naming to education. ***—nāmakaraṇa: "Name-giving" and formal entry into one or another sect of Hinduism, performed 11 to 41 days after birth. The name is chosen according to astrology, preferably the name of a God or Goddess. At this time, guardian devas are assigned to see the child through life. One who converts to or adopts Hinduism later in life would receive this same sacrament. ***—annaprāśana:*** "Feeding." The ceremony marking the first taking of solid food, held at about six months. (Breast-feeding generally continues). ***—karṇavedha:*** "Ear-piercing." The piercing of both ears, for boys and girls, and the inserting of gold earrings, held during the first, third or fifth year. ***—chūḍākaraṇa:*** "Head-shaving." The shaving of the head, for boys and girls, between the 31st day and the fourth year. ***—vidyārambha:*** Marks the beginning of formal education. The boy or girl ceremoniously writes his/her first letter of the alphabet in a tray of uncooked rice. ***—upanayana:*** Given to boys at about 12 years of age, marks the beginning of the period of *brahmacharya* and formal study of scripture and sacred lore, usually with an *āchārya* or *guru.* ***—samāvartana:*** Marks the end of formal religious study. See: *saṁskāra.*

saṁskāras* of adulthood:** From coming-of-age to marriage. ***—ṛitukāla: "Fit or proper season." Time of menses. A home blessing marking the coming of age for girls. ***—keśānta:*** Marking a boy's first beard-shaving, at about 16 years. Both of the above are home ceremonies in which the young ones are reminded of their *brahmacharya,* given new clothes and jewelry and joyously admitted into the adult community as young adults. ***—niśchitārtha*** "Settlement of aim." Also called *vāgdāna,* "word-giving." A formal engagement or betrothal ceremony in which a couple pledge themselves to one another, exchanging rings and other gifts. ***—vivāha:*** Marriage." An elaborate and joyous ceremony performed in presence of God and Gods, in which the *homa* fire is central. To conclude the ceremony, the couple take seven steps to the Northeast as the groom recites: "One step for vigor, two steps for vitality, three steps for prosperity, four steps for happiness, five steps for cattle, six steps for seasons, seven steps for friendship. To me be devoted *(Hiranyakeśi Gṛihya Sūtras* 1.6.21.2. VE)." See: *saṁskāra.*

saṁskāras* of later life: *—vānaprastha āśrama: Age 48 marks the entrance into the elder advisor stage, celebrated in some communities by special ceremony. ***—sannyāsa āśrama vrata:*** The advent of withdrawal from social duties and responsibilities at age 72 is sometimes ritually acknowledged (different from *sannyāsa dīkshā*). See: *sannyāsa dharma.* **—*antyeshṭi:*** The various funeral rites performed to guide the soul in its transition to inner worlds, including preparation of the body, cremation, bone-gathering, dispersal of ashes, home purification. See: *cremation, death, śrāddha, saṁskāra, transition.*

samyama: **सम्यम** "Constraint." Continuous meditation on a single concept to gain revelation on a particular subject or area of consciousness. As explained by Sage Patanjali, *samyama* consists of *dhāraṇā, dhyāna* and *samādhi.* See: *dhāraṇa, dhyāna, rāja yoga, samādhi.*

Sanātana Dharma: **सनातनधर्म** "Eternal religion" or "Everlasting path." It is a traditional designation for the Hindu religion. See: *Hinduism.*

sañchita karma: **सञ्चितकर्म** "Accumulated action." The accumulated consequence of an individual's actions in this and past lives. See: *karma.*

sanctum sanctorum: "Holy of holies." *Garbhagṛiha.* The most sacred part of a temple, usually a cave-like stone chamber, in which the main icon is installed. See: *temple.*

Śāṇḍilya Upanishad: **शाण्डिल्य उपनिषद्** Belongs to the *Atharva Veda.* Discusses eight forms of *yoga,* restraints, observances, breath control, meditation and the nature of Truth.

saṅga: **सङ्ग** "Association; fellowship." (Tamil: *Saṅgam*) Coming together in a group, especially for religious purposes.

Śaṅkara: **शङ्कर** "Conferring happiness; propitious." An epithet of Śiva.

Sankara (Śaṅkara), Adi: **शङ्कर** One of Hinduism's most extraordinary monks (788-820) and pre-eminent *guru* of the Smārta Sampradāya. He is noted for his monistic philosophy of Advaita Vedānta and his many scriptural commentaries. See: *Advaita Siddhānta, Vedānta.*

San Mārga: **सन्मार्ग** "True path." The straight spiritual path leading to the ultimate goal, Self Realization, without detouring into unnecessary psychic exploration or pointless development of *siddhis.* See: *pāda, sādhana mārga.*

San Marga Sanctuary: A meditation *tīrtha* at the foot of the extinct volcano, Mount Waialeale, on Hawaii's Garden Island, Kauai. Paths lead visitors to the sacred Wailua River, then up stone stairs to the Chola-style white-granite Iraivan Temple, hand-carved in Bangalore, India. In the sanctum sanctorum, the Supreme God, Śiva (Parameśvara-Parāśakti-Paraśiva), will be enshrined as a massive 700-pound, single-pointed earthkeeper quartz crystal. San Marga Sanctuary, founded in 1970, is among many public services of Saiva Siddhanta Church.

sānnidhya: **सान्निध्य** "(Divine) presence; nearness, proximity." The radiance and blessed presence of *śakti* within and around a temple or a holy person.

sannyāsa: **संन्यास** "Renunciation." "Throwing down" or "abandoning." *Sannyāsa* is the repudiation of the *dharma,* including the obligations and duties, of the householder and the assumption of the even more demanding *dharma* of the renunciate. The ancient *śāstras* recognize four justifiable motivations for entering into *sannyāsa: vidvat, vividishā, mārkaṭa* and *ātura. Vidvat* ("knowing; wise") *sannyāsa* is the spontaneous withdrawal from the world in search for Self Realization which results from *karma* and tendencies developed in a previous life. *Vividishā* ("discriminating") *sannyāsa* is renunciation to satisfy a yearning for the Self developed through scriptural study and practice. *Mārkaṭa sannyāsa* is taking refuge in *sannyāsa* as a result of great sorrow, disappointment or misfortune in worldly pursuits. (*Mārkaṭa* means "monkey-like," perhaps implying the analogy of a monkey clinging to its mother.) *Ātura* ("suffering or sick") *sannyāsa* is entering into *sannyāsa* upon one's deathbed, realizing that there is no longer hope in life. See: *sannyāsa dharma, sannyāsa dīkshā.*

sannyāsa dharma: **संन्यासधर्म** "Renunciate virtue." The life, way and traditions of those who have irrevocably renounced prerogatives and obligations of the householder, including personal property, wealth, ambitions, social position and family ties, in favor of the full-time monastic quest for divine awakening, Self Realization and spiritual upliftment of humanity. See: *sannyāsa, sannyāsa dīkshā, sannyāsin.*

sannyāsa dīkshā: **संन्यासदीक्षा** "Renunciate initiation." This *dīkshā* is a formal rite, or less often an informal blessing, ushering the devotee into renunciate monasticism, binding him for life to certain vows which include chastity, poverty and obedience, and directing him on the path to Self Realization. See: *sannyāsa dharma.*

sannyāsin: **संन्यासिन्** "Renouncer." One who has taken *sannyāsa dīkshā.* A Hindu monk, *swāmī,* and one of a world brotherhood (or holy order) of *sannyāsins.* Some are wanderers and others live in monasteries. See: *sannyāsa, sannyāsa dharma, sannyāsa dīkshā, swāmī.*

Sanskrit (Saṁskṛita): **संस्कृत** "Well-made;" "refined," "perfected." The classical sacerdotal language of ancient India, considered a pure vehicle for communication with the celestial worlds. It is the primary language in which Hindu scriptures are written, including the *Vedas* and *Āgamas.* Employed today as a liturgical, literary and scholarly language, but no longer used as a spoken vernacular.

śānti: **शान्ति** "Peace."

Śānti Mantra: **शान्ति मन्त्र** "Peace chant." So that each gathering of devotees is harmonious and productive, especially sessions of teacher and student, this *mantra* from the *Taittirīya Upanishad* (2.1.1) is recited at the outset to invoke peace, clarity and divine blessings, thus dispelling all potential enmity or confusion. It is recited again at the end as a closing benediction.

santosha: **सन्तोष** "Contentment." See: *yama-niyama.*

sapta ṛishis: **सप्तऋषि** Seven inner-plane masters who help guide the *karmas* of mankind.

sārī: **सारी** (Hindi: **साड़ी**) The traditional outer garment of Hindu women, consisting of a long, unstitched piece of cloth, usually colorful cotton or silk, wrapped around the body, forming an ankle-length skirt, and around the bosom and over the shoulder.

sarvabhūta: सर्वभूत "All living beings."

sarvada: सर्वद "For all times."

śāstra: शास्त्र "Sacred script; teaching." 1) Any religious or philosophical treatise, or body of writings. 2) A department of knowledge, a science.

sat: सत् "True, existing, good; reality, existence, truth." See: *Satchidānanda.*

Satchidānanda (Sachchidānanda): सच्चिदानन्द "Existence-consciousness-bliss." A synonym for *Parāśakti.* Lord Śiva's Divine Mind and simultaneously the pure superconscious mind of each individual soul. Perfect love and omniscient, omnipotent consciousness, the fountainhead of all existence, yet containing and permeating all existence. Also called pure consciousness, pure form, substratum of existence, and more. One of the goals of the meditator or *yogī* is to experience the natural state of the mind, Satchidānanda, subduing the *vṛittis* through *yogic* practices. See: *Parāśakti.*

satguru (sadguru): सद्गुरु "True weighty one." A spiritual preceptor of the highest attainment and authority—one who has realized the ultimate Truth, Paraśiva, through *nirvikalpa samādhi*—a *jīvanmukta* able to lead others securely along the spiritual path. He is always a *sannyāsin*, an unmarried renunciate. All Hindu denominations teach that the grace and guidance of a living *satguru* is a necessity for Self Realization. He is recognized and revered as the embodiment of God, Sadāśiva, the source of grace and of liberation. See: *guru bhakti, guru, guru-śishya system.*

satsaṅga: सत्संग Gathering in the company of good souls.

sattvic: Of, or relating to the *sattva guṇa,* the quality of goodness or purity. See: *guṇa.*

satya: सत्य "Truthfulness." See: *yama-niyama.*

Sat Yuga (Satya Yuga): सत् युग "Age of Truth," also called Kṛitā, "accomplished, good, cultivated, kind action; the winning die cast of four dots." The first in the repetitive cycle of *yugas,* lasting 1,728,000 years, representing the brightest time, when the full light of the Central Sun permeates Earth. See: *yuga.*

savikalpa samādhi: सविकल्पसमाधि "Enstasy with form" or "seed." See: *rāja yoga, samādhi.*

scripture (scriptural): "A writing." A sacred text or holy book(s) authoritative for a given sect or religion. See: *śāstra, smṛiti, śruti.*

Second World: The astral or subtle plane. Here the soul continues its activities in the astral body during sleep and after the physical body dies. It is the in-between world which includes the Devaloka and the Narakaloka. The Second world exists "within" the First World or physical plane. See: *three worlds.*

sect: A group of adherents who form a smaller association withing a larger (often religious) body. A religious denomination.

sectarian: Narrow adherence to the beliefs of a specific sect, especially in the sense that all other sects are incorrect or incomplete.

secular: Not sacred or religious; temporal or worldly.

seed *karma:* Dormant or *anārabdha karma.* All past actions which have not yet sprouted. See: *karma.*

seer: A wise person who sees beyond the limits of ordinary perception.

Self (Self God): God Śiva's perfection of Absolute Reality, Paraśiva—That which abides at the core of every soul. See: *Paramātman, Paraśiva.*

Self Realization: Direct knowing of the Self God, Paraśiva. Self Realization is known in Sanskrit as *nirvikalpa samādhi;* "enstasy without form or seed;" the ultimate spiritual attainment (also called *asamprajñata samādhi).* Esoterically, this state is attained when the mystic *kuṇḍalinī* force pierces through the *sahasrāra chakra* at the crown of the head. This transcendence of all modes of human consciousness brings the realization or "nonexperience" of That which exists beyond the mind, beyond time, form and space. But even to assign a name to Paraśiva, or to its realization is to name that which cannot be named. In fact, it is "experienced" only in its aftermath as a change in perspective, a permanent transformation, and as an intuitive familiarity with the Truth that surpasses understanding. See: *God Realization, liberation, kuṇḍalinī, Paraśiva, rāja yoga, samādhi.*

self-effacement: Modest, retiring behavior; giving all credit to God, preceptor and other persons and not accepting praise for one's accomplishments.

self-effulgent: Shining brilliantly by itself.

Semitic religions: The three faiths—Judaism, Islam and Christianity—that trace their origins to Abraham. See: *Abrahamic.*

sevā: सेवा "Service." *Karma yoga.* An integral part of the spiritual path, where the aspirant strives to serve without thought of reward or personal gain. The central practice of the *charyā pāda.* See: *yoga.*

seval: சேவல் The large, red, fighting rooster *(kukkuṭa* in Sanskrit) that adorns Lord Murugan's flag, heralding the dawn of wisdom and the conquest of the forces of ignorance. See: *Kārttikeya.*

sexuality: Hinduism has a healthy, unrepressed outlook on human sexuality, and sexual pleasure is part of *kāma,* one of the four legitimate goals of life. On matters such as birth control, sterilization, masturbation, homosexuality, bisexuality, petting and polygamy, Hindu scripture is tolerantly silent, neither calling them sins nor encouraging their practice, neither condemning nor condoning. The two important exceptions are adultery and abortion, both of which are considered to carry heavy *karmic* implications for this and future births. See: *celibacy, dissipation, odic force, ojas, tejas, transmutation.*

shaman: A priest of certain tribal societies who acts as a medium between the visible world and an invisible spirit worlds. See: *Shamanism.*

shamanism (shamanic): From a Siberian tribal word, akin to the Sanskrit *śramaṇa,* "ascetic," akin to *śram,* meaning "to exert." The religion of certain indigenous peoples of Northeast Asia, based on the belief in good and evil spirits who can be contacted and influenced by priests, or shamans, generally during a state of altered consciousness or trance. Also descriptive of many of the world's native, tribal faiths, and of various groups that today carry forward the practices and traditions of shamanism to maximize human abilities of mind and spirit for healing and problem-solving.

shaṭkoṇa: षट्कोण "Six-pointed star," formed by two interlocking triangles, the upper one representing Śiva's transcendent Being, and the lower one Śiva's manifest energy, Śakti. The *shaṭkoṇa* is part of Lord Kārttikeya's *yantra.* See: *Ardhanārīśvara, Kārttikeya.*

sheath: A covering or receptacle, such as the husk surrounding a grain of rice. In Sanskrit, it is *kośa,* philosophically the bodily envelopes of the soul. See: *kośa, soul, subtle body.*

Shintoism: The indigenous religion of Japan, based on the sacred power or God, *kami,* within a variety of forms, mainly of nature.

Shūm-Tyēīf: A Nātha mystical language of meditation revealed in Switzerland in 1968 by Sivaya Subramuniyaswami. (Pronounced *shoom-tyay-eef.*) Its primary alphabet looks like this:

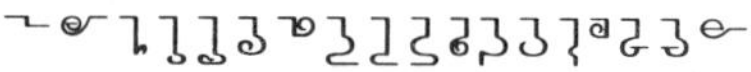

Shūm perspectives: The four perspectives of the mind: —***moolīf:*** intellectual/philosophical; —***shūmīf:*** individual awareness; —***simnīf:*** scientific/intellectual; —***dīfī:*** space travel, *devas* and Gods, inner communication. See: *defee, moolef, shūmef, simnef.*

shūmef: (Shūm) The perspective of the mind as a solid and individual awareness traveling from one area of the mind to another. Pronounced *shoom-eef.* See: *Shūm, Shūm perspectives.*

shun: To avoid or keep away from consistently. Shunning detractors or adversaries is courteously avoiding interaction and karmic entanglement with those who have shown by their actions that such interaction would not be beneficial or welcome. Shunning is a form of protection through nonengagement, building a "friendly, firm wall" while still remaining cordial.

siddha: सिद्ध A "perfected one" or accomplished *yogī,* a person of great spiritual attainment or powers. See: *siddhi.*

siddha yoga: सिद्धयोग "*Yoga* of perfected attainment, or of supernatural powers." 1) A term used in the *Tirumantiram* and other Śaiva scriptures to describe the *yoga* which is the way of life of adepts after attaining of Paraśiva. *Siddha yoga* involves the development of magical or mystical powers, or *siddhis,* such as the eight classical powers. It is a highly advanced *yoga* which seeks profound transformation of body, mind and emotions and the ability to live in a flawless state of God Consciousness. 2) The highly accomplished practices of certain alchemists. See: *siddha yogī, siddhi.*

siddha yogī: सिद्धयोगी "*Yogī* of perfection." A perfected one, adept, a realized being who is the embodiment of the most profound *yogic* states and has attained magical or mystical powers. See: *siddha yoga, siddhi.*

siddhānta: सिद्धान्त "Final attainments" or "conclusions." 1) Siddhānta refers to ultimate understanding arrived at in any given field of knowledge. 2) Especially when juxtaposed with the term *Vedānta,* it refers to the daily theistic practices of religion, as opposed to the monistic, meditative aspects; though Śaiva Siddhānta encompasses both theism and monism, Vedānta and Siddhānta, *Vedas* and *Āgamas.*

siddhānta śravaṇa (or śrāvaṇa): सिद्धान्तश्रवण "Scriptural audition." See: *yama-niyama.*

siddhi: सिद्धि "Power, accomplishment; perfection." Traditionally refers to extraordinary powers of the soul, especially psychic powers developed through consistent meditation and deliberate, *yogic sādhana.* The eight classical *siddhis* are: 1) *animā:* to be as small as an atom; 2) *mahimā:* to become infinitely large; 3) *laghimā:* super-lightness, levitation; 4) *prāpti:* pervasiveness, extension, to be anywhere at will; 5) *prakāmya:* fulfillment of desires; 6) *vashitva:* control of natural forces; 7) *iśititva:* supremacy over nature; 8) *kāma-avasayitva:* complete satisfaction.

Sikhism: "Discipleship." Religion of nine million members founded in India about 500 years ago by the saint Guru Nānak. A reformist faith which rejects idolatry and the caste system, its holy book is the *Ādi Granth,* and main holy center is the Golden Temple of Amritsar.

śilpi: शिल्पि "Craftsman." A stone worker or other traditional Hindu artrisan.

silver cord: The astral substance which connects the physical body to the astral body which is disconnected at the time of death of the physical body.

simnef: (Shūm) The perspective of the mind in its scientific, intellectual state. Pronounced *sim-neef.* See: *Shūm, Shūm perspectives.*

sin: Intentional transgression of divine law. Akin to the Latin *sons,* "guilty." Hinduism does not view sin as a crime against God, but as an act against *dharma*—moral order—and one's own self. See: *karma.*

śishya: शिष्य "A pupil" or "disciple," especially one who has proven himself and has formally been accepted by a *guru.*

Śiva: शिव The "Auspicious," "Gracious," or "Kindly one." Supreme Being of the Śaivite religion. God Śiva is All and in all, simultaneously the creator and the creation, both immanent and transcendent. As personal Deity, He is Creator, Preserver and Destroyer. He is a one Being, perhaps best understood in three perfections: Parameśvara (Primal Soul), Parāśakti (Pure Consciousness) and Paraśiva (Absolute Reality). See: *Parameśvara, Parāśakti, Paraśiva, Naṭarāja, Śaivism, Satchidānanda.*

Śiva consciousness: Śivachaitanya. A broad term naming the experience or state of being conscious of Śiva in a multitude of ways. See: *jñāna, mind (five states).*

Śivāchārya: शिवाचार्य The hereditary priests of the Śaiva Siddhānta tradition. The title of Ādiśaiva Brāhmins. An Ādiśaiva priest who has received the necessary training and *dīkshās* to perform public Śiva temple rites known as Āgamic *nitya parārtha pūjā*. A fully qualified Śivāchārya is also known as *archaka*. *Śivāchārya*, too, names the family clan of this priestly tradition. See: *brāhmin*.

Śivaliṅga: शिवलिङ्ग "Mark," "Token" or "Sign of Śiva." The most prevalent emblem of Śiva, found in virtually all Śiva temples. A rounded, elliptical, aniconic image, usually set on a circular base, or *pīṭha*. The Śivaliṅga is the simplest and most ancient symbol of Śiva, especially of Paraśiva, God beyond all forms and qualities. The *pīṭha* represents Parāśakti, the manifesting power of God. Liṅgas are usually of stone (either carved or naturally existing, *svayambhū*, such as shaped by a swift-flowing river), but may also be of metal, precious gems, crystal, wood, earth or transitory materials such as ice. See: *Śaivism*.

Śivaloka: शिवलोक "Realm of Śiva." See: *loka*.

Śivaness: Quality of being Śiva or like Śiva, especially sharing in His divine state of consciousness. See: *Śiva consciousness*.

Śivarātri: शिवरात्रि "Night of Śiva." See: Mahāśivarātri.

Śiva-Śakti: शिवशक्ति Father-Mother God, both immanent and transcendent. A name for God Śiva encompassing His unmanifest Being and manifest energy. See: *Parameśvara, Primal Soul, Śiva*.

Śivasambandha: शिवसंबन्ध "Bound together in love of Śiva." The underlying unity and harmony among devotees of Śiva, irrespective of caste or creed.

Sivathondar: சிவதொண்டர் "Servant of Śiva." Conveys the same mystic meaning as Sivanadiyar, denoting a devotee who regularly performs actions dedicated to God Śiva; selfless work in service to others. See: *karma yoga, Sivathondu*.

Sivathondu: சிவதொண்டு "Service to Śiva." Akin to the concept of *karma yoga*. See: *karma yoga*.

Śivāya Namaḥ: शिवाय नमः "Adoration to Śiva." Alternate form of *Namaḥ Śivāya*. See: *Namaḥ Śivāya*.

Skanda: स्कन्द "Quicksilver; leaping one." One of Lord Kārttikeya's oldest names, and His form as scarlet-hued warrior God. See: *Kārttikeya*.

Skanda Shashṭhī: स्कन्दषष्ठी A six-day festival in October-November celebrating Lord Kārttikeya's, or Skanda's, victory over the forces of darkness.

śloka: श्लोक A verse, phrase, proverb or hymn of praise, usually composed in a specified meter. Especially a verse of two lines, each of sixteen syllables. *Śloka* is the primary verse form of the Sanskrit epics, *Rāmāyaṇa* and *Mahābhārata*.

slothful: Lazy, disinterested in working or exerting oneself.

Smārta: स्मार्त "Of or related to *smṛiti*," the secondary Hindu scriptures. See: *Smārtism, smṛiti*.

Smārtism: स्मार्त "Sect based on the secondary scriptures (*smṛiti*)." The most liberal of the four major denominations of Hinduism, an ancient Vedic *brāhminical* tradition (ca 700 bce) which from the 9th century onward was guided and deeply influenced by the Advaita Vedānta teachings of the reformist Adi Sankara. Its adherents rely mainly on the classical *smṛiti* literature, especially the *Itihāsas (Rāmāyana* and *Mahābhārata*, the latter of which includes the *Bhagavad Gītā*), *Purāṇas* and *Dharma Śāstras*. These are regarded as complementary to and a means to understanding the *Vedas*. Smārtas adhere to Sankara's view that all Gods are but various depictions of Saguṇa Brahman. Thus, Smārtas are avowedly eclectic, worshiping all the Gods and discouraging sectarianism. The Smārta system of worship, called *pañchāyatana pūjā*, reinforces this outlook by including the major Deity of each primary Hindu sect of ancient days: Gaṇeśa, Sūrya, Vishṇu, Śiva and Śakti. In order to encompass a sixth important lineage, Sankara recommended the addition of a sixth Deity, Kumāra. Thus he was proclaimed Shaṇmata Sthapanāchārya, founder of the six-fold system. One among the six is generally chosen as the devotee's preferred Deity, Ishṭa Devatā. For spiritual authority, Smārtas look to the regional monasteries established across India by Sankara, and to their pontiffs. Within Smārtism three primary religious approaches are distinguished: ritualistic, devotional and philosophical. See: *Sankara*.

smidgen: A tiny bit, small piece or quantity.

smṛiti: स्मृति That which is "remembered;" the tradition. Hinduism's nonrevealed, secondary but deeply revered scriptures, derived from man's insight and experience. *Smṛiti* speaks of secular matters—science, law, history, agriculture, etc.—as well as spiritual lore, ranging from day-to-day rules and regulations to superconscious outpourings. From the vast body of sacred literature, *śāstra*, each sect and school claims its own preferred texts as secondary scripture, e.g., the *Rāmāyaṇa* of Vaishṇavism and Smārtism, or the *Tirumurai* of Śaiva Siddhānta. Thus, the selection of *smṛiti* varies widely from one sect and lineage to another. See: *Mahābhārata, Tirumurai*.

socialism: A system of government in which private ownership and production is superceded by community or state control.

Socrates: Greek philosopher and teacher (470-399 BCE). His method of question and answer is expressed in the dialogues of Plato, his foremost student.

solar plexus: A major physical and psychic nerve center of the body, located physically at the base of the sternum.

soul: The real being of man, as distinguished from body, mind and emotions. The soul—known as *ātman* or *purusha*—is the sum of its two aspects, the form or body of the soul and the essence of the soul (though many texts use the word *soul* to refer to the essence only). **—essence or nucleus of the soul:** Man's innermost and unchanging being—Pure Consciousness (*Parāśakti* or *Satchidānanda*) and Absolute Reality (*Paraśiva*). This essence was never created, does not change or evolve and is eternally identical with God Śiva's perfections of Parāśakti and Paraśiva.

soul body: *ānandamaya kośa* ("sheath of bliss"), also referred to as the "causal body" (*kāraṇa śarīra*), "innermost sheath" and "body of light." *Body of the* *soul*, or *soul body*, names the soul's manifest nature as an individual being—an effulgent, human-like form composed of light (quantums). The soul form evolves as its consciousness evolves, becoming more and more refined until finally it is the same intensity or refinement as the Primal Soul, Parameśvara. See: *ātman, evolution of the soul, kośa, Parāśakti, Paraśiva, purusha, Satchidānanda, spiritual unfoldment.*

spiritual unfoldment: *Adhyātma vikāsa.* The unfoldment of the spirit, the inherent, divine soul of man. The very gradual expansion of consciousness as *kuṇḍalinī śakti* slowly rises through the *sushumṇā*. The term *spiritual unfoldment* indicates this slow, imperceptible process, likened to a lotus flower's emerging from bud to effulgent beauty. When philosophical training and *sādhana* is complete, the *kuṇḍalinī* rises safely and imperceptively, without jerks, twitches, tears or hot flashes. Brings greater willpower, compassion and perceptive qualities.

śrāddha: श्राद्ध Relating to commemorative ceremonies for the deceased, held one week, one month after death, and annually thereafter, according to tradition. See: *saṁskāras of later life.*

śruti: श्रुति That which is "heard." Hinduism's revealed scriptures, of supreme theological authority and spiritual value. They are timeless teachings transmitted to *ṛishis*, or seers, directly by God thousands of years ago. *Śruti* is thus said to be *apaurusheya*, "impersonal," or rather "suprahuman." *Śruti* consists of the *Vedas* and the *Āgamas*, preserved through oral tradition and eventually written down in Sanskrit. Among the many sacred books of the Hindus, these two bodies of knowledge are held in the highest esteem. See: *Āgama, smṛiti, Veda.*

stimulants: Drugs that temporarily arouse or accelerate physiological or organic activity. Certain drugs are capable of stimulating psychic experiences, often with unpleasant consequences.

strī dharma: स्त्रीधर्म "Womanly conduct." See: *dharma.*

subconscious mind: *Saṁskāra chitta.* See: *conscience, mind (five states).*

śubha: शुभ "Auspicious," "splendid," "bright."

śubha muhūrta: शुभमुहूर्त "Auspicious time." A range of time when specified activities are most likely to thrive and succeed.

sublimate: To cause an instinctual impulse to manifest itself in a higher expression rather than a lower form. Coined after the property of some substances to transform themselves directly from a solid to a gas without becoming liquid. See: *transmutation.*

submission: Yielding to the power of another. Compliance; meekness.

Subramuniyaswami: சுப்பிரமுனியசுவாமி Current and 162nd *satguru* (1927–) of the Nandinātha Sampradāya's Kailāsa Paramparā. He was ordained Sivaya Subramuniyaswami by Sage Yogaswami on the full-moon day of May 12, 1949, in Jaffna, Sri Lanka, at 6:21 PM. This was just days after he had attained *nirvikalpa samādhi* in the caves of Jalani. The name *Subramuniya* is a Tamil spelling of the Sanskrit *Śubhramunya* (not to be confused with *Subramaṇya*). It is formed from *śubhra* meaning "light; intuition," and *muni*, "silent sage." *Ya* means "restraint; religious meditation." Thus, *Subramuniya* means a self-restrained soul who remains silent or, when he speaks, speaks out from intuition.

substratum: "Layer underneath." In philosophy, the substance or underlying force which is the foundation of any and all manifestation: Satchidānanda. See: *Parāśakti, Satchidānanda.*

subsubconscious mind: *Vāsanā chitta* ("mind of subliminal traits"). The area of the subconscious mind formed when two thoughts or experiences of the same rate of intensity are sent into the subconscious at different times and, intermingling, give rise to a new and totally different rate of vibration. This subconscious formation later causes the external mind to react to situations according to these accumulated vibrations, be they positive, negative or mixed.

subsuperconscious mind: *Anukāraṇa chitta.* See: *mind.*

subtle bodies: The various aspects of man: *prāṇic*, astral, mental and the innermost body of the soul.

subtle body: *Sūkshma śarīra*, the nonphysical, astral body or vehicle in which the soul encases itself to function in the Antarloka, or subtle world. The subtle body includes the *prāṇic*, astral and mental sheaths if the soul is physically embodied. It consists of only the astral and mental sheaths after death, when the *prāṇic* sheath disintegrates. And it consists of only the mental sheath when the astral sheath is dropped off just before rebirth or when higher evolutionary planes are entered. See: *jīva, kośa.*

śūdra: शूद्र "Worker, servant." See: caste.

śuddha: शुद्ध "Pure."

śuddha avasthā: शुद्ध अवस्था "Stage of purity." (Tamil: *avasthai.*) In Śaiva Siddhānta, the last of three stages of evolution, in which the soul is immersed in Śiva. Self Realization having been attained, the mental body is purified and thus reflects the divine soul nature, Śiva's nature, more than in the *kevala* or *sakala* state. Now the soul continues to unfold through the stages of realization, and ultimately merges back into its source, the Primal Soul. See: *avasthā, evolution of the soul, kevala avasthā, sakala avasthā, viśvagrāsa.*

Śuddha Śaiva Siddhānta: शुद्धशैवसिद्धान्त "Pure Śaiva Siddhānta," a term first used by Tirumular in the *Tirumantiram* to describe his monistic Śaiva Siddhānta and distinguish it from pluralistic Siddhānta and other forms of Siddhānta that do not encompass the ultimate monism of Vedānta.

Sufism: A mystical Islamic tradition in which Muslims seek to find the truth of divine love and knowledge through direct personal experience.

sugar, processed: In *Living with Śiva*, a number of forms of sucrose processed from sugar cane. These include "white sugar" (the most refined form of sucrose), confectioner's sugar (powdered white sugar) and brown sugar (white sugar with molasses added).

Highly refined cane sugar is unhealthy because they are stripped of all of the natural vitamins and minerals which are helpful in the digestion of sugars, causing the body to rob the same vitamins and minerals from the body's stores to assimilate them. Less refined cane sugar products, such as raw sugar, turbinado and sucanat (dried cane juice and molasses), make healthier alternatives. More nutritious sweeteners are maple syrup, date sugar (pulverized dried dates), honey, barley malt, rice syrup, jaggery and molasses.

sukarma: सुकर्म See: *karma.*

śukladāna: शुक्लदान "White, bright or pure gifts." Funds that are given freely and were earned through *dharmic* means, and thus unsullied by the negative *karmic* taint of adharmic activities. See: *yama-niyama.*

superconscious mind: *Kāraṇa chitta.* See: *mind (five states), mind (three phases), Satchidānanda.*

supernatural: Beyond or transcending the natural laws of the physical cosmos. Of or relating to an order of existence beyond the visible universe, referring to events, agencies or knowledge superseding or mystically explaining the laws of nature. See: *mysticism, shamanism.*

superstition: A belief or practice not supported by experience or reason.

supplicate (supplication): To ask for, beg humbly. To earnestly pray for.

suppressed: Subdued; ended forcibly. Kept from being revealed; inhibited. Deliberately excluded from the mind, such as with unacceptable desires or thoughts.

suppression: Desires, thoughts or memories consciously excluded from the mind. Related to repression, in which similar desires, etc., are excluded, but on a completely subconscious level.

Supreme God: Highest God, the source or creator of all other Gods, beings and all manifestation.

sushumṇā nāḍī: सुषुम्णा नाडी "Most gracious channel." Central psychic nerve current within the spinal column. See: *kuṇḍalinī, nāḍī, samādhi.*

sutala chakra: सुतल चक्र "Great abyss." Region of obsessive jealousy and retaliation. The third *chakra* below the *mūlādhāra,* centered in the knees. Corresponds to the third astral netherworld beneath the Earth's surface, called Saṁhāta ("abandoned") or Sutala. See: *chakra, hell, Naraka.*

sūtra: सूत्र "Thread." An aphoristic verse; the literary style consisting of such maxims. From 500 bce, this style was widely adopted by Indian philosophical systems and eventually employed in works on law, grammar, medicine, poetry, crafts, etc. Each *sūtra* is often accompanied by a commentary called *bhāshya* and sometimes subcommentary called *tika, vyakhyana* or *tippani.* Through the media of short, concise, easily memorized *sūtras,* vast amounts of knowledge were preserved. Reciting relevant *sūtra* texts from memory is a daily *sādhana* in various Hindu arts and sciences.

svādhishṭhāna: स्वाधिष्ठान "One's own base." See: *chakra.*

svarṇaśarīra: स्वर्णशरीर The golden actinic body formed after many experiences of Self Realization. See: *viśvagrāsa.*

swāmī (svāmī): स्वामी "Lord; owner; self-possessed." He who knows or is master of himself. A respectful title for a Hindu monk, usually a *sannyāsin,* an initiated, orange-robed renunciate, dedicated wholly to religious life. As a sign of respect, the term *swāmī* is sometimes applied more broadly to include non-monastics dedicated to spiritual work. See: *monk, sannyāsa dharma, sannyāsin.*

swastika (svastika): स्वस्तिक "It is well." The ancient Hindu symbol of auspiciousness and good fortune, representing the sun. The right-angled arms of the *swastika* denote the indirect way in which Divinity is reached—through intuition and not by intellect. It has been a prominent icon in many cultures.

sympathetic nervous system: The part of the autonomic nervous system originating in the thoracic and lumbar regions of the spinal cord that in general inhibits or opposes the physiological effects of the parasympathetic nervous system, as in tending to reduce digestive secretions, speeding up the heart, and contracting blood vessels.

syncretism: The combination of different beliefs or practices.

synthesis: Here: the application of reason to reach a particular conclusion from general concepts; also the combination of ideas to form a new idea.

T

tai chi chuan: An ancient Chinese system of slow, graceful, meditative, sequential movements. Many of the movements are originally derived from the martial arts, so in certain systems the combat aspect is a central focus. Tai chi, closely associated with acupuncture and founded in the context of Taoism, fosters the circulation and control of *chi,* "vital energy," within the body, to enhance health and vitality, physical strength and balance, and to foster a calm, tranquil mind.

tala: तल "Plane or world; level; base, bottom; abyss." Root of the name of the seven realms of lower consciousness centered in the seven *chakras* below the *mūlādhāra.* See: *chakra, hell, Naraka.*

talātala chakra: तलातल चक्र "Lower region." The fourth *chakra* below the *mūlādhāra,* centered in the calves. Region of chronic mental confusion and unreasonable stubbornness. Corresponds to the fourth astral netherworld beneath the Earth's surface, called Tāmisra ("darkness") or Talātala. This state of consciousness is born of the sole motivation of self-preservation. See: *chakra, Naraka.*

tamas(ic): तमस् "Force of inertia." The quality of denseness, inertia, contraction, resistance and dissolution. See: *guṇa.*

taṁbūrā: तंबूरा (Hindi) A long-necked, four-stringed fretless lute that provides a drone accompaniment for a singer or instrumentalist.

Tamil: தமிழ் The ancient Dravidian language of the Tamils, a Caucasoid people of South India and Northern Sri Lanka, now living throughout the world. The official language of the state of Tamil Nadu, India.

Tamil Nadu: தமிழ் நாடு State in South India, 50,000 square miles, population 55 million. Land of countless holy scriptures, saints, sages and over 40,000 magnificent temples, including Chidambaram, Madurai, Palani Hills and Rāmeśvaram.

tāṇḍava: ताण्डव "Exuberant dance." Any vigorous dance sequence performed by a male dancer. There are many forms of *tāṇḍava.* Its prototype is Śiva's dance of bliss, *ānanda tāṇḍava.* The much softer feminine dance is called *lāsya,* from *lasa,* "lively." Dance in general is *nartana.* See: *Naṭarāja.*

tantra: तन्त्र "Loom, methodology." 1) Most generally, a synonym for *śāstra,* "scripture." 2) A synonym for the Āgamic texts, especially those of the Śākta faith, a class of Hindu scripture providing detailed instruction on all aspects of religion, mystic knowledge and science. The *Tantras* are also associated with the Śaiva tradition. 3) A specific method, technique or spiritual practice within the Śaiva and Śākta traditions. For example, *prāṇāyāma* is a *tantra.* 4) Disciplines and techniques with a strong emphasis on worship of the feminine force, often involving sexual encounters, with the purported goal of transformation and union with the Divine. See: *kuṇḍalinī, sushumṇā nāḍī, tantrism.*

tantric (tāntrika): तान्त्रिक 1) Adjectival to qualify practices prescribed in the Tantra traditions. 2) Referring to the methods of directing the subtle masculine/feminine, aggressive/passive energies that flow between men and women. 3) Also names a practitioner of any of the Tantra traditions. 4) *Tantra* has today come to commonly refer to sex-based spiritual practices developed in Hinduism (known as "left-handed *tantra*") and in other faiths, including Bon, Tibetan Buddhism, Taoism, Christianity, Judaism and the New Age. See: *Śāktism, kuṇḍalinī, rāja yoga, tantra.*

Taoism: A Chinese religion, based on the doctrines of Lao-Tzu, founded 2,500 years ago, advocating simplicity, selflessness and other virtues. Taoism, a potently mystical tradition, is concerned with man's spiritual level of being. Following is estimated at 50 million, mostly in China and and other parts of Asia.

tapas: तपस् Also *tapasya.* "Warmth, heat," hence psychic energy, spiritual fervor or ardor. Austerity, asceticism, penance. State of accelerated unfoldment and working with the forces through spiritual practices. A state of humble submission to the divine forces and surrender to the processes of inner purification which occur almost automatically at certain stages. In the monastery *tapas* is administered and guided by the guru. Denotes religious austerity, severe meditation, penance, bodily mortification, special observances; connotes spiritual purification and transformation as a "fiery process" which "burns up" impurities, ego, illusions and past karmas that obstruct God Realization.

tapasvin: तपस्विन् One who performs *tapas* or is in the state of *tapas.*

tejas: तेजस् "Brilliance, fire, splendor." Heat or fire, one of the five elements—earth, water, fire, air, ether. *Tejas* also names the glow of *tapas* in the shining expression of the *tapasvin. Tejas* is increased through *brahmacharya,* control of the sexual energies by lifting the heat into the higher *chakras.* See: *celibacy, ojas, tapas, transmutation.*

temple: An edifice in a consecrated place dedicated to, the worship of God or Gods. Hindus revere their temples as sacred, magical places in which the three worlds most consciously commune—structures especially built and consecrated to channel the subtle spiritual energies of inner-world beings. The temple's psychic atmosphere is maintained through regular worship ceremonies *(pūjā)* invoking the Deity, who uses His installed image *(mūrti)* as a temporary body to bless those living on the earth plane. In Hinduism, the temple is the hub of virtually all aspects of social and religious life. It may be referred to by the Sanskrit terms *mandira, devālaya* (or Śivālaya, a Śiva temple), as well as by vernacular terms such as *koyil* (Tamil).

temptation: Something tempting, enticing or alluring.

temptress: An alluring, enchanting woman.

That: When capitalized, this simple demonstrative pronoun refers uniquely to the Ultimate, Indescribable or Nameless Absolute. The Self God, Paraśiva. It is the English equivalent of *Tat,* as in, *Tat tvam asi,* "You are That!"

theistic: The belief that God exists as a real, conscious, personal Supreme Being, creator and ruler of the universe. May also include belief in the Gods.

Third World: Śivaloka, "Realm of Śiva." The spiritual realm or causal plane of existence wherein Mahādevas and highly evolved souls live in their own self-effulgent forms. See: *Śivaloka, three worlds, loka.*

thought form: Manifestations of astral matter, or odic force, created within the aura of a person, which travel through astral space, or odic force fields, from one destination to another. They have the power to create, preserve, protect and destroy. They can also be seen, just as auras can be seen. See: *astral plane, aura, odic force, intellect.*

three worlds: The three worlds of existence, *triloka,* are the primary hierarchical divisions of the cosmos. 1) Bhūloka: "Earth world," the physical plane. 2) Antarloka: "Inner" or "in-between world," the subtle or astral plane. 3) Śivaloka: "World of Śiva," and of the Gods and highly evolved souls; the causal plane, also called Kāraṇaloka. See: *chakra, Naraka.*

tilaka: तिलक Marks made on the forehead or the brow with clay, ashes or sandalwood paste as an indication of Hindu sectarian affiliation.

time-out: A period of removing oneself or another person from a conflict to allow time to cool off. A technique of positive discipline for raising children with love rather punishment. See: *positive discipline.*

tirodhāna śakti: तिरोधानशक्ति "Concealing power." Veiling grace, or God's power to obscure the soul's divine nature. *Tirodhāna śakti* is the particular energy of Śiva that binds the three bonds of *āṇava, karma, māyā* to the soul. It is a purposeful limiting of consciousness to give the opportunity to the soul to grow and mature through experience of the world. See: *evolution of the soul, grace.*

tīrthayātrā: तीर्थयात्रा "Journey to a holy place." Pilgrimage. See: *pilgrimage.*

tiru: திரு "Sacred; holy." The exact Tamil rendition of *śrī*. Feminine equivalent is *tirumati.*

Tirukural: திருக்குறள் "Holy couplets." A treasury of Hindu ethical insight and a literary masterpiece of the Tamil language, written by Śaiva Saint Tiruvalluvar (ca 200 BCE) near Chennai. See: *Tiruvalluvar.*

Tirumantiram: திருமந்திரம் "Holy incantation." The Nandinātha Sampradāya's oldest Tamil scripture; written ca 200 BCE by Ṛishi Tirumular. It is the earliest of the *Tirumurai* texts, and a vast storehouse of esoteric *yogic* and *tantric* knowledge. It contains the mystical essence of *rāja yoga* and *siddha yoga,* and the fundamental doctrines of the 28 *Śaiva Siddhānta Āgamas,* which in turn are the heritage of the ancient pre-historic traditions of Śaivism. See: *Tirumurai, Tirumular.*

Tirumular: திருமூலர் An illustrious *siddha yogī* and *ṛishi* of the Nandinātha Sampradāya's Kailāsa Paramparā who came from the Himalayas (ca 200 BCE) to Tamil Nadu to compose the *Tirumantiram.* In this scripture he recorded the tenets of Śaivism in concise and precise verse form, based upon his own realizations and the supreme authority of the *Śaiva Āgamas* and the *Vedas.* Tirumular was a disciple of Maharishi Nandinatha. See: *Tirumantiram, Kailāsa Paramparā, Vedānta.*

Tirumurai: திருமுறை "Holy script." A twelve-book collection of hymns and writings of South Indian Śaivite saints, compiled by Saint Nambiyandar Nambi (ca 1000).

tiruvadi: திருவடி The feet of the *satguru* or his holy sandals, known in Sanskrit as *śrī pādukā,* worshiped as the source of grace. The *guru's* feet are especially sacred, being the point of contact of the divine and physical spheres. See: *pādukā.*

Tiruvalluvar: திருவள்ளுவர் "Holy weaver." Tamil weaver and householder saint (ca 200 BCE) who wrote the classic Śaivite ethical scripture Tirukural. He lived with his wife, Vasuki, famed for her remarkable loyalty and virtues, near modern-day Chennai. There a memorial park, the Valluvar Kottam, enshrining his extraordinary verses in marble. See: *Tirukural.*

tithe (tithing): In Sanskrit *daśamāṁśa,* or *makimai* in the Tamil tradition. The spiritual discipline, often a *vrata,* of giving one tenth of one's gainful and gifted income to a religious organization of one's choice, thus sustaining spiritual education and upliftment on earth. Tithing is given not as an offering, but as "God's money."

tithi: तिथि A lunar day, approximately one-thirtieth of the time it takes the moon to orbit the earth. Because of their means of calculation (based on the difference of the longitudinal angle between the position of sun and the moon), *tithis* may vary in length. There are 15 *tithis* in each fortnight (half month). The names of the *tithis* are Prathamā (new moon), Dvitīyā, Tritīyā, Chaturthī, Pañchamī, Shashṭhī, Saptamī, Ashṭamī, Navamī, Daśamī, Ekādaśī, Dvādaśī, Trayodaśī, Chaturdaśī, and lastly either Pūrṇimā (full moon) or Amāvasyā (new moon). These are sometimes prefixed to indicate either the dark *(kṛishṇa)* fortnight—when the moon is waning—or the light *(śukla)* fortnight—when the moon is waxing—e.g., Śukla-Navamī. Most Hindu festivals are calculated according to the *tithis.*

trance mediumship: In spiritualism, trance mediumship describes the phenomenon in which the medium leaves the physical body, and a disincarnate being enters or takes control of the body, often giving forth verbal messages to others in attendance, as in a seance. See: *samādhi.*

transcend: To go beyond one's limitations, e.g., "to transcend one's ego." Philosophically, to go beyond the limits of this world, or more profoundly, beyond time, form and space into the Absolute, the Self God.

transcendent: Surpassing the limits of experience or manifest form. In Śaiva Siddhānta, a quality of God Śiva as Absolute Reality, Paraśiva, the Self. Distinguished from immanent. See: *Paraśiva.*

transference: Passing something from one place (or state) to another.

transgress: To overstep or break a law or principle.

transition: Passing from one state, condition or place to another. A synonym of death which implies, more correctly, continuity of the individual rather than his annihilation.

transmigration: Reincarnation, the repeated rebirth of the soul in a succession of human bodies.

transmutation: Change from one form to another. Here, changing or transforming the sexual/instinctive energies into intellectual and spiritual ones. Transmutation means to reverse the forces that constantly flow from the *sahasrāra* downward into the *mūlādhāra.* It is lifting the force of sexual impulses that would tend to manifest in visualization, longing for affection and sensual feelings, often leading to masturbation and loss of the sacred fluids. One exception for both men and women is the occurrence of wet dreams, for here the astral, psychic vitality of the actinodic into the actinic energies rises as the odic fluids are released. However, night emissions are to be controlled and may be minimized or eliminated by taking only liquid or light foods in the evening. ¶Monks enhance transmutation by not eating after high noon, not viewing pornography, not mentally conjuring up sexually stimulating images, never joking or talking about sexuality and, of course, not flirting or interacting sensually with women or men. If sexual energies are aroused or one has erred from his disciplines, he performs the appropriate penance (such as fasting) or *tantra* (such as *prāṇāyāma)* to correct the matter. The *Tirumantiram* (verse 1948) states, "If the sacred seed is retained, life does not ebb; great strength, energy, intelligence and alertness: all these are attained." See: *actinic, celibacy, odic, ojas, tejas.*

trikoṇa: **त्रिकोण** A triangle; symbol of God Śiva as Absolute Reality. Also represents the element fire.

triple bondage: See: *mala, pāśa.*

tripuṇḍra: **त्रिपुण्ड्र** "Three marks." The Śaivite sectarian mark, consisting of three horizontal lines of *vibhūti* (holy ash) on the brow, often with a dot *(bindu)* at the third eye. The three lines represent the soul's three bonds: *āṇava, karma* and *māyā.* Holy ash, made of burnt cow dung, is a reminder of the temporary nature of the physical body and the urgency to strive for spiritual attainment and closeness to God. See: *bindu, tilaka, vibhūti.* §§

triśūla: **त्रिशूल** A three-pronged spear or trident wielded by Lord Śiva and certain Śaivite ascetics. Symbolizes God's three fundamental *śaktis* or powers—*icçhā* (desire, will, love), *kriyā* (action) and *jñāna* (wisdom).

Truth: When capitalized, ultimate knowing which is unchanging. Lower case (truth): honesty, integrity; virtue.

ultimate: Final, last. —**Ultimate Reality:** Final, highest Truth. God Śiva's Absolute Reality, Paraśiva.

unfoldment: Opening gradually, especially in stages. See: *evolution, spiritual unfoldment.*

United Nations: UN, a worldwide organization established in 1945, devoted to world peace, promoting economic, social and educational welfare and to creating cultural understanding between nations.

unmanifest: Not evident or perceivable. Philosophically, akin to *transcendent.* Śiva is unmanifest in His formless perfection, Paraśiva. See: *formless.*

unravel: To undo, to separate, disentangle something entangled.

upadeśa: **उपदेश** "Advice; religious instruction." Often given in question-and-answer form from *guru* to disciple. The *satguru's* spiritual discourses.

upadeśī: **उपदेशी** A liberated soul who chooses to teach, actively helping others to the goal of liberation. Contrasted with *nirvāṇī.* See: *nirvāṇī and upadeśī, satguru.*

Upanishad: **उपनिषद्** "Sitting near devotedly." The fourth and final portion of the *Vedas,* expounding the secret, philosophical meaning of the Vedic hymns. The *Upanishads* are a collection of profound texts which are the source of Vedānta and have dominated Indian thought for thousands of years. They are philosophical chronicles of *ṛishis* expounding the nature of God, soul and cosmos, exquisite renderings of the deepest Hindu thought. See: *śruti, Veda, Vedānta.*

vāhana: **वाहन** "Bearing, carrying or conveying." Each Hindu God is depicted as riding an animal or bird *vāhana,* which is symbolic of a function of the God. For example, Śiva rides the bull, a symbol of strength and potency. Kārttikeya rides the peacock, *mayūra,* emblem of beauty and regality.

vairāgya: **वैराग्य** "Dispassion; aversion." Freedom from passion. Distaste or disgust for worldliness because of spiritual awakening and the constant renunciation of obstacles on the path to liberation. See: *sannyāsa.*

Vaishṇavism (Vaishṇava): **वैष्णव** One of the four major religions, or denominations of Hinduism, representing roughly half of the world's one billion Hindus. It gravitates around the worship of Lord Vishṇu as Personal God, His incarnations and their consorts. The doctrine of *avatāra* (He who descends), especially important to Vaishṇavism, teaches that whenever *adharma* gains ascendency in the world, God takes a human birth to reestablish "the way." The most renowned *avatāras* were Rāma and Kṛishṇa. Vaishṇavism stresses the personal aspect of God over the impersonal, and *bhakti* (devotion) as the true path to salvation. The goal of Vaishṇavism is the attainment of *mukti,* defined as blissful union with God's body, the loving recognition that the soul is a part of Him, and eternal nearness to Him in Vaikuṇṭha, heaven.

vaiśya: **वैश्य** "Landowner; merchant." See: *caste.*

vanakkam: **வணக்கம்** The Tamil equivalent to *namaskāra.*

Varāha Upanishad: **वराह उपनिषद्** A minor *Upanishad* of the *Kṛishṇa Yajur Veda.*

vāsanā: **वासना** "Abode." Subconscious inclinations. From *vās,* "dwelling, residue, remainder." The subliminal inclinations and habit patterns which, as driving forces, color and motivate one's attitudes and future actions. *Vāsanās* are the conglomerate results of subconscious impressions *(saṁskāras)* created through experience. *Saṁskāras,* experiential impressions, combine in the subconscious to form *vāsanās,* which thereafter contribute to mental fluctuations, called *vṛitti.* The most complex and emotionally charged *vāsanās* are found in the dimension of mind called the sub-subconscious, or *vāsanā chitta.* See: *saṁskāra, mind (five states), vāsanā daha tantra, vṛitti.*

vāsanā daha tantra: **वासनादहतन्त्र** "Purification of the subconscious by fire." *Daha* means burning, *tantra* is a method, and *vāsanās* are deep-seated subconscious traits or tendencies that shape one's attitudes and motivations. *Vāsanās* can be either positive or negative. One of the best methods for resolving difficulties in life, of dissolving troublesome *vāsanās,* the *vāsanā daha tantra* is the practice of burning confessions, or even long letters to loved ones or acquaintances, describing pains, expressing confusions and registering grievances and long-felt hurts. Also called spiritual journaling, writing down problems and burning them in any ordinary fire brings them from the subconscious into the external mind, releasing the supressed emotion as the fire consumes the paper. This is a magical healing process. —***mahā vāsanā daha tantra:*** The special sādhana of looking back over and writing about the various aspects of one's life in order to clear all accumulated subconscious burdens, burning the papers as done in the periodic vāsana daha tantra. Ten pages are to be written about each year. Other aspects of this tantra include writing about people one has known (people check), all sexual experiences (sex check). See also: *vāsanā.*

vaṭa: वट The banyan tree, *Ficus indicus,* sacred to Śiva. Thought to derive from *vaṭ,* "to surround, encompass"—also called nyagrodha, "growing downwards." Ancient symbol of the Sanātana Dharma. Its relative, the *aśvattha,* or *pīpal* tree, is given in the *Upanishads* as a metaphor for creation, with the "roots above and the branches below."

Vāstu Śāstras: वास्तुशास्त्र Various ancient texts on *vāstu,* "the science of time and space," in the words of renowned Indian architect, Sri V. Ganapati Sthapati. The *Vāstu Śāstras* are categorized as part of the *Sthāpatyaveda,* science of architecture, classed among the *Upavedas,* which are secondary Vedic texts discussing such areas as statecraft, health and music. *Vāstu* unfolds the scientific principles and models of spiritual art and architecture to yield a harmonious flow of energy in the physical environment, giving rise to good health, wealth, intelligence and happiness.

Veda: वेद् "Wisdom." Sagely revelations which comprise Hinduism's most authoritative scripture. They, along with the *Āgamas,* are *śruti,* that which is "heard." The *Vedas* are a body of dozens of holy texts known collectively as the *Veda,* or as the four *Vedas: Ṛig, Yajur, Sāma* and *Atharva.* In all they include over 100,000 verses, as well as additional prose. The knowledge imparted by the *Vedas* ranges from earthy devotion to high philosophy. Each *Veda* has four sections: *Saṁhitās* (hymn collections), *Brāhmaṇas* (priestly manuals), *Āraṇyakas* (forest treatises) and *Upanishads* (enlightened discourses). The oldest portions of the *Vedas* are thought by some to date back as far as 6,000 BCE, written down in Sanskrit in the last few millennia, making them the world's most ancient scriptures. See: *śruti, Upanishad.*

Vedānta: वेदान्त "Ultimate wisdom" or "final conclusions of the *Vedas.*" Vedānta is the system of thought embodied in the *Upanishads* (ca 1500-600 BCE), which give forth the ultimate conclusions of the *Vedas.* Through history there developed numerous Vedānta schools, ranging from pure dualism to absolute monism. The Vedānta perspective elucidated in *Living with Śiva* is Advaita Īśvaravāda, "monistic theism" or panentheism, exemplified in the Vedānta-Siddhānta of Rishi Tirumular (ca 250 BCE) of the Nandinātha Sampradāya in his *Tirumantiram,* which is a perfect summation of both the *Vedas* and the *Āgamas.* See: *dvaita-advaita, monistic theism.*

Vedic-Āgamic: Simultaneously drawing from and complying with both of Hinduism's revealed scriptures *(śruti), Vedas* and *Āgamas,* which represent two complimentary, intertwining streams of history and tradition. The difference between Siddhānta and Vedānta is traditionally described in the way that while the *Vedas* represent man looking for God, the *Āgamas* hold the perspective of God looking to help man. This is reflected in the fact that while the *Vedas* are voiced by *ṛishis,* God or the Goddess is the bestower of truth in the *Āgama* texts. See: *grace, śruti.*

vegetarian: *Śakāhāra.* Of a diet which excludes meat, fish, fowl and eggs. Vegetarianism is a principle of health and environmental ethics that has been a keystone of Indian life for thousands of years. Vegetarian foods include grains, fruits, vegetables, legumes and dairy products. Natural, fresh foods, locally grown, without insecticides or chemical fertilizers, are preferred. The following foods are minimized: frozen and canned foods, highly processed foods, such as white rice, white sugar and white flour; and "junk" foods and beverages (those with abundant chemical additives, such as artificial sweeteners, colorings, flavorings and preservatives, or prepared with unwholesome ingredients).

veiling grace: *Tirobhāva śakti.* The divine power that limits the soul's perception by binding or attaching the soul to the bonds of *āṇava, karma,* and *māyā*—enabling it to grow and evolve as an individual being. See: *grace.*

vel: வேல் "Spear, lance." The symbol of Lord Kārttikeya's divine authority as Lord of *yoga* and commander of the *devas.* (Known as *śūla* in Sanskrit.) See: *Kārttikeya.*

vicarious: Empathizing or sharing in the experience of another person through feeling or imagination.

vibhūti: विभूति Powerful," "pervading," "appearing." From *bhū* "existence," or "manifestation" and *vi,* "apart." Holy ash, a whitish powder prepared by burning cow dung along with other precious substances—milk, *ghee,* honey, etc. It symbolizes purity and is one of the main sacraments offered to God and given to worshipers after *pūjā* in all Śaivite temples and shrines. Śaivites wear three stripes on the brow as a distinct sectarian mark, as do many Smārtas.

vibration: A distinctive emotional aura or atmosphere that can be instinctively sensed or experienced.

vidyārambha: विद्यारंभ "Commencement of learning." See: *saṁskāras of childhood.*

vigil: A one-hour time of *sādhana,* ideally before sunrise, a regimen of *pūjā,* chanting of the Guru Mantra, personal *japa,* scriptural study, *haṭha yoga* and meditation.

vīṇā: वीणा Large South Indian popular musical instrument usually having seven strings and two calabash gourds as resonance boxes.

Vishṇu: विष्णु "All-pervasive." Supreme Deity of the Vaishṇavite religion. God as personal Lord and Creator, the All-Loving Divine Personality, who periodically incarnates and lives a fully human life to re-establish *dharma* whenever necessary. In Śaivism, Vishṇu is Śiva's aspect as Preserver. See: *Vaishṇavism.*

viśuddha chakra: विशुद्धचक्र "Wheel of purity." The fifth *chakra.* Center of divine love. See: *chakra.*

viśvagrāsa: विश्वग्रास "Total absorption." The final merger, or absorption, of the soul in Śiva, by His grace, at the fulfillment of its evolution. It is the ultimate union of the individual soul body with the body of Śiva—Parameśvara—within the Śivaloka, from whence the soul first emanated. This occurs at the end of the soul's evolution, after the four outer sheaths—*annamaya kośa, prāṇamaya kośa, manomaya kośa* and *vijñāmaya kośa*—have been discarded. Finally, *ānandamaya kośa,* the soul form itself, merges in the Primal Soul. See: *ātman, evolution of the soul, nirvāṇī and upadeśī, samādhi, soul.*

Viśvaguru: विश्वगुरु "World as teacher." The playful personification of the world as the *guru* of those with no *guru,* headmaster of the school of hard knocks, where students are left to their own devices and learn by their own mistakes rather than by following a traditional teacher.

vital forces: The life-giving energies in the physical body.

vitala chakra: वितल चक्र "Region of negation." Region of raging anger and viciousness. The second *chakra* below the *mūlādhāra,* centered in the thighs. Corresponds to the second astral netherworld beneath the earth's surface, called Avīchi ("joyless") or Vitala. See: *chakra, Naraka.*

vivāha: विवाह "Marriage." See: *saṁskāras.*

Vivekananda, Swami: विवेकानन्द Disciple of Sri Ramakrishna who was overtaken by an ardent love of Hinduism and a missionary zeal that drove him onward. He passed into *mahāsamādhi* at the age of 39 (1863–1902).

vrata: व्रत "Vow, religious oath." Often a vow to perform certain disciplines over a period of time, such as penance, fasting, specific *mantra* repetitions, worship or meditation. *Vratas* extend from the simplest personal promise to irrevocable vows made before God, Gods, *guru* and community.

vrātyastoma: व्रात्यस्तोम "Vow pronouncement." The traditional purification rite, outlined in the *Taṇḍya Brāhmaṇa,* to welcome back into a Hindu community. It is performed for Hindus returning to India from abroad and for those who have embraced other faiths.

vṛitti: वृत्ति "Whirlpool, vortex." In *yoga* psychology, names the fluctuations of consciousness, the waves of mental activities *(chitta vṛitti)* of thought and perception. A statement from Patanjali's *Yoga Sūtras* (1.2) reads, "*Yoga* is the restraint *(nirodha)* of mental activity *(chitta vṛitti).*" In general use, *vṛitti* means: 1) course of action, mode of life; conduct, behavior; way in which something is done; 2) mode of being, nature, kind, character. See: *mind (individual), rāja yoga.*

Weaver's Widsom: Gurudeva's American English translation of the ancient Tamil ethical scripture, *Tirukural.* See: *Tirukural.*

Web browsing: Computer viewing of sites on the World Wide Web on a computer containing information posted by individuals or group or organizations.

wedding penant. See: *marriage pendant.*

wet dream: An involuntary emission of semen during sleep, usually as a result of a sexual dream. Swami Sivananda discusses wet dreams in his *Yoga Lessons for Children, Chapter 36 on Brahmacharya.* He states, "Many young boys and men suffer from wet dreams. Sri Aurobindo states that an occurrence once a week is normal. To have it more frequently indicates indulgence in sex thoughts." Sivananda advises a sattvic diet, rising early (as wet dreams usually occur in the last quarter of the night), cold showers, *haṭha yoga,* fresh fruit and raw foods, not going to bed right after a heavy meal. He says, "The actual essence does not come out during wet dreams. It is only the watery prostatic juice with a little semen. When nocturnal emission takes place, the mind which was working in the inner astral body suddenly enters the physical body vehemently in an agitated condition. That is the reason why emission takes place suddenly." He concludes, "Do not get depressed or anxious. It is best not to give too much importance to these dreams. Forget them, then they will not trouble you." See: *transmutation.*

winds of the body: The five primary *prāṇas* or forces of the physical body. When they are in perfect balance, vibrant health is experienced. See: *prāṇas.*

worldly: Materialistic, unspiritual. Devoted to or concerned with the affairs or pleasures of the world, especially excessive concern to the exclusion of religious thought and life. Connoting ways born of the lower *chakras:* jealousy, greed, selfishness, anger, guile, etc.

Yama: यम "The restrainer." Hindu God of death; oversees the processes of death transition, guiding the soul out of its present physical body. See: *death.*

yama: यम "Reining in, restraint." See: *yama-niyama.*

yama-niyama: यम नियम The first two of the eight limbs of *rāja yoga,* constituting Hinduism's fundamental ethical codes, the *yamas* and *niyamas* are the essential foundation for all spiritual progress. The *yamas* are the ethical restraints; the *niyamas* are the religious practices. Here are the ten traditional *yamas* and ten *niyamas.* —***yamas:*** 1) ***ahiṁsā:*** "Noninjury." 2) ***satya:*** "Truthfulness." 3) ***asteya:*** "Nonstealing." 4) ***brahmacharya:*** "Divine conduct." 5) ***kshamā:*** "Patience." 6) ***dhṛiti:*** "Steadfastness." 7) ***dayā:*** "Compassion." 8) ***ārjava:*** "Honesty, straightforwardness." 9) ***mitāhāra:*** "Moderate appetite." 10) ***śaucha:*** "Purity." —***niyamas:*** 1) ***hrī:*** "Remorse." 2) ***santosha:*** "Contentment." 3) ***dāna:*** "Giving." 4) ***āstikya:*** "Faith."

5) **Īśvarapūjana:** "Worship of the Lord." 6) ***siddhānta śravaṇa:*** "Scriptural audition." 7) ***mati:*** "Cognition." 8) ***vrata:*** "Sacred vows." 9) ***japa:*** "Recitation." 10) ***tapas:*** "Austerity." See: *anna dāna, jñāna dāna, kṛishṇa dāna, rāja yoga, śukla dāna.*

yantra: यन्त्र "Vessel; container." A mystic diagram composed of geometric and alphabetic designs—usually etched on small plates of gold, silver or copper. Sometimes rendered in three dimensions in stone or metal. The purpose of a *yantra* is to focus spiritual and mental energies according to a computer-like *yantric* pattern, be it for health, wealth, childbearing or the invoking of one God or another. It is usually installed near or under the temple Deity. Psychically seen, the temple *yantra* is a magnificent three-dimensional edifice of light and sound in which the *devas* work. On the astral plane, it is much larger than the temple itself.

yoga: योग "Union." From *yuj,* "to yoke, harness, unite." The philosophy, process, disciplines and practices whose purpose is the yoking of individual consciousness with transcendent or divine consciousness. One of the six *darśanas,* or systems, of orthodox Hindu philosophy. *Yoga* was codified by Patanjali in his *Yoga Sūtras* (ca 200 BCE) as the eight limbs *(ashṭāṅga)* of *rāja yoga.* It is essentially a one system, but historically, parts of *rāja yoga* have been developed and emphasized as *yogas* in themselves. Prominent among the many forms of *yoga* are *haṭha yoga* (emphasizing bodily perfection in preparation for meditation), *kriyā yoga* (emphasizing breath control), as well as *karma yoga* (selfless service) and *bhakti yoga* (devotional practices) which could be regarded as an expression of *rāja yoga's* first two limbs *(yama* and *niyama).* See: *bhakti yoga, kriyā yoga, haṭha yoga, rāja yoga.*

yoga mārga: योगमार्ग See: *pāda.*

yoga pāda: योगपाद The third of the successive stages in spiritual unfoldment in Śaiva Siddhānta, wherein the goal is Self Realization. See: *pāda, yoga.*

Yoga Sūtras: योगसूत्र The great work by Śaivite Nātha *siddha* Patanjali (ca 200 BCE), comprising some 200 aphorisms delineating *ashṭāṅga* (eight-limbed), *rāja* (kingly) or *siddha* (perfection) *yoga.* Still today, it is the foremost text on meditative *yoga.* See: *Kailāsa Paramparā, rāja yoga, yoga.*

Yogaswami: யோகசுவாமி "Master of *yoga.*" Sri Lanka's most renowned contemporary spiritual master (1872-1964), a Sivajñāni and Nātha *siddhar* revered by both Hindus and Buddhists. He was trained in and practiced *kuṇḍalinī yoga* under the guidance of Satguru Chellappaswami, from whom he received *guru dīkshā.* Sage Yogaswami was in turn the *satguru* of Sivaya Subramuniyaswami, current preceptor of the Nātha Sampradāya's Kailāsa Paramparā. Yogaswami conveyed his teachings in hundreds of songs, called *Natchintanai,* "good thoughts," urging seekers to follow *dharma* and realize God within. See: *Kailāsa Paramparā.*

yogī: योगी ***(yogin)*** One who practices *yoga,* especially *kuṇḍalinī* or *rāja yoga.* In Gurudeva's monastic community, *yogīs,* or *tapasvins,* are distinguished by their yellow robes and earnestness in the performance of *sādhana* and humble service. (Hindi and modern Indian vernaculars. Sanskrit: *yogin.*)

yoginī: योगिनी Feminine counterpart of *yogī.*

yoke: To join securely as if with a yoke; bind: partners who were yoked together for life. To force into heavy labor, bondage, or subjugation.

yoking: Joining securely or closely uniting.

young soul: A soul who has gone through only a few births, and is thus inexperienced or immature. See: *soul.*

yuga: युग "Aeon," "age." One of four ages which chart the duration of the world, our solar system, according to Hindu thought. They are: Satya (or Kṛita), Tretā, Dvāpara and Kali. In the first period, *dharma* reigns supreme, but as the ages revolve, virtue diminishes and ignorance and injustice increases. At the end of the Kali Yuga, in which we are now, the cycle begins again with a new Satya Yuga.

Zoroastrian: Of or related to Zoroastrianism, a religion founded in Persia by Spenta Zarathustra (ca 600 BCE). It has roughly 150,000 adherents today, mostly near Bombay, where they are called Parsis. The faith stresses monotheism while recognizing a universal struggle between the force of good (led by Ahura Mazda) and evil (led by Ahriman).

Zen: A school of Mahāyāna Buddhism that asserts that enlightenment can be attained through meditation, contemplation and intuition, rather than through faith and devotion.

Sanskrit Pronunciation

Saṁskṛita Ucchāraṇam

संस्कृत उच्चारणम्

VOWELS

Vowels marked like ā are sounded twice as long as the short vowels. The four dipthongs, e, ai, o, au, are always sounded long, but never marked as such.

अ a as in about
आ ा ā ...tar, father
इ ि i ...fill, lily
ई ी ī ...machine
उ ु u ...full, bush
ऊ ू ū ...allude
ऋ ृ ṛi ...merrily
ॠ ॄ ṛī ...marine
ऌ ḷṛi ...revelry
ए े e ...prey
ऐ ै ai ...aisle
ओ ो o ...go, stone
औ ौ au ...*Haus*

GUTTURAL CONSONANTS

Sounded in the throat.

क् k ...kite, seek
ख् kh ...inkhorn
ग् g ...gamble
घ् gh ...loghouse
ङ् ṅ ...sing

PALATAL CONSONANTS

Sounded at the roof of the mouth.

च् ch ...church
छ् çh ...mu*ch h*arm
ज् j ...jump
झ् jh ...he*dge*hog
ञ् ñ ...hinge

CEREBRAL CONSONANTS

Pronounced with the tongue turned up and back against the roof of the mouth. These are also known as retroflex.

ट् ṭ ...true
ठ् ṭh ...nuthook
ड् ḍ ...drum
ढ् ḍh ...redhaired
ण् ṇ ...none

DENTAL CONSONANTS

Sounded with the tip of the tongue at the back of the upper front teeth.

त् t ...tub
थ् th ...anthill
द् d ...dot
ध् dh ...adhere
न् n ...not

LABIAL CONSONANTS

Sounded at the lips.

प् p ...pot
फ् ph ...path
ब् b ...bear
भ् bh ...abhor
म् m ...map

SEMIVOWELS

य् y ...yet (palatal)
र् ् r ...road (cereb.)
ल् l ...lull (dental)
व् v ...voice (labial),

but more like *w* when following a consonant, as in the word *swāmī*.

ह् h ...hear (guttural)

SIBILANTS

श् ś ...sure (palatal)
ष् sh ...shut (cerebral)
स् s ...saint (dental)

ANUSVĀRA

The dot over Devanāgarī letters represents the nasal of the type of letter it precedes; e.g.: अंग = *aṅga.* It is transliterated as ṁ or as the actual nasal (ṅ, ñ, n, ṇ, m). At the end of words it is sometimes म् *(m).*

VISĀRGA (:) ḥ

Pronounced like *huh* (with a short, stopping sound), or *hih,* after i, ī and e.

ASPIRATES

The *h* following a consonant indicates aspiration, the addition of air, as in *nātha* or *bhakti.* Thus, *th* should not be confused with *th* in the word *then.*

SPECIAL CHARACTERS

ज्ञ् jñ ...a nasalized sound, like *gya* or *jya.*

क्ष् = क्+ ष् ksh

CONVENTIONS

1. As a rule, the root forms of Sanskṛit words are used (without case endings).
2. च्छ is transliterated as cçh, and च्च as cch.
3. Geographical and personal names (e.g., *Hardwar),* are generally marked with diacriticals only as main lexicon entries.
4. Diacritical marks are not used for Tamil words.

Index

Anukramaṇikā

अनुक्रमणिका

plane; Devaloka; Narakaloka; Pretaloka; Three worlds
Apology: for misconduct, (s)787; remorse and, 61. See also *Atonement; Penance; Remorse; Repentance*
Appetite: moderation in, 49-52, (s)710. See also *Moderation*
Appreciation: power of, 541-545
Āśrama dharma: stages of life, xxxv-xxxvi, 123, 167, 621-622, (s)748. See also *Brahmacharya āśrama; Gṛihastha āśrama; Vānaprastha āśrama; Sannyāsa āśrama*
Āśramas: coed vs. same-sex, 619; life in, 605, 612, 625; upkeep of, (s)783
Āratī: cleansing husband's aura, 253
Arbitration: role of community, (s)737
Archana: special personal *pūjā*, 587
Architecture: temple, (s)764
Argument: anger and, 226; avoidance of, 161, 189, 204, 555-557, (s)720, (s)760; effects on family, 560. See also *Antagonism; Conflict; Disharmony*
Ārjava: See *Honesty*
Arms: See *Weapons*
Arts: developing proficiency, (s)773; religious expression in, 468; traditional, (s)715
Arul: grace, as compassion, 46
Arul pāda: stage of grace, 85-86, 88-89, 100. See also *Pādas*
Āsanas: See *Haṭha yoga*
Ascetics: honoring, (s)754; in Hinduism, 619; providing service to, (s)729
Ash: See *Holy ash; Vibhūti*
Ashṭāṅga yoga: eight steps of, xix; first two limbs, 21; prerequisites for, xx. See also *The Master Course*
Asia: attitudes toward alcohol, 154; ideals of, 843
Associates: choosing wisely, 521-522, 653, 679, (s)716, (s)757; no drug proponents, (s)746. See also *Companions; Friends; Peers*
Association: men with men, (s)720; women with women, (s)722
Asteya: discussion, 31-33. See also *Covetousness; Credit; Debt; Stealing*
Āstikya: def., 88. See also *Faith.*
Astral body: appearing as ghost, 453-454; controlling, 136, 166-167; diet and, 135; disease and, 373, 532; dropping off, 450; experiences in, 165; five winds of, 124-125; *haṭha yoga* and, 793-795, 799-802; *karma* and, 802; old age and, 437; in reincarnation process, 419-420, 422, 426, 445; travel in, 431, 450. See also *Astral plane; Devas; Ghosts*
Astral plane: discussion, 445-455; *asuric* beings of, 246; communication in, 597-598; *devonic* beings of, 91; inner-plane schools, 130-131; protecting home, 266; psychic tubes, 124-128. See also *Antarloka; Astral body; Asuras; Occultism; Psychism; Three worlds*
Astrology: auspicious timing and, 142-143, (s)773; caution, (s)775; choosing profession, 335; *karma* and, 495; lifespan and, 432, 436; marriage and, 284, 293, 305-307, 558, (s)724, (s)726; parenting and, 143, 266-267, (s)731
Astronauts: experience of, 506
Asuras: anger and, 91; avoiding influence of, 58-59, 223; bad money and, 383-384; gossiping and, 376; protecting home from, 91, 246. See also *Beings*
Atheism: noninvolvement with, (s)757
Ātman: renunciate's goal, 628. See also *God Realization; Self*
Atonement: mitigating *karma*, 491-492. See also *Apology; Penance; Remorse; Repentance*
Attachment: bondage of, 490; negative, (s)774; to personality, 204; releasing, (s)699; resentment as, 530-532; to tasks, 204
Attention: path to enlightenment, (s)774; step towards concentration, 192
Attire: monastics', (s)783; *satguru's*, (s)760; traditional Hindu, (s)720, (s)722-773; for weddings, 308. See also *Clothing; Dress codes; Modesty*
Attitudes: aging and, 437; beliefs and, 23, 265, 501-502; children's absorption of, 515; clothing and, 651-652; monastic, (s)780-781; Tamil Śaiva, (s)773; television and, 141
Aum: beneficial for all, 794; chanting before meals, 140; how to chant, 115; overcoming abuse, 273
Aum Namaḥ Śivāya: importance of, 585. See also *Pañchākshara Mantra*
Aura: cleansing, 225, 253, 587-588, 671; congested, 231; effect on home, 58; extension of nerve system, 295; *karma* seen in, 802; *nāḍīs* of, 35; psychic entanglement of, 126-127; purity displayed in, 57-59; study of, (s)774. See also *Entanglement; Nāḍīs; Nervous system; Tubes*
Aurobindo, Sri: celibacy, 124; power of acceptance, 481
Austerity: discussion, 116-119; practice of, (s)711; *satguru's* guidance, (s)759. See also *Discipline; Penance; Sādhana; Tapas*
Automobile: genetics and, 247
Autopsy: guidelines, (s)750
Avasthā: soul's evolution through, 85-88
Awareness: aware of itself, 181; cognizing, 796; controlling, 174-181, 186-188, 193, 197-199; diet and, 135-136; externalized by sex, 125; *haṭha yoga* and, 795, 804-807; moving through mind, 185, 452. See also *Energy; Memories; Willpower*
Āyurveda: alcohol guidelines, 154; food guidelines, 50, 135-136, 140, (s)744; *haṭha yoga* and, 795, 798-799, 805; for illness, (s)745; life changes and, 433; resolving *karma*, 802

B

Babies: changing family dynamics, 286, 322; first 31 days, 426. See also *Birth; Pregnancy*
Backbiting: avoiding, (s)712; effects of, 376-378
Balance: in diet and life, 135-140
Bali: Śaivism in, 649
Bankruptcy: divorce likened to, 318
Barge: Philosophers', 555
Bathing: on returning home, (s)720; upon arising, (s)702, (s)723
Beads: See *Rudrāksha beads*

soul body, 451; God Śiva as, 9; *haṭha yoga* and, 794; masculine and feminine, 242, 259; seeing Śiva as, 92; sexual, 408; *sushumṇā* and, 799-800; transmutation of, 124-125, 129, 178; types of, 558; wise use of, 34-36. See also *Prāṇa; Transmutation*
Engagement: celebration of, 307
Enjoyment: obsession with, 317
Enlightenment: *brahmacharya* and, 34-35; destiny of all souls, 23; mountain-peak analogy, 569, 572-574; path to, (s)711, (s)774; perseverance and, 40. See also *Samādhi*
Enmity: abjuring, (s)739; beliefs conducive to, 23
Entanglement: not for monastics, (s)785; protecting family from, (s)730. See also *Aura; Nāḍīs; Tubes*
Entertainment: avoiding vulgarity, (s)720; television as, 141
Environment: cleanliness in, (s)703; responsibility for, 33; reverence for, (s)714. See also *Earth; Ecology; Species*
Equality: marriage and, 270
Eroticism: in Hinduism, 407, 414
Ethics: business, 523-524; household, (s)730; scientists', (s)740. See also *Ahiṁsā; Dharma; Yama-niyama*
Etiquette: complying with, (s)755
Europe: Laws against corporal punishment, 345. See also *West*
Evil: Hindu views on, 464; not intrinsic, (s)706; perception of, 23
Evolution: See *Soul; Unfoldment*
Example: teaching by, 143, 245, 343, 479, 504, 563, 605
Excellence: demanding of oneself, (s)700
Exercise: analogy of, 107; *brahmacharya* and, 36; health and, (s)745; spiritual, 13. See also *Haṭha Yoga; Sādhana*
Existentialism: noninvolvement with, (s)757; views of, 71
Exorcism: explanation, 454. See also *Possession*
Experience: faith and, 87-88; of God, xiv, xvii, 7-9, 503, 589; intellectualization vs., 101; learning from, 278, 493-494, (s)699; philosophy vs., 10; resolving, 11; of Self, 12; self-created, 489; and soul's evolution, 8; tendencies created by, 229; understanding, 217. See also *Karma; Mistakes*
Exploitation: avoidance of, 516, (s)738
Eyes: levels of consciousness and, 521; not looking into, (s)720, (s)722. See also *Third eye*

Face: loss of, 64
Failure: negativity and, 378; swearing and, 370. See also *Success*
Faith: discussion, 83-88; cultivating, (s)711; destruction of, 343, 635-639; expressions of, (s)706; protection of, (s)757; tithing as, 831
Faithfulness: in marriage, 20, 36, 126, (s)710. See also *Adultery; Marriage*
Faiths: respect for all, (s)714. See also *Religions*
Falsehood: refraining from, (s)710, (s)760
Fame: renunciation of, 627, 629
Families: joined by marriage, 291, 298, 305-308, 355, (s)726-727; monastics and, (s)784; *swāmīs* and, (s)786. See also *Family*
Family: abuse within, see *Abuse, child abuse, Spouse abuse;* agricultural vs. technological age, 243; *ahiṁsā* in, 341; alcohol and, (s)747; birth or death in, (s)755; breakdown of, 317, 693; business of, 363-364; daily meetings of, 21; destroyed by adultery, 37; domestic violence, see *Abuse, child abuse, Spouse abuse;* dowry hardship, xxxvi (see *Dowry*); extended, xxxviii-xxxix, 242, 286, 321, (s)730; followers as one, (s)729; future of humankind, 643; *guru* and, 336, 605, 615; harmony in, 557, 564; Hinduism's strengthening influences, xxx-xxxvii; ideals of, 266-268; joint, xxxvii-xxxviii; *kulaguru* and, 272; modern challenges, xxv-xxix; monastery and, (s)729; monastic's, 623-624, (s)780; Monday home evening, 282, (s)721; mother's essential role, 246, 248-249, 255-258; mutual respect in, 23; nuclear, 299; peace within, 503; predictable crises of, 298-299, 323; problems and solutions, 277-287; protection of, 517, 519; providing for, (s)735; raising monastic son, (s)769; reincarnation and, xxx, 363, 435, 446-448, 464; renunciation of, 628; respect for, 641; role in death, (s)749; *sādhana* in, 167; society and, 27, 247-248; strengthening, 294, (s)730, (s)733; teamwork in, 243, 334; unity of, 300, (s)732; worshiping together, 90. See also *Babies; Children; Daughters; Families; Father; Home; Householder; Husband; Marriage; Mother; Parenting; Parents; Sons; Spouse; Wife; Youth*
Fantasy: sexual, 128, (s)715
Farewell: traditional forms, (s)772
Fasting: guidelines, (s)745; for health, 52, (s)745; as penance, 128, 227, 410, 413, (s)745; self-willed death by, 424, (s)712; weekly religious, 159
Father: children and, 245, 300, 320; of monastic son, (s)769; role of, 247. See also *Parenting; Parents*
Faults: spouse's, (s)721, (s)723; wise handling of, 26. See also *Mistakes; Parenting*
Favors: indebtedness and, 49
Fear: not of aging, (s)748; *chakra* of, (s)746; in children, 278, 341; not of death, 465; drugs and, 149; never causing, 350, (s)712, (s)731, (s)787; overcoming, 348, (s)710; reincarnation and, 536; releasing, (s)699; sex and, 124, 126
Feeding, first: sacrament of, (s)731
Feedings: mass, 78
Feelings: *karma* and, 46
Feet: touching in respect, xxxiii, (s)754, (s)786
Feminism: *dharma* vs., (s)722
Festivals: attending temple, (s)765; Ekadaśa Rudra, 649; observances, (s)703; priests for, (s)764
Fever: body's natural defense, 798
Fickleness: flexibility vs., 41. See also *Indecision*
Finances: See *Money; Credit; Debt*
Fire: of cremation, (s)750; subconscious cleansing, 422. See also *Ārati; Flame; Homa; Prayer; Vāsanā daha tantra*
Fish: not consuming, 52-53, 510, (s)710, (s)744

Scriptural Bibliography

Śāstrīya Sandarbhagranthasūchī

शास्त्रीय सन्दर्भग्रन्थसूची

CITED BELOW ARE THE SOURCEBOOKS FROM WHICH WERE DRAWN THE SACRED EXCERPTS PUBLISHED IN "VERSES FROM SCRIPTURE" AND ELSEWHERE IN *LIVING WITH ŚIVA*. THE ABBREVIATION IS FOLLOWED BY THE EDITOR/TRANSLATOR, TITLE AND PUBLISHER.

AVG: Ralph T.H. Griffith, *Hymns of the Atharva Veda* (New Delhi, Munshiram Manoharlal Publishers Pvt. Ltd., 1985)

BO: Indicates "based on translation from..."

CJ: Rama Gose, *Candrajñānāgama* (Varanasi, Shaiva Bharati Shodha Pratishthanam 1995)

EH: Karan Singh, *Essays on Hinduism* (Delhi, Ratna Sagar Ltd., 1990)

HV: Abinash Chandra Bose, *Hymns from the Vedas* (Bombay, Asia Publishing House, 1965)

KA: R. Shamasastry, *Kauṭilya's Arthaśāstra* (Mysore, Wesleyan Mission Press, 1923)

NT: The Sivathondan Society, *Natchintanai, Songs and Sayings of Yogaswami* (Jaffna, The Sivathondan Society, 1974)

SY: Ratna Chelliah Navaratnam, *Saint Yogaswami and the Testament of Truth* (Columbuturai, Thiru Kasipillai Navaratnam, 1972)

RM: Arthur Osborne, ed., *The Collected Works of Ramana Maharshi* (London, Rider, 1959)

RVP: Swami Satya Prakash Sarasvati and Satyakam Vidyalankar, *RgVeda Samhita* (New Delhi, Veda Pratishthana, 1977)

SU: P. Ray, H. Gupta and M. Roy, *Susruta Samhita, A Scientific Synopsis* (New Delhi: Indian National Science Academy, 1980)

TM: Dr. B. Natarajan et al., *Tirumantiram, Holy Utterances of Saint Tirumular* (Hawaii, Saiva Siddhanta Church, 1982)

UPA: K. Narayanasvami Aiyar, *Thirty Minor Upanishads, Including the Yoga Upanishads* (Oklahoma, Santarasa Publications, 1980)

UPB: V.M. Bedekar and G.B. Palsule, *Sixty Upanishads of the Veda* (Delhi, Motilal Banarsidass, 1990)

UPH: Hume, Robert E., *Thirteen Principal Upanishads* (Madras: Oxford University Press, second edition, 1958)

UPM: Mascaro Juan, *The Upanishads* (Baltimore: Penguin Books Inc., 1965)

UPP: Prabhavananda, Swami; and Manchester, Frederick, *The Upanishads, Breath of the Eternal* (Hollywood: Vedanta Press, 1971)

UPR: Radhakrishnan, S., *The Principal Upanishads* (New York: Harper and Brothers, 1953)

VE: Panikkar, Raimond, *The Vedic Experience* (Delhi: Motilal Banarsidass, 1989)

VO: Herman W. Tull, *The Vedic Origins of Karma, Cosmos as Man In Ancient Indian Myth and Ritual* (Albany, State University of New York Press, 1989)

YM: Alain Danielou, *Yoga: The Method of Re-Integration* (New York, University Books, 1955)

YT: Georg Feuerstein, *Yoga, The Technology of Ecstasy* (Los Angeles, Jeremy P. Tarcher, Inc., 1989)

Index of Inspired Talks

Preraka Vārtānukramaṇī

प्रेरक वार्तानुक्रमणी

GURUDEVA HAS TRULY GIVEN HUMANITY A LEGACY OF MATCHLESS TEACHINGS. *LIVING WITH ŚIVA* WAS DRAWN FROM HALF A CENTURY OF INSPIRED TALKS. HERE WE ENDEAVOR TO BRIEFLY RECORD THE DATE AND CIRCUMSTANCES EACH TALK ISSUED FORTH.

1. See God Everywhere
See God Everywhere, comprising Monday through Friday's lessons, is an inspired talk given before a group of devotees by Gurudeva on February 28, 1984, Mahāśivarātri, Śiva's Great Night, in the Kadavul Hindu Temple, and published in *Know Thy Self* in 1993. Saturday and Sunday's lessons are *The Self God,* Gurudeva's ultimate statement on Absolute Reality, which he gave to a small group of *karma yoga* initiates at his Sacramento Street Temple in San Francisco on October 3, 1959, just before flying to Hawaii for the first time.

2–9. Noninjury and Truthfulness; Nonstealing and Other Virtues; Compassion, Honesty and Diet; Purity and Remorse; Contentment and Giving; Faith and Worship; Scriptural Study and Cognition; Vows, Incantation and Austerity: These eight chapters were composed in a series of question-and-answer sessions with Gurudeva on the Hindu restraints and observances, *yamas* and *niyamas,* from February 14 to March 26, 1990, at Kauai's Beachboy Hotel.

10. Celibacy and Fidelity
The lessons of this chapter are drawn from *Śaivite Virtue, the Power of Celibacy for Hindu Youth,* published in 1989, and from *The Book of Virtue,* a companion to the *Śaivite Śāstras* which Gurudeva dictated in 1974.

11. Physical, Mental, Emotional Foods
The first six lessons are drawn from a chapter by the same name in the 1967 *Master Course,* based on an inspired talk given March 1, 1958 in San Francisco. Sunday's lesson is Gurudeva's first published article, June 1949, from a Ceylon newspaper.

12. Chemical Chaos
This chapter begins with an inspired talk given in 1964 in San Francisco, addressing the issue of psychedelic drugs, when the drug movement was just

getting started and no one yet knew the long-term effects of these powerful substances. Additional input is from audio recordings made in February and March of 1999 for a CD published by the monastery called "Drug Free Kauai, Ten Hard Lessons on Drug Abuse."

13. Discipline for Self-Transformation
The first four lessons on *sādhana* are from an *upadeśa* given in Kadavul Hindu Temple to devotees at Kauai Aadheenam's Guru Pūrṇimā festival in 1982. The remaining three lessons are assembled from answers to questions submitted in 1999 and 2000 by cyberspace cadets on Kauai Aadheenam's daily website and from the study book published in 1982 entitled *Hindu Sādhana, The Master Course Book Two.*

14–15. The Meditator; Obstacles to Meditation
These two chapters embody a discourse by Gurudeva in October of 1972, outlining effective beginning techniques of meditation and offering insights on overcoming obstacles to successful inner life. It was first published in 1973 as *The Meditator,* in the "On the Path" series.

16. Harnessing Willpower
This chapter's first five lessons are from "Willpower and Comprehension," an unpublished manuscript dictated at the Kona Surf Hotel in the early 1970s. Saturday and Sunday present "The Consciousness of Comprehension," a Sunday inspired talk given at the San Francisco Temple sometime in 1958 or '59.

17. Life Is Meant to Be Lived Joyously
The chapter begins with a short excerpt about stress from "Problems and Solutions Confronting Śaivism in the Technological Age," an inspired talk gathered from discourses given in Sri Lanka on pilgrimage in January of 1982. The first three lessons (beginning with "Spiritual things you must understand with your heart"), are from "Facing Your Past" a talk Gurudeva gave on October 7, 1962, to devotees at his San Francisco Temple. Thursday's (beginning with "Morning *pūjās* are...") and Friday's lessons are from "Anāhata Yoga," a pamphlet published in 1964. Saturday and Sunday are from "Facing Overlapping Reactions," Gurudeva's Sunday message of June 8, 1958.

18. The Power of Penance
This unique chapter is drawn from the dictations on penance that Gurudeva gave in February of 1997 for a series of pamphlets to help devotees and students cope with subconscious obstacles and unresolvable problems.

19–20. The Hand that Rocks the Cradle Rules the World; Her Power, Her Domain: These chapters are drawn from an historic discourse given by Gurudeva on his fifty-third Jayantī, January 5, 1980, at the Kadavul Hindu Temple, enjoining the modern Hindu woman to not forsake her *dharma* but protect the home and nurture the family as her gift of love to the next generation.

21. Marriage and Family Life

The first five lessons of this chapter are from an *upadeśa* on marriage which Gurudeva gave on May 17, 1990. Saturday's lesson is from a series of talks on marital harmony given October 24-25, 1989. Sunday's lesson is from a series of talks given on *ahiṁsā*, also in October of 1989. Portions of these talks were reproduced as Publisher's Desk articles in HINDUISM TODAY entitled "Trouble in the Home, Differences within Marriage" in March, 1991, and "Marriage is Forever" in September, 1992.

22. Family Togetherness

This chapter's first three lessons on family life are from Gurudeva's October, 1997, Publisher's Desk, "Keeping Secrets: the First Step in Leaving Home," followed by "Is Your House a Home or a Hotel Room?" Publisher's Desk, November, 1999.

23. The Wisdom of Early Marriage

The first five lessons here are from "Child Marriage" an inspired talk given in the San Francisco Temple on March 14, 1963, and like other Sunday lectures of that period, reproduced on a mimeograph machine for the congregation. The last two lessons are from "Early Marriages," Gurudeva's Publisher's Desk column of July, 1993.

24. Modern Matchmakers

The first four lessons of this chapter are drawn from *Śaiva Dharma Śāstras, The Book of Discipline of Śaiva Siddhānta Church.* Friday and Saturday are from "Cross National Marriages," Gurudeva's Publisher's Desk column of August, 1993. Sunday's advice for young men and ladies was excerpted from "Growing Old," given in San Francisco on November, 26, 1960, along with an internet response given in May, 2000, to a young man's question, "I'm in love with a Christian girl..."

25. Divorce and Abuse

This chapter is drawn from four Publisher's Desk articles: "Marriage Is Forever" (September, 1992), "Divorce, Indian Style" (October, 1992), "Coping with Divorce" (January, 1991), and "It all Starts with that First Slap" (September, 1994).

26. Bringing Up Children

"Teenage Upbringing," Publisher's Desk, October, 1989, makes up Monday and Tuesday's lessons. Wednesday through Saturday are drawn from two Publisher's Desk discourses: "Who Are the Mentors—Kids or Parents?" (October 1991), and "The 'Why Don't You?' Philosophy" (June, 1991). Sunday presents *upadeśas* on chaperoning from 1996.

27. Positive Discipline

This chapter's first two lessons are from "The Problem with Taking It Out on the Children," Publisher's Desk, July 1999. Wednesday and Thursday present "Spare the Rod and Save the Child," Publisher's Desk, February 1997. Friday is drawn from Gurudeva's 1996 discussions on penance. Saturday and Sunday present the Publisher's Desk, "Time In and Time Out: Two Sides of Discipline," from April, 1997.

28. Teenage Trials
This candid advice on raising teens is from "Teenage Upbringing" Gurudeva's Publisher's Desk column, October, 1989, as well as from an *upadeśa* on commitment given at the Concord, California, Palaniswami Temple in June of 1988. Wednesday's story of heartbreak was first published in Gurudeva's Publisher's Desk, "Suicide, Parental Pressures" in December, 1996. This chapter also includes Internet *upadeśas* from 2000, particularly on short- and long-term goals and educating oneself for future objectives. Sunday, on the choice of careers for youth, is drawn from the 1995 edition of *Śaiva Dharma Śāstras.*

29. Language that Hurts
This chapter captures "Swearing, Gossip and Backbiting (Publisher's Desk, January/February, 2001) and "Verbal Abuse" (Publisher's Desk, July/August, 2001) along with excerpts from a Sunday talk given in the '60s at the San Francisco Temple entitled, "Gossip and Backbiting."

30. Bribery and Bad Money
This discussion on rightly acquired wealth brings forth "Good Money, Bad Money," Publisher's Desk, May, 1997, and "Bribery is Disruption of Society and Culture," Publisher's Desk, April, 1999.

31. What about Computers?
Two Publisher's Desk columns are the basis of this chapter: "A Cool, Calculating Computer-Educated Generation" (May, 1996), and "Games that Kill" (March, 1992), along with advice on television that Gurudeva dictated to his *maṭhavāsis* in a question-and-answer session on May 14, 1990.

32. Adultery and Pornography
This chapter presents "A Mystical View of Adultery," and "Pornography on the Internet" from Gurudeva's Publisher's Desk column (June, 1999, and June, 1998, respectively).

33. Birth, Abortion and Suicide
Monday's discussion on the timing of incarnation is drawn from a lengthy *upadeśa* on death and rebirth which Gurudeva gave at an editing session in August/September, 1989. Tuesday, Wednesday and Thursday present "Let's Talk about Abortion" (Publisher's Desk, January, 1992). Friday and Saturday bring forth "Let's Talk about Suicide" (Publisher's Desk, December, 1992). Sunday's discussion on the thirty-nine day retreat is from the 1995 edition of *Śaiva Dharma Śāstras,* with a response to a question from an Internet devotee.

34. Old and Gray

Old and Gray embodies Gurudeva's June, 1995, Publisher's Desk, "Old and Gray and in the Way" which was drawn from an *upadeśa* to his editing team on May 8, 1990. It concludes with "On Growing Old" (beginning in Friday's lesson with "In the Western World, the elderly...."), a Sunday lecture given in San Francisco on November, 26, 1960.

35. Beyond Death, Astral Life

This discussion comes from Gurudeva's August/September, 1990, *upadeśa* on death, dying, the afterlife and reincarnation.

36. The Joys of Hinduism

This chapter is excerpted from the inspired talk "Courage, Courage, Courage," given to devotees gathered before the *homa* fire in the Kadavul Hindu Temple on October 19, 1978.

37. Duty and Destiny

The first four lessons of this chapter on *dharma* are from "Courage, Courage, Courage." Friday and Sunday's lessons are from a series of lectures given in Mauritius from February 28 through March 2, 1982, in which Gurudeva ignited a spiritual revival among the large Hindu population of the island nation. Saturday's insights on the caste system are drawn primarily from answers to questions from Gurudeva's "Internet congregation."

38. The Wheel of Karma

Monday and Tuesday's lessons are from "Wheel of Karma," a talk given to devotees at the San Francisco Temple and published in pamphlet form in 1964. It is followed by "Karma and Responsibility," a talk Gurudeva gave in Kauai in 1981. Friday is from a short *upadeśa* given in 1988, and the last two lessons are from writings done while creating *Dancing with Śiva, Hinduism's Contemporary Catechism.*

39–40. To Do No Harm; War and Peace

This discourse on the Hindu view of *ahiṁsā,* noninjury, was dictated during a series of question-and-answer sessions in December, 1989, on Kauai, for the Upadeśa Series. Gurudeva dictated hundreds of pages on a host of subjects that year for the coming editions of *Living with Śiva* and *Merging with Śiva,* including *karma yoga, rāja yoga, japa yoga, haṭha yoga,* marriage, and death and dying. These were typed at the Beachboy Hotel on a Sony portable computer. Wednesday's lesson of Chapter 40 was dictated on September 9, 1990.

41. The Power Called Forgiveness

This chapter consists primarily of two Publisher's Desk columns Gurudeva wrote for HINDUISM TODAY, "Forgiveness, Resentment, Reconciliation" (November, 1997) and "Non-Retaliation" (February, 1998). Sunday is drawn from *Hindu Sādhana,* a study book published in 1982.

42. Nurture Gratitude, Be Considerate

The first three lessons capture Gurudeva's Publisher's Desk column, "Gratitude and Appreciation," June, 1997. The last paragraph of Wednesday and the first two paragraphs of Thursday capture an unpublished manuscript called "A Little Bit of Kindness," probably from the '60s. Friday through Sunday (and the last paragraph of Thursday) are from "How to Be Considerate," a Sunday lecture given at the temple in San Francisco on September 28, 1958.

43. Zero Tolerance for Disharmony

The first five lessons of this chapter bring forth Gurudeva's Publisher's Desk of June, 1996, and "How to Stop Tolerating Turmoil," published in the following issue. Saturday and Sunday are from a talk on spiritual love given in Kadavul Hindu Temple during November, 1999.

44. Why We Need Religion

A talk entitled "Vedanta" from the 1970s makes up the first four lessons of this chapter. The final three lessons, on monistic theism, were created in 1990 in response to questions from *maṭhavāsis* at an afternoon editing session.

45. Palaces of the Gods

This chapter is drawn from an inspired talk given by Gurudeva in the small island country of Mauritius during a spiritual lecture tour February 28 through March 2, 1982. The original talk was published as "Dharma, Gods and Temple Worship," an Insight Section in HINDUISM TODAY published shortly after the tour.

46. Sending Prayers to the Gods

This chapter was drawn from *Praying to the Gods, A Modern Tantra on Writing Prayers for the Sacred Temple Fire* (1990).

47. The Spirit of the Guru

Monday's lesson is an *upadeśa* Gurudeva gave to two of his *āchāryas* on September 30, 1989. The remaining lessons are "The Spirit of the Guru," a talk given in Kadavul Hindu Temple to devotees during the Guru Pūrṇimā festival in July of 1991.

48. Śiva's Monastics

This chapter was drawn primarily from the chapter in *Śaiva Dharma Śāstras, the Book of Discipline of Śaiva Siddhānta Church* (1995), in which Gurudeva records the structure, lifestyle and codes of conduct of his monastic order. Sunday is Swami Vivekananda's "Song of the Sannyāsin."

49. Passing on Our Heritage

Monday begins with "Tools for Educating the Young," the October, 1995, Publisher's Desk column. The next five lessons are drawn primarily from "Protect, Preserve and Promote the Śaiva Dharma," an inspired talk given in the temples and *āśramas* of Malaysia, Sri Lanka and South India during the Innersearch

and Tiru R.V. Subramanian of Greenbelt, Maryland, are dedicated to rendering the trilogy in Tamil, with the assistance of Kulapati Appasamy Kuppusamy of Kuala Lumpur, Malaysia, as typesetter and proofreader. As I write this colophon, these three Tamil elders are laboring on the 365 *Nandinātha Sūtras,* the core of the the entire *Master Course* trilogy.

This is the conclusion of the time-honored *Master Course.* The teachings contained within the trilogy of *Dancing, Living* and *Merging with Śiva* have inspired millions of my devotees in many counties to build temples and make orderly their lives through the past fifty years in various ways, large and small. The tireless efforts of the Saiva Swami Sangam made this all possible. With each and every one who has played a part in the creation of *The Master Course* we share a well-earned portion of the good *karmas* that will happen in the lives of all who are exposed, even a little, to these divine truths. May you bask in the glory of good accomplishment.

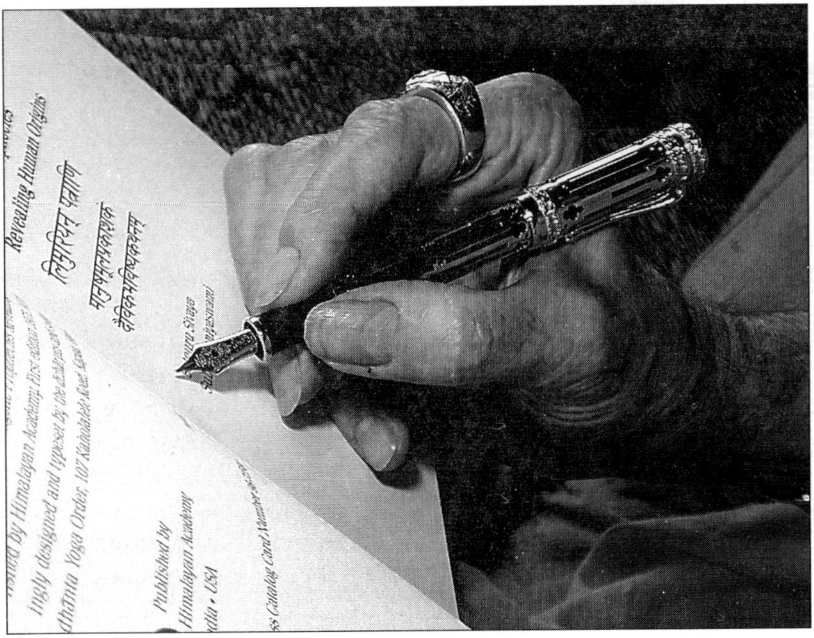

About the Author

ONCE IN A WHILE ON THIS EARTH THERE ARISES A SOUL WHO, BY LIVING HIS TRADITION RIGHTLY AND WHOLLY, PERFECTS HIS PATH AND BECOMES A LIGHT TO THE WORLD. SATGURU SIVAYA SUBRAMUNIYASWAMI (1927-2001) WAS SUCH A BEING, A SHINING example of awakening and wisdom, a leader recognized worldwide as one of Hinduism's foremost ministers. ¶In 1947, as a young man of 20, he journeyed to India and Sri Lanka and was two years later initiated into *sannyāsa* by the renowned *siddha* yogī and worshiper of Śiva, Jnanaguru Yogaswami of Sri Lanka, regarded as one of the 20th century's most remarkable mystics. For over five decades, Subramuniyaswami, affectionately known as Gurudeva, taught Hinduism to Hindus and seekers from all faiths. Known as one of the strictest gurus in the world, he was the 162nd successor of the Nandinātha Kailāsa lineage and founding *satguru* of Kauai Aadheenam, a 458-acre temple-monastery complex on Hawaii's Garden Island of Kauai. From this verdant Polynesian *āśramā* on a river bank near the foot of an extinct volcano, his monastics, under the direction of his successor, Satguru Bodhinatha Veylanswami, continue to live their cherished vision, following a contemplative and joyous existence, building a jewel-like white granite Śiva temple, meditating together in the hours before dawn, then working to promote the *dharma* together through Śaiva Siddhānta Church, Himālayan Academy and Hindu Heritage Endowment. ¶His Church nurtures its membership and local missions on five continents and serves, personally and through books and courses, the community of Hindus of all sects. Its mission is to protect, preserve and promote the Śaivite Hindu religion as expressed through three pillars: temples, *satgurus* and scripture. Its congregation is a disciplined, global fellowship of family initiates, monastics and students who are taught to follow the *sādhana mārga*, the path of yogic striving and personal transformation. The recognized hereditary *guru* of 2.5 million Sri Lankan Hindus, Gurudeva proclaimed his Church a Jaffna-Tamil-based organization which branched out from the Sri Subramuniya Ashram in Alaveddy to meet the needs of the growing Hindu diaspora of this century. It gently oversees some 40 temples worldwide. ¶HINDUISM TODAY is the influential, award-winning, international quarterly magazine founded by Gurudeva in 1979. It is a public service of his monastic order, created to strengthen all Hindu traditions by uplifting and informing followers of *dharma* everywhere. Gurudeva's numerous books present his unique and practical insights on Hindu metaphysics, mysticism, culture, philosophy and *yoga*. His *Śaivite Hindu Religion* children's course is taught in many schools, preserving the teachings among thousands of youths. Hindu Heritage Endowment is the public service trust founded by Gurudeva in 1995. It seeks to establish and maintain permanent sources of income for Hindu institutions worldwide. ¶In 1986 he founded a branch monastery in Mauritius. That same year, New Delhi's World Religious Parliament named him one of five modern-day Jagadāchāryas, world teachers, for his international efforts in promoting a Hindu renaissance. Then in 1995, in Delhi, the Parliament bestowed on him the title of Dharmachakra for his remarkable publications. The Global Forum of Spiritual and Parliamentary Leaders for Human Survival chose Subramuniyaswami as a Hindu representative at its unique conferences. At Chicago's historic centenary Parliament of the World's Religions in September, 1993, Subramuniyaswami was elected one of three presidents to represent Hinduism at the Presidents' Assembly, a core group of 25 men and women voicing the needs of world faiths. In 1996 Gurudeva upgraded the newspaper HINDUISM TODAY to a magazine, a quantum leap that placed it on newsstands everywhere. From 1996 to 2001 Gurudeva was a key member of Vision Kauai 2020, a group of inspirers (including the Mayor, county council, business and education leaders) that met to fashion the island's future based on spiritual values. On August 25, 2000, Gurudeva received the prestigious United Nations U Thant Peace Award in New York (previously awarded to the Dalai Lama, Nelson Mandela, Mikhail Gorbachev, Pope John Paul and Mother Teresa), and he addressed 1,200 spiritual leaders gathered for the UN Millennium Peace Summit. ¶Learning on October 9, 2001, that he had advanced intestinal cancer, Gurudeva decided to follow the Indian yogic practice, called *prāyopaveśa* in Sanskrit scripture, to abstain from nourishment and take water only from that day on. In the first weeks of his fast, Gurudeva seamlessly transferred his duties and responsibilities to his chosen successor, Satguru Bodhinatha Veylanswami, 59, a disciple for 37 years. He left his body peacefully on the 32nd day of his self-declared fast, at 11:54 pm on November 12, 2001, surrounded by his twenty-three monastics. ¶If you ask people what is so special about Gurudeva, they may point to his incredible power to inspire others toward God, to change their lives, to be a light on their path toward God, a father and mother to all who drew near.

Visit Gurudeva's legacy on the web: www.gurudeva.org

There are a few unusual men who have had enough of worldliness and choose to dance, live and merge with Śiva as Hindu monks.

THESE RARE SOULS FOLLOW THE PATH OF THE TRADITIONAL HINDU MONASTIC, VOWED TO POVERTY, HUMILITY, OBEDIENCE, PURITY AND CONFIDENCE. THEY PURSUE THE DISCIPLINES OF *CHARYĀ*, *KRIYĀ*, *YOGA* AND *JÑĀNA* THAT LEAD TO SELF REALIZATION. Knowing God is their only goal in life, the power that drives them tirelessly on, they live with other *maṭhavāsis* like themselves in monasteries, apart from worldliness, to worship, meditate, serve and realize the truths of the *Vedas* and *Śaiva Āgamas.*

Guided by Satguru Bodhinatha Veylanswami, successor to Satguru Sivaya Subramuniyaswami, and headquartered at Kauai Aadheenam in Hawaii, USA, on the beautiful Garden Island of Kauai, the Saiva Siddhanta Yoga Order is among the world's foremost traditional Śaivite Hindu monastic orders, accepting candidates from every nation on Earth. It is an *advaitic* Śaiva Siddhānta order, a living stream of the ancient Nandinātha Sampradāya, originally deriving from India, and in recent centuries based in Sri Lanka. Young men considering the renunciate path who strongly believe they have found their spiritual calling in this lineage are encouraged to write to Bodhinatha, sharing their personal history, spiritual aspirations, thoughts and experiences. Holy orders of *sannyāsa* may be conferred on those who qualify after ten to twelve years of training. Write to:

Satguru Bodhinatha Veylanswami
Guru Mahāsannidhānam, Kauai Aadheenam
107 Kaholalele Road, Kapaa, Hawaii 96746-9304 USA
E-mail: bodhi@hindu.org; World Wide Web: www.gurudeva.org

> *Hail, O* sannyāsin, *love's embodiment! Does any power exist apart from love? Diffuse thyself throughout the happy world. Let painful* māyā *cease and never return. Day and night give praise unto the Lord. Pour forth a stream of songs to melt the very stones. Attain the sight where night is not, nor day. See Śiva everywhere and rest in bliss. Live without interest in worldly gain. Here, as thou hast ever been, remain.* —SATGURU SIVA YOGASWAMI

The Hindu Heritage Endowment

HINDU THOUGHT AND CULTURE THREAD THROUGH ALMOST EVERY CIVILIZATION ON THE PLANET, WEAVING A SUBTLE TAPESTRY OF LOFTY PHILOSOPHY AND EARTHY, PRAGMATIC WISDOM. WHOSE LIFE HAS NOT BEEN TOUCHED? SOME HAVE BEEN raised in India and enjoy memories of warm extended families and cool temples resounding with ancient *mantras.* Others find peace of mind in Hindu *yoga* practices. Many find solace in the concepts of *karma, dharma* and reincarnation, which express their own inner findings and beliefs. If you are one who has been touched by Hindu thought and culture, you may wish to further enrich your life by giving back to Sanātana Dharma in countries around the globe and helping preserve its rich heritage for future generations. ¶Hindu Heritage Endowment (HHE) provides such an opportunity. A public charitable trust recognized by the United States government, HHE was created to maintain permanent endowments for Hindu projects and institutions worldwide. Its endowments benefit orphanages, children's schools, *āśramas* and temples. They support priests and publish books, and they are designed to continue giving that financial support year after year, decade after decade, century after century. The staff at HHE is one-pointed in their dedication to seeing that qualified donations will be used effectively for the purposes intended. Each beneficiary must give a detailed yearly report on its income from HHE and a schedule of how the next year's funds will be spent before funds are issued. We take it as a *sādhana* to see that your gifts meet their purpose. Please place Hindu Heritage Endowment in your will, your year-end giving and/or your monthly budget. Whether you are inspired to give a few dollars to support orphanages or bequest millions in your will, write, give us a call or look us up on the Internet. Find out how to enrich your life by helping to preserve the treasures of a profound heritage for generations now living or as yet unborn.

Hindu Heritage Endowment, Kauai's Hindu Monastery,
107 Kaholalele Road, Kapaa, Hawaii, 96746-9304, USA. Phone: (800) 890-1008;
outside of the US: (808) 822-3012, ext. 224; fax: (808) 822-3152;
E-mail: hhe@hindu.org World Wide Web: http://www.hheonline.org/

The Mini-Mela Bookshop

For all our books, visit www.minimela.com

Merging with Śiva

Hinduism's Contemporary Metaphysics
Book 3 of The Master Course Trilogy
By Satguru Sivaya Subramuniyaswami

Here is the ultimate text for the serious seeker. It may well go down in history as the richest and most inspired statement of meditation and God Realization ever, in any language. Yet, it's user-friendly, easy to follow, sensible and nonacademic! *Merging with Śiva* is 365 daily lessons about the core of your own being. It's about God, about the mystical realm of the fourteen *chakras,* the human aura, *karma,* force fields, thought and the states of mind, the two paths, *samādhi* and so much more. Illustrated with fifty original South Indian paintings. Second edition, 2002, 1,000 pages, 7" x 10", case bound (ISBN 0-945497-99-7), US$59.95.

Dancing with Śiva

Hinduism's Contemporary Catechism,
Book 1 of The Master Course Trilogy
By Satguru Sivaya Subramuniyaswami

This remarkable 1,000-page sourcebook covers every subject, answers every question and quenches the thirst of the soul for knowledge of God and the Self. Clearly written and lavishly illustrated, expertly woven with 600 verses from the *Vedas, Āgamas* and other holy texts, 165 South Indian paintings, 40 original graphics, a 25-page timeline of India's history and a 100-plus-page lexicon of English, Sanskṛit and Tamil. A spiritual gem and great value at twice the price. "The most comprehensive and sensitive introduction to the living spiritual tradition of Hinduism ...a feast for the heart and the mind (Georg Feuerstein)." Sixth edition, 2001, 7" x 10", case bound (ISBN 0-945497-96-2), US$59.95.

Weaver's Wisdom

Ancient Precepts for a Perfect Life
Satguru Sivaya Subramuniyaswami

A finely crafted American English translation of a beloved 2,200-year-old Tamil classic, *Tirukural*, by the weaver saint, Tiruvalluvar—yet, it's all about today's world, business, family, relationships, money, enemies, personal fears, gambling, politics, diet and health. Arguably the world's ultimate ethical guide, its pithy, often humorous, aphorisms offer an earthy assessment of human nature. In South India this scripture is sworn on in courts of law. Quote from it freely. Read from it to your children to train their minds and guide them along the path of *dharma*. Over 100 illustrations, 1,080 verses. First edition, 1999, 408 pages, 5½" x 8½", softcover (ISBN 0-945497-76-9), US$19.95. Hardcover version, US$29.85. Hardcover, full-color edition with English and modern Tamil translations, 600 pages (ISBN 81-7017-390-6), US$49.95.

How to Become a Hindu

A Guide for Seekers and Born Hindus
By Satguru Sivaya Subramuniyaswami

Hundreds of thousands of half-Hindus, having received a first name of a God or Goddess from their *yoga* teacher or a *swami*, want to enter the religion fully. Because of Hinduism's liberal doctrine, it is left to the individual as a "do-it-yourself conversion." *How to Become a Hindu* explains how the six steps of ethical conversion have enhanced the lives of many in the East and West. Here Americans, Canadians and Europeans tell their stories of passage from Western faiths to Hinduism. The book raises and convincingly settles the debate about non-Hindus entering the religion. "This elucidative book will provide immense help to those who wish to enter the Hindu fold, and also the younger generation of Hindus living outside India" (Puri Shankaracharya). First edition, 2000, 496 pages, 8½" x 5½", softcover (ISBN 0-945497-82-2), US$27.95.

Śaivite Hindu Religion

A Children's Course, Books One, Two and Three
By Satguru Sivaya Subramuniyaswami

What every Hindu parent needs: intelligent, nonviolent, traditional texts for their kids—an authentic, illustrated, seven-book series, teaching philosophy, culture and family life. Based on the holy *Vedas,* the world's oldest scripture, this course is the loving work of Sivaya Subramuniyaswami. An excellent resource for educators and parents, it explains the "why" of each belief and practice in simple terms in three languages. Prominent leaders of all sects have given enthusiastic endorsements. "A commendable, systematically conceived course useful to one and all with special significance to fortunate children who shall be led on the right path (Sri Sri Sri Tiruchi Mahaswamigal, Bangalore, India)." Book One (5- to 7-year-old level) is available in a Hindi-Tamil-English edition, softcover, 8½" x 11", 170 pages, US$9.95. Book Two (6- to 8-year-old level), English-Tamil-Malay, 196 pages, US$9.95. Book Three (7- to 9-year-old level), English-Tamil-Malay-French, 96 pages, US$4.95.

Hinduism Today

The International Magazine

Enjoy a spiritual experience with the foremost international journal on Sanātana Dharma, published by Satguru Bodhinatha Veylanswami and the *swamis* of the Saiva Siddhanta Yoga Order. Breaking news, ancient wisdom, modern trends, world-class photos, family resources, humor—you'll treasure every issue! "HINDUISM TODAY is a beautiful example of the positive possibility of the media being fulfilled, a bright ray of light in a darkened world" (Anne Shannon, Portland). Introductory offer (US only): one-year subscription, 4 stunning issues, for US$35! And yes, the author of this book founded this global magazine and guided it for 20 years. ISSN 0896-0801; UPC: 0-74470-12134-3. Visit: www.hinduismtoday.com

Loving Gaṇeśa

Hinduism's Endearing Elephant-Faced God
By Satguru Sivaya Subramuniyaswami

No book about this beloved elephant-faced God is more soul-touching. The Lord of Dharma will come to life for you in this inspired masterpiece. It makes approaching this benevolent Lord easy and inspiring. Learn about Gaṇeśa's powers, pastimes, mantras, nature, science, forms, sacred symbols, milk-drinking miracle and more. "A copy of *Loving Gaṇeśa* should be placed in every library and Hindu home"(Sri Om Prakash Sharma). Second edition, 1999, 576 pages, 5½" x 8½", softcover (ISBN 0-945497-77-6), US$29.85.

Lemurian Scrolls

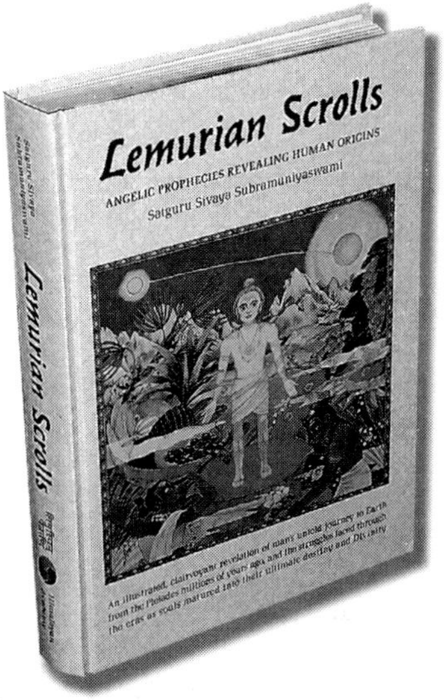

Angelic Prophecies Revealing Human Origins
By Satguru Sivaya Subramuniyaswami

Enliven your spiritual quest with this clairvoyant revelation of mankind's journey to Earth millions of years ago from the Pleiades and other planets to further the soul's unfoldment. Learn about the ensuing challenges and experiences faced in evolving from spiritual bodies of light into human form and the profound practices followed and awakenings achieved in ancient Lemuria. These angelic prophecies, read by Sivaya Subramuniyaswami from *ākāśic* records written two million years ago, will overwhelm you with a sense of your divine origin, purpose and destiny and motivate a profound rededication to your spiritual quest. An extraordinary metaphysical book which answers the great questions: Who am I? Where did I come from? Where am I going? Second Edition, 2006, 7" x 10", 400 pages, beautifully illustrated with original color paintings, hardcover (ISBN 0-945497-79-2), $39.95.

Mini Mela Bookshop Order Form

☐ Please send me free literature.
☐ Please send me an application for The Master Course Correspondence Study.
☐ I wish to subscribe to HINDUISM TODAY.
USA rates: ☐ 1 year, $35 ☐ 2 years, $65 ☐ 3 years, $95 ☐ Lifetime, $1001
(For international rates send e-mail to: subscribe@hindu.org)

I would like to order:
☐ *Dancing with Śiva,* $59.95 ☐ *Living with Śiva,* $59.95 ☐ *Merging with Śiva,* $59.95
☐ *How to Become a Hindu,* $27.95 ☐ *Lemurian Scrolls,* $39.95
☐ *Śaivite Hindu Religion:* Book 1, $9.95 ☐ Book 2, $9.95 ☐ Book 3, $4.95
☐ *Weaver's Wisdom,* $19.95 ☐ *Loving Gaṇeśa,* $29.85

Prices are in US currency. Add 20% for postage and handling in US and foreign. Foreign orders are shipped sea mail unless otherwise specified and postage is paid. For foreign airmail, add 50% of the merchandise total for postage.

☐ My payment is enclosed. Charge to: ☐ MasterCard ☐ Visa ☐ Amex

Card number: ____________________

Expiration, month: ________ year: ________ Total of purchase: ____________

Name on card: [PLEASE PRINT] ____________________

Signature: ____________________

Address: [PLEASE PRINT] ____________________

____

____

Phone: ____________________ Fax: ____________________

E-mail: ____________________

Order on the World Wide Web at www.minimela.com

Or mail, phone, fax or e-mail orders to:

Himalayan Academy Publications, Kauai's Hindu Monastery, 107 Kaholalele Road, Kapaa, Hawaii 96746-9304 USA. Phone (USA and Canada only): 1-800-890-1008; outside USA: 1-808-822-7032, ext. 238; Fax: 1-808-822-3152; E-mail: books@hindu.org

Also available through the following (write or call for prices):

Sanatana Dharma Publications, 15 Lintang Besi, Off Jalan Melawis, 41000 Klang, Selangor, Malaysia. Phone: 603-3371-9242; E-mail: silvaraj@tm.net.my

Sanathana Dharma Publications, Blk 210 #06-326, Pasir Ris Street 21, Singapore 510210. Phone: 65-9664-9001. E-mail: sanatana@mbox4.singnet.com.sg

Saiva Siddhanta Church of Mauritius, Mini Mela, La Pointe, Rivière du Rempart, Mauritius, Indian Ocean. Phone: 230-412-7177.

Iraivan Temple Carving Site, P.O. Box No. 4083, Vijayanagar Main, Bangalore, 560 040, India. Phone: 91-80-2839-7118; Fax: 91-80-2839-7119; E-mail: jiva@vsnl.com

H.H. Sri La Sri Arunagirinatha Sri Gnanasambanda Desikar Paramacharya Swamigal, Aadheenakarthar and 292nd Guru Mahasannidhanam of Madurai Aadheenam, Madurai, India

The book *Living with Siva* is the greatest book ever written. It is a book of divine instruction. It offers comfort in sorrow, guidance in perplexity, advice for our problems, rebuke for our sins and daily inspiration for our every need. This is not simply one book. It is an entire library of books covering the whole range of literature. It includes history, poetry, drama, biography, prophecy, philosophy, science and inspirational reading. ¶*Living with Siva* alone truly answers the greatest questions that men of all ages have asked: "Where have I come from?", "Where am I going?", "Why am I going?", "Why am I here?", "How can I know the Truth?" *Living with Siva* reveals the truth about God, explains the origin of man, points out the only way to salvation and eternal life and explains the age-old problem of sin and suffering. *Living with Siva* discovers sin and confronts us with it, helps cleanse us from the pollution of sin, imparts strength, provides us with a sword for victory over sin, makes our lives fruitful and gives us power to pray.

Sri Sri Swami Bua Ji Maharaj, age 112, founder and head of the Indo-American Yoga-Vedanta Society in New York, teacher of Sanatana Dharma in South America and elsewhere

The hands of a clock are powered from the center no matter where they point. Likewise, Siva's followers, wherever they are, whatever direction they look at, are powered by Siva from the universal center and guided by the satguru. But these days the digital clocks have come up. So, the center as well as the hands have become invisible. It does not mean that they do not exist. It is only more difficult to visualize the center and the hands. ¶At this juncture, there is a proclamation in the form of a book that says God is within you and you are in God. The hands have merged with the center. We see only the movements—only the dance—only the change in the digits. ¶This is an ardent attempt to break the misconception that if you worship God Siva, He will take everything away from you. This is not true. God Siva gives everything. "Living with Siva is living with love." ¶We seekers of the present day who can read English are highly fortunate since Gurudeva has decided to release this second edition wherein he has included about 800 pages of his inspired speeches which cover all the subjects on the Earth, varying from marriage, abortion, suicide, television, computers… is there anything else which is left out? ¶The traditional path of dharma is elucidated—methods and techniques which will be helpful to everyone to find God within themselves are enumerated in this book. The four progressive stages of life are defined. The normal human life span is specified as 120 years with transitions at 40 and 80. The student stage is from 12 to 24, the householder stage is from 24 to 48; the stage of respected elder is from 48 to 72 and the stage of the religious solitaire after 72 years of age. How wonderful it would be if the human race understands these stages and regulates their lives accordingly! In the modern world, there are many who become householders around twenty by losing brahmacharya and become disrespected elders around sixty-five! ¶Starting from the purpose of life, the 365 Nandinatha Sutras unfold one after the other with stunning simplicity and astonishing brightness like pearls. Defining discipline, touching on theology, they specify ethics showing care for the world, they examine life and death. There are instructions for everybody, for every situation—for men, women, parents, husbands, wives, business men, politicians, scientists—none is forgotten or left out. ¶Some have called these sutras a modern Tirukural. I would like to call these a "Parallel Tirukural"—parallel because these convey the same messages in similar formats of aram, porul, veedu and inbam in short precise sentences loaded with essence. ¶The language used is very simple, direct and does not need any interpreter. Each sutra emanates religious fragrance to Saiva followers. This book which is an excellent compilation of ethical rules, moral directives, saintly instructions and Godly guidance, should reach far and wide and become the pride possession of many, transforming this land worthy of living.

Pundit K.N. Navaratnam, M.A.F.A., F.A.A., Jaffna Tamil elder, Jyotisha Marthand and National Astrologer of Australia, Sivathondan Center, Hallam, Australia

Living with Siva is the latest monumental spiritual work from our beloved Gurudeva. In this time of spiritual darkness his teachings are like the cooling rains on a parched summer afternoon. Following directly in the lineage of Tirumular, who gave us three thousand verses of wisdom, Gurudeva has blessed us with another thousand pages of insight that is akin to being hit over the head with a hammer to awaken us from our spiritual slumber. This work is medicine for a sick and diseased world where the darkness of *maya* has led many people away from God. God consciousness cannot be explained in words but must be uncovered inside oneself by oneself. Gurudeva explains how to remove the *maya* of the world and conditioning of the mind like peeling the layers off an onion. ¶In all his works, Gurudeva shows the path that must be walked. It is a path that must be walked alone, although we can take great reassurance he is always with us like a divine guide pointing in the right direction and offering advice and encouragement. All seekers are urged to join us on this great journey. The road is tough and full of dangers and pitfalls, but once on it we must follow it to the end. It is so reassuring Gurudeva is here to provide the much needed religious insight in our technologically advanced and ever-changing world. He is like a shining diamond spreading his divine wisdom to all corners of the world.

Sri Sri Swami Pragyanand,
Founder and Patron of Sai Pragya Dham, Pragya Mission International, Pragya Mitra Pariwar and Pragya Yoga Foundation, New Delhi, and Vishwa Mata Gayatri Trust, Delhi, India

I wonder how deep is Sivaya Subramuniyaswami's knowledge about the great Hindu Gods Ganesha and Siva. These volumes have made him an institution in himself rather than an individual. While reading *Living with Siva,* I feel that Swamiji has completely engaged himself with Lord Siva and, through deep meditation, he has actually visualized what he has written in the book. He has actually attained in reality all that a saint aspires to achieve. With his thoughts and writings, Swamiji has rendered valuable service to humanity all over the world, not only to Hindus. Swamiji is a living, legendary scholar, and he has influenced the entire galaxy of saints the world over. The saintly world is highly proud of him. ¶I have not come across any other publication so deep in thought, devotion and vision as this, except Swamiji's earlier treatise *Dancing with Siva.* The book is a testimony of his communion with Lord Siva, as just a thinker, whatever his intellect, cannot give this kind of disclosure. ¶The subject matter embodied in *Living with Siva* is so diversified and comprehensive that it leaves out no aspect of present day life and the prevailing distortions in society. The book is a practical guide to individuals as to how to be pure in thoughts and actions. I would like to particularly draw the attention of the truth seeker readers to the 365 *Nandinatha Sutras* for right living. If practiced, the individual will elevate himself and the society to where there will be no misdeeds, no violence, no social tensions, no hatred, no cold wars, no fear, no greed and no lust for power. It will be a society without any kind of evil. There would be a mutual tolerance, nonviolence, unity, equality, love, international peace and brotherhood. ¶Humanity is on the brink of its self-annihilation and self-destruction. It is crying and groaning. There is darkness all around. International brutalities, terrorism and blood thrust have made the Earth a hell. The path shown by *Living with Siva* is the only hope. It is the silver lining in the thick and dark clouds.

Tiru A. Kandiah, Ph.D
Jaffna Tamil elder, Author of Malarum Manamum; Former Head of the Department of Tamil, University of Kelaniya, Sri Lanka, Former Professor at the University of London, now living in Sydney, Australia

If a person studies these lessons every day for a year, he or she will have completed a profound *sadhana,* a personal odyssey into the interior life of him or herself and into the depths of Hinduism, a practice sufficient to change their lives by transforming the way they look at life itself.

H.H. Dada J.P. Vaswani
Head of the worldwide Sadhu Vaswani Mission, renowned Sindhi religious leader and eloquent lecturer, Pune, India

Living with Siva, Hinduism's Contemporary Culture deals with some of the profound issues of our time concerning God, family life, money, food, religion and culture. The Western materialistic goal is personal fulfillment. The Eastern religious ideal is fulfillment of one's duty towards parents, children, society, country and religion. When the children of Eastern families encounter Western values, in many cases personal fulfillment overrides duty, threatening to cut at the very roots of our culture. Taking India and the West as two poles for comparison, this wonderful book analyzes the cause of the cultural crisis and its ethical, philosophical and social implications. ¶*Living with Siva* is the fruit of Satguru Sivaya Subramuniyaswami's years of study and experience. It is a reflection on the fundamentals of Hinduism, the religion which, like the sun, is ever ancient and ever new, the religion that rises up after every upheaval like a center-of-gravity doll. What does Hinduism have to say about the issues relating to traditional family life and their relevance to modern times? How far are Hinduism's ideas about God, family life, money, food and culture different from those of other faiths? This lucid, impressive and highly readable book draws our attention, among other things, to the focus of Hinduism on *dharma* and its deep-rooted faith in the theory of *karma*. When *dharma* is the shared ideal of every family member, as opposed to self-fulfillment or socio-economic objectives, it is easier to navigate troubled waters. Faith in *karma*, the law by which our thoughts, words and deeds reap their natural reactions helps hold the family together. ¶At a time when we are facing a global failure of the traditional family unit and find ourselves at a loss in coping with the by-products of such a failure, this timely book emerges as a breath of fresh air, reminding us of our rich cultural heritage. Here is a book that is waiting to embrace into its fold millions of Hindus who are waiting to be converted into true Hindus.

Shiva Pasupati
Jaffna Tamil elder, President's Counsel and Former Attorney General of Sri Lanka, President of the Australian Tamil Foundation, Sydney, Australia

One of the greatest challenges facing modern society, particularly in the more "developed" countries, is the need to reestablish the family unit, the disintegration of which has largely contributed to the increase in crime, the misuse of drugs and other evils. In *Living with Siva,* Gurudeva has revealed very lucidly all aspects of Hinduism's contemporary culture, drawing on the experiences of over 6000 years of Hindu family history. There is now an urgent need to preserve and practice the Hindu culture, which has displayed resilience and an ability to survive many of the ravages of modern society. It is not only Hindus, but all seekers of wisdom, truth and knowledge living in different parts of the world, who will be inspired and guided by this remarkable masterpiece.

V. Canaganayagam
Former manager of Gurudeva's Sri Subramuniya Ashram in Alaveddy, Sri Lanka

Living with Siva is an excellent book which lays down the *dharmic* way in which every Hindu could live his or her life from the beginning to the end. Hindu literature is so vast that it is not possible for everyone to go through it and gather the essence of it. Besides, the language in which it is enshrined may not be familiar to all. To make the spiritual treasures of Hinduism available to all who wish to avail themselves of them and the rendering of them in an international language like English is much to be appreciated. We Hindus value the words of a sage or *swami.* That the intuition and insight of Gurudeva and the *swamis* have gone into the making and publication of this book makes it all the more sacred. In a fast-moving world everyone does not find time for so many things, even to know and practice one's religion. The dedication of this book in memory of Siva Yogaswami of Jaffna makes the Jaffna man proud of his spiritual inheritance.

Sri Svami Yogananda Giri
Founder and Spiritual Head of Unione Induista Italiana, Sanatana Dharma Samgha, Gitananda Ashram, Carcare, Italy

I read *Living with Siva* by Satgurudeva with great pleasure and interest. His encyclopedic knowledge expresses its vastness and deepness in this book. It is really extraordinary how Satgurudeva deals with any subject with great ability and wisdom: from ethical to spiritual life, social life with all its sacraments *(samskaras),* emotional purity, penance *(tapas)*. Actually, every aspect of *dharma, sadhana* and Hindu religion is dealt with in an illuminating and crystal clear manner. It's a book for everyone on everything. Satgurudeva takes us by hand lesson after lesson, leading us towards full spiritual emancipation. It is surely a text that any person who aspires to reach spiritual emancipation should read and above all meditate on. May Siva give long life to this representative of Him on Earth so that he may always illumine the path.

Thiru Satkunendran
Jaffna Tamil elder, Assistant Secretary of the Sivathondan Nilayam, Toronto, Ontario, Canada

What an appropriate book to be released by Gurudeva in this Kali Yuga cycle, when the Tamil diaspora in Europe, North America and Australia are reeling aimlessly, being unable to discriminate between the good and bad, especially our youth, who are caught in the midst of the Western "culture shock." They do not know how to respect parents, *guru,* temple and teachers at school. People changing religion for mere financial benefits, breakdown in marriages, family and the dawn of a new culture… "single parent homes!" The author beautifully states that the Western materialistic goal is personal fulfillment, while the Eastern religious ideal is fulfillment of duty to one's parents, society and country, which includes tradition. However, when children of Eastern families are raised up with Western values, personal fulfillment overrides everything else. This book contains golden advice in easy to understand English, is interesting to read, as each subject is short, and the reader can simply get the message of Gurudeva without the aid of another person to provide explanation. This is written targeting the present and future generations who are desperately seeking the truth, which parents are unable to interpret in a modern way, and this is aptly seen in this brilliant work. Enlightening both to the young and old alike. For the young, all the unanswered questions have meaningful explanations and, for the old, many topics refresh the mind and, of course, answers to the questions of modern times are found only in this invaluable book. The *guru* is so kind and generous in saying that one needs to read only one lesson a day, as he appreciates our hectic lifestyle. Topics vary from *yoga* practice to computers, war and peace to reverence for the environment, tobacco and drugs to guidelines for business and money. Guru protocol is a must to be read over, as many devotees are not aware of the do's and don'ts in the presence of the *guru.* A first glance at the size of the book will make anyone think, "Oh! Where do I find enough time to read this dictionary?" But once you start reading, it motivates you to read more than one lesson a day! Thank you, Gurudeva, for this wonderful gift.

Sri Sri Swami Satchidananda, Founder and Spiritual Head of Satchidananda Ashram and its Light of Truth Universal Shrine (LOTUS), renowned yoga master and visionary, Yogaville, Virginia

Gurudeva Sri Sivaya Subramuniyaswami has done it again. Here in this book he clearly guides the reader who would want to follow the Saiva Siddhanta tradition. May all the readers benefit by this great book.

Swami Shuddhananda Brahmachari
Founder of the Lokenath Divine Life Mission, India, and Lokenath Divine Life Fellowship, USA

In this most useful handbook of daily practice, Satguru Sivaya Subramuniyaswamiji, inspires every Hindu—and seekers in general—to follow the timeless principles of Sanatana Dharma. I am sure, like his previous two books, *Dancing with Siva* and *Merging with Siva,* this final book of his creative trilogy, *Living with Siva,* will guide travelers on the path of Truth towards the ultimate destination of realizing Oneness with Siva.

Ashwinee Ragoonanan
Jyotishi from Banaras Hindu University, Publisher of Kashi ka Patra, President of the Kashika Yog and Meditation Foundation, Trinidad and Tobago

Sri Adi Sankaracharya was responsible for reestablishing the status of Sanatana Dharma when it was at its lowest ebb. Today, without a doubt, it is safe to say that Gurudeva Satguru Sivaya Subramuniyaswami is an incarnation of Adi Sankaracharya in principle and wisdom, reestablishing and redefining Sanatana Dharma for the present generation and future minds. The gamut of Sanatana Dharma could not be composed in a more lucid and comprehensive manner as it is presented in *Living with Siva.* Swamiji, in his compilation of *Living with Siva,* has caught the dynamism of Hinduism to touch the spirit and mind of both the young and the old, the ancient and the modern.

Vimala Krishnapillai, Ph.D
Lecturer at the University of Colombo, Sri Lanka, President of the Sri Ramakrishna Sarada Samithi, Colombo, Joint Trustee of the Siva Yogar Swami Thiruvadi Trust

Living with Siva is a priceless, monumental text. On reading it, I felt that Lord Siva, transcending time and space, has transmitted His gift of grace, to humanity through Satguru Sivaya Subrumuniyaswami. The presence of the direct communication of truth, so far as it can be put in words, is there on every page. Written in simple words, it is made understandable to all who aspire to walk the Saiva path, Saivaneri. Every aspect of day-to-day living, both secular and religious, family, society, food, health, money management and, above all, God, are touched upon. Step by step, Gurudeva helps one to live a balanced, harmonious life with the goal of raising one's spiritual consciousness. The tremendous energizing power of the text awakens and arouses one from his or her stupor to keep the inner light aglow. ¶The text contains in essence the whole of Hindu heritage, the *Vedas, Upanishads, Agamas* and the outpouring of saints and sages down the ages. Herein, Sanatana Dharma, the ancient and eternal path, ever fresh and vibrant, forges forth into international frontiers as the religion of the future. ¶May we express our hearts' deepest gratitude and praise to Satguru Sivaya Subramuniyaswami for placing this sacred text as *samarpanam* at the *tiruvadi,* gracious feet, of his Paramaguru Siva Yogaswamigal of Yalpanam, Sri Lanka, whom we adore and venerate as our ancestral *kulaguru.*

H.H. Swami Tejomayananda
Spiritual Head of Chinmaya Mission, Central Chinmaya Mission Trust, Sandeepany Sadhanalaya, Mumbai, India

The book becomes interesting since it touches almost all aspects of one's life, secular and spiritual. It is the lack of such information and knowledge that creates confusion in the minds of people regarding their own duties and understanding of their religion. In this context, this book plays a very important role in educating the Hindus. There are certain topics, like the wisdom of early marriage, which are quite controversial in modern time. Gurudeva has dealt with them beautifully, and I have every hope that people will appreciate the maturity of thought running through these topics.

Thillaiampalam Visuvalingam,
President of the Saiva Sidhdhantha Manram, Managing Editor of Anbu Neri, Mississauga, Ontario, Canada

Living with Siva is a divine work of Siva Consciousness. These lessons address all the issues confronting a modern person who wishes to follow Sanatana Dharma. This divine work should be in all households for the Saivite Hindus, young and old, to gain the true path of Lord God Siva realization. ¶This is a book on Siva consciousness for all Saivite Hindus, and especially for those who lack faith in themselves and whose faith is undermined by ignorance and indifference. We are all fortunate that such a book has been conceived by Gurudeva to meet the needs of modern men and women. May the almighty Lord Siva bless him with all courage and a long healthy life to continue his divine contribution.

Brahmacharini Maya Tiwari
Spiritual Head of the Wise Earth Monastery, Candler, North Carolina, and the Mother Om Mission, Guyana, South America

In this impressive guidebook, Gurudeva's beneficent voice of universal Truth unearths and reintroduces the Hindu *dharmas* for living in awareness, integrity and joy. More than a perennial wellspring of Hindu ideals, *Living with Siva* demonstrates everyday-life ways that help us to become conscious of negative habits and provides us with the means to recognize, acknowledge and rid toxic thoughts and harmful activities from our lives. This guidebook is a masterful blueprint for reclaiming physical, emotional and spiritual health or, as Gurudeva puts it, "the *ahimsa* home" wherein we may connect our inner experience to the infinite wisdom of the *rishis. Living with Siva* implies exactly that: cultivating unflinching awareness and adherence to the path of *dharma.*

Pandit Rajendra Sharma
Priest of the Hindu Worship Society, Houston, Texas

Living with Siva is not a book, but a manual of salvation for all humankind! Gurudeva has taken out the nectar supreme from Sanatana scriptures and has presented them here in simple language for the benefit of all living creatures. If I compare this manual to the great *Bhagavad Gita,* I would not be wrong. Bhagwan Sri Krishna gave the synopsis of the *Vedas* and *Upanishads* to Arjun in the simple language of the day, yonder "Prakrit," for the benefit of the simple-minded people. So has Gurudeva presented this great essence of the Sanatana Dharma for the public of today. A long time ago a great religious and social reformer was born who gave us a great treatise which is known to the modern world as *Manu Smriti,* and in this modern time we have our own Gurudeva who has made it possible for us by giving the same kind of knowledge for the common people of today. I hereby suggest that this great book of knowledge be kept in all homes and libraries on this Earth.

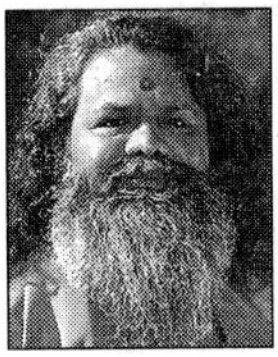

Vishwaguru Mahamandaleshwar Paramhans Swami Maheshwarananda
Spiritual Head of the Society "Yoga in Daily Life," Vienna, Austria

With this divine work, once more Gurudeva is going to inspire and uplift the consciousness of mankind, especially of the Hindus who live in different parts of the world. After the volumes *Dancing with Siva* and *Merging with Siva,* this new publication brings Lord Siva straight into our daily lives. *Living with Siva* is designed to become an integrated part of everyday life—day-by-day throughout the whole year the reader will get a divine lesson that motivates and encourages him the whole day long. I congratulate the author of this really ingenious guidebook that preserves and makes approachable the eternal values of Sanatana Dharma for our modern civilization in an easily comprehensible way. Especially, I recommend this book to Indian parents living in and outside of India. The children are the future of this Earth, and in order to reveal and establish the ethical fundamentals of Vedic culture and religion to the new generation, this book really should not be missed in any Indian family!

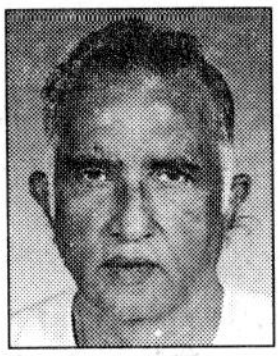

Tiru Perampalam Saravanamuthu
President of the Selangor Wilayah Persekutuan Ceylon Saivites Association, Chairman of the First National Malaysian Saiva Siddhanta Seminar, 1983, Kuala Lumpur, Malaysia

Living with Siva is not a book for keeping in the cupboard of a home library; instead, the book should form an essential item in the prayer room, taking its place with the ritual utensils used for prayer at the altar. The subjects covered are most relevant for not only the adult Saivite Hindu but more for Saivite children for whom the reading of this book should be mandatory, as the present Saivites are faced with new multifarious challenges arising from negative influences prevalent in modern society. It is only through sound knowledge of the tenets of Sanatana Dharma that the community could insulate itself from the onslaught of new-fangled practices that only cater to the base instincts and would attract many rebirths to atone for the bad *karmas* thus accumulated. *Living with Siva* is for daily use during prayers, by those present—a lesson a day would keep bad *karmas* at bay. ¶*Living with Siva* contains 365 lessons which were originally delivered to the disciples at Kauai Aadheenam and others and, as such, have been tested and tried and found to be very appropriate for all those professing or wanting to learn more about Saivite Hinduism. The author has delved deeply and systematically into the various subjects that constitute the lessons. For example, the ten *yamas* and the ten *niyamas* have been expounded upon extensively, so much so that 100 pages give detailed explanations on the ancient scriptural injunction for all aspects of human thought, attitude and behavior, giving no room for any doubts to arise in the mind of the layman. The oft repeated advice is that a family should pray together to be on the spiritual path. ¶The lessons have been flavored and garnished with the occasional Sanskrit or Tamil word to convey the exact meaning and interpretation of the tenets under discussion. But almost every Sanskrit or Tamil word used has been accompanied by its most appropriate English word or phrase. Thus, the object of introducing specific Sanskrit and Tamil words, namely to make their meanings familiar to the reader, has been achieved through this method of repeating the words and thus enabling the reader to learn the word and its meaning through minimum effort. ¶The present lifestyle of many Saivites is based on Western culture, which in some instances runs contradictory to Hindu culture. The adoption of an alien custom and tradition often results in the arousal of negative emotions which destroy not only the individual but the family and the community. The writings in this book cry out to the Saivite reader: Go back to basics. An appeal is also being made to the readers of *Living with Siva* to study the scriptures and practice the Saivite customs and traditions which have been cleansed in the fire of purification which had been fueled by the logs of love, fasts, sacrifices and experience during the past many millennia, which would lead the devotee to merge with Siva.

R. Rajathurai
Former school teacher, former president of the Senpaga Vinayagar Temple, Singapore

The release of this book at this point in time is most appropriate in view of the many challenges faced by the Saivite community. The book contains a wealth of information on various topics within its more than a thousand pages. Anyone reading the 365 lessons, which form the daily sermon for the whole year, would feel His Holiness' concerns for the multifarious problems faced by the Hindu Saivite community in general and the youth in particular. Rapid progress achieved in the fields of science and technology, especially within the second half of the 20th century, has to some extent warped human thinking. Man now thinks of "playing God" by tinkering and tampering with nature's creation to improve its quality. This illusion has produced some horrendous results—an example is the mad cow disease. Such new thinking has also affected long established institutions by creating disarray. For example, the holy matrimony normally conducted in a sanctified holy place is now sometimes conducted in odd places—while parachuting, while deep-sea diving and so on—and the consumption of non-*sattvic* food on such occasions is becoming fashionable. The legal empowerment of women has resulted in a shift of women's place in creation. God's natural empowerment of women as creators has now been surrendered to the pill and to the abortionist; the nourishment of children has now largely been surrendered to the udder of the cow, the street hawker and to the school canteen operator. And as for education, it is left entirely to the school which is unable to replace what should rightly be shared with those in the child's home. The school, furthermore, is at all times competing with the influence of the television on young minds. Beginning at a very tender age, the child could enter an empty house after school while the mother is slaving with the father for additional income to purchase luxuries in their "competition with the Jones." ¶*Living with Siva* is a powerful weapon now in the hands of Saivites to combat the evils mentioned under such a scenario, and it is hoped that every Saivite will arm himself or herself with this weapon of destruction of evil and use it every day to save not only oneself but to liberate as many souls as possible from their *prarabdha karma* by following the advice as enunciated in the lessons and in the *Nandinatha Sutras* of this book.

K.L. Seshagiri Rao, Ph.D.
Professor Emeritus at the University of Virginia, Editor of the quarterly journal *World Faiths Encounter,* Chief Editor of the forthcoming *Encyclopedia of Hinduism,* Columbia, South Carolina

On the threshold of the 21st century, Satguru Sivaya Subramuniyaswami has presented us with a special gift: *Living with Siva: Hinduism's Contemporary Culture.* It is a timely gift to the followers of Saivism and to Hindus all over the world. ¶The author underscores in this work the essential principles of Sanatana Dharma, popularly known as Hinduism, and relates them to the issues and problems of our times and society. Dharma includes a code of conduct in all its aspects: duties to God, to fellow human beings and to creation in general. Deep faith in Siva, God, provides a firm basis for individuals and groups to deal with the problems of life successfully; it leads to the wisdom that discovers right solutions and to the strength that puts them into action in individual and social life. ¶A great deal of attention is given to life and living, here and now, in this technological age. For example, the institution of the family, which is under severe attack these days, is given special attention, and the ways to restore the sacred values of the family to domestic life are discussed. It shows that spiritual life that neglects worldly duties is callous, and worldly life that neglects spiritual values is blind. In the process, many misconceptions about Hinduism are corrected. ¶Human beings become entangled in materialism under conditions of ignorance. Exclusive materialistic endeavors frequently make people aggressive, arrogant, selfish, violent and miserable. The author points out that spiritual nature illumines the intellect and dispels ignorance. Living in divine consciousness releases spiritual values such as love, compassion, service and abiding happiness, which uplift life and bring all peoples together. ¶This is a significant publication; it is not merely informative, but also transformative. While it continues to strengthen Sivasambandham in the spirit of the ancient *Tirukural*, it is also of ecumenical and contemporary interest . For anyone interested in improving the quality of life, it can serve as a valuable moral and spiritual guide on a daily basis. I hope it will receive the wide attention it deserves.

Vina Kandavanam
Patron of the the Hindu Religious Society of Ontario, Canada, editor of Athmajothy, President of the Tamil Writers Association of Canada and author of 25 literary and religious books

Experience is the key word in this holy book. There are 365 well-planned lessons, each of which is an experience. Life and books are shaken and honeyed together in a manner and style suitable for all levels of readers who are inclined towards Sanatana Dharma. By providing the right experience, Gurudeva slowly and steadily paves the way for the readers to open up their minds and elevates them to realize the Siva within themselves and to live with Him thereafter. Once this unique stage of Siva Consciousness is reached, life becomes smooth, peaceful, joyful and meaningful. ¶It is my humble opinion that this sacred book has the power to lighten up the hearts and minds of the readers and cleanse them of all forms of sin, evil thought and desire and put them on the path of Sanatana Dharma. I pray to Lord Siva that all His devotees be able to taste this Saiva fruit, a wonderful gift from Gurudeva.

Sivanesan Sinniah
School Community Advisor with Toronto School Board, President of the Association of Sri Lankan Graduates of Canada, founder member and past president of Sivathondan Center of Toronto

This treasure trove of Gurudeva should be in the hands of everyone who is eager to learn or know the Hindu way of life, which is older than five thousand years or more. The traditional Hindu way of living, which has undergone many changes with the advent of scientific advancement, is brought to light by Gurudeva forcefully and in a methodical way. His opening sentences with his *guru* Siva Yogaswami's sayings, "See God in everything; you are in God; God is within you; you must have a strong body and a pure mind," are apt and thought provoking. This book, with a wealth of knowledge and advice to all Hindus, has come out at the proper time when some Hindus are at a crossroads, having lost their roots, their culture, having been enticed by the Western culture and worldly pleasures. I am delighted to see a well-planned and well-written book of Hindu culture. Hindu philosophy is well explained by simple analogies and anecdotes. ¶This book has many valuable pieces of advice and suggestions for all Hindus to take note of. Go through the daily lessons in the book, digest the messages, follow them diligently, and you will be a different person. You will be amazed to see the wealth of knowledge this book has to offer to the readers. Most of us are ignorant of our tradition and Hindu culture. It is high time that we realize our roots and start living as true Hindus. ¶Gurudeva has written about all aspects of life and has analyzed them from various angles, traditional and modern: practical advice to parents on managing a home, rearing children, dealing with teens, managing money, eating healthy foods, praying as a family and worshiping in temples. He has explained about the *yamas* and *niyamas*, the core of the Hindu disciplines and restraints for individuals, groups, communities and nations. He speaks of untying the *malas* that bind us, namely *anava, karma* and *maya*, of purifying the intellect, transmuting willpower, about vows and *vratas*, marriage and sanctity. ¶He also speaks of marvels of meditation and consciousness, subconsciousness and superconsciousness, and a whole lot of social issues like women's liberation and mothers' neglecting children due to pressure of work in the office and at home. Hence, children miss motherly love and affection. ¶Burning problems of immigrant communities such as interfaith marriages, divorces, cross-national marriages and clashing of cultures are dealt with in this book very carefully. He also mentions about life in the inner world, astral planes, transition, death and rebirth. Lots of interesting facts are given in this book. Hence I feel that it is a must for everyone who is interested in inner peace of mind and spiritual bliss.

Rajesh K.R. Bali
Director of Manufacturing and Service for Lacent Technologies, Inc., Edmonton, Alberta, Canada

The more times I read Satguru Sivaya Subramuniyaswami's *Living with Siva,* the more attachment I have with our supreme Lord Sada Shiva. All Hindus understand the vastness of Sanatana Dharma and that there are many ways to approach that one Supreme God, Sada Siva. The way Gurudeva has explained Hinduism in his many writings is indeed unique. It allows the individuals to go deeper in their search for their personal Deity. I am certain that there are many followers of Sanatana Dharma who, by merely reading the writings of His Holiness, have been put on the fast track towards attaining liberation. ¶Having gone through some of his writings on Siva confirmed that my spiritual objective on this Earth is to attain the great devotion of Lord Sada Siva. *Living with Siva* indeed is one scripture that is written in very simple terms. The format is great and it is a practical guidebook for modern Hindus. I absolutely appreciate the 365 lessons on various aspects, e.g. *sadhana, siddhanta,* ethics, etc. It covers all aspects of human life, and it certainly is a guide in our household. I am certain this book will be well received by devotees at large.

Dr. David Frawley, O.M.D. (Pandit Vamadeva Shastri), Vedacharya, Director of the American Institute of Vedic Studies, Author of How I Became a Hindu, Santa Fe, New Mexico

Satguru Sivaya Subramuniyaswami has emerged as the most articulate living spokesman for Hindu Dharma in the West and in a modern English idiom. *Living with Siva* is the latest of his monumental texts on the world's oldest and most comprehensive religious tradition, covering its enormous depth, beauty and power with both detail and precision. ¶All who want to practice any paths in the field of Hindu Dharma will find much relevant instruction in the book. Those who want to understand what Hinduism really is will find that the book expands their horizons exponentially. In fact, anyone interested in higher knowledge will find the book to be a treasure house of wisdom illuminating all aspects of life, the universe and consciousness in a lucid and compassionate manner. It can bring the very power of Siva into your own mind and heart.

Georg Feuerstein, Ph.D.
Director of the Yoga Research Center, author of The Shambhala Encyclopedia of Yoga, Lower Lake, California

Satguru Sivaya Subramuniyaswami is today's foremost spokesman for the living spiritual tradition of Saivism. Like his earlier book *Dancing with Siva,* the complementary *Living with Siva* is yet another priceless gift to the world. This comprehensive and easy-to-read work not only gives the reader reliable and deep insight into the practice of Saivism but Hinduism as a whole. Full of wisdom and sane counsel, *Living with Siva* points a sure way out of the complexities and confusions of conventional life, drawing the reader closer to peace and inner freedom. Even non-Saivites can benefit from this masterful presentation.

Dr. Mahesh Mehta
Professor of Indian Religions and Philosophy, Department of Languages, Literatures and Cultures, University of Windsor, Canada

Living with Siva is, at its best, about living in the constant consciousness of Siva, that is, living a life divine. *Living with Siva* is a product of Subramuniyaswami's profound wisdom and realization. It is written out of a benevolent desire to enable earnest aspirants to achieve their spiritual unfoldment systematically and steadily. The lessons are both secular and spiritual instructions for the inner journey of a *sadhaka* to the ultimate goal of merging into Siva. Part One is especially significant in that it deals with the cultivation of mental and moral purification and of meditative discipline culminating in seeing the eternal dance of Siva in one's own Self and in all beings and things.

Swami Chidananda Saraswati
President of the Divine Life Society, Rishikesh, India

All the Hindus of our global Hindu brotherhood are verily indebted to Satguru Sivaya Subramuniyaswami for his super compendium of Hinduism, so carefully compiled, classified, carefully arranged, edited and published. Today it can be unhesitatingly proclaimed that he is a genius of Hinduism. He has put millions under a deep debt of gratitude by his unprecedented literary work. This marvelous practical guidebook is a most comprehensive and almost complete summary. True, books have been produced to present to the public knowledge of our religion, but most of them have been limited in scope. ¶This second edition of *Living with Siva* is a super publication which will doubtlessly girdle the globe. Once upon a time the saying that was current declared, "The sun never sets upon the British Empire." Even so, the light of Hinduism will never stop shining all over the world as long as this great book remains in circulation. The very praiseworthy feature of this book from the Hindu Monastery of Kauai is the interesting way it has been presented in four parts and in the form of 365 lessons for a systematic perusal which makes for easy reading. Satguru Sivaya Subramuniyaswami has broken new ground and become a pioneer in the field of religious and socio-cultural literature, even as Sir Edmund Hillary and the renowned Sherpa Tensing Norkay in the field of mountaineering and scaling of unscaled peaks. Nevertheless, inspite of the greatness of this achievement, it is inspiring to note his great humility as a *chela,* or disciple, of his worshipful *guru,* Satguru His Holiness Sri Siva Yogaswami of Jaffna, Sri Lanka, who was a living *guru* even till the year 1963 when he attained *mahasamadhi.* ¶What greatly enhances the value of *Living with Siva* is that its pages do not merely constitute a learned dissertation upon a subject, but rather they address themselves to the reader, i.e. the devout religious minded Hindu individual living his life in the framework of Hindu society as well as human society as a whole and carrying on his daily duties and activities as a *brahmachari,* or a *grihastha,* or a retired *vanaprasthi,* or as a monastic *sannyasin* even, in the true spirit of Saivism and of Hinduism. The ideals of all four of these stages, or *ashrams,* just mentioned are brought and presented in a nice manner so as to constitute a guideline for the individual reader to live up to it. ¶I warmly congratulate revered Satguru Sivaya Subramuniyaswami for this gift to 21st-century mankind and wish the book the widest possible circulation that it richly deserves. May God bless you. Aum Namah Sivaya.

Karan Singh, Ph.D.
Member of Parliament (Rajya Sabha), former Indian Ambassador to the US, Chancellor of the Banaras Hindu University and son of Kashmir's last Maharaja, New Delhi, India

With the publication of *Living with Siva, Hinduism's Contemporary Culture,* Sri Sivaya Subramuniyaswami has completed a remarkable trilogy which includes *Dancing with Siva* and *Merging with Siva.* These three volumes taken together comprise a rich and invaluable source of inspiration for Hindus around the world. Written with great depth of thought, clarity of exposition and based upon his personal experience, these volumes should find an honored place in Hindu homes around the world. In addition, they are a valuable source material for studies in Hinduism and comparative religion and will, therefore, be of considerable value for universities, academic institutions and public libraries around the world. I warmly commend this book to all seekers, students and *sadhakas* around the world.

Swami Asimatmananda for Srimat Swami Ranganathanandaji, President of the Belur Ramakrishna Math and Mission, West Bengal, India

Maharaj found the praise of Siva presented in the book very inspiring. He himself has been a devotee of Siva from his boyhood days when he regularly used to visit the beautiful cave temple of Siva in the village of his birth. Maharaj hopes that *Living with Siva* will inspire many people in their devotion to Siva. Maharaj conveys his love to Satguru Sivaya Subramuniyaswamiji as also to all other *mathavasis* of the Hindu Monastery at Kauai. He remembers his meeting with Satguru Yogaswami, whom he had visited along with the late Swami Prematmanandaji, the then Head of the Ramakrishna Mission, Colombo, during one of his visits to Jaffna, many years ago.